# THE COLOUR LIBRARY BOOKS

# FAMILY DOCTOR

## HOME ADVISER

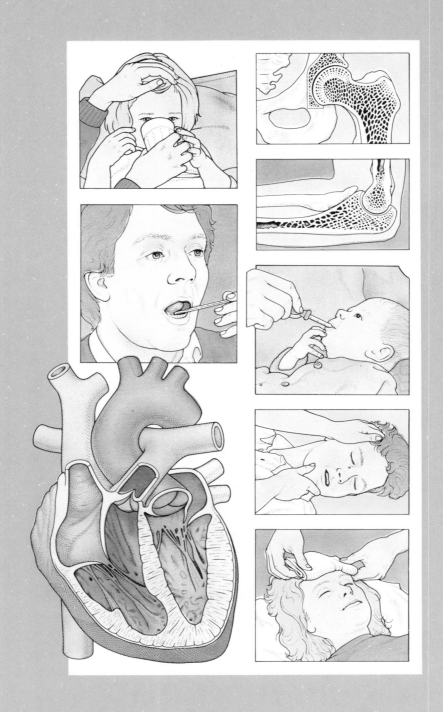

# THE COLOUR LIBRARY BOOKS

# FAMILY DOCTOR

## HOME ADVISER

Editor-in-chief  Dr Tony Smith MA BM Bch.

*Project editor*
Cathy Meeus

*Editors*
Terence Monaighan
Jillian Agar
Candace Burch

*Art editor*
Dinah Lone

*Design assistants*
Jane Tetzlaff
Sally Powell
Peter Cross
Sarah Ponder

*Editorial adviser*
Donald Berwick

*Editorial director*
Amy Carroll

CLB 2475

This 1990 edition produced exclusively for
Colour Library Books Ltd, Godalming, Surrey.

First published in Great Britain in 1986 by
Dorling Kindersley Publishers Limited.

Copyright © 1986
Dorling Kindersley Limited, London.

ISBN 0 86283 777 4

Printed in Singapore

# Foreword

Attitudes to illness have changed enormously in the last few years. People today want to know exactly what is wrong with them or their children and why, how quickly they may expect to get better, and how best to speed up that process.

At the same time, we have become more self-reliant. Most of us realise that the mass of common, minor illnesses such as a cold in the head or an attack of diarrhoea do not need expert medical assessments or complex drug treatments. These disorders are self-limiting – when we fall ill in this way we get better whatever treatment is given, even if no treatment is given.

The problem for ordinary people without medical training is that some symptoms such as a headache or a cough may be the first warning of a serious illness. And few events can be more alarming, or make a parent feel more helpless, than the sudden illness of a child – especially with children too young to describe their symptoms clearly. For how long does a sensible person treat the problem at home? When should you call your doctor? And when do you need to make an urgent visit to the hospital's emergency department?

By following the easy-to-read decision charts in this book, you can learn to tell the difference between minor problems and conditions that need immediate medical attention. We do not believe that any book can teach you how to make a medical diagnosis, and this is not a guide to being your own doctor. What it does do, however, is to tell you when and for how long you may safely wait for things to get better, when it is sensible for you to take a medicine bought over-the-counter, and when you need medical help right away. With this book you can make better use of your doctor, calling him or her only when necessary. It will also encourage you to be self-reliant when that makes sense.

The self-help decision charts contained within have been developed under medical supervision, tested on patients under real conditions, and reviewed by leading medical experts.

*Tony Smith*

**Dr. Tony Smith**
**Medical editor**

# Contents

## The human body

## The symptom charts

## Useful information

# How to use this book

The *Colour Library Books Family Doctor Home Adviser* has been designed as a ready reference to enable the reader not only to understand how his or her body works, but to determine if something has gone wrong, and what to do about it. Information is divided among three major sections, The Human Body, The Charts and Useful Information.

### The human body

The first section of the book is a look at the human body beginning with conception and fetal growth, a child's developing systems and skills, on through to the adult body, both male and female. In addition to infant growth, the developmental milestones – intellectual, physical, social and emotional – experienced by all children are set out in pictures and charts.

Each of the adult body's major systems – circulatory, respiratory, endocrine, reproductive, etc. – is illustrated to show how it works. Special symptoms boxes point out what could go wrong and list the charts that deal with those problems. Here, too, will be found a discussion of what happens in pregnancy and ways of safeguarding your own and your family's health including advice on fitness, diet, exercise and the avoidance of bad health habits.

### The charts

At the core of the book are 147 charts which concentrate on the most common and worrying symptoms experienced by men, women and children. Each chart deals with a specific symptom and then explores the possible diagnoses. Finding the probable cause is simply a matter of answering yes or no questions. You will then be advised on what to do next, for instance, consult your doctor without delay. All you need to know about the charts is found on page 38 – How to use the charts.

For ease of use, children's symptoms are confined to 53 special children's charts. And because symptoms may have different causes at different ages, they are divided among Babies under one, Children of all ages, and Adolescents.

Charts for men and women are also broken down into different sections. 60 charts cover General medical problems: men and women; Special problems: men are dealt with in 10 charts while Special problems: women including pregnancy and childbirth will be found in 24 separate charts.

There are three ways to find the chart you need – whether its from the children's, general medical or special problems sections. Pain-site maps, system-by-system chartfinders and chart indexes are individually set out for men, women and children. Refer to pages 40-48.

### Useful information

The third section contains information which will help you to deal with illness or injury at home, and to record useful medical information. Essential first aid, home nursing and a medications guide are illustrated here as are growth and height and weight charts, and a complete set of family medical records. Finally, there is room to list emergency telephone numbers so they'll always be at hand.

## The human body

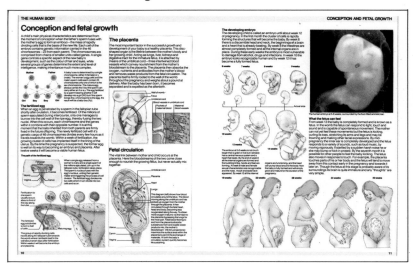

## The charts

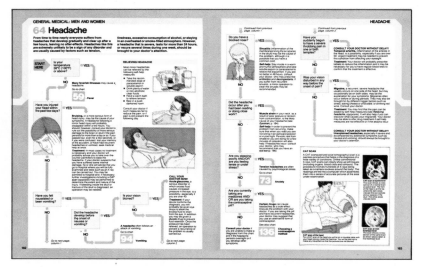

## Useful information

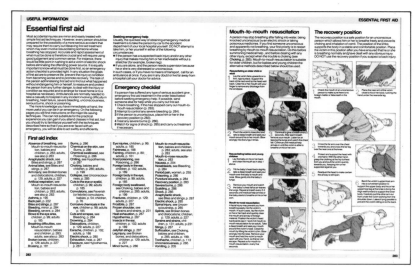

# The human body

# Conception and fetal growth

A child's main physical characteristics are determined from the moment of conception when the father's sperm fuses with the mother's egg to form a zygote – the start for the mass of rapidly dividing cells that becomes an embryo. Each cell of the embryo contains genetic information carried in the 46 chromosomes – 23 from each parent. The chromosomes are comprised from chains of smaller units called genes. A single gene controls a specific aspect of the new baby's development, such as hair colour, while several groups of genes determine the extent, height and level of intelligence, making inheritance much more complex.

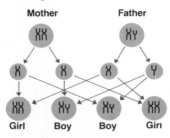

A baby's sex is determined by a single chromosome, either X (female) or y (male). The woman's egg cells and the male's sperm cells each contain 23 chromosomes only one of which is the sex chromosome. The mature egg always carries the X but the sperm can carry either an X or a y. The egg fertilized by a sperm bearing another X will develop into a girl (XX) but if the sperm brings the y chromosome to the egg, the result will be a baby boy (Xy).

## The fertilized egg

When an egg is penetrated by a sperm in the fallopian tube shortly after ovulation, it becomes fertilized. Of the millions of sperm ejaculated during intercourse, only one manages to burrow into the cell wall of the ripe egg, thereby fusing the two nuclei. When this occurs, each chromosome and the genes within it combine with their opposite number. It is at this moment that the traits inherited from both parents are firmly fixed in the future offspring. The newly fertilized cell with it's genetic cargo of 46 chromosomes divides every few hours as it travels towards the womb. Within a week of fertilization, the growing cluster of cells has implanted itself in the lining of the uterus. By the time the pregnancy is suspected, the former egg is well on its way to becoming an embryo and placenta. After twelve weeks it will become a viable human fetus.

### The path of the fertilized egg

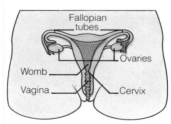

When a single egg released from a woman's ovary and a single sperm of the millions ejaculated, join up in the fallopian tube, fertilization takes place. The sperm's nucleus fuses with the egg's nucleus, uniting their genetic matter and triggering the process of cell division. The fertilized egg divides into two cells which in turn divide into two cells and so on.

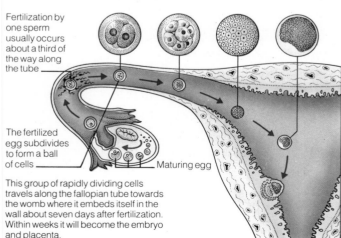

Fertilization by one sperm usually occurs about a third of the way along the tube

The fertilized egg subdivides to form a ball of cells

Maturing egg

This group of rapidly dividing cells travels along the fallopian tube towards the womb where it embeds itself in the wall about seven days after fertilization. Within weeks it will become the embryo and placenta.

## The placenta

A healthy placenta is an important factor in the successful growth and development of your baby. This disc-shaped organ is the lifeline between the mother's body and her growing child. Acting as lungs, liver, kidneys and digestive tract for the immature fetus, it is attached by means of the umbilical cord – three intertwined blood vessels which convey nourishment from the mother's bloodstream to the placenta. The placenta then absorbs the oxygen, nutrients and antibodies from the mother's blood and removes waste products from the fetal circulation. The placenta itself is firmly rooted to the wall of the womb throughout the pregnancy and weighs about a pound at delivery. After the baby has been born, it becomes separated and is expelled as the afterbirth.

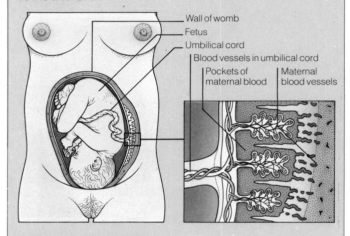

Wall of womb
Fetus
Umbilical cord
Blood vessels in umbilical cord
Pockets of maternal blood
Maternal blood vessels

## Fetal circulation

The vital link between mother and child occurs at the placenta. Here the bloodstreams of the two come close enough to nourish the growing fetus, but never actually mix together.

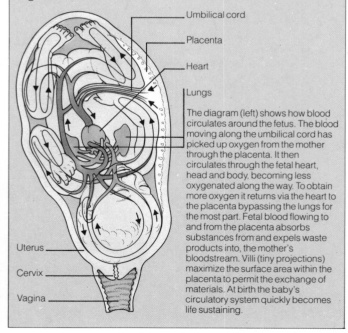

Umbilical cord
Placenta
Heart
Lungs

The diagram (left) shows how blood circulates around the fetus. The blood moving along the umbilical cord has picked up oxygen from the mother through the placenta. It then circulates through the fetal heart, head and body, becoming less oxygenated along the way. To obtain more oxygen it returns via the heart to the placenta bypassing the lungs for the most part. Fetal blood flowing to and from the placenta absorbs substances from and expels waste products into, the mother's bloodstream. Villi (tiny projections) maximize the surface area within the placenta to permit the exchange of materials. At birth the baby's circulatory system quickly becomes life sustaining.

Uterus
Cervix
Vagina

## The developing embryo

The developing child is called an embryo until about week 12 of pregnancy. In the first month the cluster of cells is rapidly forming the structures that will become the baby. By week 6 there is a discernible head and neck, the beginnings of a brain and a heart that is already beating. By week 8 the intestines are almost completely formed and all the internal organs are in place. During these early weeks the embryo is most vulnerable to damage from alcohol, drugs and infections. In week 10 the embryo looks recognizably human and by week 12 it has become a fully formed fetus.

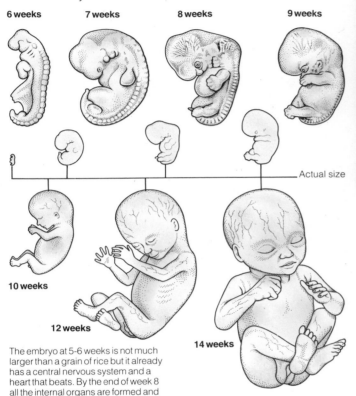

6 weeks    7 weeks    8 weeks    9 weeks

Actual size

10 weeks

12 weeks

14 weeks

The embryo at 5-6 weeks is not much larger than a grain of rice but it already has a central nervous system and a heart that beats. By the end of week 8 all the internal organs are formed and the budding limbs, hands and feet are forming. At week 9 male and female sexual characteristics are recognizable and the nose, mouth and eyes have appeared. By week 12 all the internal

organs are functioning, and the heart can pump blood around the body. Now the baby is fully formed and will simply grow and mature for the duration of the pregnancy.

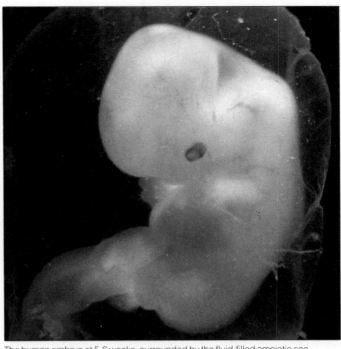

The human embryo at 5-6 weeks, surrounded by the fluid-filled amniotic sac.

## What the fetus can feel

From week 13 the baby is completely formed and is known as a fetus. In the womb the fetus can respond to light, touch and sound and is capable of spontaneous movement. The mother can not feel movements until about week 20 but well before this the fetus is kicking, curling its toes, stretching its arms and legs and may be frowning and making other facial expressions. By mid-pregnancy the inner ear is completely developed and the fetus responds to a variety of sounds, such as loud music, by moving vigorously. If startled by a sudden harsh noise he or she may bump or kick in protest. By the seventh month it is possible for other people to feel the baby kicking. The fetus also moves in response to touch. For example, the placenta touches parts of his or her body and the fetus will tend to move away from this contact early in the pregnancy and towards it later on. Though the fetus at this stage is probably aware of its surroundings its brain is quite immature and any "thoughts" are very simple.

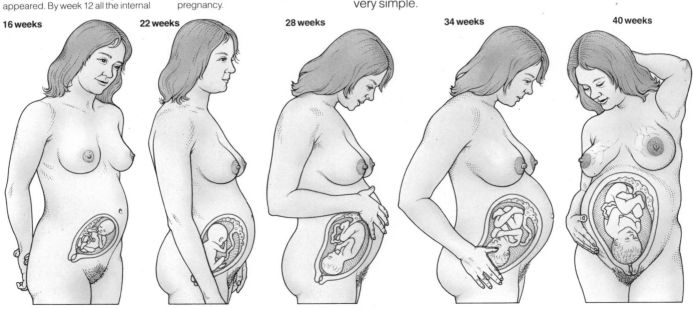

16 weeks    22 weeks    28 weeks    34 weeks    40 weeks

# The newborn baby

At birth, the placenta ceases to supply the baby with oxygen and food and to take away waste products. A baby is born with certain instincts and reflexes which help him or her to survive the first few days of life. For example, during breast-feeding, a baby will naturally attach to the mother's nipple and feed, and a baby's bladder empties automatically. A baby born early, or who is small for the time he or she has been in the womb (for example, as a result of under-nourishment), may require special treatment at birth as some of the body's systems, particularly the respiratory system, may be immature. A premature baby may have difficulty in breathing, feeding and maintaining his or her body temperature. In an incubator the baby can be carefully monitored and protected from infection until the systems become fully developed.

## The appearance of the newborn baby

The newborn baby with its oddly proportioned little body and red blotchy skin may look very different from the perfect pink bundle its parents had imagined.

### The head

The head of the newborn baby will seem far too large and heavy for its tiny body. At birth the head is a quarter the size of the trunk, by two years it is a fifth and in the eighteenth year only an eighth. A newborn rarely has a perfectly rounded head. Pressures on the head during birth and the movement of the bones in the skull for the protection of the brain, commonly lead to temporary changes in its shape. Even if the head seems slightly swollen or bumpy, the brain is safe within and will have come to no harm.

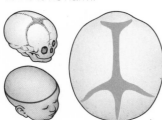

**The fontanelles**
At birth, the skull bones are made up of areas of cartilage with 'soft' areas between them. The larger of these 'soft' spots – which are areas of thick membrane – are known as the fontanelles. A baby has two main fontanelles, one at the front and one at the back of the head. During birth the areas of cartilage interlock in order to protect the brain from damage.

### The eyes

Red puffy eyes are common among newborns because of the tremendous pressure exerted during the birth. This swelling wanes within a few days. Many babies have a squinting appearance due to the folds of skin at the inner corners of the eyes. These are perfectly normal and should become less noticeable. If your baby is still squinting after 3 months consult your doctor.

### The mouth

"Sucking" blisters may appear on the newborn's upper lip or in the mouth at any time while the baby is purely milk-fed. These

are harmless and will eventually disappear. The tongue of the new baby grows from the tip during the first year so that it appears to be more firmly anchored than an adult's tongue. By the first birthday the tongue will be fully mobile.

### The skin

The skin is rarely perfect. Red or blue patches, jaundice, and small white spots are common. A baby who has been undernourished in the womb or a baby of an exceptionally long pregnancy is likely to have wrinkled skin. The skin usually clears by the end of the first month.

**The vernix:** At birth the baby is covered with a white, greasy substance called the vernix. This is a natural protection against minor skin infections and should be left to absorb naturally into the skin within a few days.

**The lanugo hair** often covers parts of the baby's body at birth. This may be a soft fuzz on the head or a very coarse layer over the shoulders and down the back. The lanugo is entirely normal and usually rubs off after 1-2 weeks.

Other aspects particular to the skin of the newborn may occur in some babies and not in others. These are discussed in the following paragraphs.

**Peeling skin:** Some babies are born with a dry peeling skin on the palms or soles of the feet. This is not eczema and will disappear in a few days.

**Cradlecap:** This is as common as peeling skin and is not related to dandruff. It will go of its own accord.

**Variable skin tone:** The newborn's hands and/or feet may appear bluish and at times the upper half of the baby's body is more pale than the lower half. This is due to immaturity of the circulation and will right itself.

**Blue patches:** Sometimes called "Mongolian blue spots", these look like bruises but in fact are temporary patches of pigment beneath the skin. They are more common in babies with dark skin tones, are completely harmless and will fade away in time.

**Birthmarks:** Most red marks on the baby's skin are from pressure exerted during birth and will fade away naturally. Sometimes small red streaks on the eyelids, forehead and nape of the neck are caused by enlarged blood vessels near the surface of the skin. These too will fade. Ask your doctor about any large or unusual birthmark.

**Weals and rashes:** Some babies will develop a rash that is red and blotchy with small white spots. The condition usually lasts only a few days and will disappear without treatment.

**Spots:** New babies get all sorts of spots, most of which form because the newborn skin and its pores do not yet function efficiently. Red spots with yellow centres and/or white spots across the nose should never be squeezed. They will disappear after a few days.

### Sexual characteristics

A slight swelling of the breasts in babies of both sexes is completely normal. This may occur in the first few days after the birth and is due to the flood of hormones intended for the mother but which may affect the baby as well. The baby's breasts may even have a tiny amount of milk in them which should be left strictly alone because of the risk of introducing infection. The swelling will go down in a few days.

The genitals of both boys and girls at birth are larger in proportion to the rest of their bodies than at any other stage in their development. The presence of maternal hormones may cause a bit of extra swelling in the first days after the birth and the vulva or scrotum may also look a bit red or inflamed. The swelling and inflammation will subside as soon as the baby's body rids itself of excess hormones from the mother.

### The umbilicus

The umbilical cord that has served as the baby's lifeline to the mother throughout its life in the uterus, is painlessly cut after the placenta has been delivered. The cord is first tied and it is then cut, leaving three or four inches of stump which shrivels and drops away within ten days or so. Sometimes the baby will develop a small bulge just near the navel which is called an umbilical hernia. Though it may protrude more when the baby cries it is not a cause for worry and usually clears up within the first year.

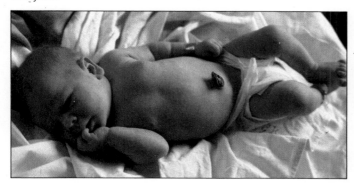

## Tests on the newborn baby

The following tests are carried out on the newborn in order to detect any congenital defects. The chances of curing defects are much greater if discovered at this age.

- Backbone-checked for a swelling or ulcer which may indicate spina bifida.
- Navel-checked for a swelling typical of an umbilical hernia
- Face-checked for a hare lip and cleft palate
- Face-checked for features of Down's syndrome: upward slanting eyes and puffy eyelids
- Anus-checked for imperforate anus
- Genitals-checked for physical defects
- Feet-checked for club foot
- Hips-checked for dislocation of the hip
- Eyes-checked for discharge and physical defects

### Blood tests on the newborn

A blood test (Guthrie test) is usually carried out on every baby one week after birth to test for phenylketonuria, a disorder in which the body lacks an essential chemical. The blood is usually taken from the heel. Additional blood tests may be carried out to check on the level of the chemical bilirubin in the body if the baby is jaundiced, or to check for any biochemical disorder known to run in the family.

## Reflexes and movements

Every newborn comes into the world with an instinctive set of reflexes intended to protect and sustain life. A baby whose breathing is blocked will struggle to free its nose and mouth, and will close its eyes when the eyelids are touched. Voluntary movements become obvious at about 3 months.

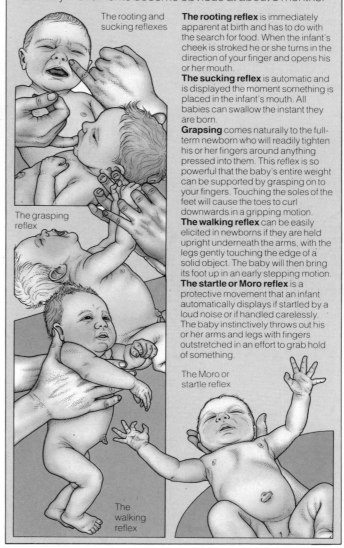

The rooting and sucking reflexes

The grasping reflex

The Moro or startle reflex

The walking reflex

**The rooting reflex** is immediately apparent at birth and has to do with the search for food. When the infant's cheek is stroked he or she turns in the direction of your finger and opens his or her mouth.

**The sucking reflex** is automatic and is displayed the moment something is placed in the infant's mouth. All babies can swallow the instant they are born.

**Grasping** comes naturally to the full-term newborn who will readily tighten his or her fingers around anything pressed into them. This reflex is so powerful that the baby's entire weight can be supported by grasping on to your fingers. Touching the soles of the feet will cause the toes to curl downwards in a gripping motion.

**The walking reflex** can be easily elicited in newborns if they are held upright underneath the arms, with the legs gently touching the edge of a solid object. The baby will then bring its foot up in an early stepping motion.

**The startle or Moro reflex** is a protective movement that an infant automatically displays if startled by a loud noise or if handled carelessly. The baby instinctively throws out his or her arms and legs with fingers outstretched in an effort to grab hold of something.

## The Apgar scale

At birth, 5 simple tests are carried out to assess the general well-being (particularly the breathing) of a newborn baby. A score between 0 and 2 is given for the following and the total is known as the Apgar score:

A score of 4 or less indicates severe breathing difficulties (asphyxia). Most babies score between 7 and 10. The test is repeated after 5 minutes, by which time the score has usually improved.

| What is tested | Points given | | |
|---|---|---|---|
| | 2 | 1 | 0 |
| Colour | Pink all over | Blue extremities | Blue all over |
| Breathing | Regular | Irregular | Absent |
| Heart rate | More than 100 beats a minute | Less than 100 beats a minute | Absent |
| Movement | Active | Some movement | Little or no movement |
| Reflex response | Cries | Whimpers | Absent |

# The growing child

At the moment of conception one complete cell is formed; this contains the genetic information – passed on or 'inherited' from each parent – which determines not only the sex of the new child but also many of his or her specific characteristics. Different genes define physical traits, such as height, build, and skin type, and the rate at which a child develops. Therefore, a child whose parents were relatively late in walking, speaking or reaching puberty is likely to follow a similar pattern of development. Physiological traits are also genetically determined – a child may inherit a susceptibility to certain diseases at conception. The effects of inherited physiological traits, however, can be modified. For example, if a child has a susceptibility to ear infections, prompt treatment each time the symptoms occur should ensure against any permanent damage. Poor or good-quality teeth are inherited; a parent can take steps to safeguard the teeth of the young child, such as buying a toothpaste containing extra fluoride.

A growing body requires both nutrients and exercise. A child who is happy, eats a well-balanced diet (see *Eating a healthy diet,* p.34, and *The components of a healthy diet,* p.119 ) and regularly plays or participates in sport (see *Getting enough exercise,* p.34) will develop normally and establish a basis for long-term good health.

## Emotional development

From birth a child has individual needs which, in infancy, reflect themselves in the baby's feeding and sleeping patterns. The infant is entirely dependent upon the parents for all his or her practical and emotional needs. Gradually this dependence lessens as children become more able to do things for themselves and begin to make friends. The environment in which a child grows plays a vital part in this development. A child is usually able to adjust to changing needs and demands (for example, at school) relatively easily if the home environment is loving and secure.

As a child develops certain skills (see *Milestones,* p.17) his or her personality begins to assert itself. For example, between the 1st and 3rd years children are often 'difficult' as they practise and build on newfound skills (see *The terrible two's,* p.88).

Some children are constantly physically and emotionally restless, and are known as hyperactive – a type of behaviour which is at one end of the spectrum of 'normal' development. Such children demand a great deal of patience and understanding, and occasionally, help from outside the family (see *Hyperactivity,* p.89).

During nursery and school years every child's environment is widened from the family as the child begins to form new relationships, independent from those formed at home. The time of greatest emotional development is during adolescence. The physical development of puberty, which marks the transition from childhood to adulthood, is accompanied by increased hormonal activity which affects all adolescents' feelings about themselves. For the teenager, adolescence is usually a time of experimentation (for example, smoking, drinking and sexual relationships are usually experienced for the first time). See also *Adolescent behaviour problems,* chart 51).

## Changing proportions and features

There are two 'growth spurts' in the development of a child, one during the first year of life, and the other during puberty. From the first year the rate of growth gradually declines to reach its lowest point immediately before puberty begins.

At birth, a baby's head is about a quarter of his or her body length, and as wide as the shoulders. The legs account for nearly half of body length. Gradually these proportions change so that by adulthood the head is about 1/8 and the legs 1/2 of the total body length.

Until puberty begins the male and female are, on average, of similar height and build. During puberty, however, differences between the male and the female become marked. On average, the male grows taller; the male's height generally increases by 11in (28cm) and the female's by 8in (20cm). Change begins in the legs and progresses to the trunk, where most of the growth occurs. Muscle bulk increases – particularly in the male, whose chest, shoulders and arms become noticeably broader. In both sexes the forehead becomes more prominent and the jaw and chin lengthen so that any 'chubby' look is lost. During adolescence, the diameter of the head grows and the skull thickens by 15%. In the adolescent female, the pelvis broadens and layers of fat are laid down on the hips so making them wider than the male's, and breast development occurs, usually as the first sign of puberty. See also chart 50, *Delayed puberty,* and *The reproductive system,* p.21.

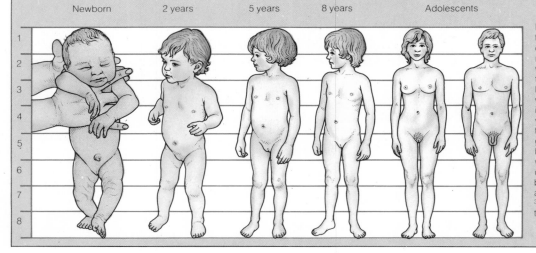

Newborn     2 years     5 years     8 years     Adolescents

During the first eighteen years of life the body is constantly growing and changing. In this time it undergoes radical change – in total body length, weight, proportions and shape. The features of the face gradually become more defined. At birth the weight of a baby equals 5 per cent of its young adult weight. In the first year alone a baby's growth rate triples. In the second year, while growth is still rapid it is slower: the baby now weighs four times the birth weight. By the age of ten, 50 per cent of the young adult weight has been reached. Between infancy and adolescence the legs change from 3/8 of the total body length to a 1/2, and the head from a 1/4 to an 1/8.

# Developing skills

From the moment an infant enters the world his or her growth is a constant process of development and maturation. Within three months, the instinctive reflexes present at birth have given way to voluntary responses and the process of thinking, learning and developing skills is well on its way. No two babies are ever the same and although the pattern of development is constant, the rate of progress varies greatly from one child to another. Your son or daughter may walk weeks later than your nephew but all children will definitely have learned to crawl first. In any case it is never wise to compare your baby with your neighbour's, each of them will eventually sit, stand, crawl and walk, each at his or her own pace. Every passing week brings new accomplishments in muscle coordination and manipulative ability.

### Hand and eye coordination

Learning to put what the eyes see, together with what the hands do, is called "hand-eye coordination". During the first eight weeks of life the infant looks at things without touching them and touches things without looking at them. At this stage, the infant has no idea that looking and touching aren't two separate things. As soon as an object passes out of the baby's limited visual range it is as though it never existed and until the hands are discovered the toy can only be passively gazed upon. The actual business of reaching out and connecting with a thing takes a while to get right. First the baby must be able to clearly see the object and want what he or she sees. Then its a matter of knowing where his or her hand is in space and being able to gauge the distance between the two. Next comes the tricky manoeuvering of hand and arm enabling the baby to actually grab hold of the object.

From about the second or third month the baby begins to link seeing with doing. Now when a rattle is spied the baby tries to keep it in view and do something with it. At first he or she can only swipe at it but later the hand opens wide and grasping fingers curl tightly around the toy. When the rattle moves it makes a noise drawing the baby's attention from the sight of the toy back to the motion of his or her hands. In this way the coordination between hand and eye is further reinforced and the baby gains a sense of his or her own power and control over objects.

Most babies enjoy being propped up in a sitting position so that they can look around and feel a part of things. You can help your baby practice sitting up by supporting the tummy and shoulders as you talk to him or her so that he or she raises the head to look up at you. In this way the muscles of the neck and shoulders are gradually strengthened. By the time the baby is eight or nine months old he or she will be able to sit up, look over a shoulder, and reach forward without losing his or her balance.

### Sitting

Most babies are not able to sit up without support until they are about eight or nine months old. It is only at this time that the baby has gained sufficient strength in the neck, shoulders and trunk to enable him or her to sit up without toppling over. Until he or she can hold the head and torso steady, you can help your child to develop the necessary strength by introducing him or her to games using the muscles needed for grasping, pulling and pushing.

### Crawling

The business of crawling demands from babies a good deal of strength, balance and complicated manoeuvering. Before they can get going they must have developed enough muscular control to hold their heads up and support their bodyweight on the forearms while lying on their tummies. Then they must get into position by tucking their knees up under them, raising their posteriors into the air and summoning enough balance to finally shove off. It is no easy task and most babies won't accomplish it until they are 8 or 9 months old.

At about 9 or 10 months a child will begin trying to stand on his or her own. Because back, leg and foot muscles still will be a bit wobbly, it helps a child to have something to pull up with and to hang on to. If this is a piece of furniture make sure it is solid and won't topple over.

When a baby is ready to start walking his or her willingness to do so may well exceed his or her balance. Walking toys can be used to great advantage by aiding effort thus reducing frustration. Even so it will be trial and error all the way and the baby must also learn to remember that when he or she moves the walker forward, so too must his or her feet move.

## Safety tips

A child's newly developed mobility means that he or she is far more vulnerable to accidents than ever before. His or her agility will most certainly exceed the ability to sense danger and parents must take sensible precautions.

### The sitting baby
Most babies from as early as six weeks like to be propped up so that they can look around. A bouncing chair is ideal but the baby must be securely fastened and the chair placed on a non-skid surface. If you prop your baby up in a regular chair or on the floor make sure he or she is surrounded by plenty of pillows so that he or she does not topple over. Beware of flimsy cots or prams that the baby might pull over when trying to stand up.

### The crawling baby
A crawling baby must be carefully watched. Make sure the area is clean, smooth surfaced and free of loose wires, sharp-edged or rickety furnishings and open fires. Trailing tablecloths, low-hanging plants, breakables and the dog's water bowl should be removed. Always have safety gates across stairways and don't let your child crawl anywhere near a door that may open. Never leave a crawling baby unsupervised.

### The walking baby
Once your child begins walking leave shoes and socks off as often as possible as they can cause a baby to slip and fall. Toddlers who walk can reach and climb so don't leave the windows wide open. Bannisters should be too narrow to squeeze through and stairways fenced off. Swinging or sliding doors should be locked and locks must be out of reach. Possible hiding places like cupboards, trunks and old kitchen appliances must be securely fastened.
   Turn all the handles of pots and pans away from the front of the cooker or install a guard around it. Never leave anything boiling or hot on a reachable surface and make sure that all sharp kitchen utensils are stowed away. Glass doors should have obvious markers and garden gates with road access must be firmly shut. Lock all medicines well away. Never leave small objects lying around that can be shoved into nose and ears and never leave your child unsupervised.

## Standing
As early as five or six months babies love to be held in a supported standing position on your lap or in a baby bouncer. By seven months they are hopping from one foot to another and at nine months are placing one foot in front of another while supported. Imagine a child's excitement when he or she discovers how to stand on his or her own two feet. It is not until the baby is 10 or 11 months old that he or she gains enough control over the lower leg muscles to stand up. By then he or she will stand squarely taking the whole of his or her bodyweight on the feet. Once a child has pulled him or herself into a standing position it may take another week or so to learn how to sit back down again.

## Walking
All babies are born with a "walking" reflex, but real walking comes much later with the baby taking his or her first unsupported steps anywhere between 9 and 15 months of age. At first the child walks clinging to the furniture or to you and later he or she begins to negotiate the space between supports. Now the baby begins to "toddle" managing a few paces in open space between one support and the next. The day that the baby strikes out alone, with legs stretched wide apart for balance and elbows all akimbo is one of great excitement and pride for all.

## Milestones

The ages below are average times by which children usually achieve certain skills. Each child develops individually and may progress slightly earlier or later.

**6 weeks**
- Smile

**10 weeks**
- Roll over from a sideways position on to the back

**4-6 months**
- Raise head and shoulders from a face down position
- Sit up unsupported

**7 months**
- Pass a toy from one hand to the other

**8 months**
- Try to feed him- or herself with a spoon

**9 months**
- Rise to a sitting position

**12 months**
- Understand simple commands
- Stand unsupported for a second or two

**18 months**
- Walk unaided

**20 months**
- Achieve bowel control

**2 years**
- Stay dry during the day

**3 years**
- Talk in simple sentences
- Stay dry during some nights

**4 years**
- Get dressed and undressed (with a little help)

**5 years**
- Draw a figure with separate body and limbs.

## Social behaviour

### Playing

Play is a childs work and toys are the tools of the trade. As much as they need food, warmth and love, children need play to enlarge their understanding of the world around them. Playthings are the stimuli that spur a child to intelligently explore his or her universe, and while it is important to provide your child with a variety of materials and activities, it is just as essential to provide the space in which to enjoy them. Children need an open place or even a quiet corner in which to play, think and dream. A clamour of toys and games will rob them of the chance to focus all their attention on one thing at a time. Give your children the space they need so that they can totally immerse themselves in the challenge of moulding clay castles or brushing Teddy's teeth.

If playing with objects teaches children how the world works then making friends and playing with other children helps them to know how they fit in. Awareness of another's existence is the first step toward learning to consider other peoples needs. The child that misses out on this interaction may find it difficult to relate to people later on and may withdraw, becoming shy and solitary. Some children are naturally reluctant to leave mummy for a new friend and it is important that they be gently encouraged and never pushed.

### Sharing

Toddlers under three years of age may not always play together in complete harmony but they will begin to learn toleration and cooperation. It is essential in life that we learn "how to play the game" and those seeds are sown in time, when a child begins to share not only toys but him or herself with another child. Play then becomes a cooperative discipline with rules and terms of honour.

### Discipline

Sensitive parents will use discipline in a positive sense to teach rather than to punish, thus helping their child balance his or her own needs in concert with others. In this sense the parent uses discipline to define clearly what is or is not acceptable behaviour enabling their child to live happily and in fellowship with others. The socially healthy child learns to share joyfully and to cultivate the art of persuasion rather than force. The child who understands how to give the same attention to another child that he or she enjoys for him or herself will never lack for friends. Children whose parents inspire imaginative thought will be able to find their own way of expressing themselves, thus sharing not only their toys but their experience of living.

# Your child's body

## The skeleton

The skeleton is the body's framework, a rigid structure consisting of 206 bones which act as levers for the muscles to pull against thus allowing movement. The skeleton is a rigid structure which gives support and protection to the body by surrounding and enclosing the vital organs contained within the head, chest and abdomen. At birth the skeleton consists mostly of cartilage which is a soft, fibrous and elastic tissue which works along with bone to build the mature skeleton.

### Structure of the bone

Within the hard structural part of the bone the cells are arranged in thousands of cylinders which help distribute the forces acting on the bones. The marrow, the fatty centre of the bone, produces most of the body's white blood cells and all of its red blood cells. In a young child all bone contains blood-producing marrow (the marrow remains active only in the trunk of the adult.) The bones contain minerals – mainly calcium and phosphate – which add to their strength and rigidity.

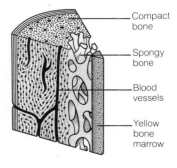

- Compact bone
- Spongy bone
- Blood vessels
- Yellow bone marrow

### How bones develop

During childhood, bone forms within the cartilage at specific developmental stages until, during adolescence, the skeleton matures to its adult state.

Bone is an active, living, but hard tissue which grows, develops and renews itself. Old bone cells are constantly reabsorbed and new ones formed. During childhood the skeleton undergoes a process of constant remodelling and strengthening. Growth of the long bones mostly takes place in one region – the epiphysis, or the 'growing' end of the bone. Injury to this region can impair growth. Both exercise and adequate supplies of vitamins (particularly vitamin D), minerals (particularly calcium) and protein in the diet encourage the growth of healthy bones. See also *Fitness and exercise,* p. 34 and *The components of a healthy diet,* p. 119.

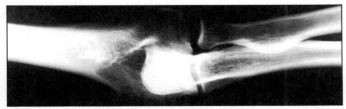

Adult's elbow joint

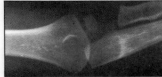

Child's elbow joint

The x-rays opposite and above show what happens to bones as they are forming. The actual shape of each bone is present at birth. The bones in the child's arm are made up of areas of cartilage (not visible on the x-ray) and bone (visible as solid areas). As a child develops, the cartilage is converted to bone. By early adult life this conversion is complete.

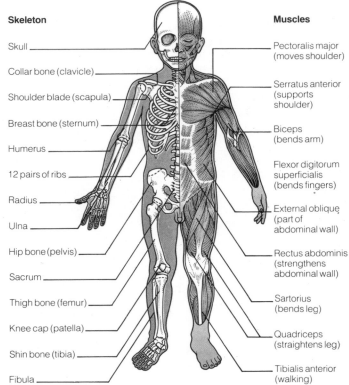

**Skeleton**
- Skull
- Collar bone (clavicle)
- Shoulder blade (scapula)
- Breast bone (sternum)
- Humerus
- 12 pairs of ribs
- Radius
- Ulna
- Hip bone (pelvis)
- Sacrum
- Thigh bone (femur)
- Knee cap (patella)
- Shin bone (tibia)
- Fibula

**Muscles**
- Pectoralis major (moves shoulder)
- Serratus anterior (supports shoulder)
- Biceps (bends arm)
- Flexor digitorum superficialis (bends fingers)
- External oblique (part of abdominal wall)
- Rectus abdominis (strengthens abdominal wall)
- Sartorius (bends leg)
- Quadriceps (straightens leg)
- Tibialis anterior (walking)

## Muscles

All movement of the body and its internal organs is carried out by the muscle. These are made up of thousands of individual muscle fibres which contract to produce movement. There are two distinct types of muscle: the voluntary muscles, which control body movements, and the involuntary muscles, which are responsible for movement within the body (such as those of the digestive tract that contract rhythmically to propel food through the gut). Muscles thrive on work; exercise improves the circulation of blood in the muscles, increases their bulk and improves their chemical efficiency (see *Getting enough exercise,* p.34). A baby is born with certain instinctive reactions known as reflex movements. Gradually these give way as the central nervous system and the muscles develop; this allows the young child to increasingly gain control over the body. (See *Brain and nervous system,* opposite page.)

### How muscles grow

A baby while still in the womb moves vigorously and continues to do so at birth, all the muscles being present. However, they are not yet fully developed and they require a nutritious diet, exercise and hormones to mature properly. After adolescence the male hormones promote the greater size and strength of a boy's muscle. Exercise is imperative for proper muscle growth; without it muscle will actually shrink. Children who are physically active have stronger more well-coordinated muscles than those who are inactive.

### Symptoms

Common problems include fracture of the bones, dislocation of joints, and muscle strains. Most injuries sustained are minor, and conditions such as bone infections and tumours are rare. Occasionally the spine tends to curve sideways, and this condition, known as scoliosis, needs early recognition for satisfactory treatment. An injured child who lies still or refuses to move a damaged limb has probably sustained a serious injury, while a child who can still use an injured arm or hand during play is unlikely to have done much damage.

See also the following diagnostic charts: **45** Painful arm or leg **46** Painful joints **47** Foot problems

### Symptoms

Muscles which are underused or overused are more susceptible to damage. When a muscle is underused it actually shrinks in size and becomes flabby. Inactivity further promotes muscle-wasting and weakness. Damage to muscles from overuse normally produces pain, stiffness and sometimes inflammation and swelling. Muscles may also become weak or painful as a result of virus infection.

See also the following diagnostic charts: **14** Fever in children **26** Rash with fever **45** Painful arm or leg **46** Painful joints **47** Foot problems.

## Heart and circulation

The heart is the centre of the body's circulatory system. It is a muscle made up of two pumps. Each pump is divided into two compartments linked by valves and the main pumping chambers are the right and left ventricles. Blood, which carries nutrients and oxygen to all parts of the body and takes away waste products, is pumped throughout the body by the heart, first to the lungs where oxygen is added and carbon dioxide eliminated. It then goes back to the heart, passes through the left atrium, down into the left ventricle and on to the brain and all body organs via the aorta. Arteries carry blood away from the heart and veins return the blood to it. When the blood returns to the heart it enters the right atrium, passing through the tricuspid valve to the right ventricle, which pumps it on to the lungs for fresh oxygen. In the fetus, two temporary paths which close shortly after birth allow the blood to bypass the non-functioning lungs. (See also *Heart and circulation in adults,* p. 24).

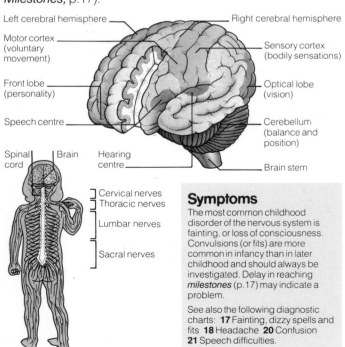

Superior vena cava — Aorta
Pulmonary arteries
Pulmonary valve
Right atrium
Tricuspid valve
Inferior vena cava
Pulmonary veins
Left atrium
Mitral valve
Aortic valve
Left ventricle
Right ventricle

### Symptoms

If there is congenital heart disease, it is generally discovered during routine tests at birth. In an infant rapid breathing and difficulty in eating, and in a child poor physical development, are occasionally symptoms of a heart disorder. Serious heart disorders in children are rare, but congenital heart disease accounts for almost half the major physical defects present at birth.

## Respiratory system

Respiration – the process of inhaling (breathing in) and exhaling (breathing out) air – enables the body to absorb the oxygen it needs to produce energy and to discharge carbon dioxide, a waste product of that process. The respiratory tract consists of the lungs and the tubes (bronchi) through which the air passes on its way to and from the lungs. Air breathed in through the nose and mouth passes down the trachea (windpipe) and enters the lungs through the bronchi and bronchioles. The lungs themselves are sponge-like organs made up of millions of air sacs called alveoli. It is through these tiny sacs that oxygen passes into the bloodstream and carbon dioxide passes out to be exhaled. Throughout this process the diaphragm – a sheet of muscle between the chest and abdomen – is rhythmically contracting and relaxing; allowing the ribcage and lungs to expand and suck in air, and then to contract and exhale the air.

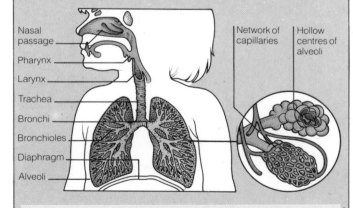

Nasal passage
Pharynx
Larynx
Trachea
Bronchi
Bronchioles
Diaphragm
Alveoli
Network of capillaries
Hollow centres of alveoli

### Symptoms

The most common breathing problems in childhood are due to infections and to asthma. Young children are particularly susceptible to viruses until they have developed immunity to the common ones; after this they catch fewer colds. Sore throat, runny nose, coughing and raised temperature often accompany a cold. Fast, noisy and difficult breathing are symptomatic of breathing disorders. An asthmatic child has attacks in which the small airways in the lung become narrow and so make breathing difficult. Asthmatic attacks tend to become less frequent as the child grows.

See also the following diagnostic charts: **3** Fever in babies **9** Feeling generally unwell **14** Fever in children **18** Headache **31** Runny or blocked nose **32** Sore throat **33** Coughing **34** Fast breathing **35** Noisy breathing

## Brain and nervous system

A child's ability to develop both physical and mental skills is largely determined by the gradual development of the nervous system. This is made up of the brain and spinal cord (central nervous system) and a network of nerves which connect with the brain (peripheral system). (See diagrams below). The nervous system controls both conscious activities and unconscious body functions, such as digestion. (see *Brain and nervous system in adults,* p. 26).

### Development of the nervous system

The nervous system is made up of billions of nerve cells which detect information from inside and outside a child's body. At birth the connections between the nerve cells are immature. In addition, the brain, which receives messages from, and transmits information to the nerves, is only partially developed. The nervous system matures gradually, enabling a young child to control internal organs (such as the bladder) and to develop a wide range of skills, including walking and speaking (see *Milestones,* p.17).

Left cerebral hemisphere
Motor cortex (voluntary movement)
Front lobe (personality)
Speech centre
Right cerebral hemisphere
Sensory cortex (bodily sensations)
Optical lobe (vision)
Cerebellum (balance and position)
Brain stem

Spinal cord
Brain
Hearing centre
Cervical nerves
Thoracic nerves
Lumbar nerves
Sacral nerves

### Symptoms

The most common childhood disorder of the nervous system is fainting, or loss of consciousness. Convulsions (or fits) are more common in infancy than in later childhood and should always be investigated. Delay in reaching *milestones* (p.17) may indicate a problem.

See also the following diagnostic charts: **17** Fainting, dizzy spells and fits **18** Headache **20** Confusion **21** Speech difficulties.

# The senses

Each of the five senses is in working order from the moment a child is born. Newborn babies are thought to have a sense of smell because they do in fact have a sense of taste and the two are inextricably linked. A newborn is able to see clearly from the moment of birth and can discriminate brightness and movement. Babies are able to sense sound vibrations in the womb and can hear at birth. Babies also react to touch in the womb moving to and from the placenta and at birth they respond with pleasure to gentle warm pressure on their backs and stomachs.

### Hearing
The ear, as described on p.103 is important both as a means of communication and as the body's centre of balance.

### Sight
The instruments of sight are the eyes, which begin in the embryo as two fledgling "buds" from the brain. A child builds up a visual vocabulary from birth. The eyeball is a complex structure consisting of three layers: the sclera is visible as the white of the eye; the choroid layer is rich in blood vessels that supply the sensitive inner lining of the eyeball; and the retina contains the light-sensitive nerve cells that pick up images and transmit the information through the optic nerve to the brain. It is in the brain that these images are decoded to allow vision.

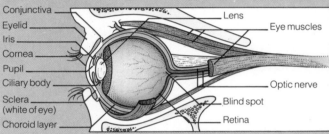

Conjunctiva
Eyelid
Iris
Cornea
Pupil
Ciliary body
Sclera (white of eye)
Choroid layer
Lens
Eye muscles
Optic nerve
Blind spot
Retina

### Touch
It is known that the fetus within the womb reacts to touch because it moves away from the surrounding placenta early in the pregnancy but towards it later on. At birth, the newborn reacts instinctively to touch by gripping any object placed within his or her hand and likewise will respond with sucking reflexes to a gentle stroking on the cheek. Most babies react with pleasure to warmth, softness and gentle pressure, and contact comfort is an essential need from the moment of birth on. By the time a child is one year old his or her sense of touch is well-developed enough to know a cuddly toy just by the feel of it.

### Taste
The child's tastebuds identify different tastes in the same manner as the adult's. Specific areas on the tongue detect particular tastes; bitterness at the back, sourness at the sides, saltiness at the front and sweet tastes on the tip. Bitter, acid or sour tastes cause a baby to grimace, turn away or cry. Babies can also distinguish between different gradations of sweetness and will suck longer and harder at a bottle of sweetened water than plain or only slightly sweetened water. By the toddler stage a child easily knows the chocolate biscuits from plain.

### Smell
The sensitive hair-like endings of the olfactory nerves project into the nasal passage. They detect odours in the air and pass the information to the olfactory bulbs which are linked directly to the brain. One of the first associations a baby makes is with his or her mother's smell. Each individual gives off a personal smell which a baby's sensitive sense can recognize. A baby responds to his or her mother's smell because he or she recognizes the source of comfort, pleasure and food.

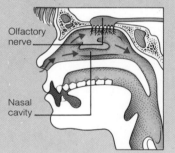

Olfactory nerve
Nasal cavity

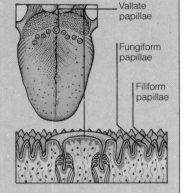

Vallate papillae
Fungiform papillae
Filiform papillae

### Symptoms
The main symptom of disorder in any of the senses is partial or total loss of sensitivity. There may be pain or other symptoms affecting the sensory organ concerned. The most common ear problem is infection and symptoms include earache, itching, a raised temperature, and discharge from the ear. Symptoms of loss of hearing are, in a baby, a failure to respond to sounds and in an older child, turning up the TV's volume. Common childhood eye problems are infections and irritations which cause pain, itchiness, redness and discharge. A neglected squint may eventually cause blindness in the affected eye.

See also the following diagnostic charts: **27** Eye problems **28** Disturbed or impaired vision **29** Painful or irritated ear **30** Deafness **31** Runny nose **32** Sore throat

# The digestive system

The series of organs responsible for carrying out the digestive process are known collectively as the digestive tract. This is a tube extending from the mouth to the anus, in which food is broken down so that the minerals, vitamins, sugars, fats and proteins that food contains can be absorbed into the body.

### Symptoms
Gastroenteritis (infection of the digestive tract) is the most common digestive disorder of childhood. Symptoms include vomiting, diarrhoea and abdominal pain. The digestive tract reacts strongly to infected foods or irritants, causing the loss of body fluid in diarrhoea. If this fluid is not replaced, a child may become seriously dehydrated.

See also the following diagnostic charts: **7** Vomiting and regurgitation **8** Diarrhoea in babies **7** Vomiting **38** Abdominal pain **39** Loss of appetite **40** Diarrhoea in children **41** Constipation **42** Abnormal-looking faeces **43** Urinary problems

### Mouth
Digestion begins in the mouth when, as food is chewed, enzymes in the saliva break down certain carbohydrates. The tongue and the muscles of the pharynx then propel the mixture of food and saliva (known as the bolus) into the oesophagus and so down into the stomach.

### Stomach
Food may spend several hours in the stomach, where it is churned and partially digested by acid and more enzymes until it has a semi-liquid consistency (called chyme). After passing into the duodenum, the chyme is further broken down by digestive juices from the liver and pancreas.

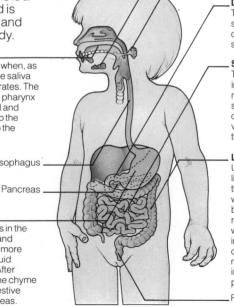

Salivary glands

### Duodenum
The duodenum is the first part of the small intestine into which the partially digested food (chyme) from the stomach passes for further break-down.

### Small intestine
The final stage of digestion is completed in the small intestine, where the nutrients are split into chemical units small enough to pass through the wall of the intestine into the network of blood vessels and lymphatics, which carry them to the liver.

### Large intestine
Undigested material passes in semi-liquid form from the small intestine into the large intestine, where most of the water content is reabsorbed into the bloodstream. The semi-solid waste that remains moves down into the rectum where it is stored until expelled at intervals from the body through the anal canal. The addition of fibre in the diet may increase the efficiency of the large intestine to properly eliminate waste products.

Oesophagus
Pancreas
Rectum

# The lymphatic system

The lymphatic system consists of the lymph glands, found mainly in the neck, armpits and groin, and the small vessels that connect them, the lymphatics. The lymph glands contain white blood cells that form antibodies to defend the body against infection. When infection occurs, the lymph glands may increase in size and become tender as they respond to the invading microorganisms. Lymphocytes (white cells) are released from the glands into the blood circulation.

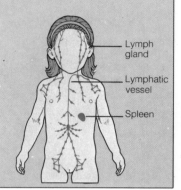

Lymph gland

Lymphatic vessel

Spleen

## Symptoms

Glands that swell during an infection are actually lymph nodes. Swollen tender glands behind the ear are a sign of ear infection, those below the ear and jaw may indicate tonsilitis, and in the back of the neck may mean German measles.

See also the following diagnostic charts: **9** Feeling sick **15** Swollen glands **26** Rash with fever **29** Painful ear **32** Sore throat **33** Coughing

# The endocrine system

The endocrine glands manufacture hormones and distribute them to all parts of the body via the bloodstream. These hormones regulate the body's internal chemistry, its responses to hunger, stress, infection and disease, and its preparation for physical activity.

### Pituitary gland
The pituitary gland is a peanut-sized organ located just beheath the brain. The most important part that the pituitary plays is to stimulate and coordinate the functions of the other endocrine glands, so that they will produce their own hormones. It also manufactures growth hormones which regulate body growth during childhood.

### Thyroid gland
The thyroid gland is situated at the front of the throat, just below the Adam's apple. It is responsible for producing the hormones that control the conversion of food into energy and regulate body temperature.

### Parathyroid glands
The parathyroids produce a hormone which controls the level of calcium and phosphorous – essential for healthy bones and efficient nerves and muscles.

### Adrenal glands
The adrenal glands lie directly above the kidneys and produce hormones, which help to regulate the amounts of sugar, salt and water in the body as well as the shape and distribution of body hair. The adrenal medulla increases the flow of blood to the muscles, heart and lungs to deal with excitement, or physical and mental threats.

### Pancreas
The pancreas lies at the back of the abdomen behind the stomach. It makes enzymes that pass down into the duodenum where they help to digest food, and it produces the hormones insulin and glycogen, which play an integral part in regulating the glucose level in the blood.

### Ovaries (female) testes (male)
The ovaries in the adolescent female and the testes in the adolescent male produce the hormones responsible for the onset of puberty. In the female the ovaries are also responsible for the production of the ova (eggs) and in the male the testes produce sperm. The hormones secreted by these glands determine the development of male and female sexual characteristics.

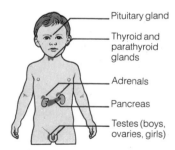

Pituitary gland

Thyroid and parathyroid glands

Adrenals

Pancreas

Testes (boys, ovaries, girls)

## Symptoms

Disorders can occur when the level of a hormone alters. Symptoms of diabetes mellitus, an upset in the level of insulin in the body, include thirst and abnormally frequent urination. Delay in the onset of puberty may be the result of a hormonal disorder. Consult your doctor.

See also the following diagnostic charts: **10** Slow growth **40** Diarrhoea in children **43** Urinary problems **50** Delayed puberty **51** Adolescent behaviour problems

# The urinary system

A baby's reflexes automatically expel urine from the bladder. A child masters control of bladder and bowels when he or she is physiologically and mentally ready to do so (see *Toilet training*, p.127). Also, a child urinates more frequently than an adult, as children have smaller bladders (see *The structure of the urinary tract*, p.125).

## Symptoms

Infection in the urethra or bladder, causing pain when your child passes urine, is the most common disorder of the urinary system. Pain or a change in the number of times your child passes urine in a day, or in its colour, may indicate an underlying disorder.

See also the following diagnostic charts: **8** Diarrhoea in babies **40** Diarrhoea in children **41** Constipation **42** Abnormal-looking faeces **43** Urinary problems **44** Toilet-training problems

# The reproductive system

### Boys
In the male fetus, the organs of reproduction, the testes, lie in the abdomen and descend into the scrotum shortly before birth. The male's reproductive system usually matures between 11 and 17 with the enlargement of the penis and the ability to ejaculate sperm.

The male reproductive system consists of the external genitalia – two testes within the scrotum, and the penis – and a series of internal organs: the prostate gland, two seminal vesicles, and two tubes known as the vas deferens. Sperm are continually manufactured in each testis and pass into the epididymis where they mature for 2-3 weeks. They then pass into the va deferens for storage before ejaculation.

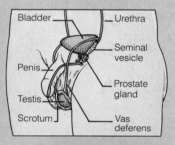

Bladder

Urethra

Seminal vesicle

Penis

Prostate gland

Testis

Scrotum

Vas deferens

### Girls
The ovaries in a young girl already contain all the eggs that will ever be produced in her fertile life. At puberty, usually between 11 and 14 years, the female sex hormones begin production which stimulates the beginning of menstruation.

The female genital system includes the vagina, the ovaries, the womb (uterus) and the fallopian tubes. The uterus does not begin to grow until puberty. The ovaries produce the female hormones and provide storage for the eggs. The fallopian tubes link the uterus with the ovaries and are positioned so that the egg, upon ovulation, can find its way inside the tube. The vagina accommodates the penis and is the birth canal.

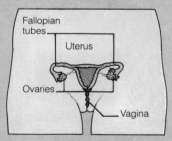

Fallopian tubes

Uterus

Ovaries

Vagina

## Symptoms

**Boys:** Symptoms of a genital disorder include pain, swelling and inflammation, and should always receive medical attention. Problems include internal damage as a result of external injury to the groin, infection of the urinary tract and less commonly, the foreskin of the penis may be too tight.

**Girls:** The most common gentital problem experienced by young girls is inflammation and irritation of the external genital area. Pain when urinating and abnormal frequency in urinating are common symptoms of a genital disorder. Delay in the onset of puberty only rarely indicates a serious underlying problem, but should be investigated in both the male and the female.

See also the following diagnostic charts: **43** Urinary problems **48** Genital problems (boys) **49** Genital problems (girls) **50** Delayed puberty

# Your body

## The skeleton

The skeleton gives form, support and protection to the body. It consists of 206 bones, supplemented by pieces of cartilage. Cartilage is a tough elastic material which forms an important complement to bone especially where a combination of strength and flexibility is required. The bones, especially the long bones of the limbs act as levers operated by the muscles, thus allowing movement. Some bones serve to protect the organs they enclose and some contain the bone marrow where red blood cells are formed. The bones are living material with cells that are constantly replacing old bone with new material. To maintain healthy bones, you need adequate amounts of protein, calcium and vitamins-particularly vitamin D- in your diet.

### Joints

The separate bones of the skeleton are interconnected by joints. There are several types of joints. Fixed (sutures) hold the bones firmly together, allowing no movement, as in the skull. Partly movable joints (cartilaginous) allow some flexibility, as in the bones of the spine. And freely movable joints (synovial) provide great flexibility in several planes of movement, as in the shoulder.

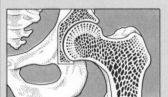

**Ball and socket joints**
Ball and socket joints as in the hip and shoulder, permit maximum range of movement. In the hip the top of the thigh bone is nearly spherical and slots into a semi-circular socket in the pelvis. The ball-and-socket principle allows movement in virtually every direction.

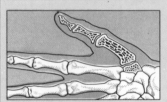

**Saddle joints**
Saddle joints allow both side-to-side and back-and-forth motion. There is a saddle joint within the thumb without which it is extremely difficult to grasp objects large or small. Without this movement in the thumb the hand would be a dummy claw.

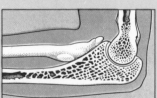

**Hinge joints**
Hinge joints which are found in the fingers, toes, elbows and knees, allow movement in one direction only. The two bones that meet at the hinge are held together by tough fibrous ligaments and the ends are cushioned in lubricating fluid.

**Gliding joints**
Gliding joints in the carpal bones of the wrists slide in similar motion to the saddle joints, side-to-side and back-and-forth, but the movement is more restricted. With age, the movement of the joints can become less smooth and increasingly difficult.

### Symptoms

Symptoms of joint problems include pain, swelling and stiffness in the area of movement. Osteoarthritis caused by wear and tear of the joints commonly affects the neck, hands, hips and knees. Rheumatoid arthritis attacks the connective tissue around the joints causing stiffness and distortion.

See also the following diagnostic charts: **108** Painful stiff neck **112** Painful swollen joints **113** Painful knee.

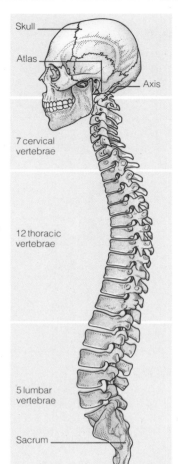

Skull

Atlas

Axis

7 cervical vertebrae

12 thoracic vertebrae

5 lumbar vertebrae

Sacrum

Coccyx

**The skull and spinal column**
At the base of the skull is an opening through which the spinal cord connects with the brain. The cord itself runs through the spinal column which is made up of over 30 separate vertebrae which form a protective casing for the spinal cord.

### Symptoms

The most common problems affecting the skeleton of people of all ages include breakage (fractures) of the bones as a result of injury and damage to the joints between bones as a result of injury or wear and tear. Bone infections and tumours are rare. Symptoms of disorders of the skeleton include pain, swelling and inflammation (redness and heat) around the affected part.

See also the following diagnostic charts: **107** Back pain **108** Painful and/or stiff neck **109** Painful arm **113** Painful knee **110** Painful leg **112** Painful and/or swollen joints **111** Foot problems

### The structure of bone

The structure of bone combines strength with lightness and a degree of flexibility. Bone itself is made up of protein hardened with mineral salts, principally those of calcium and magnesium. The outer (compact) bone contains blood and lymph vessels and the inner (spongy) bone has a honeycomb structure for lightness. In the centre of the long bones is a cylindrical cavity filled with bone marrow. The marrow inside the bones is a fatty material containing blood forming tissues that produce the red and white blood cells.

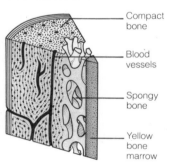

Compact bone

Blood vessels

Spongy bone

Yellow bone marrow

## Muscles

Movement of the body and its internal organs is carried out by the muscles – soft tissue arranged in fibres which can contract and relax to produce movement. There are two distinct types of muscle: the voluntary muscles, which control body movement, and the involuntary muscles, which are responsible for movement within the body – for example, those responsible for the rhythmical contraction of the digestive tract that propels food along its length.

Muscles thrive on work and normally remain in good condition if used regularly. Vigorous exercise increases the size of muscles and improves the circulation of blood to them, thereby increasing their capacity for still more strenuous activity. Conversely, inactivity can soon lead to muscle-wasting and weakness.

**Involuntary muscles**
Involuntary muscles are not under conscious control. That is, they do not contract or relax in response to your decision to make a movement. Instead they work automatically. Both types of involuntary muscle-smooth and cardiac – are in continuous use, maintaining such functions as respiration, digestion, circulation and contraction of the heart.

Heart

Intestines

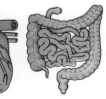

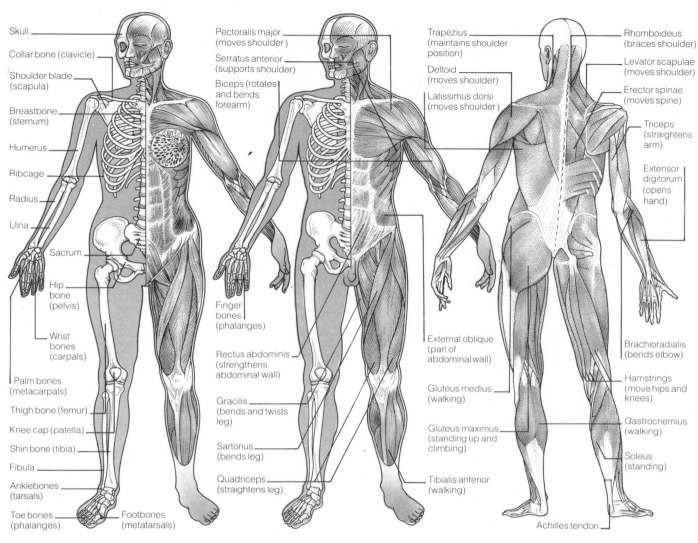

Skull

Collar bone (clavicle)

Shoulder blade (scapula)

Breastbone (sternum)

Humerus

Ribcage

Radius

Ulna

Sacrum

Hip bone (pelvis)

Wrist bones (carpals)

Palm bones (metacarpals)

Thigh bone (femur)

Knee cap (patella)

Shin bone (tibia)

Fibula

Anklebones (tarsals)

Toe bones (phalanges)

Footbones (metatarsals)

Pectoralis major (moves shoulder)

Serratus anterior (supports shoulder)

Biceps (rotates and bends forearm)

Finger bones (phalanges)

Rectus abdominis (strengthens abdominal wall)

Gracilis (bends and twists leg)

Sartorius (bends leg)

Quadriceps (straightens leg)

Trapezius (maintains shoulder position)

Deltoid (moves shoulder)

Latissimus dorsi (moves shoulder)

External oblique (part of abdominal wall)

Gluteus medius (walking)

Gluteus maximus (standing up and climbing)

Tibialis anterior (walking)

Rhomboideus (braces shoulder)

Levator scapulae (moves shoulder)

Erector spinae (moves spine)

Triceps (straightens arm)

Extensor digitorum (opens hand)

Brachioradialis (bends elbow)

Hamstrings (move hips and knees)

Gastrocnemius (walking)

Soleus (standing)

Achilles tendon

## Voluntary muscles

Voluntary muscles are those governed directly by the central nervous system. Only the skeletal muscles are under conscious control and are therefore voluntary in motion.

Skeletal muscles are attached to bone either directly or through tendons and can bend and straighten joints in response to specific stimuli.

## The upperarm

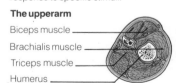

Biceps muscle

Brachialis muscle

Triceps muscle

Humerus

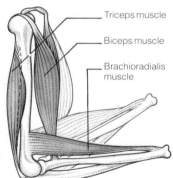

Triceps muscle

Biceps muscle

Brachioradialis muscle

## How muscles work

The muscles have been called the body's engines. They account for almost half the body weight and convert chemical energy into force which is exerted upon the tendons and through them, on the bones and joints. Most muscles usually work in groups, where the contraction of one muscle is accompanied by relaxation of another. During contraction a muscle shortens in length by as much as 40 per cent to bring closer together their points of attachment on two different bones. Most voluntary muscles are fixed to two or more adjacent bones, often by means of a fibrous tendon. When a muscle contracts, the bones to which it is attached move. In this way every movement is in effect a pull and not a push.

Relaxed muscle fibre

Contracted muscle fibre

## Muscle biopsies

A muscle biopsy is a laboratory examination of a small sample of muscle tissue for signs of disease. The photographs shown here are of very thin slices of healthy muscle, magnified 8,000 times. Each fibre is made up of fibrils bound together by a membrane. Each fibril contains two different proteins which are laid down in parallel filaments, creating the tiny dark stripes (myosin molecules) and the light stripes (actin molecules) seen in the photographs left. In a relaxed muscle (left) the stripes overlap only slightly. In a contracted muscle (lower left) they slide over each other, shortening the length of muscle.

## Symptoms

Damage to muscles from injury normally produces pain, stiffness and sometimes inflammation and swelling. Muscles may also become weak or painful as a result of virus infection.

See also the following diagnostic charts: **107** Back pain **108** Painful and/or stiff neck **109** Painful arm **113** Painful knee **110** Painful leg **112** Painful and/or swollen joints

# Heart and circulation

The heart is a muscular pump with four chambers into which enter the major blood vessels carrying blood to and from the rest of the body. As it rhythmically squeezes the chambers, making them expand and contract, blood flows in the correct direction.

Blood transports oxygen and nutrients (see *Blood analysis,* p. 146) to all parts of the body and carries away waste products. It circulates via the arteries, which carry oxygenated blood, and the veins which return "used" blood to the heart.

Good blood circulation is essential for the health of every organ in the body and this in turn depends partly on the efficient functioning of the heart muscle and partly on the ease of blood flow through the arteries.

The good health of the circulatory system depends on the blood vessels remaining free from any obstruction, such as fatty deposits or blood clots. It is also important that the pressure of the circulating blood does not exceed certain levels. High blood pressure (hypertension) may damage the blood vessels or increase the risk of blockage of the blood vessels. For advice on reducing the risks of diseases of the heart and circulation, see *Coronary heart disease,* p.221.

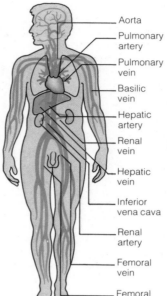

Aorta
Pulmonary artery
Pulmonary vein
Basilic vein
Hepatic artery
Renal vein
Hepatic vein
Inferior vena cava
Renal artery
Femoral vein
Femoral artery

## Symptoms

The symptoms of impaired circulation depend on the organs or region affected. Heart disease may cause chest pain, palpitations or breathlessness; poor circulation to the brain may cause fainting, dizzy spells or confusion; circulation problems in the limbs may cause pain or swelling.

See also the following diagnostic charts: **63** Faintness and fainting **65** Giddiness **66** Numbness and tingling **69** Forgetfulness and confusion **90** Difficulty in breathing **106** Chest pain **105** Palpitations **109** Painful arm **110** Painful leg

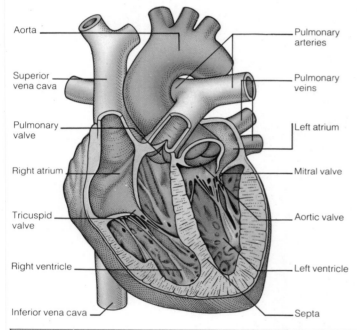

Aorta
Superior vena cava
Pulmonary valve
Right atrium
Tricuspid valve
Right ventricle
Inferior vena cava

Pulmonary arteries
Pulmonary veins
Left atrium
Mitral valve
Aortic valve
Left ventricle
Septa

### The circulatory system
The circulatory system carries blood to and from every part of the body. The centre of the system is the heart. Arteries carry blood away from the heart, veins return blood to the heart.

### Arteries and veins
The walls of arteries need to be strong because blood is forced along them under high pressure, so they are made of four layers. Arteries and their various branches (arterioles) are surrounded by muscle which allows them to dilate or contract to regulate the body temperature. Veins have less elastic, less muscular walls. Valves in the veins stop blood from flowing in the wrong direction.

### Heart vessels
The heart is divided into two by the septa. Each side has two chambers – an atrium, and a ventricle – linked by a one-way valve. The left atrium and ventricle control oxygenated blood, and those on the right de-oxygenated ("used") blood. The septa prevents the two types of blood from mixing.

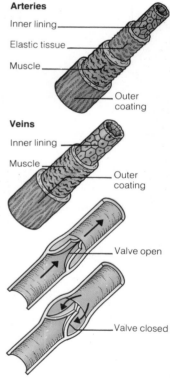

**Arteries**
Inner lining
Elastic tissue
Muscle
Outer coating

**Veins**
Inner lining
Muscle
Outer coating
Valve open
Valve closed

# Blood circulation through the heart and lungs

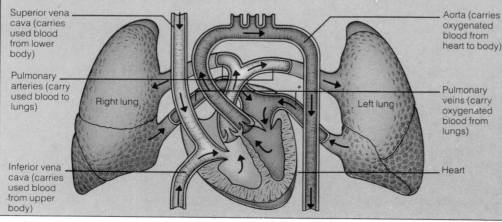

Superior vena cava (carries used blood from lower body)
Pulmonary arteries (carry used blood to lungs)
Right lung
Inferior vena cava (carries used blood from upper body)

Aorta (carries oxygenated blood from heart to body)
Left lung
Pulmonary veins (carry oxygenated blood from lungs)
Heart

De-oxygenated ("used") blood is carried back to the heart via the superior and inferior branches of the vena cava, which enters the right atrium. The blood then passes into the right ventricle from where it is pumped along the pulmonary arteries to the lungs. As blood passes through the network of small blood vessels surrounding the lungs, it absorbs oxygen from the breathed-in air and discharges waste carbon dioxide to be breathed out. The newly-oxygenated blood then returns to the heart via the pulmonary veins, enters the left atrium and then passes into the left ventricle. The oxygenated blood is then pumped through the aorta to all parts of the body.

# The respiratory system

Respiration – the process of inhaling (breathing in) and exhaling (breathing out) air – allows the blood to absorb the oxygen it needs to produce energy, and to eliminate carbon dioxide and water, the waste products of that process. Respiration involves the ribcage, diaphragm (the sheet of muscle between the chest and abdomen) and the respiratory tract which includes the lungs and the tubes (bronchi and bronchioles) through which air passes on its way to and from the lungs. Air is breathed in through the nose and mouth and passes down the trachea (windpipe) and through a branching tree of tubes – the bronchi and bronchioles to the lungs. The respiratory system will maintain its good health unless damaged by repeated exposure to tobacco smoke, pollutants in the atmosphere, car exhaust, or by infections. People who smoke and/or live in areas of severe air pollution are more likely to have chronic bronchitis, an inflammation of the mucous membranes that line the lungs.

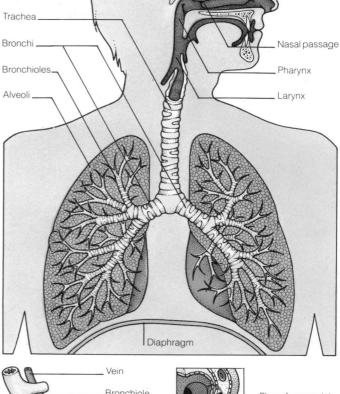

Sinuses
Trachea
Bronchi
Bronchioles
Alveoli
Nasal passage
Pharynx
Larynx
Diaphragm

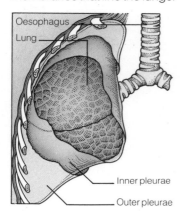

Oesophagus
Lung
Inner pleurae
Outer pleurae

### The pleurae

Each lung is surrounded by a thin membranous covering called the pleura. This is folded back upon itself to form a double layer all around each lung. There is a tiny space between the layers that contains a small amount of lubricating fluid. The inner layer is attached to the lung and the outer layer is attached to the ribcage. The main function of the pleura is to allow the lungs to expand and contract smoothly and uniformly. When you breathe in the ribcage lifts upwards and outwards. This action increases the volume of the chest enabling the lungs to expand and suck air in at the same time. The stronger the muscle action the more air enters your lungs.

## How we breathe

Air you breathe in through your nose is warmed and moistened by small blood vessels very close to the nasal cavity before it passes into the lungs. In addition tiny hairs that line the nose filter the air of foreign particles that might get into the lungs. When you breathe in, the diaphragm, which is dome shaped when relaxed, is pulled flat. At the same time, muscles between your ribs contract and pull the ribcage up and out. These movements enlarge the volume of your chest thus enabling the lungs to expand and suck in air. When you breathe out, the chest muscles and diaphragm relax, causing the ribcage to sink and the lungs to contract and squeeze out the air.

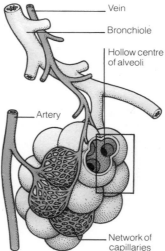

Vein
Bronchiole
Hollow centre of alveoli
Artery
Network of capillaries

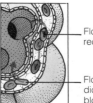

Flow of oxygen into red blood cells
Flow of carbon-dioxide from red blood cells

### How oxygen enters the blood

The lungs are sponge-like organs which are made up of millions of tiny air sacs called alveoli. The thin linings of these sacs consist of minute blood vessels, and it is here that the vital exchange of oxygen and carbon dioxide takes place. The alveoli bring the blood into close contact with the breathed-in air, allowing oxygen to pass into the bloodstream and carbon dioxide to pass out for exhalation.

## Symptoms

The most common respiratory disorders are caused by infection and lead to inflammation of the lining of the tract, or of the lung tissues themselves. This may cause chest pain or soreness in the throat, and/or result in the production of excessive amounts of mucous. Coughing is a common symptom of respiratory disorders. If the breathing mechanism is severely damaged there may be shortness of breath.

See also the following diagnostic charts: **85** Runny nose **86** Sore throat **87** Hoarseness or loss of voice **88** Wheezing **89** Coughing **90** Difficulty in breathing **106** Chest pain

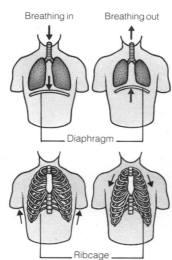

Breathing in
Breathing out
Diaphragm
Ribcage

### Bronchiogram of the lungs

A small amount of liquid visible on X-rays is trickled down the throat into the lungs, and outlines the breathing pattern of the trachea and bronchi.

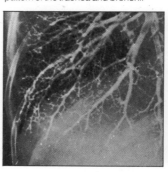

### Endoscopic view of the lungs

This view of the inside of the lungs (below right) shows the trachea dividing into the two main tubes or bronchi, which lead into the lungs.

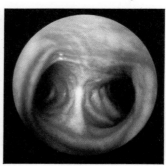

# Brain and nervous system

The brain and nervous system together provide the control mechanism for both conscious activities, such as thought and movement, and for unconscious body functions such as breathing and digestion. Nerves also provide the means by which we register sensations such as pain and temperature. The brain and nervous system require a constant supply of oxygenated blood. Disruption of the blood flow to any part of the system is one of the most common causes of malfunctioning of the brain and nervous system.

Brain cells suffer permanent damage if their blood supply stops for more than two minutes. Therefore, the prevention of circulatory trouble is of crucial importance. Ruptured or blocked blood vessels in the brain can have serious consequences including permanent disability.

Injury, infection, degeneration, tumours and diseases of unknown cause may also affect the brain and nervous system. Certain disorders may arise out of abnormal electrical activity or chemical imbalances in the brain.

### The brain

The human brain lies well protected within the rigid, bony box formed by the bones of the skull. It consists of millions of nerve cells (neurons) and nerve pathways, capable of an infinite variety of intercommunications upon which individual intelligence and creativity depend. The brain is by far the most complex organ in the body and many aspects of its structures and functions are not yet fully understood. Certain parts of the brain control different bodily functions. The two cerebral hemispheres, the cerebellum and the brain stem comprise nearly 90 percent of brain tissue and control conscious thought and movement, as well as interpretation of sensory stimuli. The cerebellum regulates subconscious activities such as coordination of movement and balance. The brain stem connects the rest of the brain to the spinal cord and contains the nerve centers that govern the "automatic" functions which sustain life such as heartbeat and respiration.

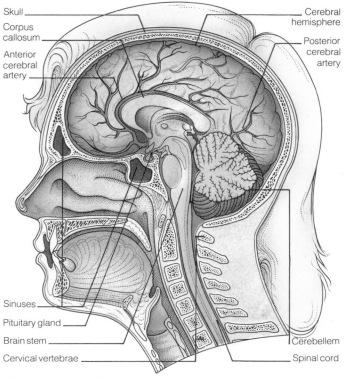

Skull — Cerebral hemisphere — Corpus callosum — Posterior cerebral artery — Anterior cerebral artery — Sinuses — Pituitary gland — Brain stem — Cerebellem — Cervical vertebrae — Spinal cord

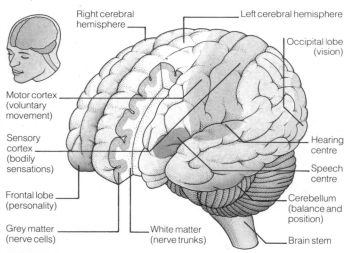

Right cerebral hemisphere — Left cerebral hemisphere — Occipital lobe (vision) — Motor cortex (voluntary movement) — Sensory cortex (bodily sensations) — Hearing centre — Speech centre — Frontal lobe (personality) — Cerebellum (balance and position) — Grey matter (nerve cells) — White matter (nerve trunks) — Brain stem

### The nervous system

The brain and nerve tracts of the spinal cord acting together make up the central nervous system, with the spinal cord serving as the nervous link between the brain and the rest of the body. Motor pathways which carry stimuli from the brain to various organs of the body descend through the spinal cord, while sensory pathways from the skin and other sensory organs ascend through the spinal cord carrying messages to the brain. A network of peripheral nerves link the central system with other parts of the body and manage the conscious control of muscles and the unconscious control of organ function.

#### The spinal cord

The spinal cord is made up of numerous bundles of nerve fibres carrying messages to and from the brain. Connected to it and running throughout is the peripheral nervous system which controls voluntary and involuntary actions. There are 12 pairs of such nerves radiating from the brain and 31 pairs from the spinal cord.

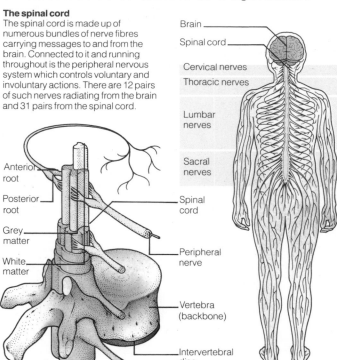

Anterior root — Posterior root — Grey matter — White matter — Brain — Spinal cord — Cervical nerves — Thoracic nerves — Lumbar nerves — Sacral nerves — Spinal cord — Peripheral nerve — Vertebra (backbone) — Intervertebral disc

## Symptoms

The symptoms of brain and nervous system disorders depend on the part of the system affected and may include pain, loss of sensation and weakness. Brain disorders may cause a variety of psychological symptoms as well as physical symptoms, such as headache, drowsiness, confusion, or hallucinations.

See also the following diagnostic charts 63 Faintness and fainting 64 Headache 65 Giddiness 66 Numbness and tingling 67 Twitching and trembling 68 Pain in the face 69 Forgetfulness and confusion 70 Difficulty in speaking 72 Depression 107 Back pain

# The senses

These are the means by which we monitor aspects of our environment. Five separate systems respond to different types of stimuli: the eyes enable us to interpret visual information; the ears monitor sound and control balance; the nose and tongue respond to different smells and tastes respectively; and the sensory nerves in the skin allow us to feel physical contact (touch), changes in temperature, and pain.

## The eyes

The instruments of sight are the eyes, which begin in the embryo as two "buds" from the brain. It is in the brain that nerve impulses from images recorded by the eyes are decoded to allow vision. The eye is directional using six separate muscles which swivel it to look at objects in different directions. Normal vision depends on the refractive, or light-bending power of the lens and cornea. Light rays entering the eye focus on the retina and the image then forms in front of it.

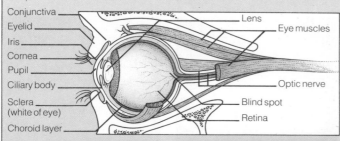

Conjunctiva
Eyelid
Iris
Cornea
Pupil
Ciliary body
Sclera (white of eye)
Choroid layer
Lens
Eye muscles
Optic nerve
Blind spot
Retina

**Opthalmoscopic view of the retina**
Vision results from the stimulation of nerve cells in the retina, signalling patterns of light intensity and colour, which are decoded by the brain. In the photo (right) the pale disc is the optic disc, where all the nerves come together and leave the eye on the way to the brain. Arteries can be seen radiating from the disc to supply the retina and other structures in the eye with blood.

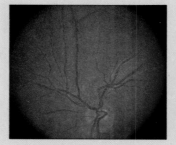

## The ears

The ear is concerned not only with hearing but with posture and balance and consists of an outer, middle and inner part. The outer ear is the visible flap which guards the auditory canal. The canal is protected by hairs and sweat glands that secrete wax to trap foreign particles. The middle ear contains the three smallest bones in the body—the hammer, anvil and stirrup—which link the eardrum to the inner ear, which contains the cochlea, the organ of hearing. Vibrations from the eardrum are converted to nerve impulses that the brain perceives as sound.

The pinna or earflap not only protects the ear but acts as a directional range finder channeling sound into the eardrum.

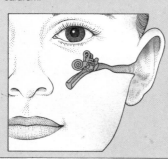

## Symptoms

The main symptom of any disorder of the senses is partial or total loss of sensitivity. There may also be pain or other symptoms affecting the sensory organ concerned.

See also the following diagnostic charts: **65** Giddiness
**66** Numbness and tingling
**80** Painful or irritated eye
**81** Disturbed or impaired vision
**82** Earache **83** Noises in the ear
**84** Deafness

## Smell

Smells are detected by the olfactory nerves. These hair-like organs project into the top of the nasal cavity and absorb and analyse molecules from the breathed-in air. The sense of smell may be damaged by smoking or temporarily impaired by colds or allergies. Permanent loss of smell may occur following nerve damage, perhaps as a result of a skull injury, or it may be caused by a disorder affecting the part of the brain which interprets smell sensations.

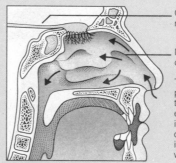

Olfactory nerve
Nasal cavity

The nasal passage is linked to three pairs of sinuses or air-filled cavities in the skull. The sensitive hair-like endings of the olfactory nerves project into the nasal passage. They detect odors in the air and pass the information to the olfactory bulbs which are linked directly to the brain.

## Taste

The main taste organs are the taste buds which are located in hair-like papillae that project from the upper surface of the tongue. They can distinguish only four basic tastes: sweet, sour, salt and bitter. The taste buds for each taste are located in a specific area of the tongue. The sense of taste is allied to the sense of smell, which helps us to differentiate a greater range of flavours. Loss of the sense of smell is the usual cause of impairment to the sense of taste, but certain drugs and occasionally zinc deficiency may have the same effect.

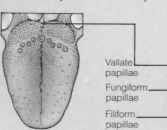

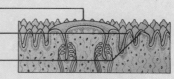

**The tongue**
Specific areas on the tongue detect particular tastes. Bitterness is at the back, sourness at the sides, saltiness at the front and sweetness on the tip.

Vallate papillae
Fungiform papillae
Filiform papillae

## Touch

The sense of touch, which includes all skin sensations, is conveyed through nerves from the sense receptors that lie under the surface of the skin. A different type of receptor is responsible for monitoring each of the main sensations. The number of sense receptors varies from one part of the body to another: the fingertips and the area around the mouth have a large number of receptors, whereas the skin of the middle back has very few. The sense of touch may be impaired by local damage to the skin's nerve endings following an injury, or any of the diseases that damage nerve fibres, or from a condition affecting the brain and/or nervous system.

Skin surface
Free nerve endings
Nerves grouped together and conducted to the spinal cord

The sensation of touch is associated with a specific type of receptor embedded at various levels within the skin. Free nerve endings respond to gentle pressure and moderate heat and cold. Enclosed nerve endings register pressure immediately and others respond to vibration and stretch. Thermo receptors respond to sensations of heat and cold signalling the hypothalamus in the brain to adjust body temperature.

# The digestive system

The series of organs responsible for carrying out the digestive process are known collectively as the digestive tract. This is a tube that extends from the mouth to the anus, in which food is broken down so that the minerals, vitamins, carbohydrates, fats and proteins it contains can be absorbed into the body.

## The mouth
Digestion begins in the mouth when, as you chew food, enzymes in the saliva break down certain carbohydrates. The tongue and the muscles of the pharynx propel the mixture of food and saliva, known as the bolus, into the oesophagus and it then travels down into the stomach.

**The digestive organs**

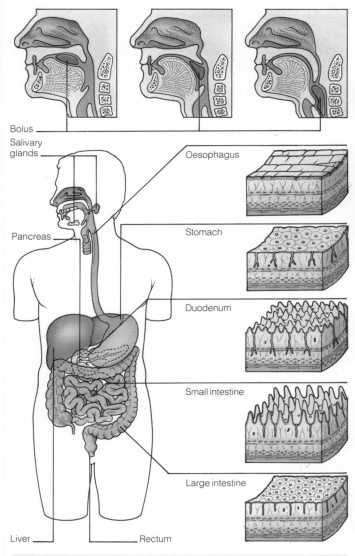

Bolus
Salivary glands
Pancreas
Liver
Rectum

Oesophagus
Stomach
Duodenum
Small intestine
Large intestine

## The stomach and duodenum
Food may spend several hours in the stomach, being churned and partially digested by acid and enzymes, until it becomes a semi-liquid consistency (chyme) which then passes into the duodenum. Here the chyme is further broken down by digestive juices from the liver and pancreas.

## The small intestine
The final stage of digestion is completed in the small intestine, where the nutrients are split into chemical units small enough to pass through the wall of the intestine into the network of blood vessels and lymphatics.

## The large intestine
Undigested food in liquid form flows from the small intestine into the large intestine, where most of the water content is absorbed back into the body. The semi-solid waste that remains moves down into the rectum where waste is stored until it is released through the anus as a bowel movement.

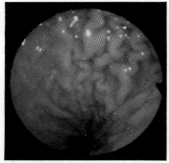

**Endoscopic view of stomach**
This photograph shows the lining of the stomach at the part adjacent to the duodenum. Its circular muscles are partially contracted.

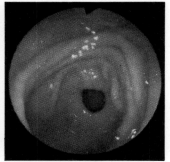

**Endoscopic view of duodenum**
It is possible to see the characteristic circular folds of membrane which make up the surface of the duodenum. See *Endoscopy*, p. 201.

## The liver
The liver is the single largest internal organ in the body. It is a dark reddish-brown colour and fills the upper right-hand part of the abdomen behind the lower ribs. The nutrients extracted from food by the digestive system are carried straight to the liver in the portal vein. The liver plays a vital role in regulating the composition of the blood and other essential chemical reactions in the body. Its functions include the breakdown of ageing red blood cells containing the red pigment hemoglobin, the production and storage of proteins, and the regulation of protein metabolism and its byproducts. Other important life-sustaining functions include the storage of sugar and fats, the neutralization of substances toxic to the body, the breakdown of drugs, the manufacture of bile (a fluid that passes into the duodenum where it helps to break down fatty food) and the manufacture and storage of red blood cell components.

## Symptoms
The lining of the intestines is renewed every 24 hours and so can cope with a wide range of substances passed through it every day. The digestive system also reacts quickly against irritants such as contaminated food and may cause vomiting and/or diarrhoea.

See also the following diagnostic charts **56** Loss of weight **94** Vomiting **95** Recurrent vomiting **96** Abdominal pain **97** Recurrent abdominal pain **98** Swollen abdomen **99** Wind **100** Diarrhoea **101** Constipation **102** Abnormal-looking faeces

## Symptoms
Symptoms of a deteriorating liver may include loss of appetite, anaemia, nausea, vomiting and weight loss. There may be abdominal discomfort and indigestion. With extensive liver destruction, the legs and abdomen may fill with fluid and jaundice may appear. The patient may become disoriented and confused.

See also the following diagnostic charts: **54** Feeling Under the Weather **55** Tiredness **56** Loss of weight **69** Forgetfulness and confusion **95** Recurrent vomiting **97** Recurrent abdominal pain.

# The lymphatic system

This consists of the lymph glands, found mainly in the neck, armpits and groin, and the small vessels that connect them, the lymphatics. The lymph glands produce lymphocytes, a type of white blood cell, and antibodies that defend the body against infection. The glands and the spleen act as barriers to the spread of infection by trapping any infection-carrying microbes that travel along the lymphatic vessels, so preventing them from reaching vital organs. If you have an infection, the lymph glands near the surface of the skin often become visibly swollen and sometimes painful. The lymphatic system is also responsible for carrying nutrients and oyxgen from the blood to every cell in the body.

## The spleen

The spleen is, in effect, a large lymph gland concerned with iron metabolism, blood cell storage, and the manufacture and destruction of blood cells. When red blood cells become old or defective the spleen aids the liver in filtering them out of the bloodstream. The spleen also produces cells that help to destroy foreign bacteria.

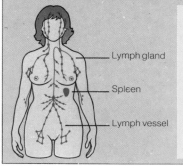

Lymph gland

Spleen

Lymph vessel

### Symptoms

In the majority of cases, any lump or swelling beneath the surface of the skin indicates that the lymphatic system is working normally – protecting your body against infection. In some cases, however, it may indicate a more serious underlying disorder.

See also the following diagnostic chart: **62** Lumps and swellings

# The endocrine system

Endocrine glands manufacture hormones and distribute them to all parts of the body via the bloodstream. These hormones help to regulate the body's internal chemistry, its responses to hunger, stress, infection and disease, and its preparation for physical activity.

**Hormone producing glands**

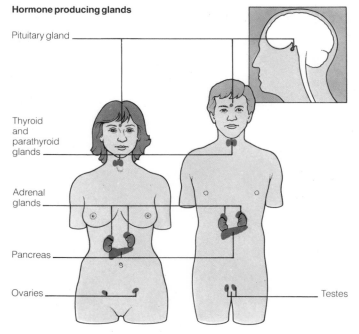

Pituitary gland

Thyroid and parathyroid glands

Adrenal glands

Pancreas

Ovaries

Testes

## The pituitary gland

This is a peanut-sized organ situated just beneath the brain. The most important part that the pituitary plays is to stimulate and coordinate the functions of the other endocrine glands, so that they produce their own hormones. It also manufactures growth hormone and hormones to control the volume of urine and the contraction of the uterus during labour. The pituitary influences the activity of other endocrine glands such as the thyroid, the adrenals, the ovaries and the testicles.

## The thyroid gland

This gland is located at the front of the throat, just below the Adam's apple. It is responsible for producing the hormones that control the body's metabolism (the conversion of food into energy) and regulates the body's internal thermostat.

## The parathyroid glands

These four glands are situated behind the thyroid. The hormone that they produce controls the levels of calcium and phosphorous which are essential for healthy bones, and for the efficient functioning of nerves and muscles.

## The adrenal glands

The adrenal glands lie directly above the kidneys. Each adrenal consists of two parts: the cortex and the medulla which have separate functions. The adrenal cortex produces steroid hormones, which help to regulate the amounts of sugar, salt and water in the body, and influences the shape and distribution of body hair. The adrenal medulla produces adrenalin and noradrenalin, the hormones that increase the flow of blood to the muscles, heart and lungs so that they are prepared to deal with excitement, or physical and/or mental stress.

## The pancreas

The pancreas lies at the back of the abdomen behind the stomach. It makes enzymes that pass down into the duodenum where they help to digest food, and it produces the hormones insulin and glycogen, which play an important part in regulating the glucose level in the blood. Glucose is the main source of energy for all the body's cells and insulin stimulates the cells to absorb it in sufficient amounts.

## The ovaries

The ovaries are two endocrine glands which produce sex hormones and ova (eggs). A woman is born with all the ova she will have, numbering approximately 400,000 at birth. The ovaries are about a centemetre thick and are bean-shaped. The fallopian tubes hang over the ovaries so that the egg can easily drop inside after ovulation.

## The testes

These hang in the pouch of skin known as the scrotum. The hormone they produce, testosterone, is responsible for the onset of puberty and determines the development of male characteristics such as a deep voice, body shape and pattern of hair growth.

### Symptoms

Disorders usually occur when the level of a particular hormone increases or decreases, upsetting the body's chemistry. Any disorder and the symptoms involved depends on which hormone is affected. For instance, if production of the hormone insulin is disrupted, the most common endocrine gland disorder may result – diabetes melitus. Changes in hormonal levels are also responsible for the natural physical changes in your body during puberty.

See also the following diagnostic charts **55** Tiredness **56** Loss of weight **57** Overweight **60** Excessive sweating

# The urinary system

The urinary system is responsible for filtering the blood and expelling the resulting waste fluid from the body. The organs of the urinary system consist of two kidneys, two ureters, the bladder and the urethra, the tube through which urine passes out of the body. The male urethra is about 25cm (10 in) long and provides an outlet for semen as well as urine. In the female, the urethra is much shorter, about 25mm (1 in) long and lies just in front of the reproductive organs. Because of its close proximity to the anus and vagina, a woman's urinary tract is much more susceptible to infection.

## How the urinary tract works

The kidneys are responsible for filtering waste substances from the blood to keep it constantly purified. The filtered liquid passes into the central section of the kidney, where certain chemicals are reabsorbed to monitor the levels of acids, salts and water in the body. The liquid that remains is urine, and this trickles down the ureters into the bladder, which is kept closed by a ring of muscles (sphincter), and then released periodically from the body through the urethra.

**The urinary tract**

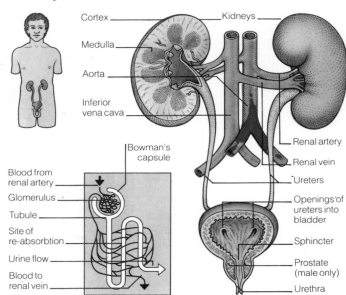

## How the kidneys filter blood

Both kidneys consist of millions of filtering units which are supplied with blood from the renal artery via a cluster of minute blood vessels called glomeruli. Each cluster is surrounded by a cup-shaped organ called a Bowman's capsule, which is joined to the tubule. This is the point where the filtration takes place – filtered material is condensed to make a small amount of urine, which then passes down to the bladder.

## Symptoms

Disorders of the urinary system are fairly common, caused in most cases by infection in or near the bladder that has led to inflammation; infections usually enter the body via the urethra. Difficulty in passing urine or any increase in the volume of urine passed may be a symptom of a more serious underlying disorder such as an obstruction. Pain when you urinate or discharge from the urethra may be caused by a sexually transmitted disease (p. 238 men, 262 women).

See also the following diagnostic charts: **104** General urinary problems, **117** Painful urination in men, **132** Painful urination in women.

# The male reproductive system

The male reproductive system is responsible for the manufacture and delivery of sperm. The organs of the reproductive system become fully developed at puberty (between the ages of 12 and 15). They are partly external – the scrotum containing the testes, and the penis, and partly internal – the prostate and various organs that collect and store sperm.

**The reproductive organs**

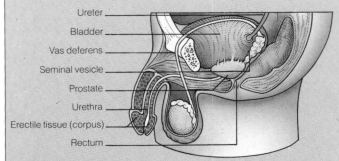

**Transverse section of penis**

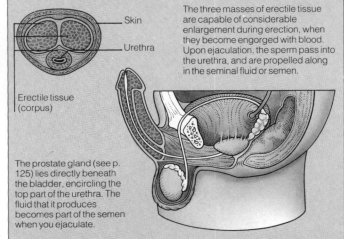

The three masses of erectile tissue are capable of considerable enlargement during erection, when they become engorged with blood. Upon ejaculation, the sperm pass into the urethra, and are propelled along in the seminal fluid or semen.

The prostate gland (see p. 125) lies directly beneath the bladder, encircling the top part of the urethra. The fluid that it produces becomes part of the semen when you ejaculate.

## The penis

The penis is the organ through which the greater part of the urethra passes. Sexual desire leads to erection of the penis. The soft spongy tissue becomes filled with blood, making the penis lengthen and stiffen. Also, partial erection may occur during sleep when you dream.

## The testes

The testes, commonly known as the testicles, have two functions: they form the sperm (see Sperm production, p. 246) and they produce the male hormone, testosterone, responsible for the development of male genitals, growth of male facial and bodily hair, and for the deepening of the male voice.

## Symptoms

Most disorders of the reproductive system affect the external organs. If you notice discharge from the urethra this is likely to be caused by a sexually transmitted disease (p. 238). Blood in the semen is usually the result of rigorous sexual activity, though in some cases it may be the result of a serious disorder such as tuberculosis. Any swelling with or without pain, or any change in the appearance of your testicles or penis, is a sign of an underlying disorder.

See also the following diagnostic charts: **116** Painful penis, **115** Painful or swollen testicles.

# Breasts

The breasts, or mammary glands are actually modified sweat glands, accessories to the major reproductive organs. The layer of skin over the breast is smoother than elsewhere on the body and the skin of the nipple and its surrounding area (aerola) is particularly thin. It is here that the sweat and sebaceous glands are contained. The nipple is cylindrical or conical in shape, and responds to sexual arousal by becoming erect. Each of a woman's breasts consists of 15 to 20 groups of milk producing glands embedded in fatty tissue. Milk ducts run from the glandular groups, through the core of the nipple and open at the tip. During pregnancy, the release of specific hormones from the placenta and the pituitary gland cause the breasts to enlarge and produce sufficient milk for feeding.

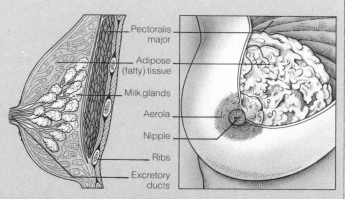

Pectoralis major
Adipose (fatty) tissue
Milk glands
Aerola
Nipple
Ribs
Excretory ducts

The breasts are supported by muscles, ligaments and fatty tissue. The milk producing glands are grouped into lobes which radiate out from the nipple. In a girl of 10 or 11 years the nipple begins to protrude while the aerola around it swells outward. Glandular tissue and fat beneath increase rapidly and the aerola flattens over the breast as it takes on a circular shape.

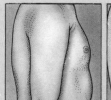 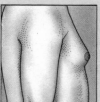 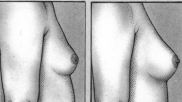 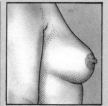

### Breast development
The exact size and shape of a woman's breasts vary from one woman to another and at different times of life when the female hormones are especially active, as during the menstrual cycle, pregnancy and lactation. They begin their development in the womb when the fetus is about 5 months old, and at birth there is a nipple with primitive milk ducts already present. Sometimes the rush of hormones surging through the mother just before delivery affects the fetus as well and the baby is born with slightly enlarged breasts. There may even be a discharge of colostrum in the first few days after birth but this and the swelling quickly subsides. In the latter part of adolescence after the menstrual cycle is established, a young girl's body begins to develop the female shape and the breasts show the first signs of sexual development. The greater part of the breast is made up of glandular tissue supported in fat. The breast has no surrounding wall and merges with the fat underneath the skin. The breasts contain no muscle at all and therefore can not be influenced in size or shape by any amount of exercise.

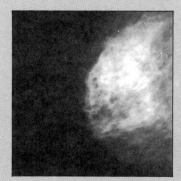

### Symptoms
Lumps or swelling in the breasts should be examined by your doctor. Most growths are benign cysts or tumours. A malignant lump may or may not be painful and the skin over it may be dimpled or creased. Sometimes there is a dark-colored discharge from the nipple.

See also the following diagnostic charts: **124** Breast problems **146** Breast feeding problems.

### Mammography
This is a painless procedure which produces an X-ray picture of the internal structures. Obvious variations in consistency and increased density, may be an indication of cancerous conditions. To have a mammogram you must place your breasts in various positions under a cone-shaped device.

# The female reproductive system

The organs of the reproductive system in women are the ovaries (two), each connected to the womb (uterus) by a fallopian tube, and the vagina, the passage that leads from the womb to the external genitalia. Every month one of the ovaries releases an egg into the fallopian tube which if fertilized, embeds itself in the womb causing pregnancy. If the egg is not fertilized, it is shed along with the lining of the womb during menstruation.

### The external organs
The genitals vary in size and shape from one woman to the next. They consist of the mons pubis, the fatty area of tissue and skin covered by pubic hair; the labia majora, two large lips of skin encircling the vaginal opening; the labia minora, two small lips of skin surrounding the clitoris and the clitoris which is exactly analgous to the male penis and is the most erotically sensitive part of the genitalia, doubling in size and becoming erect during sexual activity. This group of structures are known as the vulva.

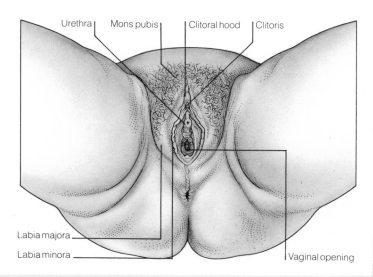

Urethra | Mons pubis | Clitoral hood | Clitoris
Labia majora
Labia minora
Vaginal opening

## The internal organs

The internal reproductive organs in a woman are encased in the bones of the pelvic girdle. They include two ovaries and fallopian tubes, the uterus, cervix and vagina. The uterus lies in the centre of the pelvis with the bladder in front and the rectum behind and is well supported in a double fold of elastic ligament.

**The vagina** is a tube about 8 centimetres long which not only serves as passage for the male penis but is the canal through which a baby is delivered into the world. In order to accommodate both of these functions the vagina is capable of great variation in size and flexibility. It contains bundles of muscles rich in blood supply which cause it to become swollen during sexual arousal.

**The cervix** is a narrow thick-walled structure, located in the lower front end of the uterus and leading to the top of the vagina. The inner part of the cervix is the opening between the uterus and the vagina.

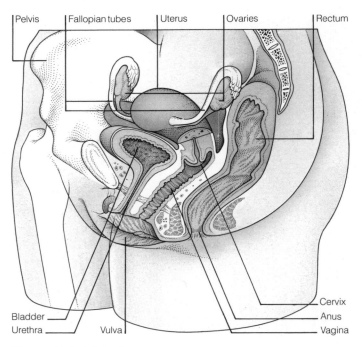

Pelvis | Fallopian tubes | Uterus | Ovaries | Rectum

Bladder | Urethra | Vulva | Cervix | Anus | Vagina

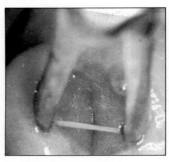

The opening of the cervix into the vagina is called the os and it is the appearance of this part of the cervix that is noted during routine pelvic examinations. During this procedure the physician surveys the cervix and vaginal walls for any abnormalities. A few cells are rubbed off the cervix and sent to a laboratory where they are examined for signs of cancer of the cervix or conditions that might lead to cancer. This is called a Pap smear or cervical smear test and should be done at least once every three years.

**The uterus** is a hollow, pear-shaped organ which lies at the front of the lower abdomen, behind the urinary bladder. It is composed of powerful muscles, the strongest in the human body, which can accomodate a fully-formed fetus, push it down the birth canal, and then shrink back to original size within six weeks. The walls of the uterus are made of solid muscle tissue, and surround the cavity called the endometrium which forms the site for implantation of the fertilized egg. If the egg is not fertilized the lining which had built up within the endometrium is shed during menstruation.

**The fallopian** tube is the site where the sperm meets the mature egg shortly after ovulation. The tube itself is about 10 centimetres in length and is funnel-shaped ending in a fringe of finger-like projections. The inner lining of the fallopian tube is covered by cells which set up a current that transport the ripe egg from the ovaries along the tube and into the uterine cavity.

**The ovaries** are endocrine glands which are situated in the abdomen below the naval. They produce eggs ready for fertilization and secrete the hormones estrogen and progesterone, which determine female characteristics and the pattern of menstruation. At birth, the ovaries contain all the eggs (approximately 400,000) a woman will ever have. Each ovary contains thousands of eggs and during a woman's fertile years, one egg ripens and is released into the fallopian tube each month. This is the process of ovulation. If the egg released by the ovary is fertilized, pregnancy results.

**Cross section of an ovary**

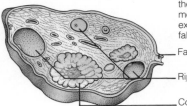

The egg ripens within a follicle inside the ovary. Halfway through the menstrual cycle the follicle ruptures, expelling the mature egg into the fallopian tube.

— Fallopian tube

— Ripening follicles

— Corpus luteum

## The menstrual cycle

The menstrual cycle usually starts in a young girl between the ages of 11 to 14 years. The first period is called the menarche and those following may be irregular for the first year or two as the process of ovulation becomes regularized. The entire cycle usually lasts about 28 days but this fluctuates from one woman to the next. Each stage in the menstrual cycle is regulated by a combination of hormones and chemicals produced in the hypothalamus of the brain, the pituitary gland and the ovaries. During the days prior to ovulation, the hormones act to thicken the lining of the uterus, which becomes engorged with blood. If a fertilized egg reaches the uterus, the lining will be ready for implantation. If the egg is not fertilized, the thickened lining is not required and is discharged about 14 days after the start of ovulation. After the age of about 45 periods become irregular and eventually cease altogether.

The month-long process of egg-ripening, egg release (ovulation) and shedding of the lining of the uterus is called the menstrual cycle.

During the few days prior to ovulation the lining of the uterus is thickening up and becoming engorged with blood. This is to prepare the womb for implantation.

Each month one of the two ovaries releases an egg. The egg travels down the fallopian tube to the uterus, or womb. This part of the cycle takes 5 days.

A woman is fertile and can become pregnant anytime within a day or two before or after ovulation occurs.

## Symptoms

The most common problems of the reproductive system are difficulties with menstrual periods, most often premenstrual tension and pain, irregular and heavy bleeding, or a change in the pattern of menstruation. Any change in the colour or consistency of vaginal discharge is often a symptom of an infection in the vagina, uterus or fallopian tubes. Additional problems can occur after

the menopause of the vaginal walls become dry and sore.

See also the following diagnostic charts: **125** Absent periods **126** Heavy periods **127** Painful periods **128** Irregular vaginal bleeding **129** Abnormal vaginal discharge **130** Genital irritation **134** Painful intercourse **137** Failure to conceive

# Pregnancy

Pregnancy and childbirth involve unique changes in the physical and emotional chemistry of every woman. An understanding of how and why these changes occur and which symptoms are normal or abnormal can help allay any anxiety over what is happening to the body. If a woman is generally healthy, she should have little difficulty during pregnancy, although most women have some symptoms (such as nausea). If you think you might be pregnant, see your physician for confirmation and arrange to have regular, prenatal checkups.

## Your changing body

Several changes take place in the body during pregnancy. The most obvious is the absence of periods. Early in pregnancy this may be accompanied by nausea or vomiting ("morning sickness").

**The breasts** will probably become enlarged and a tingling sensation may be noticed in the nipples. The skin around the nipples may darken and the small lubricating glands in this area may become more prominent, creating small bumps.

**The womb** (uterus) is normally about the size and shape of a pear. In early pregnancy, as the uterus begins to grow, it presses on the bladder. This makes the bladder want to expel urine, even in small amounts, so a pregnant woman feels the need to pass urine more frequently than usual. For the first three months of pregnancy, the size of the uterus does not change very much, but the enlargement becomes more noticeable in the fourth month. By the end of the fifth month, when the fetus is about eight inches long, the increase in size becomes more rapid. By the end of the pregnancy, the total weight of the uterus, fetus and amniotic fluid is about 16 pounds.

**The skin** also changes during pregnancy. The skin around the nipples may darken and so may the skin around the upper part of the cheeks and forehead. Some women notice a dark line extending from the naval down to the pubic hair. This colouring should fade, but may not disappear altogether affter delivery. "Stretch marks", tiny scars under the skin, may appear on the stomach, breasts, buttocks and thighs, but they usually fade and in time, become barely visible.

**The teeth** are affected by the high levels of progesterone produced during pregnancy which cause the gums to become spongy and soft, therefore inviting infection. Meticulous oral hygiene is essential during these months. A high-calcium diet low in sugar will counteract problems.

**The joints** become more pliant in pregnancy because the ligaments which bind them soften in response to hormonal action. This means that joints are more likely to stretch and ache, especially in the lower back, legs and feet. Exercise, attention to good posture and well-fitting supportive shoes, can relieve much of the discomfort.

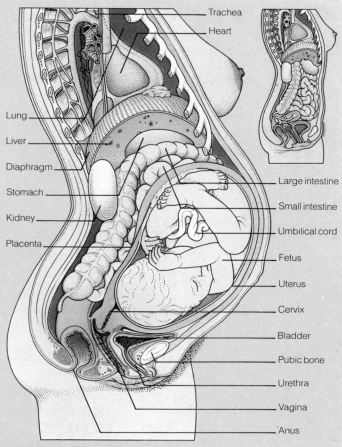

Labels: Trachea, Heart, Lung, Liver, Diaphragm, Stomach, Kidney, Placenta, Large intestine, Small intestine, Umbilical cord, Fetus, Uterus, Cervix, Bladder, Pubic bone, Urethra, Vagina, Anus

## The vital functions

During pregnancy the heart has to work harder to circulate blood through the uterus and placenta. The circulation to the breasts, kidneys, skin and even gums also increases in quantity. During pregnancy the volume of blood increases by about 2½ pints and by the end of the second trimester the heart is working 40% harder to push the extra fluids around the body.

The lungs must also work harder during pregnancy to keep the increased blood supply well-stocked with oxygen. Pressure on the lungs by the enlarging uterus may cause feelings of breathlessness, which is aggrevated by the physical effort of carrying around the extra weight of the fetus, uterus, and amniotic fluid. Breathing exercises may bring relief.

In early pregnancy the enlarging uterus may irritate the bladder and it may need emptying more often. In later pregnancy the pressure of the growing baby upon the bladder causes a renewed frequency of urination. In addition, the kidneys are cleaning and filtering 50 per cent more blood than before, resulting in greater amounts of urine for excretion.

## After childbirth

Hormonal changes affecting the muscles, which were essential for childbirth, may lead to a new mother tiring easily. For this reason, it is essential to get sufficient rest in the days and weeks following. It is quite common to feel weepy and depressed around the third or fourth day after childbirth when the milk "comes in". This is strictly owing to the action of hormones which stimulate the breasts to produce milk, causing emotional fluctuations as well. If depression worsens or persists more than two weeks consult your doctor.

## Symptoms

During pregnancy sudden high levels of hormones may cause nausea and vomiting as well as softening of the ligaments which can contribute to backache. If a pregnant woman develops an unexplained rash with fever, German measles (rubella) is a possibility. Because the virus may damage the developing fetus, consult your doctor immediately (see chart 79 Rash with fever).

See also the following diagnostic charts: **55** Tiredness **138** Nausea and vomiting in pregnancy **139** Skin changes in pregnancy **140** Back pain in pregnancy **141** Heartburn in pregnancy **142** Vaginal bleeding in pregnancy **143** Shortness of breath in pregnancy **144** Ankle swelling in pregnancy **145** Am I in labour? **146** Breast-feeding problems **147** Depression after childbirth.

# Keeping your child healthy

Children are surprisingly resilient beings. They are usually able to become and remain healthy and strong providing you give them a basic framework of care as well as encouragement to pursue healthy activities. This framework should consist of the following: a good diet, opportunity for plenty of exercise, maintenance of reasonable safety precautions both in and outside the home, and regular access to medical facilities. If you follow the advice on this page, you will not necessarily be ensuring avoidance of disease or other health problems, but you will be providing a foundation for good health that should help your child to recover quickly from any temporary illness. Good habits of care may also establish a pattern of healthy living that will continue when the child grows up.

## Eating a healthy diet

A child who has a healthy diet containing sufficient quantities of essential nutrients (see *The components of a healthy diet,* p.119) is likely to grow and develop at the expected rate and will be less susceptible to, and more likely to recover from, many of the minor complaints of childhood. Furthermore, the good eating habits established in childhood are likely to be continued in adulthood.

Your main concern should be to provide your child with all the nutrients the body needs for healthy growth and day-to-day functioning. You can start by breast-feeding (see *Breast- and bottle-feeding,* p.61). As your child grows older you can make sure that he or she has a balanced diet of a variety of nutritious foods including meat, fish, dairy produce, wholemeal grain products (including bread), fresh fruit and vegetables and a minimum of processed foods. In particular, it is wise to limit your child's consumption of sugary foods such as cakes, biscuits and confectionery, all of which can lead to obesity and tooth decay.

### A balanced day's eating

**Breakfast**
Wholegrain cereal with milk and a small amount of sugar (high fibre and vitamins); glass of natural orange juice (high vitamins); wholemeal toast spread with low fat margarine, with scrambled egg (high protein, high carbohydrate and fibre). Alternatively, serve toast with marmalade (medium protein, high carbohydrate, fibre).

**Lunch**
Peanut butter sandwiches made out of wholegrain bread (high fibre, medium carbohydrate and protein); tomato (high fibre and vitamins); wholemeal fruit cake (high fibre, high carbohydrate); wholemeal biscuits (high carbohydrate, fibre); milk (high protein and vitamins).

**Dinner**
Potato baked in its jacket with grated cheese (high protein, high carbohydrate, medium fibre and vitamins); fish fingers (high protein, medium carbohydrate); broccoli (high fibre and vitamins); bananas and custard (medium carbohydrate, fat and vitamins); fresh fruit (high fibre and vitamins); natural fruit juice (high vitamins).

**Between meal snacks**
Fresh fruit and raw vegetables (high fibre and vitamins); dried fruit (high fibre, carbohydrate and vitamins); nuts (high protein, high carbohydrate and vitamins).

## Getting enough exercise

Exercise is important for children. It helps them to gain weight and to develop muscle power and a healthy heart and lungs. Exercise can be encouraged from an early age: babies should be in a playpen or free on the floor as often as possible. A young child can be encouraged to walk and perhaps push the push-chair some of the way as an outing. Older children should be encouraged to participate in strenuous physical activities with other children of the same age in the form of sport and informal play.

## Preventive medical care

Your doctor and community health service have a vital role to play in your child's health. Regular visits to the doctor and child health clinic will give you the opportunity to discuss your child's progress and to receive advice on any matters of concern. These health checks will ensure that minor problems are noticed before they become more serious.

The most important element in preventive medical care for your child is immunization against a range of infectious diseases (see *Immunization,* p. 97). Immunization needs to be part of your regular health care programme.

## Preventing accidents

Accidents are a common cause of death in children and account for a high proportion of emergency admissions to hospital. The majority of accidents can be avoided by taking precautions to ensure that your home is safe and by making an effort to reduce the risk of accidents outside the home. The following checklist gives guidance on the basic precautions you should take.

- Keep all medicines and chemicals out of reach.
- Put guards on all fires and use a hob guard on your cooker.
- Put safety socket covers on power points.
- Fit a safety gate to the bottom and top of the stairs.
- Make sure that your child cannot interfere with electrical appliances.
- Put transfers on any clear glass to make it more obvious.
- Cover any hot radiators with towels.
- Keep garden tools locked away.
- Teach your child the safety code for crossing the road.
- Check your child's bicycle to ensure that brakes, tyres and lights are in good condition.
- Teach your child to swim.
- Provide adequate safety equipment for all sporting activities.

# Safeguarding your health

Your health and your susceptibility to disease are determined partly by your lifestyle and partly by inheritance. Whether or not you come from a long-lived, healthy family, you can improve your chances of keeping fit and free from disease by reducing the avoidable risk factors in your lifestyle – by improving your diet, reducing your alcohol intake, giving up smoking and taking more exercise. You can improve your physical well-being at any age by adopting a healthier lifestyle following the guidelines described below.

### Exercise

To be fit, a person must exercise regularly. This helps the body in three ways: maintains mobility, maintains body strength, and conditions the heart and lungs. Physical activity makes you breathe more deeply to get oxygen into your lungs, and your heart beats faster to pump blood to the muscles. There are many health benefits to be gained from exercise (see *The benefits of exercise,* p.37), and the more activities you undertake which involve a high degree of physical exertion to make you breathless and sweaty, the greater the degree of benefit. Exercise will also help you to lose weight if combined with a sensible weight-reducing diet (see *How to lose weight,* p.151). It will boost the amount of energy (calories) you burn up and will tone up slack muscles. Exercise also helps to regulate your appetite.

### Weight

Being overweight according to the chart on p.302-303 is dangerous for your health. It increases the risk of serious disorders such as diabetes and high blood pressure-related conditions (for example, heart disease and strokes), and exaggerates the symptoms of many other disorders. Most people can achieve and maintain an ideal weight if they follow a sensible weight-reducing diet (see *How to lose weight,* p.151). It is far easier to prevent yourself becoming overweight by eating a healthy, balanced diet than to lose weight, and adjusting the quality and quantity of your intake accordingly, can prevent weight gain. (see *Age and increasing weight,* p.150).

## Smoking and alcohol

If you smoke, give it up. Smoking is beyond doubt the main cause of many serious illnesses (see *The dangers of smoking,* p.196), including lung cancer and diseases of the heart and circulation. If you smoke regularly, you are probably losing around 5 minutes of life expectation for each cigarette smoked. By giving up smoking, your chances of suffering from tobacco-related diseases lessen with each successive year. The smoking habit often accompanies the use of alcohol, a drug which can damage your health if consumed in large quantities. You may be putting your health at serious risk if you regularly exceed the safe limits outlined in *The effects of alcohol,* p.146, and/or if drinking ever becomes a necessity. For example, you may risk obesity and damage to the liver (cirrhosis). However, if you drink alcohol in moderation it is unlikely that your health will suffer. The action of alcohol on the body and mind depends on the concentration of alcohol in the blood, and so varies from person to person according to their individual weight. Men, as they tend to be heavier than women, usually feel the effects of the same amount of alcohol slightly later. Factors such as the type of alcohol you drink and the speed at which you drink also affect the action of alcohol. Beer, for example, has a lower alcohol content than whisky, and slowly sipping any drink reduces its effects.

## Diet

Diet plays a fundamental part in determining general health. In order to function efficiently your body needs to receive adequate amounts of each of the various nutrients in the table below. However the main risk of eating a typical western diet is overnutrition – eating too many denatured refined foods high in "empty calories". The abuse of simple carbohydrates in the form of white flour foodstuffs and simple sugars has been linked with obesity and a host of diseases related to obesity. The intake of excessive amounts of fats and sugars has been related to increased blood pressure and the subsequent risk of stroke, as well as to heart disease. People whose diets are extremely high in fats and sugars may have elevated levels of blood cholesterol and triglyceride, the two blood fats which have been linked with obstructed blood flow and hardening of the arteries leading to the heart.

| Proteins | Carbohydrates |
|---|---|
|  |  |
| Proteins are needed for growth, repair and replacement of body tissues. Proteins are found in pulses (beans, lentils, peas) and cereals as well as in meat, fish, and in dairy products.<br><br>**Diet advice:** Try to avoid eating too much beef, lamb, and pork, which have high fat contents. Instead eat fish, poultry, and vegetable protein sources such as nuts and grains. | Carbohydrates are a major source of energy but eaten in excess they are stored in the body as fat. They are available as natural sugars and starches present in cereals, grains and root vegetables.<br><br>**Diet advice:** Eat unrefined products such as wholemeal bread and brown rice, which also contain fibre and other nutrients, and green and yellow vegetables and potatoes. Avoid eating white bread and refined cereals which have few nutrients. |

| Fats | Fibre |
|---|---|
|  |  |
| Fats are a concentrated source of energy that provide more calories than any other food. Saturated fats are found mainly in animal products, dairy products and eggs. Monounsaturated fats are most commonly found in poultry, margarine and olive oil. Polyunsaturated fats are found in fish, corn oil and safflower oil.<br><br>**Diet advice:** Intake of saturated fats should be kept to a minimum. | Fibre is the indigestible residue of plant products that passes through the digestive system.<br><br>**Diet advice:** While fibre contains no energy value or nutrients it is important for a healthy bowel action, adding bulk to the faeces. |

| Minerals | Vitamins |
|---|---|
| Minerals and certain salts are needed in minimum quantities. These include iron, potassium, calcium and sodium (found in salt).<br><br>**Diet advice:** Too much salt in the diet may be harmful. | Vitamins are complex chemical compounds needed by the body in tiny quantities to regulate metabolism and to help with the conversion of carbohydrates and fats into energy.<br><br>**Diet advice:** They may be sometimes destroyed by lengthy cooking, so eat uncooked vegetables and fruit regularly. |

# Fitness and exercise

Regular exercise brings sound benefits to health. You will sleep better, wake more refreshed, feel more alert and will be able to concentrate much longer. Exercising regularly will help you control your weight (see Exercise and weight loss, p.149) and help you to build up your stamina – that is your staying power and endurance – which will in turn improve your physical and mental capacity for everyday activities. Recent research has shown that regular strenuous physical activity can help prevent and alleviate minor depression. And there is evidence that regular (but not excessive) exercise can help to delay the process of bone thinning (osteoporosis) a disorder common in post-menopausal women (see p.252).

**The benefits of exercise**
Regular exercise has also been shown to help prevent coronry disease.

**Heart, lungs and arteries:** Regular, vigorous activity will increase the strength and resiliency of the heart and lungs helping them to become more efficient and less prone to disease. Exercise may also decrease blood pressure, thereby reducing the risk of hardening of the arteries. At the same time exercise may widen the arteries and make complete blockage, by a clot, for instance, far less likely. Recent research has linked vigorous activity with an increase in the chemical factors in the blood that actually interfere with the rate of fat deposition in the arteries.

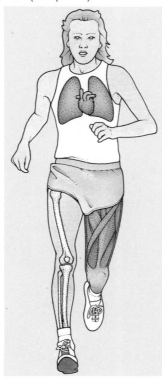

**Joints** that are regularly exercised will maintain their strength and flexibility. Under-use contributes to stiffening and weakness of the ligaments that support and protect the joints. Your muscles will also become weak and flabby with lack of use – as you will soon discover if you give up on your regular activities.

**Muscles:** Exercise increases muscle tone thereby conditioning the entire body. Because the muscles that move the legs are among the largest in the body, activities that use the legs, such as swimming, jogging or bicycling, are excellent ways to place healthy demands on the heart and lungs.

## Your exercise programme

Three 20-minute sessions a week at regular intervals should be sufficient to put you on the path to fitness and well-being. Choose a level of activity intense enough to make you sweaty, breathless, and aware of your heart beating, although you should never exert yourself to the point where you feel dizzy or faint. It is important to find an activity that you enjoy, or you may lack the motivation to continue your exercise program over a period of time.

**Sensible precautions**
If you are thinking of starting a new sport or other form of exercise training, and if you are not accustomed to regular exercise, you should remember the following points:

■ Do not be over ambitious at first in the goals you set for yourself; it is safer to try to increase your level of fitness gradually.
■ Make sure that your clothing and equipment is suitable (see opposite).
■ Always do some warm-up exercises (see right) before each session to reduce the likelihood of sprains and strains.
■ If any exercise or movement becomes painful or causes other forms of discomfort, stop at once. Pain is a sign of damage. (See Common injuries, opposite.)

## Warning

It is probably a good idea to consult your doctor before taking up any sort of strenuous activity for the first time if you belong to any of the following categories:

■ If you are over 60 years of age, or if you are over 40 and have not taken regular exercise since adulthood.
■ If you are a heavy smoker (i.e. you smoke more than 20 cigarettes a day).
■ If you are overweight (see Weight chart, p.302-303).
■ If you are under a doctor's care for a long-term health problem, such as high blood pressure, heart disease, diabetes or kidney disease.
■ If you are pregnant (see opposite).

## Warming up exercises

You can reduce the risk of pulled muscles and torn ligaments by doing some gentle exercises to stretch and loosen the muscles and ligaments before you put them under strain. Repeat the exercises described here for about 15 minutes before each exercise session, and for 5 minutes afterwards. These exercises can be practised at other times to help increase all-round fitness.

**Head and neck (1)**
Slowly roll your head in a full circle, flexing your neck backwards at the back of the circle and bending it forward at the front. Try to relax the muscles in your forehead as well as the shoulder muscles while gently rotating your head.

**Shoulders and chest (2)**
Extend both arms in front of you. Lift them above your head, placing the palms together. Keeping your arms straight, lower them towards your sides, holding them at shoulder height.

**Backs of the legs (3)**
Stand upright with your feet wide apart and hands on hips. Lean forward bending at the hips and keeping your back straight. Lower your arms towards the floor in front.

**Trunk (4)**
Stand up straight with your feet about a shoulder-width apart and with your arms by your sides. Bend sideways from the waist towards the right, allowing your right hand to slide down the leg to below the knee. Straighten up and do a similar bend to the left.

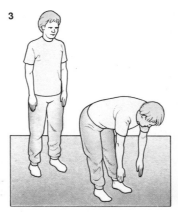

# The right equipment

Sports and other forms of exercise are important for maintaining health and general fitness (see The benefits of exercise, left), but an over ambitious program may lead to injuries and other health problems. Injuries may also be due to inadequate warming-up before exercise or failure to use the correct safety equipment or clothing. Some sports, by their very nature, carry a high risk of injury – for example boxing – where brain damage and other injuries are common. Other sports, such as football, carry a risk of accidental injury – commonly, pulled muscles and broken noses. Make sure that you are aware of the risks of any exercise activity you undertake, so that you can balance these against the likely health benefits, and so that you can take reasonable precautions to prevent injury.

## Safety equipment

In some sports you can reduce the risk of injury by the use of special safety equipment – for example, eyeguards for squash players, shin pads for footballers, and helmets for cyclists. Make sure that any equipment you buy is of good quality and meets your individual requirements. If you are unsure what equipment is necessary, seek advice from your sports club or from the appropriate sporting organization.

## Clothing

For most exercise activities, choose clothes that are comfortable and do not restrict movement. Natural fibres such as cotton are best for shirts, shorts and socks because they allow air to circulate freely, reducing the likelihood of chafing and blisters. It is a good idea, especially in cold weather, to start off wearing several layers that can be removed as you warm up. Most women will find they are more comfortable wearing a sport bra for extra support. When specialized protective clothing is required for sports such as skiing, seek expert advice before you buy. Be sure to wash your sports gear regularly to prevent the occurrence of fungal infection.

## Shoes

Wearing suitable shoes during exercise is essential if you are to avoid damage to the feet, legs and knees. Make sure that your sports shoes fit properly, allowing room for your feet to expand slightly during exercise. Your running shoes should be light-weight and have well-cushioned flexible soles with arch supports. You should have half an inch of clearance between your toes and the front of your shoe so that your toes move freely.

# Exercise and pregnancy

If you are used to taking regular exercise, and providing you do not overtire yourself, there is no reason why you should not continue to participate in most sports until well into pregnancy, when your increasing size may make certain movements difficult or uncomfortable. However, activities that carry a risk of injury, such as horse-riding, skiing or mountaineering may not be advisable. It is also unwise to take up a strenuous physical activity for the first time during pregnancy. But gentle forms of exercise will increase your feeling of well-being and help to relieve the minor aches and pains of pregnancy. Walking is a perfect way to exercise as is cycling. Swimming is excellent and is one exercise that can safely be continued until the ninth month. With any form of exercise during pregnancy remember to take it gently and to stop as soon as you feel tired or breathless. Some doctors feel that if a woman has a history of miscarriage or there are any complications she should not undertake any exercise in the first three months.

# Sports injuries

## Minor injuries

Chafing (soreness that can result from friction between clothes, equipment and skin) may be prevented by rubbing petroleum jelly into susceptible areas, or by wearing protective bandages. Blisters on the feet are usually the result of poorly-fitting shoes. Apply an adhesive plaster to protect against further rubbing.

## Strains, sprains, and pulled muscles and ligaments

These injuries occur when muscles and joints are stretched beyond their normal limits of movement, resulting in damage to muscle and ligament fibres. Such injuries are most common in those just starting exercise after a long period of inactivity and those who have not undertaken adequate warming-up exercises. Serious injuries of this type can be very painful and require first aid and professional medical attention (see *First aid for sprains and strains, children*, p.131; *adults*, p.231). Never attempt to continue exercise after such an injury, as you may do further damage. Aching in the muscles the day after unaccustomed exercise is usual and best treated by keeping mobile. In such cases, resting the affected part for a few days and gradually returning to a vigorous exercise program is advisable. Some people find that a warm bath after exercise helps to prevent such pain from developing.

## Shin splints

Shin splints are pains along the shin bone that may occur during or after exercise. Shin splints may be the result of a stress fracture, swelling of the muscles, or inflammation of the lining of the bone. If you have pain apply an ice bag, elevate your leg and rest it as much as possible. Wrapping the leg with an elastic bandage may also help.

## Stress fractures

Bones that are constantly under stress may develop hairline cracks known as stress fractures. Pain may only be slight, so there is a danger that the injury may go unnoticed and that further exercise may increase the damage. If you suspect a stress fracture, consult your doctor, who will arrange for you to be X-rayed (see *Bone X-rays*, p.225). Rest and bandaging of the affected part is the usual treatment.

## Osteoarthritis

The main long-term health problem sometimes associated with regular vigorous exercise is osteoarthritis. This often develops in later life as a result of wear and tear on joints, even in those who do not exercise excessively, but it is more likely to occur at a younger age in professional athletes. For most people the health benefits of regular exercise outweigh the risk of premature osteoarthritis, and this risk can be reduced by choosing a sport that does not overwork one set of joints – for example, swimming. If you suffer persistent joint pain following exercise, consult your doctor.

# After an injury

Muscles and their tendons can be strained or torn by any sudden violent contraction or awkward movement. Also referred to as a "pulled muscle" this is a common sports injury. If you have suffered any sort of injury after exercising it is wise to consult a doctor who may decide that an X-ray is necessary. Following treatment, you should be careful not to strain the injured part by an over-rapid return to your former exercise routine. It may be helpful to follow a program of special exercise to help restore strength to the injured part gradually. If pain or swelling recurs or persists, consult your doctor.

# How to use the charts

The 147 diagnostic charts in this book have been compiled to help you find probable reasons for your symptoms. Each chart shows in detail a single symptom – for instance, vomiting, headache or a rash – and explores the possible causes of the symptom by means of a logically organized sequence of questions, each answerable by a simple YES or NO. Your responses will lead you toward a clearly worded end point, which suggests what may be wrong and offers advice on whether your disorder requires professional attention. To see how the charts work, examine the accompanying sample chart and study the explanatory notes. In particular, make sure you understand the exact meanings of the systematized action codes that indicate the relative urgency of the need to consult a doctor (see *What the instructions mean,* opposite).

Note that every chart is numbered and bears a label defining or describing the key symptom. An introductory paragraph provides further description and explanation of the purpose of the chart. Read this paragraph carefully to make sure you have chosen the most appropriate pathway toward an analysis of your problem; then proceed as indicated in the chart itself. Always begin with the first question and follow through to the end point that fits your special situation. In many cases, extensive boxed information accompanying the chart will enhance your understanding of specific diagnoses as well as likely treatment for underlying disorders. Always read through such information texts (except, of course, in emergencies, when swift action is essential).

It is important to consult the *correct* chart at the *correct* time. For instructions on how to recognize and define your symptom and how to choose the precise chart you need, turn to p. 40.

**Chart group.**
The charts are grouped in sections according to the type of problem they cover.

**Chart number**
Each chart has a number so that it can be easily found.

**Chart cross-reference**
At the end of a pathway you may be directed to another chart.

Go to chart

**00** Chart title

**Chart title**
A short, descriptive term for the symptom heads each chart.

**Definition**
Each symptom is defined in simple, non-technical terms and an indication of when a symptom is severe enough to cause concern is given.

**The questions**
These are structured so that you follow either a YES or a NO pathway from each question. Follow the series of questions, answering as appropriate in your case. In almost all cases you will then arrive at a possible reason for your symptoms.

**The diagnosis**
Each series of questions usually leads to a possible diagnosis and the treatment you are likely to need. The diagnoses take various forms according to the potential seriousness of a complaint. For example, it takes the form of a warning in cases where you may need urgent medical attention (see *What the instructions mean,* opposite). You may be referred to other sections of the book for further information.

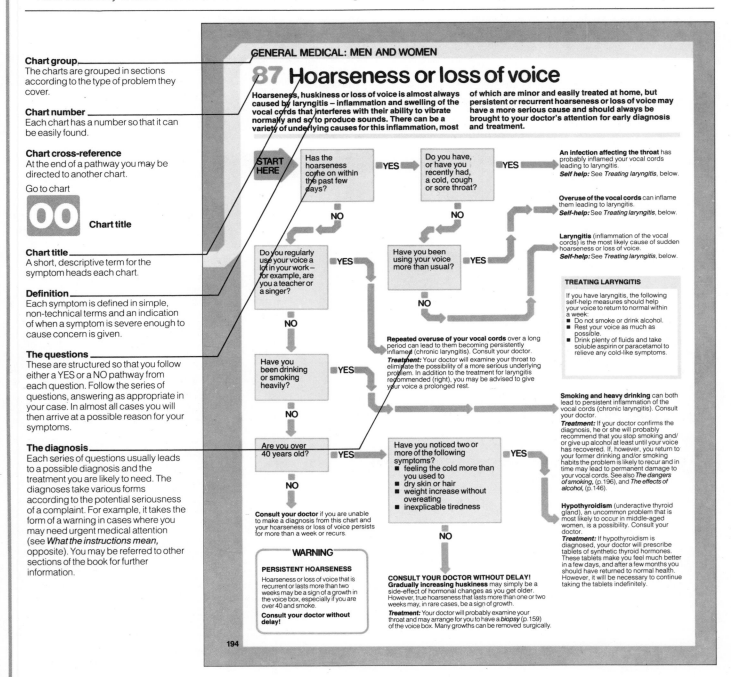

**GENERAL MEDICAL: MEN AND WOMEN**

## 87 Hoarseness or loss of voice

Hoarseness, huskiness or loss of voice is almost always caused by laryngitis – inflammation and swelling of the vocal cords that interferes with their ability to vibrate normally and so to produce sounds. There can be a variety of underlying causes for this inflammation, most of which are minor and easily treated at home, but persistent or recurrent hoarseness or loss of voice may have a more serious cause and should always be brought to your doctor's attention for early diagnosis and treatment.

START HERE

Has the hoarseness come on within the past few days? — YES → Do you have, or have you recently had, a cold, cough or sore throat? — YES → **An infection affecting the throat** has probably inflamed your vocal cords leading to laryngitis. *Self help:* See *Treating laryngitis,* below.

NO

NO

Do you regularly use your voice a lot in your work – for example, are you a teacher or a singer? — YES

Have you been using your voice more than usual? — YES → **Overuse of the vocal cords** can inflame them leading to laryngitis. *Self-help:* See *Treating laryngitis,* below.

**Laryngitis** (inflammation of the vocal cords) is the most likely cause of sudden hoarseness or loss of voice. *Self-help:* See *Treating laryngitis,* below.

NO

NO

Have you been drinking or smoking heavily? — YES

**Repeated overuse of your vocal cords** over a long period can lead to them becoming persistently inflamed (chronic laryngitis). Consult your doctor. *Treatment:* Your doctor will examine your throat to eliminate the possibility of a more serious underlying problem. In addition to the treatment for laryngitis recommended (right), you may be advised to give your voice a prolonged rest.

### TREATING LARYNGITIS

If you have laryngitis, the following self-help measures should help your voice to return to normal within a week:
■ Do not smoke or drink alcohol.
■ Rest your voice as much as possible.
■ Drink plenty of fluids and take soluble aspirin or paracetamol to relieve any cold-like symptoms.

NO

Are you over 40 years old? — YES

Have you noticed two or more of the following symptoms?
■ feeling the cold more than you used to
■ dry skin or hair
■ weight increase without overeating
■ inexplicable tiredness

— YES

**Smoking and heavy drinking** can both lead to persistent inflammation of the vocal cords (chronic laryngitis). Consult your doctor. *Treatment:* If your doctor confirms the diagnosis, he or she will probably recommend that you stop smoking and/or give up alcohol at least until your voice has recovered. If, however, you return to your former drinking and/or smoking habits the problem is likely to recur and in time may lead to permanent damage to your vocal cords. See also *The dangers of smoking,* (p.196), and *The effects of alcohol,* (p.146).

NO

**Consult your doctor** if you are unable to make a diagnosis from this chart and your hoarseness or loss of voice persists for more than a week or recurs.

### WARNING

**PERSISTENT HOARSENESS**

Hoarseness or loss of voice that is recurrent or lasts more than two weeks may be a sign of a growth in the voice box, especially if you are over 40 and smoke.

**Consult your doctor without delay!**

NO

**Hypothyroidism** (underactive thyroid gland), an uncommon problem that is most likely to occur in middle-aged women, is a possibility. Consult your doctor. *Treatment:* If hypothyroidism is diagnosed, your doctor will prescribe tablets of synthetic thyroid hormones. These tablets make you feel much better in a few days, and after a few months you should have returned to normal health. However, it will be necessary to continue taking the tablets indefinitely.

**CONSULT YOUR DOCTOR WITHOUT DELAY!**
**Gradually increasing huskiness** may simply be a side-effect of hormonal changes as you get older. However, true hoarseness that lasts more than one or two weeks may, in rare cases, be a sign of growth. *Treatment:* Your doctor will probably examine your throat and may arrange for you to have a *biopsy* (p.159) of the voice box. Many growths can be removed surgically.

194

**WARNING:** Though self-treatment is recommended for many minor disorders, remember that the charts provide only *likely* diagnoses. If you have any doubt about the diagnosis or treatment of any symptom, *always consult your doctor.*

## What the instructions mean

### EMERGENCY
### GET MEDICAL HELP NOW!

The condition may threaten life or lead to permanent disability if not given immediate medical attention. Get medical help by the fastest means possible, usually by calling an ambulance. In some cases it may be better to call your own doctor or take the patient to the hospital yourself.

### CALL YOUR DOCTOR NOW!

There is a possibility of a serious condition that may warrant immediate treatment and perhaps hospital admission. Seek medical advice immediately – day or night – usually by telephoning your doctor, who will then decide on further action. If you are unable to make contact with your doctor within an hour or so, emergency action (left) may be justified.

### CONSULT YOUR DOCTOR WITHOUT DELAY!

The condition is serious and needs urgent medical assessment, but a few hours' delay in seeking treatment is unlikely to be damaging. Seek your doctor's advice within 24 hours. This will usually mean telephoning for an appointment the same day.

### Consult your doctor

A condition for which medical treatment is advisable, but for which reasonable delay is unlikely to lead to problems. Seek medical advice as soon as practical.

### Discuss with your doctor

The condition is nonurgent and specific treatment is unlikely. However, your doctor's advice may be helpful. Seek medical advice as soon as practical.

## Boxed information

On most charts there are boxes containing important additional information to expand on either a diagnosis or a form of treatment. See the information and self-help boxes below.

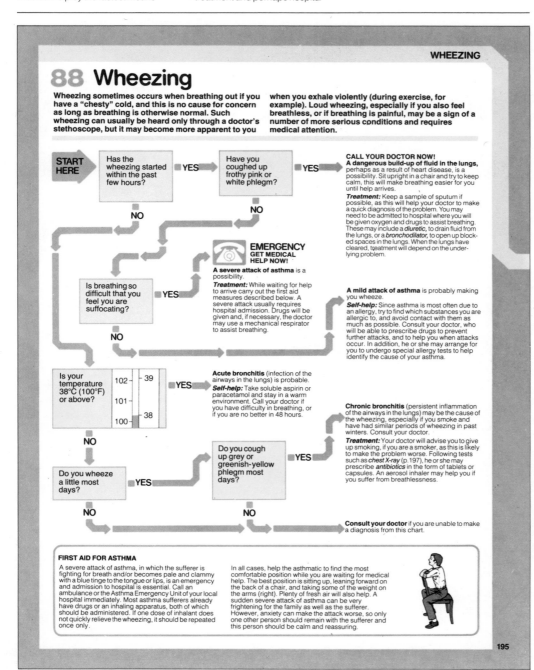

## 88 Wheezing

Wheezing sometimes occurs when breathing out if you have a "chesty" cold, and this is no cause for concern as long as breathing is otherwise normal. Such wheezing can usually be heard only through a doctor's stethoscope, but it may become more apparent to you when you exhale violently (during exercise, for example). Loud wheezing, especially if you also feel breathless, or if breathing is painful, may be a sign of a number of more serious conditions and requires medical attention.

**START HERE**

**Has the wheezing started within the past few hours?** — YES → **Have you coughed up frothy pink or white phlegm?** — YES →

**CALL YOUR DOCTOR NOW!**
**A dangerous build-up of fluid in the lungs,** perhaps as a result of heart disease, is a possibility. Sit upright in a chair and try to keep calm, this will make breathing easier for you until help arrives.
*Treatment:* Keep a sample of sputum if possible, as this will help your doctor to make a quick diagnosis of the problem. You may need to be admitted to hospital where you will be given oxygen and drugs to assist breathing. These may include a *diuretic,* to drain fluid from the lungs, or a *bronchodilator,* to open up blocked spaces in the lungs. When the lungs have cleared, treatment will depend on the underlying problem.

NO / NO

**Is breathing so difficult that you feel you are suffocating?** — YES →

**EMERGENCY**
**GET MEDICAL HELP NOW!**
**A severe attack of asthma** is a possibility.
*Treatment:* While waiting for help to arrive carry out the first aid measures described below. A severe attack usually requires hospital admission. Drugs will be given and, if necessary, the doctor may use a mechanical respirator to assist breathing.

**A mild attack of asthma** is probably making you wheeze.
*Self-help:* Since asthma is most often due to an allergy, try to find which substances you are allergic to, and avoid contact with them as much as possible. Consult your doctor, who will be able to prescribe drugs to prevent further attacks, and to help you when attacks occur. In addition, he or she may arrange for you to undergo special allergy tests to help identify the cause of your asthma.

NO

**Is your temperature 38°C (100°F) or above?** [102 / 101 / 100 — 39 / 38] — YES →

**Acute bronchitis** (infection of the airways in the lungs) is probable.
*Self-help:* Take soluble aspirin or paracetamol and stay in a warm environment. Call your doctor if you have difficulty in breathing, or if you are no better in 48 hours.

**Chronic bronchitis** (persistent inflammation of the airways in the lungs) may be the cause of the wheezing, especially if you smoke and have had similar periods of wheezing in past winters. Consult your doctor.
*Treatment:* Your doctor will advise you to give up smoking, if you are a smoker, as this is likely to make the problem worse. Following tests such as *chest X-ray* (p.197), he or she may prescribe *antibiotics* in the form of tablets or capsules. An aerosol inhaler may help you if you suffer from breathlessness.

NO

**Do you wheeze a little most days?** — YES → **Do you cough up grey or greenish-yellow phlegm most days?** — YES →

NO / NO

**Consult your doctor** if you are unable to make a diagnosis from this chart.

### FIRST AID FOR ASTHMA

A severe attack of asthma, in which the sufferer is fighting for breath and/or becomes pale and clammy with a blue tinge to the tongue or lips, is an emergency and admission to hospital is essential. Call an ambulance or the Asthma Emergency Unit of your local hospital immediately. Most asthma sufferers already have drugs or an inhaling apparatus, both of which should be administered. If one dose of inhalant does not quickly relieve the wheezing, it should be repeated once only.

In all cases, help the asthmatic to find the most comfortable position while you are waiting for medical help. The best position is sitting up, leaning forward on the back of a chair, and taking some of the weight on the arms (right). Plenty of fresh air will also help. A sudden severe attack of asthma can be very frightening for the family as well as the sufferer. However, anxiety can make the attack worse, so only one other person should remain with the sufferer and this person should be calm and reassuring.

195

### WARNING

Symptoms that indicate an immediate danger to life are highlighted in these boxes. Where appropriate, steps that can be taken while waiting for medical help to arrive are explained.

### FIRST AID

Where symptoms may require either simple first-aid or lifesaving measures, you will find boxed information on what action you should take.

### INFORMATION

These boxes expand on the possible diagnoses and likely forms of treatment for specific symptoms. For example, several of them contain an explanation of a particular medical procedure. Where applicable, self-help treatment is included.

### SELF-HELP

Where self-help measures may be effective in dealing with a symptom, advice is given on ways in which you may alleviate the problem.

# How to find the chart you need

There are three ways of finding the appropriate diagnostic chart for your symptom. You can use the *Pain-site map,* the *System-by-system* chartfinder, or the *Chart index,* depending on the nature of the symptom, where it is located, and on how easily you are able to define it in words yourself. Whichever method you choose to find your chart, you will be given the title of the appropriate chart and its number.

### 1 Pain-site map

If you are in pain, the quickest way to find the correct chart is by reference to the pain-site map for children (below), men (p. 43) and women (p. 46).

### 2 System-by-system chartfinder

If you know the body system affected but are unsure how to define your symptom, consult the system-by-system chartfinder for children (opposite), men (p. 44) and women (p. 47).

### 3 Chart index

When you have no difficulty naming your symptom, consult the chart index for children (p. 42), men (p. 45) and women (p. 48). If you are suffering from more than one symptom at the same time, concentrate on the symptom that causes you the most distress or that is most prominent.

## 1 Children's pain-site map

Consult this section to find the correct diagnostic chart for your child's symptom if he or she is suffering from pain in any part of the body. The illustrations below indicate possible areas of pain and are keyed in to the titles and numbers of the charts that deal with pain in that part of the body.

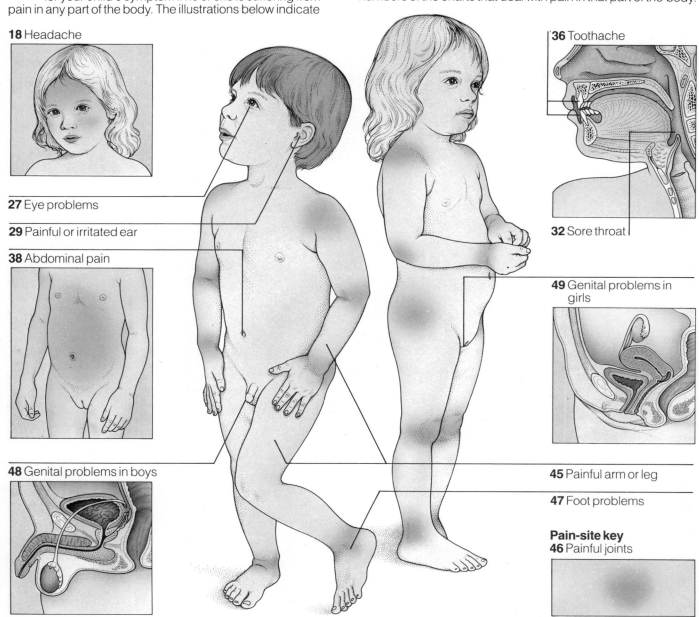

**18** Headache

**27** Eye problems

**29** Painful or irritated ear

**38** Abdominal pain

**48** Genital problems in boys

**36** Toothache

**32** Sore throat

**49** Genital problems in girls

**45** Painful arm or leg

**47** Foot problems

**Pain-site key**
**46** Painful joints

# 2 Children's system-by-system chartfinder

Consult this section if you know what part of the body or which body system your child's symptom originates in. A list of the charts that deal with each of the main body systems is given under each main heading. Select the chart that most closely seems to fit your child's symptom.

## General symptoms

**Babies under one**
1 Slow weight gain
2 Waking at night
3 Fever in babies
5 Excessive crying
6 Feeding problems

**Children of all ages**
9 Feeling generally unwell
10 Slow growth
11 Excessive weight gain
12 Sleeping problems
13 Drowsiness
14 Fever in children
15 Swollen glands

**Adolescents**
50 Delayed puberty
53 Adolescent weight problems

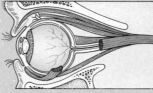

## Eyes and sight symptoms

27 Eye problems
28 Disturbed or impaired vision

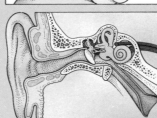

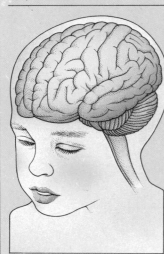

## Head, brain and psychological symptoms

**Children of all ages**
13 Drowsiness
17 Fainting, dizzy spells and fits
18 Headache
19 Clumsiness
20 Confusion
21 Speech difficulties
22 Behaviour problems
23 School difficulties

**Adolescents**
51 Adolescent behaviour problems
53 Adolescent weight problems

## Ears and hearing symptoms

29 Painful or irritated ear
30 Deafness

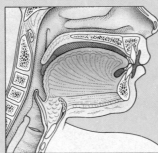

## Mouth, tongue and throat symptoms

32 Sore throat
36 Toothache

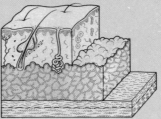

## Skin, hair and nail symptoms

**Babies under one**
4 Skin problems

**Children of all ages**
16 Itching
25 Spots and rashes
26 Rash with fever

**Adolescents**
52 Adolescent skin problems

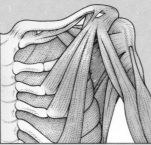

## Muscle, bone and joint symptoms

45 Painful arm or leg
46 Painful joints
47 Foot problems

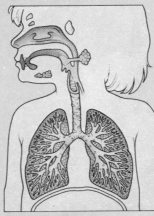

## Respiratory symptoms

31 Runny or blocked nose
32 Sore throat
33 Coughing
34 Fast breathing
35 Noisy breathing

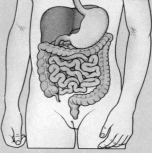

## Abdominal and digestive symptoms

**Babies under one**
7 Vomiting in babies
8 Diarrhoea in babies

**Children of all ages**
37 Vomiting in children
38 Abdominal pain
39 Loss of appetite
40 Diarrhoea in children
41 Constipation
42 Abnormal-looking faeces

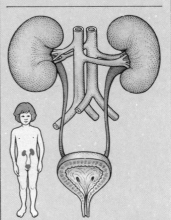

## Urinary symptoms

43 Urinary problems
44 Toilet-training problems

## Genital symptoms

48 Genital problems in boys
49 Genital problems in girls

# 3 Children's chart index

Consult this index if you think that you know the correct name for the symptom. The chart titles and their numbers are listed alphabetically together with possible, alternative names for symptoms (for example, *Raised temperature* for *Fever* or *Swellings* for *Swollen glands*). In this section you will also find the titles of information boxes dealing with symptoms that do not have a separate diagnostic chart.

## A

Abdominal pain **38**
Abnormal-looking faeces **42**
Abnormal-looking urine **43**
Acne **52**
Adolescent behaviour problems **51**
Adolescent skin problems **52**
Adolescent weight problems **53**
Aggressiveness **22**
Appetite, loss of **39, 53**
Arm, painful **45**

## B

Balance, loss of **17**
Behaviour problems, children **22, 23;** adolescents **51**
Blackheads **52;**
Blocked nose **31**
Blood in the faeces **42**
Boils **25**
Breathing, fast **34;** noisy **35**

## C

Clumsiness **19**
Confusion **20**
Constipation **41**
Convulsions **17**
Coughing **33**
Crying, excessive **5**

## D

Deafness **30**
Delayed puberty **50**
Destructiveness **22**
Diarrhoea, babies **8;** children **40**
Disobedience **22**
Disturbed vision **28**
Dizzy spells **17**
Drooping eyelid **27**
Drowsiness **13**

## E

Ear, painful or irritated **29**
Excessive crying **5**
Excessive weight gain, children **11;** adolescents **53**
Eye problems **27, 28**

## F

Faeces, abnormal-looking **42**
Fainting **17**
Fast breathing **34**
Feeding problems **6**
Feeding generally unwell **9**
Fever, babies **3;** children **14**
Fever, rash with **26**
Fits, feverish, babies **3;** children **14**
Foot problems **47**

## G

Genital problems, boys **48;** girls **49**
Glands, swollen **15**
Growth, slow **10**

## H

Hair problems **24**
Headache **18**
Hearing difficulties **30**
High temperature, babies **3;** children **14**

## I

Impaired vision **28**
Irritated ear **29**
Itching **16**

## J

Joints, painful **46**

## L

Late-rising in the morning **13**
Loss of appetite **39**
Loss of consciousness **17**
Leg, painful **45**
Lumps **15**

## N

Nail problems **24**
Nose, runny or blocked **31**
Noisy breathing **35**

## O

Overweight, children **11;** adolescent **53**

## P

Painful arm **45**
Painful ear **29**
Painful joints **46**
Painful leg **45**
Puberty, delayed **50**

## R

Raised temperature, babies **3;** children **14**
Rashes **25, 26**
Rash with fever **26**
Regurgitation **7**
Run down, feeling **9, 13**
Runny nose **31**

## S

Scalp problems **24**
School difficulties **23**
Seizures **17**
Sickness, babies **7;** children **37**
Sight, disturbed or impaired **28**
Skin problems, babies **4;** adolescents **52**

## L

Sleeping problems, babies **2;** children **12**
Slow growth **10**
Slow weight gain, babies **1;** adolescents **53**
Sore throat **32**
Speech difficulties **21**
Spots **25**
Squint **27, 28**
Stomach ache **38**
Swellings **15**
Swollen glands **15**

## T

Temperature, high babies **3;** children **14**
Throat, sore **32**
Tiredness **13**
Toilet-training problems **44**
Toothache **36**

## U

Urinary problems **43, 44**

## V

Violence **22**
Vision, disturbed or impaired **28**
Vomiting, babies **7;** children **37**

## W

Waking at night, babies **2;** children **12**
Warts **25**
Weight gain, excessive, children **11;** adolescents **53**
Weight loss, babies **1;** adolescents **53**
Weight gain, slow **1**
Wind, babies **5;** children **38**
Withdrawal **22**

# 1 Men's pain-site map

Pain in any form, whether mild or severe is the body's way of telling you that something is wrong. Pain may be 'referred', that is originating in one part of the body and felt in another, or localized at the site of an injury. In any case, pain that persists should never be ignored or masked through the indiscriminate use of pain-killing drugs. Consult this section to find the correct diagnostic chart for your symptom if you are suffering from pain in any part of your body. The illustrations below indicate possible areas of pain and are keyed in to the titles and numbers of the charts that deal with pain in that part of the body.

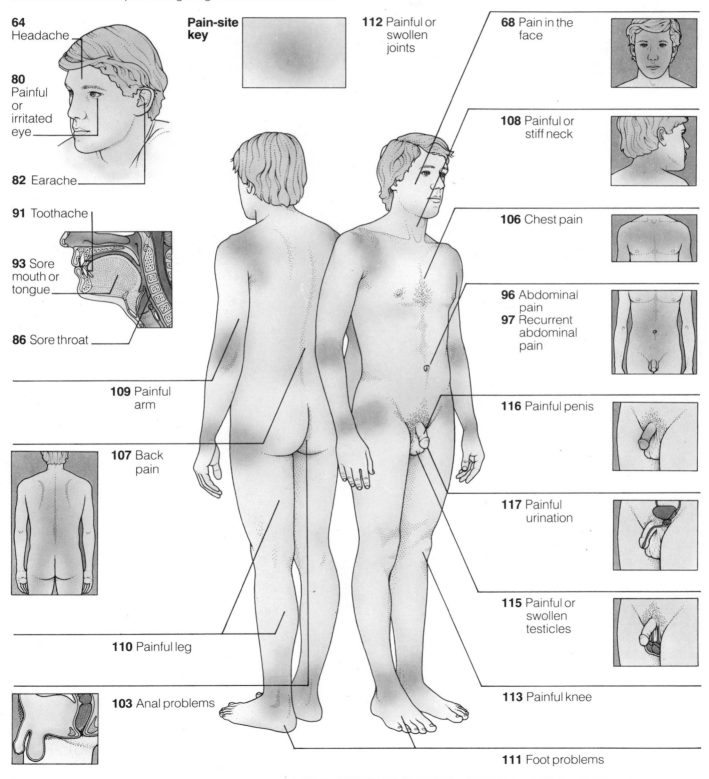

**64** Headache

**80** Painful or irritated eye

**82** Earache

**91** Toothache

**93** Sore mouth or tongue

**86** Sore throat

**Pain-site key**

**112** Painful or swollen joints

**109** Painful arm

**107** Back pain

**110** Painful leg

**103** Anal problems

**68** Pain in the face

**108** Painful or stiff neck

**106** Chest pain

**96** Abdominal pain
**97** Recurrent abdominal pain

**116** Painful penis

**117** Painful urination

**115** Painful or swollen testicles

**113** Painful knee

**111** Foot problems

# 2 Men's system-by-system chartfinder

Consult this section if you know what part of the body or which body system your symptom originates in. A list of the diagnostic charts that deal with each of the main body systems is given under each main heading. Select the chart that most closely seems to fit your symptom.

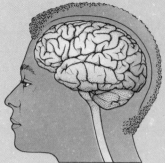

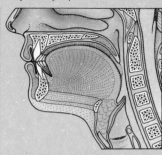

## Head, brain and psychological symptoms

**63** Faintness and fainting
**64** Headache
**65** Giddiness
**66** Numbness and tingling
**67** Twitching and trembling
**68** Pain in the face
**69** Forgetfulness and confusion
**70** Difficulty in speaking
**71** Disturbing thoughts and feelings
**72** Depression
**73** Anxiety

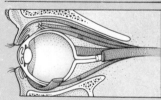

## Eyes and sight symptoms

**80** Painful or irritated eye
**81** Disturbed or impaired vision

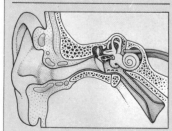

## Ears and hearing symptoms

**82** Earache
**83** Noises in the ear
**84** Deafness

## Mouth, tongue and throat symptoms

**86** Sore throat
**91** Toothache
**92** Difficulty in swallowing
**93** Sore mouth or tongue

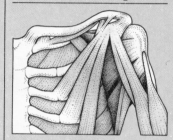

## Muscle, bone and joint symptoms

**107** Back pain
**108** Painful or stiff neck
**109** Painful arm
**110** Painful leg
**111** Foot problems
**112** Painful or swollen joints
**113** Painful knee

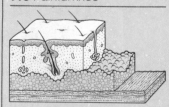

## Skin, hair and nail symptoms

**60** Excessive sweating
**61** Itching
**62** Lumps and swellings
**75** Nail problems
**76** General skin problems
**77** Spots and rashes
**78** Raised spots and lumps on the skin
**79** Rash with fever
**114** Baldness

## General symptoms

**54** Feeling under the weather
**55** Tiredness
**56** Loss of weight
**57** Overweight
**58** Difficulty in sleeping
**59** Fever

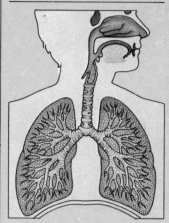

## Respiratory symptoms

**85** Runny Nose
**86** Sore throat
**87** Hoarseness or loss of voice
**88** Wheezing
**89** Coughing
**90** Difficulty in breathing
**106** Chest pain

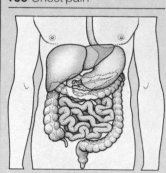

## Abdominal and digestive symptoms

**94** Vomiting
**95** Recurrent vomiting
**96** Abdominal pain
**97** Recurrent abdominal pain
**98** Swollen abdomen
**99** Excess wind
**100** Diarrhoea
**101** Constipation
**102** Abnormal-looking faeces
**103** Anal problems

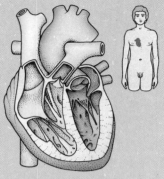

## Heart symptoms

**105** Palpitations
**106** Chest pain

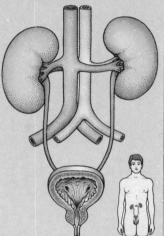

## Urinary symptoms

**104** General urinary problems
**117** Painful urination

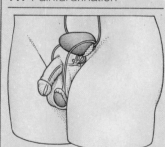

## Genital symptoms

**115** Painful or swollen testicles
**116** Painful penis

## Sexual symptoms

**118** Erection difficulties
**119** Premature ejaculation
**120** Delayed ejaculation
**121** Low sex drive
**122** Fertility problems
**123** Contraception

# 3 Men's chart index

Consult this index if you think that you know the correct name for your symptom. The chart titles and their numbers are listed alphabetically together with possible, alternative names for symptoms (for example, *Raised temperature* for *Fever*). In this section you will also find the titles of information boxes dealing with symptoms that do not have a separate diagnostic chart.

## A

Abdomen, swollen **98**
Abdominal pain **96**
Abdominal pain, recurrent **97**
Abnormal-looking faeces **102**
Abnormal-looking urine **117**
Abnormal thoughts **71**
Anal problems **103**
Anxiety **73**
Arm, painful **109**

## B

Back pain **107**
Bad breath **93**
Baldness **114**
Blood, coughing up **89**
Blood in faeces **102**
Blood in semen **116**
Blood in vomit **94, 95**
Body odour **60**
Breathing, difficulty in **90**
Breathlessness, **90**
Bruising **77**

## C

Chest pain **106**
Confusion **69**
Constipation **101**
Contraception **123**
Coughing **89**
Coughing up blood **89**

## D

Deafness **84**
Delayed ejaculation **120**
Depression **72**
Diarrhoea **100**
Difficulty in breathing **90**
Difficulty in sleeping **58**
Difficulty in speaking **70**
Difficulty in swallowing **92**
Disturbed vision **81**
Disturbed thoughts and feelings **71**
Dizziness **65**
Drowsiness **55**

## E

Ear, noises in the **83**

## E (continued)

Earache **82**
Elbow, painful **109**
Erection difficulties **118**
Ejaculation, delayed **120;** premature **119**
Excess weight **57**
Excess wind **98, 99**
Excessive sweating **60**
Eye painful or irritated **80**
Eye problems **80, 81**
Eyestrain **80**

## F

Face, pain in the **68**
Faeces, abnormal-looking **102;** blood-in **102;** hard **101;** soft **100**
Fainting **63**
Faintness **63**
Feelings, disturbing **71**
Feeling under the weather **54**
Fertility problems **122**
Fever **59**
Fever, rash with **79**
Foot problems **111**
Forgetfulness **69**

## G

General skin problems **76**
General urinary problems **104**
Giddiness **65**

## H

Hair problems **114, 74**
Headache **64**
Heart flutterings **105**
High temperature **59**
Hoarseness **87**

## I

Impaired memory **69**
Impaired vision **81**
Irritated eye **80**
Itching **61**

## J

Joints, painful or swollen **112**

## K

Knee, painful **113**

## L

Leg, painful **110**
Loss of voice **87**
Loss of weight **56**
Low sex drive **121**
Lumps **62, 78**

## M

Memory, impaired **69**
Mouth, sore **93**
Malaise, general **54**

## N

Nail problems **75**
Nausea **94**
Neck, painful or stiff **108**
Noises in the ear **83**
Nose, runny **85**
Nosebleeds **85**
Numbness **66**

## O

Overweight **57**

## P

Painful arm **109**
Painful elbow **109**
Painful eye **80**
Painful joints **112**
Painful knee **113**
Painful leg **110**
Painful neck **108**
Painful penis **116**
Painful shoulder **109**
Painful testicles **115**
Painful urination **117**
Pain in the face **68**
Palpitations **105**
Panic attacks **73**
Penis, painful **116**
Premature ejaculation **119**

## R

Raised lumps on the skin **78**
Raised spots on the skin **78**
Raised temperature **59**
Rashes **76, 77, 78**
Rash with fever **79**
Recurrent abdominal pain **97**
Recurrent vomiting **95**
Run down, feeling **54, 55**

## K (col 3)

Runny nose **85**

## S

Scalp problems **74**
Sex drive, low **121**
Shoulder, painful **109**
Sickness **94, 95**
Skin problems, general **76**
Sleeping, difficulty in **58**
Sore mouth **93**
Sore throat **86**
Sore tongue **93**
Speaking, difficulty in **70**
Spots **76, 77, 78**
Stomach ache **96, 97**
Stiff neck **108**
Stress **73**
Swallowing, difficulty in **92**
Sweating, excessive **60**
Swellings **62, 78, 115**
Swollen abdomen **98**
Swollen joints **112**
Swollen testicles **115**

## T

Temperature, high **59**
Tension **73**
Testicles, painful or swollen **115**
Thoughts, disturbing **71**
Throat, sore **86**
Tingling **66**
Tiredness **55**
Tongue, sore **93**
Toothache **91**
Trembling **67**
Twitching **67**

## U

Urination, painful **117**
Urinary problems **104**
Urine, abnormal-looking **117**

## V

Varicose veins **110**
Vision, disturbed or impaired **81**
Voice, loss of **87**
Vomiting **94, 95;** recurrent **95**

## W

Weight, excess **57;** loss of **56**
Wheezing **88**
Wind **99**
Worrying **73**

# 1 Women's pain-site map

Pain in any form, whether mild or severe is the body's way of telling you that something is wrong. Pain may be 'referred', that is originating in one part of the body and felt in another, or localized at the site of an injury. In any case, pain that persists should never be ignored or masked through the indiscriminate use of pain-killing drugs. Consult this section to find the correct diagnostic chart for your symptom if you are suffering from pain in any part of your body. The illustrations below indicate possible areas of pain and are keyed in to the titles and numbers of the charts that deal with pain in that part of the body.

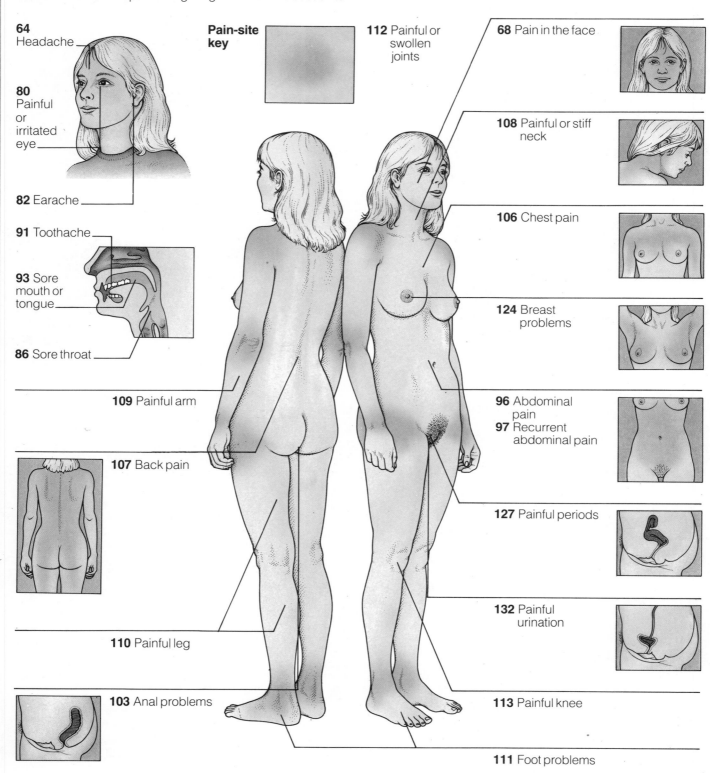

**64** Headache

**80** Painful or irritated eye

**82** Earache

**91** Toothache

**93** Sore mouth or tongue

**86** Sore throat

**Pain-site key**

**109** Painful arm

**107** Back pain

**110** Painful leg

**103** Anal problems

**112** Painful or swollen joints

**68** Pain in the face

**108** Painful or stiff neck

**106** Chest pain

**124** Breast problems

**96** Abdominal pain
**97** Recurrent abdominal pain

**127** Painful periods

**132** Painful urination

**113** Painful knee

**111** Foot problems

# 2 Women's system-by-system chartfinder

Consult this section if you know what part of the body or which body system your symptom originates in. A list of the charts that deal with each of the main body systems is given under each main heading.

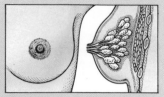

## General symptoms

**54** Feeling under the weather
**55** Tiredness
**56** Loss of weight
**57** Overweight
**58** Difficulty sleeping
**59** Fever

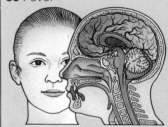

## Head, brain and psychological symptoms

**63** Faintness and fainting
**64** Headache
**65** Giddiness
**66** Numbness and tingling
**67** Twitching and trembling
**68** Pain in the face
**69** Forgetfulness and confusion
**70** Difficulty in speaking
**71** Disturbing thoughts and feelings
**72** Depression
**73** Anxiety
**147** Depression after childbirth

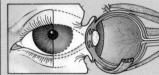

## Eyes and sight symptoms

**80** Painful or irritated eye
**81** Disturbed or impaired vision

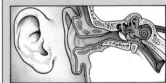

## Ears and hearing symptoms

**82** Earache
**83** Noises in the ear
**84** Deafness

## Mouth, tongue and throat symptoms

**86** Sore throat
**91** Toothache
**92** Difficulty in swallowing
**93** Sore mouth or tongue

## Skin, hair and nail symptoms

**60** Excessive sweating
**61** Itching
**62** Lumps and swellings
**74** Hair and scalp problems
**75** Nail problems
**76** General skin problems
**77** Spots and rashes
**78** Raised spots and lumps on the skin
**79** Rash with fever
**139** Skin changes in pregnancy

## Muscle, bone and joint symptoms

**107** Back pain
**108** Painful or stiff neck
**109** Painful arm
**110** Painful leg
**111** Foot problems
**112** Painful or swollen joints
**113** Painful knee
**144** Ankle-swelling in pregnancy

## Heart symptoms

**105** Palpitations
**106** Chest pain

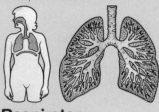

## Respiratory symptoms

**85** Runny nose
**86** Sore throat
**87** Hoarseness or loss of voice
**88** Wheezing
**89** Coughing
**90** Difficulty in breathing
**106** Chest pain

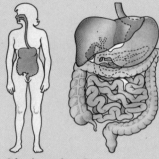

## Abdominal and digestive symptoms

**94** Vomiting
**95** Recurrent vomiting
**96** Abdominal pain
**97** Recurrent abdominal pain
**98** Swollen abdomen
**99** Wind
**100** Diarrhoea
**101** Constipation
**102** Abnormal-looking faeces
**103** Anal problems
**138** Nausea and vomiting in pregnancy
**141** Heartburn in pregnancy

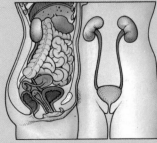

## Urinary symptoms

**131** Poor bladder control
**132** Painful urination
**133** Abnormally frequent urination

## Breast symptoms

**124** Breast problems
**146** Breast-feeding problems

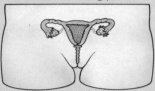

## Gynaecological symptoms

**125** Absent periods
**126** Heavy periods
**127** Painful periods
**128** Irregular vaginal bleeding
**129** Abnormal vaginal discharge
**130** Genital irritation

## Sexual symptoms

**134** Painful intercourse
**135** Loss of interest in sex
**136** Choosing a contraceptive method
**137** Failure to conceive

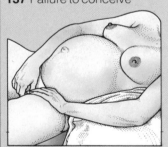

## Symptoms in pregnancy

**138** Nausea and vomiting in pregnancy
**139** Skin changes in pregnancy
**140** Back pain in pregnancy
**141** Heartburn in pregnancy
**142** Vaginal bleeding in pregnancy
**143** Shortness of breath in pregnancy
**144** Ankle-swelling in pregnancy
**145** Am I in labour?
**146** Breast-feeding problems
**147** Depression after childbirth

# 3 Women's chart index

Consult this index if you think that you know the correct name for your symptom. The chart titles and their numbers are listed alphabetically together with possible, alternative names for symptoms (for example, *Raised temperature* for *Fever*). In this section you will also find the titles of information boxes within the diagnostic charts.

## A

Abdomen, swollen **98**
Abdominal pain **96,**
    recurrent **97**
Abnormal-looking
    faeces **102**
Abnormal-looking urine **133**
Abnormally frequent
    urination **133**
Abnormal vaginal discharge
    **129**
Absent periods **125**
Acne **76**
Am I in labour? **145**
Anal problems **103**
Ankle-swelling in pregnancy
    **144**
Anxiety **73**
Arm, painful **109**

## B

Back pain **107**
Back pain in pregnancy **140**
Bad breath **93**
Balance, loss of **65**
Bladder control, lack of **131**
Bleeding, irregular vaginal
    **128,** during pregnancy **142**
Blood, coughing up **89**
Blood in faeces **102**
Blood in vomit **94**
Body odour **60**
Bowel, irritable **97**
Breast-feeding problems **146**
Breast problems **124**
Breathing, difficulty in **90**
Breathlessness, in
    pregnancy **143**
Bruising **77**

## C

Chest pain **106**
Choosing a contraceptive
    method **136**
Conceive, failure to **137**
Confusion **69**
Constipation **101**
Contraception **136**
Coughing **89**
Coughing up blood **89**

## D

Deafness **84**
Depression **72,** postnatal **147**
Depression after
    childbirth **147**
Diarrhoea **100**
Difficulty in breathing **90**
Difficulty in sleeping **58**
Difficulty in speaking **70**

Difficulty in swallowing **92**
Discharge, abnormal
    vaginal **129**
Disturbed vision **81**
Disturbing feelings **71**
Disturbing thoughts **71**
Dizziness **65**
Drowsiness **55**

## E

Ear, noises in the **83**
Earache **82**
Eczema **76, 77**
Elbow, painful **109**
Excess wind **99**
Excessive sweating **60**
Eye painful or irritated **80**
Eye problems **80, 81**
Eyestrain **80**

## F

Face, pain in the **68**
Faeces, abnormal-looking
    **102;** blood-in **102;** hard **101;**
    soft **100**
Failure to conceive **137**
Fainting **63**
Faintness **63**
Feelings, disturbing **71**
Feeling under the weather **54**
Fertility problems **137**
Fever **59**
Fever, rash with **79**
Foot problems **111**
Forgetfulness **69**

## G

General skin problems **76**
Genital irritation **130**
Giddiness **65**

## H

Haemorrhoids **103**
Hair problems **74**
Headache **64**
Heartburn in pregnancy
    **141**
Heart flutterings **105**
Heavy periods **126**
High temperature **59**
Hoarseness **87**

## I

Impaired vision **81**
Intercourse, painful **134**
Irregular vaginal bleeding **128**
Irritable bowel **97**
Irritated eye **80**
Irritation, genital **130**
Itching **61**

## J

Joints, painful or swollen **112**

## K

Knee, painful **113**

## L

Labour **145**
Lack of bladder control **131**
Leg, painful **110**
Loss of interest in sex **135**
Loss of voice **87**
Loss of weight **56**
Lumps **62, 78, 124**

## M

Memory, impaired **69**
Mouth, sore **93**

## N

Nail problems **75**
Nausea **94, 138**
Nausea in pregnancy **138**
Neck, painful or stiff **108**
Noises in the ear **83**
Nose, runny **85**
Nosebleeds **85**
Numbness **66**

## O

Overweight **57**

## P

Painful arm **109**
Painful elbow **109**
Painful eye **80**
Painful intercourse **134**
Painful joints **112**
Painful knee **113**
Painful leg **110**
Painful neck **108**
Painful periods **127**
Painful shoulder **109**
Painful urination **132**
Pain in the face **68**
Palpitations **105**
Panic attacks **73**
Periods, absent **125;** heavy
    **126;** painful **127**
Postnatal depression **147**
Pregnancy, ankle-swelling in
    **144;** back pain in **140;** heart-
    burn in **141;** nausea in **138;**
    shortness of breath in **143;**
    skin changes in **139;** vaginal
    bleeding in **142;** vomiting
    in **138**

## R

Raised lumps on the skin **78**
Raised spots on the skin **78**
Raised temperature **59**
Rashes **76, 77, 78**
Rash with fever **79**
Recurrent abdominal pain **97**
Recurrent vomiting **95**
Run down, feeling **54-55**

Runny nose **85**

## S

Scalp problems **74**
Sex, loss of interest in **135;**
    painful **134**
Shortness of breath in
    pregnancy **143**
Shoulder, painful **109**
Sickness **94, 95**
Skin changes in
    pregnancy **139**
Skin problems, general **76**
Sleeping, difficulty in **58**
Sore mouth **93**
Sore throat **86**
Sore tongue **93**
Speaking, difficulty in **70**
Spots **76, 77, 78**
Stomach ache **96, 97**
Stiff neck **108**
Stress **73**
Swallowing, difficulty in **92**
Sweating, excessive **60**
Swellings **62, 124**
Swollen abdomen **98**
Swollen joints **112**

## T

Temperature, high **59**
Tension **73**
Thoughts, disturbing **71**
Throat, sore **86**
Tingling **66**
Tiredness **55**
Tiredness in early
    pregnancy **55**
Tongue, sore **93**
Toothache **91**
Trembling **67**
Twitching **67**

## U

Urination, frequent **133;**
    painful **132;**
    uncontrolled **131**
Urine, abnormal-looking **133**

## V

Vaginal bleeding **128**
Vaginal bleeding in
    pregnancy **142**
Vaginal discharge,
    abnormal **129**
Vaginal irritation **130**
Varicose veins **110**
Vision, disturbed or
    impaired **81**
Voice, loss of **87**
Vomiting **94;** recurrent **95;**
    in pregnancy **138**

## W

Weight, excess **57;** loss of **56**
Wheezing **88**
Wind **99**
Worrying **73**

# 1 Children's charts

## Babies under one

## All ages,

## Adolescents,

# 1 Slow weight gain

It is important to keep a regular check on your baby's weight gain, because failure to put on weight can be a sign of a variety of problems. Your baby is likely to be weighed whenever you visit your local baby clinic, where any problems are likely to be quickly noticed and dealt with. However, it is also a good idea for you to keep your own chart of your baby's progress so that you can reassure yourself that your baby is developing normally. Using the growth charts on pp. 298-301.

compare your baby's weight gain and increase in head circumference with the average for babies of similar birth weight. But do not worry if your baby's progress does not exactly follow the curve shown; there can be many normal variations to this pattern (see Growth patterns in infancy, below). Only if you can find no normal explanation for your baby's failure to gain weight at the expected rate, should you consult the diagnostic chart on the facing page.

**For children over 1 year, see chart 10, Slow growth**

### GROWTH PATTERNS IN INFANCY

The growth charts on pp. 298-301 allow you to record your baby's growth and to compare his or her progress with the standard weight gain for small, average and large babies. Most babies follow these standard curves, but there are many possible variations, most of which are quite normal. The charts on this page show some common examples of how your baby's growth may differ from the usual pattern. Remember that weight and head circumference are interrelated. When your doctor assesses the size of your baby, he or she is looking at the relationship between them. Above all, do not worry if your child appears to be growing slowly; consult your doctor.

**Small mother and tall father**
A small mother is likely to have a smaller than average baby. But if the father is tall and the baby is ultimately going to take after him, the baby's growth chart is likely to show a rapid increase in both weight and head circumference in the first few months of life.

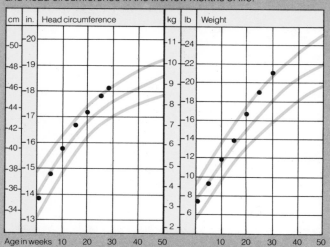

**Tall mother and small father**
A tall mother is likely to have a larger than average baby. However, if the father is small and the baby is going to take after him, the baby is likely to gain weight and increase his or her head circumference at a slower rate than normal for the first few months.

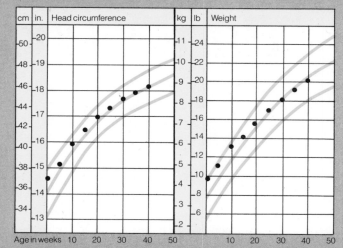

**Gaining too little weight**
This chart shows a baby who is gaining too little weight. The head is growing normally for an average-sized baby, but the weight gain curve is flattening out and approaching that for a small baby. In this case you should consult the diagnostic chart opposite.

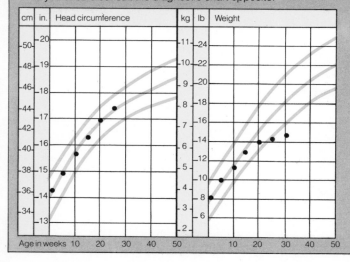

**Gaining too much weight**
This chart shows a baby who was average weight at birth, but whose weight has consistently risen at a faster rate than his or her head circumference, so that the weight curve now relates to that of a larger-than-average baby. (See chart 11, *Excessive weight gain*.)

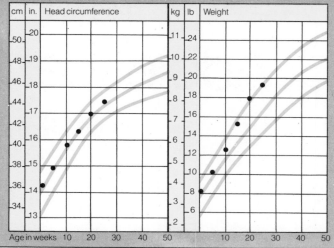

**START HERE** → Does your baby seem unwell – for example, is he or she slow to feed or does he or she seem lethargic or irritable?

**YES** → **An underlying illness** may be causing your baby's slow weight gain. Consult your doctor.

**NO** ↓

Is your baby entirely breast-fed?

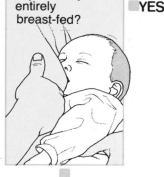

**YES** → Do you offer a feed whenever your baby cries?

**YES** → **Insufficient milk supply** may mean that your baby is not getting enough nourishment. However, if your baby is over 3 months, he or she may be ready to start on solids. Discuss the problem with your doctor or health visitor, who may recommend supplementary bottles or advise you on weaning.

**NO** ↓

Do you offer a feed whenever your baby cries?

**YES** → **Undernourishment** may be the cause of slow weight gain.

*Self-help:* Crying is your baby's way of letting you know he or she is hungry. Imposing a strict feeding routine may prevent your baby from receiving the necessary amount of milk, and may also lead to a reduction in your milk supply (see *Breast feeding* p. 61). So always offer your baby a feed when he or she cries, even if it is sometimes refused. If your baby does not start to gain weight normally within 3 weeks, consult your doctor.

**NO** ↓

**Undernourishment** may be the cause of slow weight gain.
*Self-help:* Crying is your baby's way of letting you know he or she is hungry. Imposing a strict feeding routine may prevent your baby from receiving the necessary amount of milk. So always offer a feed when your baby cries, even if it is sometimes refused. If your baby does not start to gain weight normally within 2 weeks, consult your doctor.

**NO** ↓

Is your baby bottle-fed?

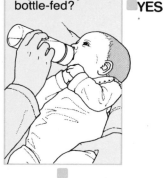

**YES** → Does your baby always finish every drop of the feed?

**YES** → Might you be adding too much water or too little milk formula when mixing the feeds?

**YES** → **Over-dilution of the feeds** may mean that your baby is not receiving adequate nourishment.
*Self-help:* Always follow the manufacturer's instructions exactly when mixing your baby's feeds. If you think your baby is thirsty offer extra boiled water separately. If your baby does not start to gain weight normally within 2 weeks, consult your doctor.

**NO** ↓ (Might you be adding too much water...)

**NO** ↓ (Does your baby always finish every drop of the feed?)

**Increasing appetite** may mean that your baby needs more food than you are offering, even if you are giving the correct amount for your baby's age.
*Self-help:* Always offer more milk than you think necessary and let your baby feed until satisfied. If your baby is over 3 months, he or she may be ready to start on solids. If your baby does not start to gain weight normally within 2 weeks, or if you need advice on weaning, consult your doctor.

**NO** (Is your baby bottle-fed?) →

**Consult your doctor** if you are unable to make a diagnosis from this chart.

---

**WEIGHT LOSS IN THE NEWBORN**

Most babies lose about 150g (5oz) in weight during the first week of life. This is perfectly normal and is not a sign that your breast-milk supply is inadequate or that your baby is underfed. Most babies start to put on weight again on the fifth day and have regained their birth weight by the time they are 10 days old. Thereafter weight gain should continue at a steady rate.

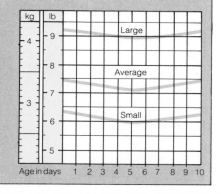

| kg | lb | | | | | | | | | | |
|---|---|---|---|---|---|---|---|---|---|---|---|
| | 9 | | | | Large | | | | | | |
| 4 | 8 | | | | | | | | | | |
| | 7 | | | | Average | | | | | | |
| 3 | 6 | | | | Small | | | | | | |
| | 5 | | | | | | | | | | |

Age in days   1  2  3  4  5  6  7  8  9  10

# 2 Waking at night

Most babies wake at regular intervals through the day and night for feeds during the first few months of life. This is perfectly normal and there is no point in trying to enforce a more convenient routine on a baby of this age.

Consult this chart only if you think your baby is waking more frequently than is normal, if you have difficulty settling your baby at night, or if a baby who has previously slept well starts to wake during the night.

**For children over 1 year, see chart 12, Sleeping problems**

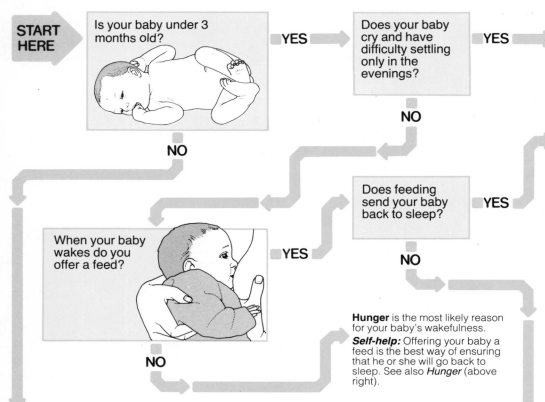

**START HERE**

Is your baby under 3 months old?

**YES** → Does your baby cry and have difficulty settling only in the evenings?

**YES** → **Evening colic** may cause such restlessness and crying.

Go to chart

**5** **Excessive crying**

**NO** ↓ (from "under 3 months")

**NO** ↓ (from "difficulty settling in evenings")

Does feeding send your baby back to sleep?

**YES** → **Hunger** is probably causing your baby to wake. The need for frequent feeds is normal in babies of this age (see *Frequency of feeds,* p.60).

*Self-help:* Attempts to prevent a young baby from waking at night through hunger – for example, by offering supplementary bottles of milk in the evening – are usually unsuccessful. It is best to resign yourself to several more weeks of disturbed nights and adjust your own routine accordingly. Try to take rests during the day when your baby is asleep. If possible, both parents should take it in turns to get up at night. If your baby is breast-fed, try expressing milk so that the father can sometimes give the baby bottle at night. If you think lack of sleep is beginning to affect your general health, or is making you resentful towards your baby, consult your doctor.

When your baby wakes do you offer a feed?

**YES** →

**NO** ↓

**NO** ↓ (from "Does feeding send your baby back to sleep?")

**Hunger** is the most likely reason for your baby's wakefulness.
*Self-help:* Offering your baby a feed is the best way of ensuring that he or she will go back to sleep. See also *Hunger* (above right).

---

## HELPING YOUR BABY TO SLEEP

### Young babies (under 4 months)
In the first few months of life a baby will sleep when fed and comfortable; the most you can do to help your baby sleep is to ensure that these basic needs of food, warmth, and comfort are provided. Concentrate on adjusting your own routine so that you sleep when your baby does, in order to prevent yourself from becoming over-tired by disturbed nights. The following suggestions may help you to cope more easily:

- Try to take rests during the day when your baby is asleep.
- Take it in turns with your partner to get up at night when your baby cries.
- If your baby is breast-fed, express some milk so that your partner can give a bottle at night sometimes.
- Move your baby into a separate room as soon as you feel ready, preferably before the age of 6 months.

### Older babies (4 to 12 months)
Most babies who are past the stage of needing frequent night feeds benefit from a fairly regular bedtime routine. A baby who has learnt to go to bed without fuss during the first year is less likely to create problems at bedtime later on. In general it is best to be firm and predictable, but

this should not prevent you from making bedtimes affectionate and fun. Your baby needs to be reassured that going to bed and being separated from you is not a form of punishment. Some suggestions for increasing the chances of problem-free bedtimes are listed here:

- Always carry out the preparations for bed in the same order – for example, supper, bath, quiet playtime, breast- or bottle-feed, and into the cot for the night.
- Avoid too much excitement in the hour or so before bed.
- Make your baby's room as inviting as possible with plenty to look at on the walls and favourite toys in the cot.
- Provide a night light if your baby seems frightened of the dark.
- Do not be too ready to go to your baby if you hear whimpering in the night. He or she may simply be making noises while asleep, and your going into the room may wake the baby unnecessarily.
- If your baby cries in the night, do whatever is necessary to settle him or her (giving a drink or change of nappy) as quickly and quietly as possible. Do not let your baby persuade you to play; otherwise he or she may learn that waking at night can be fun.

Help your baby not to feel lonely or bored in the cot by providing plenty of interesting things to look at.

*Go to next page*

*Continued from previous page*

**Has your baby previously slept well at night?** — **YES** →

**Does your baby seem unwell in any way — for example, is his or her temperature 38°C (100°F) or above?** — **YES** →

**A physical illness** can easily disrupt a baby's sleep. Depending on your baby's additional symptoms, go to the appropriate chart elsewhere in the book.

**When your baby woke was he or she crying and difficult to console?** — **YES** →

**NO** (from "Has your baby previously slept well at night?")

**NO** (from "Does your baby seem unwell")

**NO** (from "When your baby woke")

**Does your baby sleep in the same room as you?** — **YES** →

**Sharing the same room** can result in unnecessarily disturbed nights for you and your baby. This may be because you make sounds that disturb your baby or – and this is more likely – the closeness of your baby may make you overaware of his or her movements during sleep and cause you to think that little noises that babies often make in their sleep are signs of wakefulness. Many babies are restless sleepers and, if left undisturbed, will continue to sleep.
*Self-help:* If possible, move your baby into a different room. It is unlikely that you would fail to hear a true cry, but you are less likely to be disturbed by less urgent sounds.

**Earache,** possibly as a result of an infection of the middle ear, is a common cause of waking at night and of distress in a baby who has previously slept well.

Go to chart

**29** **Painful or irritated ear**

**NO** (from "Does your baby sleep in the same room")

**Is the room where your baby sleeps cold AND do you usually find the covers have been kicked off during the night?** — **YES** →

**Cold** may be waking your baby.
*Self-help:* A baby who moves a great deal while asleep and kicks off the bedclothes can be kept warm at night by a sleeping bag or warm sleep suit.

**NO** (from "Is the room where your baby sleeps cold")

**Anxiety** is a possible cause for disrupted sleep in a young baby. Even small changes in domestic routine can upset some babies.
*Self-help:* It may take several days to reassure your baby that there is no cause for anxiety. During this time try to ensure that there are no further changes of routine. When your baby wakes at night, offer a drink and a cuddle, but make sure that your baby understands that he or she will be put back in the cot, otherwise there is a danger that your baby will get into the habit of waking and expecting to play. See also *Helping your baby to sleep* (opposite).

**Has there been any domestic upheaval or possible cause for anxiety in recent weeks — for example, a move to a new house or a recent absence by the mother or father?** — **YES** →

**A need for the comfort and reassurance of your presence** is the most common explanation for waking at night when a baby is past the stage of needing night feeds.
*Self-help:* Make every effort to stick to a set routine for putting your baby to bed (See *Helping your baby to sleep,* opposite). If your baby wakes at night, offer a drink but try to avoid picking him or her up out of the cot. Do not stay with your baby any longer than is necessary to reassure him or her of your presence and to reassure yourself that all is well. If your baby cries when you leave the room, try to resist the temptation to go back. Crying for a few minues before falling asleep again will do your baby no harm.

**NO** (from "Has there been any domestic upheaval")

---

**SLEEPING PATTERNS**

No two babies have the same sleeping pattern or the same sleep requirements, so do not make the mistake of thinking that your baby is abnormal if he or she sleeps less than a friend's baby of the same age. The typical sleeping patterns described here are simply given as examples, and your own baby's routine will almost certainly be different. However, the gradual transition from spending most of the day and night asleep to spending almost the whole day awake and almost the whole night asleep is likely to apply to most babies.

**Newborn**
A newborn baby spends most of the time asleep, waking for feeds about every 3 hours. After the first few months, most babies will sleep for longer at night, perhaps only waking once. Wakeful periods in the day will probably become more prolonged.

**6 months**
By the time a baby is 6 months old, he or she is likely to sleep for most of the night, but may wake briefly for a drink in the early hours of the morning. He or she will be awake for most of the day, but will probably need a nap in the morning and in the afternoon.

**1 year**
A 1-year-old baby usually sleeps without waking throughout the night (between 10 and 12 hours on average). At this age a baby will probably need only one major nap during the day.

☐ Awake

☐ Asleep

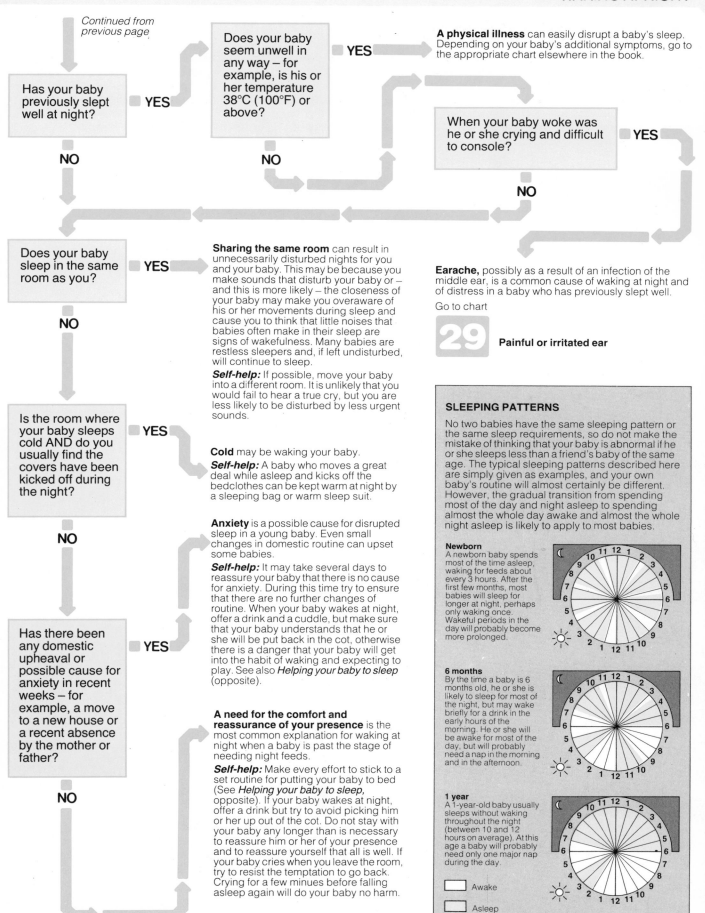

# 3 Fever in babies

A fever (above-normal body temperature) is usually caused by infection. (Viral and bacterial infections are discussed on p. 66. You may suspect that your baby has a fever if the forehead feels hot, if your baby is sweating more than usual, or if he or she seems generally unwell or irritable. Taking your baby's temperature as described in the box opposite will enable you to confirm your suspicions. Normal temperature may vary from 36 to 37.5°C (97 to 99°F). Minor fluctuations within this range are no cause for concern if your baby seems otherwise well. Consult this chart if your baby's temperature rises above this level.

For children over 1 year, see chart 14, Fever in children

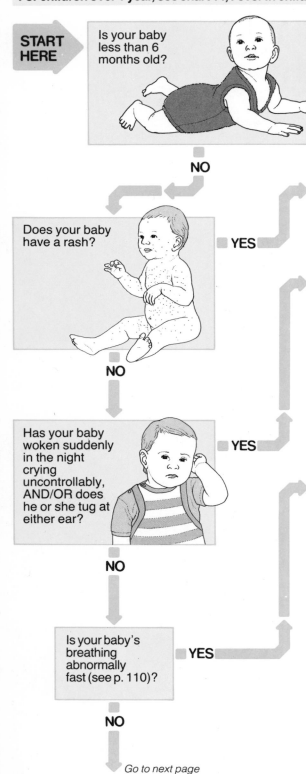

**START HERE**

Is your baby less than 6 months old?

**YES**

**NO**

Does your baby have a rash?

**YES**

Go to chart **26** Rash with fever

**NO**

Has your baby woken suddenly in the night crying uncontrollably, AND/OR does he or she tug at either ear?

**YES**

**NO**

Is your baby's breathing abnormally fast (see p. 110)?

**YES**

**NO**

*Go to next page*

**Infection of the middle ear** is a common cause of a raised temperature in babies. This diagnosis is especially likely if your baby has recently had a cold. Consult your doctor.
***Treatment:*** If this diagnosis is confirmed, your doctor will probably prescribe a course of *antibiotics*, and possibly some *decongestant* nose drops or spray. During treatment you can give liquid paracetamol to relieve pain and reduce fever.

**CALL YOUR DOCTOR NOW!**
**A chest infection** is possible, especially if your baby has had a cold within the past week.
***Treatment:*** Your doctor may decide that your baby can be treated at home with frequent doctor's visits, but in a severe case he or she is likely to recommend hospital admission. In either case treatment will probably consist of paracetamol to reduce fever and ease discomfort, and possibly *antibiotics* to fight the infection. If you are looking after your baby at home, make sure that he or she drinks plenty of fluids. Keeping the air moist – by placing a wet towel over a radiator, for example – may help to ease your baby's breathing.

---

## WARNING

**HIGH FEVER**

If your baby's temperature rises above 39°C (102°F), whatever the suspected cause, you should call your doctor at once. This is because high temperatures can lead to fits (see below) in some babies.

**CALL YOUR DOCTOR NOW!**
**Infections** at this age are unusual and may sometimes be serious.
***Treatment:*** Until your doctor arrives carry out temperature-reducing measures as described on p. 228. Your doctor will examine your baby (see *Examination by the doctor* p. 67) and make a diagnosis. Depending on whether a viral or bacterial infection (see p. 66) is diagnosed, your doctor may prescribe *antibiotics*. Admission to hospital may be advised.

**FEVERISH FITS**

Some babies suffer fits (also known as febrile convulsions) when their temperature rises above a certain point. During such a fit the arms and legs will shake uncontrolledly and the baby may go blue in the face. This may last for several seconds or longer.

**What to do**
If your baby has a feverish fit lay him or her stomach down over a pillow to prevent choking, and seek medical help at once. While waiting for medical help to arrive, attempt to reduce your baby's temperature by removing his or her clothing and sponging with tepid water as described on p. 288 if your baby vomits, clean out his or her mouth with your finger. Even if your baby quickly recovers from a fit, you should call your doctor so that any underlying problem can be diagnosed and, if necessary, treated. Sometimes tests such as *electroencephalography* (p. 81) may be recommended.

**FOREIGN TRAVEL**

If your baby develops a fever soon after a visit to a hot climate, be sure to tell your doctor. This is because your baby may have caught an illness that is rare in this country, and that your doctor might not otherwise suspect.

*Continued from previous page*

**Does your baby have a clear discharge from the nose AND/OR has he or she been coughing?**

**YES** →

**Measles** is a possibility if your baby has been in contact with the disease within the past week or so. The appearance of a rash within the next few days will confirm the diagnosis. (See also *Comparison of childhood infectious diseases,* p.97) Otherwise a generalized viral infection such as flu is likely. Consult your doctor.

***Treatment:*** For both types of illness your doctor is likely to recommend that you take steps to reduce your baby's temperature (see p. 288) while the infection runs its course for the next week or so. Call your doctor at once if your baby becomes drowsy or unresponsive, or if he or she refuses to drink.

**NO** ↓

**Is your baby unusually drowsy or irritable?**

**YES** →

**CALL YOUR DOCTOR NOW!**
**Meningitis** (inflammation of the membranes surrounding the brain, caused by viral or bacterial infection) may be the cause of such symptoms, especially if your baby has also vomited.

***Treatment:*** Your baby will probably be admitted to hospital where, after a *lumbar puncture* (p. 74) to make an exact diagnosis, he or she will be given fluids and possibly *antibiotics* (if the infection is bacterial) through an intravenous drip.

**NO** ↓

**Has your baby had diarrhoea AND/OR been vomiting?**

**YES** →

**CONSULT YOUR DOCTOR WITHOUT DELAY!**
**Gastroenteritis** (infection of the digestive tract) is the most likely cause of such symptoms.

***Treatment:*** If the diagnosis is confirmed, your doctor is likely to recommend that you follow the guidelines for treating gastroenteritis described in the box on p. 63. However, if your baby's symptoms are severe, or if there are signs of dehydration (see *Persistent vomiting*, p. 62), your doctor may advise admission to hospital, where fluids can be given by intravenous drip.

**NO** ↓

**Has your baby been refusing solid food?**

**YES** →

**A throat or mouth infection** is the most likely explanation for these symptoms.

***Self-help:*** Follow the advice on treating a sore throat on p. 107. Do not force your baby to eat if pain makes swallowing difficult, but make sure he or she drinks at least ¾ litre (1½ pints) of fluid a day. Consult your doctor if your baby is no better in 48 hours or develops any of the danger signs in the box on p. 106.

**NO** ↓

**Is your baby very warmly dressed AND/OR is he or she in warm surroundings?**

**YES** →

**Overheating,** caused by too much clothing or by excessively warm surroundings, can cause a baby's temperature to rise.

***Self-help:*** In general, babies do not need to wear much more clothing than an adult in similar conditions and will be comfortable in a room temperature of 15 to 20°C (60 to 68°F). A baby's cot should never be placed next to a radiator. If your baby has become overheated, removing any excess clothing and moving the baby to a slightly cooler (though not cold) place, will soon reduce any fever. If your baby's temperature is not down to normal within an hour, consult your doctor.

**NO** ↓

**Consult your doctor** if you are unable to make a diagnosis from this chart.

## HOW TO TAKE A BABY'S TEMPERATURE

The best way for you to take your baby's temperature is by using a clinical thermometer under the arm.

**1** Shake the thermometer with firm downward flicks of the wrist so that the mercury runs down into the bulb and reads well below the "normal" mark.

**2** Place your baby on your knee and put the thermometer bulb into the armpit.

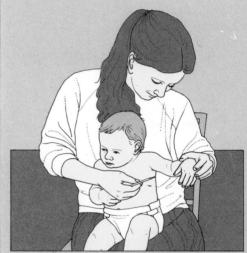

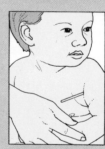

**3** Hold your baby's arm close to his or her side to keep the thermometer firmly in place for 3 minutes.

**4** Remove the thermometer and look at it, turning it until you get a clear reading.

Using this method, you can consider your baby to have a fever if his or her temperature is 38°C (100°F) or above.

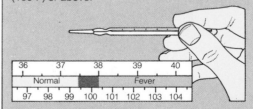

| 36 | 37 | 38 | 39 | 40 |
|---|---|---|---|---|
| Normal | | | Fever | |
| 97 | 98 | 99 | 100 | 101 | 102 | 103 | 104 |

**Temperature indicator strips**
An alternative method of taking temperature is to use a temperature indicator strip – a re-usable plastic strip that is placed against the forehead. Heat-sensitive panels change colour to give an approximate indication of body temperature. While this method has the advantage of being easy to use, particularly for babies and small children, there is a tendency for the indicator strips to under-estimate a fever and you should allow for this by adding ½°C (1°F) to a temperature-strip reading.

# 4 Skin problems

The skin of newborn babies is very sensitive and can easily become temporarily inflamed or spotty as a result of minor irritations such as prolonged contact with urine or faeces, over-heating, or rubbing on rough fabrics. Such minor rashes are usually no cause for concern although you should deal with the cause of the trouble. Rashes and other skin abnormalities that occur for no apparent reason, or that persist for more than a few days, should always be brought to your doctor's attention, especially if your baby also seems unwell.

**START HERE** ➤

**Is your baby less than 2 months old?**

**YES** ➤

**Does your baby have an inflamed scaly rash in two or more of the following places?**
- neck
- behind the ears
- face
- groin
- armpits

**YES** ➤

**Seborrhoeic dermatitis** is a possible cause of skin inflammation in these areas. It is more likely if your baby has been suffering from extensive nappy rash and/or cradle cap (below left).

**Self-help:** In mild cases of this condition no special treatment is needed, other than paying special attention to washing and drying in between the folds of skin in these areas (see *Caring for your baby's skin*, opposite). You should, however, avoid using soap, baby lotion or baby bath solution. An emulsifying ointment, available from chemists, can be used instead for cleansing and moisturizing your baby's skin. If the rash is extensive or seems to be causing discomfort, or if the skin becomes broken and starts to ooze, consult your doctor.

**NO** ↓

**NO** ↓

**Does your baby have brownish, crusty patches on the scalp?**

**YES** ➤

**Cradle cap**, a form of seborrhoeic dermatitis (above right), is a minor and harmless condition.

**Self-help:** If you find the crusts unsightly, you can remove them by rubbing your baby's scalp with baby oil or petroleum jelly and then gently washing them off. If cradle cap is extensive, consult your doctor, who may be able to prescribe a special cream to control the condition.

**NO** ↓

**Does your baby have a scaly or blistery rash on the face, inside the elbows or behind the knees?**

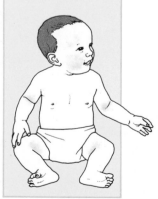

**YES** ➤

**Infantile (atopic) eczema**, an allergic condition, is possible. This diagnosis is most likely if other members of the family also suffer from eczema or other allergic conditions such as hay fever or asthma.

**Self-help:** If the rash is mild and causes your baby no discomfort, there is no need to consult a doctor. Avoid using soap, baby lotion or baby bath solution. Instead, use an emulsifying ointment, available from chemists, to clean and moisturize your baby's skin. If the rash if widespread or weepy, consult your doctor, who may prescribe *cortico steroid* or *antibiotic* creams, which you should be careful to use exactly as instructed. Your doctor may also prescribe medicine to reduce itching. Your doctor may recommend excluding certain foods from the diet, if these seem to make the condition worse.

**NO** ↓

*Go to next page* ▷

---

**BIRTHMARKS**

Every baby has a few moles and pigmented spots. Some are born with large areas of abnormally coloured skin. The sight of such marks in a new baby is often alarming for parents but, depending on the type of birthmark, these marks usually become less prominent as the child grows older and may disappear completely:

**Strawberry naevus**
This is a bright red, usually raised mark that can appear anywhere on the body. It may grow during the first few months of life, but in the second half of the first year starts to shrink.

The mark continues to shrink until about the age of 7, when in 80 per cent of cases it disappears completely. Treatment to remove the naevus is only necessary if it is near the eye and obscures vision.

**Port wine stain**
This is an area of purplish-red skin that may be slightly raised. It most commonly affects the face and limbs. This birthmark usually remains unchanged, but if it is disfiguring it can be disguised with make-up or treated by plastic surgery or lasers later in childhood.

**Large pigmented spots**
Some babies are born with several flat patches of darkened skin known as café au lait spots. They do not usually alter with age, but can be successfully disguised with cosmetics.

**Mongolian blue spots**
These are bluish bruise-like marks that sometimes appear on the skin of babies of dark-skinned races. These marks disappear without treatment before the second birthday.

*Continued from previous page*

Does your baby have an area of inflamed skin or spots confined to or spreading from the nappy area?

**YES** →

Is the rash mainly around the anus?

**YES** →

**Irritants** that occur naturally in your baby's faeces may be inflaming the skin around the anus. This type of nappy rash is most likely to occur when a baby has diarrhoea.
***Self-help:*** Change your baby's nappy as soon as it becomes soiled. Wash all traces of faeces away and apply a protective cream (see also *Caring for your baby's skin*, below). Consult your doctor if nappy rash persists for more than 10 days. If your baby is passing unusually watery or frequent faeces he or she may have an infection.

Go to chart

**8**

**Diarrhoea in babies**

**NO** ↓

**NO** ↓

Is your baby generally well and feeding normally?

**YES** →

**NO** ↓

Does your baby have a rash of spots or blotches anywhere on the body?

**YES** →

**A childhood infectious illness** such as chickenpox is possible if a baby develops a rash and seems unwell. See *Comparison of childhood infectious diseases* (p. 97) and consult your doctor.

**NO** ↓

**Consult your doctor** if you are unable to make a diagnosis from this chart.

**Unexplained rashes** in a well baby are usually due to minor skin irritations and are seldom cause for concern. Consult your doctor if the rash has not faded by the following day or your baby shows any signs of being unwell.

**Generalized nappy rash** is usually due to prolonged contact with wet nappies. Substances in the urine react with chemicals in the faeces to produce ammonia, which is irritating to a baby's skin. Sometimes there is a strong smell of ammonia from the wet nappy. This type of nappy rash is most likely if you use fabric nappies that have been inadequately sterilized.
***Self-help:*** Make sure that you change your baby's nappies frequently, and wash the nappy area thoroughly between each change. It is best to use disposable nappies, if possible, because these are certain to be sterile. If you continue to use fabric nappies do not cover them with waterproof pants except on important occasions. Leave off your baby's nappies as often as possible to help the skin to dry out and promote healing. Before putting on a clean nappy apply a protective cream (see also *Caring for your baby's skin*, below). If these measures fail to clear up the nappy rash within 10 days or if it starts to get worse, there is a possibility that the skin may have become infected by candida (thrush) – a fungus that is often present in the bowel. In this case consult your doctor, who may prescribe a special cream and possibly a medicine to treat the infection.

---

## CARING FOR YOUR BABY'S SKIN

A baby's skin is delicate and needs protection from severe cold or heat and strong sunlight or it may become inflamed, dry and sore. Regular careful washing is necessary to prevent skin infections and nappy rash.

### Washing and bathing

A baby's skin should always be kept clean; usually the best way to ensure this is to give your baby a daily bath. However, providing that you wash the nappy area thoroughly at each nappy change (see *Nappy changing*, right) and wipe away any dribbled milk, etc., less frequent bathing is adequate. When you bath your baby remember the following points:

- Make sure that the water is not too hot; check it using your elbow.
- Even when he or she can sit up unaided, never leave your baby in the bath unattended.
- Use a mild unscented soap or baby bath solution. If your baby has dry skin or any form of eczema, use emulsifying ointment and wash it away with plain water.
- When your baby's hair starts to grow thickly, wash it once a week with a mild shampoo.
- Dry your baby, using his or her own towel, making sure all the moisture is removed from the skin folds.
- If you use talcum powder, apply it to your baby's skin sparingly.

Hold your baby securely in the bath (above).

### Nappies

You can use either disposable or fabric nappies. Fabric nappies need careful washing and sterilizing and should be used with a "one-way" nappy liner to keep moisture away from the skin. Disposables are more convenient and are always sterile, but may hold less moisture than fabric nappies.

### Nappy changing

When you change your baby's nappy, wipe away all traces of urine and faeces with cotton wool moistened with water or, if your baby's skin is dry, baby oil or emulsifying ointment.

Before putting on a clean nappy, apply a protective cream such as zinc and castor oil or petroleum jelly to the nappy area.

If possible, try to set aside some time at least once a day for your baby to be without nappies. Exposure to air helps to prevent nappy rash. If your baby has a sore bottom, try leaving the nappies off for long periods, and let your baby lie in a warm room on a towel or nappy instead. This assists healing. Also, be particularly careful to change nappies regularly, especially after soiling. If the rash persists for more than 10 days, consult your doctor.

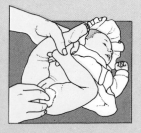

Use cotton wool moistened with water or baby lotion (above right) to clean your baby's bottom (right).

# 5 Excessive crying

Crying is a young baby's only means of communicating physical discomfort or emotional distress. All babies sometimes cry when they are hungry, wet, upset or in pain, and some babies often seem to cry for no obvious reason. Most parents learn to recognize the most common causes of their baby's crying and can deal with them according to need. Consult this chart if your baby regularly cries more often than you think is normal, or if your baby suddenly starts to cry in an unusual way or for no apparent reason.

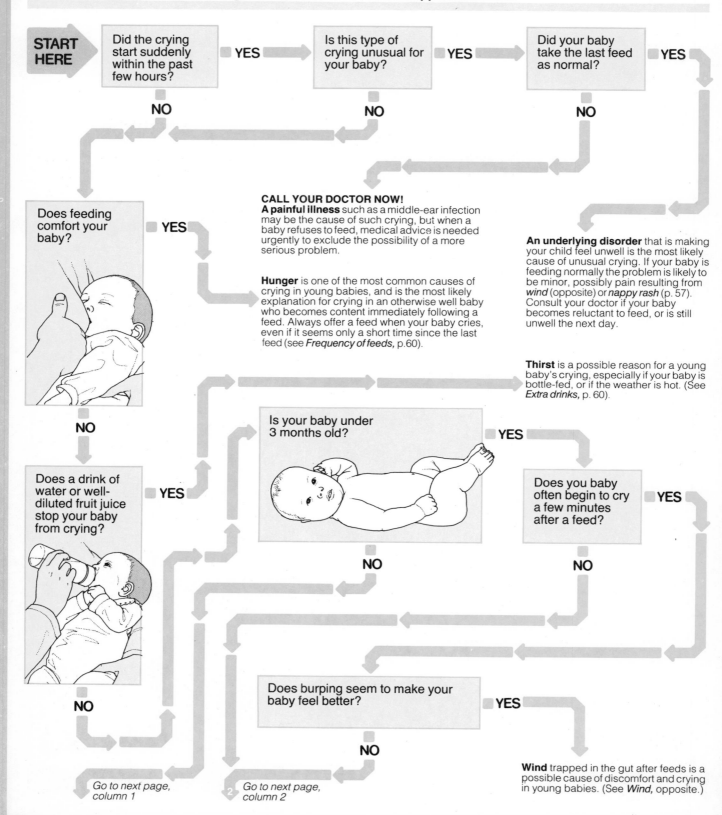

**START HERE**

Did the crying start suddenly within the past few hours? — **YES** → Is this type of crying unusual for your baby? — **YES** → Did your baby take the last feed as normal? — **YES**

**NO** ↓ (from first box)
**NO** ↓ (from second box)
**NO** ↓ (from third box)

Does feeding comfort your baby? — **YES**

**CALL YOUR DOCTOR NOW!**
**A painful illness** such as a middle-ear infection may be the cause of such crying, but when a baby refuses to feed, medical advice is needed urgently to exclude the possibility of a more serious problem.

**Hunger** is one of the most common causes of crying in young babies, and is the most likely explanation for crying in an otherwise well baby who becomes content immediately following a feed. Always offer a feed when your baby cries, even if it seems only a short time since the last feed (see *Frequency of feeds,* p.60).

**An underlying disorder** that is making your child feel unwell is the most likely cause of unusual crying. If your baby is feeding normally the problem is likely to be minor, possibly pain resulting from *wind* (opposite) or *nappy rash* (p. 57). Consult your doctor if your baby becomes reluctant to feed, or is still unwell the next day.

**Thirst** is a possible reason for a young baby's crying, especially if your baby is bottle-fed, or if the weather is hot. (See *Extra drinks,* p. 60).

Does feeding comfort your baby? **NO** ↓

Does a drink of water or well-diluted fruit juice stop your baby from crying? — **YES**

Is your baby under 3 months old? — **YES**

Does you baby often begin to cry a few minutes after a feed? — **YES**

**NO** (under drink box)
**NO** (under 3 months box)
**NO** (under cry after feed box)

Does burping seem to make your baby feel better? — **YES**

**NO** ↓

**Wind** trapped in the gut after feeds is a possible cause of discomfort and crying in young babies. (See *Wind,* opposite.)

*Go to next page, column 1*

*Go to next page, column 2*

**1** *Continued from previous page, column 1*

**2** *Continued from previous page, column 2*

**Does you baby seem content for most of the day but cry a great deal during the late afternoon and evening?**

**YES** →

**Evening (or 3-month) colic** is the term often used to describe this common type of crying. It usually starts when a baby is about 6 weeks old and ceases after the age of 3 months. There are many possible explanations for this problem, including painful spasm of the intestines, tiredness and tension in the mother, and a possible reduction in her milk supply at this time of day.

*Self-help:* There is no effective cure for evening colic. The main priority for parents is to find a way of minimizing the strain on themselves from a constantly crying baby. Try to find ways of preventing yourself from becoming too tired at the end of the day – for example, by taking an afternoon rest. Parents can take it in turns to give each other an evening off or you can sometimes ask a trusted babysitter to look after the baby. Discuss the problem with your doctor, who may be able to prescribe a medicine that helps your baby to settle and who will advise you on how to cope.

**NO**

**Does your baby usually stop crying when picked up and given your full attention?**

**YES** →

**The need for attention and physical comfort** is a common cause of crying. Some babies are quite happy when left alone in their cot or playpen, but others need the constant reassurance of their parents' presence.

*Self-help:* Cuddle your baby as much as he or she seems to want. At this age there is no danger of "spoiling", and your baby will be happier as a result of an increased feeling of security. To enable you to get on with your everyday chores, you can try putting a young baby in a carrying sling while you go about the house. An older baby may be content if placed in a bouncing cradle or propped up on some cushions where he or she can see you.

**NO**

**Are you feeling tense or over-tired OR has there been a recent major domestic, upheaval?**

**YES** →

**Sensitivity to increased tension** in the home and particularly in the mother can make a baby unsettled and liable to periods of unexplained crying.

*Self-help:* A baby will usually settle down to a new routine or in new surroundings within a week or so, although you will need to give more attention and reassurance than usual during this time. If you think that the cause of your baby's crying could be a reaction to your own tension, try to find ways of reducing any strain you are under. Discuss this with your doctor or health visitor, who may be able to suggest ways of helping. It is particularly important to seek medical advice if your baby's crying is making you angry or resentful, or causing you to have violent thoughts towards your baby so that you are in danger of losing control to the extent of shaking or hitting your baby.

**NO**

**Consult your doctor** if you are unable to make a diagnosis from this chart.

---

**WIND**

Young babies often swallow air during feeds, especially those eager feeders who gulp greedily at the start of every feed. Excess wind in the gut causes regurgitation of feeds and may be linked to discomfort and crying (colic); so it is a good idea to spend a little time helping your baby to bring up wind after each feed. Some of the best positions for burping a baby are shown below.

**Positions for burping**
When feeding your baby, make sure that he or she is supported in a semi-upright position (above). After feeding help your baby to bring up wind by holding him or her against your shoulder (left), over your knee (below left), or on your lap (below).

# 6 Feeding problems

Feeding problems are a common source of irritability and crying in young babies as well as concern in their parents. Such problems may include a reluctance to feed, constant hungry crying, and swallowing too much air, leading to regurgitation. There may also be special problems for mothers who are breast-feeding. The diagnostic chart and the boxes on these pages deal with most of the common problems that may arise.

For children over one, see chart 39, Loss of appetite

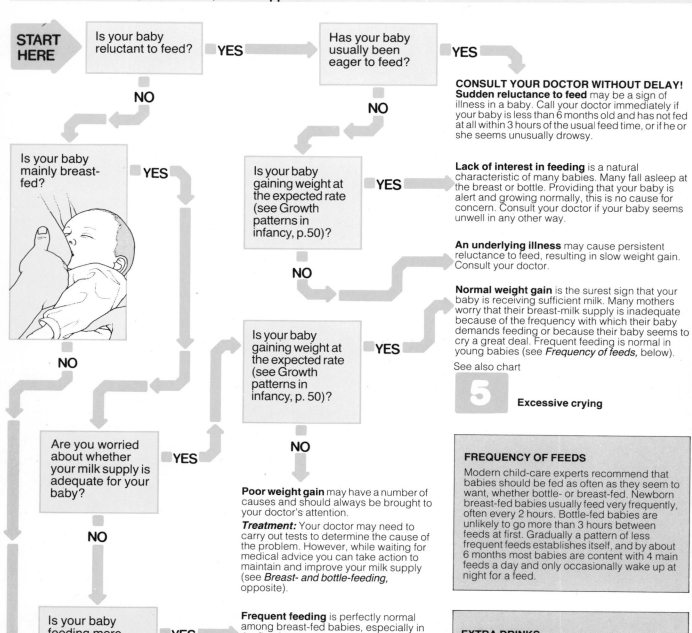

START HERE

Is your baby reluctant to feed? — YES → Has your baby usually been eager to feed? — YES →

**CONSULT YOUR DOCTOR WITHOUT DELAY!**
**Sudden reluctance to feed** may be a sign of illness in a baby. Call your doctor immediately if your baby is less than 6 months old and has not fed at all within 3 hours of the usual feed time, or if he or she seems unusually drowsy.

NO

Is your baby mainly breast-fed? — YES →

NO → Is your baby gaining weight at the expected rate (see Growth patterns in infancy, p.50)? — YES →

**Lack of interest in feeding** is a natural characteristic of many babies. Many fall asleep at the breast or bottle. Providing that your baby is alert and growing normally, this is no cause for concern. Consult your doctor if your baby seems unwell in any other way.

**An underlying illness** may cause persistent reluctance to feed, resulting in slow weight gain. Consult your doctor.

**Normal weight gain** is the surest sign that your baby is receiving sufficient milk. Many mothers worry that their breast-milk supply is inadequate because of the frequency with which their baby demands feeding or because their baby seems to cry a great deal. Frequent feeding is normal in young babies (see *Frequency of feeds,* below).

See also chart

**5** Excessive crying

NO

Is your baby gaining weight at the expected rate (see Growth patterns in infancy, p. 50)? — YES →

Are you worried about whether your milk supply is adequate for your baby? — YES →

NO

**Poor weight gain** may have a number of causes and should always be brought to your doctor's attention.
**Treatment:** Your doctor may need to carry out tests to determine the cause of the problem. However, while waiting for medical advice you can take action to maintain and improve your milk supply (see *Breast- and bottle-feeding,* opposite).

Is your baby feeding more frequently than you think is normal? — YES →

**Frequent feeding** is perfectly normal among breast-fed babies, especially in the first few weeks, and this helps build up your milk production. It is only a problem if you are becoming over-tired as a result. (see *Frequency of feeds,* above right).
**Self-help:** If you are tired from frequent night feeds, try expressing milk, which your partner can give to your baby during the night so that you can have some uninterrupted sleep. Some mothers find that it helps to have the baby in bed with them so that they need not get up at night when the baby needs feeding. If tiredness is making you depressed or irritable, consult your doctor.

NO

**FREQUENCY OF FEEDS**
Modern child-care experts recommend that babies should be fed as often as they seem to want, whether bottle- or breast-fed. Newborn breast-fed babies usually feed very frequently, often every 2 hours. Bottle-fed babies are unlikely to go more than 3 hours between feeds at first. Gradually a pattern of less frequent feeds establishes itself, and by about 6 months most babies are content with 4 main feeds a day and only occasionally wake up at night for a feed.

**EXTRA DRINKS**
Most breast-fed babies and many bottle-fed babies do not need extra drinks in the first few weeks. However, if the weather is hot or if milk does not seem to satisfy your baby, you can offer extra drinks of cooled boiled water from a sterilized bottle or spoon. Later on, especially after you have begun weaning, your baby will enjoy more frequent drinks of non-milk fluids. Remember, sweetened fruit syrups that have not been sufficiently diluted may give young babies diarrhoea, and can lead to excessive weight gain and tooth decay. Plain water and unsweetened fruit juices are preferable.

Go to next page, column 1 — Go to next page, column 2

**1** *Continued from previous page, column 1*

**2** *Continued from previous page, column 2*

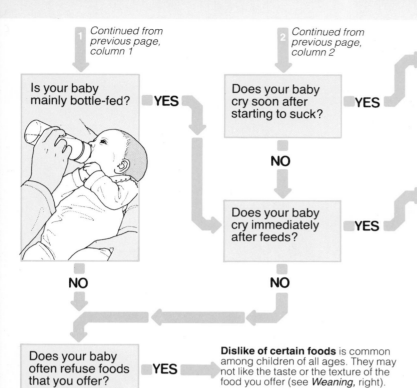

**Is your baby mainly bottle-fed?** → **YES**

**Does your baby cry soon after starting to suck?** → **YES**

NO

**Does your baby cry immediately after feeds?** → **YES**

NO — NO

**Does your baby often refuse foods that you offer?** → **YES**

NO

**Consult your doctor** if you are unable to make a diagnosis from this chart.

**Dislike of certain foods** is common among children of all ages. They may not like the taste or the texture of the food you offer (see *Weaning*, right).

**Self-help:** In the first year eating is still a new experience. So be patient and continue to offer a variety of foods (see *The components of a healthy diet*, p.119). Providing that your baby is putting on weight normally (see *Growth patterns in infancy*, p. 50), there is no need to consult your doctor.

**Delayed "let down" reflex** is often the cause of such crying. This means that milk is not immediately released from the glands in the breast when your baby starts to suck. Alternatively, the milk may be let down too forcefully.

**Self-help:** If you think that the problem is delayed let-down, the best cure is to relax. Make sure you are comfortable and undistracted during feed times. If necessary, go into a room away from the rest of the family and take the telephone off the hook. If your let-down reflex is too strong for your baby, try expressing a little milk before starting a feed.

**Wind or thirst** are possible explanations for this.

Go to chart

**5** **Excessive crying**

### WEANING
Your doctor or health visitor will give you full advice on the age at which to start to introduce your baby to solid foods and the best way to do this, but here are some broad guidelines to help you:

- Do not give non-milk foods before 3 months.
- Start slowly by giving small amounts (about one teaspoonful) of ground rice, cereal, or fruit or vegetable puree, once a day.
- Never add salt or sugar to your baby's food.
- Make sure early foods are smooth and not too thick.
- Gradually give a wider variety of tastes and textures.
- Do not give ordinary cow's milk before 6 months.
- Remember gradually to reduce your baby's milk intake as more solid food is given or your baby will become overweight.

See also *The components of a healthy diet*, p. 119.

---

## BREAST- and BOTTLE-FEEDING

### Breast-feeding
All doctors nowadays agree that where possible breast-feeding is the best way to feed a baby. Breast milk contains all the nutrients a baby needs in the ideal proportions and in the most easily digested form. In addition, a baby who is breast-fed receives substances called antibodies in the milk that protect against infection.

There are very few women who cannot or should not breast-feed their baby if they want to. And most early difficulties can be overcome with patience and determination. Some common breast-feeding problems are discussed below.

### Sore nipples
Most new mothers experience some soreness in the first few days of breast-feeding. This normally gets better without special treatment, but here are some suggestions for minimizing discomfort:

- Ensure that your baby is latching on properly (see right).
- Prevent your breasts from becoming overfull (see right).
- Keep your nipples as dry as possible between feeds.
- If necessary apply a bland, lanolin-based cream.

Consult your doctor or midwife if the skin around the nipple becomes cracked or if pain continues throughout the feed.

### Maintaining your milk supply
Most mothers produce exactly the right amount of milk to meet their baby's needs. The following measures will ensure that your milk supply remains plentiful:

- Eat a nourishing diet (you may need 800 calories a day more than usual).
- Do not allow yourself to become overtired.
- Offer your baby a feed whenever you or your baby feels the need.
- If you are temporarily unable to feed your baby express your milk at normal feed times so that you can resume normal feeding later.
- Unless there is a special reason, avoid giving your baby supplementary bottles of artificial milk; these will satisfy your baby's hunger and prevent your breasts receiving the stimulation they need to produce more milk.

**Latching on**
When you put your baby to the breast, make sure that he or she takes the whole of the nipple and areola (coloured area) into the mouth (far left) otherwise your nipples may become sore. If your breasts are overfull, latching on may be difficult (left) and you should follow the advice below.

### Overfull breasts
This can be uncomfortable for you and frustrating for your baby because it makes latching on difficult. Some suggestions for dealing with this problem are listed.

- Encourage your baby to feed frequently.
- If latching on has become difficult for your baby, express a little milk from the nipple before each feed.
- If your breasts are very full and your baby is not ready to feed, express some milk.

### Bottle-feeding
Breast milk is the ideal form of nutrition for young babies. But for those mothers who are unable or unwilling to breast-feed, modern artificial milk formulas provide a satisfactory alternative.

### Making up the feeds
Feeds should always be made up exactly according to the manufacturer's instructions. Adding too much milk formula may make the feed dangerously concentrated, and adding too little may over a long period lead to poor weight gain. Always use water that has previously been boiled. Keep feeds made up in advance in air-tight containers in a fridge for no longer than 24 hours.

### Sterilizing feeding equipment
Because germs grow very easily in inadequately washed bottles and utensils, make sure you wash all your baby's feeding equipment thoroughly after each feed and sterilize it before the next.

# 7 Vomiting in babies

**Vomiting is the forceful "throwing up" of the contents of the stomach. In young babies it is easy to confuse this with regurgitation which is the effortless bringing back of small amounts of milk during or just after a feed. Almost any minor upset can cause a baby to vomit once, but persistent vomiting can be a sign of serious disease.**

For children over 1 year, consult chart 37, Vomiting in children.

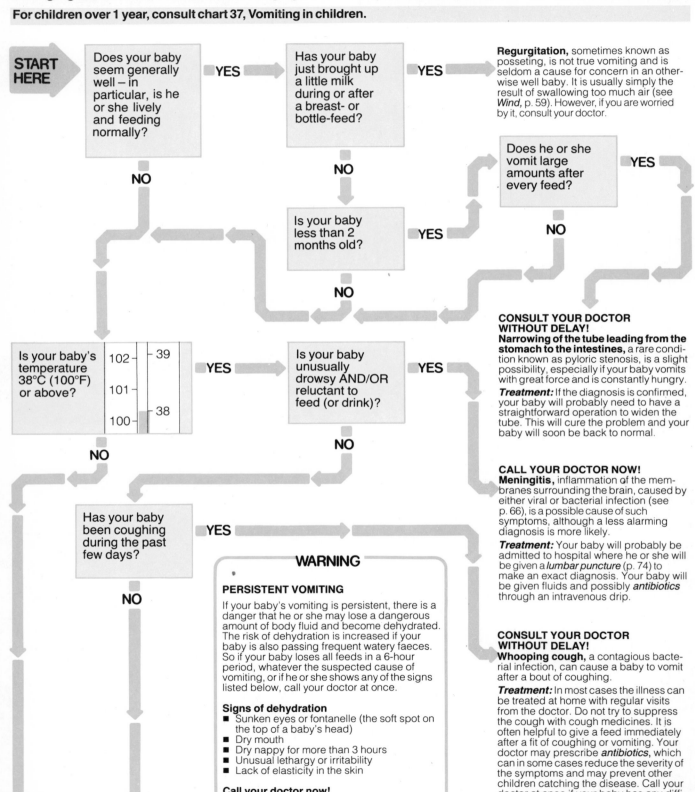

**START HERE**

Does your baby seem generally well – in particular, is he or she lively and feeding normally?

Has your baby just brought up a little milk during or after a breast- or bottle-feed?

**Regurgitation,** sometimes known as posseting, is not true vomiting and is seldom a cause for concern in an otherwise well baby. It is usually simply the result of swallowing too much air (see *Wind,* p. 59). However, if you are worried by it, consult your doctor.

Does he or she vomit large amounts after every feed?

Is your baby less than 2 months old?

Is your baby's temperature 38°C (100°F) or above?

*[thermometer: 102, 101, 100 / 39, 38]*

Is your baby unusually drowsy AND/OR reluctant to feed (or drink)?

**CONSULT YOUR DOCTOR WITHOUT DELAY!**
**Narrowing of the tube leading from the stomach to the intestines,** a rare condition known as pyloric stenosis, is a slight possibility, especially if your baby vomits with great force and is constantly hungry.

***Treatment:*** If the diagnosis is confirmed, your baby will probably need to have a straightforward operation to widen the tube. This will cure the problem and your baby will soon be back to normal.

**CALL YOUR DOCTOR NOW!**
**Meningitis,** inflammation of the membranes surrounding the brain, caused by either viral or bacterial infection (see p. 66), is a possible cause of such symptoms, although a less alarming diagnosis is more likely.

***Treatment:*** Your baby will probably be admitted to hospital where he or she will be given a *lumbar puncture* (p. 74) to make an exact diagnosis. Your baby will be given fluids and possibly *antibiotics* through an intravenous drip.

Has your baby been coughing during the past few days?

## WARNING

**PERSISTENT VOMITING**

If your baby's vomiting is persistent, there is a danger that he or she may lose a dangerous amount of body fluid and become dehydrated. The risk of dehydration is increased if your baby is also passing frequent watery faeces. So if your baby loses all feeds in a 6-hour period, whatever the suspected cause of vomiting, or if he or she shows any of the signs listed below, call your doctor at once.

**Signs of dehydration**
- Sunken eyes or fontanelle (the soft spot on the top of a baby's head)
- Dry mouth
- Dry nappy for more than 3 hours
- Unusual lethargy or irritability
- Lack of elasticity in the skin

**Call your doctor now!**

**CONSULT YOUR DOCTOR WITHOUT DELAY!**
**Whooping cough,** a contagious bacterial infection, can cause a baby to vomit after a bout of coughing.

***Treatment:*** In most cases the illness can be treated at home with regular visits from the doctor. Do not try to suppress the cough with cough medicines. It is often helpful to give a feed immediately after a fit of coughing or vomiting. Your doctor may prescribe *antibiotics*, which can in some cases reduce the severity of the symptoms and may prevent other children catching the disease. Call your doctor at once if your baby has any difficulty in breathing or turns bluish during a bout of coughing.

1 Go to next page, column 1

2 Go to next page, column 2

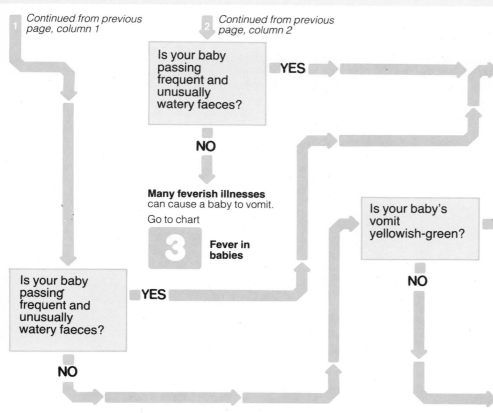

¹ Continued from previous page, column 1

² Continued from previous page, column 2

**Is your baby passing frequent and unusually watery faeces?**

**YES** → **CONSULT YOUR DOCTOR WITHOUT DELAY!**

**NO**

**Many feverish illnesses** can cause a baby to vomit.

Go to chart

**3** **Fever in babies**

**Is your baby passing frequent and unusually watery faeces?**

**YES**

**NO**

**Is your baby's vomit yellowish-green?**

**YES**

**NO**

**CONSULT YOUR DOCTOR WITHOUT DELAY!**
**Gastroenteritis,** infection of the digestive tract, is likely.

**Treatment:** If your doctor confirms the diagnosis, he or she is likely to recommend that you follow the guidelines for treating gastroenteritis described in the box below. However, if your baby's symptoms are severe, or if he or she is showing signs of dehydration (see the warning box opposite), your doctor may advise admission to hospital where fluids can be given by intravenous drip.

**CALL YOUR DOCTOR NOW!**
**A serious abdominal condition** is a possible cause of such symptoms.

**Treatment:** Your baby will probably be admitted to hospital where he or she can be properly examined and an exact diagnosis made. Treatment will depend on the underlying condition and may involve an operation.

**An isolated attack of vomiting** is unlikely to be a sign of serious illness in your baby. However, if your baby vomits more than once in a day or seems otherwise unwell, consult your doctor.

## TREATING GASTROENTERITIS IN BABIES

If your doctor decides that your baby can be safely treated at home, he or she will probably recommend that you stop all milk and solids for at least 24 hours and gradually reintroduce a normal diet over the following days. Example schemes for breast-fed, weaned and bottled-fed babies are described here. Instead of milk and other drinks you may be advised to give your baby a glucose solution (see *Making up a glucose solution,* right). While your baby is vomiting you will need to give drinks at frequent intervals (about every hour). Later on you can give drinks at your usual feed times and whenever your baby seems thirsty.

### Calculating your baby's fluid needs
Babies with gastroenteritis need to receive a carefully regulated amount of fluid each day to prevent dehydration. To calculate the correct amount for your baby, find his or her weight in the left-hand column of the table (below left) and then look across to the right-hand column to find the volume of fluid that your baby needs each day. No baby, regardless of weight, should receive less than ½ litre (¾ pint) or more than 1½ litres (2½ pints).

### Making up a glucose solution
You can make up your own glucose solution using 3 level teaspoonfuls of glucose to 200ml (7fl.oz) of boiled walter. Alternatively, you can use sachets of glucose and mineral powder, available over-the-counter from chemists, made up with cooled boiled water according to the instructions.

### Breast-fed babies
If your breast-fed baby has gastroenteritis, do not breast feed for the first 24 hours of the illness, but give the recommended amount of glucose solution. On each successive day reduce the amount of glucose solution you offer at each feed time by one fifth of the total recommended, and put your baby to the breast afterwards. During the days of treatment you can relieve the discomfort of overfull breasts by expressing the excess breast milk.

### Weaned babies
If your baby is already weaned, give no milk or dairy products for 5 days, but give the recommended amount of glucose solution for his or her weight. Give no solids on Day 1, but you can introduce gradually increased amounts of sieved fruit or vegetables from Day 2 until Day 6 when you can resume your normal feeding routine.

### Bottle-fed babies

**Day 1**
Give no milk. Instead give glucose solution at regular intervals.

**Day 2**
Give your baby a mixture of 1 part made up milk formula to 4 parts glucose solution at each feed time.

**Day 3**
Give a mixture of 2 parts milk formula to 3 parts glucose solution at each feed time.

**Day 4**
Give a mixture of 3 parts milk formula to 2 parts glucose solution at each feed time.

**Day 5**
Give a mixture of 4 parts milk formula to 1 part glucose solution at each feed time.

**Day 6**
Return to normal feeding.

**Note:** If at any time your baby's symptoms recur, go back to Day 1 and call your doctor.

| Baby's weight | | Daily fluid intake | |
|---|---|---|---|
| kg | lb | ml | fl.oz |
| under 3.5 | under 8 | 525 | 18 |
| 4 | 9 | 600 | 21 |
| 4.5 | 10 | 675 | 24 |
| 5 | 11 | 750 | 26 |
| 5.5 | 12 | 825 | 29 |
| 6 | 13 | 900 | 32 |
| 6.5 | 14 | 975 | 34 |
| 7 | 15 | 1050 | 37 |
| 7.5 | 16–17 | 1125 | 40 |
| 8 | 18 | 1200 | 42 |
| 8.5 | 19 | 1275 | 45 |
| 9 | 20 | 1350 | 48 |
| 9.5 | 21 | 1425 | 50 |
| over 10 | over 22 | 1500 | 53 |

# 8 Diarrhoea in babies

Diarrhoea is the passage of runny, watery faeces more frequently than is usual for your baby. Remember that it is quite normal for a fully breast-fed baby to pass very soft faeces and this should not be mistaken for true diarrhoea. However, if your baby has diarrhoea, it is important to prevent dehydration (see below).

**For children over 1 year, see chart 40, Diarrhoea in children**

START HERE

Is your baby's temperature 38°C (100°F) or above AND/OR is he or she vomiting?
- NO
- YES

Is your baby lethargic OR failing to feed well?
- NO
- YES

**CONSULT YOUR DOCTOR WITHOUT DELAY!**
**Gastroenteritis** is possible especially if your baby is bottle-fed.
**Treatment:** See *Treating gastroenteritis in babies,* p 63.

Have you just started to re-introduce milk into your baby's diet after a bout of gastroenteritis?
- NO
- YES

**A recurrence of gastroenteritis** is possible. Consult your doctor.
**Treatment:** You will probably be advised to resume the treatment for *gastroenteritis* (p. 63) for a few more days, and then gradually to re-introduce a normal diet.

Are you mainly bottle-feeding your baby?
- NO
- YES

Have you added sugar to the feed?
- NO
- YES

## AVOIDING GASTROENTERITIS

If anyone in your household is suffering from gastroenteritis, it is important to be careful to avoid spreading the infection to a young baby, or, if it is the baby who is affected, to avoid spreading the infection to the rest of the family.

It is sensible to take the following precautions as a matter of routine:
- Wash your hands after going to the lavatory.
- Sterilize all feeding equipment and dummies regularly and thoroughly.
- Always wash your hands before preparing your baby's feeds and after changing nappies.
- Reserve a towel for your baby's exclusive use and wash it often.

**Avoiding infections abroad**
Travel in North America and Northwestern Europe presents no more risk of gastroenteritis for babies than travel in the UK. Your usual precautions will be sufficient. However, in other parts of the world, particularly in hot climates, you will need to be especially careful. Water supplies may carry infection, so it is best to boil all drinking water and to be scrupulous when sterilizing feeding equipment. Raw fruit and vegetables are a common source of infection and are best avoided. If the weather is hot your baby – whether bottle- or breast-fed – will need extra fluids to avoid dehydration.

**Inability to digest sugar** can easily cause a baby's digestion to be upset. Always follow the manufacturer's instructions exactly when making up feeds, and never add sugar.

Has your baby been drinking more fruit juice than usual, or been drinking or eating unusually sweet things?
- NO
- YES

**Excess sugar** in fruit juice or in sweet drinks and foods can cause stomach upsets in babies. Baby orange juice should always be diluted according to the instructions on the bottle. Sugary drinks and foods do not contribute to your baby's nutrition, and are best avoided since, as well as leading to digestive upsets, they may make your baby overweight and are likely to lead to dental decay.

Has your baby been prescribed any medicine for some other disorder?
- NO
- YES

**Some medicines** for children can cause diarrhoea, often because they have a syrupy base to encourage the child to take them. Do not stop giving the medicine, but discuss the problem with your doctor.

Have you just started your baby on solids?
- NO
- YES

**Unfamiliar foods** may cause digestive upsets in babies. This is no cause for concern if it happens only occasionally and your baby's bowel movements quickly return to normal. But if the problem persists, or seems to happen only when a certain food is eaten, consult your doctor.

**Consult your doctor** if you are unable to make a diagnosis from this chart.

## PREVENTING DEHYDRATION

If your baby has persistent diarrhoea, especially if it is accompanied by vomiting, there is a danger of dehydration (loss of body fluids). So it is important to give your baby plenty of extra fluids, even if he or she does not take in any food or milk (see *Treating gastroenteritis,* p. 63).

Even if you think your baby is taking in adequate amounts of fluid, you should be on the lookout for signs of dehydration (see *Persistent vomiting,* p. 62).

**Signs of dehydration**
- Sunken eyes or fontanelle (the soft spot on the top of a baby's head)
- Dry mouth
- Dry nappy for more than 3 hours
- Unusual lethargy or irritability
- Lack of elasticity in the skin

# Children: all ages

# 9 Feeling generally unwell

A child may sometimes complain of feeling unwell without giving you a clear idea of what exactly the matter is. Or you may suspect that your child is unwell if he or she seems less lively or more irritable than usual. If this happens you may be able to find a possible explanation for the problem by looking for specific signs of illness as described in this chart. If your child is under 2 years old, see the box below.

**For unusual drowsiness, see chart 13, Drowsiness**

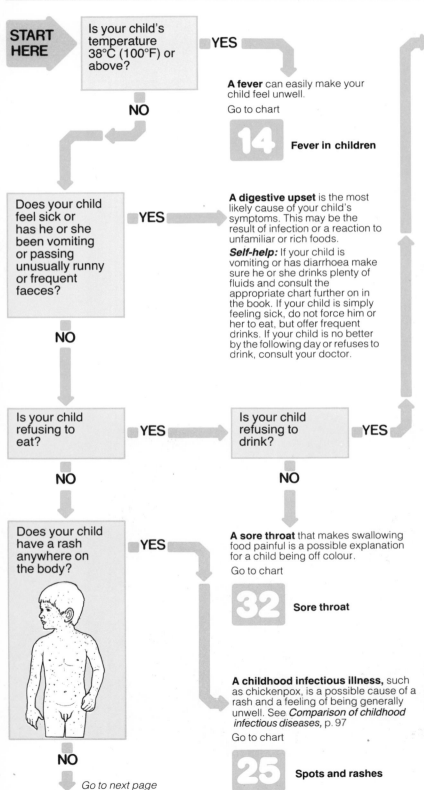

**START HERE**

Is your child's temperature 38°C (100°F) or above?

**YES** →

**A fever** can easily make your child feel unwell.

Go to chart

**14** **Fever in children**

**NO**

Does your child feel sick or has he or she been vomiting or passing unusually runny or frequent faeces?

**YES** →

**A digestive upset** is the most likely cause of your child's symptoms. This may be the result of infection or a reaction to unfamiliar or rich foods.

*Self-help:* If your child is vomiting or has diarrhoea make sure he or she drinks plenty of fluids and consult the appropriate chart further on in the book. If your child is simply feeling sick, do not force him or her to eat, but offer frequent drinks. If your child is no better by the following day or refuses to drink, consult your doctor.

**NO**

Is your child refusing to eat?

**YES** →

Is your child refusing to drink?

**YES** →

**NO**

**NO**

Does your child have a rash anywhere on the body?

**YES** →

**A sore throat** that makes swallowing food painful is a possible explanation for a child being off colour.

Go to chart

**32** **Sore throat**

**A childhood infectious illness,** such as chickenpox, is a possible cause of a rash and a feeling of being generally unwell. See *Comparison of childhood infectious diseases,* p. 97

Go to chart

**25** **Spots and rashes**

**NO**

*Go to next page*

---

**CALL YOUR DOCTOR NOW!**
**Refusal to eat or drink,** when combined with other signs of illness such as listlessness or irritability, is a serious symptom requiring urgent medical attention.

### CHILDREN UNDER TWO

It is usually easy for you to tell when your baby or young child is unwell: he or she may seem irritable, or may cry continuously and the sound of the cry may be quite different from the healthy yell you are used to. However, since a baby cannot describe his or her feelings to you, it is often quite difficult to find out the cause of the problem. In addition, illnesses in young children tend to develop much faster than in older children and adults. It is therefore usually best to seek your doctor's advice if your baby or toddler seems generally unwell for no obvious reason. You should call your doctor as a matter of urgency if your baby has any of the following symptoms:

- abnormal drowsiness or unresponsiveness
- temperature over 39°C (102°F)
- repeated vomiting
- diarrhoea for more than 24 hours
- abnormally rapid breathing (see p. 110)
- noisy breathing
- refusal to drink
- rash

### VIRAL AND BACTERIAL INFECTIONS

Childhood infections may be caused by two different types of microbe, bacteria or viruses, and these microbes and the illnesses they cause differ from each other in several important ways.

**Bacteria**
Bacteria multiply in body fluids, they are large enough to be seen under a microscope and are destroyed by *antibiotics*. A child can be infected by the same bacteria many times.

**Viruses**
Viruses are much smaller than bacteria and multiply inside body cells. They cannot be seen under a microscope and are unaffected by standard antibiotics. A single attack by a particular virus usually gives lifelong immunity and this is why children normally have mumps or chickenpox only once.

**Treatment**
A doctor examining a sick child has to decide whether the cause is likely to be a viral or bacterial infection. Often the two are difficult to distinguish without time-consuming laboratory tests. In most cases, he or she will make a diagnosis based on the test results of other local children suffering from similar symptoms. If a virus is thought to be responsible, treatment is aimed at relieving symptoms, such as pain and fever. If there is bacterial infection, or the possibility that bacterial infection may develop, your doctor may prescribe antibiotics.

*Continued from previous page*

Has your child been in contact with an infectious illness within the past 3 weeks?

**YES**

**Childhood infectious illnesses** often start by making the child feel generally unwell. The appearance of a specific symptom, such as a rash, within a few days should make diagnosis easier. (See *Comparison of childhood infectious diseases,* p. 97.) Consult your doctor if your child is no better in 24 hours or develops further symptoms.

**NO**

Does your child complain of stomach ache or does he or she cry and draw his or her legs up towards the stomach?

**YES**

**Abdominal pain** may occur in a child for a variety of reasons.

Go to chart

 **38**  **Abdominal pain**

**NO**

Can you think of any reason why your child may wish to stay at home (if he or she goes to school) or why he or she may want extra attention from you?

**YES**

**School difficulties or insecurity at home** can often make a child feel physically unwell.

*Self-help:* If this is the first time that this has happened, keep your child at home for a day and try to discover what the underlying problem is, and if possible reassure your child. If your child still feels unwell the following day, call your doctor. If your child regularly refuses to go to school, you may need special help.

Go to chart

 **23**  **School difficulties**

**NO**

**Consult your doctor** if you are unable to make a diagnosis from this chart and your child is no better in 24 hours.

---

**EXAMINATION BY THE DOCTOR**

A doctor examining a child who is unwell is following a methodical routine of assessment. First the doctor decides whether the child looks ill. He or she checks the pulse and breathing rates and then examines the different body systems in turn.

**Lymph glands**
The doctor feels along the jaw (left) and in the armpits and groin for signs of swelling that may suggest infection.

**Throat and mouth**
The inside of the mouth and throat are examined for inflammation and spots using a wooden spatula and small torch (right).

**Heart and lungs**
The health of heart and lungs are assessed by listening to the child's chest and back through a stethoscope (below).

**Ears**
*Ear examination* is described on p. 103.

**Abdomen**
The abdomen is gently pressed (palpated) to check for swelling of any of the internal organs (liver, spleen, etc.) (below).

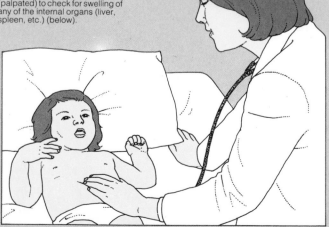

# 10 Slow growth

Many parents worry that their child is too short or too thin. Some children are naturally smaller than average as a result of heredity or other factors: serious growth disorders affecting general health are rare. The best way for you to avoid unnecessary anxiety is to keep a regular record of your child's height and weight so that you will know that your child is growing in proportion as well as at a normal rate (see the growth charts on pp. 298-301). Consult the diagnostic chart below only if your child's weight is increasing at a much slower rate than you would expect from his or her height, or if your child fails to grow in height as much as expected.

For children under 1 year, consult chart 1, Slow weight gain.

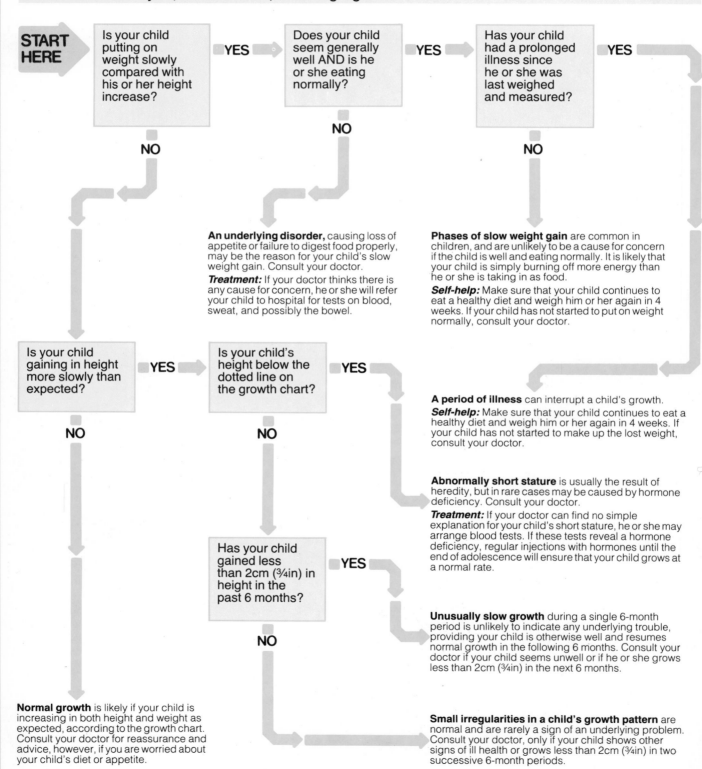

**START HERE**

Is your child putting on weight slowly compared with his or her height increase?

**YES** — Does your child seem generally well AND is he or she eating normally?

**YES** — Has your child had a prolonged illness since he or she was last weighed and measured?

**YES**

**NO** (from first box)

**NO** (from second box)

**NO** (from third box)

**An underlying disorder,** causing loss of appetite or failure to digest food properly, may be the reason for your child's slow weight gain. Consult your doctor.
**Treatment:** If your doctor thinks there is any cause for concern, he or she will refer your child to hospital for tests on blood, sweat, and possibly the bowel.

**Phases of slow weight gain** are common in children, and are unlikely to be a cause for concern if the child is well and eating normally. It is likely that your child is simply burning off more energy than he or she is taking in as food.
**Self-help:** Make sure that your child continues to eat a healthy diet and weigh him or her again in 4 weeks. If your child has not started to put on weight normally, consult your doctor.

Is your child gaining in height more slowly than expected?

**YES** — Is your child's height below the dotted line on the growth chart?

**YES**

**NO** (gaining in height)

**NO** (height below dotted line)

**A period of illness** can interrupt a child's growth.
**Self-help:** Make sure that your child continues to eat a healthy diet and weigh him or her again in 4 weeks. If your child has not started to make up the lost weight, consult your doctor.

**Abnormally short stature** is usually the result of heredity, but in rare cases may be caused by hormone deficiency. Consult your doctor.
**Treatment:** If your doctor can find no simple explanation for your child's short stature, he or she may arrange blood tests. If these tests reveal a hormone deficiency, regular injections with hormones until the end of adolescence will ensure that your child grows at a normal rate.

Has your child gained less than 2cm (¾in) in height in the past 6 months?

**YES**

**NO**

**Unusually slow growth** during a single 6-month period is unlikely to indicate any underlying trouble, providing your child is otherwise well and resumes normal growth in the following 6 months. Consult your doctor if your child seems unwell or if he or she grows less than 2cm (¾in) in the next 6 months.

**Normal growth** is likely if your child is increasing in both height and weight as expected, according to the growth chart. Consult your doctor for reassurance and advice, however, if you are worried about your child's diet or appetite.

**Small irregularities in a child's growth pattern** are normal and are rarely a sign of an underlying problem. Consult your doctor, only if your child shows other signs of ill health or grows less than 2cm (¾in) in two successive 6-month periods.

## GROWTH PATTERNS IN CHILDHOOD

The growth charts on pp. 298-301 enable you to record your child's height and weight at regular intervals and to compare his or her progress with the standard growth rates for large, average and small children.

Usually, a child's growth will remain close to the standard curves for both height and weight throughout childhood. However, sometimes growth patterns can vary, as shown below.

### Naturally slim
Some children are naturally slim. This is unlikely to be a cause for concern in a healthy child if both height and weight increase at a constant rate, and providing that the child's weight is only a little less than expected. The chart shown is that of a normal child who has always been light for his or her height.

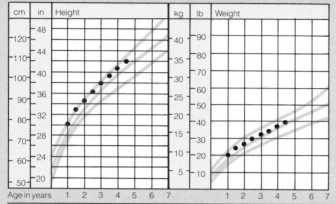

### Losing excess weight
An overweight child may at first appear to be gaining insufficient weight as he or she slims down. The chart shows a child of average height who at 2 years weighed as much as a child of above average height. Over the next 2 years he or she gained little weight so that by the age of 4, the child's weight was normal for his or her height.

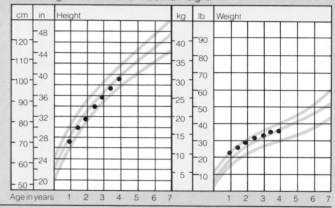

### Too light
This chart shows a tall child whose weight is increasing much slower than normal, although growing in height as expected. If your child's weight is increasing at less than the normal rate, you should consult your doctor.

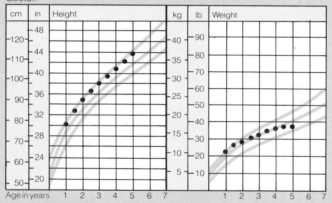

### Too small
This chart shows both weight and height increasing at a much slower rate than is normal, even for a small child. If your child's growth chart looks like this, you should seek medical advice.

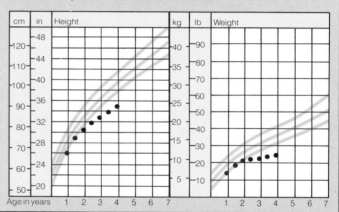

### Overweight
The chart of a child who is overweight shows a normal rate of height increase – in this example the child is just below average height – but the weight increase curve is similar to that of a much taller child. If your child's growth chart looks like this, consult diagnostic chart 11, *Excessive weight gain.*

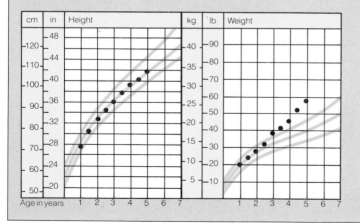

### Late puberty
A child approaching puberty who is a late developer may appear to be growing more slowly than normal, at an age when many of his or her contemporaries have reached a period of rapid growth. This is, however, no cause for concern, the child will make up for the delay later, as shown in this example. See also diagnostic chart 50, *Delayed puberty*

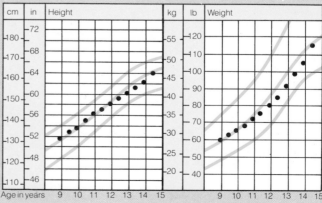

# 11 Excessive weight gain

Growing appreciation of the dangers of obesity in adults has led to an increasing awareness that the problem often starts in childhood when eating habits are established. In addition, being overweight carries particular health risks for a child and may contribute to emotional and social problems as he or she gets older. It is therefore most important for parents to be alert to the possibility of excessive weight gain in their child. The appearance of a young baby is not always a reliable sign of obesity, as babies and toddlers are naturally chubby. The best way of ensuring that you quickly notice any weight problem in your child is to keep a regular record of your child's growth (see the growth charts on p. 298-301). If your child's weight-gain curve is rising more steeply than that for increase in head circumference or for height increase, your child is probably becoming fat. Consult this diagnostic chart to find out the possible cause of the problem.

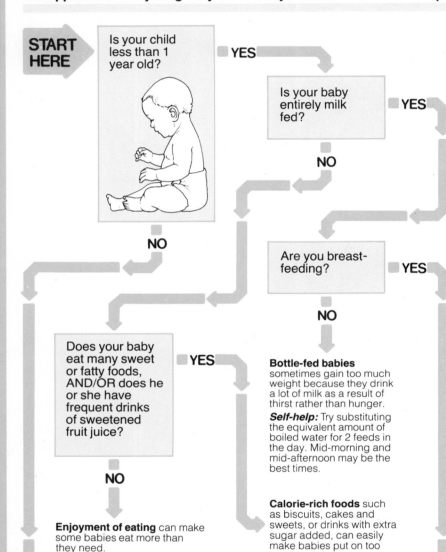

**START HERE**

Is your child less than 1 year old?

YES → Is your baby entirely milk fed?

YES → Are you breast-feeding?

YES

NO

NO

NO

Does your baby eat many sweet or fatty foods, AND/OR does he or she have frequent drinks of sweetened fruit juice?

YES

NO

**Enjoyment of eating** can make some babies eat more than they need.
***Self-help:*** Try to increase the amount of bulky, but low-calorie foods such as fruit and vegetables that you offer your baby. Commercial baby foods often contain more calories than meals you prepare yourself, so it is best to use these as little as possible. Look at your baby's milk intake. If he or she is still drinking as much milk as before you started mixed feeding you may be able to limit weight gain by substituting plain boiled water or well-diluted, unsweetened fruit juice.

*Go to next page*

**Bottle-fed babies** sometimes gain too much weight because they drink a lot of milk as a result of thirst rather than hunger.
***Self-help:*** Try substituting the equivalent amount of boiled water for 2 feeds in the day. Mid-morning and mid-afternoon may be the best times.

**Calorie-rich foods** such as biscuits, cakes and sweets, or drinks with extra sugar added, can easily make babies put on too much weight.
***Self-help:*** Cut out all sugary and fried foods from your baby's diet. They are not necessary for adequate nutrition. Try substituting more fruit and vegetables. Commercial baby foods tend to contain more calories than meals you prepare yourself, so try to avoid these. If your baby drinks large quantities of sweetened drinks, offer plain water or well-diluted unsweetened fruit juice instead. See also *The components of a healthy diet,* p. 119.

## CAUSES OF EXCESSIVE WEIGHT GAIN

The vast majority of children who become overweight do so because they regularly eat more food than they burn up to produce energy. The excess calories are then deposited under the skin as fat. Normally children will adjust their intake of food according to their energy needs. However, the body's natural appetite-regulating mechanism can be upset by a number of factors.

**Family overeating**
The most common cause of obesity in children is habitual overeating in the family, so that the child loses touch with the body's real needs. The family may eat too many of the wrong foods (mainly sugar and fat) or may simply eat too much. So if your child is overweight, look at yourself and the rest of the family; the chances are that you are all fatter than you should be. In this case the best way to help your child to slim will be for the whole family to adopt healthier eating habits.

**Enforced eating**
A child who is brought up to finish everything on the plate, regardless of appetite, may also become overweight, because he or she will become used to eating more than necessary to please his or her parents.

**Comfort eating**
Less commonly, a child may turn to eating in reaction to stress and anxiety. In this situation food is used for comfort rather than to satisfy hunger, and over a period the child may get into the habit of eating too much.

**Medical causes**
Medical problems that cause obesity are extremely rare, and should only be considered if your child shows other signs of ill health or if genuine attempts at dieting fail.

**Three golden rules for preventing your child from becoming overweight**
- Make sure that the whole family is eating a healthy diet (see *The components of a healthy diet,* p.119).
- Always be guided by your child's appetite and never force him or her to eat. He or she will not go hungry.
- Try to avoid giving or withholding food as a form of reward or punishment. This may give food emotional significance for your child which can lead to eating problems in the future.

**Breast-fed babies** often gain weight quickly between 2 and 4 months. This is perfectly normal and no special action is necessary.

*Continued from previous page*

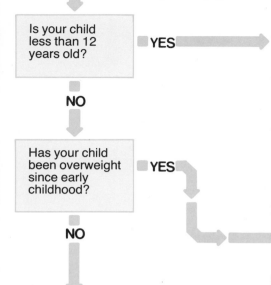

**Is your child less than 12 years old?**

**YES** →

**NO** ↓

**Has your child been overweight since early childhood?**

**YES** →

**NO** ↓

**Family overeating** is almost always the cause of excessive weight gain in this age group. See *Causes of excessive weight gain*, opposite.

**Self-help:** Suggestions for helping your child to slim are given below. Do not try to achieve a rapid weight loss or you will become over-anxious about your child's eating habits and may transmit your anxiety to your child, creating additional problems. At this age, when children have plenty of growing to do before they reach adult size, concentrate simply on preventing additional weight gain, so that your child "stretches out" as he or she gets taller. If your child is severely overweight, discuss the problem with your doctor, who will help you with diet advice, and may put you in contact with a self-help support group for overweight children in your area.

**Unhealthy eating habits** established in early childhood are likely to persist into adolescence and adulthood unless action is taken.

**Self-help:** Your child probably realizes that he or she has a weight problem and may already be suffering embarrassment because of it. Plenty of moral support from you is necessary to make any diet successful. Look at the diet suggestions below and discuss the best methods of losing weight with your child. Your child's cooperation is essential; if you try to enforce a diet – he or she will only start to eat secretly. Never encourage crash dieting. This can be harmful physically and emotionally. Gradual weight loss over many months is far more effective in the long term.

**Sudden weight gain** as a child approaches adolescence is common, particularly in girls. Slight weight gain may be the result of hormonal changes, but excessive weight gain is more likely to be the result of overeating, possibly as a result of emotional insecurity.

**Self-help:** If your child is only slightly overweight, no special action is necessary other than paying a little extra attention to providing a healthy diet. If your child has put on a lot of weight, try to find out why he or she is overeating. Does your child have any reason to feel insecure? Are there any problems in the family or at school? Tackling the underlying cause of any unhappiness as well as adopting a sensible reducing diet (see *How to help your child lose weight,* right) will help your child to feel more self-confident.

## THE DANGERS OF OBESITY IN CHILDHOOD

### Dangers to health
The principal danger to physical health of obesity in childhood is that children who become fat are statistically more likely to remain so and become fat adults, who in turn are at greater than average risk from disorders of heart and circulation and other problems. There are also risks to health for the child. Some doctors believe that overweight children suffer from more chest infections than those who are slimmer. Tooth decay is more common in overweight children who tend to eat more sugary foods than other children. A child who is overweight is likely to be less physically active than a slimmer child, making it more difficult to burn off the excess fat or to become physically fit in other ways.

### Social and psychological risks
An important risk for obese children is that of social isolation. Fat children are often the butt of other children's cruel jokes, leading to much unhappiness. And, as these children approach adolescence, they will feel more self-conscious and less secure than other children at a time when self-confidence may be low in any case, and the need for acceptance is at its greatest.

## HOW TO HELP YOUR CHILD LOSE WEIGHT

### Diet
The principal adjustment to your child's diet should be to cut out all foods that contain a lot of energy (calories) but few nutrients. Foods in this category include sugar, sweets, cakes, biscuits, most puddings, white bread, and sweetened drinks. At mealtimes substitute fresh fruit for a pudding, and encourage your child to drink plain water or unsweetened fruit juice instead of cola or pop. In many cases this change of diet alone is enough to help a child to lose weight.

You should also look at the way you cook and serve food. Fats of all types (butter, margarine, oil, lard) are all high in calories. So cut down on the amount of fat you use in cooking; grill rather than fry, bake rather than roast. Do not coat vegetables in butter and avoid heavy gravies and sauces. Spread butter and margarine very thinly on bread.

Replace the foods you have cut down on with plenty of fruit and vegetables. These will help satisfy hunger and supply vitamins without making your child fat.

### The importance of exercise
The more physically active a child is, the easier it is to burn up excess fat. Persuade your young child to walk rather than ride in the push chair, and encourage outdoor games that involve running about rather than sedentary activities. An older child may need persuasion to take part in sports at which he or she is unlikely to do well. Less competitive activities such as swimming, dancing and cycling may be more suitable for an overweight child.

### Your support
For children to lose weight successfully, they must never be made to feel different or excluded. Adopt the diet suggestions for the whole family – it will do none of you any harm. Make exercise an enjoyable part of the family routine in which you all participate. Above all, never make your child feel that the diet is a form of punishment. Assure your child of your love no matter what, and you are far more likely to succeed.

All the family can enjoy a healthy diet that helps your child to lose weight.

# 12 Sleeping problems

Most children over 1 year old will sleep through the night without interruption. The amount of sleep a child needs each night varies according to age and individual requirements from about 9 to 12 hours. Lack of sleep does not affect appetite, growth, or development. However, refusal to go to bed at what you consider to be a reasonable time, and/or waking in the middle of the night can be disruptive and sometimes distressing for the whole family. A number of factors may be responsible for such sleeping problems – among them, physical illness, emotional upset, nightmares, and failure to establish a regular bedtime routine.

**For children under 1 year, see chart 2, Waking at night.**

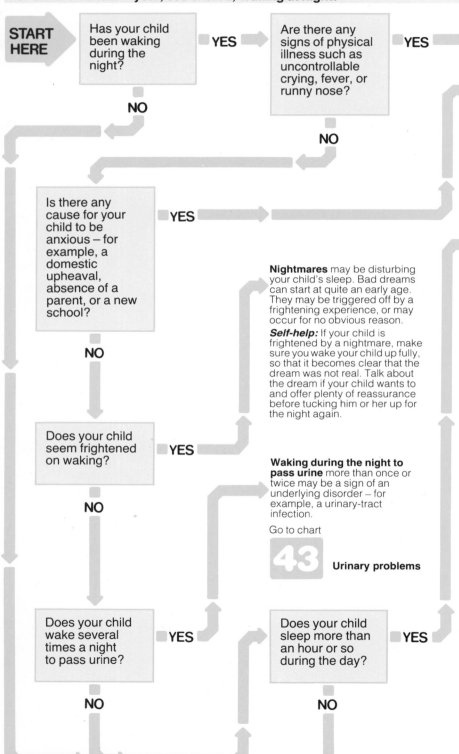

**START HERE**

Has your child been waking during the night?

**YES** →

Are there any signs of physical illness such as uncontrollable crying, fever, or runny nose?

**YES** →

**Most illnesses** will disrupt a child's sleep. Consult the appropriate diagnostic chart elsewhere in the book.

**NO**

**NO**

Is there any cause for your child to be anxious – for example, a domestic upheaval, absence of a parent, or a new school?

**YES** →

**Anxiety** can easily disrupt sleep even if your child seems untroubled during the day.

*Self-help:* Once the cause for worry has been removed, or the child has become used to the new situation, he or she should begin to sleep well again. Meanwhile, offer plenty of reassurance during the day and quietly comfort your child back to sleep again when he or she wakes at night. If there is difficulty in removing the cause of anxiety, or if your child remains disturbed for longer than you think normal, consult your doctor.

**Too much sleep during the day** may mean that your child is not tired enough to sleep properly at night. Some children, especially after the age of 2, need little sleep in the day.

*Self-help:* Try cutting down your child's daytime naps and increase the amount of physical activity during the day. This should make your child more tired and therefore more ready to sleep at night.

**NO**

**Nightmares** may be disturbing your child's sleep. Bad dreams can start at quite an early age. They may be triggered off by a frightening experience, or may occur for no obvious reason.

*Self-help:* If your child is frightened by a nightmare, make sure you wake your child up fully, so that it becomes clear that the dream was not real. Talk about the dream if your child wants to and offer plenty of reassurance before tucking him or her up for the night again.

Does your child seem frightened on waking?

**YES** →

**NO**

**Waking during the night to pass urine** more than once or twice may be a sign of an underlying disorder – for example, a urinary-tract infection.

Go to chart

**43**

**Urinary problems**

Does your child wake several times a night to pass urine?

**YES** →

Does your child sleep more than an hour or so during the day?

**YES** →

**NO**

**NO**

*Go to next page*

---

**NIGHT-TIME WANDERING**

Many children climb out of their cot or bed at night. If you do not want this to become a habit that is hard to break, it is best to deal with it quickly and firmly. If your child is still in a cot, you may be able to lower the base to make climbing out more difficult. If this is not possible, you may not be able to prevent your child from getting up, but should put him or her back to bed firmly and without hesitation each time it happens.

**Sleep-walking**
Walking while asleep is an uncommon, usually harmless problem, which mainly affects 10- to 14-year-olds. It is not known why children should do this, but it may be connected with anxiety. If you find your child sleep-walking, gently guide him or her back to bed. It is not necessary to wake the child unless you think he or she is having a nightmare as well.

*Continued from previous page*

Does your child usually cry as soon as you leave the room at night?

**YES**

**NO**

**Waking at night without obvious cause** may mean that your child has got into the habit of expecting attention from you during the night.
***Self-help:*** To re-establish a regular sleeping rhythm you will need to stick firmly to a plan such as the one described in the box on *Preventing and overcoming sleeping problems,* below. Your child will probably take up to 2 weeks to adjust to the new routine.

**Fear of being left alone** and a continuing need for the reassurance of your presence will often make a child reluctant to go to sleep at night.
***Self-help:*** You will need to accustom your child gradually to the idea of going to sleep on his or her own each night. Try the suggestions for *Preventing and overcoming sleeping problems,* below. If you think your child may be frightened of the dark, leave a night light on.

---

## PREVENTING AND OVERCOMING SLEEPING PROBLEMS

Most children need to have a predictable bedtime ritual to help them settle down for the night. The suggestions made for establishing such a routine for babies under 1 year (see *Helping your baby to sleep,* p. 52) also apply in the main to older children. However, even when there is an established bedtime routine, many young children develop sleeping problems. A child may begin to refuse to go to bed, or may regularly wake at night. This may be triggered off by an upset to the routine, such as a holiday away from home or a stay in hospital, but often may have no apparent cause. If your child has developed some bad sleeping habits, you will need to take steps to re-establish a more convenient pattern.

### Refusal to go to bed
If your child refuses to go to sleep and cries when put to bed for the night after the usual bedtime ritual, you can try one of two approaches suggested below. Whichever method you choose, you will need to ensure total consistency from both parents; any exception to the rule will undermine the progress you have already made. Both methods are likely to involve prolonged periods of crying, so it is wise to warn your neighbours of this.

### Sudden withdrawal
Once you have settled your child in the cot or bed, say goodnight and leave the room, and do not return when your child starts to cry. The first night your child may take an hour or more to go to sleep, but each successive night the period of crying should get shorter, until after a week or so he or she will go to bed without fuss. Your child will come to no harm from the crying, but many parents find this method too upsetting to persevere with.

### Gradual withdrawal
Having put your child to bed, say goodnight and leave the room. Allow your child to cry for about 5 minutes and then return for a few moments to reassure your child that you are still there, say goodnight again and then leave. Repeat this every 5 minutes, trying to reduce the amount of time you spend in the room, until your child falls asleep. This may take several hours the first night, but if you persevere, the time should get shorter until after a week or two there is no further trouble.

### Waking during the night
If your child has got into the habit of waking during the night, you can try a programme of conditioning similar to those described for refusal to go to bed. If your child only whimpers in the night, do not go into the room at once; wait a few moments, he or she may still be half-asleep and will drift off again if undisturbed. If your child is truly crying, you will need to go into the room to check that there is nothing wrong – for example, earache or a nightmare. Once you are satisfied that all is well, give a drink if wanted, tuck your child up again, and say goodnight, then leave the room as quickly and quietly as possible. After this you can either allow your child to cry him- or herself to sleep or return every 5 minutes as described for *gradual withdrawal,* above.

### How your doctor can help
If these suggestions do not work for your child, or if you are worn out by many sleepless nights, consult your doctor. He or she may prescribe a suitable sleeping drug for your child which you can give for several nights. This may break the irregular sleeping pattern; but more important, it will give you a chance to rest so that you can tackle the problem of conditioning your child with renewed vigour. A word of warning: Never give your child sleeping drugs prescribed for an adult; these can be extremely dangerous for children.

**Your child's bedroom**
It is important to make your child's room as pleasant and as welcoming as possible, so that he or she is always happy to be left there at night (right).

**Bedtime ritual**
Most young children respond to a predictable bedtime ritual, such as a bath, always followed by a story, before turning the lights out (below).

**Comfort objects**
Many children become attached to a particular toy or to another comfort item such as a blanket. Cuddling this object will often encourage sleep (below right).

# 13 Drowsiness

Drowsiness (or excessive sleepiness) is a child's natural response to lack of sleep or an unusually late night. In addition, a child who is unwell – for example, with flu – is likely to sleep more than usual. Consult this chart if your child suddenly becomes unusually sleepy or unresponsive, or if he or she is difficult to arouse from sleep, and you can find no obvious explanation. This is a serious symptom that should never be ignored.

**START HERE**

Does your child have one or more of the following symptoms?
- temperature of 38°C (100°F) or above
- vomiting without diarrhoea
- reluctance to bend the head forwards
- headache

**YES** →

**CALL YOUR DOCTOR NOW!**
**Meningitis** (inflammation of the membranes surrounding the brain) or encephalitis (inflammation of the brain itself) may be the cause of such symptoms.
***Treatment:*** Your child will probably be admitted to hospital where he or she will be given a *lumbar puncture* (below right) to make an exact diagnosis and will also be given fluids and possibly *antibiotics* – if there is bacterial infection – through an intravenous drip.

**NO**

Could your child have taken any of the following?
- drugs prescribed for an adult
- alcohol
- poisonous plants or berries

**YES** →

**EMERGENCY**
**GET MEDICAL HELP NOW!**
**Poisoning** by any of these substances can cause a child to become drowsy. See *Poisoning* (p. 286) for first aid service.

**NO**

Does your child have a rash anywhere on the body?

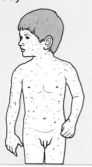

**NO**

**YES** →

Go to chart

## 25

**Spots and rashes**

Has your child suffered a blow to the head within the past few days?

**NO**

**YES** →

**EMERGENCY**
**GET MEDICAL HELP NOW!**
**A serious head injury,** resulting in bleeding inside the skull, may cause drowsiness.
***Treatment:*** Your child will probably need to have an X-ray or *CAT scan* (p. 85) of the brain. If tests reveal bleeding inside the skull, an operation may be necessary.

### LUMBAR PUNCTURE

A child who has suspected meningitis will need to have a lumbar puncture to find out whether infection by viruses or bacteria is responsible for the disease. This test involves syringeing a sample of the fluid that surrounds the brain and spinal cord (cerebrospinal fluid) from the base of the spine. The area is numbed by local anaesthetic before the needle is inserted, and most children suffer no discomfort.

The needle of the syringe is inserted between the backbones (vertebrae) at the base of the spine to enable a sample of cerebrospinal fluid to be drawn off.

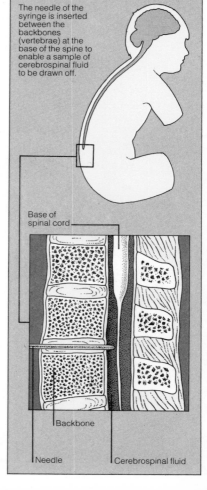

Base of spinal cord

Backbone

Needle

Cerebrospinal fluid

*Go to next page*

*Continued from previous page*

**Does your child have diarrhoea?**

**YES** →

**CALL YOUR DOCTOR NOW!**
**Dehydration** as a result of persistent diarrhoea is possible, especially if your child has been vomiting as well. This may originally have been caused by infection of the digestive tract (gastroenteritis).
***Treatment:*** If your doctor confirms the diagnosis of dehydration, your child will be admitted to hospital where fluids can be given through an intravenous drip.

**CALL YOUR DOCTOR NOW!**
**Too much sugar in the blood** as a result of diabetes can cause drowsiness. Diabetes occurs when the body fails to make sufficient quantities of the hormone insulin which helps to convert sugar into energy.
***Treatment:*** If your doctor suspects this possibility, he or she will arrange for your child to be admitted to hospital where tests on urine will confirm the diagnosis. Your child will be given immediate insulin injections and also fluids to reduce the level of sugar in the blood by intravenous drip. Life-long insulin treatment will probably be necessary.

**NO**

**Has your child been unusually thirsty lately?**

**YES** →

**Has your child been passing large amounts of urine?**

**YES**

**NO**

**NO**

**Has you child lost weight AND/OR been unusually tired during the past few weeks?**

**YES**

**Certain drugs** – especially antihistamines given for allergic disorders – may cause mild drowsiness. Discuss the problem with your doctor. If, however, your child becomes very drowsy and unresponsive, you should call your doctor at once.

**NO**

---

**DROWSINESS AND DRUG AND ALCOHOL ABUSE**

Parents of children over about 10 years of age should bear in mind the possibility of abuse of drugs (perhaps tranquillizers belonging to an adult), solvents (including glue and dry-cleaning fluids), or alcohol, if their child has episodes of unusual sleepiness or lethargy over a period of days or weeks. Additional signs may include loss of appetite, red eyes, headaches, or a falling off in school performance. There are, of course, a number of less worrying explanations for such symptoms, such as a minor infection or temporary anxiety or depression, but, whichever problem you suspect, your child's symptoms should be brought to your doctor's attention.

See also *Smoking and drug abuse,* p. 140.

---

**Is your child taking any medicines prescribed by your doctor?**

**YES**

**NO**

**Consult your doctor** without further delay if you are unable to make a diagnosis from this chart.

---

**LATE-RISING IN THE MORNING**

Children, like adults, can be divided into two groups – those who find it easy to get up and function well in the morning, and those who are at their most active in the evening and take longer to wake up in the morning. Which of these groups your child falls into will probably be apparent from the early years of childhood.

Parents of late-waking children – especially if they are early risers themselves – often worry that this reluctance to get up in the morning is a sign of lack of sleep or of a physical disorder. However, there is rarely any cause for concern if an otherwise healthy child, who is alert and energetic for most of the rest of the day, takes an hour or so to become fully awake in the morning. Enforcing an early bedtime when a child feels full of energy is unlikely to help the problem and may lead to' unnecessary conflict.

**When to consult your doctor**
While there is no cause for concern if a child is regularly sluggish in the mornings only, you should consult your doctor in the following cases:

- If your child starts to become drowsy at other times of the day.
- If a normally early-waking child is unusually drowsy in the morning for no obvious reason.

Call your doctor at once if you cannot rouse your child from sleep in the morning.

# 14 Fever in children

A fever (above-normal body temperature) is usually caused by infection either by viruses or bacteria (p. 66). However, a child may also become feverish if allowed to become overheated – for example, as a result of playing too long in hot sunshine. A raised temperature will make a child's forehead feel hot and will cause increased sweating and a general feeling of being unwell. If you suspect a fever, take your child's temperature as described opposite. Consult this chart if the temperature reading is 38°C (100°F) or above.

**For children under 1 year old, see chart 3, Fever in babies.**

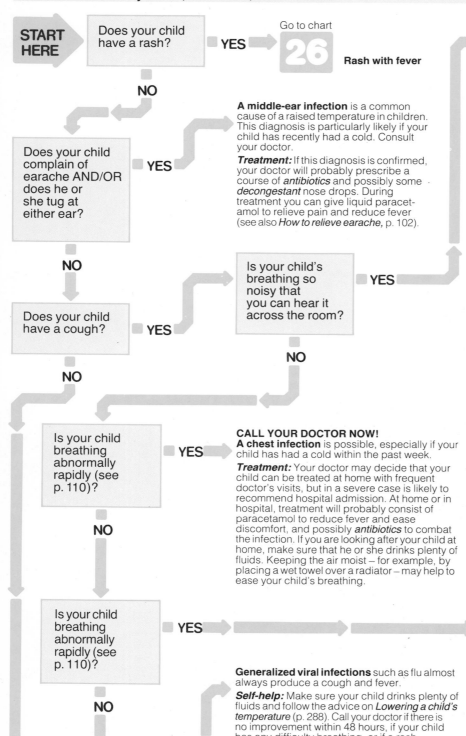

**START HERE**

**Does your child have a rash?** — **YES** → Go to chart **26** Rash with fever

**NO**

**Does your child complain of earache AND/OR does he or she tug at either ear?** — **YES** →

**A middle-ear infection** is a common cause of a raised temperature in children. This diagnosis is particularly likely if your child has recently had a cold. Consult your doctor.
**Treatment:** If this diagnosis is confirmed, your doctor will probably prescribe a course of *antibiotics* and possibly some *decongestant* nose drops. During treatment you can give liquid paracetamol to relieve pain and reduce fever (see also *How to relieve earache*, p. 102).

**NO**

**Does your child have a cough?** — **YES** →

**Is your child's breathing so noisy that you can hear it across the room?** — **YES** →

**NO**

**NO**

**Is your child breathing abnormally rapidly (see p. 110)?** — **YES** →

**CALL YOUR DOCTOR NOW!**
**A chest infection** is possible, especially if your child has had a cold within the past week.
**Treatment:** Your doctor may decide that your child can be treated at home with frequent doctor's visits, but in a severe case is likely to recommend hospital admission. At home or in hospital, treatment will probably consist of paracetamol to reduce fever and ease discomfort, and possibly *antibiotics* to combat the infection. If you are looking after your child at home, make sure that he or she drinks plenty of fluids. Keeping the air moist – for example, by placing a wet towel over a radiator – may help to ease your child's breathing.

**NO**

**Is your child breathing abnormally rapidly (see p. 110)?** — **YES** →

**Generalized viral infections** such as flu almost always produce a cough and fever.
**Self-help:** Make sure your child drinks plenty of fluids and follow the advice on *Lowering a child's temperature* (p. 288). Call your doctor if there is no improvement within 48 hours, if your child has any difficulty breathing, or if a rash develops.

**NO**

*Go to next page*

 **EMERGENCY**
**GET MEDICAL HELP NOW!**
**Narrowing of the air passages** caused by inflammation of the tissues resulting from infection is a possibility.
**Treatment:** While waiting for medical help to arrive, you may be able to ease your child's breathing by moistening the air with steam. Taking your child into a bathroom where you have turned on the hot tap or shower is often effective. Your child will probably need to be admitted to hospital where oxygen and intravenous fluids will be given. Your child may also be given *antibiotics*.

---

**FEVERISH FITS**

Some young children (under 5) suffer fits (also known as febrile convulsions) when their temperature rises beyond a certain point. During such a fit the arms and legs will shake uncontrolledly and the child may go blue in the face. This may last for several seconds or for much longer.

**What to do**
Lay the child flat on his or her stomach with the head turned to the side. If there is vomiting, clean out the mouth with your finger.
Medical help should be sought at once. While waiting for help to arrive, try to reduce your child's temperature (see p.14) but do not attempt to give anything by mouth. Even if your child quickly recovers, your doctor may wish to arrange tests such as *electroencephalography* (p. 81) to rule out any underlying problem.

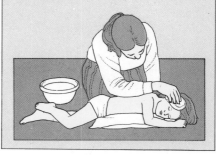

**Measles** often starts with a cough, fever, runny nose, and/or inflamed eyes. The appearance of a red rash a few days later makes this diagnosis more likely, especially if your child has not been vaccinated against the disease (see *Comparison of childhood infectious diseases*, p. 97). Consult your doctor.

**Treatment:** There is no specific treatment for measles. You will probably just be advised to keep your child's temperature down (see *Lowering a child's temperature*, p. 288). There is no need to darken your child's room as was once believed. Call your doctor at once if your child develops earache, has any difficulty in breathing, or becomes drowsy and difficult to wake. Full recovery normally takes about 10 days.

*Continued from previous page*

Is your child's face swollen between the ear and the angle of the jaw?

**YES** →

**Mumps**, a viral infection that mainly affects the salivary glands, is a possibility, especially if your child has been in contact with the disease within the past 3 weeks. (See *Comparison of childhood infectious diseases*, p. 97.) Consult your doctor.

**Treatment:** Your doctor will probably advise you to keep your child at home and give him or her paracetamol and plenty of cold drinks to relieve the discomfort. Recovery normally takes 7 to 10 days.

**NO** ↓

Does your child seem very unwell and does he or she have two or more of the following symptoms?
■ vomiting without diarrhoea
■ drowsiness
■ irritability
■ headache
■ reluctance to bend the head forwards

**YES** →

**CALL YOUR DOCTOR NOW!**
**Meningitis** (inflammation of the membranes surrounding the brain, caused by viral or bacterial infection) may be the cause of such symptoms, especially if your child has also vomited.

**Treatment:** Your child will probably be admitted to hospital where, after a *lumbar puncture* (p. 74) to make an exact diagnosis, he or she will be given fluids and possibly *antibiotics* through an intravenous drip.

**NO** ↓

Does your child have diarrhoea?  **YES** →

**Gastroenteritis** (infection of the digestive tract) is the most likely cause of such symptoms, especially if your child is also vomiting.
**Self-help:** See *Treating your child's gastroenteritis,* p. 121. Consult your doctor if your child is less than 2 years old or if he or she vomits repeatedly for more than 12 hours.

**NO** ↓

Does your child complain of a sore throat AND/OR is he or she refusing solid food?  **YES** →

**Pharyngitis and tonsillitis** (infections of the throat and tonsils respectively) are the most likely causes of a sore throat and fever.
**Self-help:** Give your child paracetamol to relieve the discomfort and reduce fever. Do not force your child to eat if pain makes swallowing difficult. Plenty of cold drinks and ice-cream will help to soothe the inflammation. Consult your doctor if your child is no better in 48 hours or develops further symptoms such as earache. Call your doctor at once if your child's breathing becomes noisy or difficult.

**NO** ↓

Has your child been passing urine more frequently than usual AND/OR complaining of pain when passing urine?  **YES** →

**A urinary-tract infection** is a possible cause of fever and frequent or painful urination. Consult your doctor.
**Treatment:** Your doctor will probably ask for a mid-stream specimen of your child's urine (see *Collecting a mid-stream specimen*, p. 125). If tests reveal an infection, your doctor will probably prescribe *antibiotics* and advise you to give your child plenty to drink. (See also *Preventing urinary-tract infections*, p. 125.)

**NO** ↓

Has your child been exposed to hot sunshine for several hours?  **YES** →

**Overheating**, leading to a rise in body temperature, can easily occur in such circumstances.
**Self-help:** Make your child lie down in a cool room with as little clothing on as possible. Sponge his or her body with tepid water and use a fan if available. Give plenty to drink along with the recommended dose of paracetamol. Seek medical help if your child's temperature has not returned to normal within an hour.

**NO** ↓

**Consult your doctor** if you are unable to make a diagnosis from this chart.

---

**TAKING YOUR CHILD'S TEMPERATURE**

The best way of determining whether your child has a fever, is to take his or her temperature using a clinical thermometer. For children under 7 years old you should place the thermometer under the arm (see *How to take your baby's temperature*, p. 55). Older children can have their temperature taken by mouth.

**Taking a temperature by mouth**
1 Shake the thermometer with firm downward flicks of the wrist so that the mercury runs down into the bulb and reads well below the normal mark.

2 Place the bulb of the thermometer inside your child's mouth under the tongue. Let it remain in place for 3 minutes.

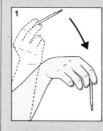 

3 Remove the thermometer and turn it until you get a clear reading.

Using this method you can consider that your child has a fever if his or her temperature is 38°C (100°F) or above. If your child's temperature rises above 39°C (102°F), whatever the suspected cause, you should call your doctor.

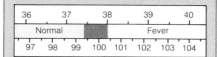

| 36 | 37 | 38 | 39 | 40 |
|----|----|----|----|----|
| Normal | | | Fever | |
| 97 | 98 | 99 | 100 | 101 | 102 | 103 | 104 |

**Temperature indicator strips**
This alternative method for measuring body temperature is described on p. 55.

---

**FOREIGN TRAVEL**

If your child develops a fever soon after a visit to a hot climate, be sure to tell your doctor. This is because your child may have caught an illness that is rare in this country, and that your doctor might not otherwise suspect.

# 15 Swollen glands

The term swollen glands usually refers to swelling (sometimes accompanied by tenderness) of one or more of the lymph glands (below). In babies under 1 year this is an unusual symptom that is difficult for the parent to diagnose, and you should therefore consult your doctor. In older children, the glands, especially those in the neck, often swell noticeably as a result of minor infections and this is rarely a cause for concern. However, persistent or generalized swelling of the glands should always be reported to your doctor.

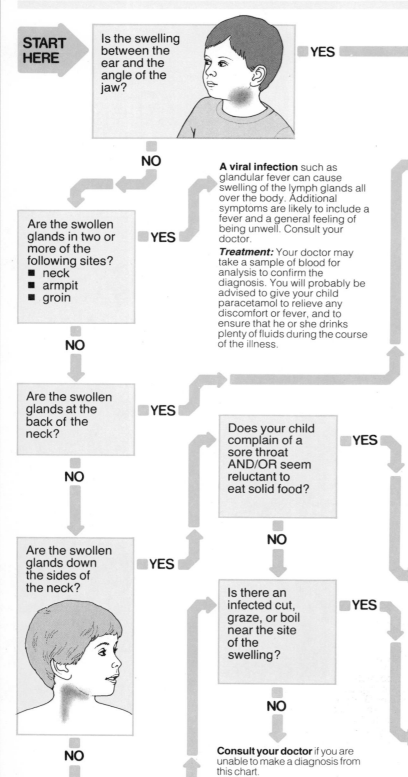

**START HERE**

Is the swelling between the ear and the angle of the jaw?

**YES** →

**NO** ↓

Are the swollen glands in two or more of the following sites?
- neck
- armpit
- groin

**YES** →

**NO** ↓

Are the swollen glands at the back of the neck?

**YES** →

**NO** ↓

Are the swollen glands down the sides of the neck?

**YES** →

**NO**

**A viral infection** such as glandular fever can cause swelling of the lymph glands all over the body. Additional symptoms are likely to include a fever and a general feeling of being unwell. Consult your doctor.

**Treatment:** Your doctor may take a sample of blood for analysis to confirm the diagnosis. You will probably be advised to give your child paracetamol to relieve any discomfort or fever, and to ensure that he or she drinks plenty of fluids during the course of the illness.

Does your child complain of a sore throat AND/OR seem reluctant to eat solid food?

**YES** →

**NO** ↓

Is there an infected cut, graze, or boil near the site of the swelling?

**YES** →

**NO** ↓

**Consult your doctor** if you are unable to make a diagnosis from this chart.

---

**Mumps,** a viral infection affecting the salivary glands, is a possibility, especially if your child has been in contact with the disease within the past 3 weeks (see *Comparison of childhood infectious diseases,* p. 97). Consult your doctor.

**Treatment:** Your doctor will probably advise you to keep your child at home and to give paracetamol and plenty of cold drinks to relieve the discomfort. Recovery normally takes 7 to 10 days.

**German measles,** or a similar viral infection, may cause these glands to swell. The appearance of a pink rash on the body within a couple of days would make German measles more likely. (See *Comparison of childhood infectious diseases,* p. 97).

**Self-help:** German measles is a mild illness and generally needs little treatment other than paracetamol if your child seems feverish. It is important, however, to keep your child at home, to avoid infecting others, especially any woman who is pregnant, because of the damage the disease can do to the unborn child. If you want to consult your doctor, telephone the surgery first, so that your doctor can visit your child at home, if necessary.

**LYMPH GLANDS**

The lymphatic system consists of the lymph glands (or nodes) linked by vessels containing a watery fluid (lymph). The glands contain large numbers of lymphocytes, a type of white blood cell that fights infection. When large numbers of microbes are present, the lymph glands – especially those near the surface of the skin – become noticeably swollen.

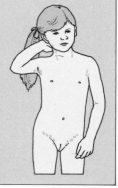

**Glands near the skin surface**
The illustration (right) shows the sites of the lymph glands that most often become obviously swollen as a result of infection in childhood.

**Tonsillitis,** inflammation of the tonsils as a result of viral or bacterial infection (see p. 66), often causes swelling of these glands.

**Self-help:** Do not force your child to eat if pain makes swallowing difficult. Follow the advice on treating a sore throat in the box on p. 107. Consult your doctor if your child is no better in 48 hours or if he or she develops any of the danger signs listed in the box on p. 106. Your doctor may prescribe *antibiotics.* An operation to remove the tonsils (see *Tonsils removal,* p. 107) is carried out only occasionally in cases of recurrent, severe tonsillitis.

**Localized infection** may cause swelling of nearby lymph glands.

**Self-help:** Keep the wound or boil clean by bathing the area daily with a mild antiseptic solution, and if necessary cover it with an adhesive plaster. Consult your doctor if a wound is persistently painful, or if swelling persists for more than a week. *Antibiotic* treatment may be needed. (See also *Warts and boils,* p.95).

# 16 Itching

This diagnostic chart deals with itching that affects either the whole body or a particular area such as the scalp or anus. A variety of disorders can cause such irritation, including external irritation and infestation by parasites. Your child is likely to scratch and, if unchecked, this may lead to the development of sore, infected areas. So it is important to deal promptly with any disorder that produces itching.

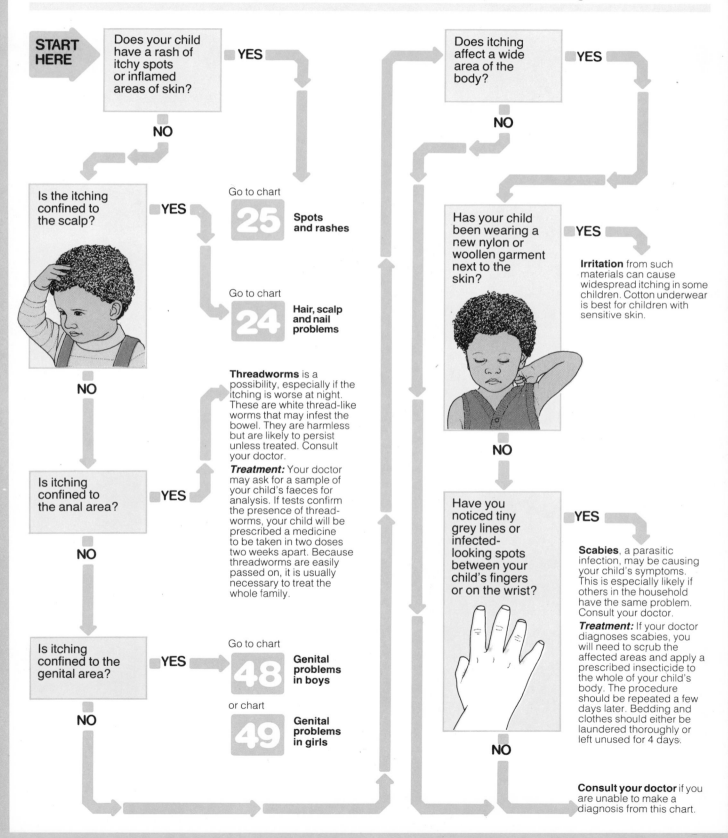

**START HERE**

**Does your child have a rash of itchy spots or inflamed areas of skin?**

YES

**Go to chart 25 Spots and rashes**

NO

**Is the itching confined to the scalp?**

YES

**Go to chart 24 Hair, scalp and nail problems**

NO

**Is itching confined to the anal area?**

YES

**Threadworms** is a possibility, especially if the itching is worse at night. These are white thread-like worms that may infest the bowel. They are harmless but are likely to persist unless treated. Consult your doctor.

*Treatment:* Your doctor may ask for a sample of your child's faeces for analysis. If tests confirm the presence of thread-worms, your child will be prescribed a medicine to be taken in two doses two weeks apart. Because threadworms are easily passed on, it is usually necessary to treat the whole family.

NO

**Is itching confined to the genital area?**

YES

**Go to chart 48 Genital problems in boys**

**or chart 49 Genital problems in girls**

NO

**Does itching affect a wide area of the body?**

YES

NO

**Has your child been wearing a new nylon or woollen garment next to the skin?**

YES

**Irritation** from such materials can cause widespread itching in some children. Cotton underwear is best for children with sensitive skin.

NO

**Have you noticed tiny grey lines or infected-looking spots between your child's fingers or on the wrist?**

YES

**Scabies**, a parasitic infection, may be causing your child's symptoms. This is especially likely if others in the household have the same problem. Consult your doctor.

*Treatment:* If your doctor diagnoses scabies, you will need to scrub the affected areas and apply a prescribed insecticide to the whole of your child's body. The procedure should be repeated a few days later. Bedding and clothes should either be laundered thoroughly or left unused for 4 days.

NO

**Consult your doctor** if you are unable to make a diagnosis from this chart.

# 17 Fainting, dizzy spells and fits

This chart deals with fainting, feelings of faintness and unsteadiness, dizzy spells and other types of loss of consciousness including fits and periods of "blankness". Many children suffer from faints from time to time and this is usually caused by anxiety or hunger, but frequent loss of consciousness or attacks during which a child suffers uncontrolled movements of the body or limbs may be a sign of an underlying disorder.

**START HERE** →

Did your child suddenly fall to the ground unconscious?

**YES** →

**NO** ↓

Is your child's temperature 38°C (100°F) or above?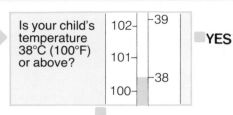

| | |
|---|---|
| 102— | ┌39 |
| 101— | |
| 100— | └38 |

**YES** →

**NO** ↓

**Grand mal epilepsy** is possible if a child suffers from episodes of loss of consciousness and twitching, especially if these attacks occur repeatedly. See the box on *Epilepsy* (opposite) and consult your doctor.

## WARNING

### PROLONGED LOSS OF CONSCIOUSNESS

Momentary loss of consciousness – fainting – is not usually a cause for concern if your child is breathing normally and regains consciousness within a minute or two. If, however, your child remains unconscious for longer, or if breathing slows or becomes irregular or noisy, get medical help at once. See *Essential first aid,* p. 282-287

Did your child's face and/or limbs twitch while he or she was unconscious?

**YES** →

**NO** ↓

**CALL YOUR DOCTOR NOW!**
**Convulsions** may be brought on by a fever in some children. See *Feverish fits in children,* p.76.

### FIRST AID FOR FAINTING

A child who feels faint or has fainted should preferably be laid down with legs raised. If this is not possible sit your child down with the head between the knees. Loosen any tight clothing and make sure that the child has plenty of fresh air and is shaded from hot sunshine. When your child regains consciousness do not allow him or her to get up for a few more minutes. A child who feels faint or has fainted may be suffering from low blood sugar as a result of not having eaten, so when he or she has regained consciousness, offer a sweet drink and a light snack. Never try to give an unconscious child anything to eat or drink.

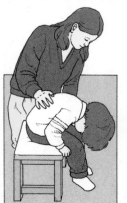

**When a child faints**
Lay your child down with feet raised (top) or sit him or her down with head lowered (left). When consciousness is regained, offer a drink and a snack (above).

Did your child pass urine, bite the tongue or suffer any other sort of injury while unconscious?

**YES** →

**NO** ↓

**Fainting** (brief loss of consciousness, usually preceded by sudden pallor and a feeling of light-headedness or dizziness) is rarely any cause for concern in an otherwise well child. It is usually caused by a sudden drop in blood pressure as a result of anxiety, or by a low level of sugar in the blood as a result of not having eaten for some time.

***Self-help:*** See *First aid for fainting* (left). Seek medical help at once if your child remains unconscious for more than a minute, or seems to have any difficulty breathing. Consult your doctor if fainting attacks recur.

*Go to next page*

*Continued from previous page*

**Has your child been suffering from dizzy spells when everything seem to be spinning around?**

**YES** → **Labyrinthitis** – viral infection of the labyrinth (see *The structure of the ear,* p. 103) – is the most common cause of dizziness in children. Consult your doctor.

**Treatment:** The disease cures itself in a week or so. Meanwhile, your doctor may prescribe drugs to relieve your child's symptoms.

**NO** ↓

**Has your child been having periods of blankness when he or she seems to "switch off" for a few seconds?**

**YES** → **Petit mal,** a mild form of epilepsy, is possible. See *Epilepsy* (below) and consult your doctor.

**NO** ↓

**Has your child felt faint or unsteady for a few moments?**

**YES** → **Feeling faint** is hardly ever a cause for concern if your child is otherwise well. Your child is probably simply suffering from anxiety, hunger, or from the effects of heat or from a combination of these factors.

**Self-help:** Offer your child a sweet drink and try to persuade him or her to lie down for a little while (see *First aid for fainting,* left). Faintness usually passes within 5 minutes. If your child still feels unsteady after 30 minutes, call your doctor.

**NO** →

**Consult your doctor** if you are unable to make a diagnosis from this chart.

---

## EPILEPSY

Epilepsy is the medical term for repeated loss of consciousness caused by abnormal electrical impulses in the brain. The underlying cause of the disorder is not known. The type and severity of symptoms may vary according to the nature of the abnormal impulses and the part of the brain affected. There are two main forms of the disease:

### Grand mal
In the form of the disease known as grand mal, the child falls to the ground suddenly and may suffer injury during the fall. He or she remains unconscious for up to several minutes, often jerking the limbs or face uncontrolledly. Gradually the movements stop and the child passes into normal sleep.

### Petit mal
In petit mal epilepsy, the child loses full consciousness but does not fall to the ground. Attacks last for 10 to 15 seconds, during which the child's face becomes vacant, and he or she stops speaking and does not hear what people are saying. Petit mal attacks often cease after adolescence.

### Treatment
If your child has attacks of loss of consciousness that lead your doctor to suspect a form of epilepsy, your child will probably be referred to a specialist (neurologist) for diagnosis and treatment. Diagnosis of the precise form of the disease and decisions about the best treatment for a child are usually made following *electro-encephalography* (EEG) (right). Most forms of epilepsy are effectively controlled by drug treatment. The neurologist will advise you about any special precautions you will need to take with regard to swimming, cycling and other activities, and will explain how to deal with attacks. You should tell your child's school teachers, and anyone else who has regular care of your child, about the disease and explain to them what to do during attacks.

### Dealing with attacks
During a grand mal attack your priorities are to prevent your child from inhaling vomit and from suffering any injury. At the first sign of an attack place the child on his or her stomach with the head to one side. Move nearby objects away from jerking arms and legs, but do not try to restrain the child from moving. Never try to place anything in the mouth of a child having an attack. Once the involuntary movements have ceased, allow him or her to sleep undisturbed.
A child having a petit mal attack needs no special treatment and should be allowed to regain normal consciousness without interference.

**Electroencephalography**
Electroencephalography (EEG) is a technique that enables doctors to monitor the electrical activity in the brain, and assists in the diagnosis of epilepsy and other conditions. A number of electrodes are placed on the scalp (right) and the signals that are picked up are recorded on a paper trace. The procedure is not painful, but it may take some time and may therefore be tiresome for a young child.

**During a grand mal attack**
A child having a grand mal attack should be gently turned on to his or her stomach with the head to one side (below). Nearby objects likely to cause injury should be moved away.

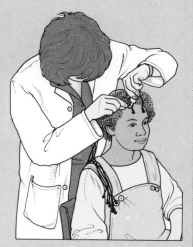

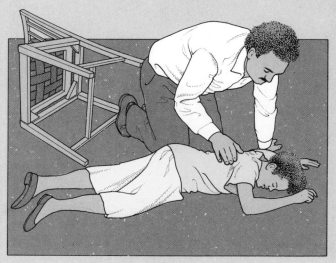

# 18 Headache

Headache includes pain on one or both sides of the head or forehead. It may vary from a dull ache to a sharp stabbing pain. Children under the age of 3 are unlikely to complain of this symptom except as a direct result of injury. Headaches can be a symptom of a number of disorders but they may also occur on their own and are usually cured by self-help measures. Always consult your doctor about severe or recurrent headaches.

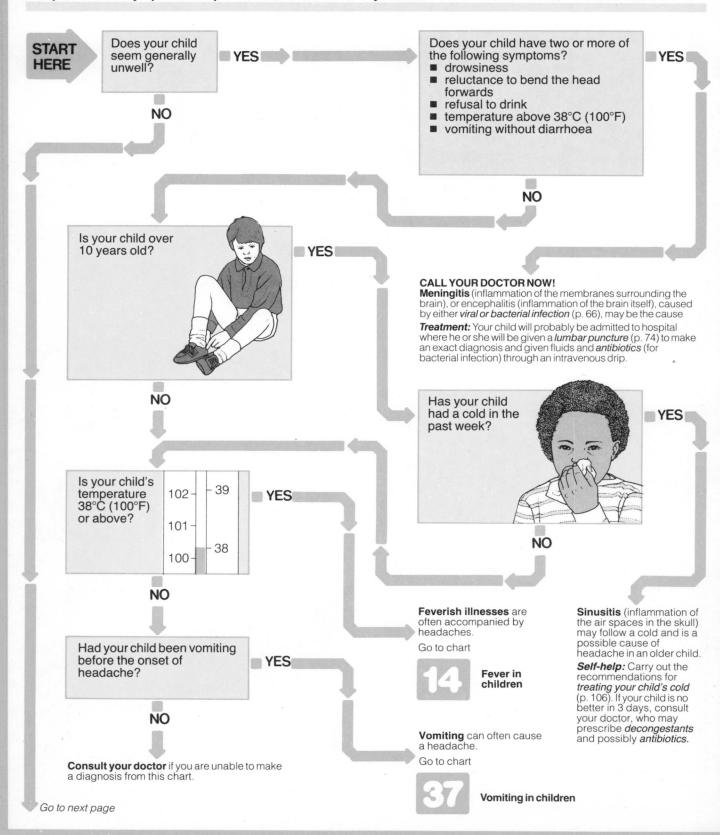

**START HERE**

**Does your child seem generally unwell?**
YES →
NO ↓

**Does your child have two or more of the following symptoms?**
- drowsiness
- reluctance to bend the head forwards
- refusal to drink
- temperature above 38°C (100°F)
- vomiting without diarrhoea

YES →
NO ↓

**Is your child over 10 years old?**
YES →
NO ↓

**CALL YOUR DOCTOR NOW!**
**Meningitis** (inflammation of the membranes surrounding the brain), or encephalitis (inflammation of the brain itself), caused by either *viral or bacterial infection* (p. 66), may be the cause
**Treatment:** Your child will probably be admitted to hospital where he or she will be given a *lumbar puncture* (p. 74) to make an exact diagnosis and given fluids and *antibiotics* (for bacterial infection) through an intravenous drip.

**Has your child had a cold in the past week?**
YES →
NO ↓

**Is your child's temperature 38°C (100°F) or above?**
102 — 39
101
100 — 38
YES →
NO ↓

**Had your child been vomiting before the onset of headache?**
YES →
NO ↓

**Feverish illnesses** are often accompanied by headaches.
Go to chart

**14** Fever in children

**Sinusitis** (inflammation of the air spaces in the skull) may follow a cold and is a possible cause of headache in an older child.
*Self-help:* Carry out the recommendations for *treating your child's cold* (p. 106). If your child is no better in 3 days, consult your doctor, who may prescribe *decongestants* and possibly *antibiotics*.

**Vomiting** can often cause a headache.
Go to chart

**37** Vomiting in children

**Consult your doctor** if you are unable to make a diagnosis from this chart.

*Go to next page*

*Continued from previous page*

**Does your child often have headaches?** —**YES**→ **Has your child had a headache every day for a week?** —**YES**→ **Frequent headaches** in a child should be brought to your doctor's attention. They may be *migraines* (see below left), especially if other members of the family suffer from them, but your doctor will want to rule out the possibility of them being caused by a more serious underlying disorder.

**NO**↓

**NO**↓

**The periodic syndrome** is a term used to describe recurrent pains in children that may be of emotional origin.

*Self-help:* Although there may be no obvious physical cause for your child's headaches, the pain is nevertheless real. Follow the advice on *relieving your child's headache* (below). Consult your doctor if such measures fail to relieve the pain, if your child develops additional symptoms, or if he or she seems generally unwell. In addition, you should seek medical advice if the headaches start to occur increasingly often.

**Did your child often suffer from unexplained abdominal pain when younger?** —**YES**→

**NO**↓

**Do headaches only seem to occur after your child has been reading or doing other close work?** —**YES**→ **Eyesight problems** – for example, short sight – may sometimes cause headaches after such activities. Consult your doctor.

*Treatment:* Your doctor will probably examine your child and may carry out a preliminary eye test (see *Eye testing,* p. 101). If your doctor suspects a visual defect, your child will be referred to an optician for further eye tests, and may eventually need to wear glasses.

**NO**↓

**Are headaches usually accompanied by nausea or vomiting AND/OR has your child ever complained of any disturbance in vision before the onset of pain?** —**YES**→ **Migraine** is the term used to describe recurrent severe headaches, which may be accompanied or preceded by additional symptoms such as nausea, vomiting and/or visual disturbance. They are more common in adulthood, but may sometimes occur in children, particularly if a close relation also suffers from this type of headache. Consult your doctor.

*Treatment:* If your doctor confirms that your child is suffering from migraine, he or she will probably ask you about any factors that seem to trigger off attacks. Certain foods such as cheese and chocolate are common causes of migraine headaches. In addition, your doctor may prescribe drugs to alleviate pain if normal self-help measures are ineffective (see *Relieving your child's headache,* right.)

**NO**↓

**Does any close relation suffer from recurrent headaches?** —**YES**→ **Can you think of any cause for your child to be tense or anxious?** —**YES**→

**NO**↓

**NO**↓

**Occasional unexplained headaches** are hardly ever a cause for concern. They may be related to tension or hunger. Follow the advice on *relieving your child's headache* (above right). Consult your doctor if pain persists or if your child seems unwell in any other way.

### RELIEVING YOUR CHILD'S HEADACHE

The vast majority of headaches in childhood can be simply treated at home in the following way:

- Give the recommended dose of liquid paracetamol.
- If your child is hungry, offer a light snack – for example, a glass of milk and a biscuit.
- Allow your child to lie down in a cool darkened room for a few hours.

The earlier you offer treatment, the greater its effectiveness. Consult your doctor if these measures fail to relieve a headache within 4 hours, or if your child seems generally unwell.

**Tension headaches** may be brought on by anxiety – for example, about schoolwork or family problems. Such headaches are generally no cause for concern.

*Self-help:* Follow the advice on *relieving your child's headache* (above). Consult your doctor if such measures fail to relieve the pain or if your child seems otherwise unwell.

# 19 Clumsiness

Children vary greatly in their level of manual dexterity, physical coordination and agility. Some children naturally have more difficulty than others in carrying out delicate tasks such as shoelace-tying, that require precise coordination between hand and eye, and may seem to be unable to prevent themselves from knocking things over. Such clumsiness is almost always present from birth and is most unlikely to be a sign of an underlying disorder. But very occasionally, severe clumsiness or the sudden onset of clumsiness in a child who has previously been well coordinated may be the result of nervous-system or muscular disorder.

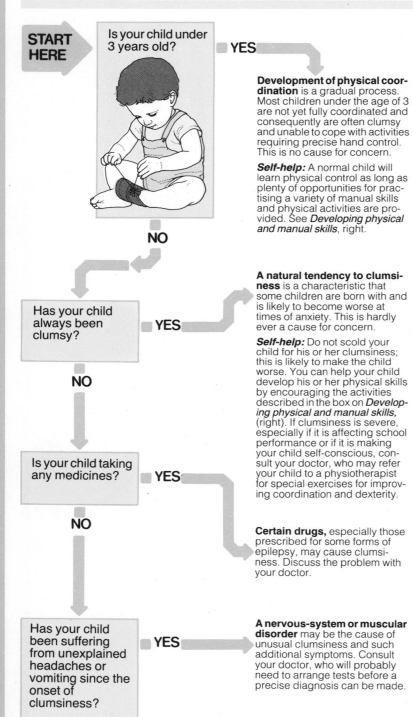

**START HERE**

**Is your child under 3 years old?**

**YES** →

**NO** ↓

**Development of physical coordination** is a gradual process. Most children under the age of 3 are not yet fully coordinated and consequently are often clumsy and unable to cope with activities requiring precise hand control. This is no cause for concern.

*Self-help:* A normal child will learn physical control as long as plenty of opportunities for practising a variety of manual skills and physical activities are provided. See *Developing physical and manual skills*, right.

**Has your child always been clumsy?**

**YES** →

**NO** ↓

**A natural tendency to clumsiness** is a characteristic that some children are born with and is likely to become worse at times of anxiety. This is hardly ever a cause for concern.

*Self-help:* Do not scold your child for his or her clumsiness; this is likely to make the child worse. You can help your child develop his or her physical skills by encouraging the activities described in the box on *Developing physical and manual skills,* (right). If clumsiness is severe, especially if it is affecting school performance or if it is making your child self-conscious, consult your doctor, who may refer your child to a physiotherapist for special exercises for improving coordination and dexterity.

**Is your child taking any medicines?**

**YES** →

**NO** ↓

**Certain drugs,** especially those prescribed for some forms of epilepsy, may cause clumsiness. Discuss the problem with your doctor.

**Has your child been suffering from unexplained headaches or vomiting since the onset of clumsiness?**

**YES** →

**NO** ↓

**A nervous-system or muscular disorder** may be the cause of unusual clumsiness and such additional symptoms. Consult your doctor, who will probably need to arrange tests before a precise diagnosis can be made.

**Consult your doctor** if you are unable to make a diagnosis from this chart.

---

### DEVELOPING PHYSICAL AND MANUAL SKILLS

Children learn to control their bodies from the first weeks of life. They soon learn skills such as following a moving object with the eyes and grasping a toy that is held out to them. Some children learn such skills much more easily than others and are naturally neater and more agile than their contemporaries. But throughout childhood you can help your child to develop muscular coordination and manual dexterity to the limit of his or her natural abilities by giving as many chances as possible for varied physical activities.

**Athletic skills**
A toddler running, hopping and jumping is learning physical skills that will help him as an older child to be good at sports and games. Swimming is a particularly good form of exercise for clumsy children. And ball games will help improve hand-and-eye coordination (see right) as well as providing opportunities for strenuous physical activity.

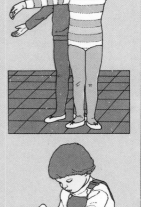

**Moving to music**
Dancing is not only fun for young children, but teaches them to coordinate their body's movements with the rhythms of the music. Disciplined forms of dancing, such as ballet, can also improve balance, physical grace and agility.

**Coordinating hand and eye**
Banging pegs into a frame with a hammer is a game that most toddlers enjoy (below right). It also helps to teach coordination between the hand and eye and will help your child to learn more sophisticated manual tasks such as sewing and woodwork later on. Similarly, scrawling on scrap-paper with crayons is an important stage in the development of the more delicate control needed for writing and drawing. Toys that are particularly good for hand-and-eye coordination include building blocks and beakers, jigsaws with large pieces, and toy telephones.

# 20 Confusion

Children who are confused may talk nonsense, appear dazed or agitated, or see and hear things that are not real. This is a serious symptom that should receive immediate medical attention.

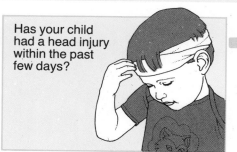

**START HERE** → Has your child had a head injury within the past few days?

**YES** → ☎ **EMERGENCY GET MEDICAL HELP NOW!**

**Pressure on the brain** from slow bleeding within the skull is possible if a child who seemed to be all right at first, becomes confused following a head injury.

*Treatment:* Your child will be admitted to hospital and will probably need to undergo tests such as a skull X-ray or a *CAT scan* (below) to determine the nature and extent of any damage to the brain or skull. An operation may be necessary.

**NO** ↓

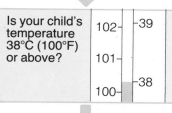

Is your child's temperature 38°C (100°F) or above?

102 – 39
101 –
100 – 38

**YES** → **CALL YOUR DOCTOR NOW!**
**Delirium** may develop in a child with a fever, especially if temperature rises above 39°C (102°F). This may in turn lead to a feverish fit (p. 76).

*Treatment:* While waiting for medical help to arrive carry out self-help measures (see *Lowering a raised temperature in a child,* p. 288).

See also chart

 **14 Fever in children**

**NO** ↓

Does your child have one or more of the following symptoms?
- headache
- vomiting without diarrhoea
- refusal to drink
- reluctance to bend the head forwards

**YES** → **CALL YOUR DOCTOR NOW!**
**Meningitis** – inflammation of the membranes surrounding the brain, caused by either *viral or bacterial infection* (p. 66) – is possible.

*Treatment:* Your child will probably be admitted to hospital where he or she will be given a *lumbar puncture* (p. 74) to make an exact diagnosis and given fluids and *antibiotics* (for bacterial infection) through an intravenous drip.

**NO** ↓

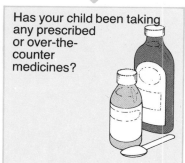

Has your child been taking any prescribed or over-the-counter medicines?

**YES** → **CALL YOUR DOCTOR NOW!**
**Certain drugs,** particularly some of those contained in travel sickness medicines, cough medicines and some drugs used in the treatment of asthma, may cause confused behaviour in some children.

**NO** ↓

**Consult your doctor** if you are unable to make a diagnosis from this chart.

---

**CAT SCAN**

A CAT (computerized axial tomography) scan is a painless procedure that helps in the diagnosis of a wide variety of conditions. Unlike conventional X-rays, CAT scans can clearly show up soft tissues (including organs, blood clots and tumours). The procedure involves hundreds of X-rays being taken as a camera revolves around the body. The readings are fed into a computer which assembles them into a series of accurate pictures of the area under examination.

**CAT scan of the head**
For a CAT scan of the head your child will lie on a movable table with his or her head resting inside the machine. Your child will be told not to make any movement so that the pictures are not blurred.

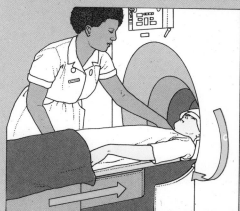

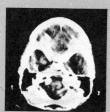

**CAT scan at eye level**
The scan (left) shows a cross-section of a child's head at eye level. The front of the head is at the top. The white areas indicate bone; the grey areas, soft tissue; and the black areas, air spaces.

**Cat scan at mid-forehead level**
The scan (left) shows a cross-section of the same head taken at mid-forehead level. The grey central area is the brain.

# 21 Speech difficulties

Consult this chart if your child has any problem with his or her speech such as delay in starting to talk, lack of clarity, defects in pronunciation, or stammering. Most forms of speech difficulty resolve themselves in time without treatment. However, in some cases a child's speech can be improved with therapy.

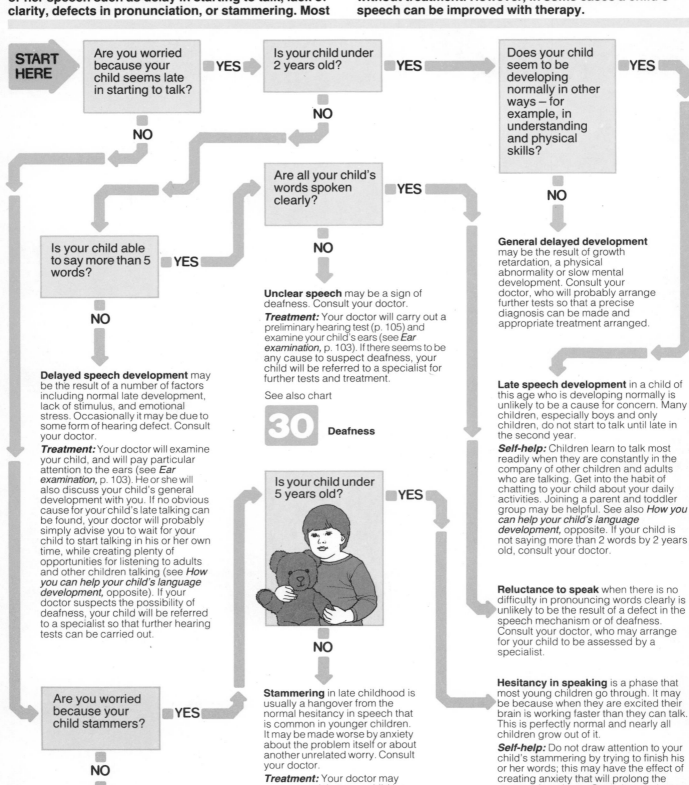

**START HERE**

**Are you worried because your child seems late in starting to talk?**

NO / YES

**Is your child under 2 years old?**

NO / YES

**Does your child seem to be developing normally in other ways – for example, in understanding and physical skills?**

NO / YES

**Is your child able to say more than 5 words?**

NO / YES

**Are all your child's words spoken clearly?**

NO / YES

**Delayed speech development** may be the result of a number of factors including normal late development, lack of stimulus, and emotional stress. Occasionally it may be due to some form of hearing defect. Consult your doctor.

**Treatment:** Your doctor will examine your child, and will pay particular attention to the ears (see *Ear examination,* p. 103). He or she will also discuss your child's general development with you. If no obvious cause for your child's late talking can be found, your doctor will probably simply advise you to wait for your child to start talking in his or her own time, while creating plenty of opportunities for listening to adults and other children talking (see *How you can help your child's language development,* opposite). If your doctor suspects the possibility of deafness, your child will be referred to a specialist so that further hearing tests can be carried out.

**Unclear speech** may be a sign of deafness. Consult your doctor.

**Treatment:** Your doctor will carry out a preliminary hearing test (p. 105) and examine your child's ears (see *Ear examination,* p. 103). If there seems to be any cause to suspect deafness, your child will be referred to a specialist for further tests and treatment.

See also chart

## 30 Deafness

**General delayed development** may be the result of growth retardation, a physical abnormality or slow mental development. Consult your doctor, who will probably arrange further tests so that a precise diagnosis can be made and appropriate treatment arranged.

**Late speech development** in a child of this age who is developing normally is unlikely to be a cause for concern. Many children, especially boys and only children, do not start to talk until late in the second year.

**Self-help:** Children learn to talk most readily when they are constantly in the company of other children and adults who are talking. Get into the habit of chatting to your child about your daily activities. Joining a parent and toddler group may be helpful. See also *How you can help your child's language development,* opposite. If your child is not saying more than 2 words by 2 years old, consult your doctor.

**Reluctance to speak** when there is no difficulty in pronouncing words clearly is unlikely to be the result of a defect in the speech mechanism or of deafness. Consult your doctor, who may arrange for your child to be assessed by a specialist.

**Is your child under 5 years old?**

NO / YES

**Are you worried because your child stammers?**

NO / YES

**Stammering** in late childhood is usually a hangover from the normal hesitancy in speech that is common in younger children. It may be made worse by anxiety about the problem itself or about another unrelated worry. Consult your doctor.

**Treatment:** Your doctor may recommend that your child be referred for speech therapy. Children who are given such therapy at an early age usually overcome their difficulties.

**Hesitancy in speaking** is a phase that most young children go through. It may be because when they are excited their brain is working faster than they can talk. This is perfectly normal and nearly all children grow out of it.

**Self-help:** Do not draw attention to your child's stammering by trying to finish his or her words; this may have the effect of creating anxiety that will prolong the stammering phase. Consult your doctor only if your child continues to stammer beyond the age of 5 years, or if the stammer is so severe that it seriously interferes with your child's speech.

*Go to next page*

*Continued from previous page*

Does your child have a lisp or another type of speech defect?

**YES** →

Is the defect so severe that strangers cannot easily understand what your child is saying OR is your child embarrassed about the problem?

**YES** →

**Serious defects** in pronunciation may be the result of a physical problem. Consult your doctor.

***Treatment:*** Your doctor will examine your child, paying special attention to the mouth and ears, and may refer your child to a speech therapist for diagnosis and treatment. Many forms of speech defect can be corrected by speech therapy.

**NO** ↓

**NO** ↓

**Minor speech defects** are common. In most cases children will gradually overcome their difficulties with various types of sound as they grow older. Trying to correct your child's speech is likely only to make your child anxious and self-conscious. Consult your doctor if the speech defect starts to cause your child embarrassment or if it interferes with communication or school performance.

**Consult your doctor** if you are unable to make a diagnosis from this chart.

---

## SPEECH DEVELOPMENT

### The first year
Children begin to communicate well before they are ready to talk. From birth they listen to and enjoy the sound of their parents' voices and learn to associate such sounds with comfort and security. From about 2 months they are learning to make a variety of their own noises, including grunting, gurgling and cooing sounds. Such noises develop during the second half of the first year into recognizable syllables such as "ma", "da" and "ga". These words gradually become more complex until your child is babbling in long strings of syllables. By the end of the first year most children are able to understand a few simple words, phrases and commands, and have usually learned to say at least one recognizable word in its proper context.

### The second year
During the early part of the second year a child's vocabulary increases rapidly, although much of a child's conversation is still babbling. Gradually, phrases of linked words joining names of people or objects to actions or commands appear – for example, "mummy go" or "doggie eat". At this stage, understanding of things that you say is also developing rapidly. And even though it may not yet be apparent in your child's speech, a broad base of vocabulary and grammatical structure is being built up.

### The third year
The third year is a time during which a child consolidates and builds on the basic knowledge of vocabulary and grammar that was learned in the second year. An apparently never-ending stream of questions about the names of objects and what they do enlarge vocabulary and increase a child's confidence in using words. By the end of this year the majority of children understand most of what an adult says as long as it is not too complex or abstract, and can communicate their wants and thoughts and hold simple conversations about everyday subjects that interest them.

---

## HOW YOU CAN HELP YOUR CHILD'S LANGUAGE DEVELOPMENT

Children learn to talk most readily when constantly exposed to the sound of voices, in particular those of their parents, from an early age. The following specific suggestions will help you ensure that your child receives plenty of stimulation and encouragement to learn to talk when he or she is ready:

- Get into the habit of talking to your child from birth.
- Look directly at your child when you speak, so that the expression on your face gives clues to the meaning of what you are saying.
- Use actions to help your child associate particular words with objects and events.
- Use simple books and nursery rhymes (perhaps on cassette) to extend your child's vocabulary and to build confidence by the repetition of familiar words and phrases.
- Provide plenty of opportunities for your child to mix with other children and adults.
- Try not to interrupt your child constantly to correct errors in grammar or pronunciation; this may undermine confidence. Instead, concentrate on providing a good example in the way you speak.

Do not worry if your child seems to be a little late in uttering his or her first words. Your child will nevertheless be listening to you talking and building up the groundwork of language. Most children who are late-talkers catch up with their early-talking contemporaries very quickly once they start.

Talk and sing to encourage speech

Word association helps understanding

Repeated words in books build confidence

Playing with other children promotes communication skills

# 22 Behaviour problems

Problems relating to your child's behaviour can be very varied; much depends on an individual parent's perception of what constitutes a problem. It is not possible to deal with all childhood behaviour problems here. This chart covers some of the common problems which cause parents distress. It will give you some idea when help from your doctor or from a specialist in child psychiatry may be advisable.

**START HERE** → Is your child over 12 years old? → **YES**

Go to chart **51** Adolescent behaviour problems

**NO** ↓

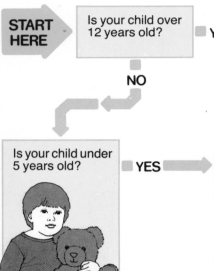

Is your child under 5 years old? → **YES** → Has your child's behaviour changed only recently — for example, has your child suddenly become destructive, disobedient, or withdrawn? → **YES**

**NO** ↓ (under 5 years)

**NO** ↓ (behaviour changed)

Is the behaviour problem mainly connected with schoolwork or behaviour at school? → **YES**

Go to chart **23** School difficulties

**NO** ↓

**Sudden changes of behaviour** in young children are almost always the result of a temporary upset or family upheaval, such as the birth of a new baby or a stay in hospital. A child may express insecurity in a variety of ways; disobedient behaviour is often just as much a plea for extra love and attention as obviously sad or distressed behaviour (see also *Types of behaviour problem,* below). In addition, many children between the ages of 1½ and 3 go through a period of difficult behaviour (see *The terrible two's,* below left).

**Self-help:** While you will obviously need to control extremes of behaviour that are unacceptable to you (see *Rules and discipline,* opposite), any action you take should be accompanied by extra love and attention when your child is behaving well. Try to discover any underlying worries and deal with them. If your child's unusual behaviour lasts longer than a few weeks, discuss the problem with your doctor or health visitor, who may be able to offer help and advice. In some cases specialist help may be advised (see *Child guidance,* opposite).

**Long-term behaviour problems** in young children may be the result of personality traits, prolonged disturbance in the home, boredom or lack of stimulation, or a combination of these factors. (See also *Types of behaviour problem,* below, and *Hyperactivity,* opposite).

**Self-help:** If you think that boredom may be part of the problem, try to find outlets for your child's interests and energy. It may help to join a playgroup or parent and toddler club. Discuss your child's behaviour with your doctor and/or health visitor. They may have some further helpful suggestions to make and may be able to arrange for specialist help, if necessary (see *Child guidance,* opposite). It is particularly important to seek help if difficult behaviour is damaging your relationship with your child and/or making you anxious or depressed.

---

**THE TERRIBLE TWO'S**

The period between 1½ and 3 years is a time during which children are beginning to appreciate their separate identity. Is often a time of alternating moments of self-assertion, including violent temper tantrums when the child's wishes are frustrated, and moments of increased dependency and insecurity, when he or she reverts to babyish habits such as thumb sucking and refuses to be separated from the parents. This type of behaviour can make the "terrible two's" a very trying time for the parents.

**Dealing with tantrums**

If your child has tantrums, it is essential to keep calm. If you can remain outwardly unmoved by your screaming child, pick up your child and hold him or her closely until he or she has calmed down. But if you are upset by the tantrums, it is better to leave the room than to shout or display other signs of distress yourself. If frequent temper tantrums are making you feel anxious and unable to cope, consult your doctor, who may be able to offer constructive help.

---

**TYPES OF BEHAVIOUR PROBLEM**

**Aggressiveness, violence and destructiveness.**
Assertiveness may be a natural part of a child's personality, but excessively aggressive or violent behaviour may be a response to worry, boredom, or lack of parental attention.

**Withdrawal**
Sudden withdrawal from social contact in a child could be a sign of anxiety or depression. If this type of behaviour persists for more than a week or so, you should try to find out the cause and, if necessary, seek medical advice.

**Stealing**
A child who steals may simply want something very badly or may do it for a thrill and to gain the admiration of friends.

It is common for an insecure child to steal in order to gain attention. Occasionally, a child may repeatedly steal small objects of little value, and this may be a sign of emotional disturbance for which you probably need to seek professional help.

**Disobedience and rudeness**
If your child persistently defies your wishes, it may be a sign that the framework of rules you have provided is too rigid and your child is using disobedience as a means of expressing independence. Or it may be that your child has not fully understood the reasons for the rules. Children may also use deliberate defiance and the use of bad or insulting language as a means of gaining attention by provoking a shocked or angry reaction.

*Go to next page*

*Continued from previous page*

Has your child's behaviour recently become any of the following?
- violent
- destructive
- withdrawn
- generally disobedient

**NO** ↓

Are you worried that your child may be doing any of the following?
- smoking
- drinking alcohol
- taking drugs
- inhaling solvents

**NO** ↓

**Consult your doctor** if you are unable to find an explanation for your child's behaviour on this chart, and if your child continues to behave in a worrying way.

**YES** →

**YES** →

Has this change in behaviour occurred following a family upset such as the birth of a new baby or separation of the parents?

**NO** ↓

**Difficult behaviour** that starts for no obvious reason may have a variety of underlying causes. There may be problems at school about which you are unaware – for example, bullying. Your child may be worried about some future event, or he or she may sense tension in the home. Alternatively, your child may be bored as a result of insufficient stimulation at school (see *Gifted children*, p. 91) or lack of constructive activities in the home. You will know best which type of explanation is most likely in your child's case. (See also *Types of behaviour problem*, opposite.)

**Self-help:** Try to channel your child's energies into demanding activities that he or she enjoys. These may include sports, family outings, or creative pastimes such as painting and model-making. Discuss the problem with your child's teacher, who may suggest ways of adjusting schoolwork to meet your child's needs more closely. If you suspect that your child is worrying about something, try to find out what the trouble is so that you can offer reassurance. If these suggestions do not work, and if you are unable to control your child's behaviour in the usual ways (see *Rules and discipline*, below), consult your doctor, who may, if needed, arrange for specialist help (see *Child guidance*, below right).

Such activities are discussed in the box on *Smoking, alcohol and drug abuse,* p. 140.

**YES** →

**Insecurity and unhappiness** can cause some children to behave in these ways. Bad behaviour is a way for children to express anger with themselves or with others and is often a signal that a child needs extra reassurance and love. (See *Types of behaviour problem*, opposite.)

**Self-help:** During this difficult time you will need to be patient, but not overindulgent towards your child. Continue to enforce your usual rules regarding behaviour (see *Rules and discipline*, below left), but you should also make every effort to talk to your child about any underlying cause of insecurity, and offer plenty of reassurance. Try to set aside a regular time each day when you give your child your undivided attention. It is also a good idea to inform a child's school teachers about any important changes in the home, so that teachers will understand about any temporary difficulties your child may have with schoolwork and will avoid tactless or hurtful comments or questions. If you find yourself unable to cope with your child's difficult behaviour, or if you are worried that it seems to be persisting too long, consult your doctor.

---

## HYPERACTIVITY

Hyperactivity is the term used to describe excessively restless physical and mental activity in a child. A hyperactive child has a short attention span, is prone to temper tantrums, has apparently boundless energy, and needs little sleep. Such behaviour can be very trying and requires much patience and understanding.

Some doctors, particularly in the United States, believe that hyperactivity is the result of brain damage so minimal that it cannot be detected by diagnostic tests. However, most British doctors view hyperactivity as one end of the spectrum of normal behaviour. Any problem arises out of the parents' reaction to such behaviour which may reflect differences in temperament within the family. Treatment will depend on your doctor's approach – perhaps family counselling to encourage greater awareness and tolerance among family members.

---

## CHILD GUIDANCE

If your family doctor feels that your child's persistent behaviour problems could benefit from specialist help, he or she may arrange for your child to visit the local child guidance clinic. This is a centre specializing in the assessment of behaviour problems in children, so that the cause of the problem may be diagnosed accurately and appropriate treatment prescribed. Its staff may include a specialist in the treatment of emotional and psychological problems in childhood (child psychiatrist), specialists in child behaviour and educational difficulties (educational psychologists), and possibly social workers to advise on practical difficulties that may contribute to, or arise out of, the child's problems.

Normally, on a first visit, the whole family will be asked to attend to discuss the problem with the clinic staff. On subsequent visits it may be necessary for the child to attend with only one parent. The child may participate in various activities such as play sessions or further discussions with the staff, depending on the child's age and the nature of the problem. This enables the staff to obtain a clear picture of the case and to advise on further action.

---

## RULES AND DISCIPLINE

Most children benefit from a clearly understood system of rules setting out the bounds of acceptable behaviour to provide a strong framework for their activities. Every family has its own standards of behaviour and language; behaviour that would not be tolerated in one family may be acceptable in another. As a parent you should be clear in your own mind why you lay down certain rules whether, for example, for reasons of safety, or for consideration for the rights and feelings of others. And you should balance the advantages of adhering to certain rigid standards against the need for the occasional confrontation to enforce them. Try to allow your child scope for making independent decisions within your rules, otherwise you may be undermining initiative and self-confidence, or provoking defiance.

### Punishment

Ideally, sanctions to enforce your wishes on your child should never be necessary. Your aim should be to avoid battles of will by using other, more positive means of gaining your child's cooperation. Such means may include encouragement of good behaviour through praise and reward, the use of example (particularly in relation to manners and language), and constant explanation of the reasons for any limitations you may want to impose.

However, every parent needs to use punishments occasionally, and most children accept and respect this. The guidelines below may help:

- Always try to make the punishment appropriate to the seriousness of the "crime". Where possible make the punishment a form of reparation.
- Any punishment should immediately follow the offence and should not be delayed.
- Never threaten a punishment that you know you will be unwilling to carry out; children can always detect empty threats.
- Make sure that it is understood that punishment is not a sign that you have ceased to love your child. For many children your anger is a punishment in itself. A peacemaking hug and words of reassurance afterwards are a good idea.
- Physical (corporal) punishment is generally an ineffective means of gaining a child's cooperation, and can often lead to resentment that produces the opposite effect. However, the occasional smack is unlikely to do lasting damage. Seek advice from your doctor, health visitor or social worker if you find yourself unable to control your anger to the extent that you fear you may harm your child.

# 23 School difficulties

**School difficulties fall into two main groups: those related principally to learning, whether of a specific subject or of schoolwork in general; and those more concerned with behaviour, including classroom behaviour and reluctance to go to school. Consult this chart if your child has difficulties of any of these kinds.**

**Such problems may be the result of emotional difficulties, physical disorders, social factors, or they may arise out of a general problem of development. Most school difficulties benefit from discussions between parents and school staff, and it is often helpful to involve the family doctor.**

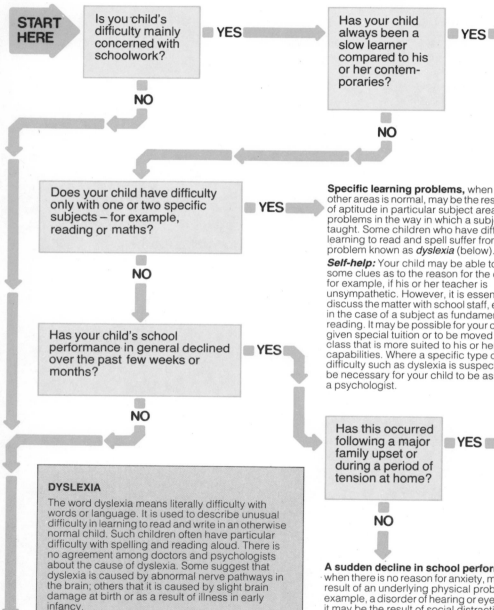

**START HERE** — Is your child's difficulty mainly concerned with schoolwork? — **YES** → Has your child always been a slow learner compared to his or her contemporaries? — **YES** →

**Slow intellectual development** may simply mean that your child is later than average at acquiring certain intellectual capabilities, but is likely to catch up with his or her fast-learning friends during the next few years. Also, a child who has had emotional problems, or who is of below average intelligence, may be expected to learn more slowly than average (see *Learning problems,* opposite).

*Self-help:* Discuss your child's progress with his or her teachers, who may be able to reassure you that your child's pace of learning is well within the normal range. It may be advisable in some cases for an intelligence test and a general physical examination to be carried out. Many children who are slow learners can be helped to catch up by attending remedial classes taught by specially trained teachers. However, in some cases it may be advisable for a child to attend a special school.

Does your child have difficulty only with one or two specific subjects – for example, reading or maths? — **YES** →

**Specific learning problems,** when ability in other areas is normal, may be the result of lack of aptitude in particular subject areas, or of problems in the way in which a subject is taught. Some children who have difficulty learning to read and spell suffer from a problem known as *dyslexia* (below).

*Self-help:* Your child may be able to give you some clues as to the reason for the difficulty – for example, if his or her teacher is unsympathetic. However, it is essential to discuss the matter with school staff, especially in the case of a subject as fundamental as reading. It may be possible for your child to be given special tuition or to be moved into a class that is more suited to his or her capabilities. Where a specific type of learning difficulty such as dyslexia is suspected, it may be necessary for your child to be assessed by a psychologist.

Has your child's school performance in general declined over the past few weeks or months? — **YES** →

Has this occurred following a major family upset or during a period of tension at home? — **YES** →

**Emotional insecurity** almost always has an effect on a child's schoolwork.

*Self-help:* Resolution of the cause of worry usually brings about an improvement. It is usually a good idea to inform teachers about any home problems that may affect a child's schoolwork so that allowances can be made and, where necessary, extra help given. If your child's work does not improve following resolution of the underlying difficulty, or if you are unable to resolve the problem, consult your doctor, who will be able to advise you on whether further specialist help is necessary.

**NO** ↓

**A sudden decline in school performance,** when there is no reason for anxiety, may be the result of an underlying physical problem – for example, a disorder of hearing or eyesight – or it may be the result of social distractions, or of a hidden cause of anxiety. Consult your doctor as well as discussing the problem with your child's teachers.

*Treatment:* Your doctor will probably do a physical examination of your child, paying particular attention to sight and hearing, and may arrange for your child to undergo further investigations. If no physical disorder is found, your doctor will probably advise further discussions with your child's schoolteachers to find out if there is any other possible cause of the difficulties. It may be necessary, following discussions with the school, to make adjustments to your child's curriculum.

**DYSLEXIA**

The word dyslexia means literally difficulty with words or language. It is used to describe unusual difficulty in learning to read and write in an otherwise normal child. Such children often have particular difficulty with spelling and reading aloud. There is no agreement among doctors and psychologists about the cause of dyslexia. Some suggest that dyslexia is caused by abnormal nerve pathways in the brain; others that it is caused by slight brain damage at birth or as a result of illness in early infancy.

**Diagnosing and treating dyslexia**

You should consider the possibility of dyslexia if your child has greater difficulty learning to read and write than would be expected for a child of his or her level of intelligence. Your child's school teachers will be able to advise you whether or not your child's progress is normal. If, after examining all aspects of your child's health and development (see *Learning problems,* opposite), the school authorities agree that dyslexia could be the problem, remedial teaching, helpful for the majority of dyslexic children, will be arranged.

*Go to next page*

*Continued from previous page*

**Has your child become reluctant to go to school?** — YES →

**Has your child only recently started school?** — YES →

NO ↓

NO ↓

**Have teachers complained about your child's behaviour at school?** — YES

**Has your child been refusing to go to school or been playing truant?** — YES

NO ↓

NO ↓

**Fear of school** is very common in children just starting a new school, especially when starting at nursery or primary school, if a child has not been used to being away from home and family for long periods.

*Self-help:* In most cases increasing familiarity with the school surroundings and growing interest in school activities will help your child to get over his or her misgivings. During the period of adjustment, try to reassure your child that being left at school is not a form of abandonment. Most nursery classes will allow parents to stay with their children for the first week or so. Make sure that there is no special cause for anxiety such as awkward lavatory facilities, and try never to be late in picking your child up from school. If fear of school persists, discuss the problem with the school authorities, who may recommend professional advice.

**School difficulties** that have not been described on this chart should be discussed with your child's teachers. Your doctor's advice may also be helpful in some cases.

**School refusal** is a sign that something is seriously wrong. It could be due to a problem at school such as bullying or a failure of the school to meet the child's individual needs, or it may be the result of the influence of friends at school. Occasionally, refusal to go to school is caused by anxiety about home life.

*Self-help:* To solve the problem of school refusal, you are likely to need the help of the school authorities and possibly your doctor, who may advise *child guidance* (p. 89). The sooner the problem is tackled the better. Make every effort to ensure that your child attends school and that the teachers concerned know that the problem exists so that unexplained absences from classes are not ignored. Meanwhile, try to discover the underlying cause of your child's refusal to go to school so that it can be dealt with if possible.

**Bad behaviour** at school can be a sign of a number of problems. It could be that the level of schoolwork is too low, leading to boredom (see *Gifted children,* below left) or it may be too high, resulting in loss of interest and leading the child to use disruptive behaviour to gain attention in class. It can also be the result of rejection of authority, often linked to the emotional changes of adolescence (see chart 51, *Adolescent behaviour problems*). In some cases it may be the result of emotional disturbance.

*Self-help:* In cases of mild misbehaviour it is often sufficient for your child to know that you are aware of the problem and invoke your usual forms of discipline (see *Rules and discipline,* p.89). However, it is also wise to discuss any possible causes for the problem with your child's teachers. Adjustments may need to be made to your child's schoolwork so that it meets your child's individual needs more closely. In cases of serious behaviour problems expert help through a *child guidance* clinic (p. 89), and occasionally special schools, may be advisable.

**Dislike of school** can arise from a variety of factors. Your child may be having difficulties with schoolwork, or may be afraid of certain teachers or of other pupils.

*Self-help:* Dislike of school should be tackled promptly before it develops into the more serious problem of *school refusal* (above). Try to find out from your child what the cause of the problem is, and discuss your child's feelings about school with his or her teachers, so that they can watch for signs of a problem such as bullying or teasing. While you are trying to resolve the problem, do not keep your child at home unless advised to do this by the school; there is a danger that this may lead your child to stay away from school in the future. Depending on the underlying cause of the problem, it may be necessary for your child to change classes or to receive special tuition.

---

## GIFTED CHILDREN

Children who are unusually gifted, whether with an exceptional talent in one area, or with a generally high level of intelligence, need special educational provision from an early age. This is because without adequate stimulation, a gifted child may become unhappy, bored and/or disruptive.

You may suspect that your child is unusually gifted if he or she learns very quickly – especially if he or she reads voraciously and complains that school is boring. In this case you should discuss the matter with your child's schoolteachers who may arrange for your child to be assessed by an educational psychologist.

If your child is found to be exceptionally intelligent, the teachers may be able to devise a learning programme that will stretch your child adequately. Alternatively, education at a special school may be the best option. If your child has a special gift for music, for example, expert tuition can usually be arranged.

Whatever educational programme you choose for your child, you will need to remember that his or her emotional and social development is unlikely to be as advanced as his or her intellectual growth. Your child should be encouraged to play with children of the same age, and to join in sports and other recreational activities, such as reading, watching television or pursuing a hobby.

---

## LEARNING PROBLEMS

In order to learn physical and intellectual skills at a normal rate, a child needs to have normal hearing, sight and intelligence. Impairment of any one of these faculties will lead to learning problems. In addition, a child's progress can be retarded by lack of sufficient stimulation in early childhood, by emotional upset, or by frequent absences from school.

### Assessing the problem
Any child who is obviously having difficulty keeping pace with his or her contemporaries at school needs to be assessed by an educational psychologist. This can be arranged by the school authorities. The psychologist will carry out intelligence tests and may also arrange tests on hearing and

vision. If a physical problem such as deafness is found, this will be treated by the family doctor. If an emotional cause for the learning difficulty is suspected, referral to a *child guidance* clinic (see p. 89) will probably be recommended. A child who seems to be of normal intelligence, but who has learning problems not caused by physical illness or emotional upset may be suffering from a specific learning difficulty known as *dyslexia* (opposite). Such children, as well as those whose difficulty is caused by lower-than-average intelligence, may be helped by special remedial classes for slow learners within an ordinary school. When intelligence is severely subnormal, it may be best for the child to be educated at a special school.

# 24 Hair, scalp and nail problems

Consult this diagnostic chart if your child has any problem affecting hair growth, including hair thinning and bald patches, or if your child's scalp is affected by itching or flaking. The most common causes of such problems are infection or parasitic infestation, which although not serious, require treatment.

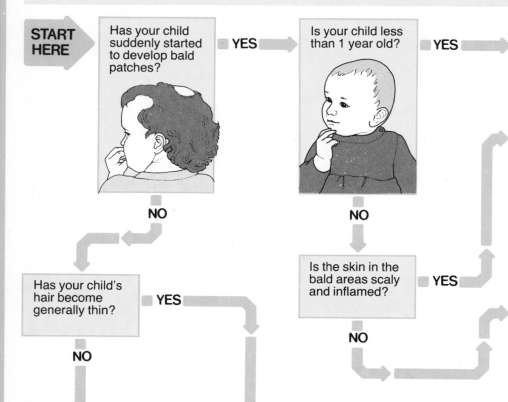

**START HERE**

Has your child suddenly started to develop bald patches?

**YES** → Is your child less than 1 year old?

**YES** → **Continual rubbing** on the bedclothes or baby seat can cause loss of a baby's delicate first hair. The bald patches will disappear as new, stronger hair grows.

**NO** ↓ (from "Has your child suddenly started to develop bald patches?")

Has your child's hair become generally thin?

**NO** ↓ (from "Is your child less than 1 year old?")

Is the skin in the bald areas scaly and inflamed?

**YES** →

**Ringworm,** a fungal infection, may cause such bald patches when it affects the scalp. Consult your doctor.

*Treatment:* If your doctor confirms the diagnosis, he or she will prescribe an *antifungal* ointment and/or medicine. To prevent reinfection, wash your child's hairbrush and comb thoroughly. Once the infection has cleared, the hair should grow back normally.

**NO** (from "Is the skin in the bald areas scaly and inflamed?")

**YES** (from "Has your child's hair become generally thin?")

**Alopecia areata** is a possible explanation for such hair loss. The cause is not fully understood, but it may be related to physical illness or to sudden emotional shocks. Consult your doctor.

*Treatment:* The condition may get better without treatment. Very occasionally permanent baldness may result.

**NO** (from "Has your child's hair become generally thin?")

## WASHING YOUR CHILD'S HAIR

Children's hair should be washed regularly (about twice a week) and thoroughly. Unless your child needs a special shampoo to control dandruff, almost any cheap shampoo will do: expensive cosmetic shampoos are unlikely to improve a child's hair in any way. However, for babies and young children it may be advisable to choose a mild (baby) shampoo that will not sting if it gets in the eyes. One application of the shampoo should be sufficient unless the hair is very dirty. Make sure that you rinse the hair thoroughly afterwards. Hair should be allowed to dry naturally if possible.

**Overcoming dislike of hair-washing**
Many young children dislike having their hair washed, because they are frightened of getting water in their eyes. It may be helpful to encourage gentle water play in the bath (left).

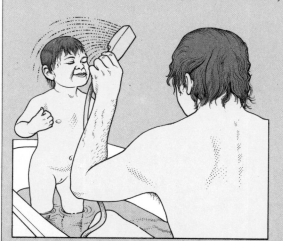

Is your child less than 1 year old?

**YES** →

**NO** ↓

**Loss of baby hair** during the first year usually results in a noticeable thinning out of hair for a brief period. Over the next few months new, stronger hair will grow, and it may be of a different colour from that with which your baby was born.

*Go to next page, column 1*

*Go to next page, column 2*

**1** *Continued from previous page, column 1*

**Is your child's scalp itchy?**

NO ↓ / YES →

**Does your child have greasy, crusty patches on the scalp?**

NO ↓ / YES →

**Is your child's scalp flaky?**

NO ↓ / YES →

**Consult your doctor** if you are unable to make a diagnosis from this chart.

**Does thorough washing relieve the itching for a few days?**

NO ↓ / YES →

**Head lice** are a possibility, especially if any of your children's friends are also affected. Head lice are easily passed from one person to another, and infestation is not the result of inadequate hair washing. Consult your doctor.

**Treatment:** The usual treatment for head lice is to wash your child's hair with a special shampoo that your doctor will prescribe. This will need to be applied several times. After each application, the hair can be combed with a fine-toothed comb to remove the eggs that remain stuck to the hair.

**Cradle cap,** a form of a harmless condition called seborrhoeic dermatitis (a type of eczema) is common in babies under 1 year.

**Self-help:** If you find the crusts unsightly you can remove them by rubbing your baby's scalp gently with baby oil or petroleum jelly and then washing the scalp to remove the crusts. If cradle cap is extensive, your doctor may be able to prescribe a special cream to control the condition.

**Dandruff** is the most likely cause of flaking of the scalp. See *Dandruff*, right.

**2** *Continued from previous page, column 2*

**Has your child been taking any medicines prescribed by your doctor?**

NO ↓ / YES →

**General thinning** of hair may be the result of illness in the past few months or may occur for no apparent reason.

**Self-help:** Other than ensuring that your child is otherwise healthy and is receiving an adequate diet (see *The components of a healthy diet,* p. 119) there is little you can do to encourage your child's hair to grow more thickly. If your child's hair is long, avoid tying it back tightly with elastic bands or pulling it into tight plaited styles. Use a soft nylon or bristle brush because hard brushes may break the hair. Your child's hair may appear thicker if cut in a short style. If you are worried, consult your doctor.

**Certain drugs** may cause temporary hair loss. Discuss the problem with your doctor.

**Dandruff,** which is sometimes caused by seborrhoeic dermatitis, a form of eczema, is the most common cause of itching of the scalp. It is also likely to lead to flaking of the scalp.

**Self-help:** Dandruff is best controlled by frequent use of one of the many over-the-counter antidandruff shampoos. If this is not effective, consult your doctor, who will prescribe another antidandruff shampoo, or a lotion to apply to the scalp.

---

## NAIL CARE

The nails of babies and children should always be kept short. In babies this prevents accidental scratching and in older children helps to prevent nail-biting and the spread of infection from dirt under the fingernails. Always use blunt-ended scissors for babies.

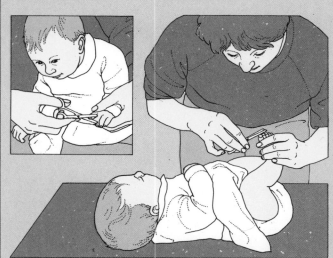

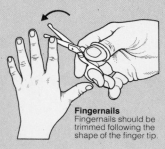

**Fingernails**
Fingernails should be trimmed following the shape of the finger tip.

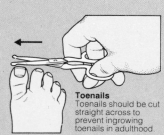

**Toenails**
Toenails should be cut straight across to prevent ingrowing toenails in adulthood.

**Nail-biting**
Nail-biting is a habit that often develops in children of primary school age. It may be copied from other children or arise as a nervous habit. It presents no risk to health, but bitten nails are unsightly and, if bitten down to the quick, may cause soreness.

If your child has a tendency to bite his or her nails, try to keep them trimmed and smooth. Encourage your child to take pride in their appearance. Buying a manicure set and applying clear nail varnish may help. Bitter-tasting paint for the nails is unlikely to have any effect and may simply make your child resentful. Most children have stopped biting their nails by the time they reach adolescence.

# 25 Spots and rashes

Spots and rashes in childhood are usually caused by inflammation of the skin as a result of infection, which may be localized or part of a generalized illness, or of an allergic reaction. Most rashes that are not accompanied by a fever or a feeling of being generally unwell are not a sign of serious illness; but if the rash is itchy or sore you should consult your doctor, who will be able to provide effective treatment.

**For children under 1 year, see chart 4, Skin problems.**

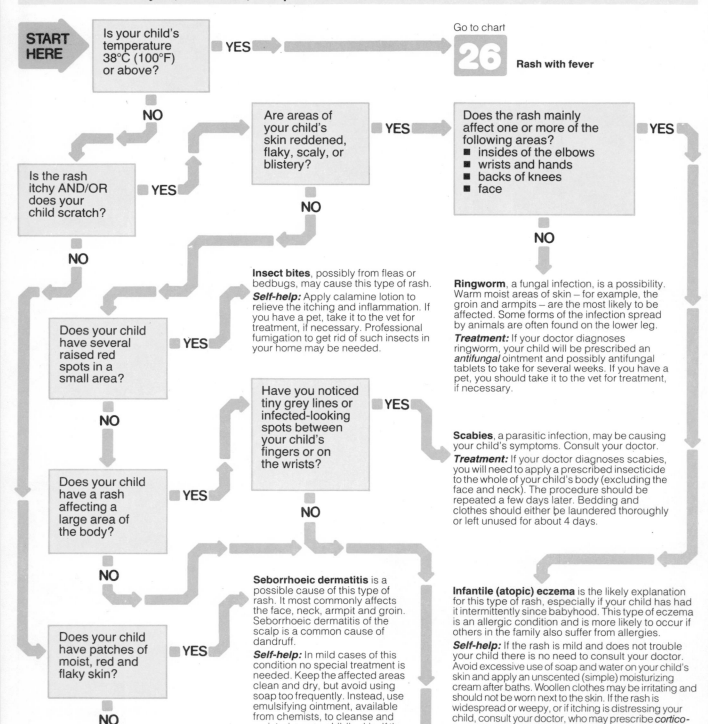

**START HERE**

Is your child's temperature 38°C (100°F) or above?

**YES** → Go to chart **26** **Rash with fever**

**NO**

Is the rash itchy AND/OR does your child scratch?

Are areas of your child's skin reddened, flaky, scaly, or blistery?

**YES**

Does the rash mainly affect one or more of the following areas?
- insides of the elbows
- wrists and hands
- backs of knees
- face

**YES**

**NO**

**YES**

**NO**

**NO**

Does your child have several raised red spots in a small area?

**YES**

**Insect bites**, possibly from fleas or bedbugs, may cause this type of rash.
**Self-help:** Apply calamine lotion to relieve the itching and inflammation. If you have a pet, take it to the vet for treatment, if necessary. Professional fumigation to get rid of such insects in your home may be needed.

**Ringworm**, a fungal infection, is a possibility. Warm moist areas of skin – for example, the groin and armpits – are the most likely to be affected. Some forms of the infection spread by animals are often found on the lower leg.
**Treatment:** If your doctor diagnoses ringworm, your child will be prescribed an *antifungal* ointment and possibly antifungal tablets to take for several weeks. If you have a pet, you should take it to the vet for treatment, if necessary.

**NO**

Does your child have a rash affecting a large area of the body?

**YES**

Have you noticed tiny grey lines or infected-looking spots between your child's fingers or on the wrists?

**YES**

**NO**

**Scabies**, a parasitic infection, may be causing your child's symptoms. Consult your doctor.
**Treatment:** If your doctor diagnoses scabies, you will need to apply a prescribed insecticide to the whole of your child's body (excluding the face and neck). The procedure should be repeated a few days later. Bedding and clothes should either be laundered thoroughly or left unused for about 4 days.

**NO**

Does your child have patches of moist, red and flaky skin?

**YES**

**Seborrhoeic dermatitis** is a possible cause of this type of rash. It most commonly affects the face, neck, armpit and groin. Seborrhoeic dermatitis of the scalp is a common cause of dandruff.
**Self-help:** In mild cases of this condition no special treatment is needed. Keep the affected areas clean and dry, but avoid using soap too frequently. Instead, use emulsifying ointment, available from chemists, to cleanse and moisturize your child's skin. If the rash is extensive or causes your child discomfort or embarrassment, consult your doctor, who may prescribe *cortico steroid* cream or ointment.

**Infantile (atopic) eczema** is the likely explanation for this type of rash, especially if your child has had it intermittently since babyhood. This type of eczema is an allergic condition and is more likely to occur if others in the family also suffer from allergies.
**Self-help:** If the rash is mild and does not trouble your child there is no need to consult your doctor. Avoid excessive use of soap and water on your child's skin and apply an unscented (simple) moisturizing cream after baths. Woollen clothes may be irritating and should not be worn next to the skin. If the rash is widespread or weepy, or if itching is distressing your child, consult your doctor, who may prescribe *corticosteroid* and possibly *antibiotic* cream. Your doctor may also prescribe medicine to reduce itching and may recommend changes in your child's diet if certain foods seem to make the rash worse.

**NO**

*Go to next page, column 1*

*Go to next page, column 2*

1 *Continued from previous page, column 1*

2 *Continued from previous page, column 2*

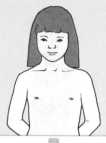

**Does your child have a rash of pink spots mainly affecting the face and/or trunk?**

**YES** → **German measles** (rubella) is possible. The disease is usually accompanied by swelling of the glands in the back of the neck and is unlikely to make your child feel very unwell. (See also *Comparison of childhood infectious diseases,* p. 97).

*Self-help:* German measles is a mild illness and generally needs little treatment other than paracetamol to reduce any fever. It is important, however, to keep your child at home to avoid infecting others, especially any woman who is pregnant, because of the damage the disease can do to the unborn child. If you want to consult your doctor, telephone the surgery first, so that your doctor can visit your child at home if necessary.

**NO** ↓

**Does your child have a blistery rash that dries up to form a golden-coloured crust?**

**YES** → **Impetigo**, a bacterial skin infection that commonly affects the face, is possible. Consult your doctor.

*Treatment:* If your doctor confirms that your child has impetigo, you will probably be advised to wash the crusts away gently with salty water and to apply *antibiotic* cream to the affected areas. While the infection persists, you should make sure that your child keeps a separate towel and other wash things to avoid infecting the rest of the family. It may be necessary to keep your child away from school.

**NO** ↓

**Is your child over 12 years old AND suffering from one or more of the following?**
- blackheads
- inflamed spots with white centres
- painful red lumps under the skin

**YES** → **Acne** is a common problem in adolescence and can occur with varying degrees of severity.

Go to chart

 **52** **Adolescent skin problems**

**NO** ↓

**Does your child have several bright-red slightly raised spots or patches with pale centres?**

**YES** → **Urticaria** (hives), an allergic reaction, produces this type of rash. It may occur as a reaction to certain foods – for example, shellfish or strawberries – or to drugs. Sometimes it occurs when the skin is exposed to certain plants or to extremes of heat or cold. In many cases no cause for the rash can be found. Occasionally, the appearance of the rash is accompanied by swelling of the face and mouth. This can be dangerous and requires urgent medical treatment.

*Self-help:* An outbreak of urticaria normally subsides within a few hours without treatment. You can apply calamine lotion to the rash to reduce any irritation. If your child suffers from repeated attacks, or if the rash persists for more than 4 hours, consult your doctor, who may prescribe *antihistamines* and may carry out tests to determine the cause of the problem.

**NO** ↓

---

### WARTS AND BOILS

**Warts**
A wart is a lump on the skin caused by virus infection. The most common type of wart is a hard, painless lump with a roughened surface. Warts may occur singly, but more often several occur together. The hands are the most commonly affected area, but flattened warts called veruccas often appear on the soles of the feet. Veruccas may cause your child pain on walking.

**Treatment**
Warts need no treatment and will disappear in their own in time. However, if your child is embarrassed by unsightly warts, or has veruccas, consult your doctor, who may recommend treatment with a lotion painted onto the wart, or may refer your child to hospital where the wart can be either burnt or frozen off. Removal of warts by freezing does not cause scarring.

**Boils**
A boil occurs when a hair follicle (a pit in the skin from which a hair grows) becomes infected by bacteria, resulting in the collection of pus in the follicle. An inflamed lump with a white centre develops under the skin. Eventually the boil bursts, releasing the pus, and the skin heals.

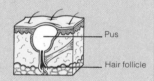

**The formation of a boil**
A boil forms when bacteria enter a hair follicle causing pus to collect there.

Pus

Hair follicle

**Treatment**
A single boil usually heals without treatment. Adding some mild antiseptic to your child's bath water will help to prevent the spread of infection. When the boil bursts, carefully wipe away the pus with cotton wool soaked in an antiseptic solution and cover with an adhesive plaster, if necessary. Consult your doctor if your child has a large painful boil, if several boils develop, or if boils recur. Your doctor may prescribe *antibiotics* or an antiseptic cream. Occasionally, it is necessary for your doctor to make a small cut in the centre of a large boil to release the pus and hasten healing.

---

**Certain drugs** may bring out a rash in susceptible children. Discuss the problem with your doctor.

**Is your child taking any medicines?**

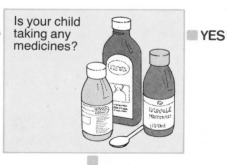

**YES** →

**NO** ↓

**Consult your doctor** if you are unable to make a diagnosis from this chart.

# 26 Rash with fever

Consult this chart if your child develops a rash anywhere on the body while suffering from a temperature of 38°C (100°F) or above. This combination of symptoms usually indicates one of the common infectious diseases of childhood. These diseases are caused by viruses and can usually be treated at home. If your child is less than a year old you should, however, consult your doctor to confirm the diagnosis.

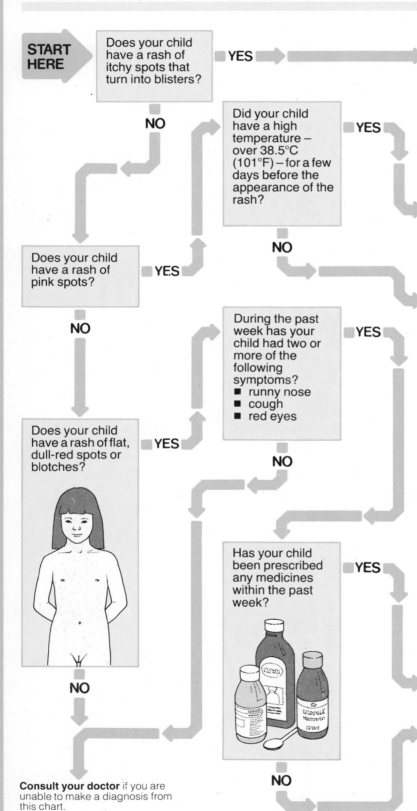

**START HERE**

Does your child have a rash of itchy spots that turn into blisters?

**YES** →

**NO**

Did your child have a high temperature — over 38.5°C (101°F) — for a few days before the appearance of the rash?

**YES** →

**NO**

Does your child have a rash of pink spots?

**YES**

**NO**

During the past week has your child had two or more of the following symptoms?
- runny nose
- cough
- red eyes

**YES** →

**NO**

Does your child have a rash of flat, dull-red spots or blotches?

**YES**

**NO**

Has your child been prescribed any medicines within the past week?

**YES** →

**NO**

**Consult your doctor** if you are unable to make a diagnosis from this chart.

**Chickenpox,** an infection caused by the herpes zoster virus, is the likely diagnosis (see *Comparison of childhood infectious diseases,* opposite). This is usually a mild disease, although an older child or adolescent may feel unwell for a few days.
***Self-help:*** Give your child paracetamol to reduce fever (see *Lowering your child's temperature,* p. 288) and apply calamine lotion to soothe the rash. Your child should be discouraged from scratching the spots because this may lead to scarring. If itching is severe, consult your doctor, who may prescribe a drug to alleviate it. Your child is no longer infectious when all the blisters have formed scabs.

**Roseola infantum,** a viral infection that commonly affects children between the ages of 6 months and 3 years, is a likely possibility (see *Comparison of childhood infectious diseases,* opposite).
***Self-help:*** Follow the advice on *Lowering your child's temperature,* p. 288. Recovery normally takes about a week.

**German measles** (rubella) is possible. The disease is usually accompanied by swelling of the glands in the neck and is unlikely to make your child feel very unwell (see *Comparison of childhood infectious diseases,* opposite).
***Self-help:*** German measles is a mild illness and generally needs little treatment other than paracetamol to reduce fever. It is important, however, to keep your child at home to avoid infecting others, especially any woman who is pregnant, because of the damage the disease can do to the unborn child. Telephone the surgery first, so that your doctor can visit your child at home, if necessary.

## WARNING

### DANGER SIGNS

In the vast majority of cases, children recover from childhood infectious diseases without special medical treatment and without experiencing complications or any long-term problems. However, in a small proportion of children, the viruses that produce these diseases may spread to the central nervous system, leading to encephalitis or meningitis, or may encourage bacterial infection of the ears and lungs. Call your doctor at once if your child develops any of the following danger signs in addition to the rash and raised temperature:

- unusual drowsiness
- refusal to drink
- earache
- abnormally fast breathing (see the box on p. 110)
- noisy breathing
- severe headache

**Certain drugs** may produce a rash in some children – in particular, *antibiotics* that are often used to treat throat and chest infections. Consult your doctor.

**Measles** is the most likely cause of such symptoms even if your child has been vaccinated against the disease (see *Comparison of childhood infectious diseases,* opposite).
***Self-help:*** There is no specific treatment for measles. Take steps to keep your child's temperature down (see *Lowering your child's temperature,* p. 288). Call your doctor at once if your child develops any of the danger signs listed in the box above. Recovery takes about 10 days.

## COMPARISON OF CHILDHOOD INFECTIOUS DISEASES

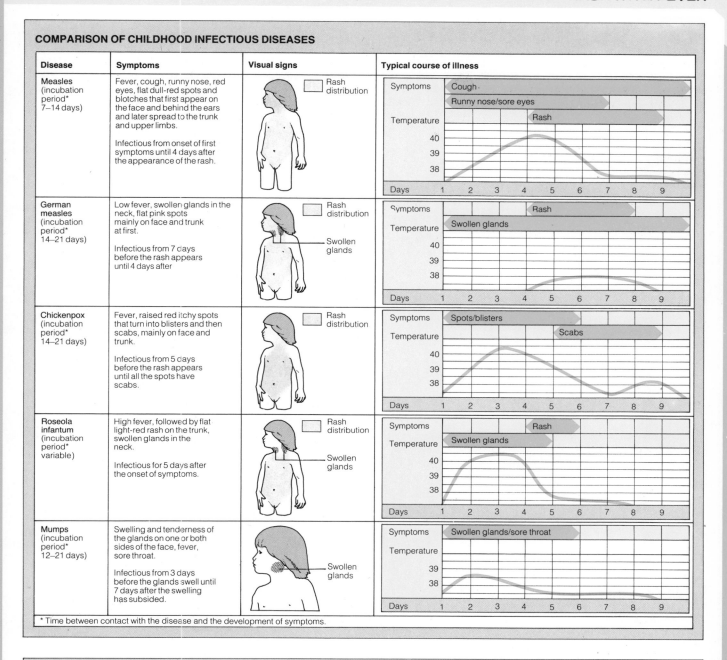

| Disease | Symptoms | Visual signs | Typical course of illness |
|---|---|---|---|
| Measles (incubation period* 7–14 days) | Fever, cough, runny nose, red eyes, flat dull-red spots and blotches that first appear on the face and behind the ears and later spread to the trunk and upper limbs.<br><br>Infectious from onset of first symptoms until 4 days after the appearance of the rash. | Rash distribution | Symptoms: Cough; Runny nose/sore eyes; Rash. Temperature 40, 39, 38. Days 1–9 |
| German measles (incubation period* 14–21 days) | Low fever, swollen glands in the neck, flat pink spots mainly on face and trunk at first.<br><br>Infectious from 7 days before the rash appears until 4 days after | Rash distribution; Swollen glands | Symptoms: Rash; Swollen glands. Temperature 40, 39, 38. Days 1–9 |
| Chickenpox (incubation period* 14–21 days) | Fever, raised red itchy spots that turn into blisters and then scabs, mainly on face and trunk.<br><br>Infectious from 5 days before the rash appears until all the spots have scabs. | Rash distribution | Symptoms: Spots/blisters; Scabs. Temperature 40, 39, 38. Days 1–9 |
| Roseola infantum (incubation period* variable) | High fever, followed by flat light-red rash on the trunk, swollen glands in the neck.<br><br>Infectious for 5 days after the onset of symptoms. | Rash distribution; Swollen glands | Symptoms: Rash; Swollen glands. Temperature 40, 39, 38. Days 1–9 |
| Mumps (incubation period* 12–21 days) | Swelling and tenderness of the glands on one or both sides of the face, fever, sore throat.<br><br>Infectious from 3 days before the glands swell until 7 days after the swelling has subsided. | Swollen glands | Symptoms: Swollen glands/sore throat. Temperature 39, 38. Days 1–9 |

\* Time between contact with the disease and the development of symptoms.

## IMMUNIZATION

Your child can be given highly effective immunity against various infectious diseases by vaccination. Some vaccines contain living microbes (in a harmless form) and these give lasting protection. Vaccines made from dead microbes or from the toxins they produce have to be given several times for best results. In each case the body is stimulated to produce substances known as antibodies to fight the disease. Immunization during childhood not only protects your child from disease, but helps to reduce the spread of disease in the community. Most forms of immunization carry little risk. However, some vaccinations may be dangerous for children who have had convulsions or if anyone in their family has suffered from fits. In these cases certain vaccinations may not be advisable and you should discuss this with your doctor. In addition, you should not have your child vaccinated when he or she is unwell. The table (right) shows a typical immunization schedule.

### TYPICAL IMMUNIZATION SCHEDULE

| Age | Disease | Method of vaccination |
|---|---|---|
| 3-6 months | Diphtheria, whooping cough, tetanus | Combined injection |
| 3-6 months | Poliomyelitis | By mouth |
| 6-8 months | Diphtheria, whooping cough, tetanus | Combined injection |
| 6-8 months | Poliomyelitis | By mouth |
| 10-14 months | Diphtheria, whooping cough, tetanus | Combined injection |
| 10-14 months | Poliomyelitis | By mouth |
| 12-24 months | Measles | Injection |
| 5 years | Diphtheria, tetanus | Combined injection |
| 5 years | Poliomyelitis | By mouth |
| 10–13 years | Tuberculosis | Injection |
| 13-14 years | German measles (girls only) | Injection |

# 27 Eye problems

This chart deals with pain, itching, redness and/or discharge from one or both eyes. In children such symptoms are most commonly the result of infection or local irritation and can often be treated at home without consulting a doctor. However, you should seek immediate medical advice about any obvious injury to the eye or for any foreign body in the eye that cannot be removed by simple first aid measures.

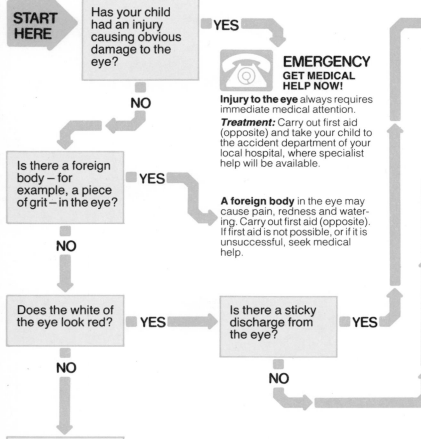

**START HERE**

**Has your child had an injury causing obvious damage to the eye?** — **YES**

**EMERGENCY GET MEDICAL HELP NOW!**

**Injury to the eye** always requires immediate medical attention.
***Treatment:*** Carry out first aid (opposite) and take your child to the accident department of your local hospital, where specialist help will be available.

**NO**

**Is there a foreign body – for example, a piece of grit – in the eye?** — **YES**

**A foreign body** in the eye may cause pain, redness and watering. Carry out first aid (opposite). If first aid is not possible, or if it is unsuccessful, seek medical help.

**NO**

**Does the white of the eye look red?** — **YES** — **Is there a sticky discharge from the eye?** — **YES**

**NO** (under "Does the white of the eye look red?")

**NO** (under "Is there a sticky discharge from the eye?")

**Are the eyelids red and itchy?** — **YES**

**Blepharitis** (inflammation of the lid margins) is the usual cause of itchy, scaly eyelids, and is most common in children who have dandruff (scaling and itching of the scalp). Consult your doctor.
***Treatment:*** Your doctor will probably prescribe an eye ointment. If your child has dandruff, treat it with an anti-dandruff shampoo.

**NO**

**Is there a red lump on one lid?** — **YES**

**A stye** (a boil-like infection at the base of an eyelash) is likely. This is a common childhood problem.
***Self-help:*** A stye will usually clear up within a week without special treatment. It will either burst, releasing pus, or dry up. If your child's stye bursts, carefully wipe away the pus with cotton wool and cooled boiled water. Use a clean piece of cotton wool each time you wipe. Consult your doctor if a stye fails to heal in a week, if the eye itself becomes red and painful, or if styes recur.

**NO**

*Go to next page*

**Conjunctivitis** (inflammation of the membrane covering the eye and lining the eyelids) caused by infection is likely. Consult your doctor.
***Treatment:*** Your doctor will probably prescribe *antibiotic* eye drops or ointment. The sticky discharge can be gently bathed away with warm boiled water. Make sure your child keeps the eyes closed, and use a clean piece of cotton wool each time you wipe. Keep a separate towel and face flannel for your child to prevent the spread of infection.

**Eye irritation** caused by fumes, chemicals (for example, in swimming pool water), or an allergic reaction (for example, to pollen) is possible. However, if other children in your area also have this problem, it may be due to viral infection (viral conjunctivitis).
***Self-help:*** If you suspect irritation from fumes or chemicals, no treatment other than avoidance of the irritant is needed. Similarly, irritation caused by allergy will subside as soon as the cause of the reaction is removed, but this is not always possible. Discuss this with your doctor. Viral conjunctivitis will clear up on its own, but you will need to take steps to prevent the spread of infection (see *Conjunctivitis,* above). In any case, consult your doctor if redness persists for more than a week or if your child complains of pain.

---

**DROOPING EYELID**

Some children have a permanently drooping upper eyelid, a condition known as ptosis. This is often present from birth, and in such cases is usually the result of weakness of the muscles in the affected eyelid. Occasionally, ptosis may develop later in childhood as a result of a nerve or muscle disorder.

**Risks**
If ptosis is so severe that the vision in that eye is blocked, and the condition is untreated, it may cause deterioration in the vision in the "lazy" eye.

**Treatment**
If your child has a drooping eyelid, consult your doctor. The condition may be treated by an operation to strengthen the muscles of the eyelid, or by special spectacles. Ptosis that is caused by a nerve or muscle disorder may be cured by treating the underlying condition. If your child has developed a lazy eye, he or she may need to wear a patch over the good eye to force the lazy eye to work harder.

Drooping eyelid in a child.

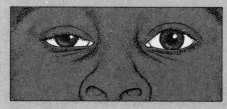

*Continued from previous page*

**Is your child less than 1 year old?**

**YES** → **A blocked tear duct,** which prevents tears from draining away normally, is possible. This is common in babies and usually corrects itself without treatment by the end of the first year. Discuss the problem with your doctor, who may show you how to massage the duct gently to remove the blockage.

**Does the eye produce tears even when your child is not crying?**

**YES** ↑

**NO** ↓

**NO** ↓

**Consult your doctor** if you are unable to make a diagnosis from this chart.

## FIRST AID FOR EYE INJURIES

If your child suffers an injury to the eye or eyelid, rapid action is essential. Except in the case of a foreign body that has been successfully removed from the eye, take your child to the accident department of your local hospital by the fastest means possible, as soon as you have carried out first aid.

### Cuts to the eye or eyelid
Cover the injured eye with a clean pad (for example, a folded handkerchief) and hold the pad lightly in place with a bandage. Apply no pressure. Cover the other eye also. Seek medical help.

### Blows to the eye area
Carry out first aid as for cuts to the eye or eyelid (above) but use a cold compress instead of a dry pad over the injured eye.

### Corrosive chemicals in the eye
If your child spills any harsh chemical (for example, bleach) in an eye, immediately flood the eye with large quantities of cold running water. Tilt your child's head with the injured eye downwards and keep the eyelids apart with your fingers (see below). When all traces of the chemical seem to have been removed, lightly cover the eye with a clean pad and seek medical help.

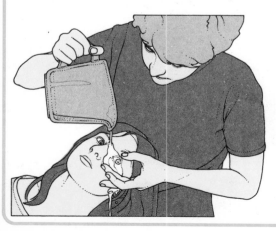

### Foreign body in the eye
Never attempt to remove any of the following from your child's eye:

- an object that is embedded in the eyeball
- a chip of metal
- a particle over the coloured part of the eye.

In any of these cases cover both eyes as recommended for cuts to the eye or eyelid (left) and seek medical help.

Other foreign bodies – for example, specks of dirt or eyelashes floating on the white of the eye or inside the lids – may be removed as follows:

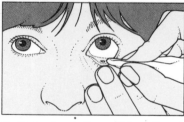

**1** If you can see the particle on the white of the eye or inside the lower lid, pick it off using the moistened corner of a clean handkerchief.

**2** If you can see nothing, hold the lashes, pull the upper lid down over the lower lid and hold it for a moment. This may dislodge the particle.

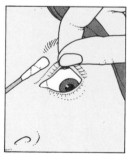

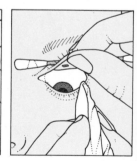

**3** If the particle remains, it may be on the inside of the upper lid. Ask your child to look down. Hold the lashes of the upper lid and pull it outwards.

**4** Place a match, cocktail stick or cotton wool bud over the upper lid and fold the lid back over it.

**5** If the particle is now visible, pick it off with the corner of a handkerchief as in step 1.

If you do not succeed in removing the foreign body, lightly cover your child's injured eye and seek medical help at once.

# 28 Disturbed or impaired vision

Defects in vision in children are usually picked up at routine eye tests. But you may suspect that your child has a problem with his or her eyesight if he or she always holds books very close to the face. Or a teacher may notice that your child performs less well if he or she sits at the back of the classroom where it may be difficult to see the blackboard. Disorders causing sudden or complete loss of vision are fortunately rare. Always consult your doctor promptly about any problems with your child's eyesight.

**START HERE**

**Has your child lost all or part of his or her vision?**

**NO** ↓

**Has your child been suffering from double vision?**

**YES** →

**Has your child had a recent head injury?**

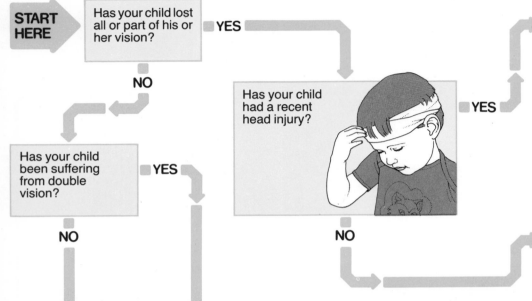

**YES** →

**EMERGENCY**
**GET MEDICAL HELP NOW!**

**Injury to the eye mechanism, or to part of the brain,** is a possibility.

*Treatment:* Your child will probably be admitted to hospital for examination by an eye specialist. Tests such as a skull X-ray, and a *CAT scan* (p. 85) will probably be necessary. Treatment will depend on the nature and extent of the damage.

**NO** ↓

**CALL YOUR DOCTOR NOW!**
**Sudden loss of vision** is always a serious symptom, even if it only lasts a few moments.

*Treatment:* Your doctor will look at your child's eyes and may arrange for him or her to be examined by an eye specialist to determine the underlying cause of the problem.

**CONSULT YOUR DOCTOR WITHOUT DELAY!**
**A squint** is possible. (See the box below.)

**NO** ↓

---

## SQUINT

A squint occurs when the eyes do not work together properly. When one eye focuses on any object, the other looks elsewhere, often inwards, but sometimes outwards, upwards or downwards (see below). The effect is usually to make the child look cross-eyed and may cause blurred or double vision.

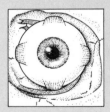

**Eye muscles**
Movement of the eyeball in the eye socket is controlled by 3 pairs of muscles (below). These are attached to the eyeball (left) and to the back of the eye socket (below left), and work together to produce the full range of eye movements.

1 Vertical muscles move the eyeball up and down.
2 Horizontal muscles move the eyeball from side to side.
3 Muscles encircling the eyeball enable it to rotate.

**Causes of squinting**
Many babies under 3 months squint occasionally as they learn to focus, and this is no cause for concern. After 3 months a squint may be the result of an imbalance in the eye muscles (left), or it may be the result of a good eye overworking to compensate for severe short or long sight in the other eye. This, if untreated, can result in further deterioration in the vision of the "lazy" eye.

Occasionally, a squint appears for the first time later on in childhood, when a disease such as measles disrupts a child's ability to compensate for a defect in vision.

**Treatment**
Always consult your doctor about squint or double vision in a child, whatever his or her age. For a squint caused by a lazy eye, the usual treatment is to prescribe spectacles to correct any defect in vision. The good eye may be covered up to force the child to use the lazy eye. This often clears up the problem in a few months. If the squint is caused by a muscular defect, an operation may be necessary.

A young child with a squint may need to wear glasses with the lens over the good eye covered.

**Types of squint**
The illustrations (left) show different types of squint in which the eye on the right is not focusing correctly. The "lazy" eye may move inwards (a), upwards (b), outwards (c), or downwards (d).

*Continued from previous page*

**Is your child's vision generally blurred?**

**YES** →

**NO** ↓

**Is either eye red and painful?**

**YES** →

**NO** ↓

**CONSULT YOUR DOCTOR WITHOUT DELAY!**
**Iritis** (inflammation of the coloured part of the eye) is possible, although uncommon in children. A less serious problem such as conjunctivitis is more likely.
***Treatment:*** If your doctor diagnoses iritis, he or she will prescribe eye drops or ointment to reduce inflammation and possibly another type of eye drops to prevent further damage. If your child has conjunctivitis, your doctor may prescribe eye drops or ointment to counter infection.

**Could your child have accidentally taken medicine prescribed for an adult?**

**YES** →

**NO** ↓

**CALL YOUR DOCTOR NOW!**
**Poisoning by certain drugs** – in particular, quinine – may cause blurring of vision. (See *Poisoning,* p. 286).

**Is your child taking any medicines?**

**YES** →

**NO** ↓

**Certain drugs** may cause blurring of vision. Discuss the problem with your doctor.

**An error of refraction,** a disorder of the focusing mechanism of the eyes, may cause blurred vision. The most common types of error in children are short sight (difficulty in seeing faraway objects), long sight (difficulty in focusing on near objects) and astigmatism (distorted vision caused by uneven curvature of the front of the eye). Consult your doctor.
***Treatment:*** If your doctor confirms the possibility of such a disorder, he or she will refer your child to an optician for a full eye test. Your child may need to wear glasses.

**EYE TESTING**
Your child's eyes and vision should be tested at regular intervals throughout childhood. In the pre-school years your family doctor will test your child's vision at routine developmental checks.

When your child goes to school his or her vision will be tested as part of a general medical examination. Most education authorities arrange for children to have several such examinations during their school years. If you are worried that your child has a defect in vision that has not been picked up at these regular checks, consult your doctor, who will, if necessary, arrange for your child to have a full eye test carried out by an optician.

**What happens**
When examining the eyes and vision of a young child, your doctor will test your child's ability to recognize small objects or pictures at a distance (below). Each eye will be tested separately while the other is covered.

A child of school age will probably be asked to read letters of gradually diminishing size on a chart from a set distance.

**Does your child have difficulty seeing distant objects?**

**YES** →

**NO** ↓

**Short sight** is likely: This means that your child's eyes have difficulty in focusing on distant objects. This type of defect is often inherited. Consult your doctor.
***Treatment:*** If your doctor thinks that your child may be short sighted, he or she will arrange for your child to have a full eye test by an optician, who may prescribe glasses.

**Has your child been seeing flashing lights or floating spots?**

**YES** →

**NO** ↓

**Has this happened on several past occasions AND does a severe headache normally follow?**

**YES** →

**NO** ↓

**Migraines** (recurrent severe headaches) may occasionally affect children. Consult your doctor.
***Treatment:*** If migraine is diagnosed, your doctor may prescribe painkillers for your child to take during attacks. Relaxing in a darkened room may also help your child's symptoms pass more quickly.

**Consult your doctor** if you are unable to make a diagnosis from this chart.

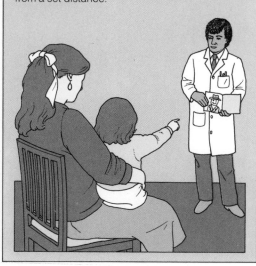

# 29 Painful or irritated ear

Ear pain is common in babies and children (up to three attacks a year is quite usual) and can be very distressing. A baby who is not old enough to tell you what the matter is may cry continuously or shriek loudly at intervals, and may pull at the affected ear. Earache is the most common explanation for waking at night in a baby who usually sleeps well. Most ear problems in childhood are due to infection.

**START HERE**

**Does your child have severe earache?** — **YES** →

**Does your child seem unwell or feverish, AND/OR does he or she have a cold?** — **YES** →

**Infection of the middle ear** is a possibility. This may have occurred as a result of germs travelling up the eustachian tube. Consult your doctor.

**Treatment:** If after examining your child the doctor confirms that the middle ear is inflamed, he or she will probably prescribe *antibiotics* and possibly some *decongestant* nose drops or spray to clear the eustachian tube. During this treatment you can help to relieve the pain by following the self-help suggestions described below.

**NO** ↓ (from severe earache)

**NO** ↓ (from unwell/feverish)

**Does your child complain of itching in the ear, OR does he or she scratch the ear?** — **YES** →

**Can you see a red lump inside the ear?** — **YES** →

**A boil** in the outer-ear canal can cause severe pain in a child. Consult your doctor.

**Treatment:** If your doctor confirms this diagnosis, he or she will probably prescribe ear drops, which usually quickly clear up the problem. The self-help suggestions below will help relieve the pain meanwhile.

**NO** ↓

**NO** ↓

**Inflammation of the outer-ear canal** is possible, especially if your child has been swimming in chlorinated water recently. Consult your doctor.

**Treatment:** Your doctor will probably prescribe ear drops to reduce inflammation and prevent infection.

**Generalized infection of the outer-ear canal** is probable. Consult your doctor.

**Treatment:** If your child's outer ear is found to be infected, your doctor will probably prescribe *antibiotic* ear drops to treat the infection and will recommend that you give your child liquid paracetamol for the pain (see *How to relieve earache*, below).

---

### FIRST AID FOR A FOREIGN BODY IN THE EAR

Young children often cause ear problems by poking small objects, such as beads or beans, into their ears. If this happens, do not try to remove the object yourself unless it is very close to the entrance of the outer-ear canal and you are quite sure that you will do no damage to the delicate lining of the outer-ear canal or to the eardrum. If you are in any doubt, consult your doctor or go to the casualty department of your local hospital.

**Insect in the ear**
If an insect gets into your child's ear, you can safely try to remove it by pouring tepid water into the ear so that it floats out. As you pour, pull the lobe of the ear gently backwards and upwards to straighten the canal. Alternatively, you may find it easier to get your child to lie back in a bath with his or her ears underwater. If these measures do not remove the insect, consult your doctor.

Pouring tepid water into your child's ear is a safe way of removing an insect trapped inside.

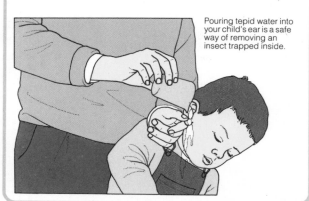

### HOW TO RELIEVE EARACHE

*Antibiotics* may take up to 24 hours before relieving the symptoms of an ear infection. During this time, you can relieve your child's earache by giving the recommended dose of paracetamol syrup or tablets (for an older child) at four-hourly intervals. It may also be comforting to place a hot-water bottle wrapped in a double thickness of towel against the ear. Do not, however, put anything (cotton wool, for example) inside the ear as this may make the problem worse.

Remember, pain-relieving measures alone will not cure the underlying disorder. You should always seek your doctor's advice about persistent earache in a child.

Go to next page

*Continued from previous page*

**Is there a discharge from the affected ear?**

— YES → **Does the pain get worse when you gently pull on your child's ear lobe?**

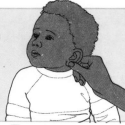

— YES →

**Infection of the outer-ear canal** may cause pain and discharge. Consult your doctor.

***Treatment:*** If your doctor finds that your child's outer-ear canal is infected, he or she will probably advise you to gently clean away the discharge from the outer ear and may prescribe *antibiotic* ear drops.

**NO** ↓ (from "Does the pain get worse...")

**Infection of the middle ear** may have caused your child's eardrum to rupture, producing pain and discharge. This is especially likely if your child has, or has recently had, a cold. Consult your doctor.

***Treatment:*** If your doctor confirms this diagnosis; he or she will probably prescribe a course of *antibiotics*. He or she may also prescribe antibiotic ear drops to prevent infection of the outer-ear canal and will probably advise you to regularly clean away the discharge from the outer ear.

**NO** ↓ (from "Is there a discharge...")

**Did your child suddenly develop earache during or immediately after a flight in an aircraft?**

— YES →

**Barotrauma,** in which the air pressure balance between the middle and the outer ear is disrupted, is a possibility.

***Self-help:*** To prevent barotrauma occurring, encourage your child to suck during take off and landing. A baby can be given a breast- or bottle-feed at these times and an older child can be offered a sweet to suck. Barotrauma is more likely to develop if your child has a blocked nose, so it is best to avoid air travel, if possible, when your child has a cold. The symptoms of barotrauma normally clear up without treatment within a few hours. However, if the pain persists or your child seems otherwise unwell, consult your doctor.

**NO** ↓

**Consult your doctor** if you are unable to make a diagnosis from this chart.

---

## EAR EXAMINATION

Your child may need to have his or her ears examined because of ear problems or as part of a routine check-up. The doctor uses an instrument called an auriscope to look inside the ear for abnormalities of the outer ear or of the eardrum. This is not usually painful, but a child with an ear infection may find the procedure uncomfortable. An older child can often be examined standing up, but a baby or young child is best examined sitting on your knee while you hold his or her head firmly against your chest to provide reassurance and prevent wriggling (below).

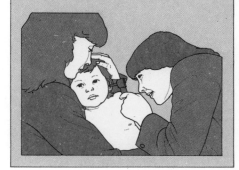

---

## THE STRUCTURE OF THE EAR

The ear is made up of three main parts:

**The outer ear** includes the external part of the ear, the pinna, which collects and funnels sound waves along the outer-ear canal to the eardrum which then vibrates.

**The middle ear** contains the eardrum and three small bones that transmit the vibrations of the eardrum to the inner ear. Air pressure in the middle ear is kept normal by means of the eustachian tube that links the middle ear cavity to the back of the throat. In children this tube is shorter and straighter than in adults, allowing infection from the throat to travel more easily into the middle ear.

**The inner ear** is filled with fluid and contains the cochlea, which converts the vibrations from the middle ear into nerve impulses. These are passed to the brain by the auditory nerve. The inner ear also contains the labyrinth which controls the body's balance.

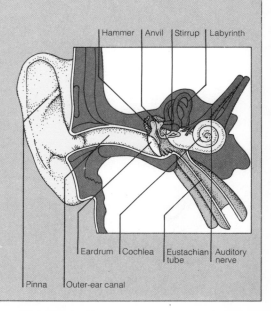

Hammer | Anvil | Stirrup | Labyrinth

Eardrum | Cochlea | Eustachian tube | Auditory nerve

Pinna | Outer-ear canal

# 30 Deafness

Deafness is often overlooked in a child. If you find that you are having to repeat things you say to your child, or if he or she always needs to have the television or radio louder than you think necessary, or if there is a sudden deterioration in school performance, you may suspect deafness. Hearing problems in babies are usually detected by the doctor during developmental checks or at other routine consultations, but you may be the first to notice that your baby is not responding to sounds or learning to speak as quickly as you think he or she should. This should always be brought to your doctor's attention.

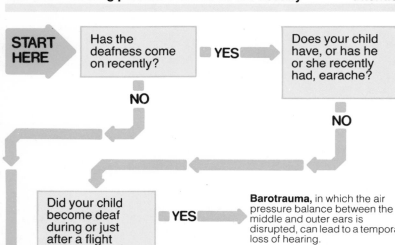

**START HERE** ▶ **Has the deafness come on recently?**

YES ▶ **Does your child have, or has he or she recently had, earache?**

YES ▶ **Infection of the middle ear or of the outer-ear canal** can cause pain and temporary deafness that may persist after the infection has cleared. Consult your doctor.

**Treatment:** Your doctor will examine your child's ear (see *Ear examination*, p. 103) and if he or she finds signs of infection will probably prescribe *antibiotics*, either as syrup (for middle-ear infections) or as ear drops (for outer-ear infections). If the infection is in the middle ear, your doctor may also prescribe *decongestant* nose drops to allow any accumulated fluid to drain away.

**NO** (from first question)

**NO** (from earache question)

**Did your child become deaf during or just after a flight in an aircraft?**

YES ▶ **Barotrauma,** in which the air pressure balance between the middle and outer ears is disrupted, can lead to a temporary loss of hearing.

**Self-help:** To prevent barotrauma occurring, encourage your child to suck and swallow during take-off and landing. A baby can be offered a breast- or bottle-feed at these times and an older child can be offered a sweet to suck. Barotrauma is more likely to develop if your child has a blocked nose, so it is best to avoid air travel, if possible, when your child has a cold. The symptoms of barotrauma normally clear up without treatment within a few hours. However, if deafness persists, call your doctor.

**NO**

**Does your child have or has he or she recently had, a cold AND/OR has he or she been sneezing?**

YES ▶ **Blockage of the eustachian tube** as a result of a cold or hay fever may account for your child's deafness. Consult your doctor.

**Treatment:** Your doctor may recommend that you simply wait for the ear to clear itself. If, however, the condition has persisted for some time, he or she may prescribe *decongestant* nose drops to clear the eustachian tube. If hay fever is the cause of the problem, your doctor may also prescribe anti-allergic medicine or spray to prevent the blockage from recurring.

**NO**

**Blockage of the outer-ear canal** by wax or perhaps by a foreign body, may be the cause of your child's deafness. Consult your doctor.

**Treatment:** If your doctor finds that your child's ears are blocked by wax, he or she will probably suggest you use wax-softening ear drops for a few days. If a foreign body is the cause of the trouble, your doctor will remove it using the auriscope (see *Ear examination,* p. 103) or by syringe.

---

### WARNING

**VIRUS INFECTIONS AND DEAFNESS**

In rare cases, virus infections in childhood, such as measles, mumps or meningitis, may cause deafness. If your child shows any sign of loss of hearing following one of these illnesses, **consult your doctor without delay.**

---

### MYRINGOTOMY AND GROMMETS

Myringotomy is a minor operation sometimes carried out in children when the eustachian tube, which runs between the middle ear and the back of the throat, is blocked and the middle ear becomes filled with fluid, a condition known as glue ear. The operation usually requires a hospital stay of 1 to 2 days and is carried out under general anaesthetic.

**What happens**
A small cut is made in the eardrum to allow the fluid to drain away. Usually a small plastic tube, called a grommet (or stopple), is then inserted into the hole to allow air to circulate freely in the middle ear and so dry out the tissues. In some cases the adenoids may be removed at the same time (see *Adenoid removal,* p. 109). The grommet usually stays in place for about six months, after which it drops out naturally. The hole in the eardrum then quickly heals. Provided symptoms do not recur, your child will not be asked to return to hospital. While the grommet is in place there is no reason to restrict swimming or other activities.

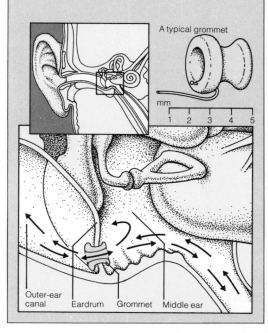

A typical grommet

mm
1  2  3  4  5

Outer-ear canal    Eardrum    Grommet    Middle ear

*Go to next page*

*Continued from previous page*

**Did the onset of deafness follow an earache?**

**YES** → **Glue ear,** accumulation of fluid in the middle ear, sometimes follows infection of the middle ear in children. Consult your doctor.

**Treatment:** If your doctor diagnoses glue ear, he or she will prescribe *decongestant* medicine or *antihistamines* to disperse the fluid and reduce swelling of the tissues. If this treatment does not work, or if the congestion is severe, your doctor may recommend myringotomy and the insertion of a grommet (see opposite). In most cases hearing is restored to normal following treatment.

**NO** ↓

**Are you worried that your child has never been able to hear properly?**

**YES** → **During pregnancy was there any possibility of contact or infection with German measles, OR was there any unexplained rash or fever?**

**YES** → **German measles during pregnancy** can cause deafness in the unborn child. Consult your doctor.

**Treatment:** If your doctor already knows that there was a possibility of German measles in pregnancy, it is likely that he or she is watching your child's progress carefully and would have noticed any hearing problems. However, if you are concerned about your child's hearing explain your fears to your doctor who will be able to arrange for your child to have a hospital hearing test. If your child is found to be deaf, you will receive advice on helping your child to talk to and to understand others from trained therapists.

**NO** ↓

**Consult your doctor** if you are unable to make a diagnosis from this chart. The problem may simply be the result of wax blockage (see *Blockage of the outer-ear canal,* opposite).

**Congenital hearing defects** are rare without a history of German measles or a family history of deafness. However, if you are worried about your child's hearing, discuss the problem with your doctor, explaining the basis for your fears.

**Treatment:** Your doctor will probably want to know about your child's general health and about the pregnancy, particularly whether any drugs were taken. If after examining your child he or she thinks there may be grounds for concern, or if you are not satisfied by his or her reassurances, your doctor can arrange for your child to have a full hospital hearing test.

---

## HEARING TESTS FOR CHILDREN

All children should have their hearing tested at regular intervals during early childhood, ideally at 8–9 months, at 3 years and at 5 years. Preliminary hearing tests are carried out by your family doctor and depend on the age of your child.

**Under 6 months** (below) The doctor will make a sudden sound and look for startled reaction.

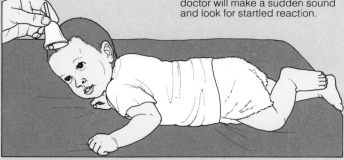

**From 6 to 12 months** (left) The best test is for one person to hold the baby's attention while another makes a soft sound such as crinkling tissue paper, to distract the baby.

**After 12 months** The doctor will assess the child's reaction to quiet speech.

If the response to any of these tests gives your doctor reason to suspect that your child may be deaf, he or she will be referred for special hospital tests which can measure the nervous response in the inner ear to sound regardless of your child's age.

## HEADPHONES AND LOUD MUSIC

Many older children and adolescents enjoy listening to loud music through headphones attached to a radio, record player or portable tape player. However, parents should be aware of the potential danger to hearing that these present.

**The risks**
At normal volumes headphones present no risk. But your child may be tempted to turn the volume up – for example, to exclude external noise – and could permanently damage his or her hearing. The sound need not be painfully loud to damage hearing, so the fact that your child insists that the volume is not uncomfortably high is not a reliable way of judging what level is safe. A useful guideline is that if others in the room can hear the music when your child is wearing headphones, it is likely that the volume is too high. Portable tape players with headphones may also increase the risk of road accidents if used when walking or cycling in traffic, because they reduce awareness of what is going on around you.

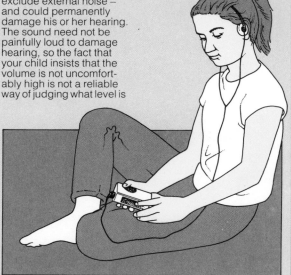

# 31 Runny or blocked nose

Runny nose is probably the most common medical symptom in childhood. All children have a runny nose (usually accompanied by sneezing) from time to time, and in the overwhelming majority of cases a common cold is responsible. A runny nose can be irritating for a child, and a blocked nose can be distressing for a baby, making sucking difficult, but neither symptom on its own is likely to be a sign of serious disease.

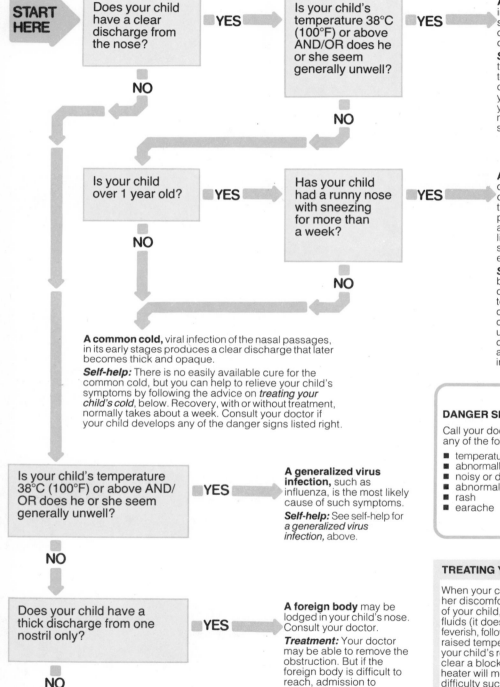

**START HERE**

**Does your child have a clear discharge from the nose?**

**YES** → **Is your child's temperature 38°C (100°F) or above AND/OR does he or she seem generally unwell?**

**YES** → **A generalized virus infection,** such as influenza, is the most likely cause of such symptoms. But there is also a possibility of measles if your child has been in contact with the disease recently.

**Self-help:** If your child is feverish, follow the advice on p. 288 for reducing a raised temperature. Make sure that he or she drinks plenty of fluids, but do not worry if your child does not feel like eating. Call your doctor if your child is less than 6 months old or develops any of the danger signs listed in the box below.

**NO** (from first box)

**NO** (from temperature box)

**Is your child over 1 year old?**

**YES** → **Has your child had a runny nose with sneezing for more than a week?**

**YES** → **Allergic rhinitis** (or hay fever) is a common cause of persistent clear discharge from the nose. The condition is the result of an allergic reaction to a particular substance, often pollen or animal fur. This diagnosis is particularly likely if you have noticed that your child's symptoms recur at the same season each year.

**Self-help:** If your child is not distressed by the symptoms there is no need to consult your doctor. But you may be able to help your child by discovering the cause of the problem so that he or she can avoid contact with it. If your child is upset by the symptoms, consult your doctor who may prescribe *antihistamines* and possibly *decongestants* to be used in moderation.

**NO** (over 1 year)

**NO** (runny nose week)

**A common cold,** viral infection of the nasal passages, in its early stages produces a clear discharge that later becomes thick and opaque.

**Self-help:** There is no easily available cure for the common cold, but you can help to relieve your child's symptoms by following the advice on *treating your child's cold*, below. Recovery, with or without treatment, normally takes about a week. Consult your doctor if your child develops any of the danger signs listed right.

**Is your child's temperature 38°C (100°F) or above AND/OR does he or she seem generally unwell?**

**YES** → **A generalized virus infection,** such as influenza, is the most likely cause of such symptoms.

**Self-help:** See self-help for *a generalized virus infection,* above.

**NO**

**Does your child have a thick discharge from one nostril only?**

**YES** → **A foreign body** may be lodged in your child's nose. Consult your doctor.

**Treatment:** Your doctor may be able to remove the obstruction. But if the foreign body is difficult to reach, admission to hospital for a minor operation to remove it may be necessary.

**NO**

**A common cold,** viral infection of the nasal passages, is the most likely cause of a thick discharge from both nostrils.

**Self-help:** See *Treating your child's cold,* right.

---

## WARNING

### DANGER SIGNS

Call your doctor at once if your child develops any of the following symptoms:

- temperature over 39°C (102°F)
- abnormally fast breathing (see the box on p. 110)
- noisy or difficult breathing
- abnormal lethargy or drowsiness
- rash
- earache

---

### TREATING YOUR CHILD'S COLD

When your child has a cold, you can reduce his or her discomfort in several ways. Whatever the age of your child, make sure he or she drinks plenty of fluids (it does not matter what). If he or she is feverish, follow the advice on p. 288 for reducing a raised temperature. Try to keep the atmosphere of your child's room warm and humid, as this helps to clear a blocked nose (a wet towel hung near a heater will moisten the air). If your young baby has difficulty sucking, you can use children's (paediatric) nose drops to clear the nose before feeding times. But you must be careful not to exceed the recommended dose or to use them any longer than is necessary. An older child can be encouraged to inhale steam from a basin of hot water and can be taught to blow his or her nose properly – one nostril at a time.

# 32 Sore throat

Sore throat is a common symptom throughout childhood. While an older child will usually tell you that his or her throat hurts, in the case of a baby or young child, your attention is most likely to be be drawn to the problem by your child's reluctance to eat because of the pain caused by swallowing. Most sore throats are the result of viral or bacterial infection and usually clear up within a few days.

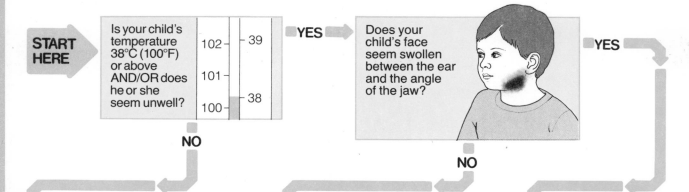

**START HERE** → Is your child's temperature 38°C (100°F) or above AND/OR does he or she seem unwell?

102 — 39
101
100 — 38

**YES** → Does your child's face seem swollen between the ear and the angle of the jaw? **YES** →

**NO**

**NO**

### TREATMENT FOR A SORE THROAT

The following measures will give a child relief from most types of sore throat:

- Giving plenty of cold drinks (preferably milk) and ice-cream.
- Giving the recommended dose of liquid paracetamol.
- For older children (over 8), gargling with a mild antiseptic diluted with water.

**Pharyngitis and tonsillitis,** infections of the throat or tonsils respectively, are the likely causes of your child's sore throat. The infection may be caused by viruses or bacteria (see p.66).

*Self-help:* Do not force your child to eat if pain makes swallowing difficult. Follow the advice on treating a sore throat, left. Consult your doctor if your child is no better in 48 hours, or develops any of the danger signs listed in the box on the chart opposite. Your doctor may prescribe *antibiotics*. An operation to remove the tonsils (below) is carried out only occasionally in cases of recurrent, severe tonsillitis.

**Mumps,** a viral infection affecting the salivary glands, is a possibility, especially if your child has been in contact with the disease within the past 3 weeks (see *Comparison of childhood infectious diseases,* p. 97). Consult your doctor.

*Treatment:* Your doctor will probably advise you to keep your child at home and to give him or her paracetamol and plenty of cold drinks to relieve the discomfort. Recovery normally takes 7 to 10 days.

**A common cold,** viral infection of the nasal passages, is the most likely cause for your child's sore throat.

*Self-help:* There is no easily available cure for the common cold but you can help to relieve the symptoms by following the advice on *treating your child's cold* (opposite). Recovery, with or without treatment, normally takes about a week. Consult your doctor if your child develops any of the danger signs listed in the box on the chart opposite.

Has your child been sneezing AND/OR does he or she have a runny nose? **YES** →

**NO**

**Inflammation of the throat,** as a result of minor infection or local irritation, is the likely cause of a sore throat with no other symptoms.

*Self-help:* Give your child plenty of cold drinks to soothe the inflammation and, if necessary, give the recommended dose of liquid paracetamol. Consult your doctor if your child develops any of the danger signs listed in the box on the chart opposite, or if the sore throat is no better in 48 hours.

### WHAT ARE TONSILS?

The tonsils are two glands at the back of the throat. They help guard against infection. They are very small at birth and enlarge gradually, reaching their maximum size when the child is 6 to 7 years old and most at risk from infections of the nose, throat and lungs. After this age the tonsils become smaller again. The tonsils are normally noticeable only when they become inflamed and swollen as a result of infection, as shown in the illustration (right).

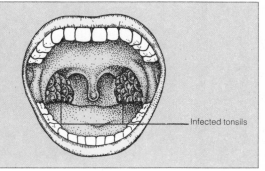

Infected tonsils

### TONSILS REMOVAL

Occasionally, when a child has repeated and severe bacterial infections of the tonsils, an operation (sometimes called tonsillectomy) to remove the tonsils is recommended. This operation used to be carried out more frequently, but the increased effectiveness of *antibiotics* against bacterial infection has meant that this operation is now only necessary when there is a risk that recurrent illnesses may interfere with the child's general health or education.

The operation usually requires a hospital stay of 2 to 3 days and is carried out under a general anaesthetic. The tonsils are cut away and sometimes the adenoids are removed at the same time (see *Adenoid removal,* p. 109). After the operation, your child's throat is likely to be very sore and there may be slight bleeding from the raw areas. Plenty of cold drinks and ice-cream will help to reduce the discomfort. Most children are back to normal within 2 weeks.

# 33 Coughing

Coughing is a perfectly normal reaction to irritation and congestion in the throat and lungs. It is simply a noisy expulsion of air from the lungs. It is an unusual symptom in babies under 6 months, and can be a sign of a serious lung infection. In older children, the vast majority of cases are due to minor infections of the nose and throat. However, occasionally a sudden cough can be a sign of a more serious blockage in the respiratory tract. You should therefore call your doctor at once if your child's breathing seems in any way abnormal.

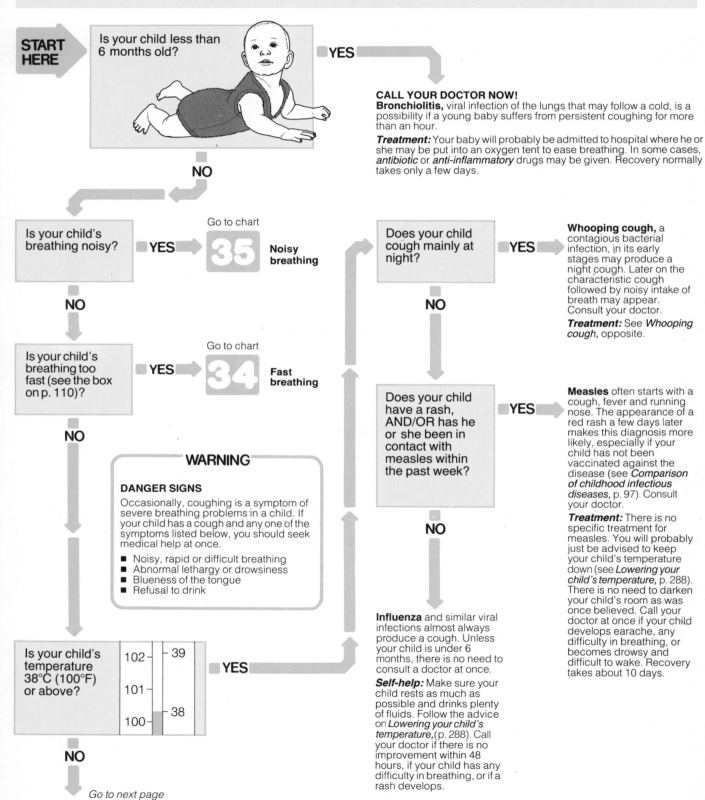

**START HERE**

**Is your child less than 6 months old?**

**YES** →

**CALL YOUR DOCTOR NOW!**
**Bronchiolitis,** viral infection of the lungs that may follow a cold, is a possibility if a young baby suffers from persistent coughing for more than an hour.

**Treatment:** Your baby will probably be admitted to hospital where he or she may be put into an oxygen tent to ease breathing. In some cases, *antibiotic* or *anti-inflammatory* drugs may be given. Recovery normally takes only a few days.

**NO** ↓

**Is your child's breathing noisy?** **YES** → Go to chart **35** Noisy breathing

**NO** ↓

**Is your child's breathing too fast (see the box on p. 110)?** **YES** → Go to chart **34** Fast breathing

**NO** ↓

### WARNING

**DANGER SIGNS**

Occasionally, coughing is a symptom of severe breathing problems in a child. If your child has a cough and any one of the symptoms listed below, you should seek medical help at once.

- Noisy, rapid or difficult breathing
- Abnormal lethargy or drowsiness
- Blueness of the tongue
- Refusal to drink

**Is your child's temperature 38°C (100°F) or above?**

| 102 – | – 39 |
| 101 – | |
| 100 – | – 38 |

**YES** →

**NO** ↓

*Go to next page*

---

**Does your child cough mainly at night?** **YES** →

**Whooping cough,** a contagious bacterial infection, in its early stages may produce a night cough. Later on the characteristic cough followed by noisy intake of breath may appear. Consult your doctor.

**Treatment:** See *Whooping cough,* opposite.

**NO** ↓

**Does your child have a rash, AND/OR has he or she been in contact with measles within the past week?** **YES** →

**Measles** often starts with a cough, fever and running nose. The appearance of a red rash a few days later makes this diagnosis more likely, especially if your child has not been vaccinated against the disease (see *Comparison of childhood infectious diseases,* p. 97). Consult your doctor.

**Treatment:** There is no specific treatment for measles. You will probably just be advised to keep your child's temperature down (see *Lowering your child's temperature,* p. 288). There is no need to darken your child's room as was once believed. Call your doctor at once if your child develops earache, any difficulty in breathing, or becomes drowsy and difficult to wake. Recovery takes about 10 days.

**NO** ↓

**Influenza** and similar viral infections almost always produce a cough. Unless your child is under 6 months, there is no need to consult a doctor at once.

**Self-help:** Make sure your child rests as much as possible and drinks plenty of fluids. Follow the advice on *Lowering your child's temperature,* (p. 288). Call your doctor if there is no improvement within 48 hours, if your child has any difficulty in breathing, or if a rash develops.

*Continued from previous page*

**Does your child have bouts of uncontrollable coughing followed by a noisy intake of breath, AND/OR is coughing often accompanied by vomiting?**

**YES** →

**Whooping cough,** a contagious bacterial infection, produces this distinctive type of cough, often with a runny nose. Consult your doctor.

***Treatment:*** In most cases the illness can be treated at home with regular visits from the doctor. Do not try to suppress the cough with cough medicines. If bouts of coughing are accompanied by vomiting, it is often helpful to give a light meal immediately after a coughing fit. Your doctor may prescribe *antibiotics*, which can in some cases reduce the severity of the symptoms and may prevent other children catching the disease. Call your doctor at once if your child has severe difficulty in breathing or turns bluish during a bout of coughing.

**NO** ↓

**Does your child have a runny or blocked nose?**

**YES** →

**NO** ↓

**A cold** is often accompanied by a cough, which is a natural reaction to mucus dripping down the back of the throat. Coughing prevents congestion in the lungs.

***Self-help:*** For the first day or so of a cold it is best to keep your child at home in a warm, but not dry, atmosphere. A blocked nose in an older child can often be eased by inhaling steam from a basin of hot water. If a young child has a severely blocked nose, your doctor may prescribe *decongestant* nose drops. For further information on treating colds, see p. 106.

**Has the cough come on only within the past week or so?**

**YES** →

**An inhaled foreign body** is a possibility if a young child suddenly develops a cough, especially if he or she has recently been eating peanuts or playing with small objects. Even an older child may have breathed in a particle of food. Consult your doctor.

***Treatment:*** If your doctor suspects that your child has a foreign body in the lung, he or she may arrange for your child to go to hospital for an examination of the lungs. If a foreign body is found, it will be removed and if there is any sign of infection, *antibiotics* will be prescribed.

**NO** ↓

**Does your child have a persistently runny nose?**

**YES** →

**Is your child's speech nasal, AND/OR does he or she suffer from recurrent ear infections?**

**YES** →

**Enlarged adenoids** (glands at the back of the nasal passage) may be encouraging infection in your child's nose, ears and throat, creating an irritating discharge. Consult your doctor.

***Treatment:*** If the adenoids are enlarged, your doctor will probably prescribe *antibiotics* to combat infection. However, if this treatment fails to cure the problem, an operation to remove the adenoids may be necessary (see *Adenoid removal*, below).

**NO** ↓

**NO** ↓

**Has your child had whooping cough within the past few months?**

**YES** →

**The after-effects of whooping cough,** a contagious bacterial infection, can often leave a child with a persistent cough. This is not usually a cause for concern. But if symptoms persist for more than 3 months after the original illness, or if your child seems ill or distressed, consult your doctor.

**Recurrent colds** can produce an irritating mucus discharge that causes the child to cough. Such colds are the result of the child being exposed to viruses to which he or she has not yet built up an immunity. See *Viral and bacterial infections,* p.66.

***Self-help:*** There is little you can do to prevent your child getting colds, but you can help to alleviate the symptoms. For general advice on the treatment of colds, see p. 106. If coughing is disturbing your child's sleep, adjusting the temperature of the room may help. A drink and a dose of cough mixture before bedtime may also soothe a troublesome cough. There is no need to consult your doctor unless your child is distressed by the cough or seems generally unwell.

**NO** ↓

**Does anyone in the home smoke OR could your child have been smoking?**

**YES** →

**Smoke** in the atmosphere and smoking itself can irritate a child's throat and lungs causing a persistent cough and increasing the likelihood of chest infections. Giving up smoking will benefit your own and your child's health. A child who is smoking should be discouraged from this habit.

Go to chart

**22**

**Behaviour problems**

**NO** ↓

**Consult your doctor** if you are unable to make a diagnosis from this chart.

---

**ADENOID REMOVAL**

The adenoids are two gland-like swellings at the back of the nose, near the tonsils. If they become so enlarged that they cause recurrent ear or throat infections, they can be removed surgically, sometimes together with the tonsils, usually when the child is 6 to 7 years old.

The operation (sometimes called adenoidectomy) is carried out under general anaesthetic and involves a hospital stay of 2 to 3 days. There are no after-affects,

but the child may have a sore throat for a few days following the operation.

Adenoids

# 34 Fast breathing

A child's breathing rate is an important indicator for determining the seriousness of any problems affecting the windpipe or lungs. If your child's breathing is faster than the normal rate shown in the box below, there may be some cause for concern, especially if he or she is under 6 months or has additional symptoms such as blueness of the tongue or excessive drowsiness, in which case you should get medical help at once.

**START HERE**

**Is your child's breathing so noisy that you can hear it from across the room?**

**YES** → Go to chart  **36** **Noisy breathing**

**NO**

**Does your child have one or more of the following symptoms?**
- blueness around the lips
- abnormal drowsiness
- inability to speak or make sounds normally

**NO**

**Is your child under 6 months old?**

**NO**

**YES** →

**EMERGENCY GET MEDICAL HELP NOW!**

**Severe breathing difficulty** may be caused by infection or inhalation of a small object or particle of food, particularly if your child seemed to be choking at first.

*Treatment:* Rapid action is essential. If you think a foreign body may be responsible, turn your child upside-down and slap him or her firmly on the back (see also *First aid for choking,* p.285). If this does not remove the object, or if you think that there is another cause, get your child to hospital at once. In hospital, any object lodged in the windpipe will be removed. If there is an infection, your child may be given *antibiotics*.

**YES** →

**CALL YOUR DOCTOR NOW!**

**Bronchiolitis,** viral infection of the lungs that may follow a cold, is a possibility, especially if your baby has also started to cough and/or seems unusually lethargic.

*Treatment:* Your baby is likely to be admitted to hospital and put in an oxygen tent. *Antibiotics* or *anti-inflammatory* drugs may be given. Recovery normally takes only a few days.

**CALL YOUR DOCTOR NOW!**

**A chest infection** is possible, especially if your child has had a cold within the last week and is coughing.

*Treatment:* Your doctor may decide that your child can be treated at home with frequent doctor's visits, but in a severe case he or she is likely to recommend that your child is admitted to hospital. At home or in hospital treatment will probably consist of paracetamol to reduce any fever and ease discomfort, and possibly *antibiotics* to fight the infection. If you are looking after your child at home; make sure that he or she drinks plenty of fluids. Keeping the air moist, by placing a wet towel over a radiator, for example, may help to ease your child's breathing.

### IS YOUR CHILD BREATHING TOO FAST?

The normal breathing rate of a child varies according to age. Count the number of breaths your child takes in a 30 second period while he or she is sitting quietly at rest. Then check the result against the graph below. If your child is taking more breaths than is normal for his or her age, he or she is breathing too fast and is likely to need medical attention.

Breaths in 30 seconds (y-axis: 30, 25, 20, 15, 10, 5)

Age in years (x-axis: 1, 2, 3, 4, 5, 6 and over)

### ALL ABOUT ASTHMA

In asthma the small airways in the lung sometimes become narrowed by swelling of their walls and production of mucus. This partially obstructs the airflow in the lungs causing difficulty in breathing. Asthma attacks can be triggered off by an allergic reaction to a particular substance, such as house-dust mites, pollen, animal fur or a certain food. However, attacks may also be triggered by infection, inhaling irritant substances, or by physical or psychological stress.

Susceptibility to asthma often runs in families, and children who suffer from hay fever (allergic rhinitis) or eczema are more likely to develop asthma. Attacks of asthma are unusual in children under the age of four and often cease after puberty.

#### Symptoms

The main symptoms of asthma are attacks of wheezing and difficulty in breathing. The severity of these attacks can vary from slight wheezing to severe and distressing shortness of breath. Some children are rarely free from wheezing, while others may go many months in normal health between attacks. Severe attacks may be life-threatening and should always be taken seriously.

#### Treatment

Treatment will depend on the frequency and severity of the attacks. If your child has only occasional breathless attacks, your doctor is likely to prescribe just a *bronchodilator*, to use when the attacks occur or before exercise. However, if your child suffers from frequent attacks of asthma or often coughs at night, your doctor may prescribe further drugs to be taken regularly to prevent attacks and reduce their severity.

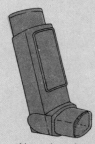

An inhalant that sprays a bronchodilator drug into the lungs is prescribed for most asthmatic children.

Nowadays there is no need for the asthmatic child to be treated as an invalid. In fact, it has been shown that physical activity is positively beneficial even if you have to increase the drug treatment to prevent attacks after exercise. So encourage your child to participate in sports such as swimming.

#### Preventing asthma attacks

If your child is asthmatic, you may be able to reduce the frequency of attacks by identifying, and then helping your child to avoid, the triggering factor(s). In many cases, however, there is no obvious cause. Your doctor may help you by arranging skin tests in which a solution of the suspected allergen is put on or injected into the skin to see if it produces an allergic response. It may also be helpful to keep a diary of your child's activities, including what food he or she ate, or if, for example, he or she has attacks in the house, but not in the open countryside, or when staying with some friends, but not with others. All this information can give valuable clues to the cause of your child's asthma.

# 35 Noisy breathing

Many children wheeze slightly when they have a "chesty" cold, and this is no cause for concern, providing the child is not distressed and is able to breathe normally. This chart deals only with breathing that is loud enough to be heard across an average-sized room. The type of sound produced may vary from loud wheezing and grunting to a harsh crowing noise that gets louder when the child breathes in. Except when a child has already been diagnosed as asthmatic and has home treatment available, such noisy breathing is always a serious symptom. In all cases you should be alert for any of the danger signs listed in the box below.

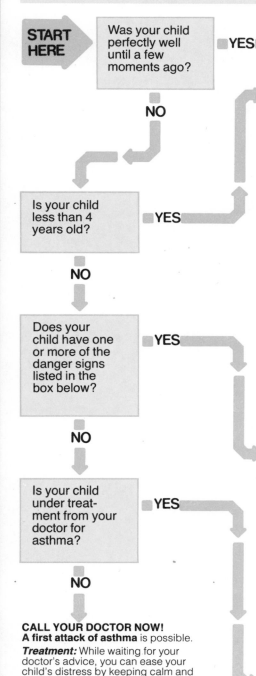

**START HERE**

Was your child perfectly well until a few moments ago?

**NO**

Is your child less than 4 years old?

**NO**

Does your child have one or more of the danger signs listed in the box below?

**NO**

Is your child under treatment from your doctor for asthma?

**NO**

**YES** → Does your child have one or more of the danger signs listed in the box below?

**YES** (age branch)

**YES** (danger signs branch)

**YES** (asthma treatment branch)

## CALL YOUR DOCTOR NOW!
**A first attack of asthma** is possible.

*Treatment:* While waiting for your doctor's advice, you can ease your child's distress by keeping calm and helping him or her to sit in an upright position, leaning forward against the back of a chair. If your doctor confirms the diagnosis, he or she will probably prescribe drugs to assist breathing. If your child develops any of the danger signs listed below, admission to hospital may be necessary. For further information on the prevention and treatment of asthma, see opposite.

## CALL YOUR DOCTOR NOW!
**Inflammation of the windpipe or lungs,** as a result of infection or an allergic reaction, is possible.

*Treatment:* While awaiting your doctor's advice, you may be able to reduce the severity of your child's symptoms by taking him or her into a moist atmosphere – for example, the bathroom where you have turned on the hot taps or shower. Your doctor may recommend admission to hospital, but some cases can be treated at home. Whether at home or in hospital, your child may be given *antibiotics* to treat any infection, or *antihistamines* if an allergic reaction is the problem.

## EMERGENCY
**GET MEDICAL HELP NOW!**

**A severe asthma attack** can cause serious breathing problems.

*Treatment:* While waiting for medical help, keep calm and reassure your child. Sitting in an upright position leaning forward against the back of a chair may help your child to breathe more easily. If you have *bronchodilator* treatment for your child available, give the recommended dose. Your child will probably need to be admitted to hospital where oxygen and drugs to ease breathing may be given. For further information on the prevention and treatment of asthma, see the box on the opposite page.

**An asthma attack** is the most likely cause of your child's noisy breathing.

*Self-help:* Help your child to sit upright in a chair and give whatever home treatment your doctor has prescribed. Further doses may be given every 4 hours. However, if your child is not improving within 6 hours or develops any of the danger signs listed in the box right, get medical help at once. For further information on the prevention and treatment of asthma, see opposite.

## EMERGENCY
**GET MEDICAL HELP NOW!**

**A foreign body** may be lodged in your child's windpipe. If your child is small enough, turn your child upside down and slap him or her firmly on the back (see also *First aid for choking,* p.285). If this does not remove the object at once call an ambulance or get your child to hospital yourself as fast as you can.

*Treatment:* If you succeed in removing the foreign body yourself, no further treatment is needed and your child should quickly return to normal. However, if your child develops a cough or fever within the next few days, it may be a sign of a lung infection and you should consult your doctor at once. In hospital, treatment for a foreign body in the windpipe is likely to consist of an emergency operation to remove the object and allow your child to breathe freely.

## EMERGENCY
**GET MEDICAL HELP NOW!**

**Narrowing of the air passages** caused by inflammation of their lining and swelling in the throat, resulting from infection or an allergic reaction (croup), is a possibility.

*Treatment:* While you are waiting for medical help to arrive, you may be able to ease your child's breathing by moistening the air with steam. Taking your child into the bathroom where you have turned on the hot tap or shower is often effective. Be prepared to carry out *mouth-to-mouth respiration* (p. 283) if your child stops breathing. Your child will probably need to be admitted to hospital where he or she may be given oxygen and intravenous fluids. If an infection is diagnosed, *antibiotics* may be given.

## WARNING

**DANGER SIGNS**

If your child's noisy breathing is accompanied by any one of the symptoms listed below, it is a sign that he or she has severe breathing problems. This is an **EMERGENCY** and you should seek medical help at once.

- Blueness of the tongue
- Abnormal drowsiness
- Inability to speak or make sounds normally
- Abnormally fast breathing (see the box on the opposite page)

# 36 Toothache

Your child's teeth are just as much living structures as any other part of the body, despite their tough appearance. They are constantly under threat from our Western diet because of the high level of sugar we consume. Bacteria act on sugar to produce acids that attack enamel, the tooth's protective layer. When this happens, it is not long before bacterial destruction (decay) spreads down the root canal to the nerve, causing inflammation and pain. Any pain coming from your child's tooth, or from the teeth and gums in general, whether it is a dull throb or a sharp twinge, should be brought to your dentist's attention for investigation and treatment.

**START HERE**

**Does your child have one of the following symptoms?**
- continuous pain
- a fever

**YES**

### CONSULT YOUR DENTIST WITHOUT DELAY!
**A tooth abscess** is possible. This is formed when pus builds up in the bone and tissue near a tooth that has had a very deep filling or cavity, or one that has been injured.

**Treatment:** Two forms of treatment are common – root canal treatment or extraction. If the dentist feels the tooth can be saved, root canal treatment may be performed. He or she will make an opening in the tooth to release the pus and relieve the pressure. Sometimes an emergency incision is made in the gum to relieve the swollen area. The dentist will then remove the diseased tissue from inside the tooth. Later, the tooth will be cleaned and a permanent filling will be placed in the tooth.

**NO**

**Does he or she have repeated bouts of throbbing pain OR is the tooth extremely sensitive to both hot and cold and does the pain continue for several minutes?**

**YES**

**Advanced dental decay, a very deep filling or an injury** may have irreversibly inflamed the pulp (nerve) in the centre of the tooth.

**Treatment:** The dentist will remove the decay and/or old filling. If the nerve is exposed, a root canal treatment may be necessary to save the tooth, or an extraction may be needed. If the pulp is not visibly exposed, the dentist may try to soothe the inflamed pulp with a temporary, medicated filling. After a few weeks, the tooth will be re-evaluated for possible root canal treatment, an extraction, or a permanent filling.

**NO**

**Has the dentist filled one or more of your child's teeth within the past few weeks?**

**YES**

**Does the tooth hurt only when he or she bites on it?**

**YES**

**NO**

**NO**

**After a filling**, especially a deep one, it is normal to have some sensitivity, especially to cold water or air. This sensitivity will be sharp, but will last for only a few seconds and then subside. If the sensitivity increases in intensity or duration, or if the tooth becomes sensitive to heat, consult your dentist for the possibility of irreversible pulp (nerve) damage.

*Go to next page*

---

### THE ORDER IN WHICH TEETH APPEAR

The ages at which teeth appear vary considerably from child to child, so the ages given here are only a rough guide. A few children have one or more teeth at birth, while others still have none at a year old. The sequence or order in which teeth erupt is more important than the age of eruption. Neither early nor late teething is cause for worry.

With the exception of the permanent (adult) molars (which do not replace primary [baby] molars), the remaining permanent teeth should appear soon after their corresponding primary teeth fall out. The first permanent molar should be the first adult tooth to appear at 6 or 7 years of age. Many parents may mistake this tooth for a baby tooth since it erupts so early and appears just behind the second primary molar. Next, the incisors (front teeth) appear, with the lowers usually preceding the uppers. Occasionally, the primary teeth must be extracted early to allow the permanent teeth to grow into the correct position. The order in which the primary cuspids (canines) and molars are lost varies considerably.

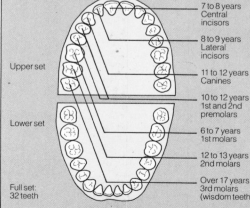

**Primary (baby) teeth**

Upper set

Lower set

Full set:
20 teeth

- 25 to 33 months 2nd molars
- 13 to 19 months 1st molars
- 16 to 22 months Canines
- 9 to 13 months Lateral incisors
- 8 to 12 months Central incisors

**Permanent (adult) teeth**

Upper set

Lower set

Full set:
32 teeth

- 7 to 8 years Central incisors
- 8 to 9 years Lateral incisors
- 11 to 12 years Canines
- 10 to 12 years 1st and 2nd premolars
- 6 to 7 years 1st molars
- 12 to 13 years 2nd molars
- Over 17 years 3rd molars (wisdom teeth)

**An uneven or "high" filling** can cause discomfort. Your dentist will adjust the filling if necessary.

*Continued from previous page*

Does the pain occur only when your child is eating something cold or sweet (ice cream or chocolate) AND does the pain go away after a few seconds?

**YES**

**Decay under an old filling, a cracked tooth or filling, or exposure of the root surface due to improper toothbrushing or gum disease** may be the cause of the pain. Consult your dentist.

*Treatment:* Your dentist may recommend replacing an old filling or remove any decay. If the problem is sensitivity, the dentist may recommend a special desensitizing toothpaste, protective fluoride applications or bonding to seal over the sensitive root area.

**NO**

Does the tooth hurt only when your child bites or chews on it?

**YES**

**A cracked filling or a cracked or fractured tooth** is probably the cause of the pain. Consult your dentist.

*Treatment:* Your child may need to have the affected tooth crowned (capped) or have a root canal treatment if the pain becomes more severe. The tooth may need to be extracted if the crack is too deep into the tooth. Pain may also be caused by acute sinus problems that make the upper back teeth ache and tender to bite on. If this is the case, your child may need to see a doctor for further treatment.

**NO**

**Dental decay** may have caused a hole (or cavity) in the tooth. Consult your dentist.

*Treatment:* Your dentist will probably clean out the affected tooth and put in a filling.

---

### HOW TO RELIEVE YOUR CHILD'S TOOTHACHE

If the toothache is not too severe, a few home remedies may be helpful temporarily while you are waiting for professional help. Paracetamol should only be swallowed. Never place a tablet in the cheek next to a bothersome tooth. This can cause a "chemical burn" to the gum tissues. Oil of cloves applied to the aching tooth may also help.

---

### OTHER DISEASES THAT CAUSE TOOTHACHES

#### Sinus problems
Often, since the roots of the upper back teeth are very near a sinus cavity, pressure on these roots from a sinus condition can simulate a dull toothache. Usually, several of these upper back teeth will hurt (not just one) when your child bites, and often he or she will experience an increased sensitivity to cold things (e.g., air or liquids). Your child may have a runny nose or congestion. When the condition clears up, the pain should subside. Consult your doctor.

#### Periodontal disease
Periodontal disease is a common disease of the gums and other structures that support the teeth. The gums are usually red and swollen and bleed easily (especially with brushing). Pain does not frequently occur in the early stages of the disease. Treatment for periodontal disease can range from calculus (tartar) removal by scaling the teeth to gum surgery. Early periodontal disease, can be cleared up with thorough brushing and, for children over the age of 8 years, flossing each day.

---

### PREVENTING DECAY

#### Fluoride
Fluoride is a naturally occurring mineral that has been shown to increase the tooth's resistance to acid attack, thereby lowering the risk of tooth decay. In many areas of the country, fluoride is added to the water supply. If the amount of flouride in your local water supply is low, your dentist may suggest that you give your child additional flouride in the form of tablets or drops. Once the tooth erupts and appears in the mouth, giving flouride in the form of toothpastes, rinses or topical applications can also be beneficial.

#### Diet
Sugar in the diet is the principal cause of tooth decay. Minimizing the amount, reducing the frequency and controlling the types of sweets (sticky sugars are worse than liquids) that your child eats are important steps in preventing tooth decay.

#### Night-time drinks
Never put an infant or young child to bed with a bottle filled with sweet liquids (juice, sugar water, milk or formula). These liquids pool around teeth and can cause serious decay. If you feel you must give your child a bottle, fill it only with plain water or use a clean dummy (one that is *not* dipped in any sweet liquid).

#### Cleaning your child's teeth
The goal of cleaning teeth is to remove the bacterial plaque (a sticky, colourless film that constantly forms, especially near the junction of the tooth and gum). Without plaque, there is no decay or periodontal disease.

You should ensure that your child's teeth are brushed and flossed thoroughly at least once a day. At first, clean your baby's teeth and gums using a clean, damp piece of gauze. You may find the best position to do this is with your baby sitting on your lap, held securely against your chest. Later on, develop your child's habit of brushing by encouraging the young child to help using a small toothbrush and a dab of toothpaste. But make sure that you follow this procedure with a thorough cleaning and rinsing. The proper position for cleaning a young child's teeth is from behind. When a child is 6 years old, he or she should be able to brush the teeth under supervison. Flossing can be done by the child, without supervision, when he or she is about 8 years old. A parent can check the effectiveness of the child's cleaning by using disclosing tablets or solutions to detect the remaining plaque.

A baby should be held against your chest (left) while you clean the teeth and gums using toothpaste on cotton swabs or a piece of damp gauze.

**Using the toothbrush** Teach your child to brush both the outer and inner surfaces of all the teeth, as well as the chewing surfaces. The brush should be angled 45° against the gums.

#### Sealants
Some children have natural deep grooves (pits or fissures) on the top surfaces of the back teeth. Your dentist may want to place a plastic resin in these grooves to help prevent decay.

# 37 Vomiting in children

Vomiting is the forceful "throwing up" of the contents of the stomach as a result of sudden contraction of the muscles around the stomach. In children, vomiting can be caused by almost any physical or emotional upset, but is most likely to be caused by an infection of the digestive tract. In rare cases, vomiting can be a symptom of a serious condition needing urgent medical attention, so you must always be on the look-out for the danger signs listed in the box below. Any child who is vomiting persistently needs to be given plenty of fluids to avoid dehydration (see What to do when your child vomits, opposite).

For children under 1 year, consult chart 7, Vomiting in babies.

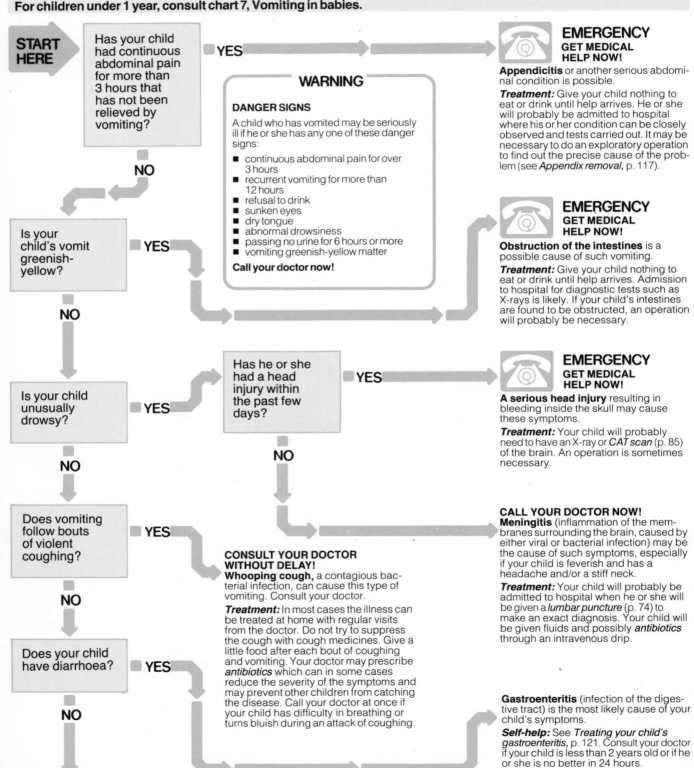

**START HERE**

**Has your child had continuous abdominal pain for more than 3 hours that has not been relieved by vomiting?**

YES →

**NO** ↓

**Is your child's vomit greenish-yellow?**

YES →

**NO** ↓

**Is your child unusually drowsy?**

YES →

**Has he or she had a head injury within the past few days?**

YES →

**NO** ↓

**NO** ↓

**Does vomiting follow bouts of violent coughing?**

YES →

**NO** ↓

**Does your child have diarrhoea?**

YES →

**NO** ↓

*Go to next page*

## WARNING

### DANGER SIGNS

A child who has vomited may be seriously ill if he or she has any one of these danger signs:

- continuous abdominal pain for over 3 hours
- recurrent vomiting for more than 12 hours
- refusal to drink
- sunken eyes
- dry tongue
- abnormal drowsiness
- passing no urine for 6 hours or more
- vomiting greenish-yellow matter

**Call your doctor now!**

## CONSULT YOUR DOCTOR WITHOUT DELAY!

**Whooping cough,** a contagious bacterial infection, can cause this type of vomiting. Consult your doctor.

*Treatment:* In most cases the illness can be treated at home with regular visits from the doctor. Do not try to suppress the cough with cough medicines. Give a little food after each bout of coughing and vomiting. Your doctor may prescribe *antibiotics* which can in some cases reduce the severity of the symptoms and may prevent other children from catching the disease. Call your doctor at once if your child has difficulty in breathing or turns bluish during an attack of coughing.

## EMERGENCY
### GET MEDICAL HELP NOW!

**Appendicitis** or another serious abdominal condition is possible.

*Treatment:* Give your child nothing to eat or drink until help arrives. He or she will probably be admitted to hospital where his or her condition can be closely observed and tests carried out. It may be necessary to do an exploratory operation to find out the precise cause of the problem (see *Appendix removal,* p. 117).

## EMERGENCY
### GET MEDICAL HELP NOW!

**Obstruction of the intestines** is a possible cause of such vomiting.

*Treatment:* Give your child nothing to eat or drink until help arrives. Admission to hospital for diagnostic tests such as X-rays is likely. If your child's intestines are found to be obstructed, an operation will probably be necessary.

## EMERGENCY
### GET MEDICAL HELP NOW!

**A serious head injury** resulting in bleeding inside the skull may cause these symptoms.

*Treatment:* Your child will probably need to have an X-ray or *CAT scan* (p. 85) of the brain. An operation is sometimes necessary.

## CALL YOUR DOCTOR NOW!

**Meningitis** (inflammation of the membranes surrounding the brain, caused by either viral or bacterial infection) may be the cause of such symptoms, especially if your child is feverish and has a headache and/or a stiff neck.

*Treatment:* Your child will probably be admitted to hospital when he or she will be given a *lumbar puncture* (p. 74) to make an exact diagnosis. Your child will be given fluids and possibly *antibiotics* through an intravenous drip.

**Gastroenteritis** (infection of the digestive tract) is the most likely cause of your child's symptoms.

*Self-help:* See *Treating your child's gastroenteritis,* p. 121. Consult your doctor if your child is less than 2 years old or if he or she is no better in 24 hours.

*Continued from previous page*

**Does your child have two or more of the following symptoms?**
- fever
- pain below the waist
- bed-wetting (when previously dry at night)
- pain on urination

**YES** →

**Urinary-tract infection** may be the cause of your child's vomiting. This diagnosis is more likely if your child is a girl (see *Structure of the urinary tract,* p. 125). Consult your doctor.

**Treatment:** If your doctor suspects a urinary-tract infection, he or she will probably ask you to provide a sample of your child's urine for analysis (see *Collecting a mid-stream specimen,* p. 125). If tests confirm the diagnosis, the usual treatment is a course of *antibiotics*.

**NO** ↓

**Did the vomiting occur while your child was very excited or before a possibly stressful event – for example, the first day at school?**

**YES** →

**Vomiting at times of emotional stress** is common among children, and most parents learn to distinguish between this type of vomiting and a physical illness.

**Self-help:** Treat the vomiting sympathetically: your child is likely to be upset by it. (See *What to do when your child vomits,* below.) If you think that worry about a particular event has caused the vomiting, do not force your child to participate if you can avoid it. However, if the problem is related to school, you will need patience to help your child overcome his or her fears. Discussing the problem with the teacher or your doctor may be useful.

See also chart

## 23 School difficulties

**NO** ↓

**Is your child passing white faeces and unusually dark urine?**

**YES** →

**Hepatitis** (viral infection of the liver) is possible. Consult your doctor.

**Treatment:** Your doctor will probably advise you to give nothing to eat while vomiting and nausea persist. Instead give frequent drinks of glucose solution (see *Treating gastroenteritis in babies,* p. 63), possibly flavoured with a little fruit juice. To prevent infection from spreading, you will need to keep your child's eating utensils and towels separate from those of the rest of the family. Your doctor may recommend that other members of the family are immunized against the disease.

**NO** ↓

**Occasional bouts of vomiting** are normal during childhood and may often have no obvious physical cause.

**Self-help:** See *What to do when your child vomits,* below.

---

## TRAVEL SICKNESS

Nausea and vomiting while travelling by car, sea or air are caused by disturbance to the balance mechanism of the inner ear by motion. Children's ears are particularly sensitive and this may be why they are especially prone to travel sickness. Most children become less susceptible to it as they get older. If your child is often travel sick, some of the following suggestions may help to prevent problems.

- Don't give heavy meals before or while travelling.
- Discourage your child from looking out of the car windows.
- Provide plenty of distractions, such as toys and games.
- Try to prevent your child from becoming overexcited.
- Keep at least one window of the car open.
- Allow frequent stops for your child to stretch his or her legs and get some fresh air.
- Travel at night when your child is more likely to sleep.
- Learn to recognize the signs of travel sickness (sudden pallor and quietness) and be prepared to stop.
- Ask your doctor to recommend a suitable medicine for preventing travel sickness.

---

## WHAT TO DO WHEN YOUR CHILD VOMITS

A child who is vomiting may be frightened and upset and, above all, needs you to be calm and sympathetic. Your child may find it reassuring if you hold his or her forehead while he or she vomits. After vomiting give your child some water to rinse out the mouth and sponge his or her face. Give a change of clothes, if necessary. Then encourage him or her to lie down and sleep. If you think that your child may vomit again have a bowl ready nearby.

If your child is vomiting persistently, you must make sure that he or she drinks plenty, especially if he or she has diarrhoea as well (as in gastroenteritis). He or she should drink at least 1 litre (1¾ pints) a day of cold clear fluids. This should preferably be a glucose solution (see *Treating gastroenteritis in babies,* p. 63). It is better if this is taken in frequent small sips, rather than in large quantities less often. While your child is feeling ill give no solids or milk products.

A hand held against the forehead while your child vomits (far left) is often comforting. After vomiting a drink (left) and a face-wash (above) will make your child feel better.

# 38 Abdominal pain

Pain between the bottom of the ribcage and the groin ("tummy ache") in a child may have a wide variety of causes both physical and emotional. Most tummy aches disappear on their own without treatment, but occasionally there is a serious physical cause, and you should be aware of the symptoms that may indicate such an illness so that you can feel confident in handling the far more likely minor conditions. The questions on this chart mainly concern children over the age of 2 because babies and toddlers are unlikely to complain of tummy ache. However, if you suspect that your child under 2 has abdominal pain, consult your doctor.

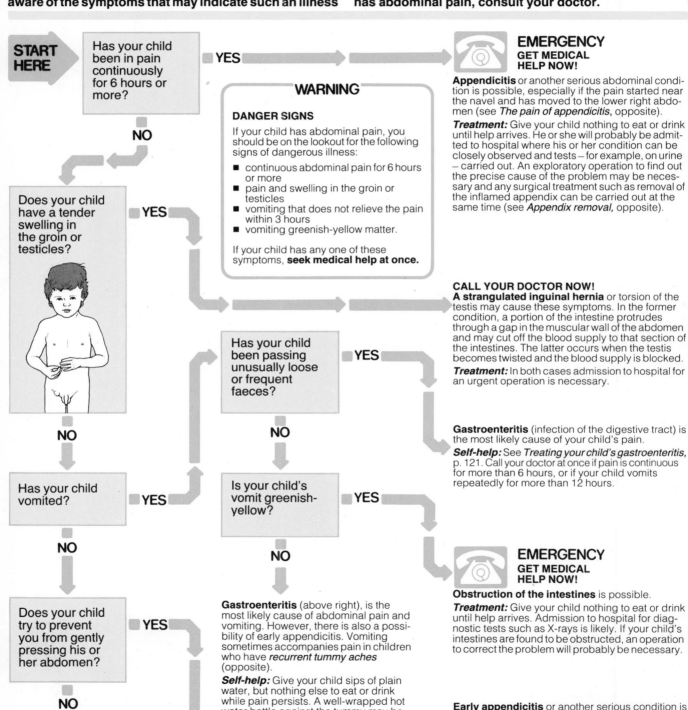

**START HERE**

Has your child been in pain continuously for 6 hours or more?

**YES** →

**NO** ↓

Does your child have a tender swelling in the groin or testicles?

**NO** ↓

Has your child vomited?

**NO** ↓

Does your child try to prevent you from gently pressing his or her abdomen?

**NO** ↓

*Go to next page*

**YES** →

Has your child been passing unusually loose or frequent faeces?

**NO** ↓

Is your child's vomit greenish-yellow?

**NO** ↓

**YES** →

---

### WARNING

**DANGER SIGNS**

If your child has abdominal pain, you should be on the lookout for the following signs of dangerous illness:

- continuous abdominal pain for 6 hours or more
- pain and swelling in the groin or testicles
- vomiting that does not relieve the pain within 3 hours
- vomiting greenish-yellow matter.

If your child has any one of these symptoms, **seek medical help at once.**

---

**Gastroenteritis** (above right), is the most likely cause of abdominal pain and vomiting. However, there is also a possibility of early appendicitis. Vomiting sometimes accompanies pain in children who have *recurrent tummy aches* (opposite).

**Self-help:** Give your child sips of plain water, but nothing else to eat or drink while pain persists. A well-wrapped hot water bottle against the tummy may be comforting. If pain persists for more than 3 hours, seek emergency help as for *appendicitis* (above). Otherwise treat as gastroenteritis (see p. 121).

---

### EMERGENCY
**GET MEDICAL HELP NOW!**

**Appendicitis** or another serious abdominal condition is possible, especially if the pain started near the navel and has moved to the lower right abdomen (see *The pain of appendicitis*, opposite).

**Treatment:** Give your child nothing to eat or drink until help arrives. He or she will probably be admitted to hospital where his or her condition can be closely observed and tests – for example, on urine – carried out. An exploratory operation to find out the precise cause of the problem may be necessary and any surgical treatment such as removal of the inflamed appendix can be carried out at the same time (see *Appendix removal*, opposite).

---

**CALL YOUR DOCTOR NOW!**

**A strangulated inguinal hernia** or torsion of the testis may cause these symptoms. In the former condition, a portion of the intestine protrudes through a gap in the muscular wall of the abdomen and may cut off the blood supply to that section of the intestines. The latter occurs when the testis becomes twisted and the blood supply is blocked.

**Treatment:** In both cases admission to hospital for an urgent operation is necessary.

---

**Gastroenteritis** (infection of the digestive tract) is the most likely cause of your child's pain.

**Self-help:** See *Treating your child's gastroenteritis*, p. 121. Call your doctor at once if pain is continuous for more than 6 hours, or if your child vomits repeatedly for more than 12 hours.

---

### EMERGENCY
**GET MEDICAL HELP NOW!**

**Obstruction of the intestines** is possible.

**Treatment:** Give your child nothing to eat or drink until help arrives. Admission to hospital for diagnostic tests such as X-rays is likely. If your child's intestines are found to be obstructed, an operation to correct the problem will probably be necessary.

---

**Early appendicitis** or another serious condition is possible, but a less alarming illness is more likely.

**Self-help:** Give your child sips of plain water, but nothing else to eat or drink. A well-wrapped hot water bottle against the tummy may be comforting. If pain persists for more than 3 hours seek emergency help as for *appendicitis* (above).

Continued from previous page

Does your child have pain below the waist AND two or more of the following symptoms?
- temperature of 38°C (100°F) or above
- bed-wetting (when previously dry at night)
- pain on urination

**YES**

**Urinary-tract infection** may be the cause of your child's pain. This diagnosis is more likely if your child is a girl (see *Structure of the urinary tract*, p. 103). Consult your doctor.

*Treatment:* If your doctor suspects a urinary-tract infection, he or she will probably want a sample of your child's urine for analysis (see *Collecting a mid-stream specimen,* p. 125). If tests confirm the diagnosis, the usual treatment is a course of *antibiotics.*

**NO**

Does your child have a cold or sore throat?

**YES**

**Upper respiratory-tract infections** in children are often accompanied by abdominal pain. Look out for any of the danger signs listed in the box opposite, but treat the cold or sore throat in the usual way (see *Treating your child's cold,* p. 106 and *How to relieve a sore throat,* p. 107).

**NO**

Did your child seem well before the onset of pain?

**YES**

Has your child had similar bouts of pain in the past few months?

**YES**

**NO**

**NO**

### THE PAIN OF APPENDICITIS

Symptoms of appendicitis in children can vary considerably. But typically the pain starts in the centre of the abdomen, near the navel, and moves towards the lower-right abdomen. If your child has this type of pain, you should be especially alert for any of the danger signs listed in the box opposite.

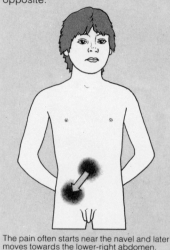

The pain often starts near the navel and later moves towards the lower-right abdomen.

**Recurrent tummy aches** (sometimes called the periodic syndrome) occur in about 10 per cent of children. They may be the result of stress or insecurity, but often there is no obvious explanation.

*Self-help:* Take the symptoms seriously; although there is unlikely to be a physical cause, your child's pain is nevertheless real. Allow him or her to rest in bed with a well-wrapped hot-water bottle. Do not force food on your child but make sure he or she drinks plenty of clear fluids. Remember that a child with recurrent tummy aches is just as likely to get a serious disease, such as appendicitis, as any other child, so be on the lookout for any of the danger signs listed in the box opposite. Call your doctor if your child's symptoms differ from his or her usual tummy aches. If you have not already done so, discuss the problem with your doctor, who will rule out the possibility of a physical disorder and try to help you discover any underlying emotional problems.

**Unexplained abdominal pain** is common in childhood. Give your child clear fluids only. A well-wrapped hot-water bottle on the tummy may ease the pain. Look out for any of the danger signs in the box opposite and consult your doctor if further symptoms develop, or if your child is still unwell the following day.

### APPENDIX REMOVAL

Appendix removal (or appendicectomy) is carried out in cases of appendicitis, when there is infection or inflammation of the appendix, a worm-shaped pouch that protrudes from the large intestine near where it meets the small intestine. The operation needs to be done as soon as symptoms suggest the possibility of appendicitis, because there is a danger that an inflamed appendix will burst, creating a dangerous generalized infection in the abdomen (peritonitis).

The operation itself is straightforward. Your child will be given a general anaesthetic and an incision will be made in the abdomen. The appendix will then be removed. In most cases recovery is rapid and there are no after-effects.

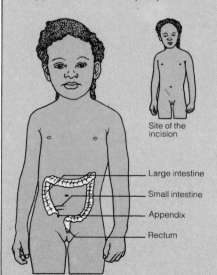

Site of the incision

- Large intestine
- Small intestine
- Appendix
- Rectum

The incision is made in the lower-right abdomen (above). The appendix is cut off at its base and removed (right).

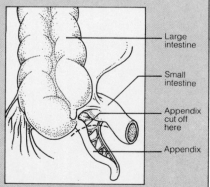

- Large intestine
- Small intestine
- Appendix cut off here
- Appendix

# 39 Loss of appetite

The appetites of children are more closely governed by their body's energy requirements than are the appetites of adults. During periods when they are active, children may consume large amounts of food, but when they use little energy they may have no appetite. In addition, a child who is going through a phase of rapid growth is likely to eat much more than a child who is going through a phase of little growth. And some children naturally burn up less energy than others. Such fluctuations in appetite are quite normal as long as your child is active and growing normally. However, there may be cause for concern if a child who has no appetite seems otherwise unwell, or is failing to grow at the expected rate (see Growth patterns in childhood, p. 69).

**For children under 1 year, go to chart 6, Feeding problems.**

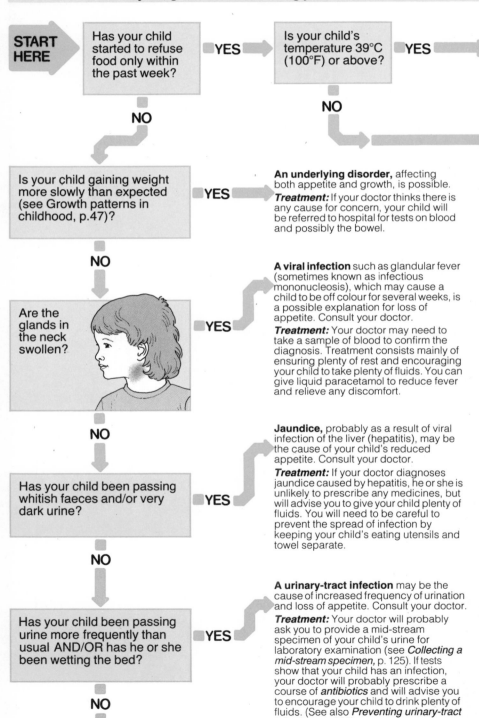

**START HERE**

**Has your child started to refuse food only within the past week?**

YES → **Is your child's temperature 39°C (100°F) or above?**

YES → **A feverish illness** can easily cause a temporary loss of appetite.

Go to chart

**14** **Fever in children**

NO ↓ (child refuse food only within the past week) NO

**Is your child gaining weight more slowly than expected (see Growth patterns in childhood, p.47)?**

YES → **An underlying disorder,** affecting both appetite and growth, is possible.

*Treatment:* If your doctor thinks there is any cause for concern, your child will be referred to hospital for tests on blood and possibly the bowel.

NO ↓

**Are the glands in the neck swollen?**

YES → **A viral infection** such as glandular fever (sometimes known as infectious mononucleosis), which may cause a child to be off colour for several weeks, is a possible explanation for loss of appetite. Consult your doctor.

*Treatment:* Your doctor may need to take a sample of blood to confirm the diagnosis. Treatment consists mainly of ensuring plenty of rest and encouraging your child to take plenty of fluids. You can give liquid paracetamol to reduce fever and relieve any discomfort.

NO ↓

**Has your child been passing whitish faeces and/or very dark urine?**

YES → **Jaundice,** probably as a result of viral infection of the liver (hepatitis), may be the cause of your child's reduced appetite. Consult your doctor.

*Treatment:* If your doctor diagnoses jaundice caused by hepatitis, he or she is unlikely to prescribe any medicines, but will advise you to give your child plenty of fluids. You will need to be careful to prevent the spread of infection by keeping your child's eating utensils and towel separate.

NO ↓

**Has your child been passing urine more frequently than usual AND/OR has he or she been wetting the bed?**

YES → **A urinary-tract infection** may be the cause of increased frequency of urination and loss of appetite. Consult your doctor.

*Treatment:* Your doctor will probably ask you to provide a mid-stream specimen of your child's urine for laboratory examination (see *Collecting a mid-stream specimen,* p. 125). If tests show that your child has an infection, your doctor will probably prescribe a course of *antibiotics* and will advise you to encourage your child to drink plenty of fluids. (See also *Preventing urinary-tract infections,* p. 125).

NO ↓

*Go to next page, column 1*

## FOOD FADS

Nearly all children go through a phase of "faddiness" about food. Sometimes a child will refuse only one or two foods, or will accept certain foods only if they are prepared in a particular way. And it is common for children suddenly to start rejecting a wide range of foods that they have previously eaten without protest.

**Is there a danger of malnutrition?**
There is little danger that a child who eats a limited diet will become deficient in essential nutrients. A child can remain healthy for a surprisingly long time on an apparently inadequate diet – for example, limited to bread and butter and a pint of milk a day.

**How to deal with the problem**
The best way to cope with a child who has become fussy about food is to ignore the problem no matter how bizarre or monotonous your child's choice of food may seem to you. Forcing your child to eat foods he or she does not like will only lead to conflict. Continue to offer a variety of foods, but do not be angry or upset if they are refused. Eventually boredom and curiosity will lead your child to accept a broader diet. Consult your doctor only if your child seems unwell or if he or she is failing to grow at the expected rate (see *Growth patterns in childhood,* p. 69).

See also chart 53, *Adolescent weight problems.*

*Go to next page, column 2*

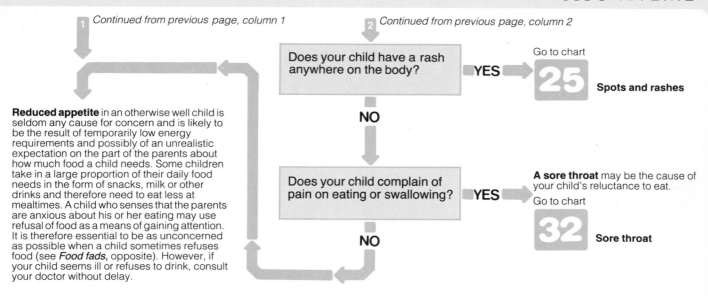

*Continued from previous page, column 1*

*Continued from previous page, column 2*

Does your child have a rash anywhere on the body?

**YES** Go to chart **25** Spots and rashes

**NO**

Does your child complain of pain on eating or swallowing?

**YES** **A sore throat** may be the cause of your child's reluctance to eat. Go to chart **32** Sore throat

**NO**

**Reduced appetite** in an otherwise well child is seldom any cause for concern and is likely to be the result of temporarily low energy requirements and possibly of an unrealistic expectation on the part of the parents about how much food a child needs. Some children take in a large proportion of their daily food needs in the form of snacks, milk or other drinks and therefore need to eat less at mealtimes. A child who senses that the parents are anxious about his or her eating may use refusal of food as a means of gaining attention. It is therefore essential to be as unconcerned as possible when a child sometimes refuses food (see *Food fads,* opposite). However, if your child seems ill or refuses to drink, consult your doctor without delay.

## THE COMPONENTS OF A HEALTHY DIET

A healthy diet is one that contains adequate amounts of each of the various nutrients that the body requires to function efficiently, repair itself and, in the case of children, to grow. The main food categories and their nutritional value are listed in the table below. In Western societies dietary deficiencies in children are rare: the main risk is of overnutrition, either in terms of total calorie intake (see below), leading to obesity, or in the provision of unnecessarily large amounts of certain types of food, in particular fats and refined carbohydrates (for example, sugar and white flour). Providing a variety of different types of food will almost certainly ensure that your child is amply nourished. Even if your child becomes fussy about eating, malnutrition is most unlikely (see *Food fads,* opposite).

| Food category | Diet advice |
|---|---|
| **Proteins** are used for growth, repair and replacement of body tissues. Animal products such as meat, fish, eggs, cheese and other milk products are high in protein, as are pulses (peas, beans, lentils, etc.). | Many protein-rich animal products are also high in fat, so make a point of sometimes offering non-animal sources of protein as an alternative. |
| **Carbohydrates** are used for energy, but eaten in excess are stored in the body as fat. Foods containing a high proportion of carbohydrates include sugar, grain products and root vegetables. | When selecting carbohydrate foods, choose unrefined products such as wholemeal bread and brown rice, which also contain fibre and other nutrients, in preference to sugar and refined cereals which provide only energy. |
| **Fats** (sometimes known as lipids) are a concentrated source of energy and provide more calories than any other food. They are found in animal products such as meat, eggs and butter, and also in certain plant products such as nuts and olives. | Nutritionists recommend that intake of fats of all kinds should be kept to the barest minimum. |
| **Fibre** is the indigestible residue of plant products that passes through the digestive system. While it contains no energy value or nutrients, it is essential for healthy bowel action. | To ensure adequate fibre intake, choose wholemeal grain products and give plenty of fruit and vegetables. |
| **Vitamins** are complex chemical compounds that are needed by the body in tiny quantities. A child receiving a normal diet is unlikely to become deficient in any vitamin. | Vitamins may sometimes be destroyed by lengthy cooking, so offer uncooked vegetables and fruit regularly. Some doctors recommend vitamin drops for children under 5, and while these are often unnecessary, they will do no harm and may reassure parents who are worried about whether their child is receiving an adequate diet. |
| **Minerals** and certain salts are needed in minute quantities. These include iron, potassium, calcium and sodium (found in table salt). A normal child is unlikely to suffer from shortages of such substances while eating a balanced diet. | Too much salt in the diet may be harmful, so use as little as possible in food. |
| **Calories** are the units used to measure the amount of energy provided by food. If a child's diet contains more calories than necessary, the excess will be stored as fat. Conversely, if a child consumes fewer calories than are being burnt up he or she will use up fat reserves and become thin. Foods containing a high proportion of fats or carbohydrates are generally high in calories. | It is important that a child's diet contains enough, but not too many, calories. Luckily, a child's natural appetite regulating mechanism normally ensures that the correct amount of calories is eaten. |

# 40 Diarrhoea in children

Diarrhoea is the passing of unusually runny faeces more frequently than is normal for your child. While diarrhoea can be worrying in young babies, in older children it is unlikely to present any risk to general health as long as you ensure that your child has plenty to drink while diarrhoea persists. The most common cause of diarrhoea is viral infection of the digestive tract (gastroenteritis). In most cases drugs are not effective; the best treatment is to allow the body to rid itself of the infection (see Treating your child's gastroenteritis, opposite).

**For children under 1 year, see chart 8, Diarrhoea in babies.**

**START HERE**

Has the diarrhoea started within the past 24 hours?

**YES**

**NO**

## WARNING

### DANGER SIGNS
A child who has diarrhoea may be seriously ill if he or she has any one of the following additional danger signs:

- continuous abdominal pain for 6 hours or more
- repeated vomiting for more than 12 hours
- refusal to drink
- sunken eyes
- abnormal drowsiness
- passing no urine for 6 hours or more

**Call your doctor now!**

### DIARRHOEA AND FOOD ALLERGIES
Allergy is associated in most people's minds with asthma, eczema and hay fever, but some cases of persistent diarrhoea may also be caused by an allergic reaction, usually to a particular food. A child is most likely to be susceptible to allergies if one or both parents are also allergic. Cow's milk protein is the most common substance in food that causes persistent diarrhoea due to an allergic reaction. Hypersensitivity to gluten, which is found in bread and other wheat products is less common. Other possible offending substances include fish, eggs, nuts, colouring and preservatives.

**Allergy tests**
A doctor may suspect that your child's diarrhoea is due to a food allergy because of the nature of the symptoms and by the exclusion of other conditions (such as infection) which produce similar effects. If the diagnosis is correct, removal of the suspected food from the diet will produce an improvement within 48 hours. The symptoms will recur on reintroduction of the food and will improve once more when the food is withdrawn again. Laboratory tests may also be helpful. These tests include skin tests in which a small amount of the substance is scratched or pricked into the skin, a raised or red area appearing within 15 to 20 minutes suggests a hypersensitive reaction to that substance. A special blood test can detect the change in the blood due to an allergic reaction. However, in some cases these tests are negative when the child is clearly allergic.

Skin tests for allergies

**Treatment**
Food allergies are usually treated by eliminating the offending food from the child's diet. However, this is practical only if your child is sensitive to one or two foods. If your child is allergic to many different substances, treatment is more difficult. Do not attempt long-term dietary treatment without medical advice. Any special diet should be supervised by an experienced dietician to prevent deficiencies of essential nutrients or vitamins.

Has your child vomited, AND/OR is his or her temperature 38°C (100°F) or above?

| 102 | 39 |
| 101 | |
| 100 | 38 |

**YES**

**NO**

Has your child complained of stomach ache?

**YES**

**NO**

Did the diarrhoea start just before a possibly stressful event — for example, an outing or an appearance in a school play?

**YES**

**NO**

**Gastroenteritis** (infection of the digestive tract) is the most likely cause of your child's symptoms.

***Self-help:*** See *Treating your child's gastroenteritis*, opposite.

**Excitement or anxiety** may cause a child to have diarrhoea.

***Self-help:*** Even though your child's symptoms may be emotional in origin, and are likely to clear up quickly without special treatment, it is advisable to follow the self-help advice for treating gastroenteritis given opposite.

*Go to next page*

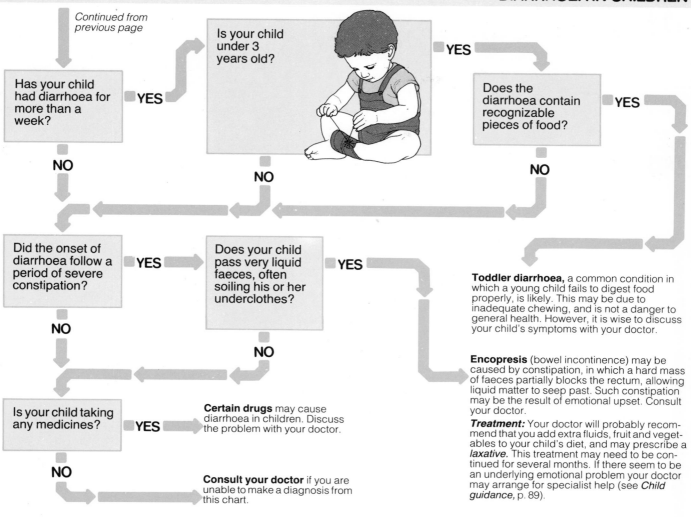

*Continued from previous page*

**Has your child had diarrhoea for more than a week?**

**Is your child under 3 years old?**

**Does the diarrhoea contain recognizable pieces of food?**

YES → YES → YES

NO ↓ NO ↓ NO ↓

**Did the onset of diarrhoea follow a period of severe constipation?**

**Does your child pass very liquid faeces, often soiling his or her underclothes?**

YES → YES →

NO ↓ NO ↓

**Toddler diarrhoea,** a common condition in which a young child fails to digest food properly, is likely. This may be due to inadequate chewing, and is not a danger to general health. However, it is wise to discuss your child's symptoms with your doctor.

**Encopresis** (bowel incontinence) may be caused by constipation, in which a hard mass of faeces partially blocks the rectum, allowing liquid matter to seep past. Such constipation may be the result of emotional upset. Consult your doctor.

**Treatment:** Your doctor will probably recommend that you add extra fluids, fruit and vegetables to your child's diet, and may prescribe a *laxative*. This treatment may need to be continued for several months. If there seem to be an underlying emotional problem your doctor may arrange for specialist help (see *Child guidance,* p. 89).

**Is your child taking any medicines?**

YES →

NO ↓

**Certain drugs** may cause diarrhoea in children. Discuss the problem with your doctor.

**Consult your doctor** if you are unable to make a diagnosis from this chart.

---

## TREATING YOUR CHILD'S GASTROENTERITIS

If you suspect that your child has gastroenteritis or a similar disorder, try the following home treatment. This allows the body to get rid of the infection while preventing dehydration. The treatment should reduce the frequency of bowel movements within 24 hours. But the faeces may remain runny for 5 to 7 days.

### General points
- Give plenty of clear fluids – 1–1½ litres (2–3 pints) a day. A glucose solution (see *Treating gastroenteritis in babies,* p. 63) is best. Alternatively, give well-diluted, unsweetened fruit juice.
- If your child is vomiting, give drinks in frequent small sips – say 30–60 ml (1–2 fl.oz) every hour.
- Give no milk products (including milk, yoghurt and cheese) for a week.
- If your child has abdominal pain, a well-wrapped hot-water bottle on the stomach may be comforting.

### Day-by-day treatment plan

**Day 1**
Give only clear fluids (see *General points,* left).

**Day 2**
Offer, in addition, vegetable and unsweetened fruit purees (for example, mashed potatoes, stewed apple, or bananas).

**Day 3**
Offer, in addition, chicken and/or soups.

**Day 4**
Offer, in addition, bread (spread with margarine, not butter), biscuits, eggs, meat and/or fish.

**Day 5**
Resume a normal diet, but continue to exclude milk products for a further 2 days.

### When to call a doctor
Consult your doctor if your child is under 2 years old, or if symptoms do not start to subside within 48 hours. Call your doctor at once if your child shows any of the danger signs listed in the box opposite.

### Preventing the spread of infection
If anyone in the house has gastroenteritis, it is important to prevent the spread of infection.

- Wash your hands thoroughly after going to the lavatory and before preparing food.

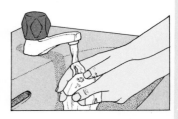

- Do not share towels, sponges, or face flannels.

# 41 Constipation

There is no rule that says a child should have a bowel movement every day. Some children defecate several times a day, others only once every three days. Both extremes are perfectly normal as long as your child is well and as long as the faeces are not so hard that they cause discomfort or straining. Temporary alteration to your child's normal bowel rhythms may be caused by a change in diet, minor illness, or emotional stress.

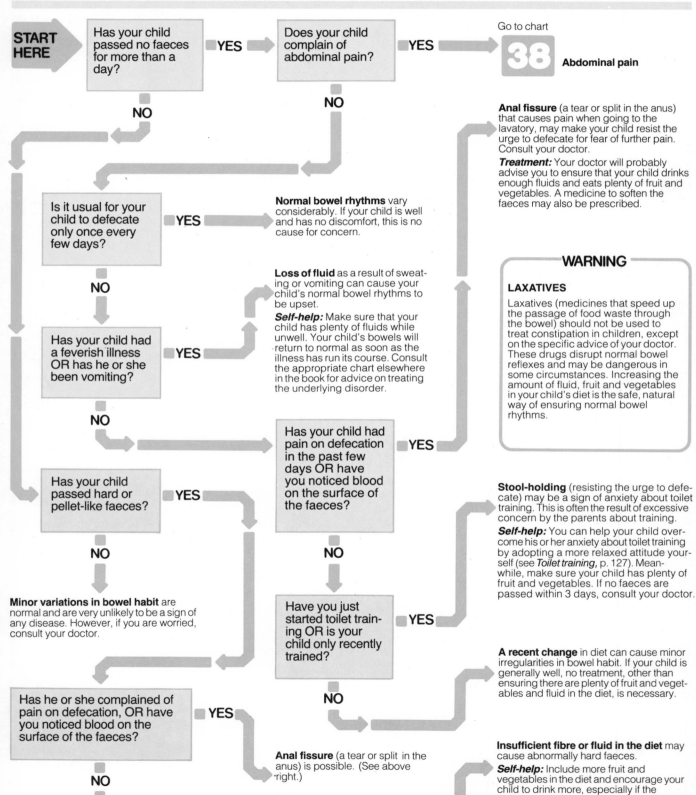

**START HERE**

**Has your child passed no faeces for more than a day?**

YES → **Does your child complain of abdominal pain?**

YES → Go to chart **38** **Abdominal pain**

NO ↓

**Is it usual for your child to defecate only once every few days?**

YES → **Normal bowel rhythms** vary considerably. If your child is well and has no discomfort, this is no cause for concern.

NO ↓

**Has your child had a feverish illness OR has he or she been vomiting?**

YES → **Loss of fluid** as a result of sweating or vomiting can cause your child's normal bowel rhythms to be upset.
*Self-help:* Make sure that your child has plenty of fluids while unwell. Your child's bowels will return to normal as soon as the illness has run its course. Consult the appropriate chart elsewhere in the book for advice on treating the underlying disorder.

NO ↓

**Has your child passed hard or pellet-like faeces?**

YES → **Has your child had pain on defecation in the past few days OR have you noticed blood on the surface of the faeces?**

YES → (Anal fissure, see right)

**Anal fissure** (a tear or split in the anus) that causes pain when going to the lavatory, may make your child resist the urge to defecate for fear of further pain. Consult your doctor.
*Treatment:* Your doctor will probably advise you to ensure that your child drinks enough fluids and eats plenty of fruit and vegetables. A medicine to soften the faeces may also be prescribed.

NO ↓

**Minor variations in bowel habit** are normal and are very unlikely to be a sign of any disease. However, if you are worried, consult your doctor.

**Has your child had pain on defecation in the past few days OR have you noticed blood on the surface of the faeces?** NO ↓

**Have you just started toilet training OR is your child only recently trained?**

YES → **Stool-holding** (resisting the urge to defecate) may be a sign of anxiety about toilet training. This is often the result of excessive concern by the parents about training.
*Self-help:* You can help your child overcome his or her anxiety about toilet training by adopting a more relaxed attitude yourself (see *Toilet training,* p. 127). Meanwhile, make sure your child has plenty of fruit and vegetables. If no faeces are passed within 3 days, consult your doctor.

NO ↓

**A recent change** in diet can cause minor irregularities in bowel habit. If your child is generally well, no treatment, other than ensuring there are plenty of fruit and vegetables and fluid in the diet, is necessary.

**Has he or she complained of pain on defecation, OR have you noticed blood on the surface of the faeces?**

YES → **Anal fissure** (a tear or split in the anus) is possible. (See above right.)

NO ↓

**Insufficient fibre or fluid in the diet** may cause abnormally hard faeces.
*Self-help:* Include more fruit and vegetables in the diet and encourage your child to drink more, especially if the weather is hot.

## WARNING

### LAXATIVES

Laxatives (medicines that speed up the passage of food waste through the bowel) should not be used to treat constipation in children, except on the specific advice of your doctor. These drugs disrupt normal bowel reflexes and may be dangerous in some circumstances. Increasing the amount of fluid, fruit and vegetables in your child's diet is the safe, natural way of ensuring normal bowel rhythms.

# 42 Abnormal-looking faeces

Minor variations in the colour of faeces are normal and are usually caused by a change in diet. Consult this chart only if there is a marked change in the appearance of your child's faeces. In most cases the cause of the trouble is something that the child has eaten, but occasionally there may be an underlying disorder that your doctor should investigate. If you decide to consult your doctor, take a sample of your child's faeces in a clean container for your doctor to look at; this will assist a rapid diagnosis.

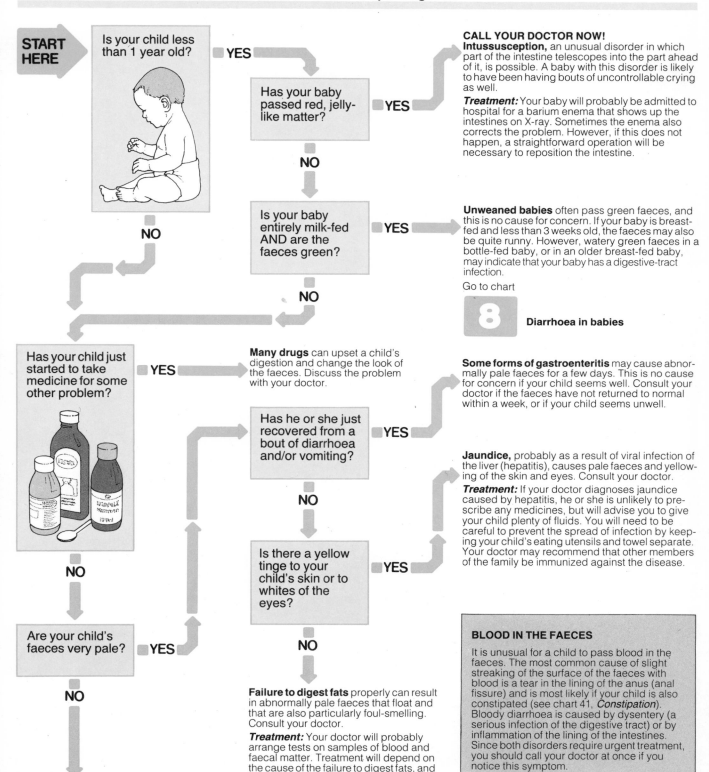

**START HERE**

**Is your child less than 1 year old?**

**YES**

**Has your baby passed red, jelly-like matter?**

**YES**

**NO**

**Is your baby entirely milk-fed AND are the faeces green?**

**YES**

**NO**

**NO**

**Has your child just started to take medicine for some other problem?**

**YES** — Many drugs can upset a child's digestion and change the look of the faeces. Discuss the problem with your doctor.

**NO**

**Are your child's faeces very pale?**

**YES**

**NO**

**Has he or she just recovered from a bout of diarrhoea and/or vomiting?**

**YES**

**NO**

**Is there a yellow tinge to your child's skin or to whites of the eyes?**

**YES**

**NO**

**CALL YOUR DOCTOR NOW!**
**Intussusception,** an unusual disorder in which part of the intestine telescopes into the part ahead of it, is possible. A baby with this disorder is likely to have been having bouts of uncontrollable crying as well.

*Treatment:* Your baby will probably be admitted to hospital for a barium enema that shows up the intestines on X-ray. Sometimes the enema also corrects the problem. However, if this does not happen, a straightforward operation will be necessary to reposition the intestine.

**Unweaned babies** often pass green faeces, and this is no cause for concern. If your baby is breast-fed and less than 3 weeks old, the faeces may also be quite runny. However, watery green faeces in a bottle-fed baby, or in an older breast-fed baby, may indicate that your baby has a digestive-tract infection.

Go to chart

**8**　**Diarrhoea in babies**

**Some forms of gastroenteritis** may cause abnormally pale faeces for a few days. This is no cause for concern if your child seems well. Consult your doctor if the faeces have not returned to normal within a week, or if your child seems unwell.

**Jaundice,** probably as a result of viral infection of the liver (hepatitis), causes pale faeces and yellowing of the skin and eyes. Consult your doctor.
*Treatment:* If your doctor diagnoses jaundice caused by hepatitis, he or she is unlikely to prescribe any medicines, but will advise you to give your child plenty of fluids. You will need to be careful to prevent the spread of infection by keeping your child's eating utensils and towel separate. Your doctor may recommend that other members of the family be immunized against the disease.

**Failure to digest fats** properly can result in abnormally pale faeces that float and that are also particularly foul-smelling. Consult your doctor.

*Treatment:* Your doctor will probably arrange tests on samples of blood and faecal matter. Treatment will depend on the cause of the failure to digest fats, and may involve the exclusion of certain foods from your child's diet.

**Consult your doctor** if you are unable to make a diagnosis from this chart.

**BLOOD IN THE FAECES**

It is unusual for a child to pass blood in the faeces. The most common cause of slight streaking of the surface of the faeces with blood is a tear in the lining of the anus (anal fissure) and is most likely if your child is also constipated (see chart 41, *Constipation*). Bloody diarrhoea is caused by dysentery (a serious infection of the digestive tract) or by inflammation of the lining of the intestines. Since both disorders require urgent treatment, you should call your doctor at once if you notice this symptom.

# 43 Urinary problems

Most children need to urinate more frequently than adults. This is because a child's bladder is smaller than that of an adult, and muscular control may be less well developed. In addition, children who drink large amounts are likely to need to pass urine more often than average. Consult this chart if your child has any pain when passing urine; if your child starts to urinate more frequently than usual without a noticeable increase in fluid intake; if your child needs to pass urine more than once an hour; or if your child has been waking several times during the night to pass urine. Most urinary problems need medical diagnosis and treatment.

**For problems of bladder or bowel control, see chart 44, Toilet-training problems.**

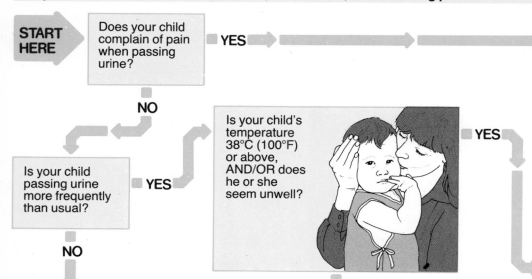

**START HERE**

**Does your child complain of pain when passing urine?**

YES →

**An infection of the urinary tract** may cause painful urination. Consult your doctor.

**Treatment:** Your doctor will probably need a specimen of your child's urine for analysis (see *Collecting a mid-stream specimen*, opposite). If your child is found to have a urinary-tract infection, he or she will probably be prescribed a course of *antibiotics*. You will probably be advised to ensure that your child drinks plenty of fluids during this treatment. (See also *Preventing urinary-tract infections*, opposite).

NO ↓

**Is your child passing urine more frequently than usual?**

YES →

**Is your child's temperature 38°C (100°F) or above, AND/OR does he or she seem unwell?**

YES →

**An infection of the urinary tract** is the most likely explanation for your child's frequency of urination. Consult your doctor.

**Treatment:** See above.

NO ↓

NO ↓

**Consult your doctor** if you are unable to make a diagnosis from this chart.

## ABNORMAL-LOOKING URINE

| Colour of urine | Possible causes | What action is necessary |
|---|---|---|
| Pink, red, or smoky | Although natural or artificial red food colourings can produce such discoloration, there is also a chance that there may be blood in the urine, possibly caused by infection or another disorder of the urinary tract. | Consult your doctor without delay. He or she may need to take samples of urine and blood for analysis in order to make a firm diagnosis. Treatment will depend on the underlying problem. |
| Dark yellow or orange | Concentration of urine caused by low fluid intake, fever, diarrhoea, or vomiting can darken the urine. | This is no cause for concern. Your child's urine will return to its normal colour as soon as the fluid intake is increased. If your child has additional symptoms such as fever, consult the appropriate chart elsewhere in the book. |
| Clear and dark brown | Jaundice caused by hepatitis (liver infection) is a possibility, especially if your child's faeces are very pale and if the skin or eyes look yellow. | Consult your doctor. He or she will take samples of urine and blood for analysis in order to make a firm diagnosis. Treatment will depend on the underlying problem. |
| Green or blue | Artificial colouring in food or medicines is almost certainly the cause of this. | This is no cause for concern; the colouring will pass through the system without harmful effects. |

*Continued from previous page*

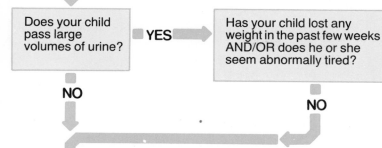

Does your child pass large volumes of urine? **YES** → Has your child lost any weight in the past few weeks AND/OR does he or she seem abnormally tired? **YES** →

**NO** ↓

**NO** ↓

### CONSULT YOUR DOCTOR WITHOUT DELAY!
**Diabetes** may cause an increase in urination. This disorder occurs when the body fails to make sufficient quantities of insulin, the hormone that helps to convert sugar into energy.

*Treatment:* Tests on your child's urine will quickly reveal the presence of this disease. If diabetes is confirmed, your child may need to have regular injections of insulin for life.

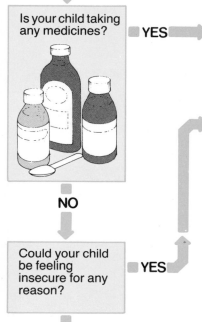

Is your child taking any medicines? **YES** →

**Certain drugs** – in particular, some that are prescribed for *asthma* (see p. 110) – may cause an increase in the frequency of urination. Discuss the problem with your doctor.

**NO** ↓

**Psychological stress** may cause a child to go to the lavatory more often than usual. This may be partly because asking for frequent drinks is an effective way of gaining attention, or it may be that going to the lavatory provides an escape from a possibly stressful situation – for example, at school. However, you should consult your doctor to rule out the possibility of an underlying disorder.

*Treatment:* Your doctor will probably want a specimen of your child's urine (see *Collecting a mid-stream specimen,* below) to eliminate the possibility of infection. If no physical cause for the problem is found, your doctor will help you discover any underlying insecurity in your child and advise you on how to overcome this.

Could your child be feeling insecure for any reason? **YES** →

**NO** ↓

**Consult your doctor** if you are unable to make a diagnosis from this chart.

### THE STRUCTURE OF THE URINARY TRACT
The urinary tract consists of 2 kidneys; 2 tubes leading from the kidneys to the bladder – the ureters; the bladder itself; and the urethra, a tube leading from the bladder to the outside. Each kidney is supplied with blood from the renal artery. As blood passes through the tiny tubes in the cortex and medulla, waste products are filtered out in the form of urine. The filtered blood is carried away via the renal vein.

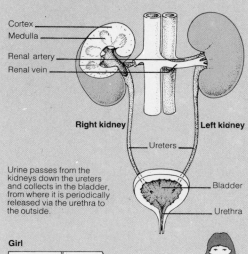

Cortex
Medulla
Renal artery
Renal vein

**Right kidney**　　　**Left kidney**

Ureters

Urine passes from the kidneys down the ureters and collects in the bladder, from where it is periodically released via the urethra to the outside.

Bladder

Urethra

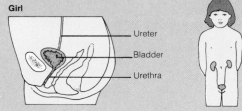

**Girl**

Ureter
Bladder
Urethra

**Boy**

Ureter
Bladder
Urethra

The female urethra is much shorter than the male urethra, allowing germs to travel up a girl's urinary tract more easily.

**Preventing urinary-tract infections**
Most urinary-tract infections are caused by germs from the bowel entering the urethra. To reduce the chances of infection, all girls should be taught always to wipe from front to back after going to the lavatory.

### COLLECTING A MID-STREAM SPECIMEN
If your doctor suspects that your child has a urinary-tract infection, you will probably be asked to provide a mid-stream specimen of the child's urine for analysis. A mid-stream specimen is a sample of urine that has been collected after some urine has already been passed.

**Boys**

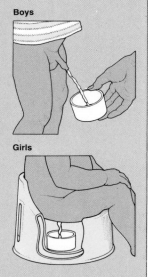

**Collecting the urine**
Your doctor will give you a clean container in which to collect the urine. Urine should be passed directly into this, not into another container – such as, a jug or pot first. The accuracy of the test depends on the specimen being free from contamination by germs that may be around the outside of the opening of the urethra, so your child should be given a bath or a thorough wash before you start to collect the sample.

**Girls**

**Boys**
A boy's urine can be collected by holding the container in the stream after a little urine has first been passed into the lavatory or pot.

**Girls**
The urine of a young girl is best collected by placing the container in the bottom of a pot (see right) before she starts to urinate. It may be easier for an older girl to hold the container under the stream while she sits well back on the toilet seat.

The method you use to collect the urine sample depends whether your child is a boy or girl.

# 44 Toilet-training problems

The process of gaining full control over bladder and bowel functions takes place over a span of about 3 years between the second and the fifth year. Few children have reliable control before the age of 2 years, and few have any problems apart from the occasional "accident" after the age of 5. Within this range there are great variations in the order and in the timing in which an individual child masters the different skills of toilet training. Serious disorders causing delay or disruption of the development of bladder or bowel control are rare in normal children; most such problems resolve themselves with time and patience. Consult this chart if you are concerned about your child's ability to control bladder or bowels.

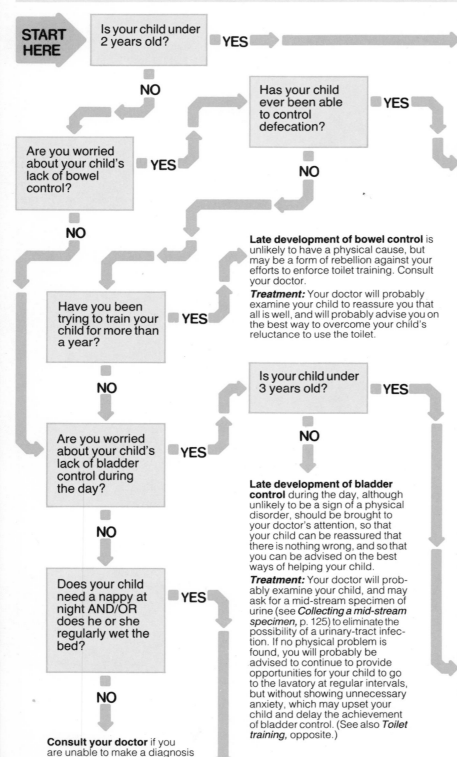

**START HERE**

Is your child under 2 years old?
**YES**

**NO**

Are you worried about your child's lack of bowel control?
**YES**

**NO**

Has your child ever been able to control defecation?
**YES**

**NO**

Have you been trying to train your child for more than a year?
**YES**

**NO**

Are you worried about your child's lack of bladder control during the day?
**YES**

**NO**

Is your child under 3 years old?
**YES**

**NO**

Does your child need a nappy at night AND/OR does he or she regularly wet the bed?
**YES**

**NO**

Does your child pass very liquid faeces, often soiling his or her underclothes?
**YES**

**NO**

**Consult your doctor** if you are unable to make a diagnosis from this chart.

**Immaturity** of the mechanisms for controlling both bladder and bowels means that many children in this age group are not yet able to prevent themselves from passing urine or faeces involuntarily.

*Self-help:* There is little you can do to speed up your child's development in this respect. Read the advice on toilet training opposite, so that when your child begins to show a readiness to learn, you are ready to help.

**Late development of bowel control** is unlikely to have a physical cause, but may be a form of rebellion against your efforts to enforce toilet training. Consult your doctor.

*Treatment:* Your doctor will probably examine your child to reassure you that all is well, and will probably advise you on the best way to overcome your child's reluctance to use the toilet.

**Late development of bladder control** during the day, although unlikely to be a sign of a physical disorder, should be brought to your doctor's attention, so that your child can be reassured that there is nothing wrong, and so that you can be advised on the best ways of helping your child.

*Treatment:* Your doctor will probably examine your child, and may ask for a mid-stream specimen of urine (see *Collecting a mid-stream specimen,* p. 125) to eliminate the possibility of a urinary-tract infection. If no physical problem is found, you will probably be advised to continue to provide opportunities for your child to go to the lavatory at regular intervals, but without showing unnecessary anxiety, which may upset your child and delay the achievement of bladder control. (See also *Toilet training,* opposite.)

**Reversion of previous toilet training** usually has an emotional cause. Your child may unconsciously be seeking attention. Such behaviour may be sparked off by anxiety – for example, about the arrival of a new baby or tension within the home. Consult your doctor.

*Treatment:* Your doctor will examine your child to rule out any physical disorder. You will probably be advised to take no immediate action other than making sure that your child has every opportunity to use the lavatory (or pot). If your child has not got over the problem within a week or so, your doctor may refer you for specialist help.

**Blockage of the rectum** by a hard mass of faeces that allows liquid matter to seep past, may cause this type of soiling. This may be the result of emotional upset. Consult your doctor.

*Treatment:* Your doctor will probably recommend that you add extra fruit and vegetables to your child's diet, and may prescribe a laxative. This treatment may need to be continued for several months. If there seems to be an underlying emotional problem, your doctor may arrange for specialist help.

**Reliable daytime control of urination or defecation** is seldom achieved by this age. Even if your child is still in nappies most of the time, there is unlikely to be any cause for concern.

*Self-help:* Follow the advice on toilet training, given opposite. Make sure that your child has plenty of opportunities to see other people – in particular, other children – using the lavatory or pot; most children learn quickest by imitation.

*Go to next page*

*Continued from previous page*

Has your child ever been dry at night for more than a week? — **YES** →

**NO** ↓

Is your child under 5 years old? — **YES** →

**NO** ↓

**Regular bed-wetting in an older child** seldom has a physical cause. However, you should discuss the problem with your doctor, who may be able to offer helpful advice.

*Treatment:* Most children are worried by their bed-wetting and need plenty of reassurance that they will soon learn to be dry at night. Try some of the suggestions for overcoming bed-wetting outlined in the box below.

**A urinary-tract infection** may cause a child who has previously been reliably dry at night to start bed-wetting. Consult your doctor.

*Treatment:* Your doctor will probably ask you to provide a specimen of your child's urine for analysis (see *Collecting a mid-stream specimen*, p. 125). If the tests reveal an infection, your child will probably be prescribed a course of *antibiotics*. You will probably be advised to ensure that your child has plenty of fluids during this treatment. If no infection is found, your doctor will help you look into any possible emotional cause for the bed-wetting.

**Lack of bladder control at night** is common in children under 5, and is hardly ever a cause for concern. Even after this age, many children continue to wet their beds occasionally.

*Self-help:* The best way to help your child is to prevent yourself from showing anxiety. If you are still putting your child in nappies continue to do so until they are often dry in the morning. If your child is out of nappies but regularly wets the bed, try lifting your child onto a pot before you go to bed yourself at night. When accidents do occur, do not reprimand your child, but deal with the wet night-clothes and bedclothes without comment. Your child is probably as anxious as you to achieve night-time control, and will do so when ready.

---

## THE DEVELOPMENT OF BLADDER AND BOWEL CONTROL

Control over passing urine and faeces depends on a child recognizing the sensation of a full bladder or rectum and then being able to hold onto or release their contents at will. Most children do not develop the capacity to do this until well into their second year. Most children learn reliable daytime control of bladder and bowel functions between the ages of 18 months and 3 years, although accidents, especially accidental urination, may continue to occur from time to time. Control over urination at night usually develops between about 2½ and 3½ years of age, but regular bed-wetting is common up to the age of 5, and may happen occasionally until a child is older.

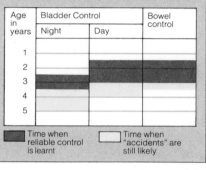

| Age in years | Bladder Control | | Bowel control |
|---|---|---|---|
| | Night | Day | |
| 1 | | | |
| 2 | | | |
| 3 | | | |
| 4 | | | |
| 5 | | | |

■ Time when reliable control is learnt   □ Time when "accidents" are still likely

---

## TOILET TRAINING

There is no single correct way of introducing your child to the use of the pot. Much will depend on your child's level of development and personality, and on your family routine. The main thing for parents to remember is not to make use of the pot a cause for conflict or tension. Your child will master control of bladder and bowels when he or she is physiologically and mentally ready. Your job is simply to provide the conditions that will make the process of learning as relaxed and easy as possible.

The guide to pot-training below is intended to provide a basic structure. Use your own judgement to adapt it to your child's needs.

### Gaining control by stages
**1 Introductions**
Buy a pot when your child is about 18 months old. Explain what it is for, but do not expect your child to use it for some time. Allow your child to go without nappies during the day as often as possible. When your child has reached the stage of being able to control urination and defecation for several hours, you can start to suggest (but never insist) that he or she uses the pot occasionally. Once your child has started to use the pot sometimes, move on to stage 2.

**2 Becoming confident**
Continue to encourage your child to use the pot whenever he or she shows the need to urinate or defecate, but do not be upset or angry when accidents occur. Conversely, do not be too effusive in your praise when your child succeeds in using the pot properly. Gradually phase out the use of nappies until you are using them only at night.

**3 Adult toilets and night-time control**
Once your child is confident with the use of a pot, you can introduce use of the toilet. Buy a special child seat that fits inside the toilet seat to make your child feel more secure. Explain that the toilet can be used in the same way as a pot. Alternate use of the pot and lavatory until your child feels equally at ease with both.

During this time look out for signs that your child is ready to go through the night without a nappy. Dry nappies on several mornings is probably the best indicator. When you decide to start leaving nappies off at night, prepare yourself mentally for the inevitable occasional wet beds. If your child's bed does not have a waterproof mattress, use a plastic undersheet. This will help you to be less concerned when your child does wet the bed. Some children can be helped to be dry at night by being lifted onto a pot a few hours after bedtime. However, if this disturbs your child so that getting back to sleep

A child seat that fits inside the adult toilet seat and a step to help your child get up onto the lavatory, are useful aids when a child is graduating from pot to adult toilet.

is difficult, it may not be worth the trouble. Restricting fluids in the evening is not usually an effective way of preventing bed-wetting.

### Bed-wetting in an older child
Many children continue to wet their beds occasionally throughout childhood. This is seldom a cause for medical concern, but if a child frequently wets the bed, it can be distressing for parents and child. Most children grow out of this habit well before adolescence, but you may be able to speed up the process in the following ways:

■ **Recording dry nights** Give your child a calendar and encourage him or her to record (for example, by using a stick-on star) any dry nights. You could try offering a reward after an agreed number of stars. Wet nights should be ignored. Increasing numbers of stars will build up your child's confidence and increase the incentive to master night-time bladder control.

■ **Bed-wetting alarms** If record-keeping fails to help the problem, your doctor may suggest the use of an alarm. This is a device fitted to a child's bed, which causes an alarm to ring as soon as any urine is passed. This wakes the child so that he or she can get up to finish urinating in the pot or lavatory. This method has a high success rate.

# 45 Painful arm or leg

As soon as children start to walk they become subject to frequent minor injuries as a result of falls, collisions, and the straining of muscles. Pain in the arm or leg in childhood is usually the result of such injuries and is seldom serious enough to warrant medical attention.

Occasionally, however, an injury may result in a broken bone (fracture) and this requires immediate medical treatment. Pain that occurs without obvious signs of injury should always be brought to your doctor's attention if it lasts more than a day or so.

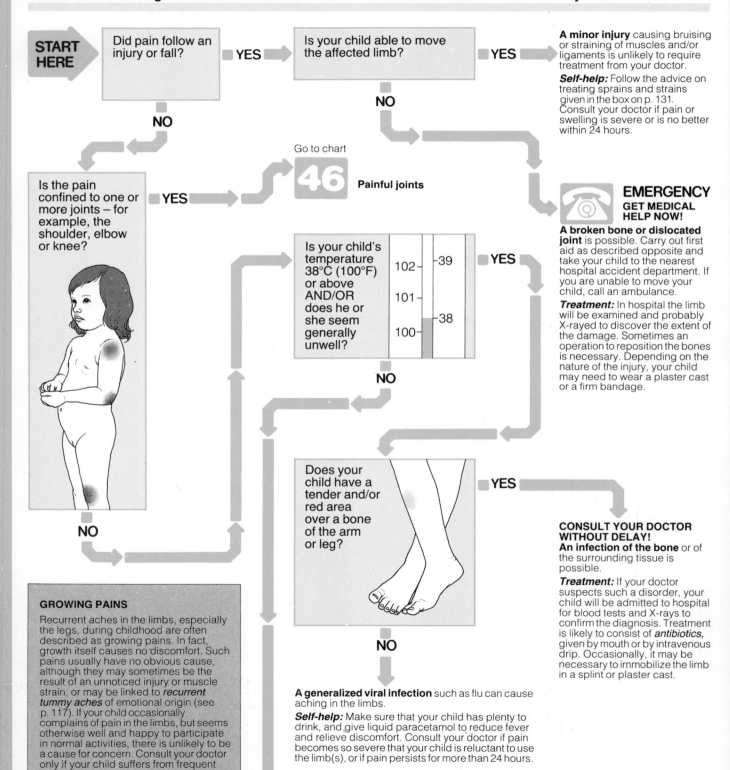

**START HERE**

**Did pain follow an injury or fall?**

**YES →** **Is your child able to move the affected limb?**

**YES →** **A minor injury** causing bruising or straining of muscles and/or ligaments is unlikely to require treatment from your doctor.

*Self-help:* Follow the advice on treating sprains and strains given in the box on p. 131. Consult your doctor if pain or swelling is severe or is no better within 24 hours.

**NO** ↓

**NO** ↓

Go to chart

**46** Painful joints

**Is the pain confined to one or more joints — for example, the shoulder, elbow or knee?**

**YES →**

**Is your child's temperature 38°C (100°F) or above AND/OR does he or she seem generally unwell?**

102 — 39
101 — 38
100 —

**YES →**

**EMERGENCY GET MEDICAL HELP NOW!**

**A broken bone or dislocated joint** is possible. Carry out first aid as described opposite and take your child to the nearest hospital accident department. If you are unable to move your child, call an ambulance.

*Treatment:* In hospital the limb will be examined and probably X-rayed to discover the extent of the damage. Sometimes an operation to reposition the bones is necessary. Depending on the nature of the injury, your child may need to wear a plaster cast or a firm bandage.

**NO** ↓

**Does your child have a tender and/or red area over a bone of the arm or leg?**

**YES →**

**CONSULT YOUR DOCTOR WITHOUT DELAY!**
**An infection of the bone** or of the surrounding tissue is possible.

*Treatment:* If your doctor suspects such a disorder, your child will be admitted to hospital for blood tests and X-rays to confirm the diagnosis. Treatment is likely to consist of *antibiotics*, given by mouth or by intravenous drip. Occasionally, it may be necessary to immobilize the limb in a splint or plaster cast.

**NO** ↓

**NO** ↓

### GROWING PAINS

Recurrent aches in the limbs, especially the legs, during childhood are often described as growing pains. In fact, growth itself causes no discomfort. Such pains usually have no obvious cause, although they may sometimes be the result of an unnoticed injury or muscle strain, or may be linked to *recurrent tummy aches* of emotional origin (see p. 117). If your child occasionally complains of pain in the limbs, but seems otherwise well and happy to participate in normal activities, there is unlikely to be a cause for concern. Consult your doctor only if your child suffers from frequent attacks of pain and/or seems reluctant to use the affected limb(s).

**A generalized viral infection** such as flu can cause aching in the limbs.
*Self-help:* Make sure that your child has plenty to drink, and give liquid paracetamol to reduce fever and relieve discomfort. Consult your doctor if pain becomes so severe that your child is reluctant to use the limb(s), or if pain persists for more than 24 hours.

*Go to next page*

*Continued from previous page*

Has your child suffered from this type of pain on several occasions in the past?

**YES**

**NO**

**Minor straining** of the muscles or ligaments as a result of vigorous play is the most likely cause of pain in the arm or leg unaccompanied by other symptoms. No special treatment is needed. Consult your doctor if your child is reluctant to use the affected limb(s), if pain persists for more than 24 hours, or if your child seems generally unwell.

**Recurrent limb pains** are common in childhood and are generally no cause for concern (see *Growing pains,* opposite). Consult your doctor if your child becomes reluctant to use the affected limb(s), if pain persists for more than 24 hours, or if your child seems generally unwell.

## FIRST AID FOR SUSPECTED BROKEN BONES AND DISLOCATED JOINTS

Your child may have broken a bone or dislocated a joint if he or she is unable to move the affected part or if it looks misshapen.

### General points
- If there is any bleeding from the wound treat this first as described on p. 284.
- Do not try to manipulate the bone or joint back into position yourself; this should be carried out only by a doctor.
- While waiting for medical help, keep the child warm and be as calm as possible.
- Give nothing to eat or drink; a general anaesthetic may be needed to reset the bone.
- If medical help is readily available, take no further action; in particular, move the child as little as possible.
- If medical help may be some time arriving, or if you have to move the child, immobilize the limb in the most comfortable position by use of bandages and splints as described below.
- As soon as you have carried out first aid, summon medical help, or if your child can be moved (as in the case of an arm injury) take him or her to the accident department of the local hospital.

### Splints
A splint is a firm support used to immobilize an injured part of the body (usually an arm or a leg) in order to reduce pain and the likelihood of further damage. In an emergency you can make an improvised splint with a household object such as a broom handle, or rolled-up newspaper (see below). Always secure the splint in at least 2 places not too close to the injury – preferably on either side of it. Use wide lengths of material or bandages (not rope or string), and be careful not to tie these too tightly (you should be able to insert one finger between the bandage and limb).

**Improvising splints**
A household object such as a rolled up newspaper (left) can serve as a splint in an emergency. Make sure that you tie it securely in at least 2 places (below left) and test that it is not too tight (below). You can provide additional support for an injured leg by securing it to the sound one with a well-padded splint in between (bottom).

### Arm injury
Gently place the injured arm in a bent position across the chest. Some padding should be placed between the arm and the chest (below left). Support the weight of the arm together with the padding in a sling along its length (below right). If the arm cannot be bent, use bandages to secure the arm to the side of the body. A splint may provide increased support.

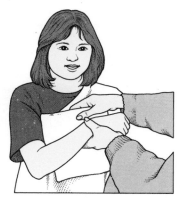

### Shoulder, collar bone or elbow injury
Support the weight of the arm in a sling in the most comfortable position for the child.

### Leg injury
Secure the injured leg to the sound one. If possible, place a well-padded splint (see below left) between them.

### Knee injury
Support the joint in the most comfortable position for the child. If the knee is bent, apply a bandage to support it in the bent position (below). If the knee is unable to bend, support the leg along its length from underneath; use a plank (or something similar) as a splint. Place padding between the knee and the splint, and around the heel.

**Bandaging a knee injury**
When an injured knee is most comfortable in the bent position, bandage it firmly to provide support in that position. Take care to extend the bandage well above and below the injured knee (below).

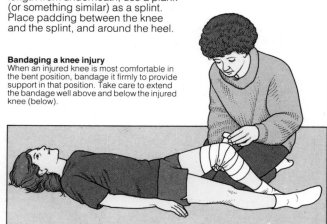

# 46 Painful joints

Pain in the joints – in particular, in those of the arm or leg – is almost always the result of injury or straining of the muscles and ligaments surrounding a joint. In children serious disorders causing pain in one or more joints are fortunately rare, but you should consult your doctor if pain is accompanied by generalized signs of being unwell, or if your child suffers from persistent or recurrent pain.

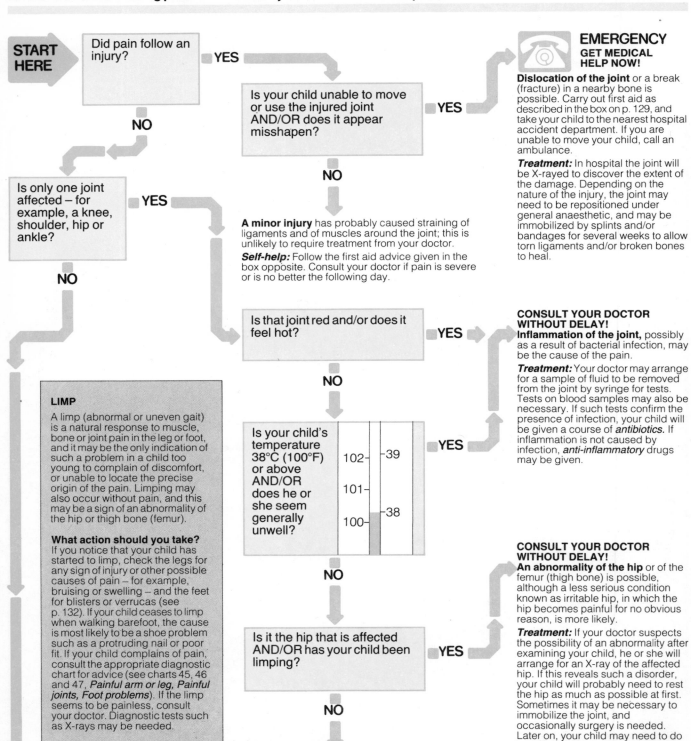

**START HERE**

Did pain follow an injury?

**YES** → Is your child unable to move or use the injured joint AND/OR does it appear misshapen?

**YES** →

### EMERGENCY
### GET MEDICAL HELP NOW!

**Dislocation of the joint** or a break (fracture) in a nearby bone is possible. Carry out first aid as described in the box on p. 129, and take your child to the nearest hospital accident department. If you are unable to move your child, call an ambulance.

**Treatment:** In hospital the joint will be X-rayed to discover the extent of the damage. Depending on the nature of the injury, the joint may need to be repositioned under general anaesthetic, and may be immobilized by splints and/or bandages for several weeks to allow torn ligaments and/or broken bones to heal.

**NO** ↓

**A minor injury** has probably caused straining of ligaments and of muscles around the joint; this is unlikely to require treatment from your doctor.
**Self-help:** Follow the first aid advice given in the box opposite. Consult your doctor if pain is severe or is no better the following day.

**NO** ↓ (from "Did pain follow an injury?")

Is only one joint affected – for example, a knee, shoulder, hip or ankle?

**YES** →

Is that joint red and/or does it feel hot?

**YES** →

### CONSULT YOUR DOCTOR WITHOUT DELAY!
**Inflammation of the joint,** possibly as a result of bacterial infection, may be the cause of the pain.

**Treatment:** Your doctor may arrange for a sample of fluid to be removed from the joint by syringe for tests. Tests on blood samples may also be necessary. If such tests confirm the presence of infection, your child will be given a course of *antibiotics.* If inflammation is not caused by infection, *anti-inflammatory* drugs may be given.

**NO** ↓

Is your child's temperature 38°C (100°F) or above AND/OR does he or she seem generally unwell?

102 — 39
101 — 
100 — 38

**YES** →

**NO** ↓

Is it the hip that is affected AND/OR has your child been limping?

**YES** →

### CONSULT YOUR DOCTOR WITHOUT DELAY!
**An abnormality of the hip** or of the femur (thigh bone) is possible, although a less serious condition known as irritable hip, in which the hip becomes painful for no obvious reason, is more likely.

**Treatment:** If your doctor suspects the possibility of an abnormality after examining your child, he or she will arrange for an X-ray of the affected hip. If this reveals such a disorder, your child will probably need to rest the hip as much as possible at first. Sometimes it may be necessary to immobilize the joint, and occasionally surgery is needed. Later on, your child may need to do exercises to strengthen the muscles of the leg. If no cause of pain is found, your doctor will probably advise rest for about a week, and avoidance of strenuous physical activity for a further week. This usually cures an irritable hip.

**NO** ↓

**A minor sprain or strain** as a result of an unnoticed injury or awkward movement is the most likely cause of joint pain in an otherwise well child.
**Self-help:** Encourage your child to rest the affected joint for a day or so. Consult your doctor if pain persists, or if your child becomes generally unwell.

**NO** ↓ (from "Is only one joint affected")

### LIMP
A limp (abnormal or uneven gait) is a natural response to muscle, bone or joint pain in the leg or foot, and it may be the only indication of such a problem in a child too young to complain of discomfort, or unable to locate the precise origin of the pain. Limping may also occur without pain, and this may be a sign of an abnormality of the hip or thigh bone (femur).

#### What action should you take?
If you notice that your child has started to limp, check the legs for any sign of injury or other possible causes of pain – for example, bruising or swelling – and the feet for blisters or verrucas (see p. 132). If your child ceases to limp when walking barefoot, the cause is most likely to be a shoe problem such as a protruding nail or poor fit. If your child complains of pain, consult the appropriate diagnostic chart for advice (see charts 45, 46 and 47, *Painful arm or leg, Painful joints, Foot problems*). If the limp seems to be painless, consult your doctor. Diagnostic tests such as X-rays may be needed.

*Go to next page*

*Continued from previous page*

Does your child have a purplish rash on the arms and/or the legs?

**YES** →

**NO** ↓

Is your child's temperature 38°C (100°F) or above AND/OR does he or she seem generally unwell?

**YES** →

**NO** ↓

**Consult your doctor** if you are unable to make a diagnosis from this chart and the affected joints remain painful for more than 24 hours.

Does your child have two or more of the following symptoms?
- headache
- cough
- sore throat

**YES** →

**NO**

### CONSULT YOUR DOCTOR WITHOUT DELAY!
**Henoch-Schönlein** purpura, an uncommon allergic disorder that causes inflammation of the joints and allows blood to leak under the skin – and sometimes into the gut causing abdominal pain – is a possible cause of such symptoms.

*Treatment:* Your child will probably need to undergo a variety of tests, including blood tests, before the diagnosis can be confirmed, and may be admitted to hospital. Treatment depends on the underlying cause of the condition and the severity of the case.

**A viral infection** such as flu is the most likely cause of such symptoms.

*Self-help:* Make sure that your child has plenty to drink, and give liquid paracetamol to reduce fever and relieve discomfort. Consult your doctor if pain in the joints becomes so severe that your child is reluctant to move his or her arms and legs, or if pain persists for more than 24 hours.

### CONSULT YOUR DOCTOR WITHOUT DELAY!
**Juvenile polyarthritis** (inflammation of the joints of unknown cause) is a possible explanation for joint pain in a child who seems generally unwell.

*Treatment:* To make a diagnosis your doctor may need to take samples of blood for analysis and may arrange for your child to have a chest X-ray. If the diagnosis is confirmed, your child will probably be given *anti-inflammatory* drugs. Regular exercise of the affected joints under the guidance of a physio-therapist is likely to be necessary, and your child may need to wear light splints at night for a few months.

---

### FIRST AID FOR SPRAINS AND STRAINS

A joint is said to be sprained when it is wrenched or twisted beyond its normal range of movement – in a fall, for example – so that some or all of the ligaments that support it are damaged. Ankles are especially prone to this type of injury. The main symptoms – which may be indistinguishable from those of a minor strain – are pain, swelling and bruising. If your child is unable to move or put weight on the injured part, if it looks misshapen, or if pain affects parts of the limb other than the joints, a broken bone or dislocated joint is possible, and you should carry out first aid as described on p. 107. In other cases try the following treatment:

**1** As soon as possible after the injury, cool the injured part (see right).

**2** Support an injured joint or limb with a firm, but not tight, bandage (below right). An arm or wrist may be more comfortable in a sling.

**3** Encourage your child to rest the injured part for a day or so. If it is a foot, leg or ankle that is injured, keep it raised whenever possible.

#### When to call your doctor
If your child has a badly sprained ankle that is still painful the day after the injury, you should go to your doctor or local hospital accident department to have the joint firmly bandaged to prevent movement while the injury is healing. In this case you should make sure that your child rests the joint for at least a week.

#### Cooling an injury
Applying cold to any injury that has caused pain, swelling and/or bruising will help to reduce inflammation and relieve pain. This is best done by use of an ice pack (a cloth bag filled with ice), but you can improvise an ice pack using a cloth pad soaked in cold water or an unopened packet of frozen vegetables. Alternatively, you could try immersing the injured part in cold water.

#### Bruises
Bruising occurs when damage to a blood vessel near the surface of the skin causes blood to leak into the surrounding tissues. This produces the characteristic purplish-blue colour of a bruise. Small bruises need no special treatment, but you can reduce the pain and severity of a large bruise by applying cold to the area immediately after the injury (see above).

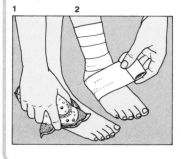

---

### BACK PROBLEMS IN CHILDHOOD

In children problems affecting the back are almost always related to injury resulting from awkward movements in sport or play, or from falls or unusual strain. Such injuries may cause pulled muscles, strained ligaments and bruising, leading to pain and stiffness. These symptoms usually disappear within a day or so without treatment.

#### Serious back injuries
If your child suffers a major injury to the back – for example, a fall from a great height **seek emergency help.** Do not attempt to move the child (see p. 285), moving the child could lead to further damage. In addition, if your child suffers from any of the following symptoms in the days following an apparently minor back injury, call your doctor at once:

- difficulty in moving a limb
- loss of bladder or bowel control
- numbness or tingling in a limb

#### Persistent back pain
If your child has persistent back pain or stiffness for more than a day or two, whether or not he or she has suffered an injury, consult your doctor.

#### Curvature of the spine
Some children are born with a sideways curvature of the spine (scoliosis) and this is usually treated in the first few years of life. However, some children develop such a curvature later on in childhood. This is particularly likely to occur in adolescence and affects girls more frequently than boys. It is important for a doctor to assess curvature of the spine as soon as possible so that, if necessary, treatment by exercises and sometimes by use of a brace on the spine can be started to correct the problem. So if you notice that your child's spine has started to curve sideways, seek medical advice. Your doctor will check the spine and if necessary send your child to a specialist for assessment.

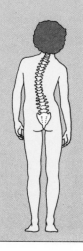

# 47 Foot problems

It is not unusual for a baby to be born with a foot or ankle that has been bent as a result of pressure within the womb. The foot can be pressed gently into position and will correct itself over the following weeks. More serious malformations, such as club foot, will be noted by the doctor at the first complete examination after birth and, if necessary, treatment will then be arranged. Consult this chart if your child develops any problem affecting one or both feet. Such problems may include pain, swelling, infection, injury, irritation or unusual appearance of the feet, such as flat feet or bent toes. Your doctor will be able to offer advice.

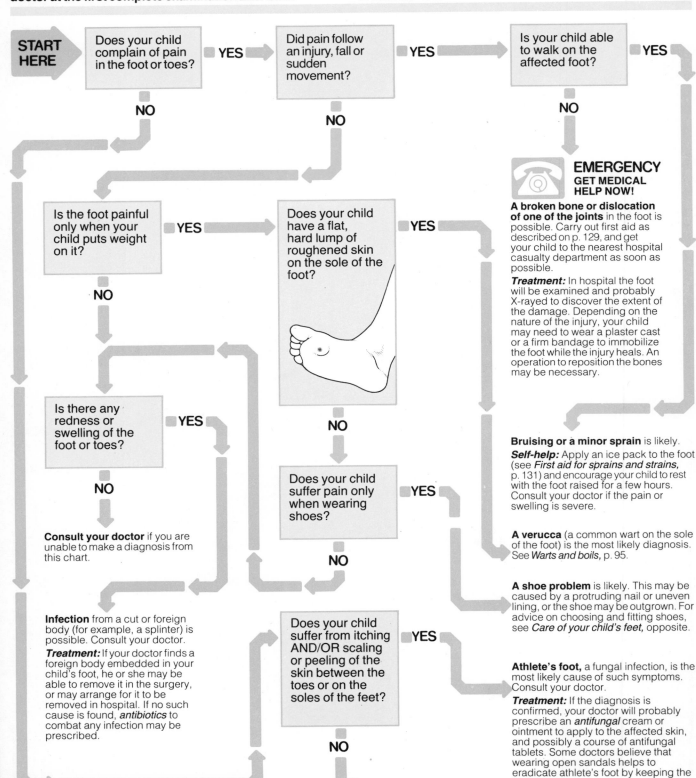

**START HERE**

Does your child complain of pain in the foot or toes? **YES** →

Did pain follow an injury, fall or sudden movement? **YES** →

Is your child able to walk on the affected foot? **YES** ↓

**NO** ↓     **NO** ↓     **NO** ↓

**EMERGENCY
GET MEDICAL HELP NOW!**

**A broken bone or dislocation of one of the joints** in the foot is possible. Carry out first aid as described on p. 129, and get your child to the nearest hospital casualty department as soon as possible.

***Treatment:*** In hospital the foot will be examined and probably X-rayed to discover the extent of the damage. Depending on the nature of the injury, your child may need to wear a plaster cast or a firm bandage to immobilize the foot while the injury heals. An operation to reposition the bones may be necessary.

Is the foot painful only when your child puts weight on it? **YES** →

Does your child have a flat, hard lump of roughened skin on the sole of the foot? **YES** →

**NO** ↓     **NO** ↓

**Bruising or a minor sprain** is likely.
***Self-help:*** Apply an ice pack to the foot (see *First aid for sprains and strains,* p. 131) and encourage your child to rest with the foot raised for a few hours. Consult your doctor if the pain or swelling is severe.

Is there any redness or swelling of the foot or toes? **YES** →

Does your child suffer pain only when wearing shoes? **YES** →

**NO** ↓     **NO** ↓

**A verucca** (a common wart on the sole of the foot) is the most likely diagnosis. See *Warts and boils,* p. 95.

**Consult your doctor** if you are unable to make a diagnosis from this chart.

**A shoe problem** is likely. This may be caused by a protruding nail or uneven lining, or the shoe may be outgrown. For advice on choosing and fitting shoes, see *Care of your child's feet,* opposite.

**Infection** from a cut or foreign body (for example, a splinter) is possible. Consult your doctor.
***Treatment:*** If your doctor finds a foreign body embedded in your child's foot, he or she may be able to remove it in the surgery, or may arrange for it to be removed in hospital. If no such cause is found, *antibiotics* to combat any infection may be prescribed.

Does your child suffer from itching AND/OR scaling or peeling of the skin between the toes or on the soles of the feet? **YES** →

**NO** ↓

**Athlete's foot,** a fungal infection, is the most likely cause of such symptoms. Consult your doctor.
***Treatment:*** If the diagnosis is confirmed, your doctor will probably prescribe an *antifungal* cream or ointment to apply to the affected skin, and possibly a course of antifungal tablets. Some doctors believe that wearing open sandals helps to eradicate athlete's foot by keeping the feet dry and cool.

*Go to next page*

*Continued from previous page*

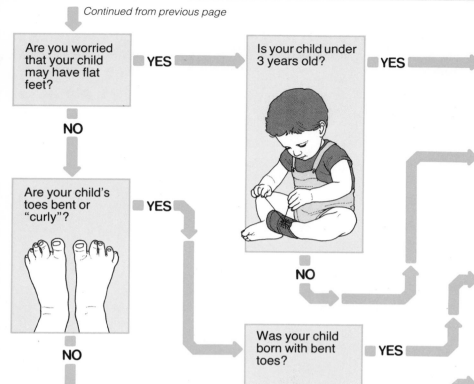

**Are you worried that your child may have flat feet?**

— YES → **Is your child under 3 years old?**

— YES → **Immaturity of the bone structure** in the foot means that the arch cannot form properly before this age. As the bones and ligaments become firmer, a normal arch will develop in most children.

NO → **Are your child's toes bent or "curly"?**

— YES →

NO →

**Flat feet** in children over 3 years old are often an inherited characteristic. This is no cause for concern as long as they cause no discomfort; flat feet should not prevent your child from participating and doing well in sports. Special exercises are almost always ineffective. If your child's feet are painful, or if you are worried, consult your doctor.

NO → **Was your child born with bent toes?**

**Congenital malformation** of the toes is rarely a cause for concern, unless it leads to pain. If the malformation is severe or seems to be troubling your child, an operation to straighten the toes may be recommended when the child is older.

— YES →

**Poorly-fitting shoes and socks** in infancy can cause a child's toes to become distorted. Make sure that you choose well-fitting shoes and socks and replace them as soon as they become too small (see *Care of your child's feet,* below).

NO →

**Consult your doctor** if you are unable to make a diagnosis from this chart.

---

## CARE OF YOUR CHILD'S FEET

The bones in the foot are not finally formed until a person is 18 years old (see right). Throughout childhood, and especially in the first 5 years of life, the bones and joints are soft and easily distorted by pressure from ill-fitting shoes and socks.

### Babies' feet
Young babies, who are not yet walking, should be left barefoot for as long as possible. If you need to cover your baby's feet to keep them warm, put on socks, soft bootees, or all-in-one suits that allow plenty of room for the toes to wriggle and stretch. Discard these as soon as the feet fill them.
   When your child starts to walk, delay buying shoes until your child is steady on his or her feet and needs shoes for protection when walking outside. Allow your child to walk barefoot inside the house whenever possible.

### Choosing and fitting your child's shoes
Well-fitting shoes in childhood are essential for healthy feet and toes in adult life. The main points to remember when choosing shoes for your child are listed below.

- Have your child's feet measured at regular intervals – at least every 3 months – throughout childhood. More frequent measuring may be necessary at times of rapid growth.
- Where possible go to a shop where the assistants are trained to fit children's shoes.
- Choose shoes that are available in a variety of width fittings and that have adjustable fastenings over the instep.
- When you buy new shoes, make sure that there is about 2cm (¾in) between the longest toe and the end of the shoe.
- Choose a style that has a straight inside edge and allows adequate room across the toes. Fashion shoes – especially those with raised heels – should be kept for special occasions only.
- If you can afford them, leather shoes are best; but even though these are expensive, do not be tempted to delay replacing them when they are outgrown. It would be better to buy cheaper shoes that you can afford to replace more often.

1 year

5 years

18 years

- Remember that tight socks may also damage young feet, and you should take care to replace socks when they become too small.
- Shoes that are painful as soon as your child puts them on or after an hour or so are probably a poor fit and are likely to be damaging your child's feet.

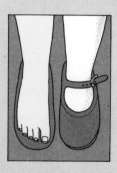

**Fitting shoes**
A salesperson will accurately measure the length and width (top left) of your child's foot and check that the shoes fit well, with about (2 cm) ¾ in. or a finger's width, to spare between the toes and the end of the shoes (top and bottom right).

### Everyday care
When you wash your child's feet, be careful to dry them thoroughly, especially between the toes, to reduce the likelihood of infections such as athlete's foot. Trim the toenails regularly (see *Nail care,* p. 93).

# 48 Genital problems in boys

Consult this chart if your son develops any pain or swelling within the scrotum (the supportive bag that encloses the testes) or in the penis. For example, your son may find urinating painful, or may complain of pain following a groin injury. In all cases consult your doctor. Severe pain in the genital area is a matter of urgency.

**START HERE**

Does your son have a painful swelling within the scrotum?

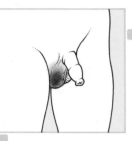

**YES** →

**NO** ↓

Has he recently had an injury to the genital area?

**YES** →

**EMERGENCY GET MEDICAL HELP NOW!**

**Internal damage** to the testes is possible if pain does not subside within a few minutes of injury to the genital area.

*Treatment:* Your son should be taken to hospital, where he will be carefully examined. In some cases no special treatment is needed, but in others an operation to repair the damage may be necessary.

**NO** ↓

Does your son have a painless swelling inside the scrotum?

**YES** →

**Painless swelling** of the scrotum may be the result of inguinal hernia, in which a portion of the intestine pushes through a weak section in the abdominal wall into the scrotum. Alternatively, it may be due to a cyst (fluid-filled sac) or to the accumulation of fluid inside the scrotum. Consult your doctor.

*Treatment:* If your doctor diagnoses a hernia, this will be corrected by a simple operation. If your child is found to have a cyst or an accumulation of fluid inside the scrotum, the fluid may be drained by syringe or removed by a minor operation.

**NO** ↓

Has your son had mumps within the past 2 weeks?

**YES** →

**Orchitis** (inflammation of the testes) may sometimes occur as a result of mumps. This is rare in young children, but occurs more frequently in adolescents. Consult your doctor.

*Treatment:* If your doctor confirms the diagnosis after examining your son, he or she will prescribe painkillers, and possibly an anti-inflammatory drug. It may be helpful to apply warmth to the genital area with a hot-water bottle wrapped in a thick towel.

**NO** ↓

Does your child have pain in the penis only during urination?

**YES** →

**An infection of the urinary tract** may cause pain in the penis during urination. Consult your doctor.

*Treatment:* Your doctor will probably need a specimen of your child's urine for analysis (see *Collecting a mid-stream specimen,* p. 125). If he is found to have a urinary tract infection, he will probably be prescribed a course of *antibiotics*. You will probably be advised to ensure that your child drinks plenty of fluids during this treatment.

**NO** ↓

**EMERGENCY GET MEDICAL HELP NOW!**

**Torsion of the testis** (twisting of the testis inside the scrotum) is a possible cause of unexplained pain and swelling. This can happen at any time, even during sleep, and may be accompanied by nausea and vomiting.

*Treatment:* Your child will need to be examined in hospital. If the diagnosis is confirmed, a doctor may try to untwist the testis by gently manipulating it. If this is not successful, emergency surgery may be necessary. The results of such surgery are usually good.

**UNDESCENDED TESTES**

Undescended testes is a condition also known as cryptorchidism, in which one or both of the testes — which normally descend into the scrotum shortly before birth — remain inside the abdomen. In such cases, the testes usually descend of their own accord within the first few years. However, if they have not descended by the time a boy is 5 years old, an operation to lower the testes into the scrotum may be necessary. Your child's future fertility and sex life should not be affected.

*Go to next page*

*Continued from previous page*

Does your child have soreness or swelling of the tip of the penis?

**YES**

**Balanitis** (inflammation of the tip of the penis) may be caused by irritation from friction with damp underclothing or over-zealous or inadequate washing. Consult your doctor.

*Treatment:* If balanitis is diagnosed, your doctor will probably prescribe a soothing cream to apply to the penis, and may advise you to add a mild antiseptic to your child's bath water. While the skin is inflamed, your son should avoid using soap to wash his penis.

**NO**

**A foreign body in the urethra** (see the box below) is the most common cause of discharge in a young child. Consult your doctor.

Does your child have a greyish-yellow discharge from the penis?

**YES**

## OVERTIGHT FORESKIN

The foreskin (the fold of skin that covers the tip of the penis) cannot normally be drawn back during the first few years of life, and you should not try to draw it back when washing your baby. Usually the foreskin becomes looser and more easily retracted as the child grows older. However, in a small proportion of cases the foreskin remains tight and may cause pain, particularly during an erection. This condition is known as phimosis and is normally treated by *circumcision* (below).

**NO**

**Consult your doctor** if you are unable to make a diagnosis from this chart.

## CIRCUMCISION

This is a surgical operation to remove the foreskin (the fold of skin that covers the tip of the penis). Occasionally the operation is carried out for medical reasons – for example, if the foreskin is overtight (see above). However, most circumcisions in infancy are performed for social and religious reasons.

Circumcision does not necessarily improve hygiene; adequate cleanliness can be maintained by ensuring that once your son is old enough, he learns to wash all secretions from beneath his foreskin. Like any operation, circumcision carries a small risk; most doctors now advise against the operation unless it is medically necessary.

## FOREIGN BODY IN THE URETHRA

Occasionally, a young child may push a small object into the urethral opening. If this is not promptly expelled during urination, it may lead to infection, which produces a greyish-yellow discharge from the penis. If you notice that your child has such a discharge consult your doctor. If there is a foreign body in the urethra, it may need to be removed by a minor operation under local anaesthetic.

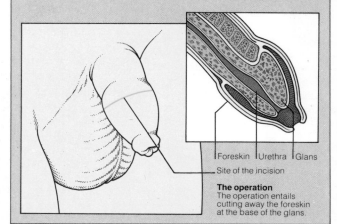

Foreskin  Urethra  Glans

Site of the incision

**The operation**
The operation entails cutting away the foreskin at the base of the glans.

# 49 Genital problems in girls

The most common genital problem in young girls is itching and inflammation of the vulva (the external genital area). This may be caused by infection or by irritation from soaps or other substances, and may lead to pain during urination. Your daughter may also be worried by an unusual vaginal discharge. Consult this diagnostic chart if you or your daughter notice any such problems.

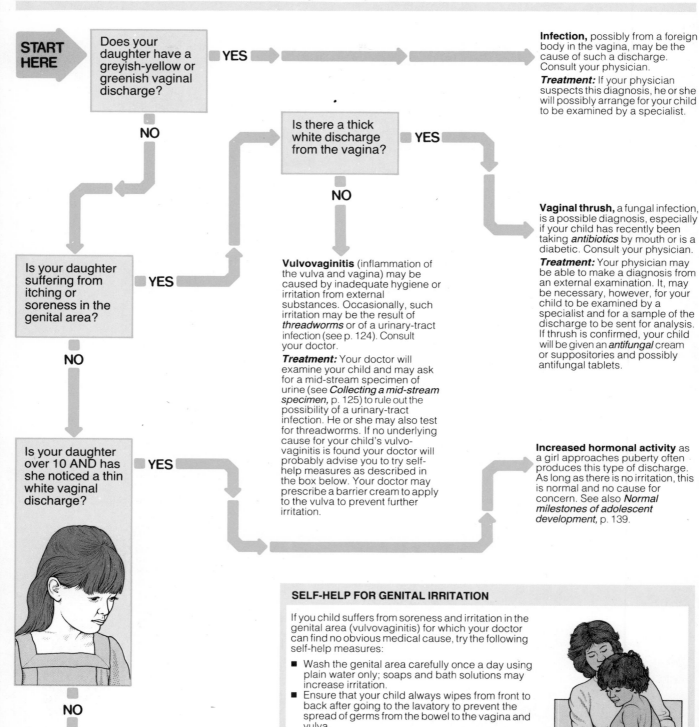

**START HERE**

**Does your daughter have a greyish-yellow or greenish vaginal discharge?**

YES → **Infection,** possibly from a foreign body in the vagina, may be the cause of such a discharge. Consult your physician.

*Treatment:* If your physician suspects this diagnosis, he or she will possibly arrange for your child to be examined by a specialist.

NO ↓

**Is there a thick white discharge from the vagina?**

YES → **Vaginal thrush,** a fungal infection, is a possible diagnosis, especially if your child has recently been taking *antibiotics* by mouth or is a diabetic. Consult your physician.

*Treatment:* Your physician may be able to make a diagnosis from an external examination. It, may be necessary, however, for your child to be examined by a specialist and for a sample of the discharge to be sent for analysis. If thrush is confirmed, your child will be given an *antifungal* cream or suppositories and possibly antifungal tablets.

NO ↓

**Is your daughter suffering from itching or soreness in the genital area?**

YES → **Vulvovaginitis** (inflammation of the vulva and vagina) may be caused by inadequate hygiene or irritation from external substances. Occasionally, such irritation may be the result of *threadworms* or of a urinary-tract infection (see p. 124). Consult your doctor.

*Treatment:* Your doctor will examine your child and may ask for a mid-stream specimen of urine (see *Collecting a mid-stream specimen,* p. 125) to rule out the possibility of a urinary-tract infection. He or she may also test for threadworms. If no underlying cause for your child's vulvo-vaginitis is found your doctor will probably advise you to try self-help measures as described in the box below. Your doctor may prescribe a barrier cream to apply to the vulva to prevent further irritation.

NO ↓

**Is your daughter over 10 AND has she noticed a thin white vaginal discharge?**

YES → **Increased hormonal activity** as a girl approaches puberty often produces this type of discharge. As long as there is no irritation, this is normal and no cause for concern. See also *Normal milestones of adolescent development,* p. 139.

NO ↓

**Consult your doctor** if you are unable to make a diagnosis from this chart.

---

**SELF-HELP FOR GENITAL IRRITATION**

If you child suffers from soreness and irritation in the genital area (vulvovaginitis) for which your doctor can find no obvious medical cause, try the following self-help measures:

- Wash the genital area carefully once a day using plain water only; soaps and bath solutions may increase irritation.
- Ensure that your child always wipes from front to back after going to the lavatory to prevent the spread of germs from the bowel to the vagina and vulva.
- Change your child's underpants daily. If possible use only those made of cotton or with a cotton gusset. Be especially careful to rinse all traces of detergent from your child's underpants when you wash them.

# Children: adolescents

# 50 Delayed puberty

Puberty is the stage of development during which children undergo the physical changes that mark their transition into adulthood. Both sexes show a marked increase in height and weight and the apocrine sweat glands become active. In girls physical changes include the development of secondary sexual characteristics such as breasts and pubic and underarm hair, as well as the onset of menstruation (monthly periods). Boys start to develop facial and other body hair, the voice deepens, and the genitals become larger. The age at which an individual child reaches puberty is primarily a matter of inheritance – for example, a girl whose mother started her periods late is also likely to be a late developer, or a boy who has been taller than average throughout childhood is likely to reach puberty sooner than shorter, less heavy boys. The ages at which the various changes of puberty usually occur in girls and boys are shown in the table opposite. In most cases, later than average onset of puberty is no cause for medical concern. However, the delay may be linked to an underlying condition. Consult this diagnostic chart if your child seems abnormally late in reaching puberty.

## GIRLS

**START HERE**

Has your daughter had her first period?

**YES** →

**The start of menstruation** is a clear sign that the hormonal activity that governs sexual development is operating normally. Any cause for medical concern is extremely unlikely, even if, for example, your daughter's breasts seem small or growth of pubic hair seems sparse. It is common for periods to be irregular at first and they may cease for several months at a time; this is not a cause for worry unless your child shows other signs of ill health.

**NO**

Has she shown either of the following signs of puberty?
- appearance of pubic hair
- breast and/or nipple enlargement

**YES** →

**Such early signs of hormonal activity** tend to precede the first period and are usually a sign that a girl is developing normally. Consult your doctor only if your daughter has not had a period by the time she is 14.

**NO**

Is she less than 14 years old?

**YES** →

**Later than average development** is generally no cause for concern in this age range. Many girls, especially if they are smaller than average, do not show marked signs of sexual development until their early teens. Consult your doctor if your daughter has not had her first period by the time she is 14, or if she is growing more slowly than expected according to the charts on p. 298-301.

**NO**

**Delay in the onset of puberty** is usually the result of a normal inherited characteristic. However, it may also be caused by poor general health, certain forms of drug treatment, and, in rare cases, hormonal or chromosomal abnormalities. Consult your doctor.

**Treatment:** Your doctor will examine your daughter – and may need to carry out an internal (vaginal) examination. He or she may also take a blood sample to assess the level of hormones and chromosomal characteristics. In most cases, your doctor will be able to reassure you that all is well. Occasionally it may be necessary to refer the child to a specialist for diagnosis and possible treatment with hormones.

## BOYS

**START HERE**

Is your son under 12 years old?

**YES** →

**Few of the changes of puberty** are obvious at this age in the majority of boys, and there is certainly no cause for concern if your boy is still child-like. He may seem to be lagging behind in development if any of his male friends are unusually early developers or in comparison with girls of the same age – girls reach puberty sooner than boys.

**NO**

Has your son shown either of the following physical signs of the onset of puberty?
- enlargement of the genitals
- growth of pubic and/or other body hair

**YES** →

**The appearance of either one of these signs** of increased hormonal activity is a sure indication that your child has entered puberty, even if other changes are not yet obvious. The different milestones do not always occur in the precise order described in the table opposite, and any variation has no effect on an adolescent's long-term development.

**NO**

Is your son under 14 years old?

**YES** →

**Late development** within a broad age range is seldom any cause for concern. It is likely that late onset of puberty is a family characteristic and/or that your child was smaller than average throughout childhood. Less common causes of late development include prolonged periods of illness in childhood and certain forms of drug treatment. Consult your doctor only if your son shows no signs of puberty by the time he is 14 or if he is growing abnormally slowly according to the charts on p. 298-301.

**NO**

**Delay in the onset of puberty** after the age of 14 is unusual and may be the result of underlying hormone deficiency or chromosomal abnormality. Consult your doctor.

**Treatment:** Your doctor will examine your son and may arrange for blood tests so that hormone levels can be measured and chromosomal characteristics checked. If such tests reveal that your son is deficient in any hormone, artificial supplements of that hormone will be prescribed. Such treatment ensures that puberty progresses normally.

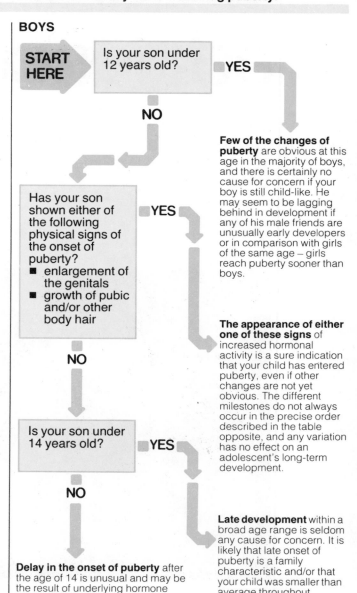

## NORMAL MILESTONES OF ADOLESCENT DEVELOPMENT

### GIRLS

| Aspect of development | Age at which change usually begins | Age at which rapid change usually ceases | Description of the changes |
|---|---|---|---|
| Increase in height and weight | 10–11 | 14–15 | In childhood growth continues at an average rate of 5cm (2in) a year. One of the earliest signs of puberty is an increase in this rate up to a maximum of about 9cm (4in) a year. The growth spurt may last for up to 4 years, but is most rapid in the first two years (see the growth charts on p. 298-301). There is a parallel increase in weight; the pelvis broadens and fat is deposited around the hips and thighs. |
| Breast development | 10–12 | 13–15 | The first stage of breast development is usually the enlargement of the nipple and areola (the coloured area surrounding the nipple). This is known as "budding". A year or so later the breasts themselves start to enlarge and the nipples and areola darken. Breast development normally ceases by the age of 15. |
| Growth of pubic and underarm hair | pubic 10–11 underarm 12–13 | Pubic 14–15 underarm 15–16 | Pubic hair normally first starts to appear as a light down around the external genital area. The hair gradually darkens and coarsens over the next 2–3 years and spreads to cover the pubic mound. Underarm hair appears 1–2 years after the emergence of pubic hair. The precise extent, colour and thickness of body hair growth depends on inheritance and racial type. |
| Development of apocrine sweat glands | 12–13 | 15–16 | Apocrine sweat glands produce a different type of sweat from that produced by the eccrine glands that are active all over the body from babyhood. Apocrine glands become active under the arms, in the groin, and around the nipples during adolescence. These produce a type of sweat that may lead to body odour if not regularly washed away. |
| Onset of menstruation | First period (menarche) 11–14 | Establishment of regular cycle 15–16 | In the UK the average age for the occurrence of the menarche (first period) is 13. It usually happens about 2 years after the start of the growth spurt and is unlikely to occur until a girl weighs at least 45kg (7 stone). A girl may notice a thin white vaginal discharge in the year preceding the menarche. In the first few years following the menarche periods are likely to be irregular and may cease altogether for several months. A regular monthly cycle has usually become established by the age of 16. |

### BOYS

| Increase in height and weight | 12 – 13 | 17 – 18 | In childhood growth continues at the rate of about 5cm (2in) a year. One of the earliest signs of puberty is an increase in this rate to up to 10cm (4in) a year for 2 – 3 years. Growth may continue at a slower rate up to the age of 20. Weight increases at a parallel rate (see the growth charts on p. 298-301). A boy's body also starts to develop adult proportions; the shoulders and chest broaden and the trunk lengthens. The muscles on the arms and legs enlarge. Parents may notice a great increase in their child's appetite during this period of rapid growth. |
|---|---|---|---|
| Genital development and ejaculation | 11 – 13 | 15 – 17 | Hormonal activity at the start of puberty stimulates the development of the male sex glands, the testes, leading to a noticeable increase in their size. The skin of the scrotum darkens and the penis lengthens and broadens. The ability to ejaculate seminal fluid usually develops within 2 years of such genital development. |
| Growth of body and facial hair | 11 – 15 | 15 – 19 | The growth of hair in the genital (pubic) area normally starts first and is followed a year or so later by the growth of hair on the face, under the arms, and, depending on inherited character-istics, in other areas of the body such as the legs, chest, and abdomen. |
| Development of apocrine sweat glands | 13 – 15 | 17 – 18 | Apocrine sweat glands produce a different type of sweat from that produced by the eccrine glands that are found all over the body from babyhood. Apocrine glands start to develop under the arms, in the groin and around the nipples during adolescence. These produce a type of sweat that may lead to body odour if not regularly washed away. |
| Deepening of the voice | 13 – 15 | 16 – 17 | The voice box (larynx) starts to enlarge and may develop into a noticeable "Adam's apple". The voice deepens ("breaks") within a year or so of such enlargement. |

## EMOTIONAL DEVELOPMENT

The physical changes of puberty are accompanied by psychological changes that are also triggered by the secretion of sex hormones. In both boys and girls these hormones stimulate interest in sexuality. Rising levels of the male hormone testosterone are thought to play a part in the increased aggression and adventurousness typical of teenage boys. The increased output of hormones by the adrenal glands also influences behaviour by increasing natural assertiveness, which helps to explain why teenagers have a tendency to be rebellious and argumentative.

Late physical development is often accompanied by delayed emotional maturity. This can cause social and psychological difficulties for the child, who has come to terms with being smaller, less physically developed, and less assertive than most of his or her contemporaries, at least for a year or two.

# 51 Adolescent behaviour problems

Adolescence, the transitional period between childhood and adulthood, is a time when difficult behaviour and conflict with parents and other people who represent authority is most likely to arise. The reasons for this may be partly physiological in that the child is experiencing new and perhaps confusing feelings as a result of the hormonal activity that starts at puberty. However, there are also social and psychological factors, including the child's need to develop both practical and emotional independence from his or her parents. Few families with adolescent children escape a certain number of arguments and misunderstandings – usually about dress, language, or general conduct – but

providing that the parents allow sufficient flexibility while retaining a recognizable and affectionate family framework, family relationships are unlikely to suffer permanent damage. Most adolescent behaviour problems can be successfully resolved within the family. However, if you feel that any behaviour problem is getting outside your control, to the extent that you fear that your adolescent child may be endangering his or her health or risking conflict with the law, it is a good idea to discuss the problem with your doctor. Although medical treatment is only rarely appropriate, the doctor may be able to offer helpful advice and/or put you in touch with relevant support services.

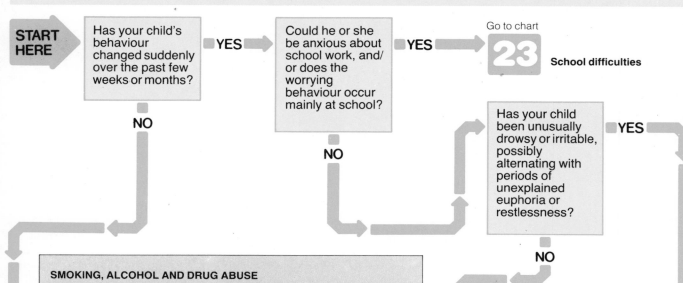

**START HERE** → Has your child's behaviour changed suddenly over the past few weeks or months? — **YES** → Could he or she be anxious about school work, and/or does the worrying behaviour occur mainly at school? — **YES** → Go to chart **23** School difficulties

(Has your child's behaviour changed...) **NO**

(Could he or she be anxious...) **NO**

Has your child been unusually drowsy or irritable, possibly alternating with periods of unexplained euphoria or restlessness? — **YES**

(Has your child been unusually drowsy...) **NO**

## SMOKING, ALCOHOL AND DRUG ABUSE

Most adolescents try smoking cigarettes at some stage, and many will also experiment with various artificial stimulants such as alcohol, drugs (including cannabis, tranquillizers, and occasionally even "hard" drugs such as heroin), and solvent fumes (including glue and cleaning fluids). Whether or not such experimentation develops into a major health risk for your child depends on a number of factors, such as the kind of example you have set your child – for instance, you smoke or drink regularly yourself – how prevalent the use of such substances is among your child's friends, and whether or not your child has an underlying emotional difficulty that may lead him or her to seek to escape through alcohol or the use of drugs.

### Cigarette smoking
Although smoking is unlikely to damage your child's health in the short term, it is one of the most serious risks to health in adult life. Because the habit is easily established in adolescence, it is essential for parents to make every effort to discourage smoking through their own example and by ensuring that their child is fully aware of the risks from an early age.

### Alcohol abuse
Alcohol can be dangerous for young people, whether as a result of a single "binge" in which too much alcohol is drunk, or as a regular habit. If you drink yourselves, it is unreasonable to try to ban your teenager from drinking at all. However, you can try to ensure that he or she learns to drink sensibly by limiting alcoholic drinks to special occasions or small amounts at some mealtimes. Drinking to excess should always be clearly discouraged.

### Drugs and solvent abuse
This is the problem that often causes parents most worry. Arm yourself and your child with the facts about the dangers of drug-taking well before you think there may be any risk of your child being tempted to try any of these substances. Advice based on sound information is likely to be treated with greater respect than reactions based on instinctive fear of the problem. And an atmosphere in which a child feels free to talk about the subject may encourage your child to confide in you if he or she feels under pressure from friends to try drugs. Always consult your doctor if you fear your child is taking drugs of any kind.

**Drug abuse, drinking alcohol, or inhaling solvents** ("glue sniffing") are all possible explanations for this type of behaviour, especially if your child always seems short of money and has any additional symptoms such as slurred speech, excessive sweating, or abnormally large or small pupils.

*Self-help:* This worrying problem for parents should always be tackled as soon as you suspect there may be any cause for concern. Talk to your child and try to find out whether or not your suspicions are correct. If your child admits to drinking or taking drugs of any kind, you will obviously try to convince him or her of the dangers of this type of behaviour. If you are unable to do this because of difficulties in communication or because you do not feel sufficiently well-informed, consult your doctor, who may be able to talk to your child more easily than you and will in any case be able to offer sound advice. If your child denies drug-taking, it is also worthwhile seeking medical advice, because this type of behaviour may also indicate an underlying emotional problem. (See also *Smoking, alcohol and drug abuse,* opposite).

1 *Go to next page, column 1*

2 *Go to next page, column 2*

**1** Continued from previous page, column 1

**2** Continued from previous page, column 2

Has your child seemed in unusually low spirits for some time, eating little, sleeping badly, and isolating him- or herself from family and friends?

**YES** →

**NO** ↓

Could your child have any cause for worry – for example, conflict between parents or other family members or difficulties in a relationship with a girlfriend or boyfriend?

**YES** →

**NO** ↓

Does your child's worrying behaviour concern his or her eating habits?

**YES** →

**NO** ↓

Are you concerned because your child seems to have few friends and spends much of his or her spare time alone?

**YES** →

**NO** ↓

Are you worried by hostility, rebelliousness and/or disregard for your feelings in your child?

**YES** →

**NO** ↓

**Consult your doctor** if the problem that worries you is not covered in this chart.

**Periods of depression** are common during adolescence and normally pass within a week or so. But prolonged depression is not normal and may be rooted in some underlying anxiety or emotional difficulty. Consult your doctor.

**Treatment:** If your doctor feels there is any cause for concern after talking to your child, he or she may recommend that the child sees a child psychiatrist. Further treatment will depend on the cause of the depression, but may include discussions involving the whole family and, occasionally, drug treatment. (See also *Child guidance,* p. 89).

**Faddishness** about food is common, particularly among adolescent girls who may either experiment with "cranky" diets or eat excessively. You need not be concerned unless your child has become either excessively thin or overweight. (See *Food fads,* p. 118).

See also chart

 **53** **Adolescent weight problems**

Are your most frequent disagreements about clothes, personal appearance and/or language?

**YES** →

**NO** ↓

**Rebelliousness** is a normal part of an adolescent's development into an independent individual, and parents must learn to accept that they cannot expect the same level of obedience in all matters from an adolescent as they can from a younger child.

**Self-help:** Trying to enforce too many rules of behaviour may only deepen and prolong any conflict, so try to limit the number of ground rules you insist on to those that are important for your child's health and safety or for the well-being of the rest of the family. Whenever possible, allow your child to make decisions and take responsibility for matters affecting his or her own life, so as to reduce potential areas of conflict and encourage independence.

**Anxiety** about a specific problem can cause an adolescent to behave out of character. Unusual behaviour may include aggressiveness, sullenness, rudeness, or at the other end of the spectrum, childishness or over-dependence on the parents.

**Self-help:** As with most adolescent behaviour problems, you should start by discussing the matter directly with your child. You may be able to discover the cause of the problem and at the same time allay any fears or take practical steps to resolve the problem yourself. However, if you are unable to help your child or if you have difficulty discovering the reason for your child's changed behaviour, consult your doctor, who will be able to offer specific advice.

**Natural shyness** or solitariness may be a normal part of your child's personality and this will not suddenly change during adolescence. However, if you suspect that there may be an underlying cause for your child's withdrawn behaviour – for example, self-consciousness about a physical problem such as severe acne or being overweight – you should try to deal with it.

**Self-help:** If your child seems shy, try to ensure that he or she has plenty of opportunity to participate in activities that he or she enjoys, perhaps with the rest of the family or where there is a chance to meet other young people who share similar interests. If the child has a skin or weight problem consult chart 53, *Adolescent weight problems* or chart 52, *Adolescent skin problems.*

**Looking and sounding like their contemporaries** is important to most adolescents. It gives them a separate identity and the security of feeling that they belong to a group. Although extremes of dress or bad language can be distressing for parents, such behaviour is rarely a cause for concern providing that it does not lead, for example, to conflict with school authorities.

**Self-help:** It is best to ignore such behaviour whenever possible, only insisting that your child conforms when it may cause offence to others. Most young people eventually learn to compromise between expressing themselves in dress and language as they like and the need in some circumstances to conform.

# 52 Adolescent skin problems

The onset of adolescence often produces marked changes in the skin. Infantile eczema, which often affects younger children, may clear up altogether during adolescence. But another form of eczema may occur for the first time as a result of contact with certain metals or cosmetics, causing an itchy red rash. In addition, certain skin problems caused by infection or infestation may become more common as a result of close contact with other teenagers. However, the most noticeable skin changes during adolescence are caused by rising levels of sex hormones which encourage the sebaceous glands in the skin to produce increasing amounts of sebum – an oily substance that helps to lubricate and protect the skin. Not only does increased sebaceous activity give the skin an oily appearance, but it encourages the development of acne, the principal skin condition affecting adolescents. There are several different types of acne and the condition may occur with varying degrees of severity. Consult this diagnostic chart if you are uncertain what, if any, treatment is feasible for your adolescent's acne or greasy skin. For other skin problems, see Chart 25, Spots and rashes.

**START HERE**

Does your child have either of the following symptoms?
■ Inflamed red spots with white centres
■ Red lumps under the skin

**YES** → Do the spots occur over a wide area of the face, chest or back?

**NO** ↓

Is your child worried by increasing oiliness of the skin?

**YES** →

**NO** ↓

**Consult your doctor** if your adolescent's problem is not covered in this chart.

**Greasy skin** is no cause for medical concern if it does not lead to acne. However, it may embarrass your child.
**Self-help:** Regular washing with mild soap and water is normally all that is needed to keep greasy skin under control. An astringent "skin freshening" lotion may also be helpful.

Do the spots occur over a wide area of the face, chest or back?

**YES** →

**NO** ↓

Do the spots seem to be leaving scars on the skin?

**YES** →

**NO** ↓

**Mild acne** can usually be controlled by self-help measures (see right).

**Severe acne,** especially if it embarrasses your child or if there is any sign of scarring, should always receive professional treatment. Consult your doctor.
**Treatment:** Your doctor will examine your child's skin and will probably recommend some of the self-help treatments described in the box opposite. In addition, depending on the severity with which your child is affected, your doctor may refer your child to a skin specialist (dermatologist) and/or prescribe *antibiotics* or other forms of treatment as outlined opposite.

## ACNE

Acne is the name used to describe a group of related skin symptoms that mainly affect the face, chest and upper back. It is caused by blockage and infection of hair follicles in the skin, principally during adolescence when hormonal activity increases the production of sebum (natural skin oil) which makes the skin more susceptible to this disorder.

**Symptoms**
There are several main types of acne spot. The following are most common:
**Blackheads:** See below left.
**Pustules:** Inflamed raised spots with white centres. They are caused by bacterial activity in sebum which has collected in a hair follicle.
**Cysts:** Tender, inflamed lumps under the skin that are caused by scar tissue forming around an inflamed area under the skin. Cystic acne spots may leave permanent scars.

**Self-help**
Mild acne can usually be controlled by means of the following preparations that are available over-the-counter from chemists:
**Antibacterial skin-washing creams, lotions, and soaps:** These may help mild acne by reducing bacterial activity in the skin.
**Sulphur or benzoyl peroxide preparations:** These can help moderately severe acne, but should be used cautiously because they can make the skin sore.
**Abrasives and keratolytics:** These remove the top layer of skin and help to clear both blocked hair follicles and blackheads. However, these products should not be used too often or too vigorously. They may not be suitable if the skin is severely inflamed.

In addition to the above treatments, many people find that exposure to sunlight helps to reduce acne.

**Professional treatment**
When self-help measures are ineffective, or if acne is severe enough to cause embarrassment or scarring, your doctor may prescribe one or more of the following treatments:
**Keratolytics:** These may be stronger than the over-the-counter preparations described above but act in a similar way.
**Antibiotics:** These are given by mouth in low doses over an extended period. They help to counter bacterial activity in the skin and often produce a marked improvement in severe cases of acne.
**Other drugs:** Various drugs including hormone and vitamin A derivatives are sometimes prescribed for adults with severe acne, but your doctor may be reluctant to prescribe them for those in their early teens.

## BLACKHEADS

Blackheads are tiny black spots that usually occur principally around the nose and chin. They are caused by dead skin cells and sebum collecting in a hair follicle and becoming discoloured by exposure to air. They may occur together with the more disfiguring forms of acne spot or on their own. If your adolescent child is affected only by blackheads, treatment is unlikely to be necessary. However, if widespread blackheads are causing embarrassment, they can be removed individually by means of a blackhead remover or by use of abrasives or keratolytic preparations (see *Acne,* right). Squeezing of blackheads by hand may lead to infection.

# 53 Adolescent weight problems

The rapid increase in height that occurs in adolescence and the development of adult body proportions can lead a teenager to appear either too thin or too fat. Adolescence is also a time when young people are likely to be particularly sensitive about their appearance, and many worry about it unnecessarily. Girls are more likely than boys to be concerned about minor changes in weight. They are also much more likely to be affected by anorexia nervosa (see below), the most serious weight-related disorder of adolescence. However, although boys less commonly become seriously underweight,

they are often overweight; in such cases helpful and sympathetic advice from parents is just as important as for girls. The best way to discover whether or not your child's changing body shape indicates unhealthy weight gain or loss is to check that both weight and height are increasing at a parallel rate as indicated in the weight charts on p. 298-301. Minor deviations from standard growth curves are unlikely to be a cause for concern, but you should consult this chart if your child is more than 3kg (5lb) heavier or lighter than would be expected for his or her age and height.

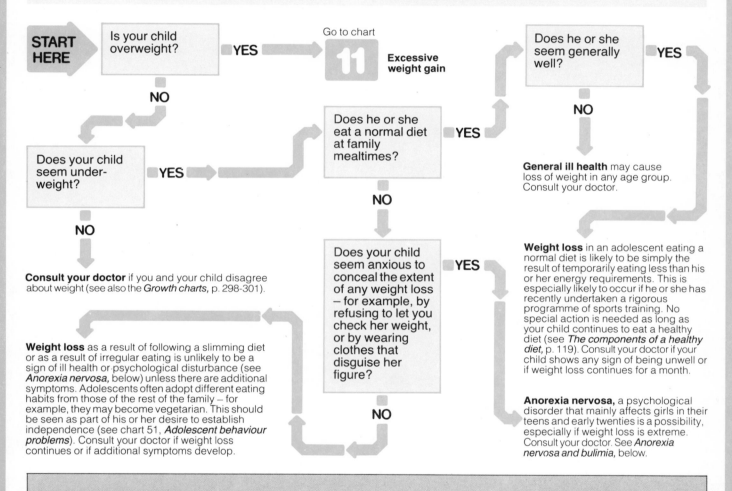

**START HERE**

**Is your child overweight?** — YES → Go to chart **11** *Excessive weight gain*

NO ↓

**Does your child seem underweight?** — YES →

NO ↓

**Consult your doctor** if you and your child disagree about weight (see also the *Growth charts,* p. 298-301).

**Weight loss** as a result of following a slimming diet or as a result of irregular eating is unlikely to be a sign of ill health or psychological disturbance (see *Anorexia nervosa,* below) unless there are additional symptoms. Adolescents often adopt different eating habits from those of the rest of the family – for example, they may become vegetarian. This should be seen as part of his or her desire to establish independence (see chart 51, *Adolescent behaviour problems*). Consult your doctor if weight loss continues or if additional symptoms develop.

**Does he or she eat a normal diet at family mealtimes?** — YES →

NO ↓

**Does your child seem anxious to conceal the extent of any weight loss – for example, by refusing to let you check her weight, or by wearing clothes that disguise her figure?** — YES →

NO ↓

**Does he or she seem generally well?** — YES →

NO ↓

**General ill health** may cause loss of weight in any age group. Consult your doctor.

**Weight loss** in an adolescent eating a normal diet is likely to be simply the result of temporarily eating less than his or her energy requirements. This is especially likely to occur if he or she has recently undertaken a rigorous programme of sports training. No special action is needed as long as your child continues to eat a healthy diet (see *The components of a healthy diet,* p. 119). Consult your doctor if your child shows any sign of being unwell or if weight loss continues for a month.

**Anorexia nervosa,** a psychological disorder that mainly affects girls in their teens and early twenties is a possibility, especially if weight loss is extreme. Consult your doctor. See *Anorexia nervosa and bulimia,* below.

---

### ANOREXIA NERVOSA AND BULIMIA

Anorexia nervosa is a psychological disturbance in which a person (most commonly a teenage girl or young woman) refuses food because of an irrational fear of putting on weight. An anorectic convinces herself that she is too fat, that she has not lost enough weight even though she has become very thin. Many girls go through a temporary phase of excessive dieting, but only a few develop anorexia nervosa.

#### The signs of anorexia
The illness usually starts with normal dieting, but an anorectic eats less and less each day and even if her figure becomes skeletal she still sees herself as plump and is terrified of putting on weight. She may be reluctant to undress or weigh herself in front of others in order to conceal her weight loss. To avoid family pressure to eat sensibly she may hide food and throw it away.

As weight loss progresses there may be hormonal disturbances that result in cessation of menstrual periods.

She may also become depressed and withdrawn.

In the variant of the disorder known as bulimia, the girl has binges of overeating in which she may consume vast amounts of ice cream, cake or soft drinks; she then makes herself vomit to avoid gaining weight. It may be very difficult for you to distinguish between bulimia and anorexia nervosa, because both disorders involve secrecy in eating habits and conflict about meals.

#### What action should you take?
If your adolescent child has an unrealistic image of herself as being too fat and seems to be dieting excessively, although already very thin, you should discuss the matter with your doctor. If, after examining your child, your doctor thinks that she may be suffering from anorexia nervosa, he or she will probably arrange for treatment by a specialist in psychological disorders. In severe cases it may be necessary to admit your child to hospital where food intake can be closely supervised.

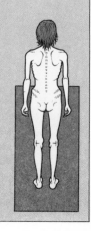

# 2 General medical: men and women

# 54 Feeling under the weather

Sometimes you may have a vague, generalized feeling of being unwell without being able to locate a specific symptom such as pain. This is usually the result of a minor infection or unhealthy lifestyle, but occasionally it may be a sign of a more serious underlying problem that requires medical treatment.

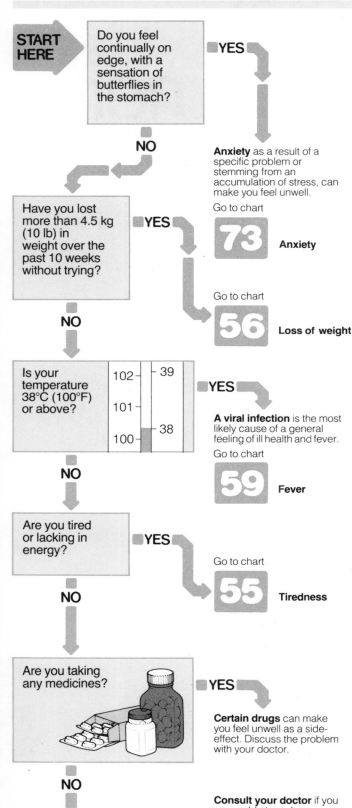

**START HERE**

Do you feel continually on edge, with a sensation of butterflies in the stomach?

**YES** → **Anxiety** as a result of a specific problem or stemming from an accumulation of stress, can make you feel unwell.

Go to chart **73** Anxiety

**NO**

Have you lost more than 4.5 kg (10 lb) in weight over the past 10 weeks without trying?

**YES** → Go to chart **56** Loss of weight

**NO**

Is your temperature 38°C (100°F) or above?

102 — 39
101 —
100 — 38

**YES** → **A viral infection** is the most likely cause of a general feeling of ill health and fever.

Go to chart **59** Fever

**NO**

Are you tired or lacking in energy?

**YES** → Go to chart **55** Tiredness

**NO**

Are you taking any medicines?

**YES** → **Certain drugs** can make you feel unwell as a side-effect. Discuss the problem with your doctor.

**NO** → **Consult your doctor** if you are unable to make a diagnosis from this chart.

## THE EFFECTS OF ALCOHOL

The main immediate effect of alcohol is to dull the reactions of the brain and nerves. In small quantities, this can produce a pleasantly relaxed feeling, but in larger amounts can lead to gross impairment of memory, judgement, coordination and emotional reactions.

Alcohol also widens the blood vessels, making you feel temporarily warm. However, body heat is rapidly lost from the dilated blood vessels and this can lead to severe chilling (hypothermia).

After a heavy drinking session, you are likely to feel tired, nauseated, and may have a headache, as a result of dehydration and the damaging effect of alcohol on the stomach and intestines.

### Long-term effects
Regular consumption of even small amounts of alcohol may cause social and family problems. Large amounts damage health.

- **Brain shrinkage** may occur in even moderate drinkers.
- **Obesity** is likely as a result of the high energy value of most alcoholic drinks.
- **Liver damage** (cirrhosis) so that the body can no longer process nutrients or drugs is almost inevitable.
- **Addiction** with accompanying social problems is a real risk for even moderate regular drinkers.

### Maximum safe alcohol intake
Women should aim to keep their alcohol consumption well below 30gm a day. This is the equivalent of 3 small glasses of wine, 3 small beers, or 3 small measures of spirits. Men should keep their consumption below 40gm a day

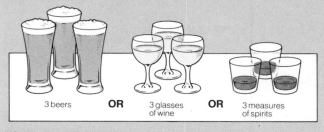

3 beers **OR** 3 glasses of wine **OR** 3 measures of spirits

### Women and alcohol
Excessive alcohol consumption has special dangers for women. It is now known that women are more susceptible than men to the harmful effects of alcohol on the liver. This is because of differences in the way their livers process alcohol. Apart from endangering their own health, women who drink during pregnancy risk damaging the unborn baby. Even small amounts of alcohol may increase the chance of a baby being born underweight and mentally retarded.

## BLOOD ANALYSIS

The blood is the principal transport medium of the body. It carries oxygen, nutrients and other vital chemicals to all the body tissues and carries waste products away from them. The blood is composed of three principal parts: the red cells, containing the red pigment (haemoglobin) which carries oxygen; the white cells and platelets, which fight infection and seal damaged blood vessels respectively; and the plasma, a yellowish fluid in which the blood cells, nutrients, chemicals and waste products are suspended.

Modern techniques for counting the numbers of different types of blood cell contained in a blood sample – a procedure known as a blood count – can help in the diagnosis of blood disorders. And examination of the chemicals in the plasma can give clues to diseases of many other parts of the body.

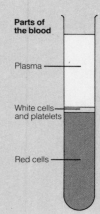

**Parts of the blood**

Plasma

White cells and platelets

Red cells

# 55 Tiredness

Consult this chart if you feel tired or lacking in energy during the day or if you spend more time asleep than normal. Lethargy is a common symptom of many disorders, some trivial and some that require medical treatment. Sudden severe drowsiness is a serious symptom and requires prompt medical attention.

**START HERE** → **Could you be short of sleep?**

**YES** → **Insufficient or disturbed sleep** for more than a few days is almost certain to make you feel tired during the day. A night or two of sound, uninterrupted sleep will probably make you feel much better. If you have difficulty in getting to sleep or if you regularly wake during the night, this may be a sign of a variety of problems.

Go to chart

**58** **Difficulty sleeping**

**NO** ↓

**Do you have one or more of the following symptoms?**
- feeling the cold more than you used to
- thinning or brittle hair
- unexplained weight gain
- dry skin

**YES** → **Hypothyroidism** (underactive thyroid gland is a possibility. The problem is most likely to occur in middle-aged women. Consult your doctor.

**Treatment:** If hypothyroidism is diagnosed, your doctor will probably prescribe tablets of synthetic thyroid hormones. These tablets will make you feel much better in a few days, and after a few months you should have returned to normal health. However, it will be necessary to keep taking tablets.

**NO** ↓

**Do you have one or more of the following symptoms?**
- paleness
- faintness
- breathlessness
- palpitations

**YES** → **Anaemia**, a disorder in which there is too little of the red pigment haemoglobin in the blood, is a possibility if your diet lacks iron or if you are a woman with heavy periods. Consult your doctor.

**Treatment:** Your doctor will probably take a sample of blood for analysis (see *Blood analysis*, opposite). If you are found to have anaemia due to iron deficiency, your doctor may give you iron in the form of tablets or injections. In addition, he or she will probably advise you to make sure that you eat plenty of iron-rich foods such as meat, wholemeal bread, dried fruits and soya beans (which are the only good vegetable source). Other forms of anaemia require laboratory investigation before treatment can be given.

**NO** ↓

**Do you regularly drink more alcohol than is recommended in the box, opposite?**

**YES** → **Regular consumption of alcohol**, even in seemingly moderate quantities can have a depresssant effect, making you feel tired (see also the box on *The effects of alcohol*, opposite).

**Self-help:** Cutting out all alcohol for a week or so and making sure that you get adequate sleep should make you feel much better. If you find it difficult to cut down or if you have difficulty in getting to sleep without the help of alcohol, consult your doctor.

**NO** ↓

*Go to next column*

---

*Continued from previous column*

**Do you have one or more of the following symptoms?**
- inability to concentrate or make decisions
- lack of interest in sex
- recurrent headaches
- feeling low in spirits

**YES** → **Depression** can make you feel tired and run down.

Go to chart

**72** **Depression**

**NO** ↓

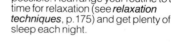

**TIREDNESS IN EARLY PREGNANCY**

Tiredness is an almost universal symptom in early pregnancy. Some women notice it even before the pregnancy has been confirmed. So if you are feeling tired for no apparent reason, and you have missed a period, consider the possibility that you may be pregnant.

Tiredness in pregnancy is a normal reaction to the major changes in your body, and does not indicate any special problem. The best way of coping with it is to take more rest. Try taking an afternoon nap or go to bed an hour or so earlier. Most women start to feel more energetic by the fourth month of pregnancy, although tiredness is likely to return in the final 6 weeks before delivery.

**Have you been working hard without a break for several weeks, either at your job or in the home?**

**YES** → **Overworking** for an extended period has probably caused your tiredness, especially if stress from problems at work or at home is making you less able to cope than usual.

**Self-help:** Try to get some help with your workload or to take some time off if possible. Rearrange your routine to allow time for relaxation (see *relaxation techniques*, p.175) and get plenty of sleep each night.

**NO** ↓

**Have you recently recovered from an infectious illness – for example, flu?**

**YES** → **Recovery** from many such illnesses can take several weeks. During this period you are likely to feel tired and depressed.

**Self-help:** Do not expect too much of yourself at first. Make sure that you eat a nourishing diet and take things easy until you feel better. If symptoms persist for more than a month, consult your doctor.

**NO** ↓

**Consult your doctor** if you are unable to make a diagnosis from this chart.

# 56 Loss of weight

Minor fluctuations in weight of only a few kilograms, as a result of temporary changes in the amount of exercise you take or the amount of food you eat, are normal. However, more severe, unintentional weight loss, especially when combined with loss of appetite or other symptoms, usually requires medical attention. Consult this chart if you have lost more than 4.5kg (10lb) in a period of 10 weeks or less, or if you have noticed any of the signs of weight loss described in the box on the facing page.

**START HERE**

**Is your appetite as good as ever?**

**YES** →

**Have you noticed two or more of the following symptoms?**
- excessive sweating
- weakness or trembling
- unexplained tiredness
- bulging eyes

**YES** →

**Thyrotoxicosis** (overactive thyroid gland), an uncommon disorder that chiefly affects women, is a possibility. Consult your doctor.

**Treatment:** If your doctor suspects the disorder, he or she will probably take some blood for tests (see *Blood analysis* p. 146) to confirm the diagnosis and you may need to have a *radio-isotope scan* of the thyroid gland (below). Treatment usually consists of drugs. In severe or recurrent cases, surgery to remove part of the gland may be necessary.

**NO**

**NO**

**Have you noticed one or more of the following symptoms?**
- unusually frequent or abundant urination
- increased thirst
- unexplained tiredness
- genital itching
- absence of periods

**YES** →

**Diabetes mellitus** is a possibility. This disorder is caused by insufficient production of the hormone insulin which is needed by the body to get energy from sugar and carbohydrate foods. Consult your doctor.

**Treatment:** Your doctor will probably arrange tests on samples of urine and blood (see *Blood analysis* p. 146). If the diagnosis is confirmed, you may need treatment with drugs or with regular injections of insulin. Your doctor will also advise you on what diet you should follow, and the importance of regular meals. You should seek special advice if you intend to have a baby because the disease carries risks for both mother and unborn baby.

**Eating less than your daily energy needs** is the most likely cause of your weight loss, if you feel well. However, you should discuss the problem with your doctor to eliminate the slight possibility of an underlying disease.

**NO**

## RADIO-ISOTOPE SCAN

Doctors use this type of scan to find out whether and how a gland or organ is malfunctioning. A radio-active chemical is injected into the bloodstream, and is absorbed by the organ being examined. This organ is then scanned with specialized equipment, to determine whether or not the chemical is being absorbed evenly and normally. The result of the scan is shown either on photographs or on a television screen.

The dark area in this scan of a thyroid gland shows a possible thyroid nodule.

## WEIGHT LOSS IN PREGNANCY

Most women lose some weight in the first 3 months of pregnancy, as a result mainly of loss of appetite, nausea and vomiting. This is not considered a problem unless you lose more than about 4kg (8lb). In this case it is advisable to consult your doctor, because it may mean that persistent vomiting is preventing you from obtaining adequate nourishment. Nausea and vomiting normally subside by the 12th week of pregnancy and by the 14th–16th week you should begin to gain about 0.5kg (1lb) a week, until about the 38th week.

### Abnormal weight loss
If you fail to gain weight at a satisfactory rate or if you lose weight after the first 3 months, you should consult your doctor. He or she will ensure that you are eating properly and may arrange tests, including urine and *blood analysis* (p. 146) and possibly an *ultra-sound scan* (p.276) to make sure that the placenta is functioning properly and that the baby is developing normally. It is therefore extremely important for you to attend the antenatal clinic regularly throughout pregnancy, so that a close watch may be kept on your weight gain and action taken when necessary.

### Pattern of weight gain and loss in pregnancy

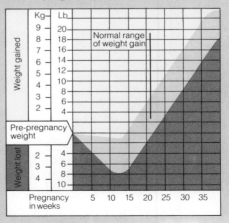

*Go to next page*

*Continued from previous page*

**Have you noticed one or more of the following symptoms?**
- recurrent bouts of diarrhoea
- recurrent constipation
- recurrent abdominal pain
- blood in the faeces

**YES**

### CONSULT YOUR DOCTOR WITHOUT DELAY!
**A digestive-tract disorder** may be causing your weight loss. Your intestines may be inflamed or you may have an ulcer, but there is also a possibility of a growth, especially if you are over 40.

**Treatment:** Your doctor will probably arrange a variety of diagnostic tests. These may include analysis of samples of blood (p. 146) and faeces, *barium X-rays* (p. 207), and possibly *sigmoidoscopy,* (p. 216).

**NO**

**Have you noticed two or more of the following symptoms?**
- profuse sweating at night
- recurrent raised temperature
- general feeling of ill health
- persistent cough
- blood in phlegm

**YES**

### CONSULT YOUR DOCTOR WITHOUT DELAY!
**A chronic lung infection** such as tuberculosis or brucellosis, or another chronic infection, is possible.

**Treatment:** Your doctor will probably take samples of blood and sputum for analysis. You may also need to have a *chest X-ray* (p. 197) and a special skin test for tuberculosis. If you are found to have tuberculosis, you will be given a long course of *antibiotics* and advised to rest as much as possible. With prompt treatment complete recovery in a few months is probable.

**NO**

**Do you have one or more of the following symptoms?**
- feeling in low spirits
- difficulty in sleeping
- lack of interest in sex
- inability to concentrate or make decisions

**YES**

**Depression** can sometimes cause a marked loss of appetite, leading to weight loss.

Go to chart

**72** Depression

**NO**

**Consult your doctor** if you are unable to make a diagnosis from this chart.

---

### SIGNS OF WEIGHT LOSS
If you lose weight without deliberately attempting to slim, you should always take the matter seriously, especially if other symptoms suggest the possibility of illness. If you do not weigh yourself regularly the following signs may indicate that you have lost weight:

- People remark on your changed appearance.
- Your cheeks become sunken.
- Your trousers (or skirts) become loose around the waist.
- Your shirt collars become loose.
- You need a smaller bra.

---

### EXERCISE AND WEIGHT LOSS
For those who are overweight (see p. 150) exercise is a useful accompaniment to a planned reducing diet. While exercise alone will not solve a serious weight problem, it will boost the amount of energy (calories) you burn and will help tone up slack muscles. But if you are already thin, further weight loss may be unhealthy. It is therefore important for those involved in strenuous physical activity – for example, dancers and athletes – to ensure that they eat an adequate diet that takes account of their increased energy requirements.

If you increase your energy output without a corresponding increase in your intake of food, the body burns up fat reserves and the result is weight loss.

| Energy output |
| Energy (food) intake |
| Weight |

---

### ANOREXIA NERVOSA AND BULIMIA
Anorexia is a psychological disturbance in which a person (most commonly a teenage girl or young woman) refuses food because of an irrational fear of putting on weight. An anorectic convinces herself that she is too fat, that she has not lost weight even though she has, and she firmly denies that there is anything wrong with her even when she has lost an excessive amount of weight. Sufferers from bulimia, a variant of anorexia, try to avoid putting on weight by forcing themselves to vomit after over-eating binges. Many young women go through a temporary phase of excessive dieting, but only a minority develop anorexia nervosa, which can lead to a dangerous loss of weight, hormonal disturbances and even death.

#### The signs of anorexia
The illness usually starts with normal dieting, but the anorectic eats less and less each day. The reason she gives for doing this may be that her arms or legs are still too fat. The less she eats, the less she wants to eat and, even if her figure becomes skeletal, she still sees herself as plump and is terrified of putting on weight. She may be reluctant to undress in front of others in order to conceal weight loss. To avoid family pressure to eat sensibly she may hide food and throw it away. Or she may make herself vomit after meals. Anorectics often take large quantities of laxatives in the mistaken belief that this will help to keep their weight down.

As weight loss progresses, most anorectics cease to have periods. Skin may become sallow and a fine down may appear on the body. Without treatment, many anorectics become severely depressed and in some cases suicidal.

#### How you can help
If you have a relative or friend who has an unrealistic image of herself as being too fat and who seems to be dieting excessively, although already painfully thin, try to persuade her to consult a doctor. While she may at first be unwilling to act on your advice, you should persevere until she does, because this can be a life-threatening condition.

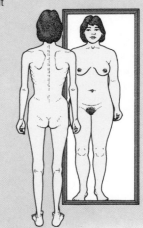

An anorectic sees herself as overweight, even though in reality she is extremely thin.

# 57 Overweight

Normally, fat accounts for between 10 and 20 per cent of the weight of an adult male, and about 25 per cent in an adult female; any more than this is both unnecessary and unhealthy, increasing the risk of diseases such as diabetes, high blood pressure and arthritis. Most people reach their ideal weight in their teens and gradually gain a little weight as they get older, reaching their heaviest at about 50. Consult this chart if you weigh more than the healthy weight for your height shown in the chart (see p.302, p.303), or if you can pinch a fold of flesh that is more than 2 inches thick on your abdomen. In most cases, weight gain is due simply to eating more than you need, and can be remedied by a balanced reducing diet, but occasionally there may be a medical reason for putting on weight.

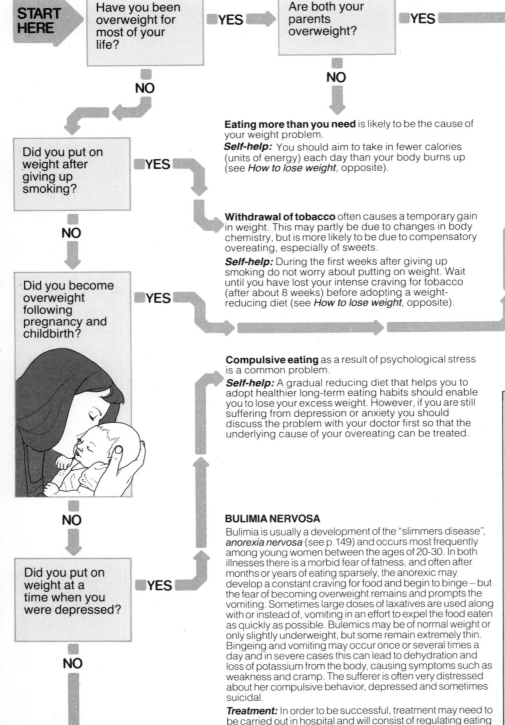

**START HERE**

**Have you been overweight for most of your life?** — **YES** → **Are both your parents overweight?** — **YES** →

**NO** ↓

**Are both your parents overweight?** **NO** ↓

**A tendency to obesity** can run in families. This may be because unhealthy eating habits tend to be passed on to the younger generation. Or it may be that some physical types naturally burn energy more slowly than others and therefore need to eat less.

**Self-help:** Adopt a sensible weight-reducing diet such as the one suggested in the box on *How to lose weight*, opposite.

**Did you put on weight after giving up smoking?** — **YES** →

**NO** ↓

**Eating more than you need** is likely to be the cause of your weight problem.
**Self-help:** You should aim to take in fewer calories (units of energy) each day than your body burns up (see *How to lose weight*, opposite).

**Did you become overweight following pregnancy and childbirth?** — **YES** →

**NO** ↓

**Withdrawal of tobacco** often causes a temporary gain in weight. This may partly be due to changes in body chemistry, but is more likely to be due to compensatory overeating, especially of sweets.
**Self-help:** During the first weeks after giving up smoking do not worry about putting on weight. Wait until you have lost your intense craving for tobacco (after about 8 weeks) before adopting a weight-reducing diet (see *How to lose weight*, opposite).

**Pregnancy** often brings about a weight gain that is difficult to lose once the baby is born, especially if you put on a lot of weight during the pregnancy.
**Self-help:** The only way to lose weight is to reduce calorie intake by following a weight-reducing diet (see *How to lose weight*, opposite). However, if you are breast-feeding make sure that there is plenty of nutritious food in your diet, and do not aim for rapid weight loss. You may also need to tone up your muscles, so adopting an exercise routine at home or joining a class will also be helpful.

**Compulsive eating** as a result of psychological stress is a common problem.
**Self-help:** A gradual reducing diet that helps you to adopt healthier long-term eating habits should enable you to lose your excess weight. However, if you are still suffering from depression or anxiety you should discuss the problem with your doctor first so that the underlying cause of your overeating can be treated.

**Did you put on weight at a time when you were depressed?** — **YES** →

**NO** ↓

**BULIMIA NERVOSA**

Bulimia is usually a development of the "slimmers disease", *anorexia nervosa* (see p.149) and occurs most frequently among young women between the ages of 20-30. In both illnesses there is a morbid fear of fatness, and often after months or years of eating sparsely, the anorexic may develop a constant craving for food and begin to binge – but the fear of becoming overweight remains and prompts the vomiting. Sometimes large doses of laxatives are used along with or instead of, vomiting in an effort to expel the food eaten as quickly as possible. Bulemics may be of normal weight or only slightly underweight, but some remain extremely thin. Bingeing and vomiting may occur once or several times a day and in severe cases this can lead to dehydration and loss of potassium from the body, causing symptoms such as weakness and cramp. The sufferer is often very distressed about her compulsive behavior, depressed and sometimes suicidal.

**Treatment:** In order to be successful, treatment may need to be carried out in hospital and will consist of regulating eating habits, psychotherapy to encourage emotional maturity and sometimes antidepressants.

*Go to next page*

## AGE AND INCREASING WEIGHT

As you get older you need less energy, partly because you become less active, partly for other reasons that are not yet clear. But many people do not reduce their food intake to correspond with their lower energy requirements as they get older. In addition, many men drink more alcohol than they did when they were younger, and alcohol contains energy in abundance. The result is a surplus of energy, causing increasing deposits of fatty flesh as old age approaches.

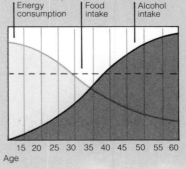

| Energy consumption | Food intake | Alcohol intake |
| --- | --- | --- |

15 20 25 30 35 40 45 50 55 60
Age

*Continued from previous page*

Did the weight gain follow a change from a physically active life to a more sedentary job or lifestyle?

**■YES**

**NO**

**Energy requirements** of the body vary according to the amount of exercise your daily routine involves. For instance, if you have a desk job your average daily calorie requirement may be only 2000 (women) to 2500 (men), but if you have a more physically active job you may require five to eight hundred calories more each day.

**Self-help:** Adjusting your food intake to take account of your reduced energy requirements should help you to lose the weight you have put on. This may mean changing eating habits you have developed over many years and it may take a little while for you to become accustomed to your new diet. See *How to lose weight*, right, for some advice on a healthy reducing diet. You should also try to incorporate some physical exercise into your new routine to help keep your muscles firm and to boost weight loss.

Have you noticed two or more of the following symptoms since you began to put on weight?
■ feeling the cold more than you used to
■ thinning or brittle hair
■ dry skin
■ unexplained tiredness

**■YES**

**NO**

**Hypothyroidism** (underactive thyroid gland), a disorder that is most common in middle-aged women, is a possibility. Consult your doctor.

**Treatment:** If hypothyroidism is diagnosed, your doctor will probably prescribe tablets of synthetic thyroid hormones. These tablets will help your body to burn up excess fat and after a few months you should return to your normal weight. However, it will be necessary to keep on taking the tablets indefinitely.

Are you taking any medicines?

**■YES**

**NO**

**Certain drugs**, particularly steroids prescribed for problems such as asthma or rheumatoid arthritis, can cause weight gain as a side-effect. Discuss the problem with your doctor.

Are you over 40 years old?

**■YES■**

**NO**

## HOW TO LOSE WEIGHT

If you are fat, it is because your body is not using all the energy you feed it. To lose weight you must expend more energy than you take in, first by changing your diet, second by exercising more. It is best to avoid crash diets, which have no lasting effect because they do not encourage you to adopt healthy new habits. You will find it more helpful to follow this step-by-step diet, which is designed to help you change your eating habits over time.

**1** Try to cut out, or at least cut down on, all foods in group 1, the sweet or rich foods. Reduce your daily alcohol intake to no more than one pint of beer (or 2 glasses of wine or 2 measures of spirits), or the equivalent. If you drink spirits, use low-calorie mixers or unsweetened fruit juices. Eat normal portions of food from groups 2 and 3. You should begin to notice a change in your weight within a fortnight.

**2** If you have not lost any weight after 2 weeks, stop having any group 1 foods, halve your helpings of group 2 foods and eat as much as you want from group 3. Cut down further on (or eliminate) your consumption of alcohol.

**3** If you fail to lose weight after 2 more weeks, halve your helpings of group 3 foods and eat as little as possible from group 2. Consult your doctor if you fail to lose weight after 4 more weeks.

| Meat | Vegetables | Dairy foods | Fish | Other |
|---|---|---|---|---|
| **Group 1 foods** | | | | |
| Visible fat on any meat<br>Bacon<br>Duck, goose<br>Sausages<br>salami<br>Pâtés | | Butter<br>Cream<br>Ice cream | | Thick gravies or sauces<br>Fried food<br>Sugar, chocolate<br>Cakes, pies, biscuits<br>Puddings<br>Canned fruits in syrup<br>Dried fruits<br>Nuts<br>Jams, honey, syrups<br>Sweet drinks |
| **Group 2 foods** | | | | |
| Lean beef<br>Lamb<br>Pork | Beans<br>Lentils | Eggs<br>Cheeses (other than cottage cheese)<br>Whole milk | Oily fish (e.g., herring, mackerel, sardines, tuna packed in oil) | Pasta or rice<br>Thick soups<br>Bread, crispbreads<br>Unsweetened cereals<br>Margarine<br>Polyunsaturated vegetable oils |
| **Group 3 foods** | | | | |
| Poultry other than duck or goose (not including the skin)<br>Tongue, liver, kidney etc. | Potatoes<br>Vegetables (raw or lightly cooked)<br>Clear or vegetable-only soups | Skimmed milk<br>Yoghurt<br>Cottage cheese | Nonoily fish, (e.g., haddock, perch, cod)<br>Shellfish (e.g., crab, shrimp)<br>Tuna packed in water | Bran<br>Fresh fruit<br>Unsweetened fruit juice |

**Growing older** is often accompanied by a gradual gain in weight. This is more than likely because you begin to take less exercise at a time in your life when your body is beginning to take longer to burn up food.

**Self-help:** Reduce your food intake to correspond with your lower energy consumption (see *How to lose weight*, above).

**Overeating** is the likely cause of your excess weight.

**Self-help:** Follow a sensible reducing diet (see *How to lose weight*, above). If after a month you fail to lose weight, consult your doctor, who will find out if the problem is due to any underlying disorder.

# 58 Difficulty in sleeping

It is quite common to have an occasional night when you find it difficult to get to sleep or to stay asleep and this need not cause concern. Consult this chart if you regularly have difficulty in falling asleep at night or if you wake during the night or too early in the morning — a problem sometimes known as insomnia.

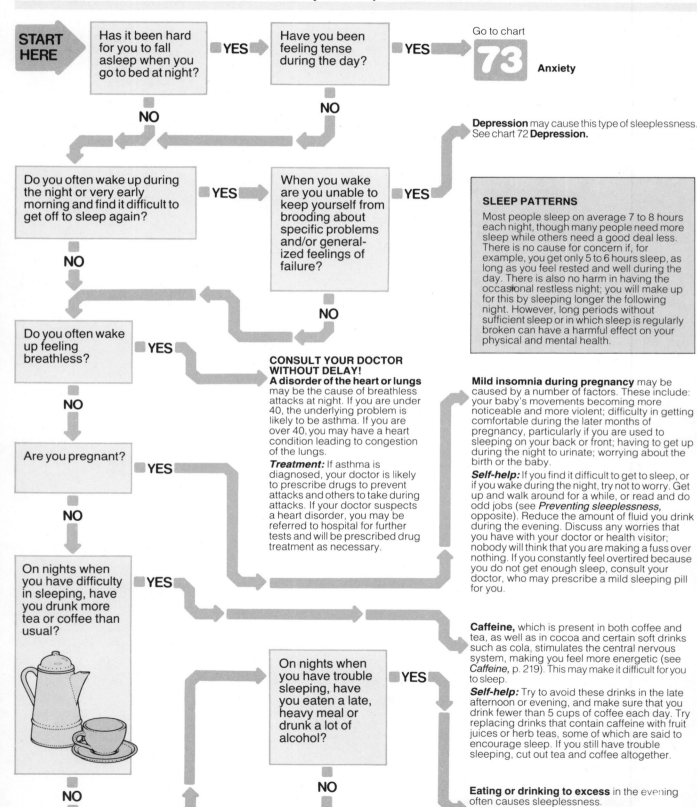

**START HERE**

**Has it been hard for you to fall asleep when you go to bed at night?**

YES → **Have you been feeling tense during the day?**

YES → **Go to chart 73** Anxiety

NO ↓     NO ↓

**Depression** may cause this type of sleeplessness. See chart 72 **Depression.**

**Do you often wake up during the night or very early morning and find it difficult to get off to sleep again?**

YES → **When you wake are you unable to keep yourself from brooding about specific problems and/or general-ized feelings of failure?**

YES →

### SLEEP PATTERNS

Most people sleep on average 7 to 8 hours each night, though many people need more sleep while others need a good deal less. There is no cause for concern if, for example, you get only 5 to 6 hours sleep, as long as you feel rested and well during the day. There is also no harm in having the occasional restless night; you will make up for this by sleeping longer the following night. However, long periods without sufficient sleep or in which sleep is regularly broken can have a harmful effect on your physical and mental health.

NO ↓     NO ↓

**Do you often wake up feeling breathless?**

YES →

### CONSULT YOUR DOCTOR WITHOUT DELAY!
**A disorder of the heart or lungs** may be the cause of breathless attacks at night. If you are under 40, the underlying problem is likely to be asthma. If you are over 40, you may have a heart condition leading to congestion of the lungs.

**Treatment:** If asthma is diagnosed, your doctor is likely to prescribe drugs to prevent attacks and others to take during attacks. If your doctor suspects a heart disorder, you may be referred to hospital for further tests and will be prescribed drug treatment as necessary.

**Mild insomnia during pregnancy** may be caused by a number of factors. These include: your baby's movements becoming more noticeable and more violent; difficulty in getting comfortable during the later months of pregnancy, particularly if you are used to sleeping on your back or front; having to get up during the night to urinate; worrying about the birth or the baby.

**Self-help:** If you find it difficult to get to sleep, or if you wake during the night, try not to worry. Get up and walk around for a while, or read and do odd jobs (see *Preventing sleeplessness,* opposite). Reduce the amount of fluid you drink during the evening. Discuss any worries that you have with your doctor or health visitor; nobody will think that you are making a fuss over nothing. If you constantly feel overtired because you do not get enough sleep, consult your doctor, who may prescribe a mild sleeping pill for you.

NO ↓

**Are you pregnant?**

YES →

NO ↓

**On nights when you have difficulty in sleeping, have you drunk more tea or coffee than usual?**

YES →

**Caffeine,** which is present in both coffee and tea, as well as in cocoa and certain soft drinks such as cola, stimulates the central nervous system, making you feel more energetic (see *Caffeine,* p. 219). This may make it difficult for you to sleep.

**Self-help:** Try to avoid these drinks in the late afternoon or evening, and make sure that you drink fewer than 5 cups of coffee each day. Try replacing drinks that contain caffeine with fruit juices or herb teas, some of which are said to encourage sleep. If you still have trouble sleeping, cut out tea and coffee altogether.

**On nights when you have trouble sleeping, have you eaten a late, heavy meal or drunk a lot of alcohol?**

YES →

NO ↓     NO ↓

*Go to next page*

**Eating or drinking to excess** in the evening often causes sleeplessness.

**Self-help:** Try eating your evening meal earlier and reducing your alcohol intake.

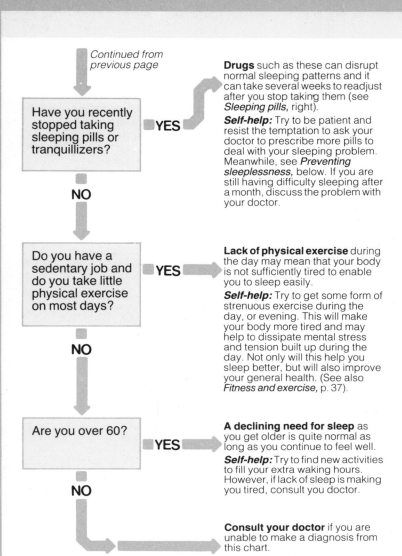

*Continued from previous page*

**Have you recently stopped taking sleeping pills or tranquillizers?**

**YES** → **Drugs** such as these can disrupt normal sleeping patterns and it can take several weeks to readjust after you stop taking them (see *Sleeping pills,* right).

**Self-help:** Try to be patient and resist the temptation to ask your doctor to prescribe more pills to deal with your sleeping problem. Meanwhile, see *Preventing sleeplessness,* below. If you are still having difficulty sleeping after a month, discuss the problem with your doctor.

**NO** ↓

**Do you have a sedentary job and do you take little physical exercise on most days?**

**YES** → **Lack of physical exercise** during the day may mean that your body is not sufficiently tired to enable you to sleep easily.

**Self-help:** Try to get some form of strenuous exercise during the day, or evening. This will make your body more tired and may help to dissipate mental stress and tension built up during the day. Not only will this help you sleep better, but will also improve your general health. (See also *Fitness and exercise,* p. 37).

**NO** ↓

**Are you over 60?**

**YES** → **A declining need for sleep** as you get older is quite normal as long as you continue to feel well.

**Self-help:** Try to find new activities to fill your extra waking hours. However, if lack of sleep is making you tired, consult you doctor.

**NO** ↓

**Consult your doctor** if you are unable to make a diagnosis from this chart.

---

## SLEEPING PILLS

If you have difficulty in sleeping at night your doctor may prescribe sleeping pills. These are particularly useful if you cannot sleep because of pain after an injury or during an illness, or at times of emotional stress – for example, following a bereavement.

**What drugs are used?**
There are two main types of drug used to treat sleeplessness: benzodiazepines and barbiturates. Both act in a similar way, but doctors rarely prescribe barbiturates because of the dangers of addiction and overdosage. Almost all prescribed sleeping pills nowadays are benzodiazepines.

**How do sleeping drugs work?**
All sleeping drugs work by suppressing brain function in some way. This means that the sleep you get when taking a sleeping drug is not normal and may leave you less rested than a natural night's sleep. This also means that if you stop taking sleeping pills after having used them regularly, you may sleep restlessly and have vivid dreams while your brain readjusts to normal.

**Are sleeping pills dangerous?**
Sleeping pills that are taken on your doctor's advice and according to the dosage prescribed are unlikely to do you any harm, even if taken for many years. However, you may become dependent on these drugs if you take them regularly. Therefore, it is a good idea to discuss the alternatives with your doctor. In addition, you should consult your doctor if you have difficulty waking up in the morning after taking a pill or if you find that your sleeping pills no longer work effectively; you may need a change of drug. People who take sleeping pills should always remember the following safety rules:

- Never take a larger dose than your doctor has prescribed.
- Never drive or operate machinery before the effects of sleeping drugs have worn off.
- Never take alcohol less than 1 hour before or less than 8 hours after taking sleeping drugs.
- Never give your sleeping pills to others, especially children.
- Never keep your tablets on your bedside table; there is a danger that you may accidentally take an additional dose when half asleep.

---

## PREVENTING SLEEPLESSNESS

If you find that you cannot get to sleep as soon as you go to bed, try not to worry about it; worry will only make matters worse. Even if you just relax or doze for a few hours you will probably be getting enough rest. The following suggestions may help:

- Try to do some form of physical exercise during the day so that your body needs rest because it is tired. A short, gentle stroll in the open air an hour or so before going to bed may help.
- A full stomach is not conducive to sleep, but a light snack and a warm, milky drink or even a small whisky at bedtime may help you to feel sleepy. Do not go to bed within 3 hours of eating a full meal.

- Avoid heavy drinking.
- A warm bath is often relaxing. A shower may not be a good idea if it is too invigorating.
- Reading that is not associated with work or study often makes people sleepy.
- Make sure that you are neither too hot nor too cold. Most people sleep best in a room temperature of 16 to 18°C (60 to 65°F).
- Make your environment as conducive to sleep as possible. Make sure that there are no irritating, dripping taps or knocking radiators.
- A comfortable bed will help (see *Preventing back pain,* p. 223).

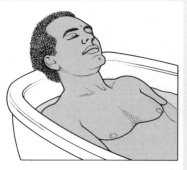

# 59 Fever

A fever (abnormally high body temperature) can be a symptom of many diseases, but usually is a sign that your body is fighting infection. You may suspect that you have a fever if you feel hot, or alternately hot and shivery, and if you feel generally unwell. To determine whether you have a fever, take your temperature as described below. Consult this chart if your temperature is 38°C (100°F) or above. Consult your doctor if your temperature remains raised for longer than 48 hours, or rises above 40°C (104°F).

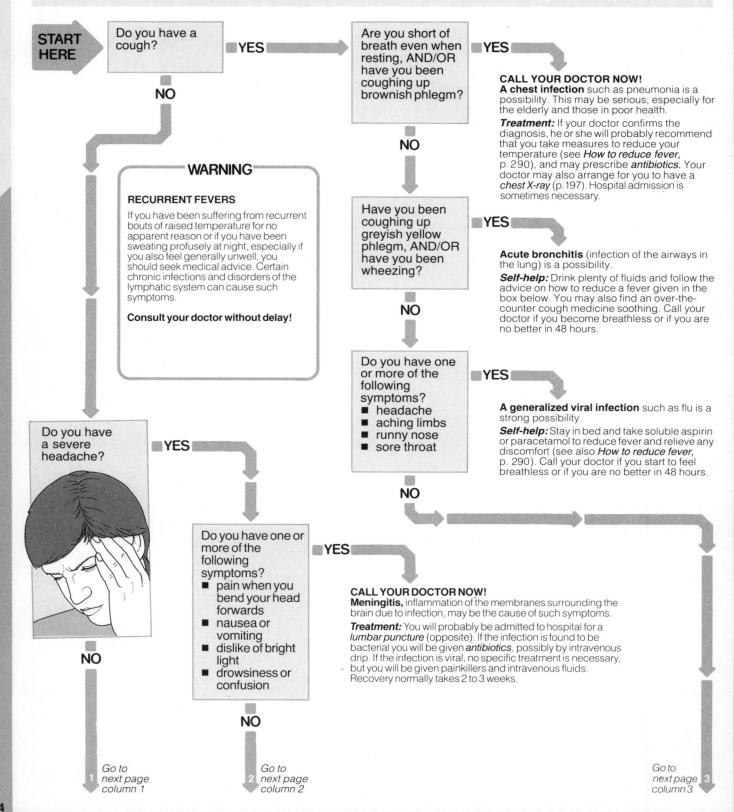

**START HERE**

**Do you have a cough?**

**NO** ↓

**YES** →

**Are you short of breath even when resting, AND/OR have you been coughing up brownish phlegm?**

**YES** →

**CALL YOUR DOCTOR NOW!**
**A chest infection** such as pneumonia is a possibility. This may be serious, especially for the elderly and those in poor health.

**Treatment:** If your doctor confirms the diagnosis, he or she will probably recommend that you take measures to reduce your temperature (see *How to reduce fever*, p. 290), and may prescribe *antibiotics.* Your doctor may also arrange for you to have a *chest X-ray* (p.197). Hospital admission is sometimes necessary.

**NO** ↓

**Have you been coughing up greyish yellow phlegm, AND/OR have you been wheezing?**

**YES** →

**Acute bronchitis** (infection of the airways in the lung) is a possibility.

**Self-help:** Drink plenty of fluids and follow the advice on how to reduce a fever given in the box below. You may also find an over-the-counter cough medicine soothing. Call your doctor if you become breathless or if you are no better in 48 hours.

**NO** ↓

**Do you have one or more of the following symptoms?**
- headache
- aching limbs
- runny nose
- sore throat

**YES** →

**A generalized viral infection** such as flu is a strong possibility.

**Self-help:** Stay in bed and take soluble aspirin or paracetamol to reduce fever and relieve any discomfort (see also *How to reduce fever*, p. 290). Call your doctor if you start to feel breathless or if you are no better in 48 hours.

**NO** ↓

### WARNING

#### RECURRENT FEVERS

If you have been suffering from recurrent bouts of raised temperature for no apparent reason or if you have been sweating profusely at night, especially if you also feel generally unwell, you should seek medical advice. Certain chronic infections and disorders of the lymphatic system can cause such symptoms.

**Consult your doctor without delay!**

**Do you have a severe headache?**

**YES** →

**NO** ↓

**Do you have one or more of the following symptoms?**
- pain when you bend your head forwards
- nausea or vomiting
- dislike of bright light
- drowsiness or confusion

**YES** →

**CALL YOUR DOCTOR NOW!**
**Meningitis,** inflammation of the membranes surrounding the brain due to infection, may be the cause of such symptoms.

**Treatment:** You will probably be admitted to hospital for a *lumbar puncture* (opposite). If the infection is found to be bacterial you will be given *antibiotics*, possibly by intravenous drip. If the infection is viral, no specific treatment is necessary, but you will be given painkillers and intravenous fluids. Recovery normally takes 2 to 3 weeks.

**NO** ↓

**NO** ↓

*Go to*
**1** *next page column 1*

*Go to*
**2** *next page column 2*

*Go to*
**3** *next page column 3*

*Continued from previous page, column 1*  **1**

*Continued from previous page, column 2*  **2**

*Continued from previous page, column 3*  **3**

Do you have one or more of the following symptoms?
- aching limbs
- runny nose
- sore throat

**■ YES** →

**A generalized viral infection** such as flu is a strong possibility.

***Self-help:*** Stay in bed and take soluble aspirin or paracetamol to reduce fever and relieve any discomfort (see also *How to reduce fever,* p. 290). Call your doctor if you start to feel breathless or if you are no better in 48 hours.

**NO**

---

Do you have a sore throat?

**■ YES** →

Go to chart

**86** **Sore throat**

**NO**

---

Have you recently returned from a stay in a hot country?

**■ YES** →

**CONSULT YOUR DOCTOR WITHOUT DELAY!**

**A tropical disease** that is rare in this country – for example, malaria or typhoid – is a possibility.

***Treatment:*** If your doctor suspects such a disease after examining you, he or she may arrange for you to be admitted to hospital for tests. These may include *blood analysis* (p.146) and tests on faecal material. Treatment will depend on the eventual diagnosis.

**NO**

---

Do you have one or more of the following symptoms?
- pain in the small of the back
- abnormally frequent urination
- pain when passing urine
- pink or cloudy urine

**■ YES** →

**CONSULT YOUR DOCTOR WITHOUT DELAY!**

**An acute infection of the kidney or bladder** may be the cause of this.

***Treatment:*** Your doctor will examine you and take a specimen of your urine and may prescribe *antibiotics.* He or she may also arrange for you to have a special X-ray of the kidneys (see *Intravenous pyelography,* p.238 *men*; 262 *women*) to try to find the underlying cause of the problem. Further treatment will depend on the results of the test.

**NO**

---

Have you spent most of the day in strong sunlight or in very hot conditions?

**■ YES** →

**Exposure to heat** may have caused your temperature to rise. In most cases your temperature will return to normal after you have rested for an hour or so in a cool room. Call your doctor at once if the fever continues to rise.

**NO**

---

Are you a woman?

**■ YES** →

Have you had a baby within the past 2 weeks?

**■ YES** →

**CALL YOUR DOCTOR NOW!**

**Puerperal infection,** although rare nowadays, is a possible cause of fever following childbirth. This occurs when the womb and/or vagina become infected after delivery. If, however, you also have pain or redness in the breast, you may have a breast infection (see chart 146, *Breast-feeding problems*).

***Treatment:*** If your doctor thinks that you may have a puerperal infection, he or she may take a sample of discharge from your vagina for analysis. Treatment consists of a course of *antibiotics*.

**NO**

Do you have pain in the lower abdomen AND/OR have you had an unusually heavy or unpleasant-smelling vaginal discharge?

**■ YES** →

**An infection of the fallopian tubes** (sometimes known as salpingitis) is a possible cause of such symptoms. Consult your doctor.

***Treatment:*** Your doctor will probably give you a vaginal examination (p.258), and will take a sample of vaginal discharge for analysis. If tests confirm the diagnosis you will probably be given a course of *antibiotics*.

**NO**

**NO**

**Consult your doctor** if you are unable to make a diagnosis from this chart and your temperature has not returned to normal within 48 hours, or if it rises again.

---

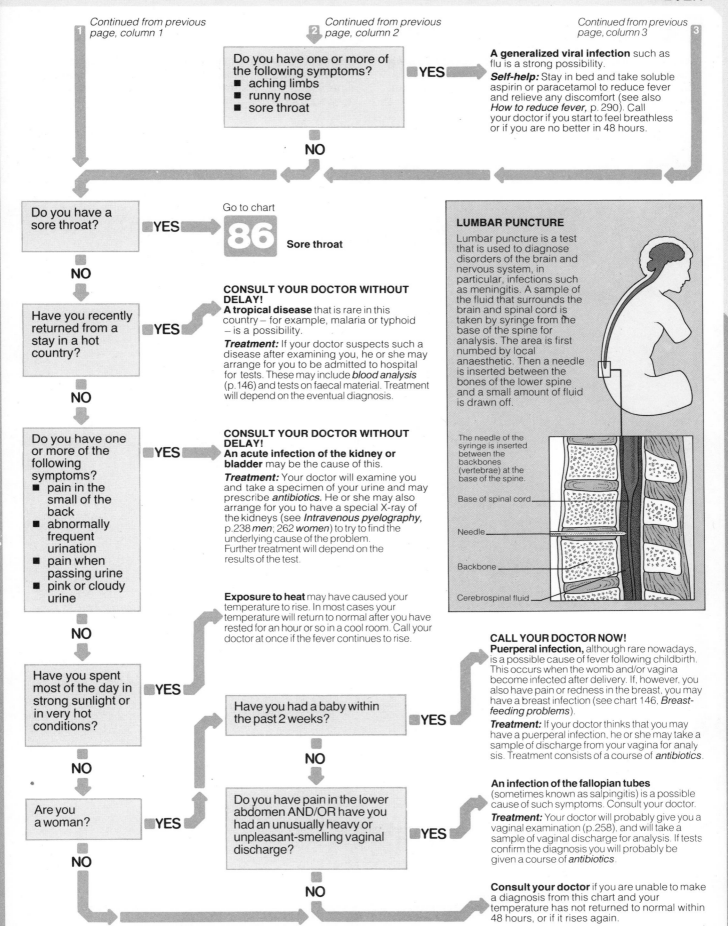

**LUMBAR PUNCTURE**

Lumbar puncture is a test that is used to diagnose disorders of the brain and nervous system, in particular, infections such as meningitis. A sample of the fluid that surrounds the brain and spinal cord is taken by syringe from the base of the spine for analysis. The area is first numbed by local anaesthetic. Then a needle is inserted between the bones of the lower spine and a small amount of fluid is drawn off.

The needle of the syringe is inserted between the backbones (vertebrae) at the base of the spine.

Base of spinal cord

Needle

Backbone

Cerebrospinal fluid

# 60 Excessive sweating

Sweating is a natural mechanism for regulating body temperature and is the normal response to hot conditions or strenuous exercise. Some people naturally sweat more than others, so if you have always sweated profusely there is unlikely to be anything wrong. However, sweating that is not brought on by heat or exercise or that is more profuse than you are used to may be a sign of a number of medical conditions.

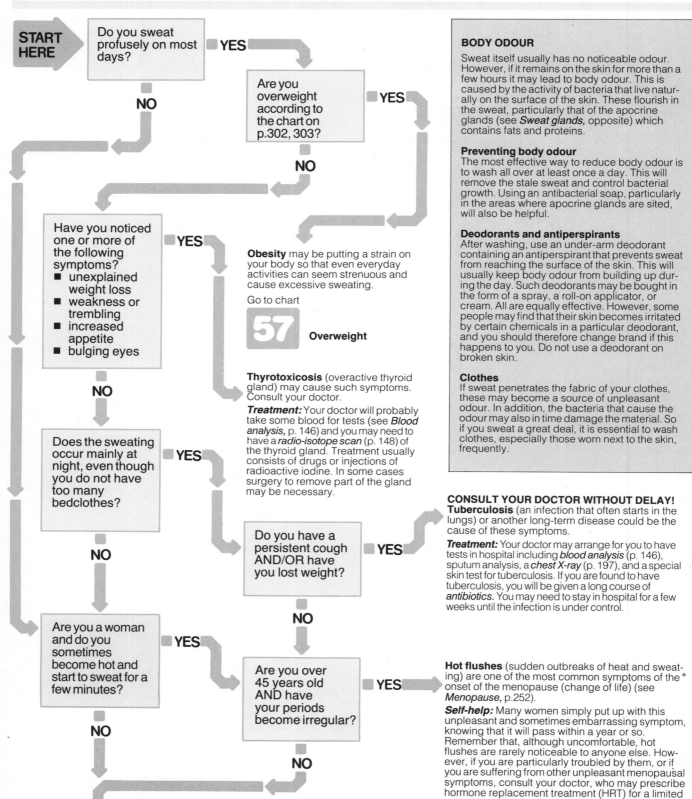

**START HERE**

**Do you sweat profusely on most days?**

NO → **Have you noticed one or more of the following symptoms?**
- unexplained weight loss
- weakness or trembling
- increased appetite
- bulging eyes

YES → **Are you overweight according to the chart on p.302, 303?**

YES → **Obesity** may be putting a strain on your body so that even everyday activities can seem strenuous and cause excessive sweating.

Go to chart

**57** Overweight

YES → **Thyrotoxicosis** (overactive thyroid gland) may cause such symptoms. Consult your doctor.

**Treatment:** Your doctor will probably take some blood for tests (see *Blood analysis,* p. 146) and you may need to have a *radio-isotope scan* (p. 148) of the thyroid gland. Treatment usually consists of drugs or injections of radioactive iodine. In some cases surgery to remove part of the gland may be necessary.

NO → **Does the sweating occur mainly at night, even though you do not have too many bedclothes?**

YES → **Do you have a persistent cough AND/OR have you lost weight?**

YES → **CONSULT YOUR DOCTOR WITHOUT DELAY!**
**Tuberculosis** (an infection that often starts in the lungs) or another long-term disease could be the cause of these symptoms.

**Treatment:** Your doctor may arrange for you to have tests in hospital including *blood analysis* (p. 146), sputum analysis, a *chest X-ray* (p. 197), and a special skin test for tuberculosis. If you are found to have tuberculosis, you will be given a long course of *antibiotics*. You may need to stay in hospital for a few weeks until the infection is under control.

NO → **Are you over 45 years old AND have your periods become irregular?**

YES → **Hot flushes** (sudden outbreaks of heat and sweating) are one of the most common symptoms of the onset of the menopause (change of life) (see *Menopause,* p.252).

**Self-help:** Many women simply put up with this unpleasant and sometimes embarrassing symptom, knowing that it will pass within a year or so. Remember that, although uncomfortable, hot flushes are rarely noticeable to anyone else. However, if you are particularly troubled by them, or if you are suffering from other unpleasant menopausal symptoms, consult your doctor, who may prescribe hormone replacement treatment (HRT) for a limited period (see p.252).

NO → **Are you a woman and do you sometimes become hot and start to sweat for a few minutes?**

NO → *Go to next page*

---

**BODY ODOUR**

Sweat itself usually has no noticeable odour. However, if it remains on the skin for more than a few hours it may lead to body odour. This is caused by the activity of bacteria that live naturally on the surface of the skin. These flourish in the sweat, particularly that of the apocrine glands (see *Sweat glands,* opposite) which contains fats and proteins.

**Preventing body odour**
The most effective way to reduce body odour is to wash all over at least once a day. This will remove the stale sweat and control bacterial growth. Using an antibacterial soap, particularly in the areas where apocrine glands are sited, will also be helpful.

**Deodorants and antiperspirants**
After washing, use an under-arm deodorant containing an antiperspirant that prevents sweat from reaching the surface of the skin. This will usually keep body odour from building up during the day. Such deodorants may be bought in the form of a spray, a roll-on applicator, or cream. All are equally effective. However, some people may find that their skin becomes irritated by certain chemicals in a particular deodorant, and you should therefore change brand if this happens to you. Do not use a deodorant on broken skin.

**Clothes**
If sweat penetrates the fabric of your clothes, these may become a source of unpleasant odour. In addition, the bacteria that cause the odour may also in time damage the material. So if you sweat a great deal, it is essential to wash clothes, especially those worn next to the skin, frequently.

*Continued from previous page*

**Is your temperature 38°C (100°F) or above?** → **YES**

Sweating is a normal response to fever.

Go to chart

**59** **Fever**

**NO**

↓

**Are you a woman and does the excessive sweating occur only during your periods?** → **YES**

**Changes in the hormone balance** cause increased sweating during menstruation in some women. This is no cause for concern, but consult your doctor if it troubles you.

**NO**

---

**Did you notice the sweating after you had been drinking alcohol or taking large doses of aspirin?** → **YES**

**Alcohol or aspirin** can cause increased sweating.

*Self-help:* If alcohol seems to be causing the problem, cut down on your drinking (see *The effects of alcohol,* p. 146). If aspirin taken for some other problem seems to be the cause of your sweating, ask your doctor for advice.

**NO**

↓

**Are you wearing clothes (or do you have bedclothes) made of nylon or other man-made materials?** → **YES**

**Synthetic materials** often cause a noticeable increase in sweating. This is because they do not absorb moisture or allow your skin to breathe.

*Self-help:* Try wearing natural fibres such as cotton or wool as often as possible. In addition, make sure that your clothing is loose; this will increase the circulation of air and allow the sweat to evaporate more quickly.

**NO**

↓

**Is the excessive sweating confined to your feet or hands?** → **YES**

**A high concentration of sweat glands** on the hands and feet (see *Sweat glands,* left) makes these parts of the body react most noticeably to increases in temperature. This is no cause for concern.

*Self-help:* If your hands are sweaty, wash them frequently. The problem is likely to become worse if you worry, so try to relax. Make sure that you wash and dry your feet carefully at least once a day. It is best to avoid wearing shoes, tights and socks made of synthetic materials. If the problem is severe, or causes embarrassment, consult your doctor.

**NO**

↓

**Do you notice the sweating only when you are anxious or excited?** → **YES**

**Emotional stress** can easily cause an increase in sweating. This in itself is not a cause for concern, but if it happens regularly or causes embarrassment, consult your doctor.

*Treatment:* Your doctor will advise you on the best methods of controlling the sweating. He or she will also discuss possible causes of any underlying anxiety with you and may recommend drug treatment. (See also chart 73, *Anxiety.*)

**NO**

↓

**Are you in your teens?** → **YES**

**The development of apocrine sweat glands** (see *Sweat glands,* left) during puberty usually causes an increase in sweating that is particularly noticeable under the arms. This is normal.

*Self-help:* There is no need to be embarrassed about increased sweating. However, you will need to wash regularly and you may want to use an antiperspirant deodorant to reduce wetness and to prevent unpleasant body odour (see *Body odour,* opposite).

**NO**

↓

**Consult your doctor** if you are unable to make a diagnosis from this chart and your excessive sweating continues to worry you. There is, however, unlikely to be a serious cause for this symptom.

---

## SWEAT GLANDS

Sweat glands are found under the skin and release moisture (sweat) through pores in the surface of the skin (see the illustration, right). There are two types of sweat glands – eccrine glands and apocrine glands – and these produce different kinds of sweat.

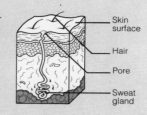

Skin surface

Hair

Pore

Sweat gland

### Eccrine glands

Eccrine glands are found all over the body and are active from birth onwards. The sweat from these glands is a clear, salty fluid containing various waste chemicals. This evaporates on the surface of the skin to reduce body temperature as necessary. The eccrine glands may also produce sweat in response to anxiety or fear. Eccrine glands are most concentrated on the forehead, palms, and soles of the feet (see below), and profuse sweating is likely to become apparent first in these areas.

### Apocrine glands

Apocrine glands become active during adolescence. They are mainly concentrated in the armpit, the groin, and around the nipples (see below). These glands produce a sticky, milky fluid that contains fats and proteins. The scent from this type of gland is thought to play a role in attracting the opposite sex. However, if it is allowed to remain on the skin for long it may interact with bacteria to produce a particularly pungent type of body odour (see *Body odour,* opposite).

**Distribution of sweat glands**

■ High concentration of eccrine glands

□ Apocrine glands

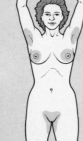

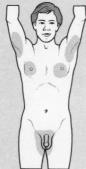

# 61 Itching

Itching (irritation of the skin that makes you want to scratch) is usually produced by contact with certain types of fabric or with a substance to which you are sensitive. Many skin disorders that produce a rash also cause itching. Occasionally, itching is a sign of an underlying disease or of psychological stress. Removal of natural oils by excessive washing may cause itching, especially in older people.

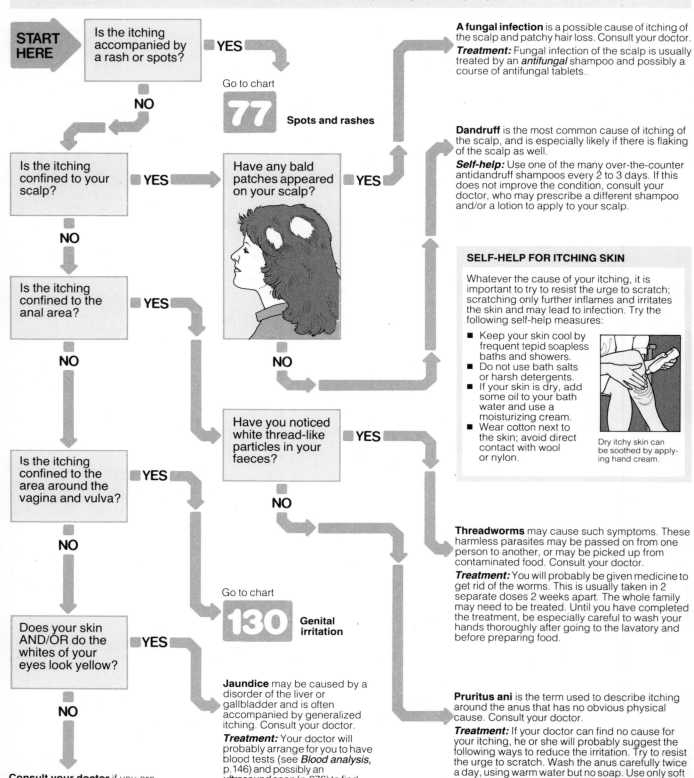

**START HERE**

**Is the itching accompanied by a rash or spots?**

YES → Go to chart **77** Spots and rashes

NO ↓

**Is the itching confined to your scalp?**

YES → **Have any bald patches appeared on your scalp?**

YES →

**A fungal infection** is a possible cause of itching of the scalp and patchy hair loss. Consult your doctor.
*Treatment:* Fungal infection of the scalp is usually treated by an *antifungal* shampoo and possibly a course of antifungal tablets.

NO (bald patches) →

**Dandruff** is the most common cause of itching of the scalp, and is especially likely if there is flaking of the scalp as well.
*Self-help:* Use one of the many over-the-counter antidandruff shampoos every 2 to 3 days. If this does not improve the condition, consult your doctor, who may prescribe a different shampoo and/or a lotion to apply to your scalp.

NO ↓

**Is the itching confined to the anal area?**

YES → **Have you noticed white thread-like particles in your faeces?**

YES →

### SELF-HELP FOR ITCHING SKIN

Whatever the cause of your itching, it is important to try to resist the urge to scratch; scratching only further inflames and irritates the skin and may lead to infection. Try the following self-help measures:

- Keep your skin cool by frequent tepid soapless baths and showers.
- Do not use bath salts or harsh detergents.
- If your skin is dry, add some oil to your bath water and use a moisturizing cream.
- Wear cotton next to the skin; avoid direct contact with wool or nylon.

Dry itchy skin can be soothed by applying hand cream.

NO ↓

**Threadworms** may cause such symptoms. These harmless parasites may be passed on from one person to another, or may be picked up from contaminated food. Consult your doctor.
*Treatment:* You will probably be given medicine to get rid of the worms. This is usually taken in 2 separate doses 2 weeks apart. The whole family may need to be treated. Until you have completed the treatment, be especially careful to wash your hands thoroughly after going to the lavatory and before preparing food.

NO ↓

**Is the itching confined to the area around the vagina and vulva?**

YES → Go to chart **130** Genital irritation

NO ↓

**Does your skin AND/OR do the whites of your eyes look yellow?**

YES →

**Jaundice** may be caused by a disorder of the liver or gallbladder and is often accompanied by generalized itching. Consult your doctor.
*Treatment:* Your doctor will probably arrange for you to have blood tests (see *Blood analysis,* p.146) and possibly an *ultrasound scan* (p.276) to find the cause of the trouble. Treatment will depend on the nature of the underlying disorder.

**Pruritus ani** is the term used to describe itching around the anus that has no obvious physical cause. Consult your doctor.
*Treatment:* If your doctor can find no cause for your itching, he or she will probably suggest the following ways to reduce the irritation. Try to resist the urge to scratch. Wash the anus carefully twice a day, using warm water but no soap. Use only soft toilet paper and wipe gently. Avoid tight underpants made of artificial fibres; cotton is best. Your doctor may also prescribe a soothing ointment.

NO ↓

**Consult your doctor** if you are unable to make a diagnosis from this chart and your itching persists for longer than 3 days.

# 62 Lumps and swellings

Consult this chart if you notice one or more swollen areas or lumps beneath the surface of the skin. In most cases such swellings are the result of enlargement of the lymph glands, which is a natural response to the presence of infection. You should always consult your doctor about a painful or persistent swelling.

For lumps and swellings in the breasts see chart 124, or in the testes see chart 115.

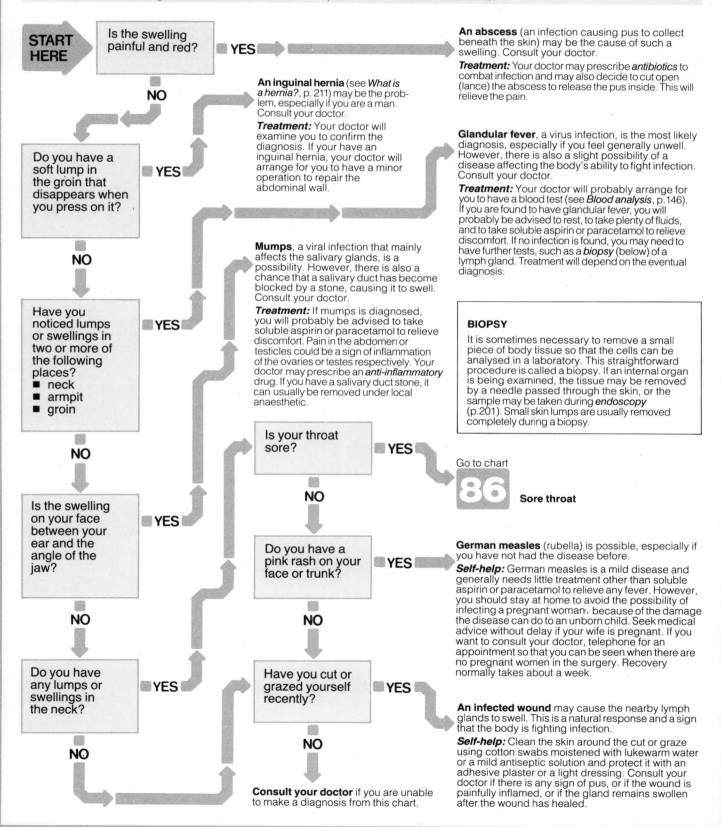

**START HERE**

**Is the swelling painful and red?**

YES →

**An abscess** (an infection causing pus to collect beneath the skin) may be the cause of such a swelling. Consult your doctor.

*Treatment:* Your doctor may prescribe *antibiotics* to combat infection and may also decide to cut open (lance) the abscess to release the pus inside. This will relieve the pain.

**NO**

**Do you have a soft lump in the groin that disappears when you press on it?**

YES →

**An inguinal hernia** (see *What is a hernia?*, p. 211) may be the problem, especially if you are a man. Consult your doctor.

*Treatment:* Your doctor will examine you to confirm the diagnosis. If your have an inguinal hernia, your doctor will arrange for you to have a minor operation to repair the abdominal wall.

**NO**

**Have you noticed lumps or swellings in two or more of the following places?**
- neck
- armpit
- groin

YES →

**Mumps**, a viral infection that mainly affects the salivary glands, is a possibility. However, there is also a chance that a salivary duct has become blocked by a stone, causing it to swell. Consult your doctor.

*Treatment:* If mumps is diagnosed, you will probably be advised to take soluble aspirin or paracetamol to relieve discomfort. Pain in the abdomen or testicles could be a sign of inflammation of the ovaries or testes respectively. Your doctor may prescribe an *anti-inflammatory* drug. If you have a salivary duct stone, it can usually be removed under local anaesthetic.

**Glandular fever**, a virus infection, is the most likely diagnosis, especially if you feel generally unwell. However, there is also a slight possibility of a disease affecting the body's ability to fight infection. Consult your doctor.

*Treatment:* Your doctor will probably arrange for you to have a blood test (see *Blood analysis*, p.146). If you are found to have glandular fever, you will probably be advised to rest, to take plenty of fluids, and to take soluble aspirin or paracetamol to relieve discomfort. If no infection is found, you may need to have further tests, such as a *biopsy* (below) of a lymph gland. Treatment will depend on the eventual diagnosis.

**NO**

**BIOPSY**

It is sometimes necessary to remove a small piece of body tissue so that the cells can be analysed in a laboratory. This straightforward procedure is called a biopsy. If an internal organ is being examined, the tissue may be removed by a needle passed through the skin, or the sample may be taken during *endoscopy* (p.201). Small skin lumps are usually removed completely during a biopsy.

**Is the swelling on your face between your ear and the angle of the jaw?**

YES →

**Is your throat sore?**

YES →

Go to chart

**86** **Sore throat**

**NO**

**NO**

**Do you have a pink rash on your face or trunk?**

YES →

**German measles** (rubella) is possible, especially if you have not had the disease before.

*Self-help:* German measles is a mild disease and generally needs little treatment other than soluble aspirin or paracetamol to relieve any fever. However, you should stay at home to avoid the possibility of infecting a pregnant woman, because of the damage the disease can do to an unborn child. Seek medical advice without delay if your wife is pregnant. If you want to consult your doctor, telephone for an appointment so that you can be seen when there are no pregnant women in the surgery. Recovery normally takes about a week.

**Do you have any lumps or swellings in the neck?**

YES →

**NO**

**Have you cut or grazed yourself recently?**

YES →

**An infected wound** may cause the nearby lymph glands to swell. This is a natural response and a sign that the body is fighting infection.

*Self-help:* Clean the skin around the cut or graze using cotton swabs moistened with lukewarm water or a mild antiseptic solution and protect it with an adhesive plaster or a light dressing. Consult your doctor if there is any sign of pus, or if the wound is painfully inflamed, or if the gland remains swollen after the wound has healed.

**NO**

**NO**

**Consult your doctor** if you are unable to make a diagnosis from this chart.

# 63 Faintness and fainting

Fainting – a brief loss of consciousness – is usually preceded by a sensation of lightheadedness or dizziness, and you may go pale and feel suddenly cold or clammy. Such feelings of faintness may sometimes occur on their own without loss of consciousness. Faintness is usually the result of a sudden drop in blood pressure – as a result, for example, of emotional shock – or it may be caused by an abnormally low level of sugar in the blood. Isolated episodes of fainting with no other symptoms are hardly ever a cause for concern, but if you suffer repeated fainting attacks or have additional symptoms you should seek medical advice.

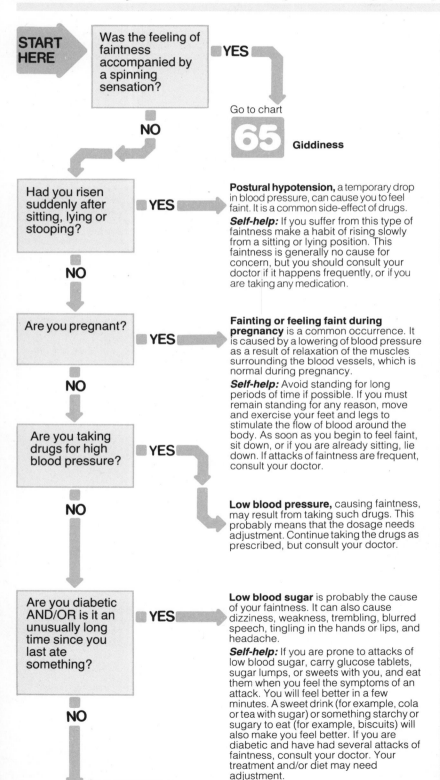

**START HERE**

Was the feeling of faintness accompanied by a spinning sensation?

**YES** ▶ Go to chart **65** Giddiness

**NO**

Had you risen suddenly after sitting, lying or stooping?

**YES** ▶ **Postural hypotension,** a temporary drop in blood pressure, can cause you to feel faint. It is a common side-effect of drugs.
***Self-help:*** If you suffer from this type of faintness make a habit of rising slowly from a sitting or lying position. This faintness is generally no cause for concern, but you should consult your doctor if it happens frequently, or if you are taking any medication.

**NO**

Are you pregnant?

**YES** ▶ **Fainting or feeling faint during pregnancy** is a common occurrence. It is caused by a lowering of blood pressure as a result of relaxation of the muscles surrounding the blood vessels, which is normal during pregnancy.
***Self-help:*** Avoid standing for long periods of time if possible. If you must remain standing for any reason, move and exercise your feet and legs to stimulate the flow of blood around the body. As soon as you begin to feel faint, sit down, or if you are already sitting, lie down. If attacks of faintness are frequent, consult your doctor.

**NO**

Are you taking drugs for high blood pressure?

**YES** ▶ **Low blood pressure,** causing faintness, may result from taking such drugs. This probably means that the dosage needs adjustment. Continue taking the drugs as prescribed, but consult your doctor.

**NO**

Are you diabetic AND/OR is it an unusually long time since you last ate something?

**YES** ▶ **Low blood sugar** is probably the cause of your faintness. It can also cause dizziness, weakness, trembling, blurred speech, tingling in the hands or lips, and headache.
***Self-help:*** If you are prone to attacks of low blood sugar, carry glucose tablets, sugar lumps, or sweets with you, and eat them when you feel the symptoms of an attack. You will feel better in a few minutes. A sweet drink (for example, cola or tea with sugar) or something starchy or sugary to eat (for example, biscuits) will also make you feel better. If you are diabetic and have had several attacks of faintness, consult your doctor. Your treatment and/or diet may need adjustment.

**NO**

*Go to next page*

## WARNING

### PROLONGED LOSS OF CONSCIOUSNESS

Momentary loss of consciousness – fainting – is not usually a cause for concern if the person is breathing normally and regains consciousness within a minute or two. If someone in your presence remain unconscious for longer, or if breathing slows or becomes irregular or noisy, get medical help at once. While waiting for medical help to arrive place the person on her stomach as shown.

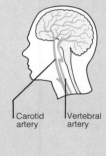

### HOW BLOOD FLOWS TO THE BRAIN

The brain is more dependent on a constant supply of oxygenated blood than any other organ in the body. Temporary interruption in this supply is likely to cause the brain to malfunction, and more serious disruption to the blood flow may cause lasting damage to brain cells.

View of the brain from beneath.

View of the brain from the side.

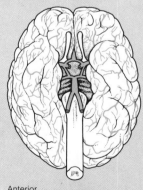

Carotid artery

Vertebral artery

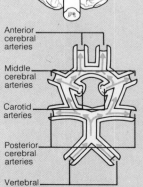

Anterior cerebral arteries

Middle cerebral arteries

Carotid arteries

Posterior cerebral arteries

Vertebral arteries

**The main arteries of the brain**
The brain is supplied with blood by 2 pairs of arteries in the neck: the vertebral arteries and the carotid arteries. At the bottom of the brain they join to form a circular junction from which other arteries – the anterior cerebral, the middle cerebral, and the posterior cerebral – run to all parts of the brain.

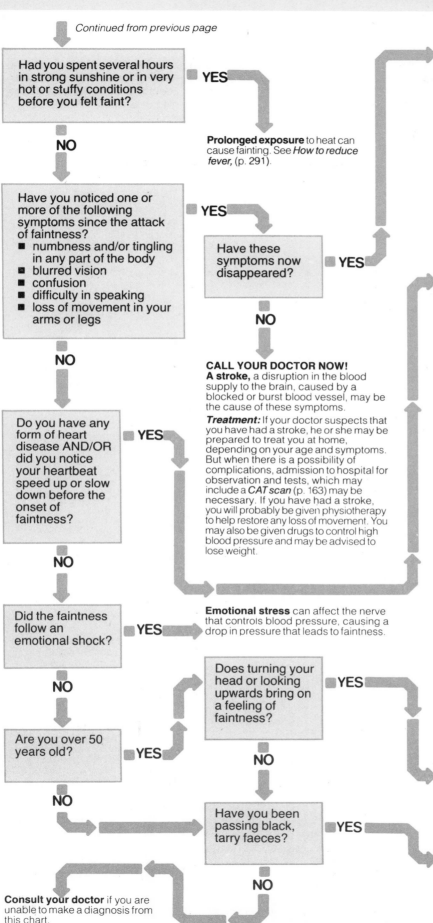

*Continued from previous page*

Had you spent several hours in strong sunshine or in very hot or stuffy conditions before you felt faint?

**YES** → **Prolonged exposure** to heat can cause fainting. See *How to reduce fever,* (p. 291).

**NO** ↓

Have you noticed one or more of the following symptoms since the attack of faintness?
- numbness and/or tingling in any part of the body
- blurred vision
- confusion
- difficulty in speaking
- loss of movement in your arms or legs

**YES** → Have these symptoms now disappeared?

**YES** →

**NO** ↓

**CALL YOUR DOCTOR NOW!**
**A stroke,** a disruption in the blood supply to the brain, caused by a blocked or burst blood vessel, may be the cause of these symptoms.

*Treatment:* If your doctor suspects that you have had a stroke, he or she may be prepared to treat you at home, depending on your age and symptoms. But when there is a possibility of complications, admission to hospital for observation and tests, which may include a *CAT scan* (p. 163) may be necessary. If you have had a stroke, you will probably be given physiotherapy to help restore any loss of movement. You may also be given drugs to control high blood pressure and may be advised to lose weight.

**NO** ↓

Do you have any form of heart disease AND/OR did you notice your heartbeat speed up or slow down before the onset of faintness?

**YES** →

**NO** ↓

Did the faintness follow an emotional shock?

**YES** → **Emotional stress** can affect the nerve that controls blood pressure, causing a drop in pressure that leads to faintness.

**NO** ↓

Are you over 50 years old?

**YES** → Does turning your head or looking upwards bring on a feeling of faintness?

**YES** →

**NO** ↓

**NO** ↓

Have you been passing black, tarry faeces?

**YES** →

**NO** ↓

**Consult your doctor** if you are unable to make a diagnosis from this chart.

**CONSULT YOUR DOCTOR WITHOUT DELAY!**
**A transient ischaemic attack** – a temporary interruption in the blood supply to the brain, sometimes linked to a narrowing of the carotid arteries (see *How blood flows to the brain,* opposite) – may have caused your symptoms.

*Treatment:* If your doctor suspects that this is the problem, he or she may simply reassure you or may refer you to a specialist for tests including *electrocardiography* (p. 219) and a *chest X-ray* (p. 197). At a later stage you may need to undergo *angiography* (p. 227) of the carotid arteries. Treatment consists of taking steps to reduce factors that may contribute to narrowing of the arteries. These are discussed in the box on *coronary heart disease* (p. 221). You may also be prescribed drugs to control high blood pressure, if you have it, and further drugs to prevent the formation of blood clots. Surgery may be necessary.

**CONSULT YOUR DOCTOR WITHOUT DELAY!**
**An Adams-Stokes attack** (sudden slowing of the heartbeat rate) could have caused the fainting. Such attacks may be a sign of an underlying disorder of heart rate or rhythm.

*Treatment:* If your doctor suspects the possibility of such a disorder, he or she will arrange for you to undergo *electrocardiography* (p. 219). If this shows abnormal heart rhythms, you will probably need treatment with an electrical pacemaker to maintain the heart in normal heart rhythm.

---

**FIRST AID FOR FAINTING**

**Dealing with faintness**
If you feel faint, lie down with your legs raised (below) or, if this is not possible, sit with your head between your knees (right) until you feel better.

**Dealing with fainting**
To help somebody who has fainted, first check that breathing is normal. Lay the person on her back with legs raised as high as possible above the level of the head. Hold the legs up, or rest them on a chair. Loosen any tight clothing (collar, waistband, etc.) and make sure that she gets plenty of fresh air. If you are indoors, open the windows to allow air to circulate. If you are outdoors, make sure that the person is in the shade. When she regains consciousness it is important that she remains lying down for a few minutes before attempting to get up.

---

**Cervical spondylosis** – arthritis of the bones in the neck – can cause feelings of faintness. Consult your doctor.

*Treatment:* See *Cervical spondylosis,* (p. 224).

**CALL YOUR DOCTOR NOW!**
**Bleeding in the digestive tract,** perhaps from a stomach ulcer, is a possibility.

*Treatment:* Your doctor will probably arrange for you to have investigations such as *endoscopy* (p. 201) a *barium X-ray* (p. 207) and a *biopsy* (p. 159) of the stomach lining. These tests should reveal the underlying cause of your symptoms.

# 64 Headache

From time to time nearly everyone suffers from headaches that develop gradually and clear up after a few hours, leaving no after-effects. Headaches like this are extremely unlikely to be a sign of any disorder and are usually caused by factors such as tension, tiredness, excessive consumption of alcohol, or staying in an overheated or smoke-filled atmosphere. However, a headache that is severe, lasts for more than 24 hours, or recurs several times during one week, should be brought to your doctor's attention.

**START HERE**

**Is your temperature 38°C (100°F) or above?**

**YES** → **Many feverish illnesses** may cause a headache.

Go to chart **59** **Fever**

**NO** ↓

**Have you injured your head within the past few days?**

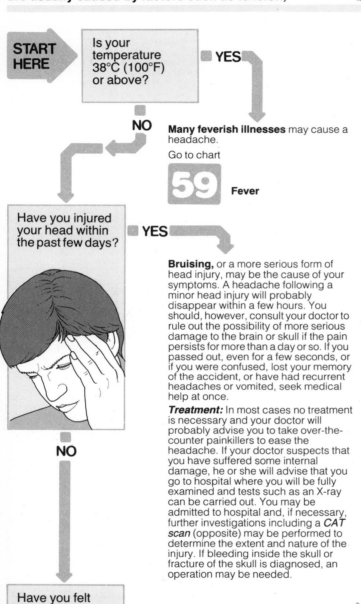

**YES** → **Bruising,** or a more serious form of head injury, may be the cause of your symptoms. A headache following a minor head injury will probably disappear within a few hours. You should, however, consult your doctor to rule out the possibility of more serious damage to the brain or skull if the pain persists for more than a day or so. If you passed out, even for a few seconds, or if you were confused, lost your memory of the accident, or have had recurrent headaches or vomited, seek medical help at once.

*Treatment:* In most cases no treatment is necessary and your doctor will probably advise you to take over-the-counter painkillers to ease the headache. If your doctor suspects that you have suffered some internal damage, he or she will advise that you go to hospital where you will be fully examined and tests such as an X-ray can be carried out. You may be admitted to hospital and, if necessary, further investigations including a *CAT scan* (opposite) may be performed to determine the extent and nature of the injury. If bleeding inside the skull or fracture of the skull is diagnosed, an operation may be needed.

**NO** ↓

**Have you felt nauseated or been vomiting?**

**YES** → **Did the headache develop before the onset of nausea or vomiting?**

**NO** ↓

Go to next page, column 1

**NO** → 

**YES** → **Is your vision blurred?**

**A headache** often follows an attack of vomiting.

Go to chart **94** **Vomiting**

**NO** ↓

### RELIEVING HEADACHE

Most minor headaches can be relieved by the following self-help measures:

- Take the recommended dose of paracetamol or soluble aspirin.
- Drink plenty of water or non-alcoholic clear fluids.
- Have a warm bath to relieve tension.
- Rest in a quiet, darkened room.

Consult your doctor if such measures fail to reduce the pain, or if pain is still present the following day.

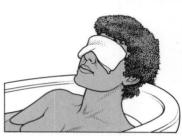

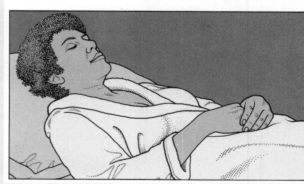

**Is your vision blurred?**

**YES** → **CALL YOUR DOCTOR NOW!** **Acute glaucoma,** a serious disorder in which excess fluid causes increased pressure in the eye, is a possibility, especially if you are over 40.

*Treatment:* If your doctor confirms the diagnosis, you will probably be given eye drops to allow the excess fluid to drain from the eye. In addition you may be given a *diuretic* drug to prevent fluid retention. Once the pressure has been relieved, an operation to prevent a recurrence of the problem is usually carried out.

Go to next page, column 2

**1** *Continued from previous page, column 1*

## Do you have a blocked nose?

**YES**

**Sinusitis** (inflammation of the membranes lining the air spaces in the skull) may be the cause of this problem, although it is possible that you have a common cold.

*Self-help:* Stay inside in a warm and humid atmosphere and take soluble aspirin or paracetamol to relieve the discomfort. If you are no better in 48 hours, consult your doctor, who may prescribe *antibiotics* and *decongestants*. If you suffer from recurrent sinusitis, a minor operation to clear the sinuses may be recommended.

**NO**

## Did the headache occur after you had been reading or doing close work?

**YES**

**Muscle strain** in your neck, as a result of poor posture or tension from concentration, is the likely cause of your headache (see *Eyestrain,* p. 184).

*Self-help:* In order to prevent the problem from recurring, make sure that when you read you are not sitting in an awkward position or in poor light. Periodic rest from whatever you are doing for a few minutes of relaxation will also help. If headaches recur, consult your doctor, who may recommend that you have an *eye test* (p. 186).

**NO**

## Are you sleeping poorly AND/OR are you feeling tense or under stress?

**YES**

**Tension headaches** are often caused by psychological stress.

Go to chart

 **73** Anxiety

**NO**

## Are you currently taking any medicines AND/OR are you taking the contraceptive pill?

**YES**

**Certain drugs** can cause headaches as a side-effect. Discuss the problem with your doctor. If you are taking the pill and have recurrent headaches, your doctor may suggest that you use an alternative form of contraception.

See also chart

 **136** Choosing a contraceptive method

**NO**

**Consult your doctor** if you are unable to make a diagnosis from this chart and if the headache persists overnight or if you develop other symptoms.

**2** *Continued from previous page, column 2*

## Have you suddenly begun to have a severe throbbing pain in one or both temples?

**YES**

**CONSULT YOUR DOCTOR WITHOUT DELAY!**
**Temporal arteritis,** inflammation of the arteries in the head, is a possibility, especially if you are over 50. Urgent treatment may be needed to prevent this condition from affecting your eyesight.

*Treatment:* Your doctor will probably prescribe tablets to reduce the inflammation and it may be necessary for you to have regular blood tests to confirm that the treatment is effective.

**NO**

## Was your vision disturbed in any way before the onset of pain?

**YES**

**Migraine,** a recurrent, severe headache that usually occurs on one side of the head, but may occasionally be on both sides, may be the explanation for your symptoms. Migraines often occur before or during periods. They may also be brought on by different trigger factors such as stress, eating cheese or chocolate, or drinking red wine. Consult your doctor.

*Treatment:* You may find that the pain can be eased by self-help measures (see *Relieving headache,* opposite). It will also help if you can discover what causes your migraines. Your doctor may be able to offer drug treatment if self-help measures are not effective or if the attacks recur.

**NO**

**CONSULT YOUR DOCTOR WITHOUT DELAY!**
**Unexplained headaches,** especially if severe and accompanied by additional symptoms such as nausea and vomiting, should always be brought to your doctor's attention.

### CAT SCAN

A CAT (computerized axial tomography) scan is a painless procedure that helps in the diagnosis of a wide variety of conditions. Unlike conventional X-rays, CAT scans can clearly show up soft tissues (including organs, blood clots and tumours). The procedure involves hundreds of X-rays being taken as a camera revolves around the body. The readings are fed into a computer which assembles them into a series of accurate pictures of the area under examination.

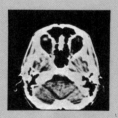

**CAT scan at eyelid level**
This scan shows a cross-section of a normal brain at eyelid level. The front of the head is at the top, where the dark areas indicate the eye sockets and air spaces in the skull. The white areas indicate bone.

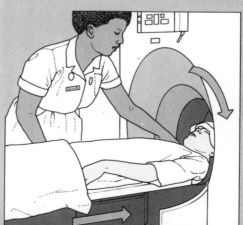

**CAT scan of the head**
For a CAT scan of the head you will lie on a movable table with your head resting inside the machine. You will be told not to make any movement so that the pictures are not blurred.

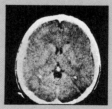

**CAT scan at mid-forehead level**
This scan shows a cross-section of the same brain as shown above taken at mid-forehead level.

# 65 Giddiness

**Giddiness is a feeling that everything around you is spinning. This usually occurs only when you have been rotating rapidly, for example, on a merry-go-round. But** if you feel giddy for no obvious reason, it may be a symptom of an underlying disorder and should be brought to your doctor's attention.

**START HERE**

Have you noticed one or more of the following symptoms since the attack of giddiness?
- difficulty in speaking
- temporary total or partial loss of vision in one or both eyes
- weakness in your arms or legs
- numbness and/or tingling in any part of your body

**YES** →

Have all your symptoms now disappeared?

**YES** →

**NO** ↓

**NO** ↓

Have you been vomiting AND/OR finding it difficult to keep your balance?

**YES** →

**NO** ↓

Have you noticed some loss of hearing AND/OR noises in the ear?

**YES** →

**NO** ↓

Does turning your head or looking upwards bring on giddiness?

**YES** →

**NO** ↓

**Consult your doctor** if you are unable to make a diagnosis from this chart.

## CONSULT YOUR DOCTOR WITHOUT DELAY!

**A transient ischaemic attack** – a temporary interruption in the blood supply to the brain, sometimes linked to a narrowing of the carotid arteries (see *How blood flows to the brain,* p. 160) – may have caused your symptoms.

**Treatment:** If your doctor suspects that this is the problem, he or she may simply reassure you or may refer you to a specialist for tests including *electrocardiography* (p. 219) and a *chest X-ray* (p. 197). At a later stage you may need to undergo *angiography* (p. 227) of the carotid arteries. Treatment consists of taking steps to reduce factors that may contribute to narrowing of the arteries. These are discussed in the box on *coronary heart disease* (p. 221). You may also be prescribed drugs to control high blood pressure, if you have it, and further drugs to prevent the formation of blood clots. Surgery may be necessary.

## CALL YOUR DOCTOR NOW!

**A stroke,** a disruption in the blood supply to the brain, caused by a blocked or burst blood vessel, may be the cause of these symptoms.

**Treatment:** If your doctor suspects that you have had a stroke, he or she may be prepared to treat you at home, depending on your age and the severity of your symptoms. But when there is a possibility of complications, admission to hospital for observation and tests, which include a *CAT scan* (p. 163), may be necessary. If you are found to have had a stroke, you will probably be given physiotherapy to restore any loss of movement. You may also be given drugs to control high blood pressure and may be advised to lose weight.

**Labyrinthitis,** inflammation of part of the inner ear (see *How you keep your balance,* right) due to viral infection, may cause these symptoms. Consult your doctor.

**Treatment:** Your doctor will examine your ears with an auriscope. If labyrinthitis is diagnosed, you will probably be prescribed drugs to alleviate your symptoms and you will be advised to rest quietly in bed. Most cases clear up within 3 weeks.

**Ménière's disease** may be the problem. This is an uncommon disorder that occurs when there is an increase in the amount of fluid in the labyrinth (see *How you keep your balance,* right). Ménière's disease is most common in middle age. Consult your doctor.

**Treatment:** Your doctor will probably arrange for you to undergo tests in hospital to confirm the diagnosis. If you are found to have Ménière's disease, you will probably be given a drug to reduce the amount of fluid in the labyrinth. Your doctor may also advise you to cut down your intake of salt to reduce the frequency of further attacks. Very occasionally an operation is recommended.

**Cervical spondylosis,** a disorder of the bones in the neck that may cause them to press on nearby nerves and blood vessels, may be the cause of this, especially if you are over 50. Consult your doctor.

**Treatment:** Your doctor may arrange for you to have an X-ray of the bones in your neck. If he or she thinks that your giddiness is due to this disorder, you may be given a supportive collar to wear for about 3 months to reduce the mobility of your neck and to relieve pressure on the nerves and blood vessels. Soluble aspirin or paracetamol can be taken to relieve any discomfort.

## HOW YOU KEEP YOUR BALANCE

The brain relies on information from a structure in the inner ear called the labyrinth, to help you to keep your balance. The labyrinth sends messages about your movements to the brain, where they are coordinated with other information from your eyes, limbs and muscles, to assess your exact position so that your body can make adjustments to keep balanced.

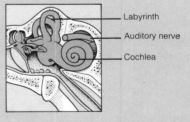

- Labyrinth
- Auditory nerve
- Cochlea

**The semi-circular canals**
Each of the three fluid-filled semi-circular canals that make up the labyrinth lies at a right angle to the other two (above), so that whichever way you move your head – whether you shake it, nod it, or tilt it – one of the canals will detect this movement and relay the information to the brain.

# 66 Numbness and tingling

It is normal to experience numbness or tingling if you are cold or sitting in an awkward position. This is commonly known as "pins and needles", and can occur in any part of the body. The feeling disappears as soon as you move around. Numbness or tingling that occurs without apparent cause may need medical treatment.

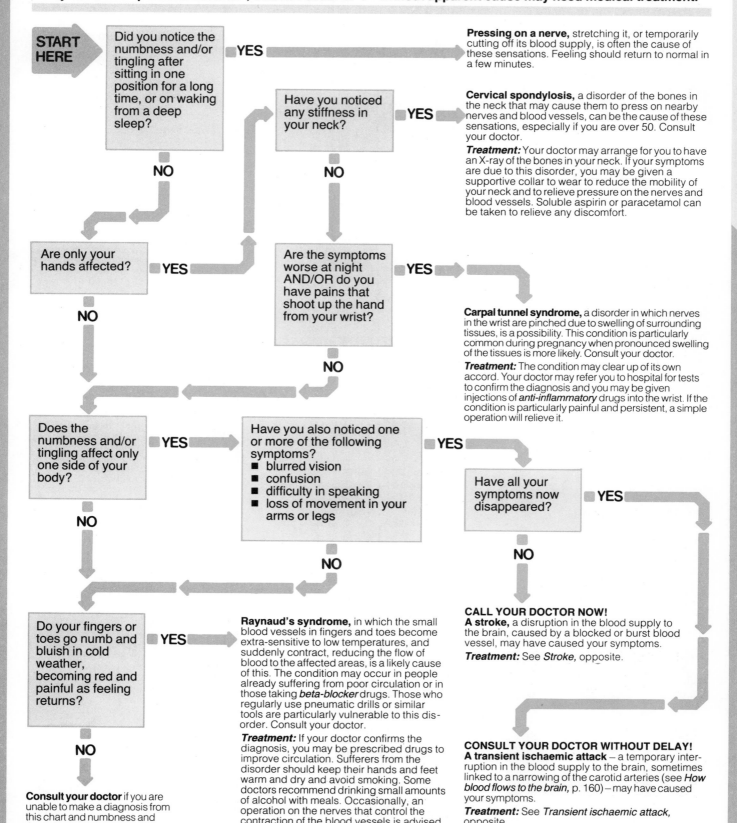

**START HERE**

**Did you notice the numbness and/or tingling after sitting in one position for a long time, or on waking from a deep sleep?**

**YES** → **Pressing on a nerve,** stretching it, or temporarily cutting off its blood supply, is often the cause of these sensations. Feeling should return to normal in a few minutes.

**NO**

**Have you noticed any stiffness in your neck?**

**YES** → **Cervical spondylosis,** a disorder of the bones in the neck that may cause them to press on nearby nerves and blood vessels, can be the cause of these sensations, especially if you are over 50. Consult your doctor.

*Treatment:* Your doctor may arrange for you to have an X-ray of the bones in your neck. If your symptoms are due to this disorder, you may be given a supportive collar to wear to reduce the mobility of your neck and to relieve pressure on the nerves and blood vessels. Soluble aspirin or paracetamol can be taken to relieve any discomfort.

**NO**

**Are only your hands affected?** **YES**

**NO**

**Are the symptoms worse at night AND/OR do you have pains that shoot up the hand from your wrist?**

**YES** → **Carpal tunnel syndrome,** a disorder in which nerves in the wrist are pinched due to swelling of surrounding tissues, is a possibility. This condition is particularly common during pregnancy when pronounced swelling of the tissues is more likely. Consult your doctor.

*Treatment:* The condition may clear up of its own accord. Your doctor may refer you to hospital for tests to confirm the diagnosis and you may be given injections of *anti-inflammatory* drugs into the wrist. If the condition is particularly painful and persistent, a simple operation will relieve it.

**NO**

**Does the numbness and/or tingling affect only one side of your body?** **YES**

**Have you also noticed one or more of the following symptoms?**
- blurred vision
- confusion
- difficulty in speaking
- loss of movement in your arms or legs

**YES**

**Have all your symptoms now disappeared?** **YES**

**NO**

**NO**

**NO**

**Do your fingers or toes go numb and bluish in cold weather, becoming red and painful as feeling returns?** **YES**

**Raynaud's syndrome,** in which the small blood vessels in fingers and toes become extra-sensitive to low temperatures, and suddenly contract, reducing the flow of blood to the affected areas, is a likely cause of this. The condition may occur in people already suffering from poor circulation or in those taking *beta-blocker* drugs. Those who regularly use pneumatic drills or similar tools are particularly vulnerable to this disorder. Consult your doctor.

*Treatment:* If your doctor confirms the diagnosis, you may be prescribed drugs to improve circulation. Sufferers from the disorder should keep their hands and feet warm and dry and avoid smoking. Some doctors recommend drinking small amounts of alcohol with meals. Occasionally, an operation on the nerves that control the contraction of the blood vessels is advised.

**NO**

**Consult your doctor** if you are unable to make a diagnosis from this chart and numbness and tingling persists.

**CALL YOUR DOCTOR NOW!**
**A stroke,** a disruption in the blood supply to the brain, caused by a blocked or burst blood vessel, may have caused your symptoms.
*Treatment:* See *Stroke,* opposite.

**CONSULT YOUR DOCTOR WITHOUT DELAY!**
**A transient ischaemic attack** – a temporary interruption in the blood supply to the brain, sometimes linked to a narrowing of the carotid arteries (see *How blood flows to the brain,* p. 160) – may have caused your symptoms.
*Treatment:* See *Transient ischaemic attack,* opposite.

# 67 Twitching and trembling

Consult this chart if you experience any involuntary or uncontrolled movements of any part of your body. Such movements may range from slight twitching to persistent trembling or shaking – for example, of the hands, arms, or head. In many cases such movements are no cause for concern, being simply the result of tiredness or stress, or of an inherited tendency.

Occasionally, however, the symptoms may be caused by problems that require medical treatment, such as excessive consumption of alcohol or a neurological disorder. Involuntary movements that are accompanied by weakness of the affected part of the body should always be brought to your doctor's attention without delay. Diagnostic tests may be needed.

**START HERE**

**Is your trouble confined to brief flickering movements of one small part of the body – an eyelid, for example?**

**YES**

**Tiredness or tension** can often cause such minor twitching. This in itself is most unlikely to be a cause for concern.

**NO**

**Have you been suffering from trembling or shaking movements of any part of the body?**

**YES**

**Are you over 55 AND is the trembling worse when the affected part of the body is at rest?**

**YES**

**Parkinson's disease** may cause such trembling. This is a disorder of the nerve centres in the brain that control body movement. Consult your doctor.

**Treatment:** If your doctor confirms the diagnosis, he or she will probably want to see you every few months to monitor the progress of your condition. In mild cases specific treatment may not be necessary, but if trembling is severe, you may be prescribed drugs to relieve your symptoms.

**NO**

**Have you recently cut down your alcohol intake after a period of heavy drinking?**

**YES**

**Sudden withdrawal of alcohol** can lead to uncontrolled shaking. This is a sign that you have become dependent on alcohol. Consult your doctor. (See also *The effects of alcohol*, p.146).

**Treatment:** Your doctor will advise you on the best way of controlling your drinking and may prescribe drugs to relieve unpleasant withdrawal symptoms. You may also be advised to contact a self-help group for alcoholics such as Alcoholics Anonymous.

**NO**

**NO**

**Consult your doctor** if you are unable to make a diagnosis from this chart.

**Have you drunk more than 5 cups of coffee or 10 cups of tea within the past 12 hours?**

**YES**

**Caffeine poisoning** in a mild form is a possibility. See *Caffeine*, p.219.

**Self-help:** Drink no more tea or coffee for the next few hours and your body should return to normal. If you regularly suffer from such symptoms after drinking tea and coffee, or if you have trouble sleeping, it may be advisable to cut down permanently on your regular caffeine intake.

## RADIO-ISOTOPE SCAN

Doctors use this type of scan to find out whether and how a gland or organ is malfunctioning. A radioactive chemical is injected into the bloodstream, and is absorbed by the organ being examined. This organ is then scanned with specialized equipment, to determine whether or not the chemical is being absorbed evenly and normally. The result of the scan is shown either on photographs or on a television screen.

The dark area in this scan of a thyroid gland shows a possible thyroid nodule.

**NO**

**Have you noticed two or more of the following symptoms?**
- excessive sweating
- inexplicable tiredness
- bulging eyes
- unexplained weight loss

**YES**

**Thyrotoxicosis** (overactive thyroid gland) may cause trembling and shaking. Consult your doctor.

**Treatment:** Your doctor will probably take some blood for tests (see *Blood analysis*, p.146) and you may need to have a *radio-isotope scan* (p.148) of the thyroid gland. Treatment usually consists of drugs or of injections of radioactive iodine. In some cases surgery to remove part of the gland may be necessary.

**NO**

**A tendency to tremble or shake** may be inherited. The symptoms may be brought on by stress or anxiety. Consult your doctor.

**Treatment:** Your doctor will probably check your general health to reassure you that nothing is wrong. If necessary, he or she may prescibe an *anti-anxiety* drug to relieve your symptoms.

# 68 Pain in the face

Consult this chart if you have pain or discomfort that is limited to the area of the face and/or forehead. Facial pain may be dull and throbbing or sharp and stabbing, and is usually caused by infection or inflammation of the underlying tissues and, although it may be distressing, it is rarely a sign of a serious disorder.

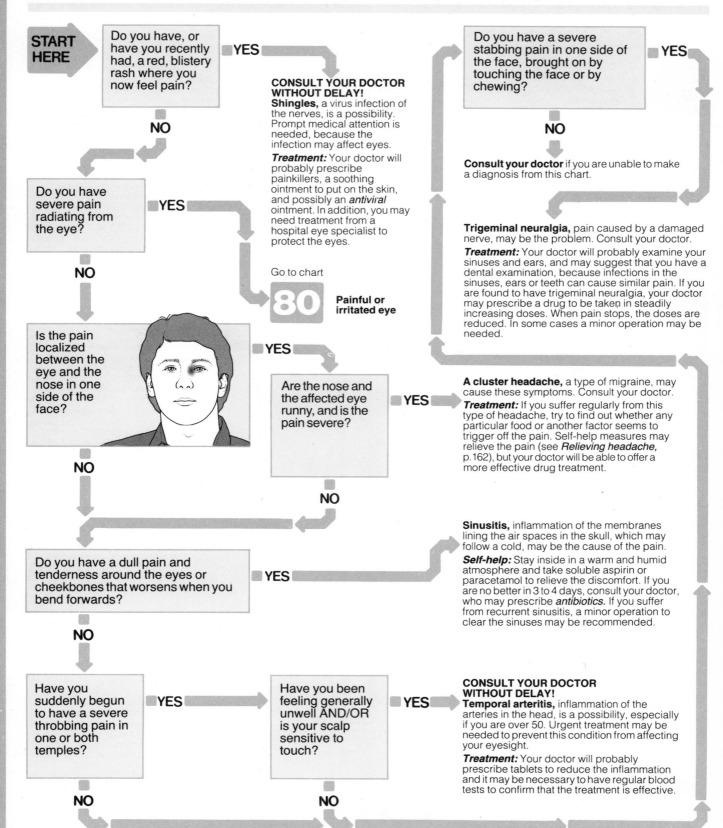

**START HERE**

**Do you have, or have you recently had, a red, blistery rash where you now feel pain?**

YES →

**CONSULT YOUR DOCTOR WITHOUT DELAY!**
**Shingles,** a virus infection of the nerves, is a possibility. Prompt medical attention is needed, because the infection may affect eyes.
**Treatment:** Your doctor will probably prescribe painkillers, a soothing ointment to put on the skin, and possibly an *antiviral* ointment. In addition, you may need treatment from a hospital eye specialist to protect the eyes.

NO ↓

**Do you have severe pain radiating from the eye?**

YES →

Go to chart
**80** **Painful or irritated eye**

NO ↓

**Is the pain localized between the eye and the nose in one side of the face?**

YES →

**Are the nose and the affected eye runny, and is the pain severe?**

YES →

**A cluster headache,** a type of migraine, may cause these symptoms. Consult your doctor.
**Treatment:** If you suffer regularly from this type of headache, try to find out whether any particular food or another factor seems to trigger off the pain. Self-help measures may relieve the pain (see *Relieving headache,* p.162), but your doctor will be able to offer a more effective drug treatment.

NO ↓

NO ↓

**Do you have a dull pain and tenderness around the eyes or cheekbones that worsens when you bend forwards?**

YES →

**Sinusitis,** inflammation of the membranes lining the air spaces in the skull, which may follow a cold, may be the cause of the pain.
**Self-help:** Stay inside in a warm and humid atmosphere and take soluble aspirin or paracetamol to relieve the discomfort. If you are no better in 3 to 4 days, consult your doctor, who may prescribe *antibiotics*. If you suffer from recurrent sinusitis, a minor operation to clear the sinuses may be recommended.

NO ↓

**Have you suddenly begun to have a severe throbbing pain in one or both temples?**

YES →

**Have you been feeling generally unwell AND/OR is your scalp sensitive to touch?**

YES →

**CONSULT YOUR DOCTOR WITHOUT DELAY!**
**Temporal arteritis,** inflammation of the arteries in the head, is a possibility, especially if you are over 50. Urgent treatment may be needed to prevent this condition from affecting your eyesight.
**Treatment:** Your doctor will probably prescribe tablets to reduce the inflammation and it may be necessary to have regular blood tests to confirm that the treatment is effective.

NO

NO

**Do you have a severe stabbing pain in one side of the face, brought on by touching the face or by chewing?**

YES →

NO ↓

**Consult your doctor** if you are unable to make a diagnosis from this chart.

**Trigeminal neuralgia,** pain caused by a damaged nerve, may be the problem. Consult your doctor.
**Treatment:** Your doctor will probably examine your sinuses and ears, and may suggest that you have a dental examination, because infections in the sinuses, ears or teeth can cause similar pain. If you are found to have trigeminal neuralgia, your doctor may prescribe a drug to be taken in steadily increasing doses. When pain stops, the doses are reduced. In some cases a minor operation may be needed.

# 69 Forgetfulness and confusion

We all suffer from mild forgetfulness and, to a lesser extent, confusion from time to time, especially after the age of 50 when such "absent-mindedness" is a natural part of ageing. Often it happens because we are preoccupied with something else and is no cause for concern. However, if confusion comes on suddenly or if forgetfulness and confusion are so severe that they disrupt everyday life, there may be an underlying medical disorder. This chart deals with sudden or severe confusion or forgetfulness that you are aware of in yourself or in a relative or friend who may not be aware of the problem.

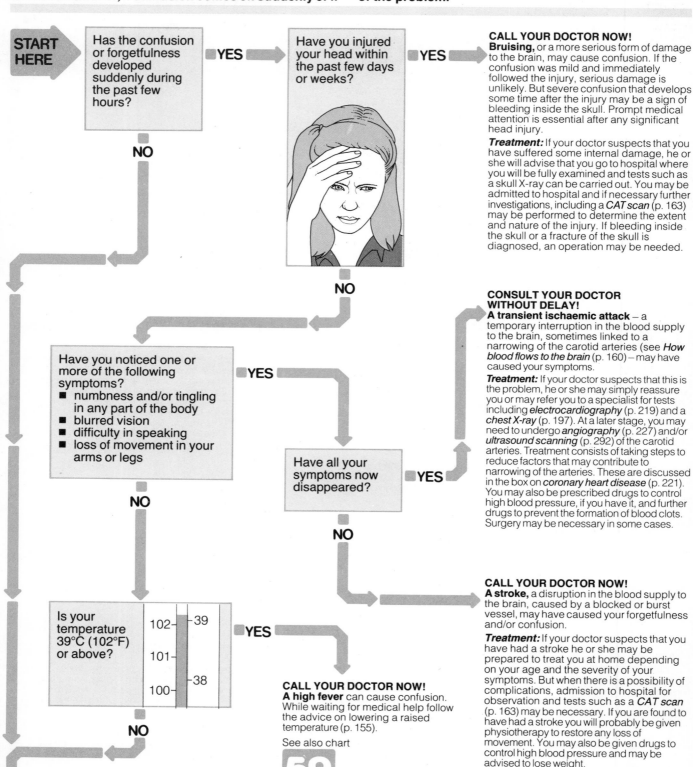

**START HERE**

**Has the confusion or forgetfulness developed suddenly during the past few hours?**

**YES** →

**Have you injured your head within the past few days or weeks?**

**YES** →

**CALL YOUR DOCTOR NOW!**
**Bruising,** or a more serious form of damage to the brain, may cause confusion. If the confusion was mild and immediately followed the injury, serious damage is unlikely. But severe confusion that develops some time after the injury may be a sign of bleeding inside the skull. Prompt medical attention is essential after any significant head injury.

**Treatment:** If your doctor suspects that you have suffered some internal damage, he or she will advise that you go to hospital where you will be fully examined and tests such as a skull X-ray can be carried out. You may be admitted to hospital and if necessary further investigations, including a *CAT scan* (p. 163) may be performed to determine the extent and nature of the injury. If bleeding inside the skull or a fracture of the skull is diagnosed, an operation may be needed.

**NO** (from first box)

**NO** (from head injury box)

**Have you noticed one or more of the following symptoms?**
- numbness and/or tingling in any part of the body
- blurred vision
- difficulty in speaking
- loss of movement in your arms or legs

**YES** →

**Have all your symptoms now disappeared?**

**YES** →

**CONSULT YOUR DOCTOR WITHOUT DELAY!**
**A transient ischaemic attack** – a temporary interruption in the blood supply to the brain, sometimes linked to a narrowing of the carotid arteries (see *How blood flows to the brain* (p. 160) – may have caused your symptoms.

**Treatment:** If your doctor suspects that this is the problem, he or she may simply reassure you or may refer you to a specialist for tests including *electrocardiography* (p. 219) and a *chest X-ray* (p. 197). At a later stage, you may need to undergo *angiography* (p. 227) and/or *ultrasound scanning* (p. 292) of the carotid arteries. Treatment consists of taking steps to reduce factors that may contribute to narrowing of the arteries. These are discussed in the box on *coronary heart disease* (p. 221). You may also be prescribed drugs to control high blood pressure, if you have it, and further drugs to prevent the formation of blood clots. Surgery may be necessary in some cases.

**NO** (symptoms box)

**NO** (symptoms disappeared)

**Is your temperature 39°C (102°F) or above?**

102 — 39
101 —
100 — 38

**YES** →

**CALL YOUR DOCTOR NOW!**
**A high fever** can cause confusion. While waiting for medical help follow the advice on lowering a raised temperature (p. 155).

See also chart

**59** Fever

**CALL YOUR DOCTOR NOW!**
**A stroke,** a disruption in the blood supply to the brain, caused by a blocked or burst vessel, may have caused your forgetfulness and/or confusion.

**Treatment:** If your doctor suspects that you have had a stroke he or she may be prepared to treat you at home depending on your age and the severity of your symptoms. But when there is a possibility of complications, admission to hospital for observation and tests such as a *CAT scan* (p. 163) may be necessary. If you are found to have had a stroke you will probably be given physiotherapy to restore any loss of movement. You may also be given drugs to control high blood pressure and may be advised to lose weight.

**NO**

*Go to next page*

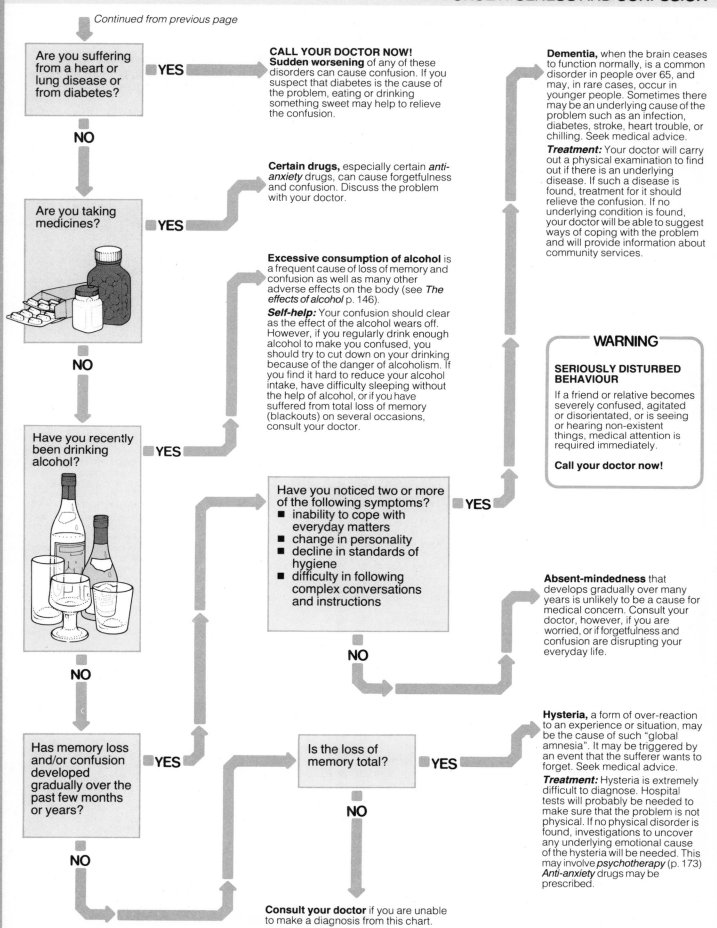

*Continued from previous page*

**Are you suffering from a heart or lung disease or from diabetes?**

**YES** → **CALL YOUR DOCTOR NOW!**
**Sudden worsening** of any of these disorders can cause confusion. If you suspect that diabetes is the cause of the problem, eating or drinking something sweet may help to relieve the confusion.

**NO**

**Are you taking medicines?**

**YES** → **Certain drugs,** especially certain *anti-anxiety* drugs, can cause forgetfulness and confusion. Discuss the problem with your doctor.

**NO**

**Have you recently been drinking alcohol?**

**YES** → **Excessive consumption of alcohol** is a frequent cause of loss of memory and confusion as well as many other adverse effects on the body (see *The effects of alcohol* p. 146).
**Self-help:** Your confusion should clear as the effect of the alcohol wears off. However, if you regularly drink enough alcohol to make you confused, you should try to cut down on your drinking because of the danger of alcoholism. If you find it hard to reduce your alcohol intake, have difficulty sleeping without the help of alcohol, or if you have suffered from total loss of memory (blackouts) on several occasions, consult your doctor.

**NO**

**Have you noticed two or more of the following symptoms?**
■ inability to cope with everyday matters
■ change in personality
■ decline in standards of hygiene
■ difficulty in following complex conversations and instructions

**YES** → **Dementia,** when the brain ceases to function normally, is a common disorder in people over 65, and may, in rare cases, occur in younger people. Sometimes there may be an underlying cause of the problem such as an infection, diabetes, stroke, heart trouble, or chilling. Seek medical advice.

*Treatment:* Your doctor will carry out a physical examination to find out if there is an underlying disease. If such a disease is found, treatment for it should relieve the confusion. If no underlying condition is found, your doctor will be able to suggest ways of coping with the problem and will provide information about community services.

**NO**

**Has memory loss and/or confusion developed gradually over the past few months or years?**

**YES** → (to symptoms box)

**NO**

**Is the loss of memory total?**

**YES** → **Hysteria,** a form of over-reaction to an experience or situation, may be the cause of such "global amnesia". It may be triggered by an event that the sufferer wants to forget. Seek medical advice.

*Treatment:* Hysteria is extremely difficult to diagnose. Hospital tests will probably be needed to make sure that the problem is not physical. If no physical disorder is found, investigations to uncover any underlying emotional cause of the hysteria will be needed. This may involve *psychotherapy* (p. 173) *Anti-anxiety* drugs may be prescribed.

**NO**

**Absent-mindedness** that develops gradually over many years is unlikely to be a cause for medical concern. Consult your doctor, however, if you are worried, or if forgetfulness and confusion are disrupting your everyday life.

---

**WARNING**

**SERIOUSLY DISTURBED BEHAVIOUR**

If a friend or relative becomes severely confused, agitated or disorientated, or is seeing or hearing non-existent things, medical attention is required immediately.

**Call your doctor now!**

---

**Consult your doctor** if you are unable to make a diagnosis from this chart.

# 70 Difficulty in speaking

Consult this chart if you have or have had difficulty in finding, using or defining words, or if your speech becomes slurred or unclear. Such speech difficulties may be related to disorders or drugs affecting the speech centres in the brain or they may be due to a disorder affecting the mouth or tongue.

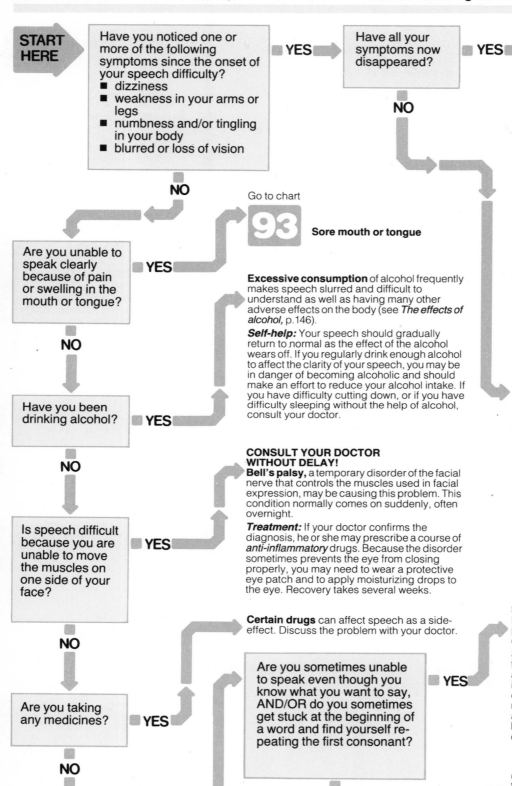

**START HERE**

Have you noticed one or more of the following symptoms since the onset of your speech difficulty?
- dizziness
- weakness in your arms or legs
- numbness and/or tingling in your body
- blurred or loss of vision

**YES** → Have all your symptoms now disappeared?

**YES** →

**CONSULT YOUR DOCTOR WITHOUT DELAY!**
**A transient ischaemic attack** – a temporary interruption in the blood supply to the brain, sometimes linked to a narrowing of the carotid arteries (see *How blood flows to the brain,* p.160) – may have caused your symptoms.

*Treatment:* If your doctor suspects that this is a problem, he or she may simply reassure you or may refer you to a specialist for tests including *electro-cardiography* (p. 219) and a *chest X-ray* (p. 197). You may also need to undergo *angiography,* (p.227) and/or *ultrasound scanning* (p.292,293) of the carotid arteries. Treatment consists of taking steps to reduce factors that may contribute to narrowing of the arteries. These are discussed in the box on *coronary heart disease* (p. 221). You may also be prescribed drugs to control high blood pressure, if you have it, and further drugs to prevent the formation of blood clots. Surgery may be necesary in some cases.

**NO** (below symptoms box)

Go to chart

**93**

**Sore mouth or tongue**

Are you unable to speak clearly because of pain or swelling in the mouth or tongue?

**YES** →

**Excessive consumption** of alcohol frequently makes speech slurred and difficult to understand as well as having many other adverse effects on the body (see *The effects of alcohol,* p.146).
*Self-help:* Your speech should gradually return to normal as the effect of the alcohol wears off. If you regularly drink enough alcohol to affect the clarity of your speech, you may be in danger of becoming alcoholic and should make an effort to reduce your alcohol intake. If you have difficulty cutting down, or if you have difficulty sleeping without the help of alcohol, consult your doctor.

**NO**

Have you been drinking alcohol?

**YES** →

**CALL YOUR DOCTOR NOW!**
**A stroke,** a disruption in the blood supply to the brain, caused by a blocked or burst blood vessel may be the cause of these symptoms.

*Treatment:* If your doctor suspects that you have had a stroke, he or she may be prepared to treat you at home, depending on your age and the severity of your symptoms. But when there is a possibility of complications, a *CAT scan* (p.163) may be necessary. If you are found to have had a stroke, you will probably be given speech therapy to help overcome your speech difficulty. You may also be given drugs to control high blood pressure and may be advised to lose weight.

**NO**

**CONSULT YOUR DOCTOR WITHOUT DELAY!**
**Bell's palsy,** a temporary disorder of the facial nerve that controls the muscles used in facial expression, may be causing this problem. This condition normally comes on suddenly, often overnight.

*Treatment:* If your doctor confirms the diagnosis, he or she may prescribe a course of *anti-inflammatory* drugs. Because the disorder sometimes prevents the eye from closing properly, you may need to wear a protective eye patch and to apply moisturizing drops to the eye. Recovery takes several weeks.

Is speech difficult because you are unable to move the muscles on one side of your face?

**YES** →

**NO**

**Certain drugs** can affect speech as a side-effect. Discuss the problem with your doctor.

Are you taking any medicines?

**YES** →

Are you sometimes unable to speak even though you know what you want to say, AND/OR do you sometimes get stuck at the beginning of a word and find yourself repeating the first consonant?

**YES** →

**Stammering** or stuttering may be brought on or made worse by anxiety, particularly if you had this trouble in early childhood.
*Self-help:* Many stammerers find that their speech improves if they try to relax and speak more slowly. If your stammer is so severe that it makes communication difficult, consult your doctor, who may prescribe drugs and/or refer you to a speech therapist. Even those who have had this problem for many years can often be helped.

**NO**

**NO**

**CONSULT YOUR DOCTOR WITHOUT DELAY!**
**Unexplained difficulty in speaking** may be an early sign of an underlying disorder of the brain or nervous system, and early treatment is important.

# 71 Disturbing thoughts and feelings

Consult this chart if you begin to have thoughts and feelings that worry you or that seem to you or to others to be abnormal or unhealthy. Such feelings may include aggressive or sexual thoughts and/or unfamiliar or uncontrolled emotions. If your thoughts and feelings continue to worry you, whatever your particular problem, talk to your doctor about them. He or she may be able to help you put your feelings into proper context by discussing them with you and may also offer treatment if he or she thinks that this is appropriate.

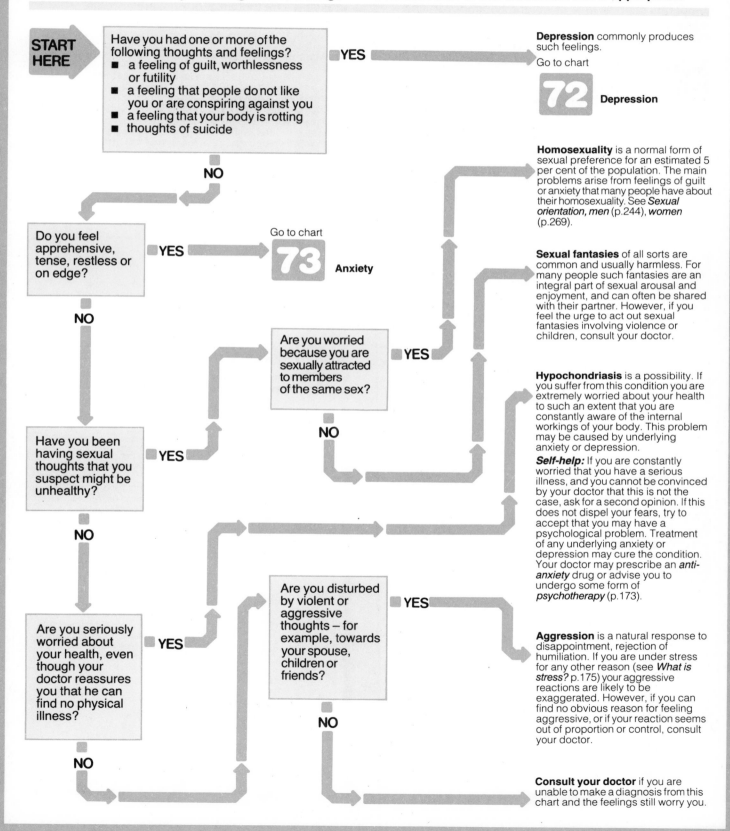

**START HERE**

Have you had one or more of the following thoughts and feelings?
- a feeling of guilt, worthlessness or futility
- a feeling that people do not like you or are conspiring against you
- a feeling that your body is rotting
- thoughts of suicide

**YES** — **Depression** commonly produces such feelings.
Go to chart **72** Depression

**NO**

Do you feel apprehensive, tense, restless or on edge?

**YES** — Go to chart **73** Anxiety

**NO**

Have you been having sexual thoughts that you suspect might be unhealthy?

**YES** — Are you worried because you are sexually attracted to members of the same sex?

**YES** — **Homosexuality** is a normal form of sexual preference for an estimated 5 per cent of the population. The main problems arise from feelings of guilt or anxiety that many people have about their homosexuality. See *Sexual orientation, men* (p.244), *women* (p.269).

**NO** (sexually attracted) —

**Sexual fantasies** of all sorts are common and usually harmless. For many people such fantasies are an integral part of sexual arousal and enjoyment, and can often be shared with their partner. However, if you feel the urge to act out sexual fantasies involving violence or children, consult your doctor.

**NO**

Are you seriously worried about your health, even though your doctor reassures you that he can find no physical illness?

**YES** — **Hypochondriasis** is a possibility. If you suffer from this condition you are extremely worried about your health to such an extent that you are constantly aware of the internal workings of your body. This problem may be caused by underlying anxiety or depression.
*Self-help:* If you are constantly worried that you have a serious illness, and you cannot be convinced by your doctor that this is not the case, ask for a second opinion. If this does not dispel your fears, try to accept that you may have a psychological problem. Treatment of any underlying anxiety or depression may cure the condition. Your doctor may prescribe an *anti-anxiety* drug or advise you to undergo some form of *psychotherapy* (p.173).

Are you disturbed by violent or aggressive thoughts – for example, towards your spouse, children or friends?

**YES** —

**Aggression** is a natural response to disappointment, rejection of humiliation. If you are under stress for any other reason (see *What is stress?* p.175) your aggressive reactions are likely to be exaggerated. However, if you can find no obvious reason for feeling aggressive, or if your reaction seems out of proportion or control, consult your doctor.

**NO**

**Consult your doctor** if you are unable to make a diagnosis from this chart and the feelings still worry you.

# 72 Depression

Most people have minor ups and downs in mood, feeling particularly good one day but low in spirits the next. This is often due to an identifiable cause and quickly passes. More severe depression, characterized by feelings of futility and guilt, and often with physical symptoms such as loss of weight, constipation and headaches, is sometimes brought on by some major event such as bereavement, divorce, or loss of a job. Depression may also be brought on by physical illness. Some people, however, are prone to repeated attacks of depression that have no apparent cause. Also, there are certain times when we are more susceptible to depression – for instance, during adolescence, after having a baby, during middle age, and at retirement.

**START HERE**

As well as feeling in low spirits, do you have two or more of the following symptoms?
- difficulty in sleeping
- loss of appetite
- loss of energy
- loss of interest in sex
- recurrent headaches

**YES**

**A depressive illness** is a possibility. This often develops with no apparent cause, and in the most severe cases it may be accompanied by feelings of persecution, guilt and worthlessness. Sleeping poorly, and especially early waking, are common symptoms of depression. A severely depressed person may contemplate suicide (see *Suicide,* below). Consult your doctor.

**Treatment:** This depends on the type and severity of your symptoms. It is likely to consist of a combination of drugs and *psychotherapy* (opposite). *Antidepressants,* if prescribed, usually begin to relieve mild depression in 2 or 3 weeks. If you are severely depressed, it may be necessary for you to spend some time in hospital. Electroconvulsive therapy (ECT), in which electric currents are passed through the brain under general anaesthetic, may be advised.

**NO**

Did the onset of depression follow a bereavement?

**YES**

**Grief** over the death of someone you have loved may naturally lead to a period of depression. This time of mourning is an essential part of the process of adjustment to the loss and should not be unnaturally hurried by well-meaning family and friends. During this period many people think they see or hear the dead person and this is perfectly normal.

**Self-help:** Do not expect yourself to return to normal within a few days or weeks. Many people take months to accept their loss. Do not, however, believe that you must not give in or that admitting to unhappiness is a sign of weakness. If depression is preventing you from coping with everyday life, or if you have difficulty in sleeping, consult your doctor. *Antidepressants* or *anti-anxiety* drugs may be helpful.

**NO**

---

**WARNING**

**SUICIDE**

Suicide threats should always be taken seriously, even if they have been made before. So if you know someone who is so depressed that he or she feels that life is no longer worthwhile, or if he or she has contemplated suicide or discussed it with others, try to persuade the person to seek medical help. The Samaritans, a voluntary organization specializing in helping people contemplating suicide, are available on the telephone 24 hours a day to offer support.

**Seek medical help without delay!**

---

Have you been under strain at work or at home?

**YES**

**Generalized stress** (see *What is stress?*, p.175) may be the cause of your depression, especially if you have felt under pressure for a prolonged period.

**Self-help:** Try to keep stress to a minimum by avoiding major upheavals in your life as much as possible. Discuss your feelings with a close friend and listen to his or her advice about how you might cope with your problems. Devote some time every day to physical relaxation that diverts your mind from day-to-day strain and worry. Keep your alcohol consumption down. Consult your doctor if you feel that the self-help measures are not working, or if your depression seems to be getting worse.

**NO**

Did your depression follow a distressing event, such as divorce or losing your job?

**YES**

**Distressing events** are often followed by a period of depression. This is known as "reactive depression". Some people react more severely than others. If your depression makes life unbearable, prevents you from coping with everyday life, begins to get worse, or if your friends are clearly worried about you, consult your doctor.

**Treatment:** This depends on the type and the severity of your symptoms. Your doctor may prescribe *antidepressants,* which will usually relieve a mild depression in 2-3 weeks. If you are severely depressed, you may be referred to a specialist for treatment, which is likely to consist of a combination of drugs and *psychotherapy* (opposite). In some cases, it may be necessary to spend some time in hospital where treatment can be supervised.

**NO**

Are you a woman AND have you recently had a baby?

**YES**

Go to chart

# 146

**Depression after childbirth**

**NO**

*Go to next page*

*Continued from previous page*

**Are you a woman AND do you feel depressed or irritable in the days before your period?**

**YES** →

**Premenstrual depression** is a common occurrence. It can vary from anything as mild as a feeling of moderate unhappiness to depression so severe that it affects all bodily functions. It is often accompanied by increased irritability, aggression and such physical symptoms as a slight increase in weight, headaches, bloated stomach and swollen ankles, which make matters worse (see *The menstrual cycle*, p.253). If your symptoms are severe enough to interfere with your day-to-day routine, consult your doctor.

**Treatment:** Your doctor will reassure you and advise you to keep pre-menstrual days as non-stressful as possible. He or she may also prescribe drugs to counteract the physical symptoms (see *Treatment of menstrual problems*, p.255).

**NO** ↓

**Have you recently recovered from an infectious illness such as flu or glandular fever?**

**YES** →

**Infectious illnesses** are often followed by a period of depression.

**Self-help:** Do not try to return to your normal routine too quickly after you have had such an illness. Make sure that you eat well and get plenty of sleep to allow your strength to build up. If your depression lasts longer than 2 weeks, consult your doctor, who may prescribe an *antidepressant.*

**NO** ↓

**Have you been drinking alcohol every day for a prolonged period?**

**YES** →

**Regular consumption of alcohol,** even in seemingly moderate amounts, over a period of time has a depressive effect on the body and mind and this may persist on days when you have had no alcohol (see *The effects of alcohol*, p.146).

**Self-help:** Your depression should clear if you stop drinking alcohol. If you find it difficult to cut down on the amount you drink, or your depression persists or begins to get worse, consult your doctor.

**NO** ↓

**Emotional instability** in the middle years of life when children begin to leave home and old age approaches, often leads to depression. In women the problem is often related to the menopause and the tremendous hormonal upheaval that takes place during this period. Sometimes called the "mid-life crisis", this can be a trying time for men as well as women when faltering career goals, declining health and growing sexual anxieties may all contribute to depression.

**Self-help:** Your doctor may recommend anti-depressants and/or hormone replacement therapy for women (see *Menopause,* p. 252), but there is much you can do to get through this difficult period. Try to discuss your feelings openly with friends and family and to accept the aging process as a fact of life. Find new interests and hobbies or take on a job if you've not been working. Take care of your physical health by eating and drinking moderately and getting plenty of sleep. Try to incorporate regular exercise into your routine (see *Fitness and exercise,* p. 36, 37). Many specific sexual problems can be treated, so discuss these with your partner as well as your doctor. If you still find that you can not cope, have your doctor examine you to rule out any underlying condition.

**Are you aged between 40 and 55?**

**YES** →

**NO** ↓

**Are you taking medicines?**

**YES** →

**Certain drugs** can cause depression. Discuss the problem with your doctor.

**NO** ↓

**Consult you doctor** if you are unable to find a cause for your depression from this chart.

---

## PSYCHOTHERAPY

Psychotherapy is the treatment of psychological problems by a therapist who encourages you to talk about your feelings and fears, and who can provide expert help and advice. This process may range from talking about your troubles with your own doctor, to an extended course of psychoanalysis with a specialist. The more common forms of psychotherapy are described below.

### Group therapy
This involves a number of sessions, during which the therapist guides a discussion between a group of people with a problem in common. The advantage of group psychotherapy is that the members of the group gain strength from knowing that other people have a similar problem and they can learn from each other's experiences. There is also a certain amount of group pressure to develop a healthier attitude to personal problems and group support for this attitude to continue.

### Behaviour therapy
This is usually used in the treatment of specific phobias, such as fear of flying, or fear of dogs or spiders. In one form of behaviour therapy known as desensitization, the sufferer is helped by the therapist to overcome the fear gradually. For example, in the case of fear of flying, the therapist encourages you to imagine the events preceding the flight – taking a train to the airport, waiting in the terminal, going through passport control, boarding, and finally sitting on the plane while it taxis on the runway and takes off and then lands. Later, when you actually come to fly, you should feel as through you have been through it before and it should then hold no fear for you.

Another method, called flooding, involves a confrontation, under the supervision of your therapist, with the object you fear in an extreme form – for example, a visit to a dogs' home as treatment for fear of dogs. Experiencing the worst imaginable degree of exposure helps you to realize that all along there has been no real danger involved and your fear has been exaggerated. Both methods should only be attempted under the guidance of a trained therapist.

### Psychoanalysis
This form of psychotherapy, based on the belief that much human behaviour is determined by early childhood conflicts, was developed in the late 19th and early 20th Centuries. Psychoanalysis involves a series of meetings with a psychoanalyst during which he or she will encourage you to talk at will. The psychoanalyst may ask occasional questions to guide the direction of your thoughts. By listening to your recollections, thoughts and feelings, he or she may be able to pinpoint the root cause of your problem; then, by discussion, the analyst enables you to reach a better understanding of yourself and this may help you to reconcile any internal conflicts.

# 73 Anxiety

If you are suffering from anxiety you will probably feel apprehensive and tense, unable to concentrate, to think clearly or to sleep well. Some people have such physical symptoms as headaches, chest pains, palpitations, backache and a general feeling of tiredness. This is often a natural reaction to a stressful situation and is only temporary. Sometimes, however, anxiety may come on without apparent cause.

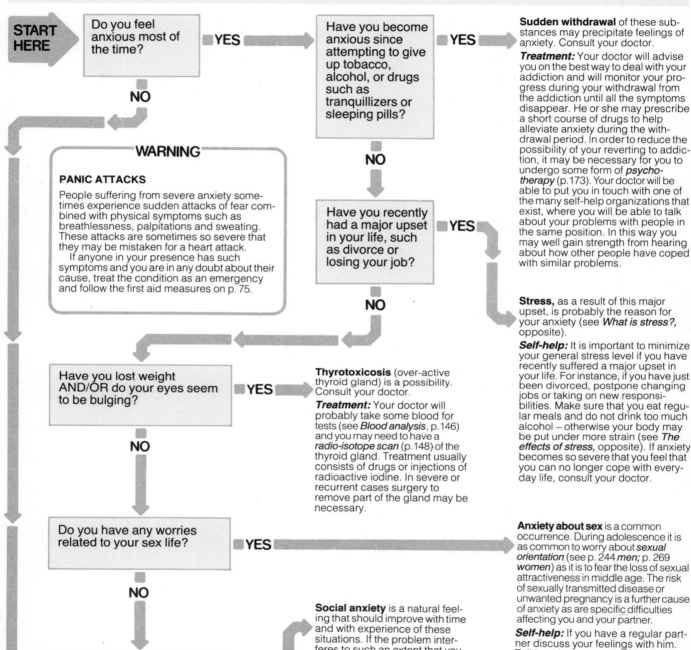

**START HERE**

**Do you feel anxious most of the time?**

YES →

**Have you become anxious since attempting to give up tobacco, alcohol, or drugs such as tranquillizers or sleeping pills?**

YES →

**Sudden withdrawal** of these substances may precipitate feelings of anxiety. Consult your doctor.

*Treatment:* Your doctor will advise you on the best way to deal with your addiction and will monitor your progress during your withdrawal from the addiction until all the symptoms disappear. He or she may prescribe a short course of drugs to help alleviate anxiety during the withdrawal period. In order to reduce the possibility of your reverting to addiction, it may be necessary for you to undergo some form of *psychotherapy* (p.173). Your doctor will be able to put you in touch with one of the many self-help organizations that exist, where you will be able to talk about your problems with people in the same position. In this way you may well gain strength from hearing about how other people have coped with similar problems.

NO ↓

NO ↓

**Have you recently had a major upset in your life, such as divorce or losing your job?**

YES →

**Stress,** as a result of this major upset, is probably the reason for your anxiety (see *What is stress?,* opposite).

*Self-help:* It is important to minimize your general stress level if you have recently suffered a major upset in your life. For instance, if you have just been divorced, postpone changing jobs or taking on new responsibilities. Make sure that you eat regular meals and do not drink too much alcohol – otherwise your body may be put under more strain (see *The effects of stress,* opposite). If anxiety becomes so severe that you feel that you can no longer cope with everyday life, consult your doctor.

NO ↓

## WARNING

### PANIC ATTACKS

People suffering from severe anxiety sometimes experience sudden attacks of fear combined with physical symptoms such as breathlessness, palpitations and sweating. These attacks are sometimes so severe that they may be mistaken for a heart attack.

If anyone in your presence has such symptoms and you are in any doubt about their cause, treat the condition as an emergency and follow the first aid measures on p. 75.

**Have you lost weight AND/OR do your eyes seem to be bulging?**

YES →

**Thyrotoxicosis** (over-active thyroid gland) is a possibility. Consult your doctor.

*Treatment:* Your doctor will probably take some blood for tests (see *Blood analysis,* p.146) and you may need to have a *radio-isotope scan* (p.148) of the thyroid gland. Treatment usually consists of drugs or injections of radioactive iodine. In severe or recurrent cases surgery to remove part of the gland may be necessary.

NO ↓

**Do you have any worries related to your sex life?**

YES →

**Anxiety about sex** is a common occurrence. During adolescence it is as common to worry about *sexual orientation* (see p. 244 *men;* p. 269 *women*) as it is to fear the loss of sexual attractiveness in middle age. The risk of sexually transmitted disease or unwanted pregnancy is a further cause of anxiety as are specific difficulties affecting you and your partner.

*Self-help:* If you have a regular partner discuss your feelings with him. Talking about sex openly is often the best way to solve and alleviate feelings of anxiety that you may have. It is important for you to be aware of your partner's feelings and vice versa. If this does not help because you are unable to communicate satisfactorily with each other or because you do not have a regular partner with whom you can talk, consult your doctor, who will be able to offer helpful advice or possibly refer you for *sex counselling* (p.268). For diagnosis of specific sex problems, see *Special problems: Men, Women,* p.233-272.

NO ↓

**Do you feel anxious in certain social situations – for instance, meeting people, going to parties, or during job interviews?**

YES →

**Social anxiety** is a natural feeling that should improve with time and with experience of these situations. If the problem interferes to such an extent that you avoid certain types of social contact because of anxiety, consult your doctor.

*Treatment:* He or she may prescribe a mild *anti-anxiety* drug to be taken just before you enter any social situation where you will feel anxious until you gain enough confidence to do without. If your doctor feels that your anxiety is severe, he or she may suggest that you undergo *psychotherapy* (p.173) to help you overcome the problem.

NO ↓

*Go to next page*

*Continued from previous page*

Do you feel anxious only when confronted with specific objects of fear or if you are prevented from doing things in your usual way?

**YES**

**NO**

**A phobia or a compulsive disorder** may be the cause of your anxiety. A phobia is an irrational fear of a specific object or situation. For instance, you may have a fear of enclosed spaces (claustrophobia). If you have a compulsive disorder, you feel an irresistible need to behave in a certain fashion, even though you may know that it is unreasonable. For example, you may feel that you have to always walk to work on the same side of the street, and if this becomes no longer possible, you become excessively anxious. Consult your doctor.

**Treatment:** Your doctor will try to discover the underlying cause of the problem and may be able to reassure you that although your worries and fears are understandable, it is possible to come to terms with them. He or she may decide that *antidepressants* or *anti-anxiety* drugs will help. If your symptoms are severe, he or she may refer you for *psychotherapy* (p.173) or for another form of specialist treatment.

**Consult your doctor** if you are unable to make a diagnosis from this chart and unexplained anxiety persists for more than a few days.

## WHAT IS STRESS?

Stress refers to physical or mental demands that require an increased response from the body. Stress can be caused by changes in daily routine, including changes for the better – getting married or having a baby – as well as for the worse – losing a job or getting divorced. The greater the change, the more stress you will suffer. A single major event such as the death of a close relative may on its own equal the stress resulting from an accumulation of smaller changes such as a new job, a move to a new house or a trip abroad.

### The effects of stress

A certain amount of stress can be beneficial when it excites and stimulates the body and so improves performance. However, as stress levels continue to rise, helpful stimulation becomes replaced by fatigue and, if stress is not reduced, may increase susceptibility to physical and mental illness. Everybody has a different level of tolerance to stress; some people never seem to suffer harmful effects from seemingly high levels of stress in their lives, while others can only cope with a few changes at any one time without becoming anxious, depressed or physically ill.

Some of the most common disorders that may be caused by or made worse by stress are listed below.
- Mental and emotional problems including anxiety and depression
- Asthma
- Mouth ulcers
- Angina and some other heart conditions
- Stomach or duodenal ulcers
- Ulcerative colitis
- Irritable bowel (see p.211)
- Stammering
- Skin problems including eczema and psoriasis
- Cessation of periods
- Certain forms of hair loss

## RELAXATION TECHNIQUES

Some people manage to remain relaxed and easygoing no matter how much strain they are under at work or at home. Others become tense and worried as a result of even minor stresses (see *What is stress?*, above). If you are one of the latter type, learning to relax may help to mitigate the harmful effects of stress, and may enable you to cope with problems more easily. Try practising some of the simple relaxation techniques described below. If stress leads to sleeplessness, see also *Preventing sleeplessness* (p.153).

### Breathing exercises

Try taking deep rather than shallow breaths. To develop the habit, sit or lie in a comfortable position, and breathe deeply and slowly for one minute, counting the number of breaths you take. Try to reduce your breathing rate, so that you take half as many breaths as you do normally. Practise this twice daily.

### Meditation

Meditation involves emptying the mind of all distractions, thoughts and worries. Try the following method:

1 Find a quiet part of the house and sit in a comfortable chair with your eyes closed.

2 Without moving your lips, repeat a word silently to yourself, paying attention only to this action. Do not choose a word that has any emotional overtones for you. If your mind wanders, do not fight this new train of thought but continue to focus your attention on the unspoken sound of the word. (Some people find it easier to concentrate on something visual – a door knob or a vase of flowers – rather than a word).

3 Do this for 5 minutes twice a day for a week, then gradually increase the meditation period until you can manage about 20 minutes at each session.

**Muscle relaxation exercises**
Try these exercises each evening or at other times if you feel tense. Wear comfortable clothes that enable you to move freely.

1 Lie on the floor, face up, eyes closed.

2 Screw up your face muscles and then let them relax.

3 Lift your head and let it fall gently back. Keep your neck and jaw relaxed so that you can feel your throat opening.

4 Press your shoulders down to the floor and then relax them.

5 Stretch out your arms and fingers. Hold them rigid for a moment before easing the strain completely.

6 Lift your buttocks and let them fall, feeling your spine stretch and relax as you do so.

7 Keep your heels together, stretch your legs and toes. Then relax completely.

Continue these exercises, one after the other, for 8–10 minutes. Next, lie totally limp for a further few minutes.

# 74 Hair and scalp problems

Hair grows over the whole surface of the human body with the exception of the palms and soles, and grows especially thickly on the head, in the armpits and around the genital area. Your hair colour and type are inherited, but its condition may be affected by your overall state of health and other factors such as diet. This chart deals with some of the more common problems affecting the growth of hair on the head and the condition of the scalp.

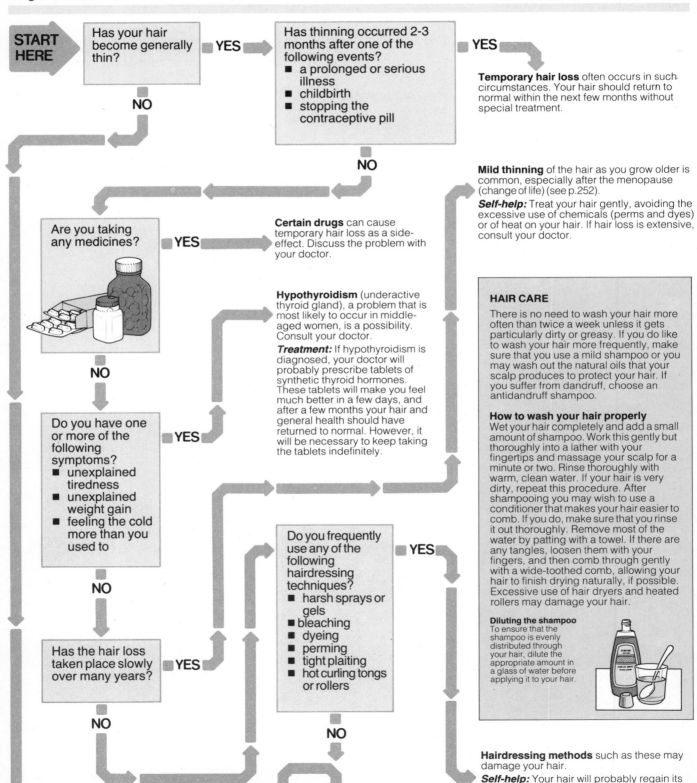

**START HERE**

**Has your hair become generally thin?**

YES →

**Has thinning occurred 2-3 months after one of the following events?**
- a prolonged or serious illness
- childbirth
- stopping the contraceptive pill

YES →

**Temporary hair loss** often occurs in such circumstances. Your hair should return to normal within the next few months without special treatment.

NO ↓

NO ↓

**Mild thinning** of the hair as you grow older is common, especially after the menopause (change of life) (see p.252).

**Self-help:** Treat your hair gently, avoiding the excessive use of chemicals (perms and dyes) or of heat on your hair. If hair loss is extensive, consult your doctor.

**Are you taking any medicines?**

YES →

**Certain drugs** can cause temporary hair loss as a side-effect. Discuss the problem with your doctor.

NO ↓

**Do you have one or more of the following symptoms?**
- unexplained tiredness
- unexplained weight gain
- feeling the cold more than you used to

YES →

**Hypothyroidism** (underactive thyroid gland), a problem that is most likely to occur in middle-aged women, is a possibility. Consult your doctor.

**Treatment:** If hypothyroidism is diagnosed, your doctor will probably prescribe tablets of synthetic thyroid hormones. These tablets will make you feel much better in a few days, and after a few months your hair and general health should have returned to normal. However, it will be necessary to keep taking the tablets indefinitely.

NO ↓

**Has the hair loss taken place slowly over many years?**

YES →

**Do you frequently use any of the following hairdressing techniques?**
- harsh sprays or gels
- bleaching
- dyeing
- perming
- tight plaiting
- hot curling tongs or rollers

YES →

NO ↓

NO ↓

*Go to next page*

### HAIR CARE

There is no need to wash your hair more often than twice a week unless it gets particularly dirty or greasy. If you do like to wash your hair more frequently, make sure that you use a mild shampoo or you may wash out the natural oils that your scalp produces to protect your hair. If you suffer from dandruff, choose an antidandruff shampoo.

**How to wash your hair properly**
Wet your hair completely and add a small amount of shampoo. Work this gently but thoroughly into a lather with your fingertips and massage your scalp for a minute or two. Rinse thoroughly with warm, clean water. If your hair is very dirty, repeat this procedure. After shampooing you may wish to use a conditioner that makes your hair easier to comb. If you do, make sure that you rinse it out thoroughly. Remove most of the water by patting with a towel. If there are any tangles, loosen them with your fingers, and then comb through gently with a wide-toothed comb, allowing your hair to finish drying naturally, if possible. Excessive use of hair dryers and heated rollers may damage your hair.

**Diluting the shampoo**
To ensure that the shampoo is evenly distributed through your hair, dilute the appropriate amount in a glass of water before applying it to your hair.

**Hairdressing methods** such as these may damage your hair.

**Self-help:** Your hair will probably regain its former thickness if you adopt a more natural hairstyle. It may be advisable to cut your hair short if it is severely damaged.

Continued from previous page

**Have one or more bald patches suddenly developed?**

**YES**

**Patchy hair loss** may be the result of fungal infection (especially if the scalp is inflamed and itchy) or of alopecia areata (a condition that may be related to emotional stress). Consult your doctor.

*Treatment:* Fungal infection of the scalp is usually treated by an *antifungal* shampoo and possibly a course of antifungal tablets. Alopecia areata often clears up without treatment and new hair grows within 6 to 9 months.

**NO**

**Is your scalp flaky and/or itchy?**

**YES**

**Dandruff** is the name used to describe excessive flaking and itching of the scalp. It is usually caused by seborrhoeic dermatitis (see *Eczema*, p.181).

*Self-help:* Use one of the many over-the-counter antidandruff shampoos every 2 to 3 days. If this does not improve the condition, consult your doctor, who may prescribe a different shampoo and/or a lotion to apply to your scalp.

**NO**

**Consult your doctor** if you are unable to make a diagnosis from this chart.

# 75 Nail problems

**Fingernails and toenails are made of hard, dead tissue called keratin, which protects the sensitive tips of the fingers and toes from damage. Any abnormalities or diseases affecting the nails may be unsightly, irritating, and sometimes painful, but they are not generally harmful to health.**

**START HERE**

**Is the skin around or underneath the nail swollen or inflamed and painful?**

**YES**

**Is only your big toe affected?**

**YES**

**An ingrowing toenail** may be the cause of the problem.

Go to chart

**111** **Foot problems**

**NO**

**NO**

**Paronychia,** an infection of the skin adjacent to the nail, may be the cause of this problem. This is particularly likely if you spend a lot of time with your hands in water. Consult your doctor.

*Treatment:* Your doctor may prescribe an *antibiotic* or *antifungal* cream or paint to apply to the affected nail after each time you wash your hands. Avoid putting your hands in water too often. Wear rubber gloves, if necessary. Your nails and cuticles should return to normal after a few months.

**Do you have a nail that has become discoloured, thickened and flaky?**

**YES**

**A fungal infection** of the nail is a possibility, especially if one or more of your toenails are affected. Consult your doctor.

*Treatment:* Your doctor may send a sample of nail clipping to be examined in a laboratory to confirm the diagnosis. The usual treatment is a long course of *antifungal* tablets, and possibly antifungal cream.

**NO**

**Have your nails become pitted or dimpled?**

**YES**

**Psoriasis** of the nails may cause this. In severe cases the nail is loosened from the nail bed. The skin may also be affected by the disease, which causes thick patches of silvery-white scaly skin to appear. Consult your doctor.

*Treatment:* Your doctor will probably advise you to keep your nails short. The application of nail varnish will disguise unsightly nails and may protect them from further damage. If your skin is also affected your doctor may prescribe one of several possible drugs and sometimes treatment with ultraviolet light.

**A tendency to brittle nails** is usually inherited, but may be exacerbated by excessive exposure to water, detergents and harsh chemicals.

*Self-help:* Wear rubber gloves whenever you have to put your hands in water or handle chemicals or detergents. Keep your nails short and, if you like, apply a protective coat of nail varnish. Regular applications of hand cream may help.

**Do your nails crack or break easily?**

**YES**

**NO**

**NO**

**Consult your doctor** if you are unable to make a diagnosis from this chart.

# 76 General skin problems

Many different types of disorders may affect the skin, including infections, inflammation, abnormal cell growth and abnormal skin colouration. Such disorders may be the result of an internal disease, exposure to an irritant or some other external factor. Symptoms may include blemishes, lumps, rashes, change in skin colouring or texture, itching or discomfort. Consult this chart if your symptom is not covered elsewhere in this book.

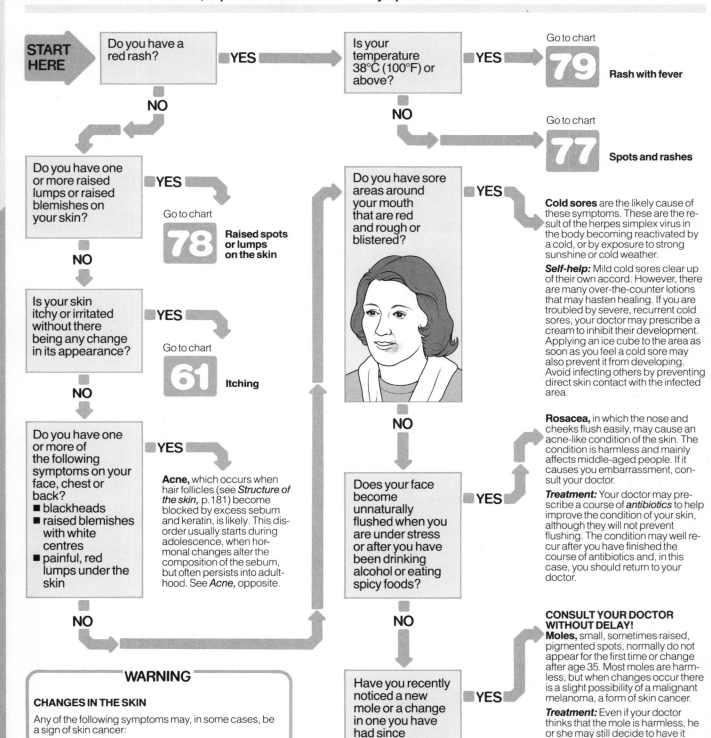

**START HERE**

**Do you have a red rash?** — **YES** → **Is your temperature 38°C (100°F) or above?** — **YES** → Go to chart **79** **Rash with fever**

**NO** (from temperature) → Go to chart **77** **Spots and rashes**

**NO** (from red rash) →

**Do you have one or more raised lumps or raised blemishes on your skin?** — **YES** → Go to chart **78** **Raised spots or lumps on the skin**

**NO** →

**Is your skin itchy or irritated without there being any change in its appearance?** — **YES** → Go to chart **61** **Itching**

**NO** →

**Do you have one or more of the following symptoms on your face, chest or back?**
■ blackheads
■ raised blemishes with white centres
■ painful, red lumps under the skin

— **YES** →

**Acne,** which occurs when hair follicles (see *Structure of the skin,* p.181) become blocked by excess sebum and keratin, is likely. This disorder usually starts during adolescence, when hormonal changes alter the composition of the sebum, but often persists into adulthood. See *Acne,* opposite.

**NO** →

**Do you have sore areas around your mouth that are red and rough or blistered?** — **YES** →

**Cold sores** are the likely cause of these symptoms. These are the result of the herpes simplex virus in the body becoming reactivated by a cold, or by exposure to strong sunshine or cold weather.

*Self-help:* Mild cold sores clear up of their own accord. However, there are many over-the-counter lotions that may hasten healing. If you are troubled by severe, recurrent cold sores, your doctor may prescribe a cream to inhibit their development. Applying an ice cube to the area as soon as you feel a cold sore may also prevent it from developing. Avoid infecting others by preventing direct skin contact with the infected area.

**NO** →

**Does your face become unnaturally flushed when you are under stress or after you have been drinking alcohol or eating spicy foods?** — **YES** →

**Rosacea,** in which the nose and cheeks flush easily, may cause an acne-like condition of the skin. The condition is harmless and mainly affects middle-aged people. If it causes you embarrassment, consult your doctor.

*Treatment:* Your doctor may prescribe a course of *antibiotics* to help improve the condition of your skin, although they will not prevent flushing. The condition may well recur after you have finished the course of antibiotics and, in this case, you should return to your doctor.

**NO** →

**Have you recently noticed a new mole or a change in one you have had since childhood?** — **YES** →

**CONSULT YOUR DOCTOR WITHOUT DELAY!**
**Moles,** small, sometimes raised, pigmented spots, normally do not appear for the first time or change after age 35. Most moles are harmless, but when changes occur there is a slight possibility of a malignant melanoma, a form of skin cancer.

*Treatment:* Even if your doctor thinks that the mole is harmless, he or she may still decide to have it removed and examined under a microscope see *Biopsy,* (p.159) for signs of cancerous cells. If cancer is confirmed, the growth will be removed, together with a wide margin of adjacent skin. A skin graft to cover the whole area will probably be carried out at the same time.

**NO** → *Go to next page*

---

## WARNING

**CHANGES IN THE SKIN**

Any of the following symptoms may, in some cases, be a sign of skin cancer:

■ an open sore that has not healed within 3 weeks
■ a slowly growing lump
■ a change in a long-standing mole
■ a newly pigmented spot or patch

**Consult your doctor without delay!**

*Continued from previous page*

Have flat patches of very pale or very dark skin developed on your skin? **YES** →

**NO** ↓

Are you pregnant? **YES** →

Go to chart

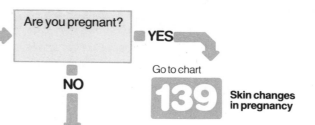

**139** **Skin changes in pregnancy**

**NO** ↓

**Uneven skin pigmentation** is usually the result of abnormal formation of the cells that produce skin pigment or of an abnormal rate of pigment production. This may sometimes be caused by a fungal infection. Consult your doctor.

***Treatment:*** Most disorders of skin pigment are harmless and require no treatment. You can disguise any disfiguring patches with make-up. If your doctor suspects a fungal infection, you will be prescribed an *antifungal* cream, which will soon clear up the condition.

## ACNE

Acne is the name used to describe a group of skin symptoms mainly affecting the face, chest and back, caused by blockage and infection of hair follicles (see *Structure of the skin* p.181). There are 3 main types of symptoms:

### Blackheads

These are tiny black spots caused by excess skin pigment overlying trapped sebum and skin debris in a hair follicle.

### Pustules

Pustules are tender, red blemishes that develop raised, white centres. They occur when excess keratin blocks a hair follicle and becomes inflamed (see below).

**The development of a pustule**

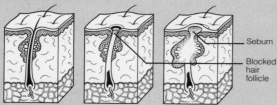

Sebum

Blocked hair follicle

### Cysts

These are painful, red, fluid-filled lumps under the skin. They persist for several weeks and are more likely than other types of blemishes to lead to scarring.

### Self-help

Mild acne with blackheads and the occasional pustule needs no special treatment other than ensuring that you wash your face thoroughly twice a day. Exposure to sunlight or careful use of an ultraviolet lamp often improves the condition. Avoid squeezing blemishes, as this is likely to increase the risk of infection and scarring. There are many over-the-counter preparations for acne. You may find some of these helpful. But you should avoid using anything too vigorously; this may lead to permanent skin damage.

### Professional treatment

If your acne is severe enough to embarrass you, if you have cystic blemishes or if there is any sign of scarring, consult your doctor. Various treatments may be advised, depending on the type of acne. You may be prescribed a lotion that gently removes the top layer of skin, clearing blocked pores and preventing further blemishes from forming. Or you may be prescribed a long course of low-dose *antibiotics* that counters bacterial activity in the skin. Less commonly, a medication that alters the composition of the sebum may be prescribed. This treatment needs to be monitored carefully because of possible side-effects.

Do you have one or more red patches covered with silvery-white, flaky skin? **YES** →

**NO** ↓

**Psoriasis,** a disorder in which the skin cells grow unusually rapidly and form scales, is a possibility. The most common sites for this to occur are the scalp, elbows and knees, though scaly patches can also appear in the armpits, on the trunk or around the anus. Consult your doctor.

***Treatment:*** Your doctor may prescribe one of several possible drugs and sometimes treatment with ultraviolet light.

Has a blistery rash appeared on one side of your body in a place in which there has been a burning sensation for a day or two? **YES** →

**NO** ↓

**Shingles,** a virus infection of the nerves, is a possibility. Consult your doctor. This is a matter of urgency if the rash is on your face because it may affect your eyes.

***Treatment:*** Your doctor will probably prescribe painkillers and a soothing ointment to put on the skin and, possibly, an antiviral agent. If there is any possibility of damage to the eyes, you will probably be referred to a specialist for treatment.

Do you have one or more open sores on your skin? **YES** →

**NO** ↓

**Skin ulcers** are usually caused by injury or infection, but may in some cases be encouraged by an underlying disorder such as poor circulation or diabetes.

***Self-help:*** Keep the sore area clean, dry and, if necessary, protect it with an adhesive bandage or light dressing. Consult your doctor if the sore has not healed within 3 weeks or if ulcers recur. Tests may be needed to determine the underlying cause of the trouble and determine treatment.

**Consult your doctor** if you are unable to make a diagnosis from this chart.

# 77 Spots and rashes

Groups of inflamed spots or blisters, or larger areas of inflamed skin, are usually caused by infection, irritation, or an allergic reaction to something you have eaten or come into contact with. Such a rash may come up suddenly or develop over a period of days and may, or may not, cause discomfort or itching. If a rash persists for more than a day, it is wise to consult your doctor for diagnosis and treatment where necessary.

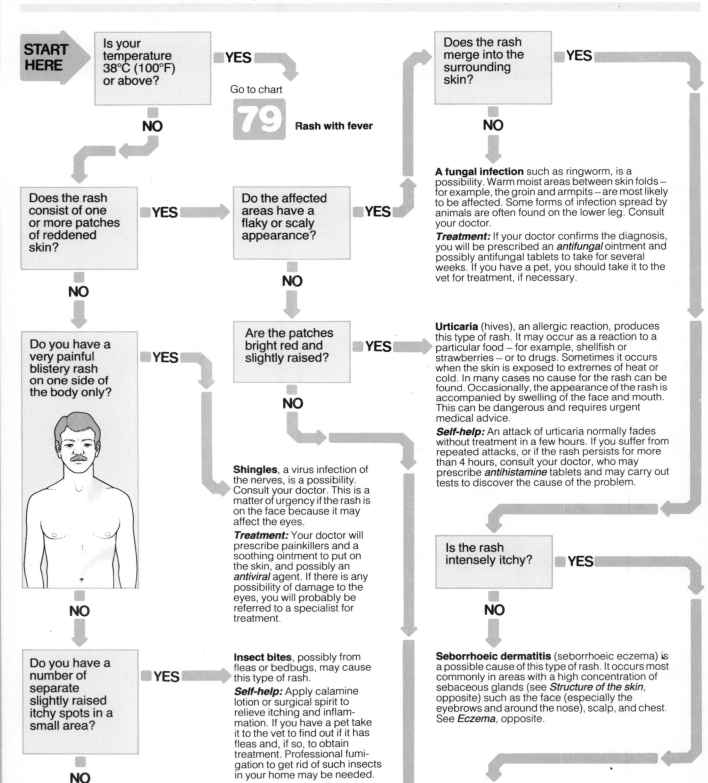

**START HERE**

Is your temperature 38°C (100°F) or above?

**YES** → Go to chart **79** Rash with fever

**NO**

Does the rash consist of one or more patches of reddened skin?

**YES** → Do the affected areas have a flaky or scaly appearance?

**YES** → Does the rash merge into the surrounding skin?

**YES** → **A fungal infection** such as ringworm, is a possibility. Warm moist areas between skin folds – for example, the groin and armpits – are most likely to be affected. Some forms of infection spread by animals are often found on the lower leg. Consult your doctor.

**Treatment:** If your doctor confirms the diagnosis, you will be prescribed an *antifungal* ointment and possibly antifungal tablets to take for several weeks. If you have a pet, you should take it to the vet for treatment, if necessary.

**NO** (for merge)

**NO** (for flaky/scaly)

Are the patches bright red and slightly raised?

**YES** → **Urticaria** (hives), an allergic reaction, produces this type of rash. It may occur as a reaction to a particular food – for example, shellfish or strawberries – or to drugs. Sometimes it occurs when the skin is exposed to extremes of heat or cold. In many cases no cause for the rash can be found. Occasionally, the appearance of the rash is accompanied by swelling of the face and mouth. This can be dangerous and requires urgent medical advice.

**Self-help:** An attack of urticaria normally fades without treatment in a few hours. If you suffer from repeated attacks, or if the rash persists for more than 4 hours, consult your doctor, who may prescribe *antihistamine* tablets and may carry out tests to discover the cause of the problem.

**NO**

Do you have a very painful blistery rash on one side of the body only?

**YES** → **Shingles**, a virus infection of the nerves, is a possibility. Consult your doctor. This is a matter of urgency if the rash is on the face because it may affect the eyes.

**Treatment:** Your doctor will prescribe painkillers and a soothing ointment to put on the skin, and possibly an *antiviral* agent. If there is any possibility of damage to the eyes, you will probably be referred to a specialist for treatment.

**NO**

Is the rash intensely itchy?

**YES** →

**NO**

**Seborrhoeic dermatitis** (seborrhoeic eczema) is a possible cause of this type of rash. It occurs most commonly in areas with a high concentration of sebaceous glands (see *Structure of the skin*, opposite) such as the face (especially the eyebrows and around the nose), scalp, and chest. See *Eczema*, opposite.

Do you have a number of separate slightly raised itchy spots in a small area?

**YES** → **Insect bites**, possibly from fleas or bedbugs, may cause this type of rash.

**Self-help:** Apply calamine lotion or surgical spirit to relieve itching and inflammation. If you have a pet take it to the vet to find out if it has fleas and, if so, to obtain treatment. Professional fumigation to get rid of such insects in your home may be needed.

**NO**

1 Go to next page, column 1

Go to next page, column 2 2

**Eczema** (dermatitis) is the likely cause of your rash. This group of skin disorders may be brought on by a variety of factors. See *Eczema*, opposite.

*Continued from previous page, column 1*

*Continued from previous page, column 2*

**Do you have a widespread itchy rash?**

**YES**

**Have you noticed tiny grey lines or red infected-looking spots between your fingers or on your wrists?**

**YES**

**NO**

**NO**

**Scabies,** a parasitic infection, may be causing these symptoms. This is especially likely if others in the household have the same problem. Consult your doctor.

***Treatment:*** If your doctor diagnoses scabies, you will need to apply a prescribed insecticide to the whole of your body. The procedure should be repeated a few days later. Bedding and clothing should either be thoroughly laundered or left unused for about 4 days.

**Have you recently started to take any medicines?**

**YES**

**Certain drugs** may cause rashes as a side-effect. Discuss the problem with your doctor.

**NO**

**Consult your doctor** if you are unable to make a diagnosis from this chart.

## STRUCTURE OF THE SKIN

Skin consists of two layers. The surface layer is known as the epidermis. Active cells at its base are continuously dividing to produce new cells, which gradually die as they fill up with a hard substance, keratin. As each cell dies, it moves up towards the surface of the skin, to be shed or worn away. This production of cells at the base of the epidermis is carefully balanced with the loss of cells at the surface of the skin. If the rate of cell replacement is altered, a skin problem develops. For instance, in psoriasis there is an abnormal build-up of surface cells being produced and pushed up from the base of the epidermis.

The underlying layer, the dermis, contains the many specialist structures that allow the skin to function properly. Here, sebaceous glands produce sebum, a waxy substance that helps to keep the surface of the skin supple. Sweat glands produce perspiration to cool you when you are hot (*Sweat glands*, p.157). And the small blood vessels dilate in hot weather so that the body can lose heat and contract in cold weather to retain heat.

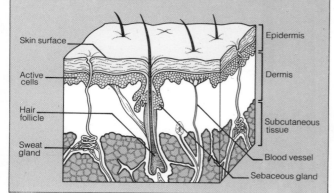

Skin surface · Epidermis
Active cells · Dermis
Hair follicle
Sweat gland · Subcutaneous tissue
Blood vessel
Sebaceous gland

## BRUISING

A bruise is a discoloured area of skin caused by blood leaking into the dermis (see *Structure of the skin*, above) from a blood vessel damaged by injury. A bruise is usually blue, purple or black at first, but gradually fades to yellow before disappearing completely.

### Self-help

If you have a bruise, do not rub or massage the bruised area; this may make matters worse. Applying an ice-pack (or an unopened packet of frozen vegetables) immediately after the injury may reduce the extent of bruising. If you have bruised your leg, resting with your feet up may assist healing.

### When to consult your doctor

Consult your doctor in any of the following circumstances:

- If you feel severe pain, or if movement is restricted.
- If bruises appear without injury.
- If you bruise frequently and easily.

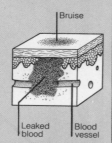

Bruise
Leaked blood · Blood vessel

**Formation of a bruise**
A bruise forms when blood from a damaged blood vessel leaks under the skin (above).

## ECZEMA

Eczema, sometimes referred to as dermatitis, is the name given to a group of related conditions in which the skin becomes inflamed and itchy. The main types of eczema are described below.

### Infantile (atopic) eczema

This is an allergic condition which usually appears for the first time in early infancy. Infantile eczema usually affects the wrists, insides of the elbows and backs of the knees, but in severe cases the whole body may be affected. The usual treatment is to avoid harsh soaps and detergents and to use instead a special soap substitute and to put oil in the bath. A rich moisturizing cream should be applied to the affected areas. If itching is severe, your doctor may prescribe drugs to alleviate this. Mild *steroid* creams are recommended in some cases and, if the eczema becomes infected, a mixed steroid and *antibiotic* cream or antibiotics by mouth are necessary. Skin tests may be carried out to try to identify factors which trigger outbreaks of eczema. Sometimes one or more foods may make eczema worse; your doctor will advise you if a special diet is necessary.

### Contact eczema

This type of eczema is caused by a reaction to contact with a substance to which you are allergic. Certain plants, such as primula or, in America, poison ivy are common causes. The skin becomes red and itchy and blisters that break and crust over may form. Milder forms of contact eczema may be caused by contact with certain metals – for example, nickel used in jewellery or on a watch. The rash will clear up in a day or so if the cause of the trouble is removed.

### Irritant eczema

As the name suggests, this type of rash is caused by contact with irritant chemicals – for example, harsh detergents or industrial chemicals in your place of work. The skin becomes dry, red, rough and itchy. The condition usually clears up if you avoid contact with the irritants by protecting your hands with gloves. A moisturizing hand cream should soothe the affected skin, but it is advisable to consult your doctor, who may prescribe a mild steroid cream to clear up the rash.

### Seborrhoeic dermatitis

The tendency to develop this type of eczema is probably inherited. Flaky, red, but not especially itchy, patches appear in areas with a high concentration of sebaceous glands (see *Structure of the skin,* above left), such as the nose and hairy parts of the face, or on scalp and chest. Seborrhoeic dermatitis on the scalp is the commonest cause of dandruff. If you suffer from this condition, keep the affected skin clean and dry, but avoid using harsh soaps or detergents on the skin. If the rash is extensive or worries you, consult your doctor, who may prescribe a mild cream or ointment.

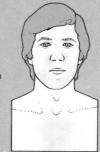

# 78 Raised spots or lumps on the skin

Consult this chart if you develop any raised lumps, whether they are skin coloured or pigmented (brown). In the majority of cases, such lumps are the harmless result of virus infection. Your doctor will be willing to give you advice on the problems if skin lumps persist or cause you discomfort or embarrassment.

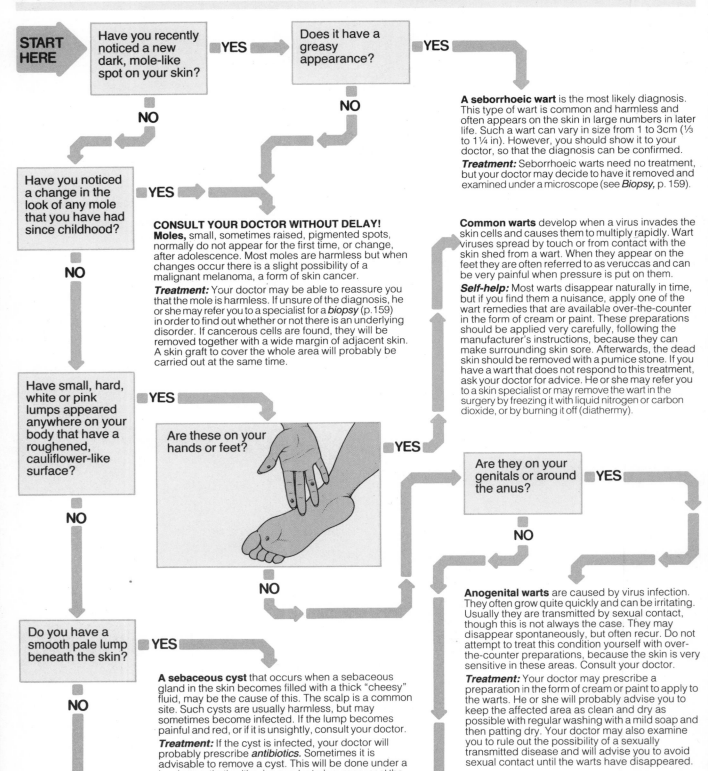

**START HERE**

Have you recently noticed a new dark, mole-like spot on your skin?

**YES** → Does it have a greasy appearance? **YES** →

**NO**

Have you noticed a change in the look of any mole that you have had since childhood?

**YES** →

**NO**

**NO**

**A seborrhoeic wart** is the most likely diagnosis. This type of wart is common and harmless and often appears on the skin in large numbers in later life. Such a wart can vary in size from 1 to 3cm (⅓ to 1¼ in). However, you should show it to your doctor, so that the diagnosis can be confirmed.

*Treatment:* Seborrhoeic warts need no treatment, but your doctor may decide to have it removed and examined under a microscope (see *Biopsy,* p. 159).

**CONSULT YOUR DOCTOR WITHOUT DELAY!**
**Moles,** small, sometimes raised, pigmented spots, normally do not appear for the first time, or change, after adolescence. Most moles are harmless but when changes occur there is a slight possibility of a malignant melanoma, a form of skin cancer.

*Treatment:* Your doctor may be able to reassure you that the mole is harmless. If unsure of the diagnosis, he or she may refer you to a specialist for a *biopsy* (p.159) in order to find out whether or not there is an underlying disorder. If cancerous cells are found, they will be removed together with a wide margin of adjacent skin. A skin graft to cover the whole area will probably be carried out at the same time.

**Common warts** develop when a virus invades the skin cells and causes them to multiply rapidly. Wart viruses spread by touch or from contact with the skin shed from a wart. When they appear on the feet they are often referred to as veruccas and can be very painful when pressure is put on them.

*Self-help:* Most warts disappear naturally in time, but if you find them a nuisance, apply one of the wart remedies that are available over-the-counter in the form of cream or paint. These preparations should be applied very carefully, following the manufacturer's instructions, because they can make surrounding skin sore. Afterwards, the dead skin should be removed with a pumice stone. If you have a wart that does not respond to this treatment, ask your doctor for advice. He or she may refer you to a skin specialist or may remove the wart in the surgery by freezing it with liquid nitrogen or carbon dioxide, or by burning it off (diathermy).

Have small, hard, white or pink lumps appeared anywhere on your body that have a roughened, cauliflower-like surface?

**YES** →

**NO**

Are these on your hands or feet?

**YES** →

**NO**

Are they on your genitals or around the anus? **YES** →

**NO**

Do you have a smooth pale lump beneath the skin?

**YES** →

**NO**

**A sebaceous cyst** that occurs when a sebaceous gland in the skin becomes filled with a thick "cheesy" fluid, may be the cause of this. The scalp is a common site. Such cysts are usually harmless, but may sometimes become infected. If the lump becomes painful and red, or if it is unsightly, consult your doctor.

*Treatment:* If the cyst is infected, your doctor will probably prescribe *antibiotics*. Sometimes it is advisable to remove a cyst. This will be done under a local anaesthetic either in your doctor's surgery or at the outpatient department of your local hospital.

**Anogenital warts** are caused by virus infection. They often grow quite quickly and can be irritating. Usually they are transmitted by sexual contact, though this is not always the case. They may disappear spontaneously, but often recur. Do not attempt to treat this condition yourself with over-the-counter preparations, because the skin is very sensitive in these areas. Consult your doctor.

*Treatment:* Your doctor may prescribe a preparation in the form of cream or paint to apply to the warts. He or she will probably advise you to keep the affected area as clean and dry as possible with regular washing with a mild soap and then patting dry. Your doctor may also examine you to rule out the possibility of a sexually transmitted disease and will advise you to avoid sexual contact until the warts have disappeared.

**Consult your doctor** if you are unable to make a diagnosis from this chart.

# 79 Rash with fever

Consult this chart if you notice any spots or discoloured areas of skin and also have a temperature of 38°C (100°F) or above. You may well have one of the infectious diseases that are more common in childhood.

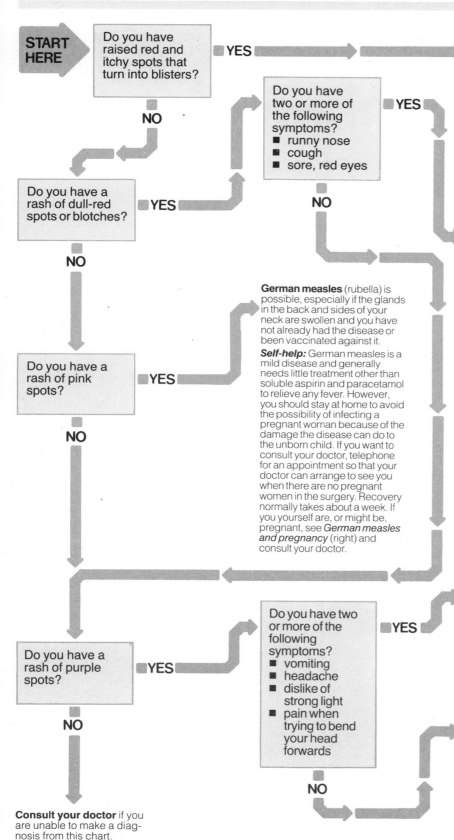

**START HERE**

**Do you have raised red and itchy spots that turn into blisters?**

NO

YES

**Do you have a rash of dull-red spots or blotches?**

YES

NO

**Do you have two or more of the following symptoms?**
- runny nose
- cough
- sore, red eyes

YES

NO

**Do you have a rash of pink spots?**

YES

NO

**German measles** (rubella) is possible, especially if the glands in the back and sides of your neck are swollen and you have not already had the disease or been vaccinated against it.

*Self-help:* German measles is a mild disease and generally needs little treatment other than soluble aspirin and paracetamol to relieve any fever. However, you should stay at home to avoid the possibility of infecting a pregnant woman because of the damage the disease can do to the unborn child. If you want to consult your doctor, telephone for an appointment so that your doctor can arrange to see you when there are no pregnant women in the surgery. Recovery normally takes about a week. If you yourself are, or might be, pregnant, see *German measles and pregnancy* (right) and consult your doctor.

**Do you have a rash of purple spots?**

YES

NO

**Do you have two or more of the following symptoms?**
- vomiting
- headache
- dislike of strong light
- pain when trying to bend your head forwards

YES

NO

**Consult your doctor** if you are unable to make a diagnosis from this chart.

**Chickenpox,** a childhood infectious disease caused by the herpes zoster virus, is the likely cause of such symptoms. The rash usually starts on the face and trunk, but may spread to the limbs.

*Self-help:* Drink plenty of fluids and take soluble aspirin or paracetamol to relieve any feverish symptoms. Apply calamine lotion to the rash to relieve itching. Try to resist the urge to scratch because scratching leads to scarring. Consult your doctor if you are, or might be, pregnant, if temperature rises above 40°C (104°F), if you develop a severe cough, if your eyes become painful, or if you find it hard not to scratch. Remember that you are infectious until all the blisters have formed scabs (after about a week).

**Measles,** a highly contagious viral disease, may be the cause of such symptoms, especially if you did not have measles as a child.

*Self-help:* There is no specific treatment for measles. Stay at home, drink plenty of fluids, and take soluble aspirin or paracetamol to reduce fever. Consult your doctor if you are, or might be, pregnant, if you develop a severe headache or earache, or if your cough starts to get worse.

**GERMAN MEASLES AND PREGNANCY**

The virus responsible for German measles may cross the placenta of a pregnant woman and damage the developing fetus, causing defects such as deafness, blindness and heart problems. The likelihood of damage occurring is strongest if the disease develops in the first 12 weeks of pregnancy. If you are pregnant or trying to become pregnant it is therefore vitally important to avoid contracting this disease.

In most cases you will be given a blood test in early pregnancy to check whether you are immune. If this test shows that you are at risk from the disease, you should be careful to avoid anyone who has the disease or has recently been in contact with it.

**CALL YOUR DOCTOR NOW!**
**Meningitis,** inflammation of the membranes surrounding the brain due to viral or bacterial infection, may be the cause of such symptoms.

*Treatment:* You will probably be admitted to hospital for a *lumbar puncture* (p.154). If the infection is found to be bacterial you will be given *antibiotics*, possibly by intravenous drip. If the infection is viral, no specific treatment is necessary, but you will be given painkillers and intravenous fluids. Recovery normally takes 2 to 3 weeks.

**CONSULT YOUR DOCTOR WITHOUT DELAY!**
**Purpura,** a type of rash caused by blood leaking from blood vessels under the skin, may be produced by an allergic reaction to a food or drug, or by infection. Call your doctor at once if your temperature rises to 40°C (104°F), or if you are suffering from a headache, stiff neck and/or vomiting.

*Treatment:* You will probably be admitted to hospital for a blood test (see *Blood analysis*, p.146) and possibly a *lumbar puncture* (p.154) to determine the exact nature of the disorder. Further treatment will depend on the results of these tests.

# 80 Painful or irritated eye

Pain or irritation in or around the eye may be caused by injury to the eye area or disorders of the eye or surrounding tissues. Infection and inflammation are the most common causes of eye discomfort. Disorders that threaten sight or that endanger health are uncommon, but should always be ruled out by your doctor.

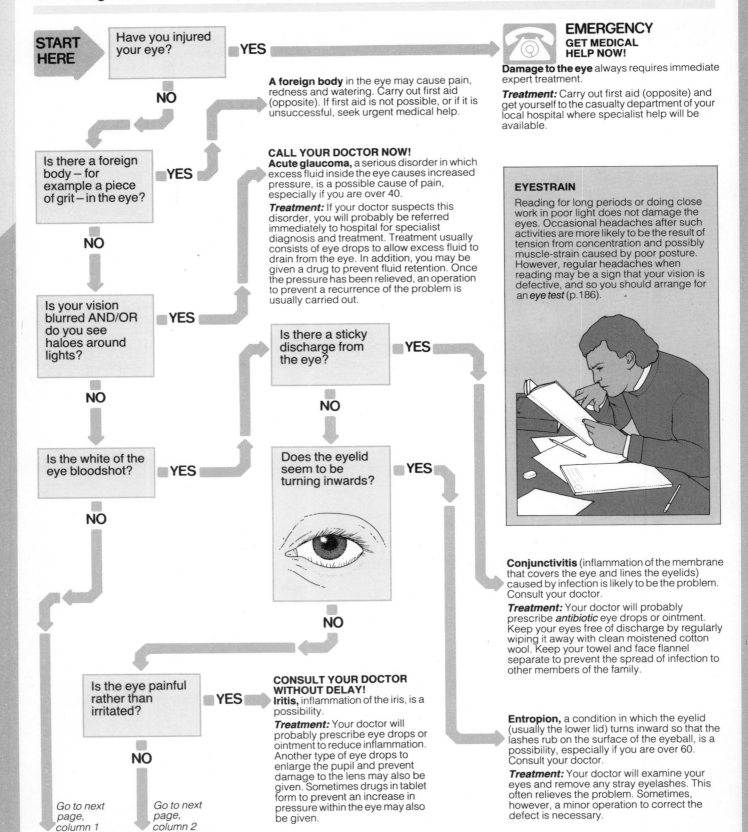

**START HERE** → **Have you injured your eye?** — **YES** →

**A foreign body** in the eye may cause pain, redness and watering. Carry out first aid (opposite). If first aid is not possible, or if it is unsuccessful, seek urgent medical help.

### EMERGENCY
**GET MEDICAL HELP NOW!**

**Damage to the eye** always requires immediate expert treatment.

***Treatment:*** Carry out first aid (opposite) and get yourself to the casualty department of your local hospital where specialist help will be available.

**NO** ↓

**Is there a foreign body – for example a piece of grit – in the eye?** — **YES** →

**CALL YOUR DOCTOR NOW!**
**Acute glaucoma,** a serious disorder in which excess fluid inside the eye causes increased pressure, is a possible cause of pain, especially if you are over 40.

***Treatment:*** If your doctor suspects this disorder, you will probably be referred immediately to hospital for specialist diagnosis and treatment. Treatment usually consists of eye drops to allow excess fluid to drain from the eye. In addition, you may be given a drug to prevent fluid retention. Once the pressure has been relieved, an operation to prevent a recurrence of the problem is usually carried out.

**NO** ↓

**Is your vision blurred AND/OR do you see haloes around lights?** — **YES** →

**Is there a sticky discharge from the eye?** — **YES** →

### EYESTRAIN

Reading for long periods or doing close work in poor light does not damage the eyes. Occasional headaches after such activities are more likely to be the result of tension from concentration and possibly muscle-strain caused by poor posture. However, regular headaches when reading may be a sign that your vision is defective, and so you should arrange for an *eye test* (p.186).

**NO** ↓

**Is the white of the eye bloodshot?** — **YES** →

**NO** ↓ (sticky discharge)

**Does the eyelid seem to be turning inwards?** — **YES** →

**NO** ↓

**Conjunctivitis** (inflammation of the membrane that covers the eye and lines the eyelids) caused by infection is likely to be the problem. Consult your doctor.

***Treatment:*** Your doctor will probably prescribe *antibiotic* eye drops or ointment. Keep your eyes free of discharge by regularly wiping it away with clean moistened cotton wool. Keep your towel and face flannel separate to prevent the spread of infection to other members of the family.

**Is the eye painful rather than irritated?** — **YES** →

**CONSULT YOUR DOCTOR WITHOUT DELAY!**
**Iritis,** inflammation of the iris, is a possibility.

***Treatment:*** Your doctor will probably prescribe eye drops or ointment to reduce inflammation. Another type of eye drops to enlarge the pupil and prevent damage to the lens may also be given. Sometimes drugs in tablet form to prevent an increase in pressure within the eye may also be given.

**Entropion,** a condition in which the eyelid (usually the lower lid) turns inward so that the lashes rub on the surface of the eyeball, is a possibility, especially if you are over 60. Consult your doctor.

***Treatment:*** Your doctor will examine your eyes and remove any stray eyelashes. This often relieves the problem. Sometimes, however, a minor operation to correct the defect is necessary.

**NO** ↓

*Go to next page, column 1*

*Go to next page, column 2*

*Continued from previous page, column 1*

**Are your eyelids red and itchy?**

**YES** ▶

**NO** ▼

**Blepharitis** (inflammation and scaling of the lid margins) may cause itchy eyelids. This usually occurs with *dandruff* (p.177). Consult your doctor.

***Treatment:*** Your doctor will probably prescribe ointment to apply to the lids.

**Do you have a red lump on the eyelid?**

**YES** ▶

**NO** ▼

**A stye** (a boil-like infection at the base of an eyelash) is likely.

***Self-help:*** A stye will usually either burst, and release pus, or dry up within a week without special treatment. If the stye bursts, carefully wipe away the pus using a clean piece of moistened cotton wool each time you wipe. Consult your doctor if a stye fails to heal within a week, the eye itself becomes red and painful, or if styes recur.

*Continued from previous page, column 2*

**Has your eye been watering?**

**YES** ▶

**NO** ▼

**Dry eye,** a condition in which the eye fails to produce enough tears, is possible. Consult your doctor.

***Treatment:*** If dry eye is confirmed, your doctor will prescribe eye drops of artificial tears, which you can use as frequently as you like in order to reduce discomfort.

**Consult your doctor** if you are unable to make a diagnosis from this chart.

**Eye irritation** may be caused by exposure to chemical fumes, or by an allergic reaction (for example, to pollen), or it may be caused by viral conjunctivitis.

***Self-help:*** There is no specific treatment for any of these conditions. Avoiding the irritant in the first two cases will bring relief. However, it may be difficult to trace an allergen. Your doctor may be able to help. Viral conjunctivitis will get better without treatment, but while it persists you will need to be careful to avoid spreading the infection to others. So keep a separate towel and face flannel.

---

## FIRST AID FOR EYE INJURIES

If you suffer an injury to your eye or eyelid rapid action is essential. Except in the case of a foreign body that has been successfully removed from the eye, go to the accident department of your local hospital by the fastest means possible, as soon as you have carried out first aid.

### Cuts to the eye or eyelid

Cover the injured eye with a clean pad (such as a folded hankerchief) and hold it lightly in place with a bandage. Apply no pressure. Cover the other eye to stop movement of the eyeball. Seek medical help.

### Blows to the eye area

Carry out first aid as for a cut eye (above) but use a cold compress instead of a dry pad over the eye.

### Corrosive chemicals in the eye

If you spill any harsh chemical (for example, bleach or household cleaner) in the eye, immediately flood the eye with large quantities of cold running water. Tilt your head with the injured eye downwards so that the water runs from the inside outwards. Keep the eyelids apart with your fingers. When all traces of the chemical seem to have been removed, lightly cover the eye with a clean pad and seek medical help.

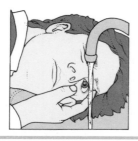

### Foreign body in the eye

Never attempt to remove any of the following:

- an object that is embedded in the eyeball
- a chip of metal
- a particle over the coloured part of the eye

In any of these cases cover both eyes as described for cuts to the eye or eyelid (left) and seek medical help. Other foreign bodies – for example, specks of dirt or eyelashes floating on the white of the eye or inside the lids – may be removed as follows –

**1** If you can see the particle on the white of the eye or inside the lower lid, pick it off using the moistened corner of a clean handkerchief (below) or cotton-tipped swab.

**2** If you cannot see the particle, pull the upper lid down over the lower lid and hold it for a moment (far right). This may dislodge the particle. If the particle remains, it may be on the inside of the upper lid. If you are alone, seek medical help. Another person may be able to remove the foreign body as in step 3.

**3** Ask the sufferer to look down. Hold the lashes of the upper lid and pull it down. Place a match, cocktail stick or cotton wool bud over the upper lid and fold the lid back over it (right). If the particle is now visible, carefully pick it off as in step 1 (far right).

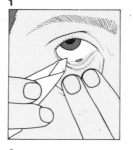
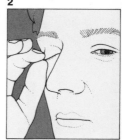
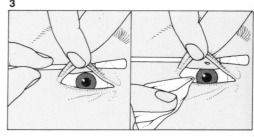

If you do not succeed in removing the foreign body, lightly cover the injured eye and seek medical help.

# 81 Disturbed or impaired vision

This chart deals with any change in your vision, including blurring, seeing double, seeing flashing lights or floating spots, and loss of part or all of your field of vision. Any such change in vision should be brought to your doctor's attention promptly to rule out the possibility of a sight-threatening eye disorder. Successful treatment of many such disorders may depend on catching the disease in its early stages.

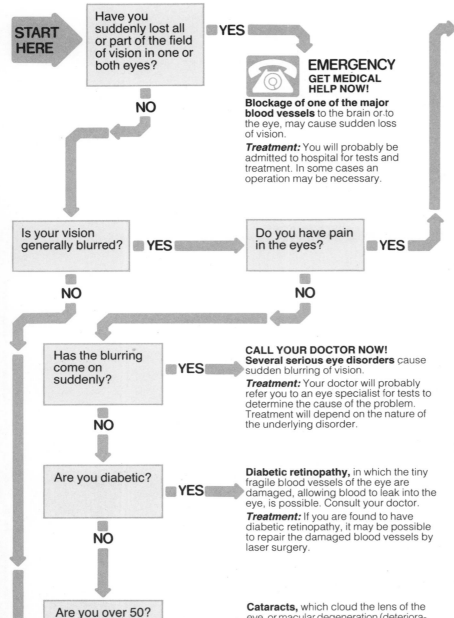

**START HERE**

**Have you suddenly lost all or part of the field of vision in one or both eyes?**

YES →

**EMERGENCY GET MEDICAL HELP NOW!**

**Blockage of one of the major blood vessels** to the brain or to the eye, may cause sudden loss of vision.

***Treatment:*** You will probably be admitted to hospital for tests and treatment. In some cases an operation may be necessary.

NO ↓

**Is your vision generally blurred?** — YES → **Do you have pain in the eyes?** — YES →

**CALL YOUR DOCTOR NOW!**
**Acute glaucoma,** is a possibility, especially if you are over 40. In this serious disorder obstruction to the normal draining mechanism causes a build-up of fluid, and a consequent increase in pressure in the eye.

***Treatment:*** If your doctor suspects this disorder, you will probably be referred to a specialist for treatment. Treatment usually consists of drugs to help lower the pressure within the eye and to relieve pain. You will also probably be given eye drops to help fluid drain from the eye. Later on you may need to have an operation to prevent a recurrence of the problem.

NO ↓     NO ↓

**Has the blurring come on suddenly?** — YES →

**CALL YOUR DOCTOR NOW!**
**Several serious eye disorders** cause sudden blurring of vision.

***Treatment:*** Your doctor will probably refer you to an eye specialist for tests to determine the cause of the problem. Treatment will depend on the nature of the underlying disorder.

NO ↓

**Are you diabetic?** — YES →

**Diabetic retinopathy,** in which the tiny fragile blood vessels of the eye are damaged, allowing blood to leak into the eye, is possible. Consult your doctor.

***Treatment:*** If you are found to have diabetic retinopathy, it may be possible to repair the damaged blood vessels by laser surgery.

NO ↓

**Are you over 50?** — YES →

**Cataracts,** which cloud the lens of the eye, or macular degeneration (deterioration of part of the retina) are both possible causes of blurred vision in this age group. Consult your doctor.

***Treatment:*** If you have a mild cataract, you may need only to have special glasses. In more severe cases, an operation to remove the affected lens is often recommended. Following this operation, you will be given a replacement plastic lens or be supplied with special glasses. Macular degeneration can, in some cases, be halted by laser surgery. In other cases, special glasses may improve vision.

NO ↓

**A variety of eye disorders** may cause blurring of vision. Consult your doctor, who may refer you to an eye specialist for treatment.

*Go to next page*

## EYE TESTING

You should have your eyes tested every 2 years after the age of 40. The optician will examine your eyes (see below) and will test the sharpness of your vision by asking you to read letters on a Snellen chart (named after its inventor). The result of the test is given as two figures. The first refers to the distance in metres – usually 6m (about 20 feet) at which you are asked to read the letters. The second figure refers to the lowermost row of letters that you were able to read correctly, and indicates the optimum distance in metres at which a person with normal vision could read that row. So the result 6/12 means that the lowest row of letters that you were able to read at a distance of 6m is one that a person with normal vision would read at 12m. The optician will also examine the eye to make sure that there are no signs that suggest a general disorder such as high blood pressure or diabetes. He or she will also check the eyes for any squint. Also, he or she will test the balance of the muscles that control the movement of the eyes.

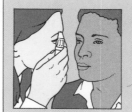

**Eye examination**
The optician looks at each eye through an instrument called an ophthalmoscope (left). With this, he or she can check that the back of the eye looks normal and that there are no signs of an underlying condition.

## COLOUR BLINDNESS

Colour blindness is a term used to describe the hereditary inability to distinguish between certain colours. All the colours we see are made up of combinations of red, green and blue – the basic colours in the light rays that enter our eyes. Literal colour blindness in which everything is seen in shades of grey is rare. The most common defect, which primarily affects men, is an inability to distinguish between red and green. Most people learn to live with this minor disability without problems. However, perfect colour vision is required for certain jobs – for example, that of an airline pilot – and anyone applying for such a job will be required to have a full eye examination, including tests for colour vision.

*Continued from previous page*

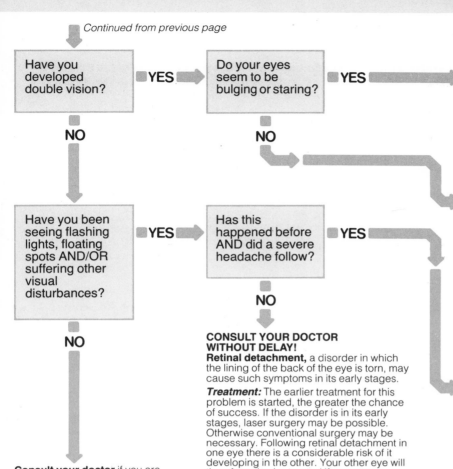

**Have you developed double vision?** → **YES** → **Do your eyes seem to be bulging or staring?** → **YES**

**Exophthalmos,** a condition in which the eyes protrude, is a possibility. Consult your doctor.

***Treatment:*** Your doctor will probably arrange tests to find out if an underlying disorder such as an overactive thyroid gland (thyrotoxicosis) is causing this condition. Treatment for thyrotoxicosis may consist of a course of drugs, injections of radioactive iodine, or surgery to remove part of the gland.

Have you developed double vision? → **NO**

Do your eyes seem to be bulging or staring? → **NO**

**A squint** may have developed. This is the result of lack of coordination between the muscles controlling the movement of both eyes. Consult your doctor.

***Treatment:*** Your doctor will probably arrange for you to have tests to find the underlying cause of the squint. These may include measuring your blood pressure, blood and urine analysis, a skull X-ray, and possibly a *CAT scan* (p.163) of the brain. While you are awaiting the results of such tests, your doctor may suggest that you wear a patch over one eye to prevent double vision. Long-term treatment will depend on the underlying cause of the squint.

**Have you been seeing flashing lights, floating spots AND/OR suffering other visual disturbances?** → **YES** → **Has this happened before AND did a severe headache follow?** → **YES**

Has this happened before AND did a severe headache follow? → **NO**

**CONSULT YOUR DOCTOR WITHOUT DELAY!**
**Retinal detachment,** a disorder in which the lining of the back of the eye is torn, may cause such symptoms in its early stages.

***Treatment:*** The earlier treatment for this problem is started, the greater the chance of success. If the disorder is in its early stages, laser surgery may be possible. Otherwise conventional surgery may be necessary. Following retinal detachment in one eye there is a considerable risk of it developing in the other. Your other eye will therefore also be treated if necessary.

**Migraine** (recurrent severe headaches) may be preceded by a warning period in which you experience disturbance to your vision. Consult your doctor.

***Treatment:*** If you suffer from migraines regularly, try to find out if any particular food or other factor seems to trigger off the headaches, so that you can avoid it. The self-help measures suggested on p. 38 may help to relieve the pain. Your doctor will be able to offer more effective drug treatment if the attacks recur.

Have you been seeing flashing lights... → **NO**

**Consult your doctor** if you are unable to make a diagnosis from this chart.

---

## THE STRUCTURE OF THE EYE

The eye is a complex and delicate structure. The eyeball itself consists of 3 layers:

**The sclera,** the tough outer layer, is visible as the white of the eye. It is continuous with the cornea, the transparent covering of the front of the eye. The visible sclera is protected at the front by the conjunctiva, a clear membrane containing blood vessels that also lines the inner surface of the eyelids.

**The choroid layer** beneath the sclera is rich in blood vessels that supply the sensitive inner lining of the eyeball. At the front of the eye, the choroid layer thickens to form the ciliary body, a circle of muscle that supports and controls the lens. In front of the ciliary body, lies the iris which contains coloured muscular fibres that control the amount of light that passes through the lens. The area between the iris and the cornea, is filled with watery fluid known as aqueous humour.

**The retina** is the innermost layer of the eyeball. This contains the light-sensitive nerve cells that pick up images and transmit the information through the optic nerve to the brain. The inner part of the eyeball is filled with a thick jelly-like substance called vitreous humour.

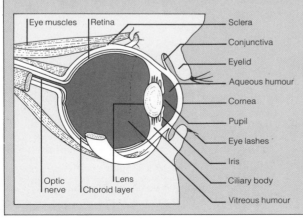

Eye muscles | Retina
Sclera
Conjunctiva
Eyelid
Aqueous humour
Cornea
Pupil
Eye lashes
Iris
Optic nerve | Lens | Choroid layer
Ciliary body
Vitreous humour

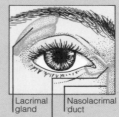

Lacrimal gland | Nasolacrimal duct
Lacrimal sac

**Tear glands and ducts**
Tears are produced in the lacrimal glands above each eyeball and drain away along tear ducts into the lacrimal sac, and via the nasolacrimal duct into the nose.

## CONTACT LENSES

In recent years, contact lenses have become a popular alternative to spectacles as a means of correcting defects in vision such as short or long sight. There are 2 main types of lens: the hard lens which is made of hardwearing plastic, but may be uncomfortable for some people; and the soft lens which is often more comfortable, but is more easily damaged and not so long lasting. Your optician will help you decide which type of lens is most suitable.

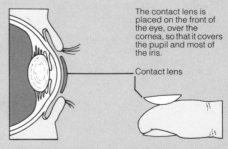

The contact lens is placed on the front of the eye, over the cornea, so that it covers the pupil and most of the iris.

Contact lens

**Care of contact lenses**
All types of contact lens need regular and careful cleaning to remove dirt and prevent the build-up of protein deposits on the lens. If this is not done there is a danger of infection and permanent damage to the eye. Always use the special cleaning and soaking solutions recommended for your type of lens, and follow your optician's detailed advice on the care of your lenses precisely.

# 82 Earache

Earache may vary from a dull, throbbing sensation to a sharp, stabbing pain that can be most distressing. It is a very common symptom in childhood, but occurs much less frequently in adults. Pain in the ear is usually caused by infection and normally requires medical attention and antibiotic treatment.

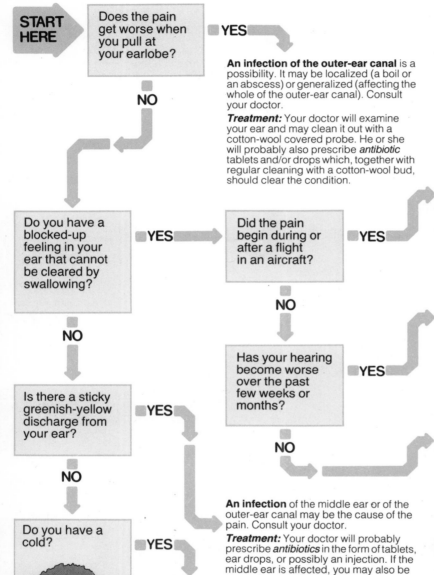

**START HERE** → **Does the pain get worse when you pull at your earlobe?**

**YES** →

**An infection of the outer-ear canal** is a possibility. It may be localized (a boil or an abscess) or generalized (affecting the whole of the outer-ear canal). Consult your doctor.

***Treatment:*** Your doctor will examine your ear and may clean it out with a cotton-wool covered probe. He or she will probably also prescribe *antibiotic* tablets and/or drops which, together with regular cleaning with a cotton-wool bud, should clear the condition.

**NO** ↓

**Do you have a blocked-up feeling in your ear that cannot be cleared by swallowing?**

**YES** → **Did the pain begin during or after a flight in an aircraft?**

**YES** →

**Barotrauma,** in which the air pressure balance between the middle and outer ear is disrupted, is a possibility, especially if you had a cold or a blocked nose when you travelled.

***Self-help:*** Try blowing through your nose while pinching the nostrils closed. In many cases this brings relief. If the trouble persists for more than 24 hours, consult your doctor.

**NO** ↓

**Has your hearing become worse over the past few weeks or months?**

**YES** →

**Wax blockage** may be causing the pain.

***Self-help:*** To remove wax yourself, soften it with over-the-counter ear drops for several days. Then lie in a warm bath with your ears submerged to loosen it. The wax should work its way out of the outer ear canal by itself. If you cannot remove the wax yourself, or if pain persists, consult your doctor, who may flush (syringe) the ear with warm water to wash away the blockage. Never attempt to lever the wax out yourself by poking a pointed instrument into your ear.

**NO** ↓

**An acute infection of the middle ear** is a possibility. This may have occurred as a result of blockage of the eustachian tube. Consult your doctor.

***Treatment:*** Your doctor may prescribe *decongestant* nose drops or spray, to help unblock the eustachian tube and to allow air to circulate. In addition, you may be given a course of *antibiotics* to clear up the infection.

**NO** ↓

**Is there a sticky greenish-yellow discharge from your ear?**

**YES** →

**An infection** of the middle ear or of the outer-ear canal may be the cause of the pain. Consult your doctor.

***Treatment:*** Your doctor will probably prescribe *antibiotics* in the form of tablets, ear drops, or possibly an injection. If the middle ear is affected, you may also be given *decongestants* to clear the eustachian tube.

**NO** ↓

**Do you have a cold?**

**YES** →

**Colds** that are accompanied by a severely blocked up nose often cause mild earache. However, severe earache is more likely to be the result of an acute infection of the middle ear.

***Self-help:*** If the pain is mild, follow the advice on *treating a cold,* (p.192). If pain persists or becomes severe, consult your doctor who may prescribe *decongestant* nose drops or spray and possibly a course of *antibiotics*.

**NO** ↓

**Consult your doctor** if you are unable to make a diagnosis from this chart.

---

### HOW TO RELIEVE EARACHE

In any case of earache, you will be able to relieve the pain by taking the recommended dose of soluble aspirin or paracetamol. It may also be comforting to place a covered hot-water bottle against the ear. But remember that these measures alone will not cure the underlying disorder. You should always consult your doctor about persistent pain in the ear.

---

### EAR PIERCING

Many people have holes pierced in their ears for earrings. If done properly, this is a perfectly safe and painless procedure, but unfortunately in many cases it is carried out inexpertly, leading to discomfort and sometimes infection. If you want to have your ears pierced, go to a reputable jeweller or department store. Ask what method of ear-piercing they use. The usual technique is by a special ear punch with a local anaesthetic. Other methods may not be reliable. Make sure that the conditions look reasonably clean and that all the instruments and earrings are sterilized before use. When you have had your ears pierced, you should wear only earrings of high-carat gold for the first month and these should not be removed for the first two weeks. You will need to bathe the earlobe with mild antiseptic twice a day during this time. Do not have your ears pierced if you have any skin infection affecting the earlobes. If either earlobe becomes inflamed or if there is any pus after having your ears pierced, consult your doctor.

# 83 Noises in the ear

If you sometimes hear noises inside your ears such as buzzing, ringing or hissing, you are probably suffering from a symptom known as tinnitus. This symptom can indicate a variety of ear disorders.

**START HERE** → **Did the noises start during or after a flight in an aircraft?**

**YES** →

**Barotrauma,** in which the air pressure balance between the middle and outer ear is disrupted, is a possibility, especially if you had a cold or a blocked nose when you travelled.

***Self-help:*** Try blowing through your nose while pinching the nostrils closed. In many cases this restores hearing to normal. If the trouble persists for more than 24 hours, consult your doctor.

**NO** ↓

**Have you noticed any loss of hearing?**

**YES** →

**Deafness** often occurs together with noises in the ear.

Go to chart

**84** **Deafness**

**NO** ↓

**Are you taking, or have you recently taken any prescribed or over-the-counter medicines?**

**YES** →

**Certain drugs** can cause noises in the ear as a side-effect. Discuss the problem with your doctor.

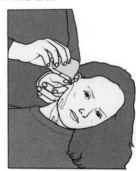

**FIRST AID FOR AN INSECT IN THE EAR**

If an insect has become trapped in your ear, you can safely try to remove it by tilting your head so that the affected side is uppermost and then pouring tepid water into the ear (it is easiest if someone helps to do this). The insect should then float out. Alternatively, you can simply lie back in a bath with your ears submerged. If these measures do not succeed in removing the insect, consult your doctor.

As you pour water into the ear, gently pull the earlobe up and back.

**An insect,** or other foreign body, may have become trapped in your outer-ear canal.

***Self-help:*** Carry out the first aid suggestions described above. If these are not effective, consult your doctor. Never attempt to remove anything by inserting an object into the ear.

**NO** ↓

**Do you have a tickling sensation in the ear?**

**YES** →

**NO** ↓

**Consult your doctor** if you are unable to make a diagnosis from this chart, especially if noises in the ear are accompanied by hearing loss, dizziness or headache.

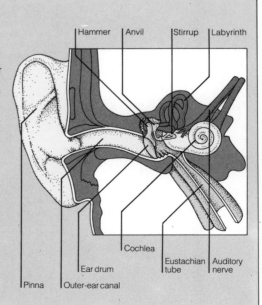

**THE STRUCTURE OF THE EAR**

The ear is made up of three main parts:

**The outer ear** includes the external part of the ear, the pinna, which collects and funnels sound waves along the outer-ear canal to the eardrum which then vibrates.

**The middle ear** contains the eardrum and three small bones (hammer, anvil and stirrup) that transmit the vibrations of the eardrum to the inner ear. Air pressure in the middle ear is kept normal by means of the eustachian tube that links the middle-ear to the back of the throat.

**The inner ear** is filled with fluid and contains the cochlea which converts the vibrations from the middle ear into nerve impulses. These are passed to the brain by the auditory nerve. The inner ear also contains the labyrinth which controls the body's balance see *How you keep your balance* (p.164).

Hammer | Anvil | Stirrup | Labyrinth

Cochlea

Ear drum

Eustachian tube | Auditory nerve

Pinna | Outer-ear canal

# 84 Deafness

Deafness – deterioration in the ability to hear some or all sounds – may come on gradually over a period of months or years, or may occur suddenly over a matter of days or hours. One or both ears may be affected. In most cases, deafness is the result of infection or wax blockage and can be treated.

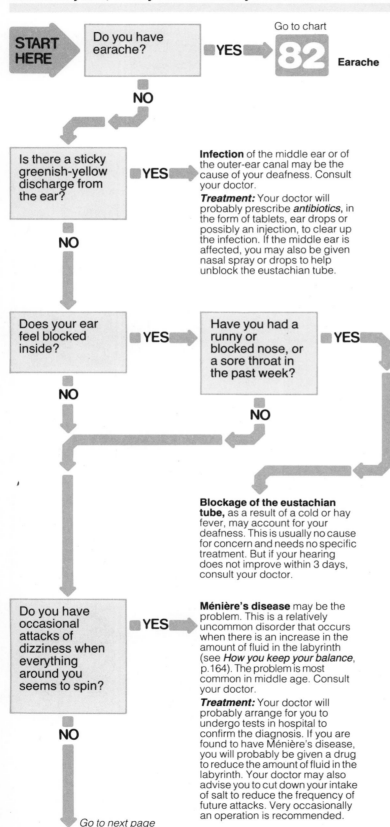

**START HERE** → Do you have earache? → **YES** → Go to chart **82** Earache

**NO**

Is there a sticky greenish-yellow discharge from the ear? → **YES** →

**Infection** of the middle ear or of the outer-ear canal may be the cause of your deafness. Consult your doctor.
**Treatment:** Your doctor will probably prescribe *antibiotics*, in the form of tablets, ear drops or possibly an injection, to clear up the infection. If the middle ear is affected, you may also be given nasal spray or drops to help unblock the eustachian tube.

**NO**

Does your ear feel blocked inside? → **YES** → Have you had a runny or blocked nose, or a sore throat in the past week? → **YES**

**NO** **NO**

**Blockage of the eustachian tube,** as a result of a cold or hay fever, may account for your deafness. This is usually no cause for concern and needs no specific treatment. But if your hearing does not improve within 3 days, consult your doctor.

Do you have occasional attacks of dizziness when everything around you seems to spin? → **YES** →

**Ménière's disease** may be the problem. This is a relatively uncommon disorder that occurs when there is an increase in the amount of fluid in the labyrinth (see *How you keep your balance*, p.164). The problem is most common in middle age. Consult your doctor.
**Treatment:** Your doctor will probably arrange for you to undergo tests in hospital to confirm the diagnosis. If you are found to have Ménière's disease, you will probably be given a drug to reduce the amount of fluid in the labyrinth. Your doctor may also advise you to cut down your intake of salt to reduce the frequency of future attacks. Very occasionally an operation is recommended.

**NO**

*Go to next page*

## HEARING TESTS

If, after examining you, your doctor suspects that your hearing is impaired, he or she may refer you to hospital for specialized hearing tests known as audiometry and acoustic impedance testing.

**Audiometry**
The first part of this test measures your ability to hear sounds conducted through the air. You are asked to listen through headphones, one ear at a time, to different pitches of sound. Each sound is played first at an inaudible level, then the volume is gradually increased until you signal that you can hear it.

The second part of the test measures your ability to hear the same sounds conducted through the bones in your head. For this test you wear a special head set that vibrates against your skull, usually behind the ear.

The results of both tests are recorded on an audiogram and show exactly what type of sounds you have most difficulty hearing.

In the first part of the test your ability to hear sound through headphones is measured (above). In the second part of the test you wear a special headset behind your ears that transmits vibrations through the bones in your skull (right).

**Acoustic impedance testing**
Acoustic impedance testing is used to assess the movement of the eardrum, which may be impaired as a result of a disorder of the middle ear. A special probe containing a sound transmitter is inserted into the outer-ear canal (below). Air is pumped through the probe and the ability of the eardrum to reflect sound emitted by the sound transmitter at different air pressure levels is measured. From the results it is possible to assess any impairment to the mobility of the eardrum and its possible cause.

*Continued from previous page*

Do you regularly spend time listening to loud music – for example, at rock concerts or discotheques, or through headphones – or are you often exposed to loud noise at work; or are you often exposed to loud noise through hobbies involving power tools?

**YES** → **Repeated exposure to loud noise** has probably caused your loss of hearing. Even noise levels that do not cause discomfort can result in permanent damage to your hearing. Headphones can be particularly dangerous as it is easy to have the volume too high, in order to overcome external noises such as traffic, without realizing it.

*Self-help:* Take whatever measures you can to prevent your hearing deteriorating further. Keep well away from the speakers at rock concerts and discos, and reduce the volume through your headphones so that others in the same room cannot hear the music. If you work in very noisy surroundings – in a factory, for example – your employer should supply you with ear muffs, or you can buy your own ear plugs. You should consult your doctor, who will probably arrange for you to have special hearing tests and, if necessary, supply a hearing aid.

**NO** ↓

Have you recently taken any prescribed or over-the-counter medicines?

**YES** → **Certain drugs** can cause deafness as a side-effect. Discuss the problem with your doctor.

**NO** ↓

Has your hearing been getting worse over a period of several weeks or more?

**NO** ↓

**YES** →

Have other members of your family suffered from gradual hearing loss?

**YES** →

**NO** ↓

**Wax blockage** may be the cause of your deafness.

*Self-help:* To remove wax yourself, soften it with over-the-counter ear drops for several days. Then lie in a warm bath with your ears submerged to loosen it. The wax should then work its way out of the outer ear by itself. If you cannot remove the wax this way do not attempt to lever it out by poking a pointed instrument into your ear, but consult your doctor, who will flush (syringe) the ear with warm water, to wash away the blockage.

Are you over 50 years old?

**YES** →

**NO** ↓

**Otosclerosis,** a disorder that affects the working of the bones in the middle ear, may be the problem. This type of deafness mainly affects young adults and is especially common in women. The disorder may get worse during pregnancy (see *Deafness and pregnancy,* below). Consult your doctor.

*Treatment:* If your doctor suspects otosclerosis, he or she will probably arrange for you to undergo *hearing tests* (opposite). If only one ear is affected, it is usual to prescribe a hearing aid. In cases where there is serious loss of hearing in one or both ears, or where this seems likely to develop, an operation, known as *stapedectomy* (above), may be recommended.

**Presbycusis,** gradual loss of hearing as you get older, is common, especially if other members of your family have become deaf in old age. Consult your doctor.

*Treatment:* Your doctor may refer you for *hearing tests* (opposite). If these confirm the diagnosis, you will probably be offered a hearing aid.

---

**STAPEDECTOMY**

Stapedectomy is an operation on the bones in the middle ear that is often carried out in severe cases of otosclerosis. Usually the operation produces a marked improvement in hearing, but unfortunatley in a small proportion of cases, it results in complete deafness in that ear. For this reason, often only one ear is operated on, so that if the operation fails, some hearing is retained in the other ear.

**The operation**
During the operation, the eardrum is pierced and the stirrup, one of the three tiny bones in the middle ear that is damaged by the disease, is replaced by a metal or plastic substitute. This improves the conduction of sound through the middle ear.

Stapedectomy normally involves a hospital stay of 1 to 2 weeks and convalescence at home for a further week or so. You may feel dizzy for a few days following the operation.

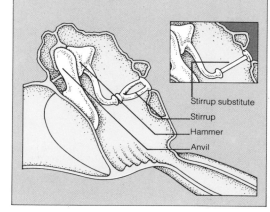

Stirrup substitute
Stirrup
Hammer
Anvil

---

**DEAFNESS AND PREGNANCY**

If you notice any loss of hearing during pregnancy, you should always seek your doctor's advice. This is because otosclerosis, a middle ear disorder resulting in progressive deafness, can sometimes appear for the first time or get worse during pregnancy. The disorder tends to run in families.

---

**Consult your doctor** if you are unable to make a diagnosis from this chart.

# 85 Runny nose

Congestion of the nose by a thick or watery discharge is probably one of the most familiar symptoms. It is nearly always caused by irritation of the delicate mucous membrane lining of the nose. This is usually the result of infection, but may sometimes occur as an allergic reaction or as a result of local irritation.

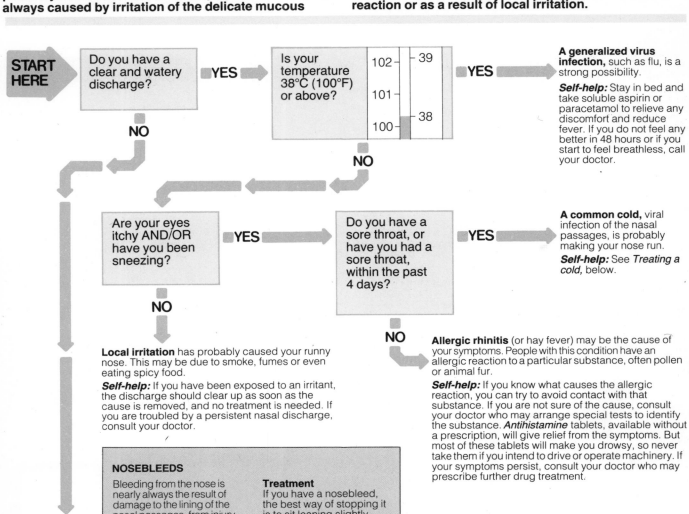

**START HERE** → **Do you have a clear and watery discharge?** → YES → **Is your temperature 38°C (100°F) or above?**

(Thermometer scale: 102 / 39, 101 / 38, 100)

→ YES →

**A generalized virus infection,** such as flu, is a strong possibility.

*Self-help:* Stay in bed and take soluble aspirin or paracetamol to relieve any discomfort and reduce fever. If you do not feel any better in 48 hours or if you start to feel breathless, call your doctor.

**NO** (from clear and watery discharge)

**NO** (from temperature)

**Are your eyes itchy AND/OR have you been sneezing?** → YES → **Do you have a sore throat, or have you had a sore throat, within the past 4 days?** → YES →

**A common cold,** viral infection of the nasal passages, is probably making your nose run.

*Self-help:* See *Treating a cold,* below.

**NO** (from eyes itchy)

**NO** (from sore throat)

**Local irritation** has probably caused your runny nose. This may be due to smoke, fumes or even eating spicy food.

*Self-help:* If you have been exposed to an irritant, the discharge should clear up as soon as the cause is removed, and no treatment is needed. If you are troubled by a persistent nasal discharge, consult your doctor.

**Allergic rhinitis** (or hay fever) may be the cause of your symptoms. People with this condition have an allergic reaction to a particular substance, often pollen or animal fur.

*Self-help:* If you know what causes the allergic reaction, you can try to avoid contact with that substance. If you are not sure of the cause, consult your doctor who may arrange special tests to identify the substance. *Antihistamine* tablets, available without a prescription, will give relief from the symptoms. But most of these tablets will make you drowsy, so never take them if you intend to drive or operate machinery. If your symptoms persist, consult your doctor who may prescribe further drug treatment.

## NOSEBLEEDS

Bleeding from the nose is nearly always the result of damage to the lining of the nasal passages, from injury or inflammation. Nosebleeds can happen when you have a cold and are particularly common in pregnancy when the increase in blood supply makes the tiny blood vessels in the nose more likely to rupture. Nosebleeds are never a sign of high blood pressure in pregnancy.

**Treatment**
If you have a nosebleed, the best way of stopping it is to sit leaning slightly forward and to pinch the end of your nose firmly between the thumb and forefinger for 5 minutes while keeping your mouth open. An ice pack or cold sponge applied to the nose may also be helpful. If the bleeding continues for more than 20 minutes, consult your doctor or go to hospital.

## TREATING A COLD

If you have a cold, stay at home in a warm, but not overheated room. Moisten the atmosphere with steam from a basin of hot water or a kettle. Drink plenty of fluids, preferably fruit juice, and take soluble aspirin or paracetamol to relieve feverish symptoms. Patent medicines may give temporary relief. If you are prone to ear infections or to bronchitis, if your nose is still running after 10 days, or if the infection seems to have spread beyond the nose and throat, consult your doctor.

**Do you have a thick and opaque discharge?** → YES → **Does your face feel painful or tender just above or below the eyes?** → YES →

**Sinusitis** (inflammation of the membranes lining the air spaces in the skull) may be the cause.

*Self-help:* Stay inside in a warm and humid atmosphere and take soluble aspirin or paracetamol to relieve the discomfort. If you are no better in 48 hours, consult your doctor, who may prescribe *antibiotics* and *decongestants.* If you suffer from recurrent sinusitis, your doctor may recommend a minor operation to clear the sinuses.

**NO** (from thick and opaque)

**NO** (from face painful)

**Consult your doctor** if you are unable to make a diagnosis from this chart.

**A common cold,** viral infection of the nasal passages, is probably making your nose run.

*Self-help:* See *Treating a cold,* above.

# 86 Sore throat

**Most people suffer from a painful, rough or raw feeling in the throat from time to time. This is usually the result** **of a minor infection or local irritation, and almost always disappears within a few days.**

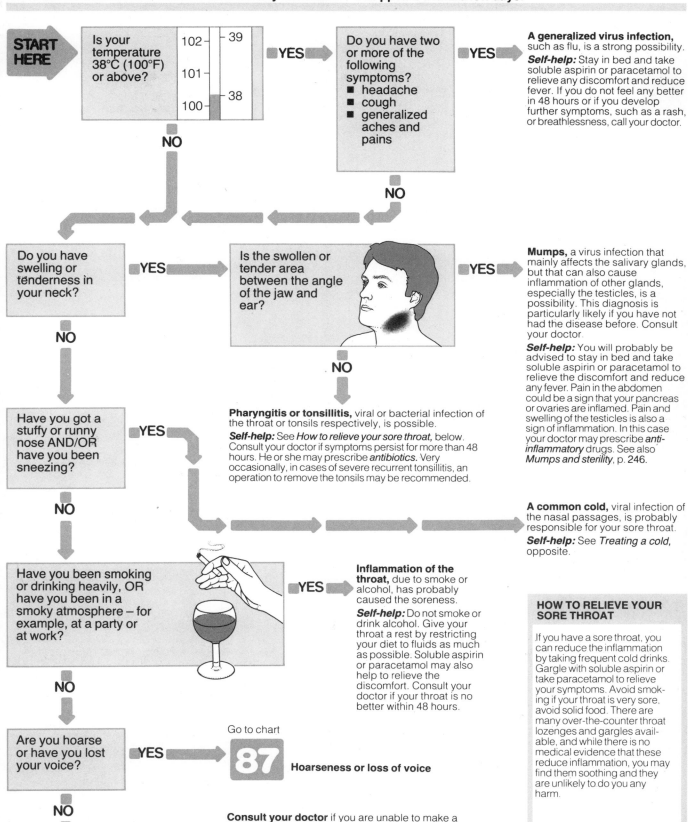

**START HERE**

Is your temperature 38°C (100°F) or above?

102 — 39

101 —

100 — 38

**YES** → Do you have two or more of the following symptoms?
- headache
- cough
- generalized aches and pains

**YES** → **A generalized virus infection,** such as flu, is a strong possibility.
*Self-help:* Stay in bed and take soluble aspirin or paracetamol to relieve any discomfort and reduce fever. If you do not feel any better in 48 hours or if you develop further symptoms, such as a rash, or breathlessness, call your doctor.

**NO** ↓

**NO** ↓

Do you have swelling or tenderness in your neck?

**YES** → Is the swollen or tender area between the angle of the jaw and ear?

**YES** → **Mumps,** a virus infection that mainly affects the salivary glands, but that can also cause inflammation of other glands, especially the testicles, is a possibility. This diagnosis is particularly likely if you have not had the disease before. Consult your doctor.
*Self-help:* You will probably be advised to stay in bed and take soluble aspirin or paracetamol to relieve the discomfort and reduce any fever. Pain in the abdomen could be a sign that your pancreas or ovaries are inflamed. Pain and swelling of the testicles is also a sign of inflammation. In this case your doctor may prescribe *anti-inflammatory* drugs. See also *Mumps and sterility,* p. 246.

**NO** ↓

**NO** ↓

Have you got a stuffy or runny nose AND/OR have you been sneezing?

**YES** → **Pharyngitis or tonsillitis,** viral or bacterial infection of the throat or tonsils respectively, is possible.
*Self-help:* See *How to relieve your sore throat,* below. Consult your doctor if symptoms persist for more than 48 hours. He or she may prescribe *antibiotics.* Very occasionally, in cases of severe recurrent tonsillitis, an operation to remove the tonsils may be recommended.

**A common cold,** viral infection of the nasal passages, is probably responsible for your sore throat.
*Self-help:* See *Treating a cold,* opposite.

**NO** ↓

Have you been smoking or drinking heavily, OR have you been in a smoky atmosphere – for example, at a party or at work?

**YES** → **Inflammation of the throat,** due to smoke or alcohol, has probably caused the soreness.
*Self-help:* Do not smoke or drink alcohol. Give your throat a rest by restricting your diet to fluids as much as possible. Soluble aspirin or paracetamol may also help to relieve the discomfort. Consult your doctor if your throat is no better within 48 hours.

**NO** ↓

Are you hoarse or have you lost your voice?

**YES** → Go to chart **87** **Hoarseness or loss of voice**

**NO** ↓

**Consult your doctor** if you are unable to make a diagnosis from this chart and your sore throat persists for more than 48 hours.

---

**HOW TO RELIEVE YOUR SORE THROAT**

If you have a sore throat, you can reduce the inflammation by taking frequent cold drinks. Gargle with soluble aspirin or take paracetamol to relieve your symptoms. Avoid smoking if your throat is very sore, avoid solid food. There are many over-the-counter throat lozenges and gargles available, and while there is no medical evidence that these reduce inflammation, you may find them soothing and they are unlikely to do you any harm.

# 87 Hoarseness or loss of voice

Hoarseness, huskiness or loss of voice is almost always caused by laryngitis – inflammation and swelling of the vocal cords that interferes with their ability to vibrate normally and so to produce sounds. There can be a variety of underlying causes for this inflammation, most of which are minor and easily treated at home, but persistent or recurrent hoarseness or loss of voice may have a more serious cause and should always be brought to your doctor's attention for early diagnosis and treatment.

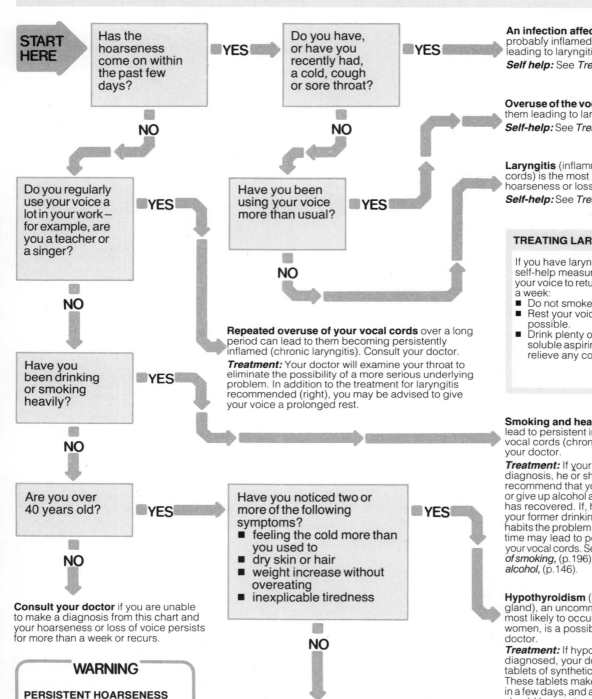

**START HERE**

**Has the hoarseness come on within the past few days?**

— YES → **Do you have, or have you recently had, a cold, cough or sore throat?**

— YES → **An infection affecting the throat** has probably inflamed your vocal cords leading to laryngitis.
*Self help:* See *Treating laryngitis*, below.

NO ↓ (from "Do you have...") **Have you been using your voice more than usual?**

— YES → **Overuse of the vocal cords** can inflame them leading to laryngitis.
*Self-help:* See *Treating laryngitis*, below.

NO ↓ (from first question) **Do you regularly use your voice a lot in your work – for example, are you a teacher or a singer?**

**Laryngitis** (inflammation of the vocal cords) is the most likely cause of sudden hoarseness or loss of voice.
*Self-help:* See *Treating laryngitis*, below.

— YES → **Repeated overuse of your vocal cords** over a long period can lead to them becoming persistently inflamed (chronic laryngitis). Consult your doctor.
*Treatment:* Your doctor will examine your throat to eliminate the possibility of a more serious underlying problem. In addition to the treatment for laryngitis recommended (right), you may be advised to give your voice a prolonged rest.

NO ↓ **Have you been drinking or smoking heavily?**

— YES → **Smoking and heavy drinking** can both lead to persistent inflammation of the vocal cords (chronic laryngitis). Consult your doctor.
*Treatment:* If your doctor confirms the diagnosis, he or she will probably recommend that you stop smoking and/ or give up alcohol at least until your voice has recovered. If, however, you return to your former drinking and/or smoking habits the problem is likely to recur and in time may lead to permanent damage to your vocal cords. See also *The dangers of smoking,* (p.196), and *The effects of alcohol,* (p.146).

NO ↓ **Are you over 40 years old?**

— YES → **Have you noticed two or more of the following symptoms?**
- feeling the cold more than you used to
- dry skin or hair
- weight increase without overeating
- inexplicable tiredness

— YES → **Hypothyroidism** (underactive thyroid gland), an uncommon problem that is most likely to occur in middle-aged women, is a possibility. Consult your doctor.
*Treatment:* If hypothyroidism is diagnosed, your doctor will prescribe tablets of synthetic thyroid hormones. These tablets make you feel much better in a few days, and after a few months you should have returned to normal health. However, it will be necessary to continue taking the tablets indefinitely.

NO ↓ (from "Are you over 40") **Consult your doctor** if you are unable to make a diagnosis from this chart and your hoarseness or loss of voice persists for more than a week or recurs.

NO ↓ (from symptoms box) **CONSULT YOUR DOCTOR WITHOUT DELAY!**
**Gradually increasing huskiness** may simply be a side-effect of hormonal changes as you get older. However, true hoarseness that lasts more than one or two weeks may, in rare cases, be a sign of growth.
*Treatment:* Your doctor will probably examine your throat and may arrange for you to have a *biopsy* (p.159) of the voice box. Many growths can be removed surgically.

---

**TREATING LARYNGITIS**

If you have laryngitis, the following self-help measures should help your voice to return to normal within a week:
- Do not smoke or drink alcohol.
- Rest your voice as much as possible.
- Drink plenty of fluids and take soluble aspirin or paracetamol to relieve any cold-like symptoms.

---

### WARNING

**PERSISTENT HOARSENESS**

Hoarseness or loss of voice that is recurrent or lasts more than two weeks may be a sign of a growth in the voice box, especially if you are over 40 and smoke.

**Consult your doctor without delay!**

# 88 Wheezing

Wheezing sometimes occurs when breathing out if you have a "chesty" cold, and this is no cause for concern as long as breathing is otherwise normal. Such wheezing can usually be heard only through a doctor's stethoscope, but it may become more apparent to you when you exhale violently (during exercise, for example). Loud wheezing, especially if you also feel breathless, or if breathing is painful, may be a sign of a number of more serious conditions and requires medical attention.

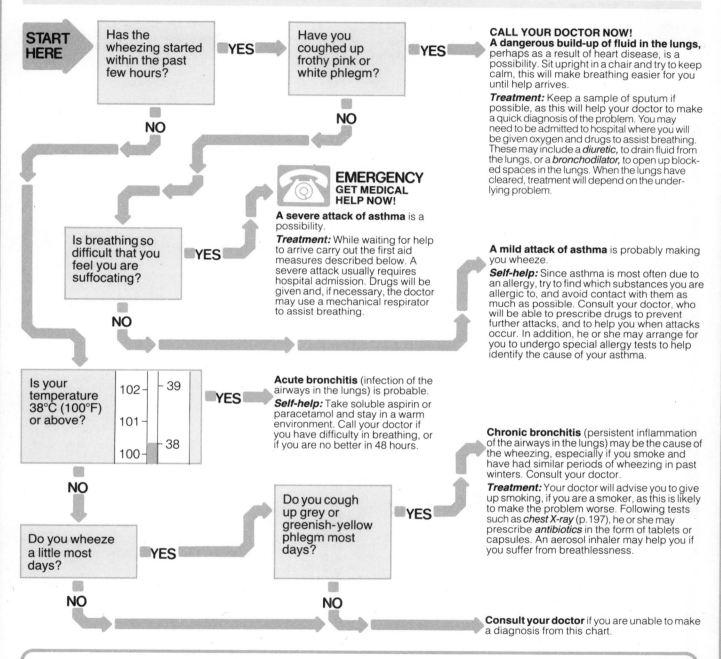

**START HERE**

**Has the wheezing started within the past few hours?**

YES → **Have you coughed up frothy pink or white phlegm?**

YES →

**CALL YOUR DOCTOR NOW!**
**A dangerous build-up of fluid in the lungs,** perhaps as a result of heart disease, is a possibility. Sit upright in a chair and try to keep calm, this will make breathing easier for you until help arrives.

*Treatment:* Keep a sample of sputum if possible, as this will help your doctor to make a quick diagnosis of the problem. You may need to be admitted to hospital where you will be given oxygen and drugs to assist breathing. These may include a *diuretic,* to drain fluid from the lungs, or a *bronchodilator,* to open up blocked spaces in the lungs. When the lungs have cleared, treatment will depend on the underlying problem.

**NO** / **NO**

**Is breathing so difficult that you feel you are suffocating?**

YES → **EMERGENCY GET MEDICAL HELP NOW!**

**A severe attack of asthma** is a possibility.
*Treatment:* While waiting for help to arrive carry out the first aid measures described below. A severe attack usually requires hospital admission. Drugs will be given and, if necessary, the doctor may use a mechanical respirator to assist breathing.

**A mild attack of asthma** is probably making you wheeze.

*Self-help:* Since asthma is most often due to an allergy, try to find which substances you are allergic to, and avoid contact with them as much as possible. Consult your doctor, who will be able to prescribe drugs to prevent further attacks, and to help you when attacks occur. In addition, he or she may arrange for you to undergo special allergy tests to help identify the cause of your asthma.

**NO**

**Is your temperature 38°C (100°F) or above?**

102 — 39
101 —
100 — 38

YES → **Acute bronchitis** (infection of the airways in the lungs) is probable.
*Self-help:* Take soluble aspirin or paracetamol and stay in a warm environment. Call your doctor if you have difficulty in breathing, or if you are no better in 48 hours.

**Chronic bronchitis** (persistent inflammation of the airways in the lungs) may be the cause of the wheezing, especially if you smoke and have had similar periods of wheezing in past winters. Consult your doctor.

*Treatment:* Your doctor will advise you to give up smoking, if you are a smoker, as this is likely to make the problem worse. Following tests such as *chest X-ray* (p.197), he or she may prescribe *antibiotics* in the form of tablets or capsules. An aerosol inhaler may help you if you suffer from breathlessness.

**NO**

**Do you wheeze a little most days?**

YES → **Do you cough up grey or greenish-yellow phlegm most days?**

YES →

**NO** / **NO**

**Consult your doctor** if you are unable to make a diagnosis from this chart.

---

**FIRST AID FOR ASTHMA**

A severe attack of asthma, in which the sufferer is fighting for breath and/or becomes pale and clammy with a blue tinge to the tongue or lips, is an emergency and admission to hospital is essential. Call an ambulance or the Asthma Emergency Unit of your local hospital immediately. Most asthma sufferers already have drugs or an inhaling apparatus, both of which should be administered. If one dose of inhalant does not quickly relieve the wheezing, it should be repeated once only.

In all cases, help the asthmatic to find the most comfortable position while you are waiting for medical help. The best position is sitting up, leaning forward on the back of a chair, and taking some of the weight on the arms (right). Plenty of fresh air will also help. A sudden severe attack of asthma can be very frightening for the family as well as the sufferer. However, anxiety can make the attack worse, so only one other person should remain with the sufferer and this person should be calm and reassuring.

# 89 Coughing

A cough may produce phlegm or be "dry". It is the body's natural response to any foreign body or congestion, or irritation in the lungs or the throat – for instance, as a result of a cold, smoking or an allergy. Sometimes, however, coughing signals a more serious disorder in the respiratory tract.

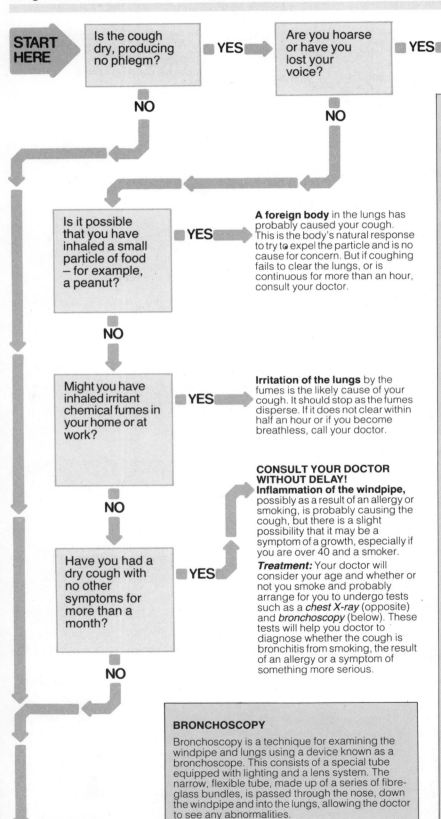

**START HERE**

**Is the cough dry, producing no phlegm?**

YES → **Are you hoarse or have you lost your voice?**

YES → Go to chart **87** Hoarseness or loss of voice

NO ↓ (from "Is the cough dry")

NO ↓ (from "Are you hoarse")

**Is it possible that you have inhaled a small particle of food – for example, a peanut?**

YES → **A foreign body** in the lungs has probably caused your cough. This is the body's natural response to try to expel the particle and is no cause for concern. But if coughing fails to clear the lungs, or is continuous for more than an hour, consult your doctor.

NO ↓

**Might you have inhaled irritant chemical fumes in your home or at work?**

YES → **Irritation of the lungs** by the fumes is the likely cause of your cough. It should stop as the fumes disperse. If it does not clear within half an hour or if you become breathless, call your doctor.

NO ↓

**Have you had a dry cough with no other symptoms for more than a month?**

YES → **CONSULT YOUR DOCTOR WITHOUT DELAY!**
**Inflammation of the windpipe,** possibly as a result of an allergy or smoking, is probably causing the cough, but there is a slight possibility that it may be a symptom of a growth, especially if you are over 40 and a smoker.
*Treatment:* Your doctor will consider your age and whether or not you smoke and probably arrange for you to undergo tests such as a *chest X-ray* (opposite) and *bronchoscopy* (below). These tests will help you doctor to diagnose whether the cough is bronchitis from smoking, the result of an allergy or a symptom of something more serious.

NO ↓

*Go to next page*

## BRONCHOSCOPY

Bronchoscopy is a technique for examining the windpipe and lungs using a device known as a bronchoscope. This consists of a special tube equipped with lighting and a lens system. The narrow, flexible tube, made up of a series of fibre-glass bundles, is passed through the nose, down the windpipe and into the lungs, allowing the doctor to see any abnormalities.

## THE DANGERS OF SMOKING

If you smoke, you should be aware of the facts about the effects that smoking has on your body. Tobacco smoke contains three highly dangerous substances: tar, nicotine and carbon monoxide.

**Tar** in tobacco smoke collects as a sticky deposit that clogs and irritates the lungs and other parts of the respiratory tract, leading to diseases such as chronic bronchitis and emphysema, and in some cases causing lung cancer, a life-threatening disease that is almost unknown in non-smokers. The toxic chemicals in tar are also absorbed into the bloodstream and then excreted in the urine. The presence of such irritant substances in the bladder is known to contribute to the development of bladder cancer.

**Nicotine** is a highly addictive drug that acts on the nervous system, increasing the heart rate and the risk of developing abnormal heart rhythms.

**Carbon monoxide,** absorbed into the bloodstream from tobacco smoke, reduces the ability of the red blood cells to carry oxygen to the body cells and therefore exaggerates the effects of any circulatory disorder. In addition, carbon monoxide seems actively to encourage the formation of substances that may block the arteries and cause fatal heart attacks and disabling circulation problems in the legs. This last effect means that women who smoke are more at risk from possible dangerous side-effects of the contraceptive pill and many doctors are reluctant to prescribe the pill for heavy smokers.

### Smoking and pregnancy

There are special dangers associated with smoking during pregnancy because nicotine and carbon monoxide in your bloodstream make the blood vessels in the placenta constrict so that less oxygen and fewer nutrients reach your baby. This can seriously impair the growth of your baby in the womb and may mean that he or she will be born underweight and will have to spend time in a special care baby unit after the birth.

### Reducing the risks

Some brands of cigarette contain less tar and nicotine than others. But switching to a low tar brand is not an effective way of reducing the risks. Most heavy smokers simply smoke more and inhale more deeply. The best way to avoid smoking-related disease is to give it up. If you succeed, the chances of developing the problems outlined here diminish with every year.

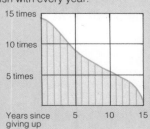

**Your risk of lung cancer compared with a non-smoker**
An average smoker is 15 times more likely to die of lung cancer than a non-smoker. The chances of developing the disease diminish after giving up smoking until after 15 years the risk is equal to that of a non-smoker.

*Continued from previous page*

**Has the cough started within the past week?** — **YES** →

**NO** ↓

**Is your temperature 38°C (100°F) or above?**

| 102 – | 39 |
| 101 – | |
| 100 – | 38 |

— **YES** →

**NO** ↓

**Are you breathless?** — **YES** →

**NO** ↓

**Do you have a runny nose AND/OR a sore throat?** — **YES** →

**NO** ↓

**A common cold,** viral infection of the nasal passages, has probably caused these symptoms.

***Self-help:*** For advice on the treatment of colds, see p.192.

**Acute bronchitis** (infection of the airways in the lungs) is a possibility.

***Self-help:*** Take soluble aspirin or paracetamol and cough medicine according to the instructions on the labels. Stay in a warm environment but it is not necessary to go to bed. Call your doctor if you have difficulty in breathing, or if you are no better in 48 hours.

**Are you short of breath, even when you have not been exercising?** — **YES** →

Go to chart

# 90

**Difficulty in breathing**

**NO** ↓

**CALL YOUR DOCTOR NOW!**
**Pneumonia** is a possibility. This is an infection of the lungs which can be dangerous, especially for the elderly and those in poor health.

***Treatment:*** Your doctor will probably recommend that you take soluble aspirin or paracetamol to reduce your fever and relieve any discomfort. He or she may prescribe ***antibiotics*** and in a severe case may advise admission to hospital.

**Do you cough up thick, grey or greenish-yellow phlegm most days?** — **YES** →

**Chronic bronchitis** (persistent inflammation of the airways to the lungs) may be the cause of a cough that brings up phlegm, especially if you smoke and have had similar periods of persistent coughing in past winters. Consult your doctor.

***Treatment:*** Your doctor may prescribe *antibiotics* in the form of tablets or capsules. An aerosol inhaler may help you if you are suffering from breathlessness. However, the problem is likely to get worse over the years unless you stop smoking.

**NO** ↓

**CONSULT YOUR DOCTOR WITHOUT DELAY!**
**A serious lung disorder** such as tuberculosis or lung cancer may cause persistent coughing although a simpler explanation such as an allergy or chronic bronchitis is more likely.

***Treatment:*** Your doctor will probably arrange for tests to find out which underlying disorder is causing the symptoms. You will probably be asked to give blood and sputum samples for analysis. A *chest X-ray* (below) and *bronchoscopy* (opposite) may also be needed.

**Have you had your cough for several weeks or months AND has it been getting more severe?** — **YES** →

**NO** ↓

**Consult your doctor** if you are unable to make a diagnosis from this chart.

**CHEST X-RAY**

A chest X-ray is an effective way of examining the lungs and is used by chest specialists as their main diagnostic test. It will show up infections, tumours and other lung disorders, fluid or air in the chest cavity, and damage to the ribcage.

This chest x-ray shows a condition called pericardial effusion in which fluid collects around the heart.

**COUGHING UP BLOOD**

Phlegm that is coloured or streaked bright red or rusty brown may contain blood. Coughing up a little blood may simply mean that you have ruptured a small blood vessel in the lung, it may also indicate congestion of the lungs, an infection such as pneumonia or tuberculosis, or a tumour. If you feel entirely well and cough up blood on a single occasion you need not feel alarmed; but if it happens more than once, or if you have any of the additional symptoms described, then it may indicate one of the following serious problems and you should seek medical advice without delay.

**A chest infection** such as pneumonia – if your temperature is above 38°C (100°F).

**A blood clot in the lung** – which is most likely if you have recently had an operation or been confined to bed by an injury or illness. This is an EMERGENCY.

**Lung cancer or tuberculosis** – especially if you have had a cough for many weeks or months.

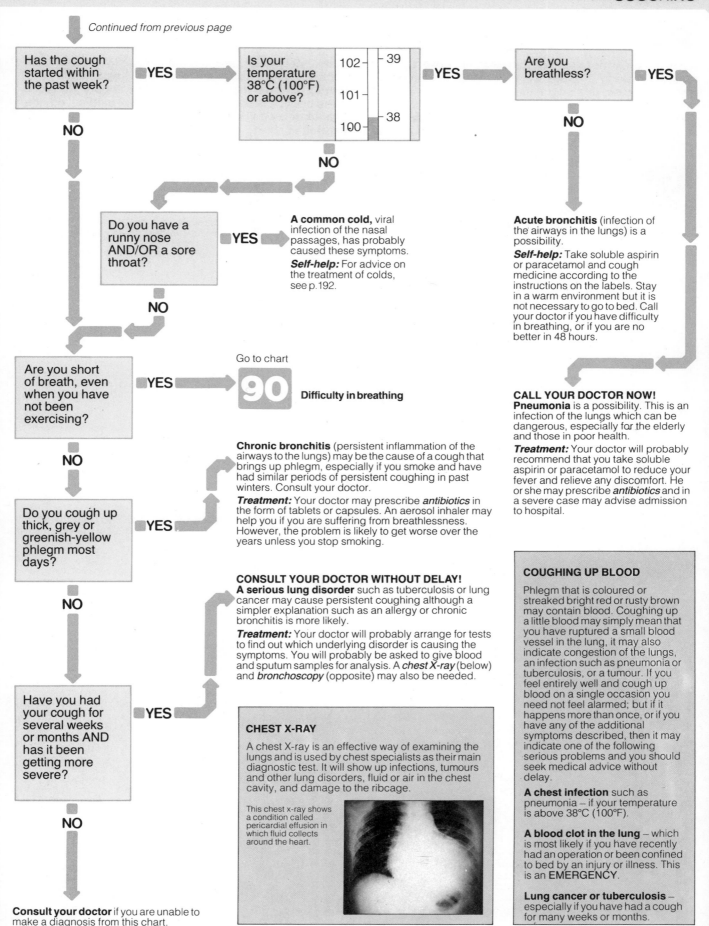

# 90 Difficulty in breathing

If you are breathless to the extent that you are breathing rapidly or "puffing" either at rest or after some form of gentle exercise, this suggests the possibility of a problem affecting the heart or the respiratory system. The sudden onset of difficulty in breathing while eating is more likely to be caused by choking and you should immediately follow the first aid instructions described in the box opposite. Because there is the possibility of a serious disorder that may threaten the supply of oxygen to the body, it is very important to seek medical advice without delay if you notice any of the symptoms in this diagnostic chart.

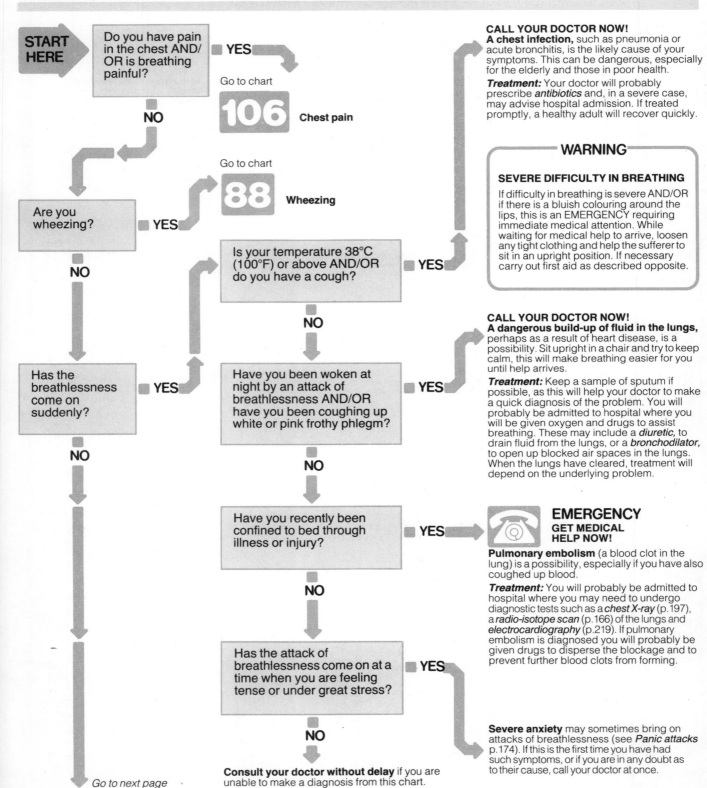

**START HERE** → Do you have pain in the chest AND/OR is breathing painful? — **YES** → Go to chart **106** Chest pain

**NO** ↓

Are you wheezing? — **YES** → Go to chart **88** Wheezing

**NO** ↓

Has the breathlessness come on suddenly? — **YES** → Is your temperature 38°C (100°F) or above AND/OR do you have a cough? — **YES** →

**NO** ↓

Is your temperature 38°C (100°F) or above AND/OR do you have a cough? — **NO** ↓

Have you been woken at night by an attack of breathlessness AND/OR have you been coughing up white or pink frothy phlegm? — **YES** →

**NO** ↓

Have you recently been confined to bed through illness or injury? — **YES** →

**NO** ↓

Has the attack of breathlessness come on at a time when you are feeling tense or under great stress? — **YES** →

**NO** ↓

*Go to next page*

**Consult your doctor without delay** if you are unable to make a diagnosis from this chart.

---

**CALL YOUR DOCTOR NOW!**
**A chest infection,** such as pneumonia or acute bronchitis, is the likely cause of your symptoms. This can be dangerous, especially for the elderly and those in poor health.

*Treatment:* Your doctor will probably prescribe *antibiotics* and, in a severe case, may advise hospital admission. If treated promptly, a healthy adult will recover quickly.

---

**WARNING**

**SEVERE DIFFICULTY IN BREATHING**

If difficulty in breathing is severe AND/OR if there is a bluish colouring around the lips, this is an EMERGENCY requiring immediate medical attention. While waiting for medical help to arrive, loosen any tight clothing and help the sufferer to sit in an upright position. If necessary carry out first aid as described opposite.

---

**CALL YOUR DOCTOR NOW!**
**A dangerous build-up of fluid in the lungs,** perhaps as a result of heart disease, is a possibility. Sit upright in a chair and try to keep calm, this will make breathing easier for you until help arrives.

*Treatment:* Keep a sample of sputum if possible, as this will help your doctor to make a quick diagnosis of the problem. You will probably be admitted to hospital where you will be given oxygen and drugs to assist breathing. These may include a *diuretic,* to drain fluid from the lungs, or a *bronchodilator,* to open up blocked air spaces in the lungs. When the lungs have cleared, treatment will depend on the underlying problem.

---

**EMERGENCY**
**GET MEDICAL HELP NOW!**

**Pulmonary embolism** (a blood clot in the lung) is a possibility, especially if you have also coughed up blood.

*Treatment:* You will probably be admitted to hospital where you may need to undergo diagnostic tests such as a *chest X-ray* (p.197), a *radio-isotope scan* (p.166) of the lungs and *electrocardiography* (p.219). If pulmonary embolism is diagnosed you will probably be given drugs to disperse the blockage and to prevent further blood clots from forming.

---

**Severe anxiety** may sometimes bring on attacks of breathlessness (see *Panic attacks* p.174). If this is the first time you have had such symptoms, or if you are in any doubt as to their cause, call your doctor at once.

*Continued from previous page*

**Do you cough up thick grey or greenish-yellow phlegm most days?**

**YES** →

**Do you, or have you, worked in a dusty atmosphere—for example in a mine or quarry?**

**YES** →

**NO** ↓

**NO** ↓

**Chronic bronchitis** (persistent inflammation of the airways in the lungs) may be the cause of your breathing difficulty, especially if you smoke and have had similar periods of coughing in the past winter. If your work involves regular exposure to mineral dusts, an industrial lung disease such as pneumoconiosis is also possible. Consult your doctor.

*Treatment:* Your doctor will advise you to give up smoking, if you are a smoker, as this is likely to make the problem worse. Following tests such as a *chest X-ray* (p.197), he or she may prescribe *antibiotics* in the form of tablets or capsules. An aerosol inhaler may help to relieve breathlessness.

**Does your work involve regular contact with grain or other crops AND/OR caged birds or animals?**

**YES** →

**NO** ↓

**Pneumoconiosis,** a reaction to coal-dust in the lungs or another dust disease, is a possibility. Consult your doctor.

*Treatment:* A *chest X-ray* (p.197) will indicate how seriously your lungs have been affected. Your doctor may advise you to change your job and, if you are a smoker, to give up smoking.

**Farmer's lung,** an allergic reaction to fungus in mouldy grain or hay or a similar sort of allergy to bird or animal droppings, can cause breathless attacks, often with coughing. Consult your doctor.

*Treatment:* Your doctor will probably arrange for you to have diagnostic tests including a *chest X-ray* (p.197) and skin tests for allergic sensitivity. If the diagnosis is confirmed, you will probably be advised to avoid further exposure to the substance causing the reaction by changing your job or by wearing a protective mask at work. You may also be given drugs to reduce inflammation of the lung.

**Are you pregnant?**

**YES** →

Go to chart

**143** **Shortness of breath in pregnancy**

**NO** ↓

**Consult your doctor without further delay** if you are unable to make a diagnosis from this chart.

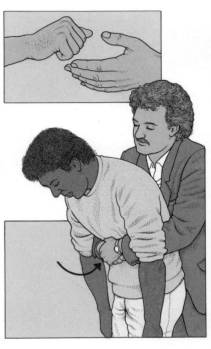

### FIRST AID FOR CHOKING

When severe breathing difficulty comes on while eating, and if the victim is unable to cough up the obstruction, carry out the following steps:

**1** Hold the victim up from behind in a standing position, pressing one fist (with thumb inward) against the waist. Hold your other hand over the fist and thrust hard in and up under the rib cage. If this does not clear the blockage, repeat 3 more times.

**2** If this does not clear the obstruction, lay the victim on his or her back. Tilt the head back (chin up), open the mouth and sweep deeply into the mouth with hooked finger (you may need to remove dentures).

**3** If obstruction is still not dislodged, repeat steps 1 and 2.

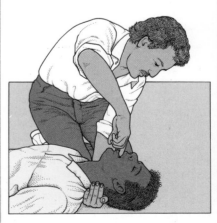

**4** If breathing does not restart following removal of the blockage, carry out mouth-to-mouth resuscitation (p.283).

# 91 Toothache

Teeth are just as much living structures as any other part of the body, despite their tough appearance. They are constantly under threat from our diet because of the high level of sugar we consume. Bacteria act on sugar to produce acids that attack enamel, the tooth's protective layer. When this happens, bacterial destruction (decay) spreads down the root canal to the nerve, causing inflammation and pain. Any pain in one tooth or from teeth and gums in general, whether it is a dull throb or a sharp twinge, should be brought to your dentist's attention.

**START HERE**

**Do you have one or more of the following symptoms?**
- continuous pain
- a tooth that feels long or high
- a tooth that feels loose
- a fever

**YES** →

**NO** ↓

**CONSULT YOUR DENTIST WITHOUT DELAY!**

**A tooth abscess** is possible. This is formed when pus builds up in the bone and tissue near a tooth that has had a very deep filling or cavity, or one that has been injured.

*Treatment:* Two forms of treatment are common – root canal treatment or extraction. If the dentist feels the tooth can be saved, root canal treatment may be performed. The dentist will make an opening in the tooth to release the pus and relieve the pressure. Sometimes an emergency incision is made in the gum. The diseased tissue is then removed from the inside of the tooth. Later, a permanent filling is placed in the root canal and the tooth is sealed and crowned. About six months later, an X-ray will be needed to ensure that the bone and tissue have grown back to normal around the root of the tooth. Extraction of an abscessed tooth may be suggested as an alternative to root canal treatment. A bridge or partial denture will be needed to keep other teeth from shifting.

**Do you have repeated bouts of throbbing pain OR is the tooth extremely sensitive to hot and cold AND does the pain continue for several minutes?**

**YES** →

**NO** ↓

**Advanced dental decay,** a very deep filling or an injury may have irreversibly inflamed the pulp (nerve) in the centre of the tooth.

*Treatment:* The dentist will remove the decay and/or old filling. If the nerve is exposed, a root canal or extraction may be needed. If the pulp is not visibly exposed, the dentist may try to soothe the inflamed pulp with a temporary, medicated filling. After a few weeks, the tooth will be re-evaluated for possible root canal treatment, extraction, or permanent filling.

**Has the dentist filled one or more of your teeth within the past few weeks?**

**YES** → **Does the tooth hurt only when you bite on it?** **YES** →

**NO** ↓

**NO** ↓

**After a filling,** especially a deep one, it is normal to have some sensitivity, especially to cold water or air. This sensitivity will be sharp, but will last for only a few seconds and then subside. If the sensitivity increases in intensity or duration, or if the tooth becomes sensitive to heat, consult your dentist for the possibility of irreversible pulp (nerve) damage.

**Does the pain only occur when you are eating something cold or sweet (ice cream or chocolate) AND does the pain go away after a few seconds?**

**YES** →

**NO** ↓

**Decay under an old filling, a cracked tooth or filling, or exposure of the root surface due to improper toothbrushing or gum disease** may be the cause of the pain. Consult your dentist.

*Treatment:* Your dentist may recommend replacing an old filling or remove any decay. If the problem is sensitivity, the dentist may recommend a special de-sensitizing toothpaste, protective flouride applications or bonding to seal the sensitive root area.

**An uneven or "high" filling** can cause discomfort. Your dentist will adjust the filling if necessary.

**Does the tooth hurt only when you bite or chew on it?** **YES** →

**NO** ↓

**Dental decay** may have caused a hole (or cavity) to form in your tooth. Consult your dentist.

*Treatment:* Your dentist will probably clean out the affected tooth and put in a filling.

**A cracked filling or a cracked or fractured tooth** is probably the cause of the pain. Consult your dentist.

*Treatment:* You may need to have the affected tooth crowned (capped) or have a root canal if the pain becomes more severe. The tooth may need to be extracted if the crack is too deep into the tooth. Pain may also be caused by acute sinus problems that make the upper back teeth ache and tender to bite on. If this is the case, you may need to see a doctor for further treatment.

---

**CARE OF YOUR TEETH**

**Brushing**
Several tooth brushing techniques are acceptable as long as you manage to remove all traces of food and plaque from the back, front and biting surfaces of your teeth. If you use a toothbrush with a small head you will be able to get at the difficult areas more easily. The toothbrush should have soft, rounded bristles unless your dentist suggests another type of brush.

**Dental floss**
Daily use of dental floss helps remove debris and plaque from between your teeth and under your gums. Your dentist will teach you how to floss your teeth correctly.

**Diet**
Sugary foods are the main cause of tooth decay, so try to keep your consumption of sweet foods to a minimum. If you need to eat snacks during the day, they should consist of cheese or nuts. If you find it hard to do without sweet foods, confine them to mealtimes and finish the meal with cheese, as this tends to neutralize acid formation.

# 92 Difficulty in swallowing

Difficulty in swallowing is most often the result of an infection causing soreness, swelling and the production of excess mucus at the back of the throat. However, difficulty or pain when swallowing that is not related to a sore throat may be a sign of a more serious disorder and should be brought to your doctor's attention.

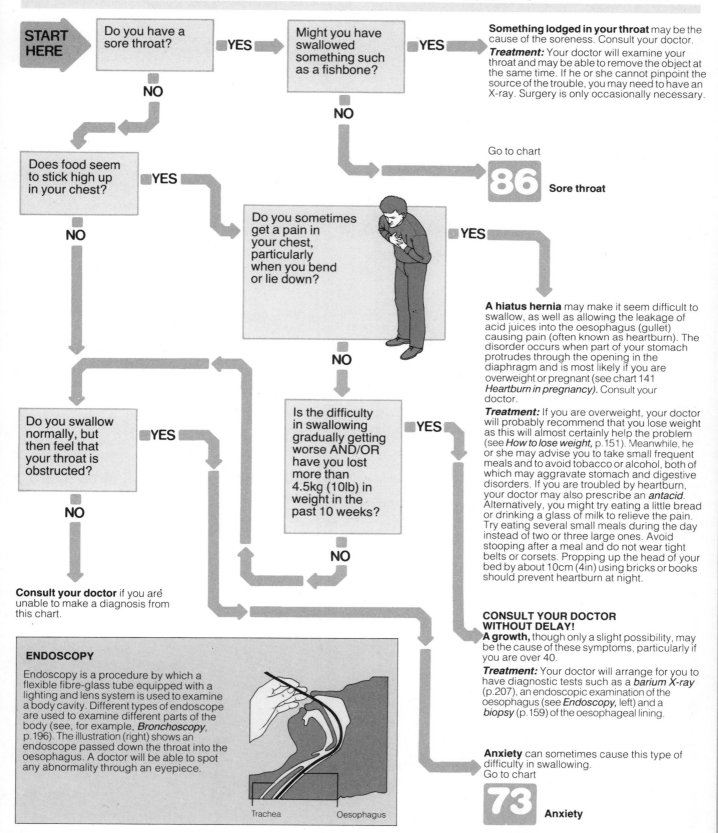

**START HERE**

**Do you have a sore throat?** → **YES** → **Might you have swallowed something such as a fishbone?** → **YES** → **Something lodged in your throat** may be the cause of the soreness. Consult your doctor.
*Treatment:* Your doctor will examine your throat and may be able to remove the object at the same time. If he or she cannot pinpoint the source of the trouble, you may need to have an X-ray. Surgery is only occasionally necessary.

**NO**

**Does food seem to stick high up in your chest?** — **YES**

**NO**

Go to chart **86** Sore throat

**Do you sometimes get a pain in your chest, particularly when you bend or lie down?** — **YES**

**NO**

**A hiatus hernia** may make it seem difficult to swallow, as well as allowing the leakage of acid juices into the oesophagus (gullet) causing pain (often known as heartburn). The disorder occurs when part of your stomach protrudes through the opening in the diaphragm and is most likely if you are overweight or pregnant (see chart 141 *Heartburn in pregnancy*). Consult your doctor.

*Treatment:* If you are overweight, your doctor will probably recommend that you lose weight as this will almost certainly help the problem (see *How to lose weight,* p.151). Meanwhile, he or she may advise you to take small frequent meals and to avoid tobacco or alcohol, both of which may aggravate stomach and digestive disorders. If you are troubled by heartburn, your doctor may also prescribe an *antacid.* Alternatively, you might try eating a little bread or drinking a glass of milk to relieve the pain. Try eating several small meals during the day instead of two or three large ones. Avoid stooping after a meal and do not wear tight belts or corsets. Propping up the head of your bed by about 10cm (4in) using bricks or books should prevent heartburn at night.

**Do you swallow normally, but then feel that your throat is obstructed?** — **YES**

**NO**

**Is the difficulty in swallowing gradually getting worse AND/OR have you lost more than 4.5kg (10lb) in weight in the past 10 weeks?** — **YES**

**NO**

**Consult your doctor** if you are unable to make a diagnosis from this chart.

**CONSULT YOUR DOCTOR WITHOUT DELAY!**
**A growth,** though only a slight possibility, may be the cause of these symptoms, particularly if you are over 40.

*Treatment:* Your doctor will arrange for you to have diagnostic tests such as a *barium X-ray* (p.207), an endoscopic examination of the oesophagus (see *Endoscopy,* left) and a *biopsy* (p.159) of the oesophageal lining.

### ENDOSCOPY

Endoscopy is a procedure by which a flexible fibre-glass tube equipped with a lighting and lens system is used to examine a body cavity. Different types of endoscope are used to examine different parts of the body (see, for example, *Bronchoscopy,* p.196). The illustration (right) shows an endoscope passed down the throat into the oesophagus. A doctor will be able to spot any abnormality through an eyepiece.

Trachea          Oesophagus

**Anxiety** can sometimes cause this type of difficulty in swallowing.
Go to chart **73** Anxiety

# 93 Sore mouth or tongue

Painful areas on the lips, tongue and gums are usually symptoms of minor conditions. Most minor problems heal within a week. Any condition that persists for longer than 3 weeks should be seen by your doctor or dentist. It is important to keep your gums and the delicate mucous membrane that lines the inside of the mouth healthy by maintaining good oral hygiene at all times (see Care of your teeth, p.200).

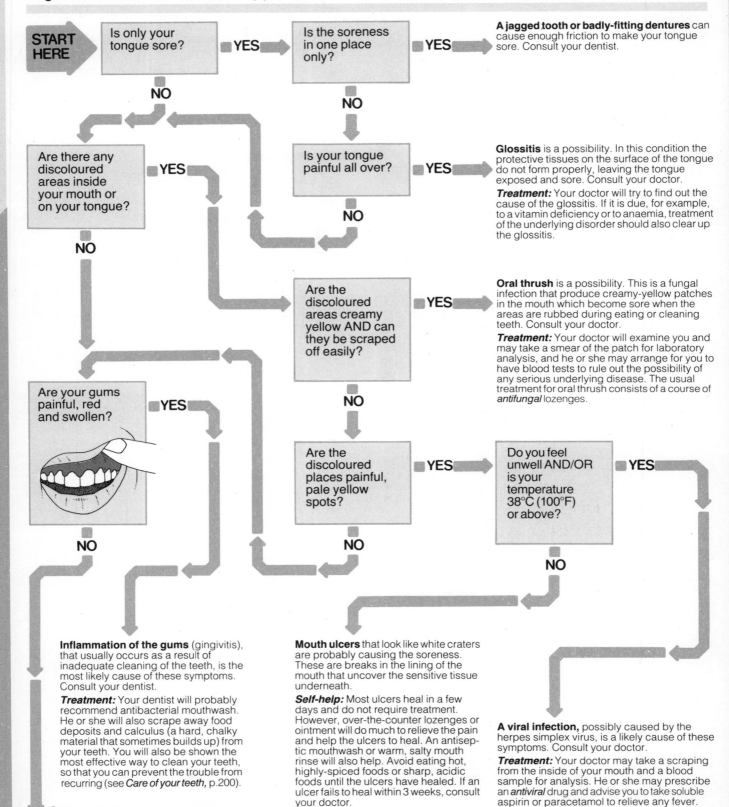

**START HERE**

**Is only your tongue sore?** — YES → **Is the soreness in one place only?** — YES → **A jagged tooth or badly-fitting dentures** can cause enough friction to make your tongue sore. Consult your dentist.

NO ↓ (from "Is only your tongue sore?")

NO ↓ (from "Is the soreness in one place only?")

**Are there any discoloured areas inside your mouth or on your tongue?** — YES → **Is your tongue painful all over?** — YES → **Glossitis** is a possibility. In this condition the protective tissues on the surface of the tongue do not form properly, leaving the tongue exposed and sore. Consult your doctor.

*Treatment:* Your doctor will try to find out the cause of the glossitis. If it is due, for example, to a vitamin deficiency or to anaemia, treatment of the underlying disorder should also clear up the glossitis.

NO ↓ (from "Are there any discoloured areas...")

NO ↓ (from "Is your tongue painful all over?")

**Are the discoloured areas creamy yellow AND can they be scraped off easily?** — YES → **Oral thrush** is a possibility. This is a fungal infection that produce creamy-yellow patches in the mouth which become sore when the areas are rubbed during eating or cleaning teeth. Consult your doctor.

*Treatment:* Your doctor will examine you and may take a smear of the patch for laboratory analysis, and he or she may arrange for you to have blood tests to rule out the possibility of any serious underlying disease. The usual treatment for oral thrush consists of a course of *antifungal* lozenges.

NO ↓ (from "Are the discoloured areas creamy yellow...")

**Are your gums painful, red and swollen?** — YES →

**Are the discoloured places painful, pale yellow spots?** — YES → **Do you feel unwell AND/OR is your temperature 38°C (100°F) or above?** — YES →

NO ↓ (from "Are your gums painful, red and swollen?")

NO ↓ (from "Are the discoloured places painful...")

NO ↓ (from "Do you feel unwell...")

**Inflammation of the gums** (gingivitis), that usually occurs as a result of inadequate cleaning of the teeth, is the most likely cause of these symptoms. Consult your dentist.

*Treatment:* Your dentist will probably recommend antibacterial mouthwash. He or she will also scrape away food deposits and calculus (a hard, chalky material that sometimes builds up) from your teeth. You will also be shown the most effective way to clean your teeth, so that you can prevent the trouble from recurring (see *Care of your teeth,* p.200).

*Go to next page*

**Mouth ulcers** that look like white craters are probably causing the soreness. These are breaks in the lining of the mouth that uncover the sensitive tissue underneath.

*Self-help:* Most ulcers heal in a few days and do not require treatment. However, over-the-counter lozenges or ointment will do much to relieve the pain and help the ulcers to heal. An antiseptic mouthwash or warm, salty mouth rinse will also help. Avoid eating hot, highly-spiced foods or sharp, acidic foods until the ulcers have healed. If an ulcer fails to heal within 3 weeks, consult your doctor.

**A viral infection,** possibly caused by the herpes simplex virus, is a likely cause of these symptoms. Consult your doctor.

*Treatment:* Your doctor may take a scraping from the inside of your mouth and a blood sample for analysis. He or she may prescribe an *antiviral* drug and advise you to take soluble aspirin or paracetamol to relieve any fever.

*Continued from previous page*

**Do you have sore places on or around the lips?** —**YES**→ **Did the sores start as painful blisters?** —**YES**→

**Cold sores** are the likely cause of these symptoms. These are the result of the herpes simplex virus in the body becoming reactivated by a cold or by exposure to strong sunshine or to cold weather.

***Self-help:*** Mild cases of cold sores clear up of their own accord. However, there are many over-the-counter lotions that may hasten healing. If you are troubled by severe recurrent cold sores, your doctor may prescribe a cream for you to apply when a sore is in its early stages to inhibit its development.

**NO** (from "Do you have sore places") → 

**NO** (from "Did the sores start as painful blisters?") ↓

**Do you have cracks at the corners of your mouth?** —**YES**→

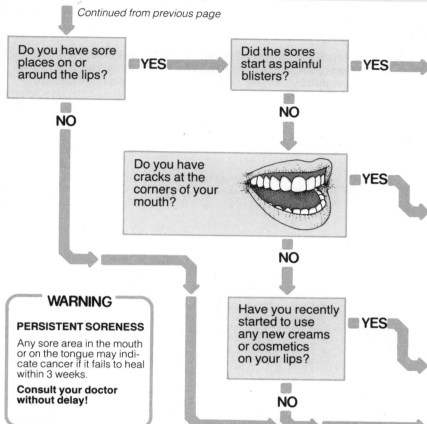

**Angular stomatitis** is the name given to these cracks, which may be due to iron deficiency in the diet. Consult your doctor. Another cause is poorly-fitting dentures. If you wear dentures consult your dentist.

***Treatment:*** If there is a possibility of vitamin deficiency, your doctor will ask you about your diet and examine you to eliminate the possibility of any underlying disease. You may be prescribed vitamin supplements. If dentures are the problem, your dentist may adjust your old base-plate or supply a new set. He or she may also prescribe lozenges to relieve the soreness.

**NO** ↓

**WARNING**

**PERSISTENT SORENESS**

Any sore area in the mouth or on the tongue may indicate cancer if it fails to heal within 3 weeks.

**Consult your doctor without delay!**

**Have you recently started to use any new creams or cosmetics on your lips?** —**YES**→

**An allergic reaction** to one of the ingredients is a possibility. (See also *Eczema,* p.181).

***Self-help:*** Avoid contact with the substance that causes the reaction. If the soreness continues, consult your doctor, who may prescribe an ointment or cream.

**NO** ↓

**Consult your doctor** if you are unable to make a diagnosis from this chart.

---

## BAD BREATH

You are unlikely to notice that you have bad breath unless it is pointed out to you by somebody else. The following are the most common causes of bad breath:

**Sore mouth**
Infection or ulceration of the mouth, gums or tongue may cause bad breath. Rinsing out your mouth with an antiseptic mouthwash usually clears up the problem within a few days. If bad breath persists, consult your doctor.

**Inadequately cleaned teeth or dentures**
If you do not clean your teeth (or dentures, if you wear them) thoroughly, at least twice a day, decaying food particles may lodge between the teeth or stick to the dentures causing bad breath. (See *Care of your teeth* p. 200 and *Looking after your dentures*, right).

**Garlic, onions and alcohol**
These foods contain volatile substances which, when absorbed into the bloodstream and then released into the lungs, may cause bad breath. Alcohol may also be responsible for bad breath in much the same way. Your breath should return to normal within 24 hours after consuming these foods.

**Smoking**
Smoking always causes bad breath. (See also *The dangers of smoking* p. 196).

If your bad breath continues for some time, you should consult your doctor.

## LOOKING AFTER YOUR DENTURES

Always remove your dentures at night and keep them in a glass of water containing a cleansing agent so that they do not dry out and warp. This will also give the gum tissues a regular rest period. Brush your dentures thoroughly every day. Your dentist will show you the best way to do this. It is also important to remember to clean any remaining natural teeth thoroughly, especially where teeth and gums meet. Partial dentures may feel a little tight when inserted in the morning, but this is normal and the feeling disappears in a few minutes. The useful life of dentures varies greatly — from 6 months to 5 years or more — depending on how well your gums and jaws keep their shape. If you have a full set of dentures, you should visit the dentist every 2 years. If you still have some natural teeth you should go for a check-up every 6 months.

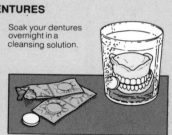

Soak your dentures overnight in a cleansing solution.

Brush your dentures daily on both sides to remove all food deposits. Rinse thoroughly before replacing them in your mouth.

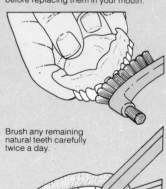

Brush any remaining natural teeth carefully twice a day.

# 94 Vomiting

Vomiting occurs when the muscles around the stomach suddenly contract and "throw up" the stomach contents. This is usually the result of irritation of the stomach from infection or over-indulgence in rich food or alcohol, but may also occur as a result of disturbance elsewhere in the digestive tract. Occasionally, a disorder affecting the nerve signals from the brain, or from the balance mechanism in the inner ear can also produce vomiting. Victims of recurrent migraine recognize their attacks, but otherwise when vomiting is accompanied by severe headache or severe abdominal pain, urgent medical attention is needed.

**For attacks of vomiting, see chart 95, Recurrent vomiting**

**START HERE** → Have you vomited on several days in the past week or more? — **YES** → **Repeated attacks of vomiting** may have a number of causes. See chart 95, *Recurrent vomiting*.

**NO** ↓

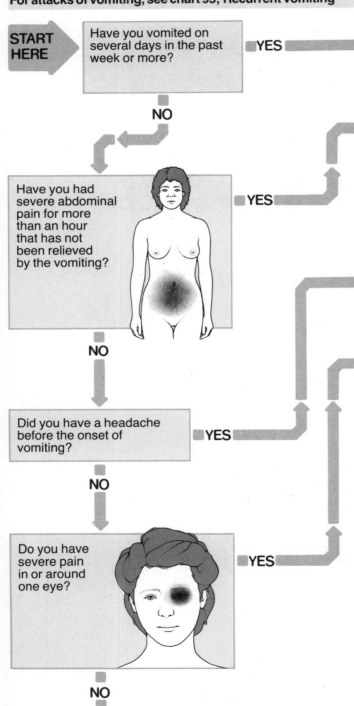

Have you had severe abdominal pain for more than an hour that has not been relieved by the vomiting? — **YES** →

**EMERGENCY GET MEDICAL HELP NOW!**

**A serious abdominal condition,** such as appendicitis or a perforated duodenal ulcer, may cause such symptoms.

***Treatment:*** Eat and drink nothing until medical help arrives. Immediate hospital admission is usually required. After observation of your symptoms, an exploratory operation may be carried out to find the precise cause of the pain and vomiting. At the same time any necessary surgical treatment, for example, removal of the appendix or repair of an ulcer, can be carried out.

Go to chart

# 64 Headache

**NO** ↓

Did you have a headache before the onset of vomiting? — **YES** →

**CALL YOUR DOCTOR NOW!**

**Acute glaucoma,** in which excess fluid causes increased pressure in the eye, is a possibility, especially if you are over 40.

***Treatment:*** If your doctor confirms the diagnosis, you will probably be given eye drops to allow the excess fluid to drain from the eye. In addition, you may be given a *diuretic* drug to prevent fluid retention. Once the pressure has been relieved, an operation to prevent a recurrence of the problem is usually carried out.

**NO** ↓

Do you have severe pain in or around one eye? — **YES** →

**NAUSEA**

Most disorders which can cause vomiting may also cause nausea (a sensation of impending vomiting) either before or instead of vomiting. So if you are suffering from nausea, you can find a possible explanation for your symptoms by consulting this self-diagnosis chart for vomiting.

**Self-help**
If you feel nauseated, do not eat, but take frequent sips of plain water and lie down until the sensation fades or until vomiting relieves it.

**NO** ↓

*Go to next page*

*Continued from previous page*

**Do you have diarrhoea OR is your temperature 38°C (100°F) or above?**

| 102 — | — 39 |
| 101 — | |
| 100 — | — 38 |

**YES** →

**Gastroenteritis** (inflammation of the digestive tract caused by infection or food poisoning) is probable.
**Self-help:** See *Self-help for gastroenteritis,* p.214. If you are no better in 24 hours, call your doctor. He or she may prescribe drugs to relieve your symptoms.

**NO** ↓

**In the past few hours, have you done any of the following?**
- over-eaten
- eaten large amounts of rich, creamy, or spicy food
- drunk a large amount of alcohol

**YES** →

**Food poisoning,** either from food contaminated by bacteria or by poisonous chemicals, or from food to which you are allergic, may be responsible for your vomiting.
**Self-help:** Follow the advice on treating vomiting (above right). If you are no better in 24 hours, or if you develop further symptoms, consult your doctor.

**NO** ↓

**Have you eaten anything that may have gone bad or to which you may be allergic?**

**YES** →

**NO** ↓

**Before you vomited, did everything around you seem to spin?**

**YES** →

**A disorder of the inner ear** may cause vomiting and dizzy spells. Consult your doctor.
**Treatment:** Your doctor may refer you to hospital for *hearing tests* (p. 190). If you are found to have an inner ear disorder, you will probably be given drugs to relieve the symptoms.

**NO** ↓

**Are you taking any medicines?**

**YES** →

**NO** ↓

---

**Gastritis,** inflammation of the stomach lining, can easily occur as a result of such "over-indulgence".
**Self-help:** Follow the advice on treating vomiting, (above). An over-the-counter *antacid* medicine will help to relieve any pain. Consult your doctor if you are no better in 24 hours.

**Does your skin or do the whites of your eyes look yellow?**

**YES**

**NO**

**Jaundice,** as a result of a liver or gallbladder disorder, is a possibility. Consult your doctor.
**Treatment:** Your doctor will probably arrange for you to have blood tests (see *Blood analysis,* p.146) and possibly an *ultrasound scan* (p.292, 293) and a *CAT scan* (p.163) to find the cause of the trouble. Treatment will depend on the nature of the underlying disorder.

---

### TREATMENT FOR VOMITING

If you have been vomiting, providing you suspect no serious cause, try the following self-help measures:
- Eat no solid food until your nausea and vomiting subside.
- Drink plenty of clear (non-alcoholic) fluids in small sips even if you cannot keep anything down for long.
- Do not smoke.
- Do not take aspirin.

If you vomit repeatedly for more than 24 hours, or if you develop further symptoms, consult your doctor.

---

### VOMITING AND THE PILL

If you are taking the contraceptive pill and suffer from an attack of vomiting, your protection against conception may be reduced. Continue to take your pills as usual, but use an alternative form of contraception as well until you start a new packet.

**Certain drugs** can cause vomiting as a side-effect. Discuss the problem with your doctor.

**Consult your doctor** if you are unable to make a diagnosis from this chart.

---

### WARNING

#### RED OR BLACK BLOOD IN VOMIT

Violent or recurrent vomiting can cause damage to the lining of the oesophagus (gullet) and this can result in streaks of red blood appearing in your vomit. Consult your doctor if this happens to you. If your vomit contains larger quantities of red blood or any black or dark brown matter like coffee grounds (partly digested blood) *seek medical help at once*; you may have a serious abdominal condition such as a bleeding stomach ulcer. It will assist rapid diagnosis of the problem if you keep the vomit containing the blood for the doctor to examine.

# 95 Recurrent vomiting

Consult this chart if you have vomited (or felt nauseated) on several days in the past week or more. Apart from the nausea and vomiting of early pregnancy, most cases of recurrent vomiting are caused by ulceration or persistent inflammation of the stomach lining. It is important to seek medical advice promptly so that you can obtain effective treatment and to eliminate the slight possibility of a more serious underlying disorder.

**For isolated attacks of vomiting, see chart 94, Vomiting.**

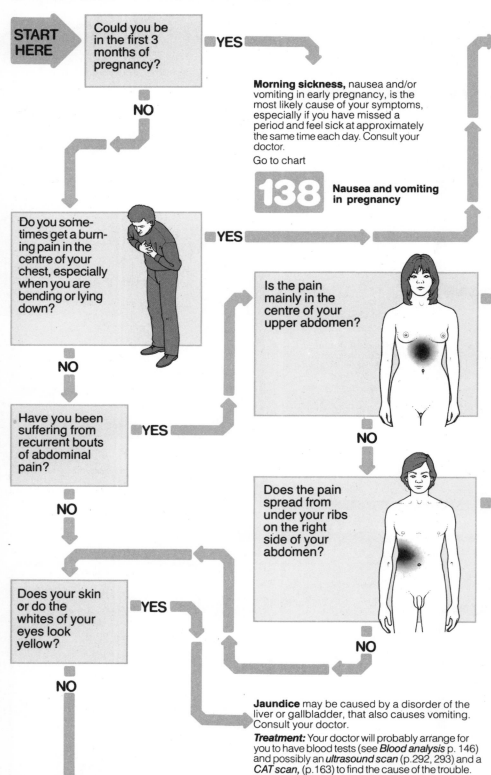

**START HERE**

**Could you be in the first 3 months of pregnancy?**

**YES** →

**Morning sickness,** nausea and/or vomiting in early pregnancy, is the most likely cause of your symptoms, especially if you have missed a period and feel sick at approximately the same time each day. Consult your doctor.

Go to chart

**138** **Nausea and vomiting in pregnancy**

**NO** ↓

**Do you sometimes get a burning pain in the centre of your chest, especially when you are bending or lying down?**

**YES** →

**Is the pain mainly in the centre of your upper abdomen?**

**NO** ↓

**Have you been suffering from recurrent bouts of abdominal pain?**

**YES** →

**NO** ↓

**Does the pain spread from under your ribs on the right side of your abdomen?**

**Does your skin or do the whites of your eyes look yellow?**

**YES** →

**NO** ↓

**NO**

*Go to next page*

**A hiatus hernia** may cause regurgitation of food and leakage of acid juices into the oesophagus (gullet) causing pain (often known as heartburn). The disorder occurs when part of the stomach protrudes through the opening in the diaphragm and is most likely if you are overweight or in the last months of pregnancy (see chart 141, *Heartburn in pregnancy*). Consult your doctor.

**Treatment:** If you are overweight, your doctor will probably recommend that you lose weight; this will almost certainly help the problem (see *How to lose weight*, p.151). Meanwhile, he or she may advise you to take small, frequent meals and to avoid tobacco and alcohol, both of which may aggravate stomach and digestive disorders. Your doctor may prescribe an *antacid* or recommend that you eat a little bread or drink a glass of milk to relieve the pain. Avoid stooping after meals and do not wear tight belts or corsets.

**YES** →

**An ulcer** in the stomach or duodenum (the tube connecting the stomach to the small intestine) is a common cause of such symptoms. Consult your doctor.

**Treatment:** Your doctor may simply give you advice and drugs which will encourage any ulcer to heal. Or he may arrange for you to undergo tests such as *endoscopy* (p.201) or a *barium X-ray* (opposite) to locate the exact site of the ulcer. Your doctor is likely to advise you to rest, to avoid tobacco and alcohol, and to eat small, frequent meals. He or she may also prescribe an *antacid* or drugs to reduce the amount of acid in the stomach.

**YES** →

**Gallstones** in the tube connecting the gallbladder to the digestive tract may be the cause of such symptoms. Consult your doctor.

**Treatment:** Your doctor may arrange for you to undergo *cholecystography* (p. 293) or an *ultrasound scan* (p.292, 293). If gallstones are diagnosed you will be advised to avoid fatty foods and may be prescribed muscle-relaxants for the pain. If symptoms persist, you may need to have an operation (see *Gallbladder removal,* opposite). In some cases drugs to dissolve the stones may be given.

**Jaundice** may be caused by a disorder of the liver or gallbladder, that also causes vomiting. Consult your doctor.

**Treatment:** Your doctor will probably arrange for you to have blood tests (see *Blood analysis* p. 146) and possibly an *ultrasound scan* (p.292, 293) and a *CAT scan,* (p.163) to find the cause of the trouble. Treatment will depend on the nature of the underlying disorder.

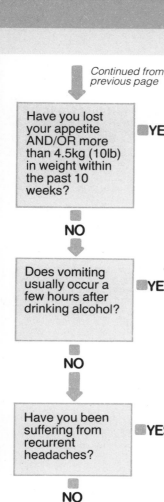

*Continued from previous page*

Have you lost your appetite AND/OR more than 4.5kg (10lb) in weight within the past 10 weeks?

**YES** → **CONSULT YOUR DOCTOR WITHOUT DELAY!**
**An ulcer** in the stomach or duodenum or gastritis are the most likely causes of your symptoms, but there is a slight possibility of stomach cancer.

*Treatment:* Your doctor will probably arrange for you to have a barium meal (see *Barium X-rays*, right) and possibly *endoscopy*, (p.201). Treatment will depend on the underlying disorder.

**NO** ↓

Does vomiting usually occur a few hours after drinking alcohol?

**YES** → **Chronic gastritis** (persistent inflammation of the lining of the stomach), a disorder that is aggravated by drinking alcohol, is a possibility (see also *The effects of alcohol,* p.146). Consult your doctor.

*Treatment:* Your doctor will probably advise you to eat nothing while vomiting persists and to drink plenty of clear (non-alcoholic) fluids (see *Treatment for vomiting,* p.205). As you start to feel better he or she will probably suggest that you gradually introduce some bland foods. If you suffer from abdominal pain, your doctor will probably prescribe an *antacid*. And he or she may advise you to cut down your regular alcohol intake.

**NO** ↓

Have you been suffering from recurrent headaches?

**YES** → Do you vomit without preceding nausea?

**YES** → **CONSULT YOUR DOCTOR WITHOUT DELAY!**
**Pressure on the brain** as a result of bleeding or a growth is possible.

*Treatment:* Your doctor will probably arrange for tests such as a *CAT scan,* (p.163) and a *radio-isotope scan* (p.148) of the brain tissues. Treatment usually consists of either surgery or drugs to reduce the pressure and relieve symptoms.

**NO** ↓

**NO** ↓

Are you taking any medicines?

**YES** → **Certain drugs** can cause nausea and vomiting as a side-effect. Discuss the problem with your doctor.

**NO** ↓

**Consult your doctor** if you are unable to make a diagnosis from this chart.

## BARIUM X-RAYS

Barium sulphate is a metallic salt that is visible on X-ray pictures. In medicine it is used to show up areas of the digestive tract that need investigation. If you need to have an X-ray of the oesophagus (gullet), stomach or small intestine, you will probably be given barium in the form of a drink (a barium *swallow* or *meal*). X-rays will then be taken when the liquid reaches the relevant part of the digestive tract (after about 10 minutes for the oesophagus, after 2 to 3 hours for the small intestine). If the large intestine (colon and rectum) is being examined, barium will be given in the form of an *enema* and the X-rays will be taken immediately. Normally, you will be told to eat nothing after midnight on the day before your barium meal or enema. If you are having an enema, you may also be given a laxative to clear the bowel.

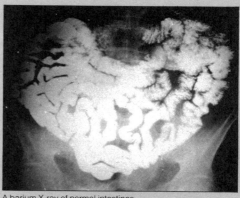

A barium X-ray of normal intestines

## GALLBLADDER REMOVAL

When gallstones or another disorder of the gallbladder cause serious symptoms, the gall-bladder is often removed surgically. The operation is performed under general anaesthetic, and the surgeon will also explore the bile duct and remove any stones found there.

Immediately after the operation, you will be on a drip feed, but after a few days you will be able to eat and drink normally. You should be able to return home about two weeks after the operation.

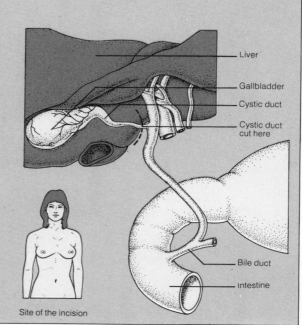

**The operation**
A cut is made in the right side of the abdomen (right). The gallbladder is then removed by cutting the cystic duct near where it joins the bile duct as shown in the diagram (above right). After the operation bile drains straight into the intestine instead of first collecting in the gallbladder.

Site of the incision

Liver
Gallbladder
Cystic duct
Cystic duct cut here
Bile duct
Intestine

# 96 Abdominal pain

Pain between the bottom of the ribcage and the groin can be a sign of a wide number of different disorders of the digestive tract, urinary tract or reproductive organs.

Most cases of abdominal pain are due to minor digestive upsets, but severe and persistent pain should always receive prompt medical attention.

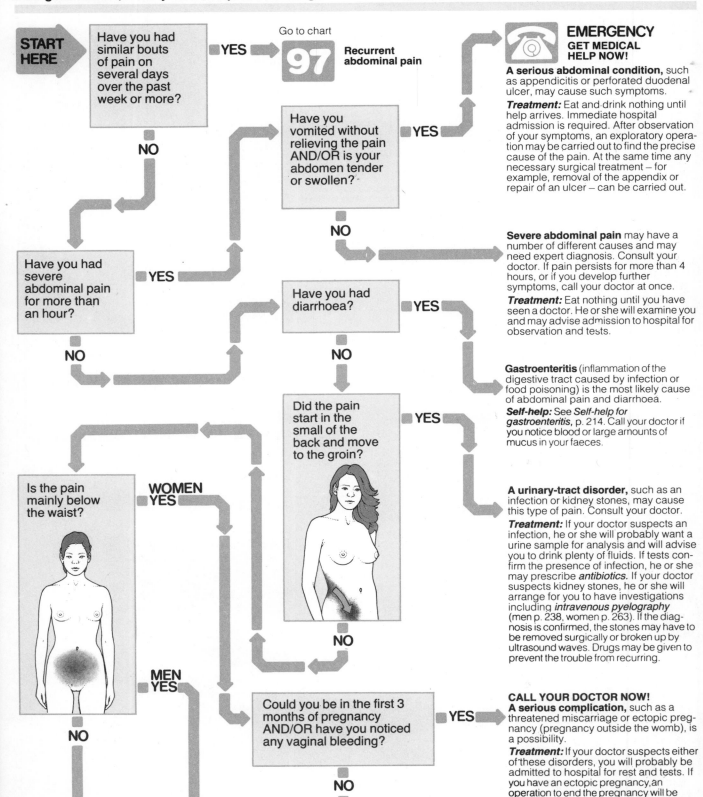

**START HERE**

**Have you had similar bouts of pain on several days over the past week or more?**

**YES** → **Go to chart 97 Recurrent abdominal pain**

**NO** ↓

**Have you had severe abdominal pain for more than an hour?**

**Have you vomited without relieving the pain AND/OR is your abdomen tender or swollen?**

**YES** → **EMERGENCY GET MEDICAL HELP NOW!**

**A serious abdominal condition,** such as appendicitis or perforated duodenal ulcer, may cause such symptoms.

*Treatment:* Eat and drink nothing until help arrives. Immediate hospital admission is required. After observation of your symptoms, an exploratory operation may be carried out to find the precise cause of the pain. At the same time any necessary surgical treatment – for example, removal of the appendix or repair of an ulcer – can be carried out.

**NO** ↓

**YES** (from Have you had severe abdominal pain)

**Have you had diarrhoea?**

**YES** → **Severe abdominal pain** may have a number of different causes and may need expert diagnosis. Consult your doctor. If pain persists for more than 4 hours, or if you develop further symptoms, call your doctor at once.

*Treatment:* Eat nothing until you have seen a doctor. He or she will examine you and may advise admission to hospital for observation and tests.

**NO** ↓

**Did the pain start in the small of the back and move to the groin?**

**YES** → **Gastroenteritis** (inflammation of the digestive tract caused by infection or food poisoning) is the most likely cause of abdominal pain and diarrhoea.

*Self-help:* See *Self-help for gastroenteritis*, p. 214. Call your doctor if you notice blood or large amounts of mucus in your faeces.

**NO** ↓

**Is the pain mainly below the waist?**

**WOMEN YES**

**A urinary-tract disorder,** such as an infection or kidney stones, may cause this type of pain. Consult your doctor.

*Treatment:* If your doctor suspects an infection, he or she will probably want a urine sample for analysis and will advise you to drink plenty of fluids. If tests confirm the presence of infection, he or she may prescribe *antibiotics*. If your doctor suspects kidney stones, he or she will arrange for you to have investigations including *intravenous pyelography* (men p. 238, women p. 263). If the diagnosis is confirmed, the stones may have to be removed surgically or broken up by ultrasound waves. Drugs may be given to prevent the trouble from recurring.

**MEN YES**

**Could you be in the first 3 months of pregnancy AND/OR have you noticed any vaginal bleeding?**

**YES** → **CALL YOUR DOCTOR NOW!**
**A serious complication,** such as a threatened miscarriage or ectopic pregnancy (pregnancy outside the womb), is a possibility.

*Treatment:* If your doctor suspects either of these disorders, you will probably be admitted to hospital for rest and tests. If you have an ectopic pregnancy, an operation to end the pregnancy will be carried out. See also *Miscarriage*, p. 276.

**NO** ↓

*Go to next page, column 1*

*Go to next page column 2*

**NO** ↓

*Go to next page, column 2*

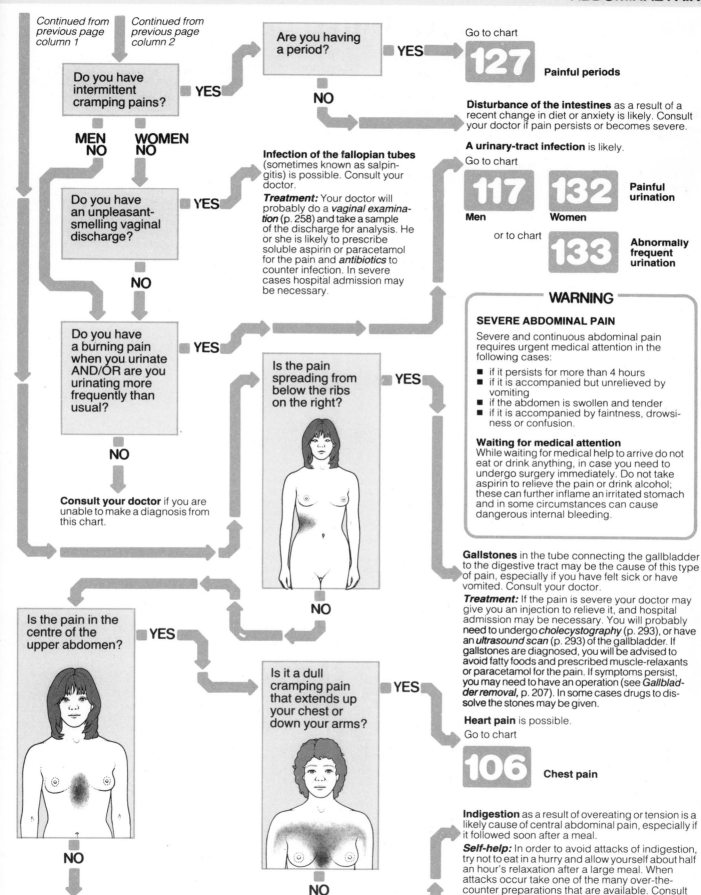

Continued from previous page column 1

Continued from previous page column 2

**Do you have intermittent cramping pains?**

**Are you having a period?** — **YES** →

Go to chart **127** Painful periods

MEN NO / WOMEN NO

**NO**

**Disturbance of the intestines** as a result of a recent change in diet or anxiety is likely. Consult your doctor if pain persists or becomes severe.

**Do you have an unpleasant-smelling vaginal discharge?** — **YES** →

**Infection of the fallopian tubes** (sometimes known as salpingitis) is possible. Consult your doctor.

***Treatment:*** Your doctor will probably do a *vaginal examination* (p. 258) and take a sample of the discharge for analysis. He or she is likely to prescribe soluble aspirin or paracetamol for the pain and *antibiotics* to counter infection. In severe cases hospital admission may be necessary.

**NO**

**A urinary-tract infection** is likely. Go to chart

**117** Men  **132** Women  Painful urination

or to chart **133** Abnormally frequent urination

**Do you have a burning pain when you urinate AND/OR are you urinating more frequently than usual?** — **YES** →

**NO**

**Consult your doctor** if you are unable to make a diagnosis from this chart.

**Is the pain spreading from below the ribs on the right?** — **YES** →

**NO**

## WARNING

### SEVERE ABDOMINAL PAIN

Severe and continuous abdominal pain requires urgent medical attention in the following cases:

- if it persists for more than 4 hours
- if it is accompanied but unrelieved by vomiting
- if the abdomen is swollen and tender
- if it is accompanied by faintness, drowsiness or confusion

### Waiting for medical attention

While waiting for medical help to arrive do not eat or drink anything, in case you need to undergo surgery immediately. Do not take aspirin to relieve the pain or drink alcohol; these can further inflame an irritated stomach and in some circumstances can cause dangerous internal bleeding.

**Gallstones** in the tube connecting the gallbladder to the digestive tract may be the cause of this type of pain, especially if you have felt sick or have vomited. Consult your doctor.

***Treatment:*** If the pain is severe your doctor may give you an injection to relieve it, and hospital admission may be necessary. You will probably need to undergo *cholecystography* (p. 293), or have an *ultrasound scan* (p. 293) of the gallbladder. If gallstones are diagnosed, you will be advised to avoid fatty foods and prescribed muscle-relaxants or paracetamol for the pain. If symptoms persist, you may need to have an operation (see *Gallbladder removal*, p. 207). In some cases drugs to dissolve the stones may be given.

**Is the pain in the centre of the upper abdomen?** — **YES** →

**NO**

**Consult your doctor** if you are unable to make a diagnosis from this chart.

**Is it a dull cramping pain that extends up your chest or down your arms?** — **YES** →

**NO**

**Heart pain** is possible. Go to chart **106** Chest pain

**Indigestion** as a result of overeating or tension is a likely cause of central abdominal pain, especially if it followed soon after a meal.

***Self-help:*** In order to avoid attacks of indigestion, try not to eat in a hurry and allow yourself about half an hour's relaxation after a large meal. When attacks occur take one of the many over-the-counter preparations that are available. Consult your doctor if the pain becomes severe or if attacks occur frequently.

# 97 Recurrent abdominal pain

Consult this chart if you have pain in the abdomen (between the bottom of the ribcage and the groin) of a similar type on several days in the course of a week or more. Most cases of recurrent abdominal pain are the result of long-standing digestive problems, and can be remedied by drugs prescribed by your doctor, possibly combined with a change in eating habits. However, early professional diagnosis is always necessary to eliminate the slight possibility of serious underlying disease of the stomach, bowel or other abdominal organs.

For isolated attacks of abdominal pain, see chart 96, Abdominal pain.

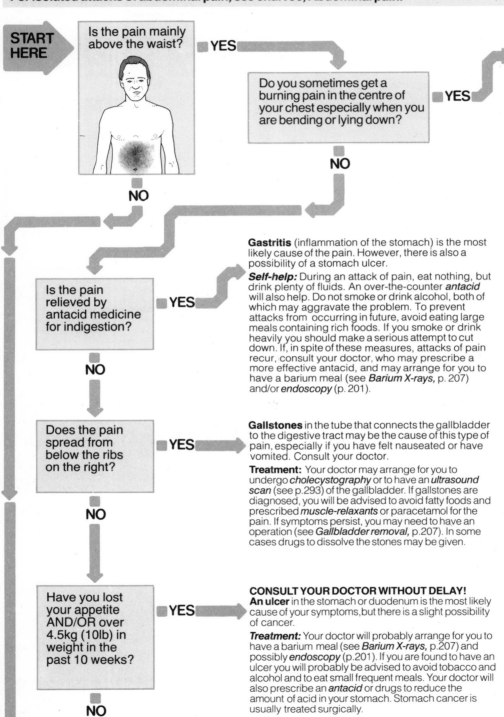

**START HERE**

**Is the pain mainly above the waist?**

**YES** → **Do you sometimes get a burning pain in the centre of your chest especially when you are bending or lying down?**

**YES** →

**A hiatus hernia** may cause leakage of acid juices into the oesophagus (gullet) causing pain (often known as heartburn). The disorder occurs when part of the stomach protrudes through the opening in the diaphragm and is most likely if you are overweight. Consult your doctor.

**Treatment:** If you are overweight, your doctor will probably recommend that you lose weight as this will almost certainly help the problem (see *How to lose weight,* p. 151). Meanwhile, he or she may also advise you to take small, frequent meals and to avoid tobacco or alcohol, both of which may aggravate stomach and digestive disorders. If you are troubled by heartburn, your doctor may also prescribe an *antacid.* Alternatively, you might try eating a little bread or drinking a glass of milk to relieve the pain. Avoid stooping after meals and do not wear tight belts. Propping up the head of your bed by about 10cm (4in) using bricks or books should prevent heartburn at night.

**NO** (from chest pain question)

**NO** (from above the waist question)

**Gastritis** (inflammation of the stomach) is the most likely cause of the pain. However, there is also a possibility of a stomach ulcer.

**Self-help:** During an attack of pain, eat nothing, but drink plenty of fluids. An over-the-counter *antacid* will also help. Do not smoke or drink alcohol, both of which may aggravate the problem. To prevent attacks from occurring in future, avoid eating large meals containing rich foods. If you smoke or drink heavily you should make a serious attempt to cut down. If, in spite of these measures, attacks of pain recur, consult your doctor, who may prescribe a more effective antacid, and may arrange for you to have a barium meal (see *Barium X-rays,* p. 207) and/or *endoscopy* (p. 201).

**Is the pain relieved by antacid medicine for indigestion?**

**YES** →

**NO** ↓

**Does the pain spread from below the ribs on the right?**

**YES** →

**Gallstones** in the tube that connects the gallbladder to the digestive tract may be the cause of this type of pain, especially if you have felt nauseated or have vomited. Consult your doctor.

**Treatment:** Your doctor may arrange for you to undergo *cholecystography* or to have an *ultrasound scan* (see p.293) of the gallbladder. If gallstones are diagnosed, you will be advised to avoid fatty foods and prescribed *muscle-relaxants* or paracetamol for the pain. If symptoms persist, you may need to have an operation (see *Gallbladder removal,* p.207). In some cases drugs to dissolve the stones may be given.

**NO** ↓

**Have you lost your appetite AND/OR over 4.5kg (10lb) in weight in the past 10 weeks?**

**YES** →

**CONSULT YOUR DOCTOR WITHOUT DELAY!**
**An ulcer** in the stomach or duodenum is the most likely cause of your symptoms, but there is a slight possibility of cancer.

**Treatment:** Your doctor will probably arrange for you to have a barium meal (see *Barium X-rays,* p.207) and possibly *endoscopy* (p.201). If you are found to have an ulcer you will probably be advised to avoid tobacco and alcohol and to eat small frequent meals. Your doctor will also prescribe an *antacid* or drugs to reduce the amount of acid in your stomach. Stomach cancer is usually treated surgically.

**NO** ↓

*Go to next page*

---

**IRRITABLE BOWEL**

Many people who suffer from recurrent cramping pains in the lower abdomen with or without intermittent diarrhoea and/or constipation have no serious underlying disorder and are diagnosed as having an irritable bowel (or spastic colon). It is thought that the disorder is caused by abnormally strong and irregular muscle contractions in the bowel. This may be due to sensitivity to the passage of matter through the intestines, but it may also be linked to psychological stress (see *What is stress?,* p. 174). A large proportion of those with this complaint are anxious, and attacks seem to be made worse by worry. Most sufferers learn to live with the problem without specific treatment. A high-fibre diet (p. 215) often relieves th symptoms. Those who suffer from severe pain may be prescribed *anti-spasmodic* drugs.

*Continued from previous page*

**Is the pain mainly below the waist?**

**YES** →

**Do you have any swelling or discomfort in the groin that is made worse by coughing or lifting heavy objects?**

**YES** →

**A hernia** (see *What is a hernia?,* below) may be the cause of such pain. Consult your doctor.

***Treatment:*** Your doctor will examine you to confirm the diagnosis. If you have a hernia, it may be necessary for you to have a minor operation to repair the abdominal wall.

**NO**

**NO**

### WHAT IS A HERNIA?

A hernia occurs when soft tissue in the abdomen bulges through a weak area in the abdominal wall. Hernias may occur in various places. In men, one of the most common sites is the groin, where the abdominal organs either push aside the weak muscles of the groin or protrude down the inguinal canal (the tube down which the testes descend before birth).

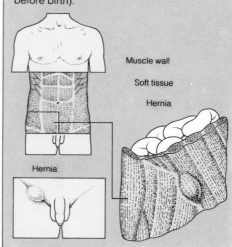

Muscle wall

Soft tissue

Hernia

Hernia

**Have you been intermittently constipated?**

**YES** →

**NO**

**Have you been having bouts of diarrhoea?**

**YES** →

**NO**

**Crohn's disease or ulcerative colitis** may cause lower abdominal pain and diarrhoea. The former is patchy inflammation of the intestines, the latter is inflammation and ulceration of the large intestine. Consult your doctor. Seek medical help without delay if you have passed any blood in your faeces.

***Treatment:*** A severe attack of ulcerative colitis may require hospital admission. In any case you will probably need to have tests such as a *barium X-ray* (p. 207), *sigmoidoscopy* (p. 216) and analysis of samples of faecal material. If you are found to have either Crohn's disease or ulcerative colitis, you will probably be put on a bland diet and may be given a course of *anti-inflammatory* drugs.

**CONSULT YOUR DOCTOR WITHOUT DELAY!**
**Irritable bowel** (see below) or diverticular disease (in which swellings develop on the walls of the large intestine) may be the cause of your symptoms. However, the slight possibility of bowel cancer also needs to be ruled out.

***Treatment:*** To make an exact diagnosis, your doctor may need to arrange tests such as a barium enema (see *Barium X-rays,* p. 207) and *endoscopy* (p. 201). The long-term treatment for both irritable bowel and diverticular disease is based on a high-fibre diet (p. 215). Your doctor may also prescribe drugs to relieve your symptoms.

**Are you a woman?**

**YES** →

**Do you have an unpleasant-smelling vaginal discharge?**

**YES** →

**NO**

**NO**

**Infection of the fallopian tubes** (sometimes known as salpingitis) is possible. Consult your doctor.

***Treatment:*** Your doctor will probably do a *vaginal examination* (p. 258) and take a sample of the discharge from your vagina for analysis. He or she is likely to prescribe soluble aspirin or paracetamol for the pain and *antibiotics* to counter infection. In severe cases hospital admission may be necessary.

**Are you pregnant?**

**YES** →

**NO**

**Periodic tightening of the muscles around the womb,** known as Braxton Hicks contractions, occurs throughout pregnancy. These make your abdomen feel hard and tense for about 30 seconds, but should not cause actual pain. Call your doctor if contractions are accompanied by vaginal bleeding, or if they are painful. In late pregnancy, an increase in the frequency and strength of these contractions may signal the start of labour (see chart 145, *Am I in labour?*)

**Consult your doctor** if you are unable to make a diagnosis from this chart.

# 98 Swollen abdomen

A generalized swelling over the whole abdomen (the area between the bottom of the ribcage and the groin) suggests a condition affecting the digestive or reproductive organs. If your abdomen is painful as well as swollen, this is an emergency and you should seek medical advice immediately.

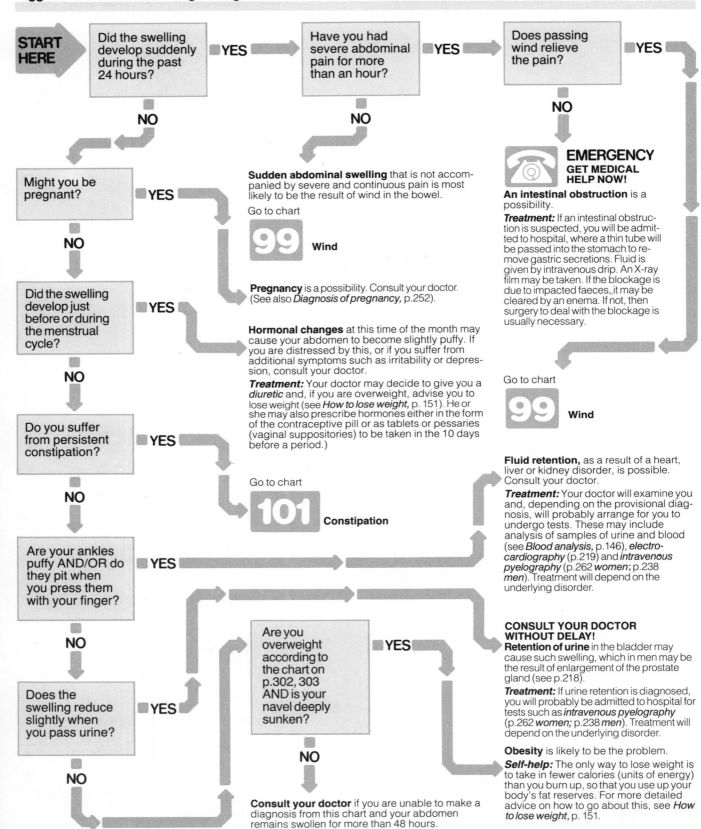

**START HERE** → Did the swelling develop suddenly during the past 24 hours? — **YES** → Have you had severe abdominal pain for more than an hour? — **YES** → Does passing wind relieve the pain? — **YES**

**Did the swelling develop suddenly during the past 24 hours? — NO**

**Might you be pregnant?** — **YES**

**Might you be pregnant? — NO**

**Sudden abdominal swelling** that is not accompanied by severe and continuous pain is most likely to be the result of wind in the bowel.

Go to chart

## 99 Wind

**Pregnancy** is a possibility. Consult your doctor. (See also *Diagnosis of pregnancy,* p.252).

**Did the swelling develop just before or during the menstrual cycle?** — **YES**

**Did the swelling develop just before or during the menstrual cycle? — NO**

**Hormonal changes** at this time of the month may cause your abdomen to become slightly puffy. If you are distressed by this, or if you suffer from additional symptoms such as irritability or depression, consult your doctor.

**Treatment:** Your doctor may decide to give you a *diuretic* and, if you are overweight, advise you to lose weight (see *How to lose weight,* p. 151). He or she may also prescribe hormones either in the form of the contraceptive pill or as tablets or pessaries (vaginal suppositories) to be taken in the 10 days before a period.)

**Does passing wind relieve the pain? — NO**

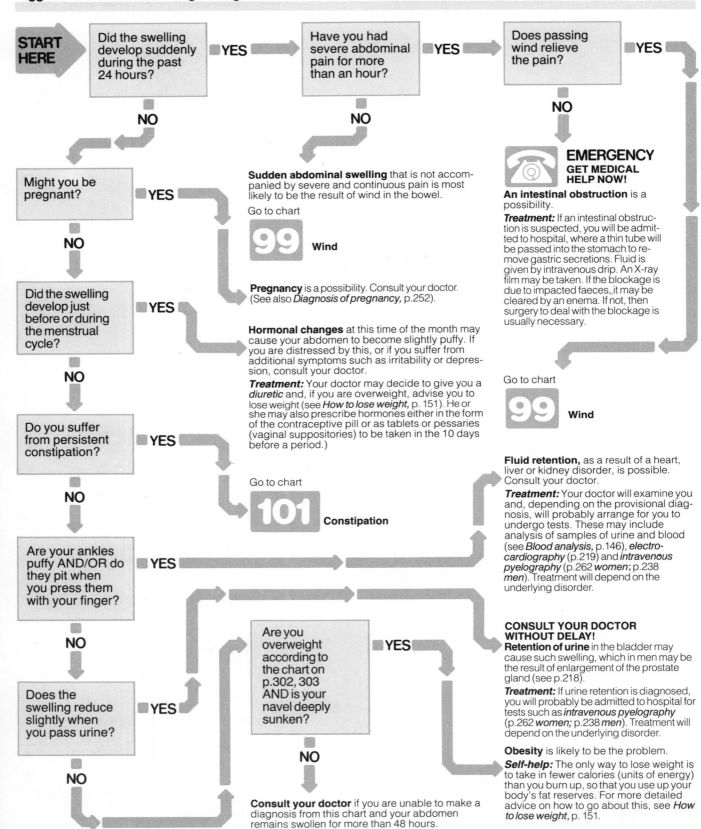

**EMERGENCY GET MEDICAL HELP NOW!**

**An intestinal obstruction** is a possibility.

**Treatment:** If an intestinal obstruction is suspected, you will be admitted to hospital, where a thin tube will be passed into the stomach to remove gastric secretions. Fluid is given by intravenous drip. An X-ray film may be taken. If the blockage is due to impacted faeces, it may be cleared by an enema. If not, then surgery to deal with the blockage is usually necessary.

Go to chart

## 99 Wind

**Do you suffer from persistent constipation?** — **YES**

**Do you suffer from persistent constipation? — NO**

Go to chart

## 101 Constipation

**Fluid retention,** as a result of a heart, liver or kidney disorder, is possible. Consult your doctor.

**Treatment:** Your doctor will examine you and, depending on the provisional diagnosis, will probably arrange for you to undergo tests. These may include analysis of samples of urine and blood (see *Blood analysis,* p.146), *electrocardiography* (p.219) and *intravenous pyelography* (p.262 *women;* p.238 *men*). Treatment will depend on the underlying disorder.

**Are your ankles puffy AND/OR do they pit when you press them with your finger?** — **YES**

**Are your ankles puffy AND/OR do they pit when you press them with your finger? — NO**

**Are you overweight according to the chart on p.302, 303 AND is your navel deeply sunken?** — **YES**

**Are you overweight according to the chart on p.302, 303 AND is your navel deeply sunken? — NO**

**CONSULT YOUR DOCTOR WITHOUT DELAY!**
**Retention of urine** in the bladder may cause such swelling, which in men may be the result of enlargement of the prostate gland (see p.218).

**Treatment:** If urine retention is diagnosed, you will probably be admitted to hospital for tests such as *intravenous pyelography* (p.262 *women;* p.238 *men*). Treatment will depend on the underlying disorder.

**Obesity** is likely to be the problem.

**Self-help:** The only way to lose weight is to take in fewer calories (units of energy) than you burn up, so that you use up your body's fat reserves. For more detailed advice on how to go about this, see *How to lose weight,* p. 151.

**Does the swelling reduce slightly when you pass urine?** — **YES**

**Does the swelling reduce slightly when you pass urine? — NO**

**Consult your doctor** if you are unable to make a diagnosis from this chart and your abdomen remains swollen for more than 48 hours.

# 99 Wind

Excess wind (or gas) in the digestive system can cause an uncomfortable distended feeling in the abdomen and may produce rumbling noises in the intestines. Expulsion of wind either through the mouth or anus generally relieves these symptoms. Although it may be embarrassing, passing wind is rarely a sign of an under-lying disease. In most cases it is caused by swallowing air or by certain foods not being properly broken down by the digestive juices, leaving a residue that ferments, producing gas in the intestines. Different foods affect different people in different ways – though onions, cabbage and beans are common causes of wind.

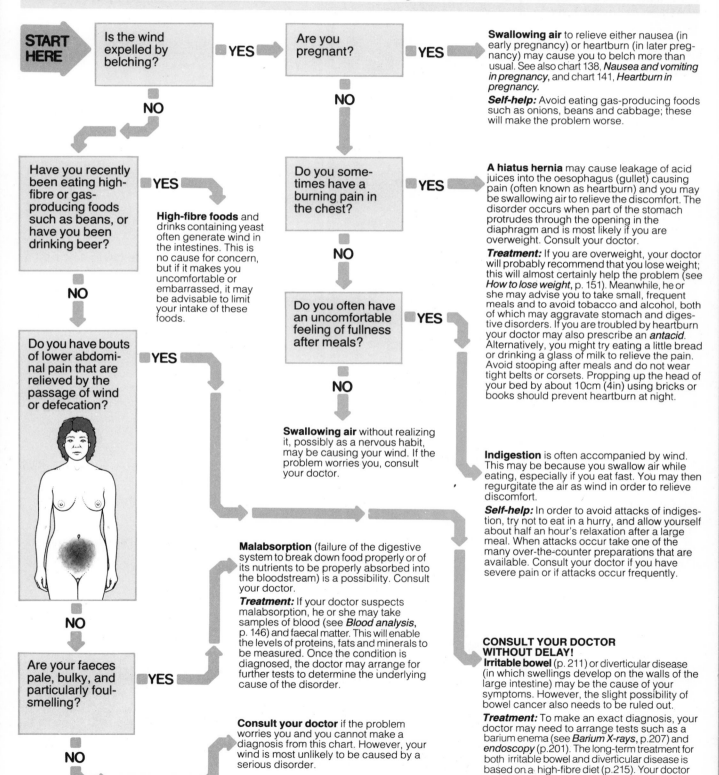

**START HERE**

**Is the wind expelled by belching?**

**YES** →

**Are you pregnant?**

**YES** →

**Swallowing air** to relieve either nausea (in early pregnancy) or heartburn (in later pregnancy) may cause you to belch more than usual. See also chart 138, *Nausea and vomiting in pregnancy*, and chart 141, *Heartburn in pregnancy.*

**Self-help:** Avoid eating gas-producing foods such as onions, beans and cabbage; these will make the problem worse.

**NO** (from belching)

**NO** (from pregnant)

**Have you recently been eating high-fibre or gas-producing foods such as beans, or have you been drinking beer?**

**YES** →

**High-fibre foods** and drinks containing yeast often generate wind in the intestines. This is no cause for concern, but if it makes you uncomfortable or embarrassed, it may be advisable to limit your intake of these foods.

**Do you sometimes have a burning pain in the chest?**

**YES** →

**A hiatus hernia** may cause leakage of acid juices into the oesophagus (gullet) causing pain (often known as heartburn) and you may be swallowing air to relieve the discomfort. The disorder occurs when part of the stomach protrudes through the opening in the diaphragm and is most likely if you are overweight. Consult your doctor.

**Treatment:** If you are overweight, your doctor will probably recommend that you lose weight; this will almost certainly help the problem (see *How to lose weight*, p. 151). Meanwhile, he or she may advise you to take small, frequent meals and to avoid tobacco and alcohol, both of which may aggravate stomach and digestive disorders. If you are troubled by heartburn your doctor may also prescribe an *antacid*. Alternatively, you might try eating a little bread or drinking a glass of milk to relieve the pain. Avoid stooping after meals and do not wear tight belts or corsets. Propping up the head of your bed by about 10cm (4in) using bricks or books should prevent heartburn at night.

**NO**

**NO**

**Do you have bouts of lower abdominal pain that are relieved by the passage of wind or defecation?**

**YES** →

**Do you often have an uncomfortable feeling of fullness after meals?**

**YES** →

**Indigestion** is often accompanied by wind. This may be because you swallow air while eating, especially if you eat fast. You may then regurgitate the air as wind in order to relieve discomfort.

**Self-help:** In order to avoid attacks of indigestion, try not to eat in a hurry, and allow yourself about half an hour's relaxation after a large meal. When attacks occur take one of the many over-the-counter preparations that are available. Consult your doctor if you have severe pain or if attacks occur frequently.

**NO**

**Swallowing air** without realizing it, possibly as a nervous habit, may be causing your wind. If the problem worries you, consult your doctor.

**Malabsorption** (failure of the digestive system to break down food properly or of its nutrients to be properly absorbed into the bloodstream) is a possibility. Consult your doctor.

**Treatment:** If your doctor suspects malabsorption, he or she may take samples of blood (see *Blood analysis*, p. 146) and faecal matter. This will enable the levels of proteins, fats and minerals to be measured. Once the condition is diagnosed, the doctor may arrange for further tests to determine the underlying cause of the disorder.

**NO**

**Are your faeces pale, bulky, and particularly foul-smelling?**

**YES** →

**CONSULT YOUR DOCTOR WITHOUT DELAY!**
**Irritable bowel** (p. 211) or diverticular disease (in which swellings develop on the walls of the large intestine) may be the cause of your symptoms. However, the slight possibility of bowel cancer also needs to be ruled out.

**Treatment:** To make an exact diagnosis, your doctor may need to arrange tests such as a barium enema (see *Barium X-rays*, p.207) and *endoscopy* (p.201). The long-term treatment for both irritable bowel and diverticular disease is based on a high-fibre diet (p.215). Your doctor may also prescribe drugs to relieve pain.

**NO**

**Consult your doctor** if the problem worries you and you cannot make a diagnosis from this chart. However, your wind is most unlikely to be caused by a serious disorder.

# 100 Diarrhoea

Diarrhoea is the passing of unusually loose and frequent faeces. It is rarely a dangerous symptom, but it may cause discomfort and is often accompanied by cramping pains in the lower abdomen. In this country, most attacks of diarrhoea are the result of virus infection and last no more than 48 hours. No special treatment other than ensuring that you drink plenty of fluids is

usually needed. However, if diarrhoea persists or recurs it should be reported to your doctor. Remember, if you are taking the contraceptive pill and have diarrhoea for more than 24 hours, your protection against pregnancy may be reduced, and you should use another means of contraception for the remainder of your cycle (see chart 136, Choosing a contraceptive method).

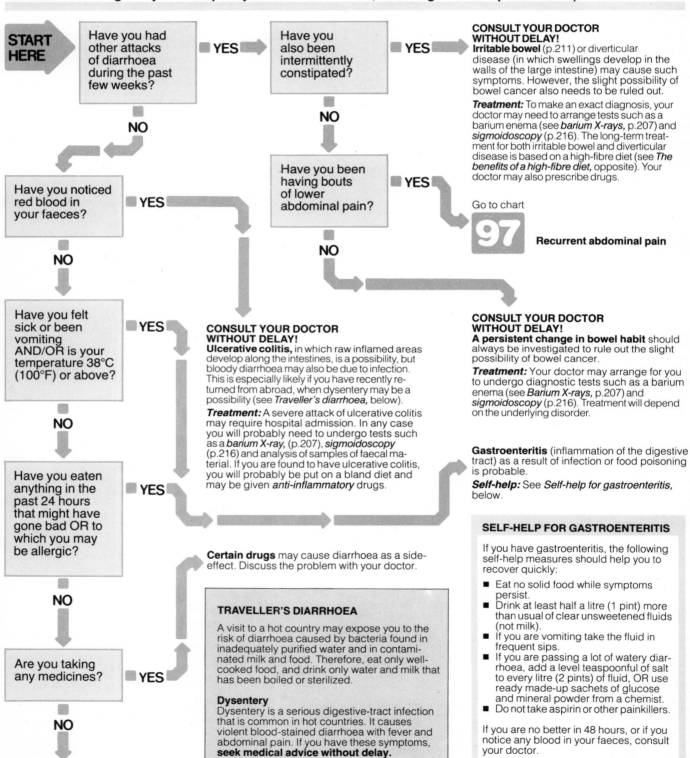

**START HERE**

**Have you had other attacks of diarrhoea during the past few weeks?** — YES → **Have you also been intermittently constipated?** — YES → **CONSULT YOUR DOCTOR WITHOUT DELAY!**
**Irritable bowel** (p.211) or diverticular disease (in which swellings develop in the walls of the large intestine) may cause such symptoms. However, the slight possibility of bowel cancer also needs to be ruled out.

*Treatment:* To make an exact diagnosis, your doctor may need to arrange tests such as a barium enema (see *barium X-rays*, p.207) and *sigmoidoscopy* (p.216). The long-term treatment for both irritable bowel and diverticular disease is based on a high-fibre diet (see *The benefits of a high-fibre diet,* opposite). Your doctor may also prescribe drugs.

NO ↓ (from first box)

**Have you also been intermittently constipated?** NO ↓

**Have you been having bouts of lower abdominal pain?** — YES →

Go to chart **97** **Recurrent abdominal pain**

**Have you noticed red blood in your faeces?** — YES →

NO ↓

**Have you been having bouts of lower abdominal pain?** NO ↓

**CONSULT YOUR DOCTOR WITHOUT DELAY!**
**A persistent change in bowel habit** should always be investigated to rule out the slight possibility of bowel cancer.

*Treatment:* Your doctor may arrange for you to undergo diagnostic tests such as a barium enema (see *Barium X-rays*, p.207) and *sigmoidoscopy* (p.216). Treatment will depend on the underlying disorder.

**Have you felt sick or been vomiting AND/OR is your temperature 38°C (100°F) or above?** — YES →

**CONSULT YOUR DOCTOR WITHOUT DELAY!**
**Ulcerative colitis,** in which raw inflamed areas develop along the intestines, is a possibility, but bloody diarrhoea may also be due to infection. This is especially likely if you have recently returned from abroad, when dysentery may be a possibility (see *Traveller's diarrhoea,* below).

*Treatment:* A severe attack of ulcerative colitis may require hospital admission. In any case you will probably need to undergo tests such as a *barium X-ray,* (p.207), *sigmoidoscopy* (p.216) and analysis of samples of faecal material. If you are found to have ulcerative colitis, you will probably be put on a bland diet and may be given *anti-inflammatory* drugs.

**Gastroenteritis** (inflammation of the digestive tract) as a result of infection or food poisoning is probable.

*Self-help:* See *Self-help for gastroenteritis,* below.

NO ↓

**Have you eaten anything in the past 24 hours that might have gone bad OR to which you may be allergic?** — YES →

NO ↓

**Certain drugs** may cause diarrhoea as a side-effect. Discuss the problem with your doctor.

**Are you taking any medicines?** — YES →

NO ↓

**Gastroenteritis** (above right) is likely.

### TRAVELLER'S DIARRHOEA

A visit to a hot country may expose you to the risk of diarrhoea caused by bacteria found in inadequately purified water and in contaminated milk and food. Therefore, eat only well-cooked food, and drink only water and milk that has been boiled or sterilized.

**Dysentery**
Dysentery is a serious digestive-tract infection that is common in hot countries. It causes violent blood-stained diarrhoea with fever and abdominal pain. If you have these symptoms, **seek medical advice without delay.**

### SELF-HELP FOR GASTROENTERITIS

If you have gastroenteritis, the following self-help measures should help you to recover quickly:

- Eat no solid food while symptoms persist.
- Drink at least half a litre (1 pint) more than usual of clear unsweetened fluids (not milk).
- If you are vomiting take the fluid in frequent sips.
- If you are passing a lot of watery diarrhoea, add a level teaspoonful of salt to every litre (2 pints) of fluid, OR use ready made-up sachets of glucose and mineral powder from a chemist.
- Do not take aspirin or other painkillers.

If you are no better in 48 hours, or if you notice any blood in your faeces, consult your doctor.

# 101 Constipation

Bowel habits vary from person to person — many people have one or more movements a day, but a few have four or five a day. These variations are quite normal if this is your usual pattern. Constipation occurs only when the faeces are hard and painful or difficult to pass, or more infrequent than you are used to.

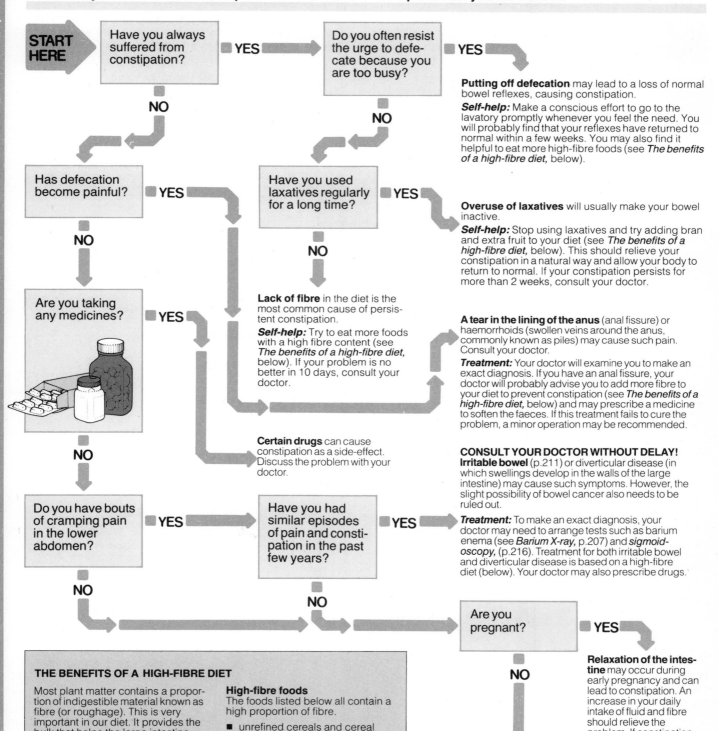

**START HERE**

**Have you always suffered from constipation?**
- YES → **Do you often resist the urge to defecate because you are too busy?**
  - YES → **Putting off defecation** may lead to a loss of normal bowel reflexes, causing constipation.
    **Self-help:** Make a conscious effort to go to the lavatory promptly whenever you feel the need. You will probably find that your reflexes have returned to normal within a few weeks. You may also find it helpful to eat more high-fibre foods (see *The benefits of a high-fibre diet,* below).
  - NO → **Have you used laxatives regularly for a long time?**
    - YES → **Overuse of laxatives** will usually make your bowel inactive.
      **Self-help:** Stop using laxatives and try adding bran and extra fruit to your diet (see *The benefits of a high-fibre diet,* below). This should relieve your constipation in a natural way and allow your body to return to normal. If your constipation persists for more than 2 weeks, consult your doctor.
    - NO → **Lack of fibre** in the diet is the most common cause of persistent constipation.
      **Self-help:** Try to eat more foods with a high fibre content (see *The benefits of a high-fibre diet,* below). If your problem is no better in 10 days, consult your doctor.

- NO → **Has defecation become painful?**
  - YES → **A tear in the lining of the anus** (anal fissure) or haemorrhoids (swollen veins around the anus, commonly known as piles) may cause such pain. Consult your doctor.
    **Treatment:** Your doctor will examine you to make an exact diagnosis. If you have an anal fissure, your doctor will probably advise you to add fibre to your diet to prevent constipation (see *The benefits of a high-fibre diet,* below) and may prescribe a medicine to soften the faeces. If this treatment fails to cure the problem, a minor operation may be recommended.
  - NO → **Are you taking any medicines?**
    - YES → **Certain drugs** can cause constipation as a side-effect. Discuss the problem with your doctor.
    - NO → **Do you have bouts of cramping pain in the lower abdomen?**
      - YES → **Have you had similar episodes of pain and constipation in the past few years?**
        - YES → **CONSULT YOUR DOCTOR WITHOUT DELAY!**
          **Irritable bowel** (p.211) or diverticular disease (in which swellings develop in the walls of the large intestine) may cause such symptoms. However, the slight possibility of bowel cancer also needs to be ruled out.
          **Treatment:** To make an exact diagnosis, your doctor may need to arrange tests such as barium enema (see *Barium X-ray,* p.207) and *sigmoidoscopy,* (p.216). Treatment for both irritable bowel and diverticular disease is based on a high-fibre diet (below). Your doctor may also prescribe drugs.
        - NO → **Are you pregnant?**
          - YES → **Relaxation of the intestine** may occur during early pregnancy and can lead to constipation. An increase in your daily intake of fluid and fibre should relieve the problem. If constipation persists avoid taking laxatives and consult your doctor.
          - NO → **Lack of fibre** in the diet is the most likely cause of constipation (see *The benefits of a high-fibre diet,* left). If your bowel habits have not returned to normal within 10 days, consult your doctor.
      - NO → (continues to "Are you pregnant?")

## THE BENEFITS OF A HIGH-FIBRE DIET

Most plant matter contains a proportion of indigestible material known as fibre (or roughage). This is very important in our diet. It provides the bulk that helps the large intestine carry away body waste and keeps the faeces soft. Those who eat plenty of fibre in their diet are less likely to develop cancer of the large intestine and other bowel problems. Finally, a high-fibre diet may help you to lose weight, because fibre fills you up without providing extra calories.

**High-fibre foods**
The foods listed below all contain a high proportion of fibre.

- unrefined cereals and cereal products such as brown rice and wholemeal bread
- fruit and vegetables
- beans and other pulses

# 102 Abnormal-looking faeces

Most minor changes in the colour, shape and consistency of your faeces are due to a recent change in diet or temporary digestive upset. But if the faeces are signifi- cantly darker or lighter in colour than usual, or if they are streaked with blood, this may indicate something more serious and you should consult your doctor.

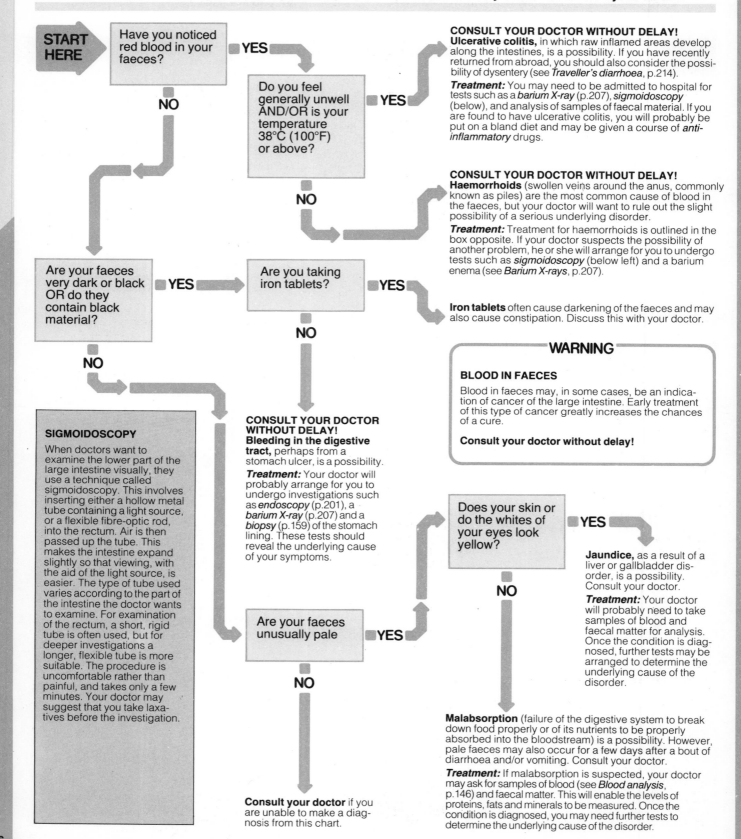

**START HERE**

**Have you noticed red blood in your faeces?** — **YES** → **Do you feel generally unwell AND/OR is your temperature 38°C (100°F) or above?** — **YES** →

**NO** ↓

**CONSULT YOUR DOCTOR WITHOUT DELAY!**
**Ulcerative colitis,** in which raw inflamed areas develop along the intestines, is a possibility. If you have recently returned from abroad, you should also consider the possibility of dysentery (see *Traveller's diarrhoea*, p.214).

***Treatment:*** You may need to be admitted to hospital for tests such as a *barium X-ray* (p.207), *sigmoidoscopy* (below), and analysis of samples of faecal material. If you are found to have ulcerative colitis, you will probably be put on a bland diet and may be given a course of *anti-inflammatory* drugs.

**NO** ↓

**CONSULT YOUR DOCTOR WITHOUT DELAY!**
**Haemorrhoids** (swollen veins around the anus, commonly known as piles) are the most common cause of blood in the faeces, but your doctor will want to rule out the slight possibility of a serious underlying disorder.

***Treatment:*** Treatment for haemorrhoids is outlined in the box opposite. If your doctor suspects the possibility of another problem, he or she will arrange for you to undergo tests such as *sigmoidoscopy* (below left) and a barium enema (see *Barium X-rays*, p.207).

**Are your faeces very dark or black OR do they contain black material?** — **YES** → **Are you taking iron tablets?** — **YES** →

**Iron tablets** often cause darkening of the faeces and may also cause constipation. Discuss this with your doctor.

**NO** ↓

**NO** ↓

---

**WARNING**

**BLOOD IN FAECES**

Blood in faeces may, in some cases, be an indication of cancer of the large intestine. Early treatment of this type of cancer greatly increases the chances of a cure.

**Consult your doctor without delay!**

---

**SIGMOIDOSCOPY**

When doctors want to examine the lower part of the large intestine visually, they use a technique called sigmoidoscopy. This involves inserting either a hollow metal tube containing a light source, or a flexible fibre-optic rod, into the rectum. Air is then passed up the tube. This makes the intestine expand slightly so that viewing, with the aid of the light source, is easier. The type of tube used varies according to the part of the intestine the doctor wants to examine. For examination of the rectum, a short, rigid tube is often used, but for deeper investigations a longer, flexible tube is more suitable. The procedure is uncomfortable rather than painful, and takes only a few minutes. Your doctor may suggest that you take laxatives before the investigation.

**CONSULT YOUR DOCTOR WITHOUT DELAY!**
**Bleeding in the digestive tract,** perhaps from a stomach ulcer, is a possibility.
***Treatment:*** Your doctor will probably arrange for you to undergo investigations such as *endoscopy* (p.201), a *barium X-ray* (p.207) and a *biopsy* (p.159) of the stomach lining. These tests should reveal the underlying cause of your symptoms.

**Does your skin or do the whites of your eyes look yellow?** — **YES** →

**Jaundice,** as a result of a liver or gallbladder disorder, is a possibility. Consult your doctor.
***Treatment:*** Your doctor will probably need to take samples of blood and faecal matter for analysis. Once the condition is diagnosed, further tests may be arranged to determine the underlying cause of the disorder.

**NO** ↓

**Are your faeces unusually pale** — **YES** →

**NO** ↓

**Malabsorption** (failure of the digestive system to break down food properly or of its nutrients to be properly absorbed into the bloodstream) is a possibility. However, pale faeces may also occur for a few days after a bout of diarrhoea and/or vomiting. Consult your doctor.
***Treatment:*** If malabsorption is suspected, your doctor may ask for samples of blood (see *Blood analysis*, p.146) and faecal matter. This will enable the levels of proteins, fats and minerals to be measured. Once the condition is diagnosed, you may need further tests to determine the underlying cause of the disorder.

**Consult your doctor** if you are unable to make a diagnosis from this chart.

# 103 Anal problems

The anus is a short tube that leads from the last part of the digestive tract (rectum) to the outside. The anus is closed by a ring of muscles (or sphincters). The most common disorder affecting this area is swelling of the veins around the anus (haemorroids). This is often related to painful constipation.

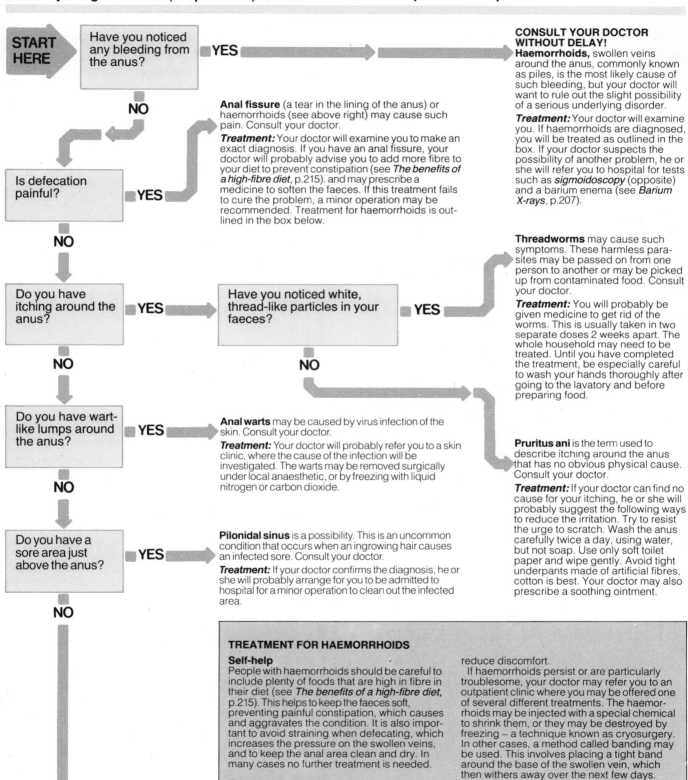

**START HERE**

**Have you noticed any bleeding from the anus?**

**YES** →

**CONSULT YOUR DOCTOR WITHOUT DELAY!**
**Haemorrhoids,** swollen veins around the anus, commonly known as piles, is the most likely cause of such bleeding, but your doctor will want to rule out the slight possibility of a serious underlying disorder.

**Treatment:** Your doctor will examine you. If haemorrhoids are diagnosed, you will be treated as outlined in the box. If your doctor suspects the possibility of another problem, he or she will refer you to hospital for tests such as *sigmoidoscopy* (opposite) and a barium enema (see *Barium X-rays*, p.207).

**NO**

**Is defecation painful?**

**YES** →

**Anal fissure** (a tear in the lining of the anus) or haemorrhoids (see above right) may cause such pain. Consult your doctor.

**Treatment:** Your doctor will examine you to make an exact diagnosis. If you have an anal fissure, your doctor will probably advise you to add more fibre to your diet to prevent constipation (see *The benefits of a high-fibre diet*, p.215). and may prescribe a medicine to soften the faeces. If this treatment fails to cure the problem, a minor operation may be recommended. Treatment for haemorrhoids is outlined in the box below.

**NO**

**Do you have itching around the anus?**

**YES** →

**Have you noticed white, thread-like particles in your faeces?**

**YES** →

**Threadworms** may cause such symptoms. These harmless parasites may be passed on from one person to another or may be picked up from contaminated food. Consult your doctor.

**Treatment:** You will probably be given medicine to get rid of the worms. This is usually taken in two separate doses 2 weeks apart. The whole household may need to be treated. Until you have completed the treatment, be especially careful to wash your hands thoroughly after going to the lavatory and before preparing food.

**NO**

**NO**

**Do you have wart-like lumps around the anus?**

**YES** →

**Anal warts** may be caused by virus infection of the skin. Consult your doctor.

**Treatment:** Your doctor will probably refer you to a skin clinic, where the cause of the infection will be investigated. The warts may be removed surgically under local anaesthetic, or by freezing with liquid nitrogen or carbon dioxide.

**Pruritus ani** is the term used to describe itching around the anus that has no obvious physical cause. Consult your doctor.

**Treatment:** If your doctor can find no cause for your itching, he or she will probably suggest the following ways to reduce the irritation. Try to resist the urge to scratch. Wash the anus carefully twice a day, using water, but not soap. Use only soft toilet paper and wipe gently. Avoid tight underpants made of artificial fibres, cotton is best. Your doctor may also prescribe a soothing ointment.

**NO**

**Do you have a sore area just above the anus?**

**YES** →

**Pilonidal sinus** is a possibility. This is an uncommon condition that occurs when an ingrowing hair causes an infected sore. Consult your doctor.

**Treatment:** If your doctor confirms the diagnosis, he or she will probably arrange for you to be admitted to hospital for a minor operation to clean out the infected area.

**NO**

**Consult your doctor** if you are unable to make a diagnosis from this chart.

---

### TREATMENT FOR HAEMORRHOIDS

**Self-help**
People with haemorrhoids should be careful to include plenty of foods that are high in fibre in their diet (see *The benefits of a high-fibre diet,* p.215). This helps to keep the faeces soft, preventing painful constipation, which causes and aggravates the condition. It is also important to avoid straining when defecating, which increases the pressure on the swollen veins, and to keep the anal area clean and dry. In many cases no further treatment is needed.

**Professional treatment**
Your doctor will probably prescribe a cream or suppositories to shrink the haemorrhoids and reduce discomfort.

If haemorrhoids persist or are particularly troublesome, your doctor may refer you to an outpatient clinic where you may be offered one of several different treatments. The haemorrhoids may be injected with a special chemical to shrink them, or they may be destroyed by freezing – a technique known as cryosurgery. In other cases, a method called banding may be used. This involves placing a tight band around the base of the swollen vein, which then withers away over the next few days.

Surgical removal of haemorrhoids (haemorrhoidectomy) under general anaesthetic is now only rarely carried out.

# 104 General urinary problems

Consult this chart if you notice a change in your urinary habits – for instance, a change in the number of times you need to pass urine daily – or if you have difficulty in starting or controlling the flow of urine.

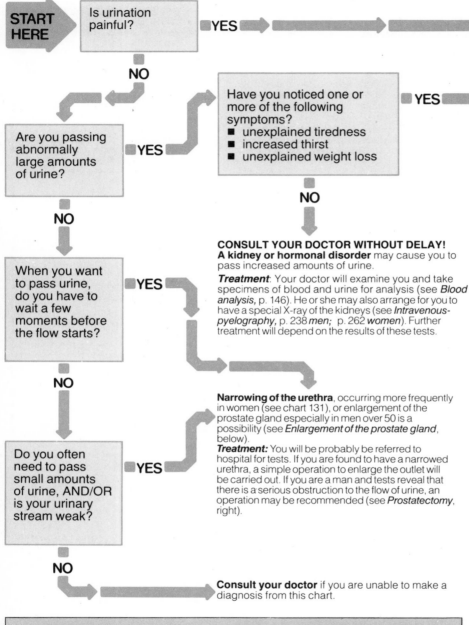

**START HERE**

**Is urination painful?**

**YES** → Go to chart **117** Men **132** Women **Painful urination**

**NO** ↓

**Are you passing abnormally large amounts of urine?**

**YES** → **Have you noticed one or more of the following symptoms?**
- unexplained tiredness
- increased thirst
- unexplained weight loss

**YES** → **Diabetes mellitus** is a possibility. This disorder is caused by insufficient production of the hormone insulin. Consult your doctor.
**Treatment:** If tests on blood (see *Blood analysis*, p.146) and urine confirm the diagnosis, you may need treatment with drugs or with regular injections of insulin. Your doctor will also advise you on diet.

**NO** ↓ (from symptoms box)

**CONSULT YOUR DOCTOR WITHOUT DELAY!**
**A kidney or hormonal disorder** may cause you to pass increased amounts of urine.
*Treatment*: Your doctor will examine you and take specimens of blood and urine for analysis (see *Blood analysis*, p. 146). He or she may also arrange for you to have a special X-ray of the kidneys (see *Intravenous-pyelography*, p. 238 *men*; p. 262 *women*). Further treatment will depend on the results of these tests.

**NO** ↓ (from large amounts box)

**When you want to pass urine, do you have to wait a few moments before the flow starts?**

**YES** →

**NO** ↓

**Do you often need to pass small amounts of urine, AND/OR is your urinary stream weak?**

**YES** → **Narrowing of the urethra**, occurring more frequently in women (see chart 131), or enlargement of the prostate gland especially in men over 50 is a possibility (see *Enlargement of the prostate gland*, below).
*Treatment:* You will be probably be referred to hospital for tests. If you are found to have a narrowed urethra, a simple operation to enlarge the outlet will be carried out. If you are a man and tests reveal that there is a serious obstruction to the flow of urine, an operation may be recommended (see *Prostatectomy*, right).

**NO** ↓

**Consult your doctor** if you are unable to make a diagnosis from this chart.

---

## WARNING

### INABILITY TO PASS URINE
If you find that you are unable to urinate even though you feel the urge, you may have a blocked urethra. This requires urgent medical attention to prevent damage to the bladder and kidneys. While waiting for medical help to arrive, try taking a warm bath; this may enable you to pass some urine.

### SUDDEN LOSS OF BLADDER CONTROL
Sudden inability to control urination may be a sign of damage to the spinal cord or nervous system, especially if you have recently had a back injury or if you have experienced weakness in your legs.

**Seek medical help at once!**

---

### PROSTATECTOMY
When the prostate gland becomes so enlarged that it seriously interferes with the flow of urine, an operation to remove part or all of the gland is usually necessary. This is known as prostatectomy. There are two main alternative types of operation available. The choice of methods depends on the details of the case. Both methods successfully relieve urinary symptoms of an enlarged prostate, but occasionally impotence or sterility results. Your doctor will discuss these risks with you. Both methods require a general anaesthetic.

### Traditional surgery
In a traditional prostatectomy, access to the gland is gained through an incision in the lower abdomen. The surgeon can then remove tissue from the gland as necessary.

### Transurethral resection (TUR)
In this form of prostatectomy, a tube is passed up the urethra from the penis to the prostate. This tube is fitted with a lens system and a cutting tool so that the surgeon can see the gland and cut away as much tissue as necessary.

---

### ENLARGEMENT OF THE PROSTATE GLAND
Nearly every man over the age of 50 has some degree of enlargement of the prostate, although this rarely becomes troublesome before the age of 55. It is a natural effect of ageing. As the gland becomes larger it tends to distort the urethra (the tube that carries the urine away from the bladder). This may make the flow of urine weak and, in extreme cases, may block it altogether.

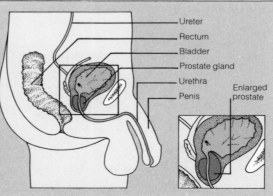

Ureter
Rectum
Bladder
Prostate gland
Urethra
Penis
Enlarged prostate

# 105 Palpitations

Palpitations is a term used to describe unusually rapid, strong, or irregular beating of the heart. It is normal for the heart rate to speed up during strenuous exercise and you may feel your heart "thumping" for some minutes after. This is no cause for concern. Consult this chart if you have palpitations unconnected with physical exertion. In most cases such palpitations are caused by nicotine and caffeine, or by anxiety. But in a small proportion of cases they are a symptom of an underlying illness. Palpitations that recur on several days or that are connected with pain or breathlessness should always be brought to your doctor's attention.

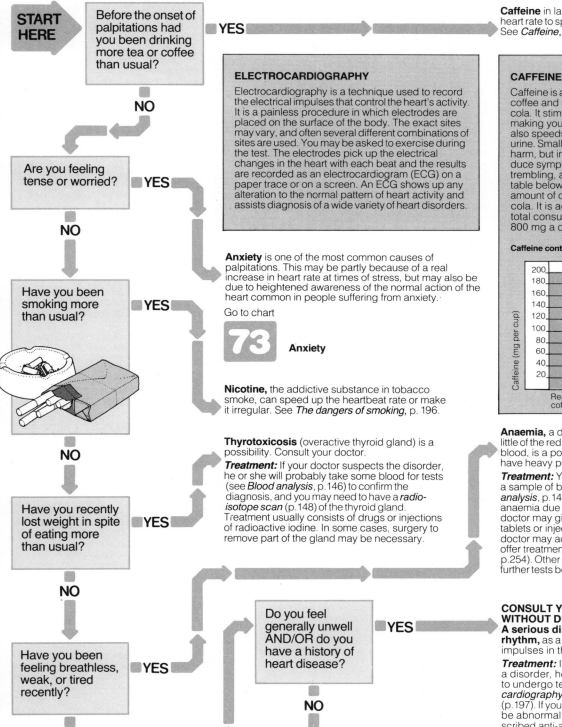

**START HERE**

**Before the onset of palpitations had you been drinking more tea or coffee than usual?**

**YES** → **Caffeine** in large doses can cause the heart rate to speed up or become irregular. See *Caffeine*, below.

**NO**

**Are you feeling tense or worried?**

**YES** → **Anxiety** is one of the most common causes of palpitations. This may be partly because of a real increase in heart rate at times of stress, but may also be due to heightened awareness of the normal action of the heart common in people suffering from anxiety.

Go to chart

**73** Anxiety

**NO**

**Have you been smoking more than usual?**

**YES** → **Nicotine,** the addictive substance in tobacco smoke, can speed up the heartbeat rate or make it irregular. See *The dangers of smoking*, p. 196.

**NO**

**Have you recently lost weight in spite of eating more than usual?**

**YES** → **Thyrotoxicosis** (overactive thyroid gland) is a possibility. Consult your doctor.

*Treatment:* If your doctor suspects the disorder, he or she will probably take some blood for tests (see *Blood analysis*, p.146) to confirm the diagnosis, and you may need to have a *radio-isotope scan* (p.148) of the thyroid gland. Treatment usually consists of drugs or injections of radioactive iodine. In some cases, surgery to remove part of the gland may be necessary.

**NO**

**Have you been feeling breathless, weak, or tired recently?**

**YES** → **Do you feel generally unwell AND/OR do you have a history of heart disease?**

**YES** → **CONSULT YOUR DOCTOR WITHOUT DELAY!**
**A serious disorder of heart rate or rhythm,** as a result of abnormal electrical impulses in the heart, is possible.

*Treatment:* If your doctor suspects such a disorder, he or she will arrange for you to undergo tests including *electro-cardiography* (above) and a *chest X-ray* (p.197). If your heart rhythms are found to be abnormal, you will probably be prescribed anti-arrhythmic drugs to regulate the heart's activity.

**NO**

**NO** → **Consult your doctor** if you are unable to make a diagnosis from this chart.

---

### ELECTROCARDIOGRAPHY

Electrocardiography is a technique used to record the electrical impulses that control the heart's activity. It is a painless procedure in which electrodes are placed on the surface of the body. The exact sites may vary, and often several different combinations of sites are used. You may be asked to exercise during the test. The electrodes pick up the electrical changes in the heart with each beat and the results are recorded as an electrocardiogram (ECG) on a paper trace or on a screen. An ECG shows up any alteration to the normal pattern of heart activity and assists diagnosis of a wide variety of heart disorders.

---

### CAFFEINE

Caffeine is a substance present in tea, coffee and some soft drinks, notably cola. It stimulates the nervous system, making you feel more energetic and also speeds up the production of urine. Small amounts of caffeine do no harm, but in large doses it may produce symptoms such as palpitations, trembling, and sleeplessness. The table below shows the average amount of caffeine in coffee, tea and cola. It is advisable to keep your total consumption of caffeine below 800 mg a day.

**Caffeine content of common drinks**

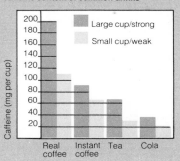

Caffeine (mg per cup): 200, 180, 160, 140, 120, 100, 80, 60, 40, 20

Large cup/strong
Small cup/weak

Real coffee · Instant coffee · Tea · Cola

---

**Anaemia,** a disorder in which there is too little of the red pigment haemoglobin in the blood, is a possibility, especially if you have heavy periods. Consult your doctor.

*Treatment:* Your doctor will probably take a sample of blood for analysis (see *Blood analysis*, p.146). If you are found to have anaemia due to iron deficiency, your doctor may give you iron in the form of tablets or injections. In addition, your doctor may advise you on diet and may offer treatment for heavy periods (see p.254). Other causes of anaemia require further tests before treatment can be given.

# 106 Chest pain

Pain in the chest (anywhere between the neck and the bottom of the rib cage) may be dull and persistent, sharp and stabbing, or crushing. Although it may be alarming, most chest pain does not have a serious cause. However, severe, crushing central chest pain, or pain that is associated with breathlessness or irregular heartbeat, may be a sign of a serious disorder of the heart or lungs and may warrant emergency treatment.

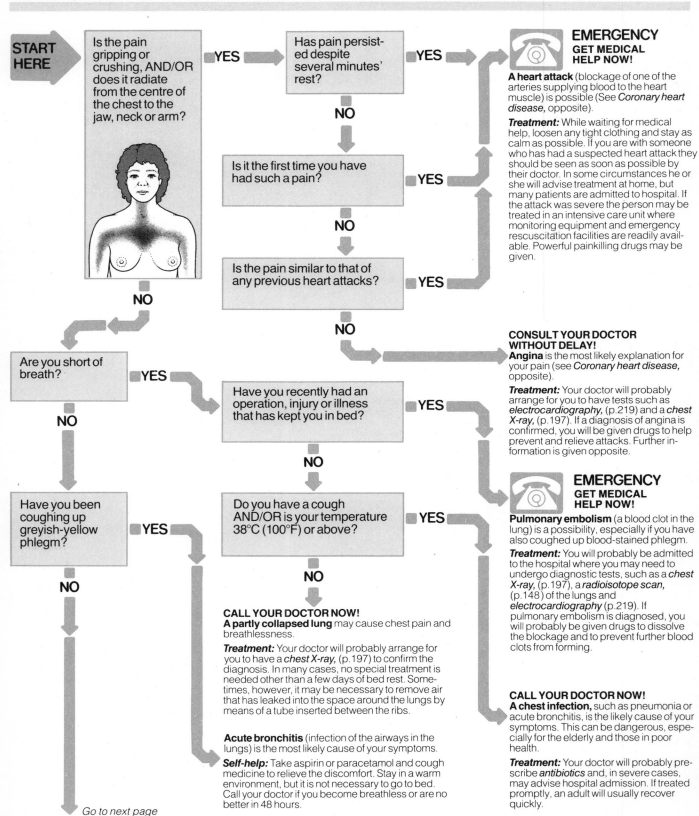

**START HERE**

**Is the pain gripping or crushing, AND/OR does it radiate from the centre of the chest to the jaw, neck or arm?**

YES → **Has pain persisted despite several minutes' rest?**

YES → **EMERGENCY GET MEDICAL HELP NOW!**

NO →

**Is it the first time you have had such a pain?**

YES →

NO →

**Is the pain similar to that of any previous heart attacks?**

YES →

NO →

NO →

**Are you short of breath?**

YES → **Have you recently had an operation, injury or illness that has kept you in bed?**

YES → **CONSULT YOUR DOCTOR WITHOUT DELAY!**

NO →

NO →

**Do you have a cough AND/OR is your temperature 38°C (100°F) or above?**

YES → **EMERGENCY GET MEDICAL HELP NOW!**

NO →

**Have you been coughing up greyish-yellow phlegm?**

YES →

NO →

*Go to next page*

## EMERGENCY GET MEDICAL HELP NOW!

**A heart attack** (blockage of one of the arteries supplying blood to the heart muscle) is possible (See *Coronary heart disease,* opposite).

***Treatment:*** While waiting for medical help, loosen any tight clothing and stay as calm as possible. If you are with someone who has had a suspected heart attack they should be seen as soon as possible by their doctor. In some circumstances he or she will advise treatment at home, but many patients are admitted to hospital. If the attack was severe the person may be treated in an intensive care unit where monitoring equipment and emergency rescuscitation facilities are readily available. Powerful painkilling drugs may be given.

## CONSULT YOUR DOCTOR WITHOUT DELAY!

**Angina** is the most likely explanation for your pain (see *Coronary heart disease,* opposite).

***Treatment:*** Your doctor will probably arrange for you to have tests such as *electrocardiography,* (p.219) and a *chest X-ray,* (p.197). If a diagnosis of angina is confirmed, you will be given drugs to help prevent and relieve attacks. Further information is given opposite.

## EMERGENCY GET MEDICAL HELP NOW!

**Pulmonary embolism** (a blood clot in the lung) is a possibility, especially if you have also coughed up blood-stained phlegm.

***Treatment:*** You will probably be admitted to the hospital where you may need to undergo diagnostic tests, such as a *chest X-ray,* (p.197), a *radioisotope scan,* (p.148) of the lungs and *electrocardiography* (p.219). If pulmonary embolism is diagnosed, you will probably be given drugs to dissolve the blockage and to prevent further blood clots from forming.

## CALL YOUR DOCTOR NOW!

**A chest infection,** such as pneumonia or acute bronchitis, is the likely cause of your symptoms. This can be dangerous, especially for the elderly and those in poor health.

***Treatment:*** Your doctor will probably prescribe *antibiotics* and, in severe cases, may advise hospital admission. If treated promptly, an adult will usually recover quickly.

## CALL YOUR DOCTOR NOW!

**A partly collapsed lung** may cause chest pain and breathlessness.

***Treatment:*** Your doctor will probably arrange for you to have a *chest X-ray,* (p.197) to confirm the diagnosis. In many cases, no special treatment is needed other than a few days of bed rest. Sometimes, however, it may be necessary to remove air that has leaked into the space around the lungs by means of a tube inserted between the ribs.

**Acute bronchitis** (infection of the airways in the lungs) is the most likely cause of your symptoms.

***Self-help:*** Take aspirin or paracetamol and cough medicine to relieve the discomfort. Stay in a warm environment, but it is not necessary to go to bed. Call your doctor if you become breathless or are no better in 48 hours.

*Continued from previous page*

**Is there a burning pain in the centre of the chest that gets worse when you bend over or lie down?**

**YES** →

**A hiatus hernia** may accompany leakage of acid juices (reflux) into the oesophagus, causing pain. The disorder occurs when part of the stomach protudes through the opening in the diaphragm and is more likely if you are overweight or in the last months of pregnancy (see chart 141, *Heartburn in pregnancy*). However, reflux may occur in the absence of hiatus hernia. Consult your doctor.

*Treatment:* See *Hiatus hernia,* (p.210).

**NO** ↓

**Do you have a pain in the middle of the chest that came on soon after eating?**

**YES** →

**Indigestion** is the most likely explanation for such pain. This may occur as a result of overeating or tension.

*Self-help:* In order to avoid attacks of indigestion, try not to eat in a hurry and allow yourself about half an hour's relaxation after a large meal. When attacks occur, take one of the many over-the-counter preparations that are available. Consult your doctor if pain becomes severe, or if attacks occur frequently.

**NO** ↓

**Is the pain on one side only?**

**YES** →

**NO** ↓

**Consult your doctor** without delay if you are unable to make a diagnosis from the chart.

**Have you recently had a chest injury or a severe cough?**

**YES** →

**NO** ↓

**Is the pain region tender to the touch?**

**YES** →

**A pulled muscle** or injury to the ligaments and cartilages of the rib cage are the most likely causes of your pain.

*Self-help:* Try not to strain the muscle further while you are feeling pain. A painkiller, such as aspirin or an aspirin substitute, will give relief, but, if pain persists for more than 48 hours, consult your doctor who may arrange for you to have a *chest X-ray,* (p.197) to rule out the possibility of a broken rib.

**NO** ↓

**Do you have a burning pain in the skin that is unaffected by breathing?**

**YES** →

**Shingles,** a virus infection of the nerves, is a possibility. The appearance of a blistery rash along the site of the pain a few days after the onset of pain will confirm the diagnosis. Consult your doctor.

*Treatment:* Your doctor will probably prescribe a painkiller and a soothing ointment to put on the skin. He or she may also prescribe an *antiviral* agent to hasten healing.

**NO** ↓

**Consult your doctor** without delay if you are unable to make a diagnosis from this chart.

---

## CORONARY HEART DISEASE

Coronary heart disease occurs when fatty deposits, or plaques, called atheroma, build up on the inside walls of the arteries that supply oxygenated blood to the heart muscle. This causes them to become narrowed and disturbs the flow of blood.

Coronary heart disease may cause chest pain (angina). This can occur after exertion or emotional stress, when the increased oxygen needs of the heart cannot be supplied through the narrowed coronary arteries. However, many people with coronary heart disease have no symptoms. Often the first indication of the disease is when they experience a heart attack, which occurs when a blood clot or build-up of atheroma blocks a coronary artery, cutting off the blood supply to part of the heart muscle. This can be fatal and even if it is not usually results in some permanent damage to the heart muscle.

### What is the treatment?
If you are found to have coronary heart disease, you will probably be advised to change any aspects of your life-style that seem to be contributing to the disease (see *Preventing coronary heart disease,* right). You will probably be given medicines to reduce the likelihood of angina attacks and others to take if attacks do occur. If you are found to have high blood pressure, this may also need drug treatment.

### Coronary artery bypass surgery
If your coronary arteries are found to be dangerously narrowed, you may be advised to have an operation in which the diseased sections of the coronary arteries are bypassed using healthy veins from the leg or an artery in the chest wall. This is a major operation, but the prospects for an active life and relief of chest pain are good.

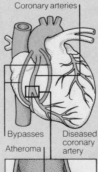

Coronary arteries

Bypasses — Diseased coronary artery

Atheroma

If surgery is necessary, the disease sections of the coronary ateries containing atheroma are bypassed, usually with multiple bypass sections.

### Preventing coronary heart disease
There are may factors that are known to increase the risk of developing coronary heart disease – notably, the tendency for the disease to run in families. But anyone who has a family history of heart disease can reduce the risk of developing serious problems by avoiding the factors listed below.

- **Smoking** Smokers are at least twice as likely to die of a heart attack than non-smokers. This is because substances in tobacco smoke increase the level of atheroma-forming fats in the bloodstream.

- **Obesity** Overweight people tend to eat higher-than-average amounts of fat, increasing the risk of atheroma build-up. Carrying too much weight places an increased strain on the heart, making it less able to withstand any restriction of its blood supply.

- **Too much fat in the diet** The tendency for atheroma to form in the arteries seems to be related to the level of certain types of fat in the bloodstream, which in turn is related partly to heredity, and partly to the amount of fat in the diet. Cutting down on all types of fat should help to reduce your risk of developing coronary heart disease.

- **Lack of exercise** Regular strenuous exercise increases the efficiency of the heart, so that it needs less oxygen to function well. If you gradually increase your physical fitness, your heart will be under less strain should its blood supply be reduced by coronary heart disease.

# 107 Back pain

Your backbone (or spine) extends from the base of your skull to the buttocks. Also known as the spinal column, it consists of more than 30 separate bones called vertebrae stacked on top of one another. In between each pair of vertebrae is a flexible disc. The vertebrae and discs are held together by ligaments. Through the centre of the spinal column is a space containing the spinal cord and the nerves that run from it to the rest of the body. Most people suffer from mild back pain from time to time, the exact cause of which may be difficult to diagnose. Back pain is usually a sign that you have damaged one or more joints, ligaments or discs by overstretching or twisting your back into an awkward position. Severe pain, however, may be the result of pressure on nerves from misalignment of the bones in the back and should receive medical attention.

**START HERE**

Did the pain follow an injury, fall or violent movement?

**YES**

Is it accompanied by one or more of the following?
- loss of bladder or bowel control
- difficulty in moving any limb
- numbness or tingling in any limb

**YES**

**EMERGENCY**
**GET MEDICAL HELP NOW!**

**Damage to the spinal cord** is possible. While waiting for medical help to arrive, a person with such symptoms should be kept warm, but not moved.

**Treatment:** In hospital, following a physical examination, spine X-rays (see *Bone X-rays*, p.225) may be carried out in order to determine the site and extent of any damage. Further treatment will depend on the results of these tests and doctors' observations. In some cases resting in bed will be sufficient to allow healing. In other cases surgery may be necessary.

**NO**

Do you have pain in one side of the small of your back just above the waist, AND do you feel generally unwell?

**YES**

**NO**

**Bruising or straining** has probably caused your backache.
**Self-help:** Take soluble aspirin or paracetamol to relieve the pain. You may also find that a hot-water bottle wrapped in a towel and placed on the painful site is helpful. The pain should clear up of its own accord, but if it is severe, or lasts more than 12 hours, or if you develop further symptoms, consult your doctor.

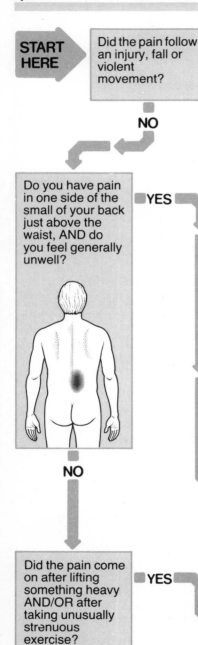

---

## SELF-HELP FOR BACK PAIN

If you are suffering from back pain that is caused by a minor strain or that has no obvious cause (non-specific backache), try the following self-help measures:

- Take the recommended dose of soluble aspirin or paracetamol.
- Lie on your back (or whichever position is most comfortable) on a firm mattress for as long as pain persists, only getting up when necessary.
- To help relieve your pain, try applying a hot-water bottle to your back.

If pain becomes severe, or is no better in 24 hours, consult your doctor, who may recommend that you consult a trained osteopath.

---

## WARNING

### PERSISTENT BACK PAIN

Whatever type of back pain you are suffering from, consult your doctor if it shows no signs of improvement after 12 hours' rest or immediately, if it is accompanied by loss of bowel or bladder control, or weakness, numbness or tingling in an arm or leg.

**NO**

**CONSULT YOUR DOCTOR WITHOUT DELAY!**
**An acute infection of the kidneys** may be the cause of this pain. This diagnosis is particularly likely if you also have a raised temperature.

**Treatment:** Your doctor will examine you and take a specimen of your urine. If a kidney infection is suspected, you may be given *antibiotics*. Your doctor may also arrange for you to have a special X-ray of the kidneys (see *Intravenous pyelography,* p.263 *women*; p.238 *men*) to find out whether or not there is an underlying cause of the problem.

Did the pain come on after lifting something heavy AND/OR after taking unusually strenuous exercise?

**YES**

Does the pain prevent you from moving OR does it shoot down one leg?

**YES**

**A prolapsed (slipped) disc** pressing on a nerve may cause such pain.

**Self-help:** Try the measures suggested under *Self-help for back pain* (above). If pain persists, consult your doctor, who may arrange for you to undergo tests. If you are found to have a prolapsed disc, your doctor may simply advise rest, recommend manipulation of the spine, or suggest that you wear a specially-fitted support corset. In severe cases of prolapsed disc, surgery may be recommended.

**NO**

**NO**

**Straining** of some of the muscles and/or ligaments in the back may be the cause of the pain. See *Types of back pain,* opposite.
**Self-help:** See *Self-help for back pain,* above right.

*Go to next page*

*Continued from previous page*

**Has your back gradually become stiff as well as painful over a period of months or years?**

YES → **Are you over 45?**

YES → **Is the pain mainly between the shoulder blades?**

YES →

NO ↓ (Has your back...)

NO ↓ (Are you over 45?)

NO ↓ (Is the pain mainly...)

**Ankylosing spondylitis** (inflammation of the joints between the vertebrae so that the spinal column gradually becomes hard and inflexible) may be the cause of this, especially if you are between 20 and 40. Consult your doctor.

*Treatment:* Your doctor will examine you and arrange for you to have a blood test (see *Blood analysis*, p.146) and an X-ray of your back and pelvic area (see *Bone X-rays*, p.225). If you are found to have ankylosing spondylitis, you will probably be given *anti-inflammatory* drugs. You will also be referred to a physiotherapist, who will teach you exercises that will help to keep your back mobile. Such mobility exercises are an essential part of the treatment for this disorder and can be supplemented by other physical activities such as swimming.

**Lumbar spondylosis,** a form of arthritis, is a possible diagnosis. This normally occurs as a result of wear and tear on the spine as you grow older. Consult your doctor.

*Treatment:* Your doctor will examine you and possibly arrange for you to have an X-ray (see *Bone X-rays*, p.225) and possibly a blood test (see *Blood analysis*, p.146) to check that no other disorder is responsible for these symptoms. If the diagnosis is confirmed, you will probably be prescribed painkillers and advised to practise exercises to strengthen the muscles in your back. You may be advised to wear a specially-fitted support corset. If you are overweight, your doctor will probably advise you to go on a weight-reducing diet (see *How to lose weight*, p.151).

**Did the pain come on suddenly after an extended stay in bed or confinement to a wheelchair, OR are you over 60?**

YES →

NO ↓

**CONSULT YOUR DOCTOR WITHOUT DELAY!**
**Sudden compression of a bone** in the spine as a result of thinning of the bones (osteoporosis) is possible.

*Treatment:* Your doctor will examine you and arrange for you to have an X-ray of the spine (see *Bone X-rays*, p.225) to confirm the diagnosis and to help him or her to determine the treatment that should follow. Your doctor will also probably advise you to eat a diet rich in calcium to keep your bones healthy. If you are in pain, he or she will prescribe painkillers and you may be prescribed other drugs to try to slow down the thinning process.

**Cervical spondylosis,** arthritis of the bones in the neck as a result of wear and tear, may be the cause of this pain. Consult your doctor.

*Treatment:* Your doctor will examine you and may arrange for you to have an X-ray of the bones in your neck (see *Bone X-rays*, p.225). If he or she thinks that the symptoms are due to this disorder, you may be given a supportive collar to wear to reduce neck mobility. Soluble aspirin or paracetamol can be taken to relieve the discomfort. If these measures fail to help, your doctor may send you to a physiotherapist for further treatment.

Go to chart

**140** **Back pain in pregnancy**

**Are you pregnant?**

YES →

NO ↓

**PREVENTING BACKACHE**

There are several practical ways in which you can minimize the amount of strain on your back to help prevent backaches. Feeling comfortable in any movement or position is a general guide to whether or not you are putting strain on your back. Below are some precautions you can take.

**Sitting correctly**
When sitting for any length of time, try to keep your back straight and avoid slumping. Choose a chair that has a firm, upright back that will support the length of your spine. You should be able to rest your feet flat on the floor with your knees bent at a right angle.

**Posture**
The correct way to stand to avoid placing unnecessary strain on your back is with your head, trunk and legs aligned.

**Sleeping**
Sleep on a firm mattress or put a board under your existing mattress. Use a single, flat pillow to support your head. These measures will support your back and prevent your spine from sagging into an unhealthy bend.

**Lifting**
When lifting a heavy object, get as close to it as possible. Keep your back straight and bend your knees so that your leg muscles, not the weaker back muscles, take the strain.

**Consult your doctor** if you are unable to make a diagnosis from this chart and if your back pain has not improved within 12 hours.

# 108 Painful or stiff neck

A stiff or painful neck is most often the result of a muscle stiffness brought on by sitting in a cold draught, sleeping in an uncomfortable position, or doing some form of exercise or activity to which you are not accustomed. This type of problem should resolve itself within a day or so. If pain and/or stiffness persist or become severe, ask your doctor for advice; you may require medical treatment.

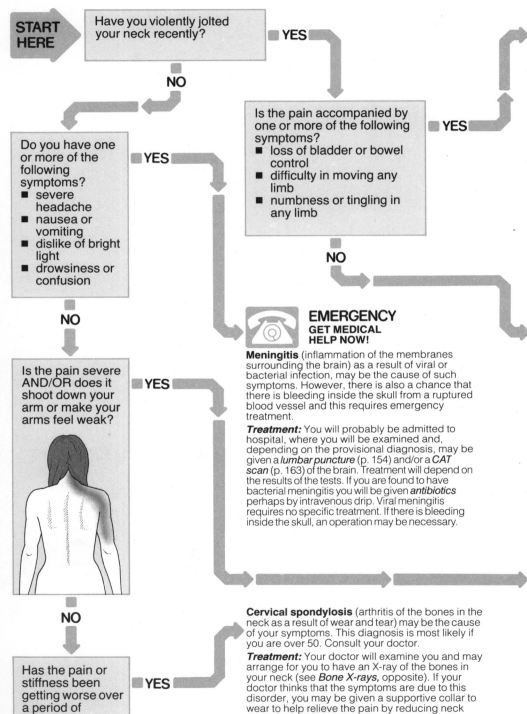

**START HERE**

Have you violently jolted your neck recently?

**NO**

**YES**

Do you have one or more of the following symptoms?
- severe headache
- nausea or vomiting
- dislike of bright light
- drowsiness or confusion

**YES**

**NO**

Is the pain accompanied by one or more of the following symptoms?
- loss of bladder or bowel control
- difficulty in moving any limb
- numbness or tingling in any limb

**YES**

**NO**

Is the pain severe AND/OR does it shoot down your arm or make your arms feel weak?

**YES**

**NO**

Has the pain or stiffness been getting worse over a period of months?

**YES**

**NO**

## EMERGENCY
### GET MEDICAL HELP NOW!

**Damage to the spinal cord** is possible. While waiting for medical help to arrive keep warm and do not move around.

***Treatment:*** You will probably be admitted to hospital, where *bone X-rays* (opposite) may be carried out in order to determine the extent of the damage. Further treatment will depend on the results of these tests and doctors' observations. In some cases resting in bed will be sufficient to allow healing. If there is little or no improvement, or if damage is severe, surgery may be necessary.

## EMERGENCY
### GET MEDICAL HELP NOW!

**Meningitis** (inflammation of the membranes surrounding the brain) as a result of viral or bacterial infection, may be the cause of such symptoms. However, there is also a chance that there is bleeding inside the skull from a ruptured blood vessel and this requires emergency treatment.

***Treatment:*** You will probably be admitted to hospital, where you will be examined and, depending on the provisional diagnosis, may be given a *lumbar puncture* (p. 154) and/or a *CAT scan* (p. 163) of the brain. Treatment will depend on the results of the tests. If you are found to have bacterial meningitis you will be given *antibiotics* perhaps by intravenous drip. Viral meningitis requires no specific treatment. If there is bleeding inside the skull, an operation may be necessary.

**A whiplash-type injury** can strain the muscles and ligaments in the neck causing pain and stiffness.

***Self-help:*** To rest your neck, lie down on a firm bed without a pillow. Take soluble aspirin or paracetamol for the pain. If you are no better in 24 hours, consult your doctor, who may recommend that you wear a supportive collar until the injury has healed. If you develop any of the symptoms described in the question above, call your doctor at once.

**A prolapsed (slipped) disc** in the neck may be the cause of this type of pain. This condition occurs when part of one disc between your vertebrae becomes displaced and presses against a nerve. Consult your doctor.

***Treatment:*** Your doctor will examine you and may arrange for you to have an X-ray of the bones in the neck (see *Bone X-rays,* opposite) to confirm the diagnosis. In the meantime your doctor may give you a supportive collar to wear to reduce neck mobility and to relieve pressure on the nerves. He or she will probably prescribe painkillers to ease discomfort. If the symptoms do not improve after these measures, you may be admitted to hospital for observation. In some cases surgery may be necessary.

**Cervical spondylosis** (arthritis of the bones in the neck as a result of wear and tear) may be the cause of your symptoms. This diagnosis is most likely if you are over 50. Consult your doctor.

***Treatment:*** Your doctor will examine you and may arrange for you to have an X-ray of the bones in your neck (see *Bone X-rays,* opposite). If your doctor thinks that the symptoms are due to this disorder, you may be given a supportive collar to wear to help relieve the pain by reducing neck mobility and relieving pressure on nearby nerves.

**Consult your doctor** if you are unable to make a diagnosis from this chart.

# 109 Painful arm

Pain in the arm is almost always the result of injury or straining of the muscles and ligaments that hold the various bones and joints in place. Such injuries are particularly likely to occur after any unaccustomed strenuous physical activity, such as playing a sport for the first time in many years. The pain should disappear if you rest your arm. However, if pain is recurrent or persistent, you should consult your doctor.

**START HERE**

**Did the pain immediately follow an injury, fall, or violent movement?**

YES →

**Are you unable to move your arm AND/OR is the pain severe even when resting?**

YES →

NO

**Is the pain mainly in the upper arm and does it come on only when you move your arm in a certain way?**

YES →

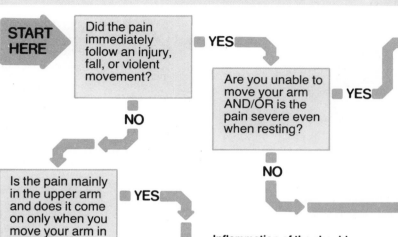

NO

**Do you have pain down the length of your arm?**

NO

**Do you also have "pins and needles" in your hand, especially at night?**

YES →

NO

## EMERGENCY
### GET MEDICAL HELP NOW!

**A fracture, dislocation or serious injury** to the muscles or ligaments may be causing this pain. See *First aid for suspected broken bones and dislocated joints*, p. 227.

***Treatment:*** In hospital the limb will be examined and probably X-rayed (see *Bone X-rays*, below) to discover the extent of the damage. Sometimes an operation to reposition the bones is necessary. Depending on the nature of the injury, you may need to wear a plaster cast or a firm bandage.

NO

**Injury to the soft tissues** (muscles, ligaments and cartilages) such as a sprain or strain, or bruising of the arm, is probably causing this pain.

***Self-help:*** Follow the advice on treating such injuries given in the box on p. 231. Consult your doctor if the pain is severe, or is no better in 24 hours. See also *Fitness and exercise*, p. 36, 37.

**Inflammation of the shoulder joint** (bursitis) as a result of injury or strain is the most likely cause of such pain, although certain forms of arthritis can also cause similar symptoms.

***Self-help:*** Take soluble aspirin or an over-the-counter *anti-inflammatory* drug to relieve the pain. Rest the arm while pain persists. Consult your doctor if you are no better in 3 days.

**Pressure on a nerve** as a result of displacement of a vertebral disc in your neck (see *Prolapsed disc*, opposite) or of arthritis (see *Cervical spondylosis*, opposite) is the most likely cause of such pain, especially if you also have numbness in the hand. Consult your doctor. However, if the pain came on with exercise and disappeared with rest, there is also the possibility of *angina* (p. 220) and in this case you should consult your doctor without delay.

YES →

**Carpal tunnel syndrome** is likely. In this disorder the nerves in the wrist are pinched due to swelling of surrounding tissues, resulting in pains in the arm and numbness and tingling in the hand. This condition is particularly common during pregnancy. Consult your doctor.

***Treatment:*** The condition often clears up of its own accord. Your doctor may refer you for tests to confirm the diagnosis and you may be given injections of *steroids* into the wrist. If the condition is persistent, a simple operation will relieve it.

### BONE X-RAYS

Because X-rays pass through soft tissues such as muscle and fat and clearly show up areas of bone, X-ray pictures are often used to diagnose the extent and nature of damage to any bones from injury or disease. This helps doctors to decide on the best form of treatment and, in the case of a broken (fractured) bone, whether or not an operation to reposition the pieces is necessary.

This bone X-ray shows a fracture in one of the bones in the lower arm. This type of break is difficult to diagnose without an X-ray.

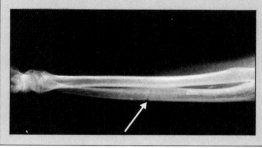

**Does the pain mainly affect your joints – for example, your shoulder, elbow or finger joints?**

YES →

Go to chart

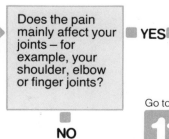

**112** **Painful or swollen joints**

NO

**Consult your doctor** if you are unable to make a diagnosis from this chart and if the pain is severe or persists for more than 24 hours.

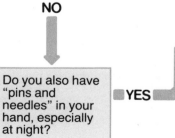

# 110 Painful leg

Pain or discomfort in the leg is almost always the result of injury or straining of the muscles and ligaments that hold the various joints in place. Such injuries are particularly likely if you take part in any unaccustomed activity, such as participating in a sport for the first time in many years. Such pain or discomfort should disappear if you rest your leg. However, persistent or recurrent pain may indicate an underlying disorder.

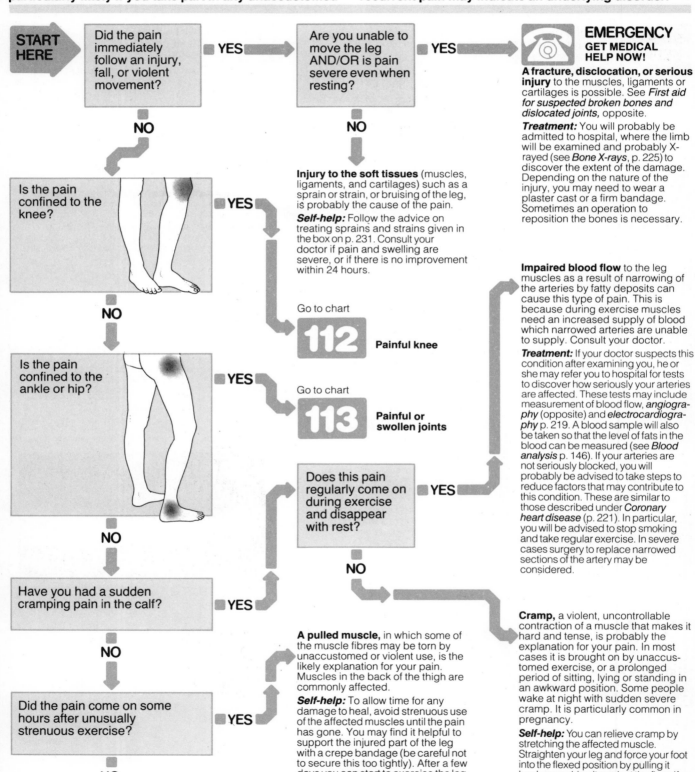

**START HERE**

**Did the pain immediately follow an injury, fall, or violent movement?**

— **YES** → **Are you unable to move the leg AND/OR is pain severe even when resting?** — **YES** →

## EMERGENCY
### GET MEDICAL HELP NOW!

**A fracture, dislocation, or serious injury** to the muscles, ligaments or cartilages is possible. See *First aid for suspected broken bones and dislocated joints,* opposite.

**Treatment:** You will probably be admitted to hospital, where the limb will be examined and probably X-rayed (see *Bone X-rays,* p. 225) to discover the extent of the damage. Depending on the nature of the injury, you may need to wear a plaster cast or a firm bandage. Sometimes an operation to reposition the bones is necessary.

**NO** ↓

**Is the pain confined to the knee?** — **YES** →

**NO** ↓ (first question)

**Injury to the soft tissues** (muscles, ligaments, and cartilages) such as a sprain or strain, or bruising of the leg, is probably the cause of the pain.

**Self-help:** Follow the advice on treating sprains and strains given in the box on p. 231. Consult your doctor if pain and swelling are severe, or if there is no improvement within 24 hours.

Go to chart

## 112
**Painful knee**

**NO** ↓

**Is the pain confined to the ankle or hip?** — **YES** →

Go to chart

## 113
**Painful or swollen joints**

**Impaired blood flow** to the leg muscles as a result of narrowing of the arteries by fatty deposits can cause this type of pain. This is because during exercise muscles need an increased supply of blood which narrowed arteries are unable to supply. Consult your doctor.

**Treatment:** If your doctor suspects this condition after examining you, he or she may refer you to hospital for tests to discover how seriously your arteries are affected. These tests may include measurement of blood flow, *angiography* (opposite) and *electrocardiography* p. 219. A blood sample will also be taken so that the level of fats in the blood can be measured (see *Blood analysis* p. 146). If your arteries are not seriously blocked, you will probably be advised to take steps to reduce factors that may contribute to this condition. These are similar to those described under *Coronary heart disease* (p. 221). In particular, you will be advised to stop smoking and take regular exercise. In severe cases surgery to replace narrowed sections of the artery may be considered.

**NO** ↓

**Does this pain regularly come on during exercise and disappear with rest?** — **YES** →

**NO** ↓

**Have you had a sudden cramping pain in the calf?** — **YES** →

**NO** ↓

**A pulled muscle,** in which some of the muscle fibres may be torn by unaccustomed or violent use, is the likely explanation for your pain. Muscles in the back of the thigh are commonly affected.

**Self-help:** To allow time for any damage to heal, avoid strenuous use of the affected muscles until the pain has gone. You may find it helpful to support the injured part of the leg with a crepe bandage (be careful not to secure this too tightly). After a few days you can start to exercise the leg again to prevent stiffness. If pain is severe, or if the leg becomes swollen, consult your doctor. (See also *Fitness and exercise,* p. 36, 37.

**Did the pain come on some hours after unusually strenuous exercise?** — **YES** →

**Cramp,** a violent, uncontrollable contraction of a muscle that makes it hard and tense, is probably the explanation for your pain. In most cases it is brought on by unaccustomed exercise, or a prolonged period of sitting, lying or standing in an awkward position. Some people wake at night with sudden severe cramp. It is particularly common in pregnancy.

**Self-help:** You can relieve cramp by stretching the affected muscle. Straighten your leg and force your foot into the flexed position by pulling it back or pushing it against the floor. If you suffer from frequent attacks of cramp, consult your doctor, who may prescribe muscle relaxant drugs.

**NO** ↓

*Go to next page*

*Continued from previous page*

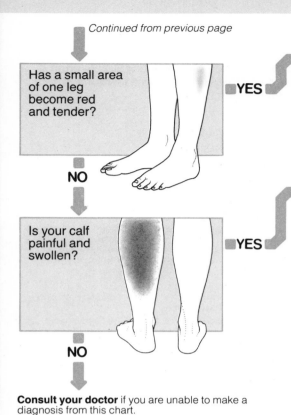

Has a small area of one leg become red and tender?

**YES** → **Thrombophlebitis** (inflammation of a superficial vein) is the likely cause of such symptoms. Consult your doctor.

**Treatment:** If your doctor confirms the diagnosis, he or she will probably prescribe painkillers and *anti-inflammatory* drugs. A sample of blood may be taken for analysis (see *Blood analysis*, p. 146) to find out if there is an underlying reason why you have developed this disorder.

**NO** ↓

Is your calf painful and swollen?

**YES** → **CONSULT YOUR DOCTOR WITHOUT DELAY!**
**Deep-vein thrombosis,** a condition in which a blood clot (thrombus) blocks a vein in the leg, may be the cause of such symptoms. This disorder is also likely to cause swelling of the ankle. People who have been immobilized by injury or illness for a long period, are particularly susceptible as are women who take the contraceptive pill or receive hormone replacement therapy (see *The menopause*, p. 252).

**Treatment:** Your doctor will examine you and if he or she confirms the possibility of deep-vein thrombosis, will probably arrange for you to be admitted to hospital for tests such as venography (see *Angiography*, below) to verify the diagnosis. Treatment for the condition consists of *anticoagulant* drugs to disperse and prevent blood clots. If you are taking the contraceptive pill, your doctor will advise you on the alternatives (see chart 136. *Choosing a contraceptive method*).

**NO** ↓

**Consult your doctor** if you are unable to make a diagnosis from this chart.

see chart 136. *Choosing a contraceptive method*

---

## VARICOSE VEINS

Varicose veins are swollen leg veins caused by poor circulation in the legs, usually as a result of damage to the valves in the veins. Women often develop varicose veins during pregnancy because of pressure on the pelvic veins from the growing baby. The veins in the back of the calf and along the inside of the leg are most commonly affected. Varicose veins are likely to cause aching of the leg and swelling of the ankle, especially after long periods of standing.

**Self-help measures**
If you think that you may be susceptible to varicose veins, especially if you are pregnant, or if you already have swollen veins in the leg, try to keep your weight off your feet as much as possible. Sit with your legs up on a footstool whenever you can, to help the blood to flow back up your leg. If you have to spend long periods standing up, flex your calf muscles every so often to help blood circulate in your leg. Wear support stockings or elastic bandages (your doctor or nurse will show you how to put these on). Consult your doctor if your varicose veins trouble you, or if the surrounding skin is cracked or sore.

**Professional treatment**
Your doctor may arrange for you to have tests such as venography (see *Angiography*, below). If varicose veins are severe and the self-help measures are not helpful, your doctor may recommend surgery to remove the affected veins, or they may be sealed off by the injection of a chemical agent.

---

## FIRST AID FOR SUSPECTED BROKEN BONES AND DISLOCATED JOINTS

A limb or joint that is very painful, that looks misshapen, or that will not move following an injury or fall may be broken and/or dislocated. Go to your local hospital accident department by the fastest means possible. If no help is readily available and/or if you are unable to move, summon an ambulance.

**General points**
- If there is bleeding from the wound, cover it firmly with a clean dressing.
- Do not try to manipulate the bone or joint back into position yourself; this should only be attempted by a doctor.
- While waiting for medical aid to arrive, a helper should try to keep the injured person warm and as calm as possible.
- A person with a suspected broken bone or dislocated joint should not eat or drink anything in case a general anaesthetic will be needed later in order to reset the bone.
- If you have to wait some time for medical attention, immobilize the limb in the most comfortable position, using bandages and splints as described below right.

**Arm injury**
Gently place the injured arm in the most comfortable position across the chest. Some padding should be placed between the arm and chest. Support the weight of the arm along its length together with the padding. If the arm cannot be bent, use bandages to secure the arm to the side of the body. A splint (right) may help to provide increased support.

**Shoulder, collar bone, or elbow injury**
Support the weight of the arm in a sling in the most comfortable position.

**Leg injury**
Secure the injured leg to the undamaged one. If possible, place a well-padded splint (below) between them.

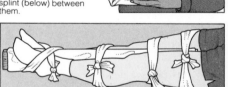

**Knee injury**
Support the joint in the most comfortable position. If the knee is bent, support it in the bent position. If the knee is unable to bend, support the leg along its length from underneath; use a plank or something similar as a splint. Place padding between the knee and the splint and around the heel.

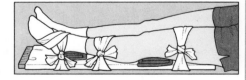

**Splints**
A splint is a firm support used to immobilize an injured part of the body (usually an arm or a leg) in order to reduce pain and minimize the likelihood of further damage. In an emergency you can make an improvised splint with a broom handle or rolled up newspaper. Secure a splint (not too tightly) on either side of the injury using wide lengths of material.

---

## ANGIOGRAPHY

This procedure allows doctors to take X-ray pictures of blood vessels that may have become narrowed or blocked. When an artery is under investigation the procedure is known as arteriography; examination of a vein is called venography.

**What happens**
During angiography, for which you may be given a sedative drug, a solution that is visible on X-ray is injected into the bloodstream. This is done either by injecting the solution directly into the blood vessel concerned, or by means of a fine tube (catheter) inserted through an incision in an accessible blood vessel. The catheter is passed along the blood vessel until it reaches the area to be examined. The solution is then released and X-rays taken.

# 111 Foot problems

Problems with feet rarely arise from a serious underlying disorder or disease. Most foot problems are the result of injury or failure to take good care of the feet (see Caring for your feet, below). Consult this chart if you have any pain, irritation, or itching in your feet, or if they become deformed in any way.

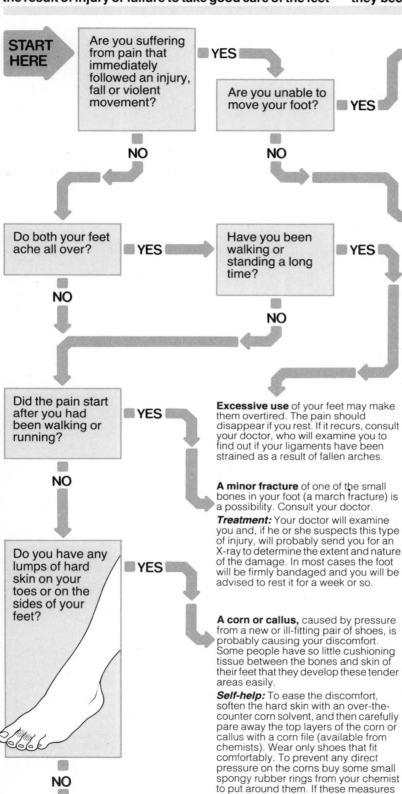

**START HERE**

Are you suffering from pain that immediately followed an injury, fall or violent movement? — **YES** → Are you unable to move your foot? — **YES** →

**EMERGENCY**
**GET MEDICAL HELP NOW!**

**A fracture, dislocation, or serious injury** to the ligaments or muscles may be causing this pain. Carry out the first aid measures for suspected broken bones and dislocated joints as described on p. 227.
**Treatment:** In hospital your foot will be examined and probably X-rayed to discover the extent of the damage. Sometimes an operation to reposition the bones is necessary. Depending on the nature of the injury, you may need to wear a plaster cast or a firm bandage.

**NO** ↓ (from first question)
**NO** ↓ (from "unable to move your foot")

**A soft tissue injury** such as a sprain, strain or bruising is probably causing this pain.
**Self-help:** Follow the advice on treating such injuries given in the box on p. 231. Consult your doctor if the pain is severe or is no better within 24 hours.

Do both your feet ache all over? — **YES** → Have you been walking or standing a long time? — **YES** →

**NO** ↓ (from "ache all over")
**NO** ↓ (from "walking or standing a long time")

Did the pain start after you had been walking or running? — **YES** →

**Excessive use** of your feet may make them overtired. The pain should disappear if you rest. If it recurs, consult your doctor, who will examine you to find out if your ligaments have been strained as a result of fallen arches.

**NO** ↓

Do you have any lumps of hard skin on your toes or on the sides of your feet? — **YES** →

**A minor fracture** of one of the small bones in your foot (a march fracture) is a possibility. Consult your doctor.
**Treatment:** Your doctor will examine you and, if he or she suspects this type of injury, will probably send you for an X-ray to determine the extent and nature of the damage. In most cases the foot will be firmly bandaged and you will be advised to rest it for a week or so.

**A corn or callus,** caused by pressure from a new or ill-fitting pair of shoes, is probably causing your discomfort. Some people have so little cushioning tissue between the bones and skin of their feet that they develop these tender areas easily.
**Self-help:** To ease the discomfort, soften the hard skin with an over-the-counter corn solvent, and then carefully pare away the top layers of the corn or callus with a corn file (available from chemists). Wear only shoes that fit comfortably. To prevent any direct pressure on the corns buy some small spongy rubber rings from your chemist to put around them. If these measures do not help and the corns or calluses persist for several weeks, consult your doctor, who may put you in touch with a foot specialist (chiropodist).

**NO** ↓

*Go to next page*

---

**CARING FOR YOUR FEET**

Ill-fitting shoes can sometimes lead to distortion of the toes and may lead to the development of painful conditions such as bunions and corns. When buying shoes take care to ensure that they fit properly, allowing enough space for the toes to spread out. Shoes with pointed toes and high heels should only be worn when you do not expect to be standing or walking for long periods. They are likely to damage the feet and make you adopt an unnatural posture that may lead to backaches and headaches.

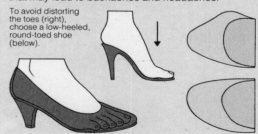

To avoid distorting the toes (right), choose a low-heeled, round-toed shoe (below).

**Foot hygiene**
Wash your feet daily, drying thoroughly between the toes to reduce the risk of fungal infection (athlete's foot). Wear socks made of natural fibres such as cotton or wool – they absorb moisture better than man-made fibres. If the skin of your feet is dry or cracked, apply a hand cream to the affected area.

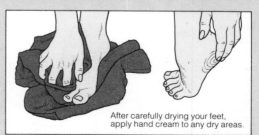

After carefully drying your feet, apply hand cream to any dry areas.

**Toenails**
Trim your toenails regularly, but do not cut them too short as this may damage the skin underneath. Always cut your toenails straight across.

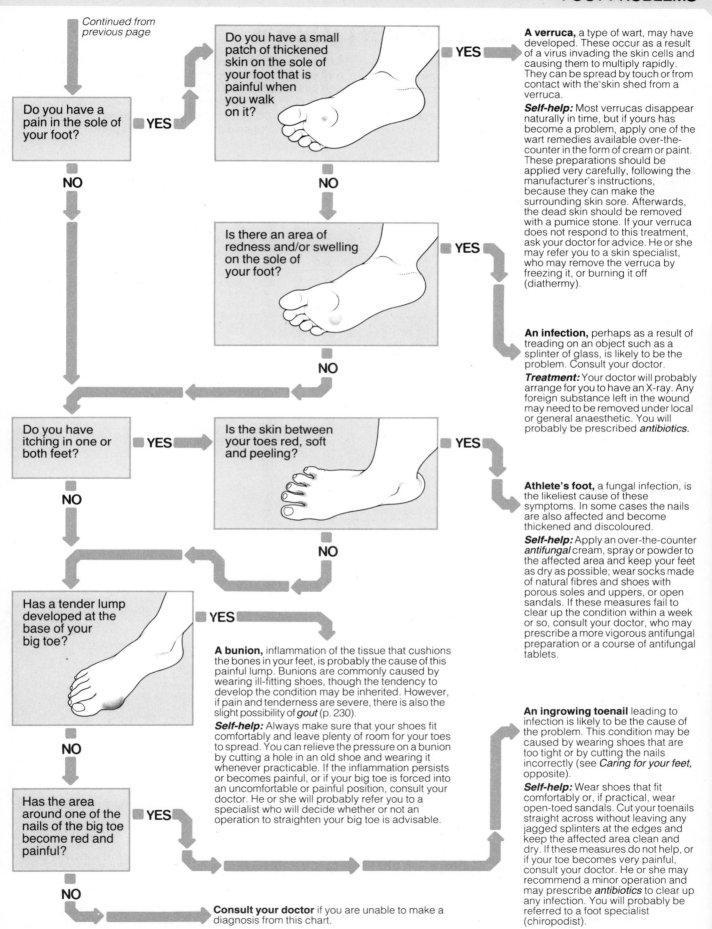

*Continued from previous page*

Do you have a small patch of thickened skin on the sole of your foot that is painful when you walk on it?

Do you have a pain in the sole of your foot?

**NO**

**YES**

**NO**

**YES**

**A verruca,** a type of wart, may have developed. These occur as a result of a virus invading the skin cells and causing them to multiply rapidly. They can be spread by touch or from contact with the skin shed from a verruca.

*Self-help:* Most verrucas disappear naturally in time, but if yours has become a problem, apply one of the wart remedies available over-the-counter in the form of cream or paint. These preparations should be applied very carefully, following the manufacturer's instructions, because they can make the surrounding skin sore. Afterwards, the dead skin should be removed with a pumice stone. If your verruca does not respond to this treatment, ask your doctor for advice. He or she may refer you to a skin specialist, who may remove the verruca by freezing it, or burning it off (diathermy).

Is there an area of redness and/or swelling on the sole of your foot?

**NO**

**YES**

**An infection,** perhaps as a result of treading on an object such as a splinter of glass, is likely to be the problem. Consult your doctor.

*Treatment:* Your doctor will probably arrange for you to have an X-ray. Any foreign substance left in the wound may need to be removed under local or general anaesthetic. You will probably be prescribed *antibiotics.*

Do you have itching in one or both feet?

**NO**

**YES**

Is the skin between your toes red, soft and peeling?

**NO**

**YES**

**Athlete's foot,** a fungal infection, is the likeliest cause of these symptoms. In some cases the nails are also affected and become thickened and discoloured.

*Self-help:* Apply an over-the-counter *antifungal* cream, spray or powder to the affected area and keep your feet as dry as possible; wear socks made of natural fibres and shoes with porous soles and uppers, or open sandals. If these measures fail to clear up the condition within a week or so, consult your doctor, who may prescribe a more vigorous antifungal preparation or a course of antifungal tablets.

Has a tender lump developed at the base of your big toe?

**NO**

**YES**

**A bunion,** inflammation of the tissue that cushions the bones in your feet, is probably the cause of this painful lump. Bunions are commonly caused by wearing ill-fitting shoes, though the tendency to develop the condition may be inherited. However, if pain and tenderness are severe, there is also the slight possibility of *gout* (p. 230).

*Self-help:* Always make sure that your shoes fit comfortably and leave plenty of room for your toes to spread. You can relieve the pressure on a bunion by cutting a hole in an old shoe and wearing it whenever practicable. If the inflammation persists or becomes painful, or if your big toe is forced into an uncomfortable or painful position, consult your doctor. He or she will probably refer you to a specialist who will decide whether or not an operation to straighten your big toe is advisable.

Has the area around one of the nails of the big toe become red and painful?

**NO**

**YES**

**An ingrowing toenail** leading to infection is likely to be the cause of the problem. This condition may be caused by wearing shoes that are too tight or by cutting the nails incorrectly (see *Caring for your feet,* opposite).

*Self-help:* Wear shoes that fit comfortably or, if practical, wear open-toed sandals. Cut your toenails straight across without leaving any jagged splinters at the edges and keep the affected area clean and dry. If these measures do not help, or if your toe becomes very painful, consult your doctor. He or she may recommend a minor operation and may prescribe *antibiotics* to clear up any infection. You will probably be referred to a foot specialist (chiropodist).

**Consult your doctor** if you are unable to make a diagnosis from this chart.

# 112 Painful or swollen joints

Joints occur at the junction of two or more bones and usually allow movement between these. The degree and type of movement allowed depends on the structure of the joint. Major joints, such as the hips, knees, and ankles, undergo constant wear and tear, and so minor degrees of discomfort or stiffness may occur from time to time. However, severe pain, swelling, or limitation of movement may be the result of damage to the bones or soft tissues of the joint from injury, or may indicate an underlying disorder of the joints or skeletal system. Consult this chart if you suffer to any extent from pain, stiffness and/or swelling in or around a joint.

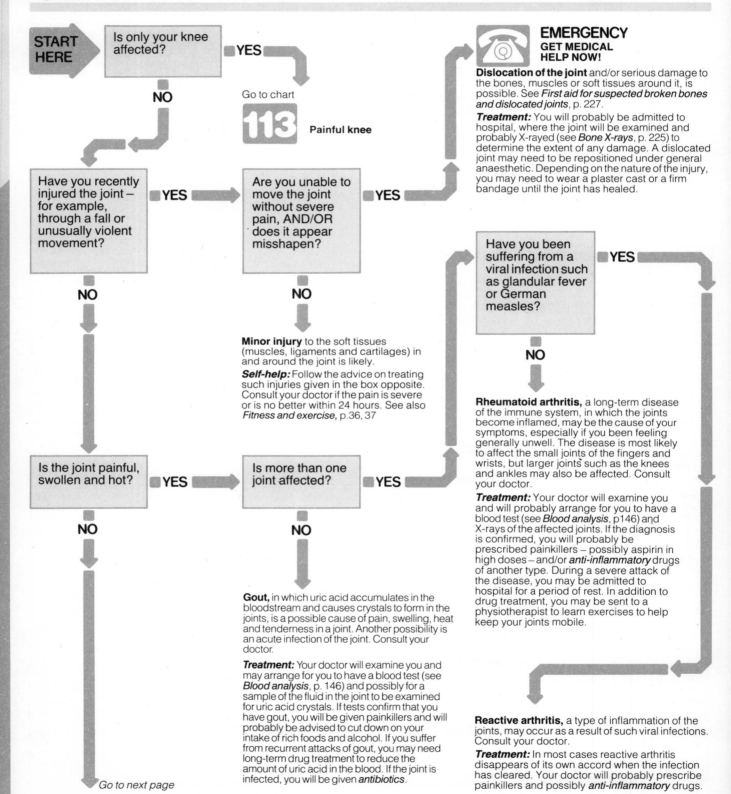

**START HERE**

**Is only your knee affected?** → **YES**

Go to chart **113** Painful knee

**NO**

**Have you recently injured the joint — for example, through a fall or unusually violent movement?** → **YES**

**Are you unable to move the joint without severe pain, AND/OR does it appear misshapen?** → **YES**

**NO**

**NO**

Minor injury to the soft tissues (muscles, ligaments and cartilages) in and around the joint is likely.
**Self-help:** Follow the advice on treating such injuries given in the box opposite. Consult your doctor if the pain is severe or is no better within 24 hours. See also *Fitness and exercise*, p.36, 37

**Is the joint painful, swollen and hot?** → **YES**

**Is more than one joint affected?** → **YES**

**NO**

**NO**

**Have you been suffering from a viral infection such as glandular fever or German measles?** → **YES**

**NO**

### EMERGENCY
**GET MEDICAL HELP NOW!**

**Dislocation of the joint** and/or serious damage to the bones, muscles or soft tissues around it, is possible. See *First aid for suspected broken bones and dislocated joints*, p. 227.

**Treatment:** You will probably be admitted to hospital, where the joint will be examined and probably X-rayed (see *Bone X-rays*, p. 225) to determine the extent of any damage. A dislocated joint may need to be repositioned under general anaesthetic. Depending on the nature of the injury, you may need to wear a plaster cast or a firm bandage until the joint has healed.

**Rheumatoid arthritis,** a long-term disease of the immune system, in which the joints become inflamed, may be the cause of your symptoms, especially if you been feeling generally unwell. The disease is most likely to affect the small joints of the fingers and wrists, but larger joints such as the knees and ankles may also be affected. Consult your doctor.

**Treatment:** Your doctor will examine you and will probably arrange for you to have a blood test (see *Blood analysis*, p146) and X-rays of the affected joints. If the diagnosis is confirmed, you will probably be prescribed painkillers – possibly aspirin in high doses – and/or *anti-inflammatory* drugs of another type. During a severe attack of the disease, you may be admitted to hospital for a period of rest. In addition to drug treatment, you may be sent to a physiotherapist to learn exercises to help keep your joints mobile.

**Gout,** in which uric acid accumulates in the bloodstream and causes crystals to form in the joints, is a possible cause of pain, swelling, heat and tenderness in a joint. Another possibility is an acute infection of the joint. Consult your doctor.

**Treatment:** Your doctor will examine you and may arrange for you to have a blood test (see *Blood analysis*, p. 146) and possibly for a sample of the fluid in the joint to be examined for uric acid crystals. If tests confirm that you have gout, you will be given painkillers and will probably be advised to cut down on your intake of rich foods and alcohol. If you suffer from recurrent attacks of gout, you may need long-term drug treatment to reduce the amount of uric acid in the blood. If the joint is infected, you will be given *antibiotics*.

**Reactive arthritis,** a type of inflammation of the joints, may occur as a result of such viral infections. Consult your doctor.

**Treatment:** In most cases reactive arthritis disappears of its own accord when the infection has cleared. Your doctor will probably prescribe painkillers and possibly *anti-inflammatory* drugs.

*Go to next page*

*Continued from previous page*

**Have you been suffering from pain and stiffness in one joint, particularly when you move it?**

**YES** →

**Has this come on gradually over a period of months or years?**

**YES** →

**Osteoarthritis,** as a result of wear and tear on the joint, is a possible cause of such pain, especially if you are over 50 or if you have regularly overused the joint at work or playing sport. Consult your doctor.

***Treatment:*** Your doctor will examine you and may arrange for you to have a blood test (see *Blood analysis*, p. 146) to exclude other possible causes of pain, and you may need to have an X-ray of the joint. If these investigations confirm the diagnosis, your doctor will prescribe painkillers. If you are overweight, it will help if you try to lose weight (see *How to lose weight*, p. 151). In some cases exercises supervised by a physiotherapist and/or heat treatment may be helpful.

**NO** ↓

**NO** ↓

**Bursitis,** inflammation of the soft fluid-filled cushions around the joint, may be the cause of your trouble.

***Self-help:*** Take soluble aspirin or paracetamol for the pain, and rest the joint as much as possible. This usually clears up the problem. If pain persists or becomes severe, consult your doctor, who will examine the joint and may inject it with a mixture of *anti-inflammatory* and painkilling drugs.

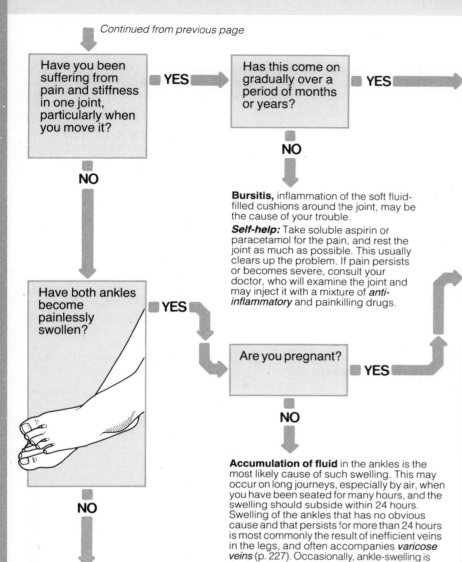

**Have both ankles become painlessly swollen?**

**YES** →

Go to chart

**144**

**Ankle-swelling in pregnancy**

**Are you pregnant?**

**YES** →

**NO** ↓

**NO** ↓

**FROZEN SHOULDER**

Frozen shoulder is a condition that sometimes occurs following a minor injury to the shoulder, or a condition such as bursitis (left). The shoulder becomes stiff and sometimes painful, and this leads to a reduction in its range of movement. Disuse can then lead to further stiffness and further limitation of movement. Frozen shoulder often persists for many months.

**Treatment**

If you think you have frozen shoulder or if you have recently suffered from a painful shoulder condition, it is important to keep the shoulder mobile by regular exercise. Take painkillers such as soluble aspirin or paracetamol, if necessary. Consult your doctor, who may prescribe *anti-inflammatory* drugs by mouth or in the form of an injection into the shoulder. Exercises under the supervision of a physiotherapist may also be recommended.

**Accumulation of fluid** in the ankles is the most likely cause of such swelling. This may occur on long journeys, especially by air, when you have been seated for many hours, and the swelling should subside within 24 hours. Swelling of the ankles that has no obvious cause and that persists for more than 24 hours is most commonly the result of inefficient veins in the legs, and often accompanies *varicose veins* (p. 227). Occasionally, ankle-swelling is the result of a heart or kidney condition. Consult your doctor about any persistent ankle-swelling. Do this without delay if you have noticed additional symptoms such as breathlessness, unusual fatigue, or swelling in any other part of the body.

**Consult your doctor** if you are unable to make a diagnosis from this chart and the pain and/or swelling is severe or persists for more than 48 hours.

---

**FIRST AID FOR SPRAINS AND STRAINS**

A joint is said to be sprained when it is wrenched or twisted beyond its normal range of movement – in a fall, for example – so as to tear some or all of the ligaments that support it. Ankles are especially prone to this type of injury. The main symptoms – which may be indistinguishable from those of a minor strain – are pain, swelling and bruising. If you are unable to move the injured part, or if it looks misshapen, a broken bone or dislocated joint is possible, and you should carry out first aid as described on p. 227. In other cases try the following first aid treatment:

**1** As soon as possible after the injury, cool the injured part (see below right).

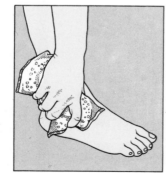

**2** Support an injured joint or limb with a firm, but not overtight, bandage. An arm or wrist may be more comfortable in a sling.

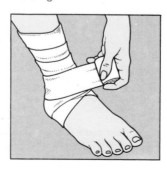

If you have a badly sprained ankle that is still painful 24 hours after the injury, you should go to your doctor or local hospital accident department to have the joint firmly bandaged to prevent movement while the joint is healing. In this case you should make sure that you rest the joint for at least a week.

**Cooling an injury**
Applying cold to any injury causing pain, swelling and/or bruising will help to reduce inflammation and relieve pain. This is best done by use of an ice pack (a cloth bag filled with ice), but you can improvise such a pack by using an unopened packet of frozen vegetables. Alternatively, you can try immersing the injured part in cold water.

**3** Rest the injured part for a day or so. If it is a foot, leg or ankle that is injured, keep it raised whenever possible.

# 113 Painful knee

The knee is one of the principal weight-bearing joints in the body and is subject to much wear and tear in an averagely active person. If your work involves a great deal of bending or squatting, the risk of damage to the knee through overuse and/or injury is increased. Consult this chart if you have pain in one or both knees.

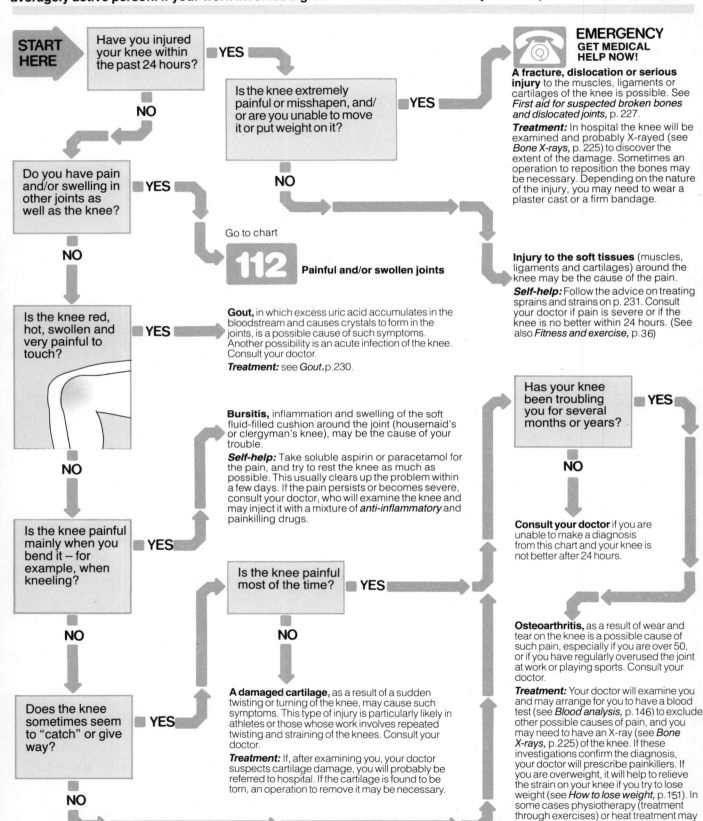

**START HERE**

**Have you injured your knee within the past 24 hours?** → **YES**

**Is the knee extremely painful or misshapen, and/or are you unable to move it or put weight on it?** → **YES** → **EMERGENCY GET MEDICAL HELP NOW!**

**A fracture, dislocation or serious injury** to the muscles, ligaments or cartilages of the knee is possible. See *First aid for suspected broken bones and dislocated joints,* p. 227.

**Treatment:** In hospital the knee will be examined and probably X-rayed (see *Bone X-rays,* p. 225) to discover the extent of the damage. Sometimes an operation to reposition the bones may be necessary. Depending on the nature of the injury, you may need to wear a plaster cast or a firm bandage.

(From "Is the knee extremely painful...") **NO** →

Go to chart **112** **Painful and/or swollen joints**

**Injury to the soft tissues** (muscles, ligaments and cartilages) around the knee may be the cause of the pain.

**Self-help:** Follow the advice on treating sprains and strains on p. 231. Consult your doctor if pain is severe or if the knee is no better within 24 hours. (See also *Fitness and exercise,* p.36)

(From START, if "Have you injured...") **NO** →

**Do you have pain and/or swelling in other joints as well as the knee?** → **YES** (go to chart 112)

**NO** ↓

**Is the knee red, hot, swollen and very painful to touch?** → **YES** →

**Gout,** in which excess uric acid accumulates in the bloodstream and causes crystals to form in the joints, is a possible cause of such symptoms. Another possibility is an acute infection of the knee. Consult your doctor.
**Treatment:** see *Gout,* p.230.

**NO** ↓

**Is the knee painful mainly when you bend it – for example, when kneeling?** → **YES** →

**Bursitis,** inflammation and swelling of the soft fluid-filled cushion around the joint (housemaid's or clergyman's knee), may be the cause of your trouble.
**Self-help:** Take soluble aspirin or paracetamol for the pain, and try to rest the knee as much as possible. This usually clears up the problem within a few days. If the pain persists or becomes severe, consult your doctor, who will examine the knee and may inject it with a mixture of *anti-inflammatory* and painkilling drugs.

**NO** ↓

**Does the knee sometimes seem to "catch" or give way?** → **YES** →

**Is the knee painful most of the time?** → **YES** →

**NO** ↓ (from "Is the knee painful most of the time?")

**A damaged cartilage,** as a result of a sudden twisting or turning of the knee, may cause such symptoms. This type of injury is particularly likely in athletes or those whose work involves repeated twisting and straining of the knees. Consult your doctor.
**Treatment:** If, after examining you, your doctor suspects cartilage damage, you will probably be referred to hospital. If the cartilage is found to be torn, an operation to remove it may be necessary.

**Has your knee been troubling you for several months or years?** → **YES** →

**NO** ↓

**Consult your doctor** if you are unable to make a diagnosis from this chart and your knee is not better after 24 hours.

**Osteoarthritis,** as a result of wear and tear on the knee is a possible cause of such pain, especially if you are over 50, or if you have regularly overused the joint at work or playing sports. Consult your doctor.
**Treatment:** Your doctor will examine you and may arrange for you to have a blood test (see *Blood analysis,* p. 146) to exclude other possible causes of pain, and you may need to have an X-ray (see *Bone X-rays,* p.225) of the knee. If these investigations confirm the diagnosis, your doctor will prescribe painkillers. If you are overweight, it will help to relieve the strain on your knee if you try to lose weight (see *How to lose weight,* p.151). In some cases physiotherapy (treatment through exercises) or heat treatment may help.

(bottom: Does the knee... "catch or give way?") **NO**

# 3 Special problems: men

# 114 Baldness

Male pattern baldness is the term used to describe the type of hair loss that affects many men as they grow older. It is a natural and irreversible part of the ageing process. Some men start to lose their hair as early as 20, and the majority have lost their hair to some extent by the age of 60, although some men retain a full head of hair until old age. In most cases hair loss is first noticed when the hairline at the front starts to recede.

**START HERE** → **Have one or more bald patches suddenly developed?**

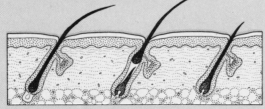

**YES** → **Is the skin in the bald areas scaly and inflamed?**

**YES** → **A fungal infection** such as ringworm is the possible cause of this problem. Consult your doctor.
*Treatment:* If your doctor confirms the diagnosis, you will be prescribed an *antifungal* shampoo and possibly a course of antifungal tablets. Your hair should return to normal in a few months. In the meantime, wash your hairbrush and comb thoroughly to prevent reinfection.

**NO** ↓

**Is your front hairline receding AND/OR is the hair on top of your head particularly thin?**

**YES** → **Alopecia areata** may be the reason for sudden patchy hair loss. This disease is not fully understood but it may be connected with tension or other emotional factors such as depression and anxiety. Consult your doctor to confirm the diagnosis, but often the condition disappears without treatment and new hair grows within 6 to 9 months.

**Hormonal changes** may cause this type of baldness. See *Male pattern baldness,* below.

**NO** (under first box) ↓

**NO** (under second box) ↓

**Consult your doctor** if you are unable to make a diagnosis from this chart.

---

## THE CAUSES OF MALE PATTERN BALDNESS

Male pattern baldness occurs when the rate of hair loss in certain areas exceeds the rate of hair replacement. The exact cause of this is not known, although it may be related to an increased production of androgen, a male sex hormone that is thought to limit hair growth. The tendency to lose hair at a certain age is probably inherited. You may inherit this tendency from one or both sides of your family. If men on both sides of your family have become bald at an early age, you are also likely to lose your hair early. However, if early baldness runs only on one side of the family, your chances of retaining your hair longer are increased.

### Concealing hair loss
Because male pattern baldness is irreversible, there is no cure for such hair loss. There is no proof that changes in diet, or that taking large doses of vitamins or minerals, can do anything to reverse or slow down hair loss. Most men simply accept their changing appearance and adopt a new hairstyle to take account of this hair loss.

If you wish to conceal baldness, there are several alternatives with varying degrees of effectiveness. The most straightforward and least risky alternative is a simple hairpiece (toupée). Hair weaving is another possibility. It involves attaching a hairpiece to existing hair on the scalp. The weave requires maintenance throughout its life as and when your natural hair, which anchors the weave in place, grows. Hair transplantation (below) is an expensive and often unsatisfactory alternative.

**The development of male pattern baldness**

1

2

3

### The cycle of hair loss and growth

1 When a hair stops growing, the root forms a bulb shape and becomes detached from the base of the follicle.
2 The old hair then moves up the follicle and is shed. A new hair starts to form at the bottom of the follicle.
3 The hair may remain in the growing phase for several years.

**Wearing a toupée**

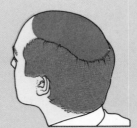

### Hair transplantation
In most types of hair transplant, hair from an area of thick growth (donor site) – often the back of the head – is implanted in the bald area (recipient site). This is a lengthy and painful process. Always seek medical advice first.

■ Recipient site

■ Donor site

# 115 Painful or swollen testicles

The commonly-used term, testicles, or testes, refers both to the sperm-producing glands and to the supportive bag that encloses them – the scrotum. Consult this chart if you feel any pain or notice a lump or swelling in or around one or both of your testes or in the whole area within the scrotum. It is important, that you also seek your doctor's advice, because early treatment of an underlying disorder reduces the risk of infertility.

**START HERE**

Have one or both testicles suddenly become painful?

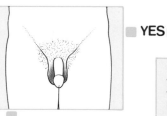

**YES**

Have you injured your genitals within the past 48 hours?

**YES**

**NO**

**NO**

Have you recently had mumps?

**YES**

**NO**

### WARNING

**LUMPS AND SWELLINGS**

Any lump or swelling in the testicles may be a symptom of disease even if it causes no pain.

**Consult your doctor without delay!**

## EMERGENCY GET MEDICAL HELP NOW!

**Internal damage to the testes** as a result of injury may have caused the pain, especially if there is also swelling.

***Treatment:*** You may need to spend some time in hospital, where your problem can be treated surgically, if necessary. If you need to have an operation, full recovery normally takes a few weeks.

**Orchitis,** a fairly common cause of swelling of one or both testes, is probably the cause of this. In rare cases, the disorder may cause infertility (see *Mumps and sterility,* p. 246). Consult your doctor.

***Treatment:*** Your doctor will examine you to rule out the possibility of your having a more serious infection of the lymph glands. He or she will probably prescribe painkillers for you to take to relieve the pain and advise you to rest in bed. It may be helpful to wear a jock strap. The pain and swelling normally subside within 2 weeks without aftereffects.

### SELF-EXAMINATION OF THE TESTES

Cancer of the testis, although rare in comparison with other cancers, is one of the most easily treated if diagnosed early. It is therefore a good idea to examine yourself regularly for any abnormalities.

**Self-examination technique**
About once a month, after you have had a hot bath or shower, when the skin of your scrotum is soft, examine your scrotum and testes following the guidelines below. Look for any change in size, shape or consistency of the testes. After doing this for a while you will get to know this part of your body well enough to detect any changes at an early stage.

1  Examine each testis by placing your index and middle fingers beneath the testis with your thumb on top as illustrated (below).

2  Gently roll each testis beneath your fingers and thumb, backward and forward and then sideways.

If you notice a new lump, (whether or not it is painful) any increased sensitivity in the scrotum, or any change in the skin, consult your doctor, who will refer you, if necessary, to a urologist for further tests.

## EMERGENCY GET MEDICAL HELP NOW!

**Torsion of the testes** (twisting of the testes inside the scrotum) is possible. This can happen at any time, even during sleep, and may be accompanied by nausea and vomiting.

***Treatment:*** You will be examined in hospital. If the diagnosis is confirmed, a doctor may try to untwist the testis by gently manipulating it. If this does not prove successful, or if the problem recurs, emergency surgery may be necessary.

**CONSULT YOUR DOCTOR WITHOUT DELAY!**
**A cyst** (fluid-filled sac) may have formed inside the scrotum. Although such cysts are harmless and can grow quite large before causing any discomfort, it is nevertheless important to see your doctor so that he or she can rule out the possibility of a tumour. Cysts are most common in men over the age of 40, although they can occur at any age.

***Treatment:*** Your doctor will examine you and probably refer you to a specialist for tests including a *biopsy* (p.35). If the swelling is caused by a cyst, further treatment is unnecessary unless the cyst grows too big for comfort, in which case it will be cut away in a minor operation. If tests reveal a tumour, surgery is the usual treatment.

Is one of your testes enlarged?

**YES**

**NO**

Do you have generalized, painless swelling of the scrotum?

**YES**

**NO**

**Hydrocele** – accumulation of a clear, thin fluid between the fibrous layers that cover the testes – may be causing this. The condition is quite common, especially in older men, though it can happen at any age. Consult your doctor.

***Treatment:*** Your doctor will examine you to decide whether or not you may need to have the fluid drawn off by needle under local anaesthetic at the outpatient department of your local hospital. If the problem recurs, your doctor may advise you to have a minor operation to tighten or remove one of the fibrous layers so that the fluid can no longer accumulate.

**Consult your doctor** if you are unable to make a diagnosis from this chart

# 116 Painful penis

Pain in the penis or soreness of the overlying skin can signal a variety of different disorders of the penis itself or of the urinary tract. Many painful conditions of the penis are the result of minor injuries such as bruising or abrasion – perhaps incurred while engaged in active sports – or from friction with clothing. Nevertheless, it is important that any pain or change in the appearance of your penis not attributable to an injury of this kind should be diagnosed by your doctor at an early stage, so that any treatment can be started promptly.

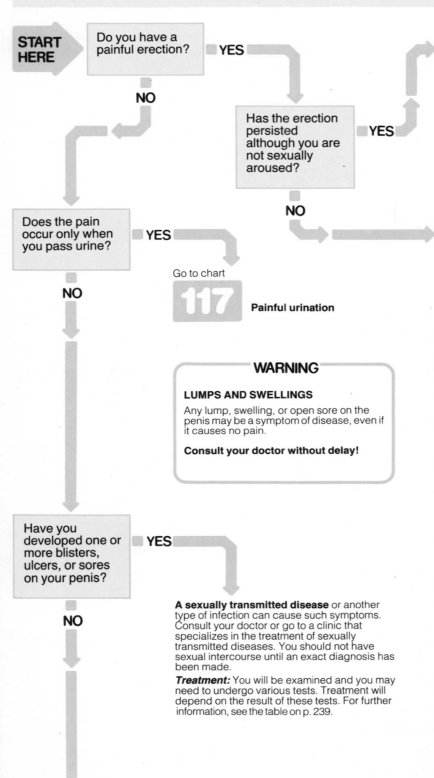

**START HERE**

**Do you have a painful erection?**

NO

YES

**Has the erection persisted although you are not sexually aroused?**

YES

NO

**Does the pain occur only when you pass urine?**

YES

NO

Go to chart

**117**

**Painful urination**

**EMERGENCY**
**GET MEDICAL HELP NOW!**

**Priapism,** a condition caused by sudden obstruction of the blood vessels so that blood cannot flow away from the erect penis, is possible.

**Treatment:** You will be examined in hospital. In some cases surgery is necessary to restore normal blood flow. In other cases the condition can be treated by drugs. If priapism is relieved quickly, you should be able to have normal erections again and return to a normal sex life.

**An overtight foreskin** may be the cause of such pain. Do not try to force the foreskin back over the penis. Consult your doctor.

**Treatment:** Your doctor will examine you and may suggest that you have a minor operation to have the foreskin removed (see *Circumcision*, below).

---

## WARNING

**LUMPS AND SWELLINGS**

Any lump, swelling, or open sore on the penis may be a symptom of disease, even if it causes no pain.

**Consult your doctor without delay!**

---

**Have you developed one or more blisters, ulcers, or sores on your penis?**

YES

NO

Go to next page

**A sexually transmitted disease** or another type of infection can cause such symptoms. Consult your doctor or go to a clinic that specializes in the treatment of sexually transmitted diseases. You should not have sexual intercourse until an exact diagnosis has been made.

**Treatment:** You will be examined and you may need to undergo various tests. Treatment will depend on the result of these tests. For further information, see the table on p. 239.

---

**CIRCUMCISION**

This is a surgical operation to remove the fold of skin, known as the foreskin, that covers the tip (glans) of the penis. Occasionally, the operation is carried out for medical reasons – for example, if the foreskin becomes tight or uncomfortable and is difficult to roll back. However, most circumcisions are done for social and religious reasons in infancy.

Circumcision has no significant effect on sexual performance – in particular, there is no firm evidence to suggest that it reduces sensitivity at the tip of the penis during intercourse or that it delays orgasm. Neither is it necessarily more hygienic to have the foreskin removed. By paying careful attention when washing to remove all secretions from beneath the foreskin (see *Genital hygiene*, opposite) you will ensure adequate cleanliness. Circumcision, like any operation, carries a small risk, and for this reason, most doctors now advise against the operation unless it is medically necessary.

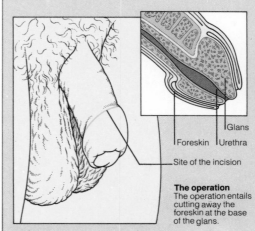

Glans
Foreskin  Urethra
Site of the incision

**The operation**
The operation entails cutting away the foreskin at the base of the glans.

*Continued from previous page*

**Do you have one or more hard, skin-coloured lumps on your penis?** — **YES**

**Anogenital warts,** caused by virus infection, are likely. These often grow quite quickly and can be irritating. They are usually transmitted by sexual contact, but this is not always the case. They may disappear spontaneously, but often recur. Do not attempt to treat this condition yourself with over-the-counter preparations, because the skin of the penis is very sensitive. Consult your doctor.

**Treatment:** Your doctor may prescribe a preparation in the form of a cream or paint to apply to the warts. He or she will probably advise you to keep the affected area as clean and dry as possible with regular washing, using a mild soap and then gently patting dry. Your doctor will also examine you to rule out the possibility of a sexually transmitted disease (p. 239) and will also advise you to avoid sexual contact until the warts have disappeared.

**NO**

**Can you see any redness or swelling on the tip (glans) of your penis?** — **YES**

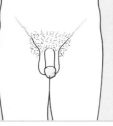

**Balanitis,** inflammation of the foreskin or tip of the penis (glans), is likely. This is usually caused by irritation from infection, clothing, or from skin secretions (smegma) collecting under the foreskin. In some cases soreness and swelling make it difficult to draw the foreskin back to clean underneath. Consult your doctor.

**Treatment:** Your doctor will examine you and may prescribe an **antibiotic** cream or tablets to relieve the inflammation. You will need to pay careful attention to washing underneath the foreskin, but should avoid using soap while inflammation persists. If your foreskin does not draw back easily to allow you to wash thoroughly, your doctor may recommend **circumcision** (opposite). See also **Genital hygiene,** right.

**NO**

**Does pain occur only on intercourse?** — **YES**

**Friction during intercourse** may cause pain, especially if your partner's vagina seems dry and if she also complains of discomfort.

**Self-help:** Try to ensure that your partner is relaxed and aroused before attempting intercourse. You may find it helpful to use an over-the-counter lubricating jelly. If the problem persists, you and your partner should consult your doctor, who will examine you both to find out if there is any physical cause for the discomfort. Sometimes **sex counselling** (p. 240) is helpful.

**NO**

**Does the tip of your penis become sore after intercourse?** — **YES**

**NO**

**Consult your doctor** if you are unable to make a diagnosis from this chart.

---

**BLOOD IN THE SEMEN**

Pinkish, reddish or brownish streaks in your semen may be caused by the presence of blood. This uncommon condition is known as haemospermia. It is caused by the rupture of small veins in the upper part of the urethra during an erection. These heal themselves within a few minutes, although the semen may continue to be slightly discoloured for a few days afterwards.

**What should be done?**

Blood in the semen is usually no cause for concern, but you should consult your doctor, he or she may wish to arrange for tests to see whether or not you have an infection of the urinary tract or an abnormality of the blood.

---

**GENITAL HYGIENE**

Minor complaints and irritations of the penis can be avoided by paying attention to genital hygiene, especially if you are sexually active. However, there is no need to be over-zealous in your approach to this; the genitals need no more attention than the rest of the body. Washing your penis with warm water and mild soap each time you have a bath or shower is sufficient to maintain hygiene. If you have not been circumcised (see *Circumcision,* opposite), be sure to draw back your foreskin to clean accumulated secretion from the glans (tip) of your penis.

**Cleaning under the foreskin**

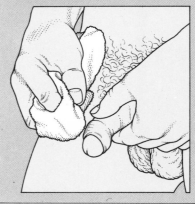

**An allergic reaction** – for example, to a contraceptive cream or douching solution used by your partner – may be the cause of soreness after intercourse. If you use a sheath, there is a possibility that you may be allergic to rubber.

**Self-help:** Soreness should disappear if you avoid contact with whatever you think may be causing the reaction. It may be necessary for you to choose an alternative form of contraception (see p. 248). If you can find no obvious cause for the soreness, or if soreness persists, consult your doctor.

# 117 Painful urination

**Consult this chart if you feel pain or discomfort when passing urine. This may be a symptom of infection or** **inflammation, or may follow injury to the urinary tract, and should be brought to your doctor's attention.**

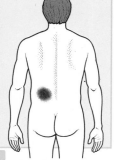

**START HERE** → Do you have pain in one side of the small of your back just above the waist?

**YES**

**NO**

Do you have an unusual discharge from your penis?

**YES**

**NO**

**CONSULT YOUR DOCTOR WITHOUT DELAY!**
**An acute infection of the kidneys** may be the cause of the pain.

*Treatment:* Your doctor will examine you and may take a specimen of your urine for analysis. If your doctor suspects a kidney infection, he or she may prescribe *antibiotics*. He or she may also arrange for you to have a special X-ray of the kidneys (see *intravenous pyelography,* right) to find out if there is an underlying cause of the problem. Further treatment will depend on the results of the tests.

## INTRAVENOUS PYELOGRAPHY

Intravenous pyelography (IVP) provides the doctor with a series of X-ray pictures of the urinary tract. A special liquid that shows up on X-ray pictures is injected into the bloodstream. It travels round your body until it reaches your kidneys, where it is excreted as waste matter through the ureters and into the bladder. During this process, which takes several hours, X-ray pictures are taken at regular intervals.

An intravenous pyelogram of a normal urinary tract.

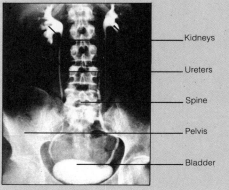

- Kidneys
- Ureters
- Spine
- Pelvis
- Bladder

**An infection** that may have been transmitted sexually may cause pain during urination and discharge from the penis. See *Sexually transmitted diseases* (opposite) and consult your doctor.

## ABNORMAL-LOOKING URINE

| Colour of urine | Possible causes | What action is necessary |
| --- | --- | --- |
| Pink, red or smoky | There is a chance that you may have blood in the urine, possibly caused by infection, inflammation, or a growth in the urinary tract. However, natural or artificial food colourings can also pass into the urine to cause such discoloration. | Consult your doctor without delay. He or she may need to take samples of urine and blood for analysis (see *Blood analysis,* p. 146) in order to make a firm diagnosis. Treatment will depend on the underlying problem. |
| Dark yellow or orange | If you have not been drinking much fluid, your urine may have become more concentrated and therefore darker than usual. Loss of fluid caused by diarrhoea, vomiting, or sweating can also make your urine more concentrated than normal. In addition, substances in senna-based laxatives and in rhubarb can darken your urine temporarily. | This is no cause for concern; as soon as you compensate for any loss of fluid by drinking, your urine will return to its normal colour. Substances in laxatives and rhubarb will pass through your system within 24 hours. |
| Clear and dark brown | Jaundice caused by a disorder of the liver or gall-bladder (most commonly hepatitis) is a possibility, especially if your faeces are very pale and your skin or the whites of your eyes look yellow. | Consult your doctor who will need to take samples of urine and blood for analysis (see *Blood analysis,* p. 146) in order to make a firm diagnosis. Treatment will depend on the underlying problem. |
| Green or blue | Artificial colouring in food or medicines is almost certainly the cause. | This is no cause for concern; the colouring will pass through without harmful effects. |

*Go to next page*

*Continued from previous page*

Do you feel a pain between your legs when you pass urine AND/OR is your temperature 38°C (100°F) or above?

**YES** →

**Prostatitis** (inflammation of the prostate gland that is usually caused by infection) is a possibility. Consult your doctor.

*Treatment:* Your doctor will probably feel your prostate gland by inserting a finger into your rectum, to find out whether the gland is swollen and tender. You will be asked to provide a urine sample for analysis. If the diagnosis is confirmed, your doctor will probably advise you to rest and may prescribe *antibiotics* to clear the infection.

**NO** →

**A urinary-tract infection** is the most likely cause of painful urination with no other symptoms. Consult your doctor.

*Treatment:* If your doctor suspects infection, he or she may take a sample of urine for analysis. In some cases further tests such as *intravenous pyelography* (opposite) are necessary. Treatment for infection in the urinary tract is likely to consist of *antibiotics*. You will also be advised to drink plenty of fluids.

## SEXUALLY TRANSMITTED DISEASES

Infections passed from one person to another during sexual contact (including sexual intercourse, anal and oral sex) are known as sexually transmitted (or venereal) diseases. If you think you have caught a sexually transmitted disease, consult your doctor, or go to a clinic that specializes in such diseases, where you will be treated in the strictest confidence. It is important to seek medical advice promptly because of the risk that you may unknowingly pass on the infection to someone else. Also, an infection may be less easy to eradicate if there is any delay in starting treatment. If you are found to have a sexually transmitted disease, you will be asked to inform any recent sexual partners, so that they too may seek treatment if necessary. You should avoid sex until treatment has cleared your symptoms.

| Disease | Incubation period* | Symptoms | Treatment |
|---|---|---|---|
| Gonorrhoea | 2 to 10 days | Discomfort when passing urine and usually discharge of pus from the tip of the penis. | The doctor will take a sample of the discharge for laboratory examination. The usual treatment is *antibiotics* by mouth or by injection. |
| Non-specific urethritis | 1 to 5 weeks | A slight tingling at the base of the penis – sometimes only felt when urinating first thing in the morning. The tingling may be accompanied by a scanty, clear discharge, which becomes slightly thicker and heavier if not treated. | The doctor will take a sample of urethral discharge for laboratory examination. The usual treatment is a course of *antibiotics*. |
| Syphilis | 9 to 90 days | In the first stage a highly infectious, painless sore called a chancre develops on the penis (or in some cases the anus). This disappears after a few weeks. In the second stage a rash which does not itch appears all over the body, including the palms and soles. There may also be painless swelling of the lymph glands and infectious wart-like lumps around the anus and maybe the armpits. | The disease is diagnosed by blood tests and samples taken from any sores. The usual treatment is a 2-week course of *antibiotic* injections. You will need to have regular blood tests for 2 years after treatment to check that the disease has not re-appeared. |
| Herpes genitalis | 7 days or less | There is usually an itching feeling on the shaft of the penis followed by the appearance of a crop of small painful blisters. Sometimes these also appear on the thighs and buttocks. The blisters burst after 24 hours leaving small, red, moist, painful ulcers which sometimes crust over. The glands in the groin may become enlarged and painful. This may be accompanied by a feeling of being unwell and a raised temperature. Outbreaks of blisters are likely to recur. | There is no complete cure for this disorder. Your doctor may prescribe an *antiviral* drug or ointment to make the ulcers less sore and to speed healing. You will be advised to avoid close sexual contact while you have blisters or sores so that you do not transmit the infection to your partner. |
| Pubic lice (crabs) | | Many people have no symptoms while others experience itching in the pubic region, particularly at night. You may be able to see the lice; they are brown and 1 to 2mm long. | Your doctor will give you a lotion or ointment which kills lice and their eggs. At the same time he or she will check that you do not have any other sexually transmitted disease. |
| AIDS (acquired immune deficiency syndrome) | | This rare disorder affects the body's natural defence (immune) system, which becomes unable to protect the body against infections and some forms of cancer. Symptoms of AIDS include recurrent fevers, respiratory and digestive-tract infections, a constant feeling of tiredness, loss of weight, swollen glands (in the neck, behind the ears, under the arms, at the elbows, and in the groin), and skin blotches or rashes. To date the disease has mainly affected male homosexuals and people who have been in contact with contaminated blood. | You will probably need to spend some time in hospital undergoing extensive tests. Treatment depends on symptoms and may consist of *antibiotics* and/or *cytotoxic* drugs. Research into cures for this disease is continuing. |

*Time between contact with the disease and appearance of symptoms

# 118 Erection difficulties

Most men fail to get an erection from time to time, despite feeling sexually aroused in other ways, for any one of a number of reasons, including psychological factors, physical factors, or a combination of both. Some men can get an erection only while masturbating or during oral sex, but not when they are trying to have sexual intercourse. Others can get an erection with one woman, and not with another. Consult this chart if you are beginning to feel that you are having problems with getting or maintaining an erection.

**START HERE** →

**Have you little or no desire for sex either in general or with your current partner?**

YES →

**Lack of sexual desire** often reduces a man's ability to get or maintain an erection.

Go to chart

121 **Low sex drive**

NO ↓

**Do you fail to get an erection only occasionally?**

YES →

**Does this usually happen at the start of a relationship?**

YES →

**Nervousness and anxiety** at the thought of intercourse with a new partner, and perhaps about your performance, may cause a temporary inability to have an erection. This is quite normal and as the relationship develops it usually becomes less of a problem.

*Self-help:* Discuss the problem with your partner. You may well find that she does not feel that enjoyable sex depends on your having an erection immediately and that she also enjoys forms of sexual contact other than sexual intercourse, such as oral sex or stimulation by hand. As you find it easier to relax you will probably find that your ability to have an erection gradually returns.

NO ↓

NO ↓

## SEX COUNSELLING

Sex counselling can take many different forms. Most family doctors have experience in dealing with the more common types of sexual difficulty and so, if you have a problem you should first consult your own doctor for advice. Depending on the nature of the problem and his or her experience in this field, your doctor may either suggest treatment him- or herself or may refer you to a specialist sex counsellor. Such counsellors may or may not be medically qualified – often they are specialists in psychology. Some large medical practices have sex counsellors attached to them. In other cases you may be referred to a clinic or hospital outpatient department.

**Treatments for sexual difficulties**
Treatment for all types of sexual difficulty has a greater chance of success if both partners attend counselling sessions. Usually a course of counselling starts with a discussion with the counsellor about the nature of the problem. In many cases this provides a couple with their first experience of talking together frankly about their sexual feelings, and this is often in itself of great help in clearing up misunderstandings and reducing anxiety. The counsellor may later suggest techniques for overcoming specific difficulties – for example, the *squeeze technique* (p. 242) if premature ejaculation is a problem. Or he or she may give more generalized advice on sexual technique. The counsellor will also, if necessary, guide you through a prolonged therapy programme to be carried out at home, such as the sensate focus technique described under *Reducing sexual anxiety* (opposite).

The success rate for couples who overcome their embarrassment sufficiently to seek sex counselling is high. So even if you feel that your problem is insoluble, it is worthwhile to seek your doctor's advice.

A qualified sex counsellor can be a great help to couples who are having difficulty in working out their sexual problems by listening to each partner and offering suggestions for self-help.

**Occasional inability to have an erection** is quite normal. This may occur if you are not in the mood for intercourse, perhaps because you are tired or under stress for some other reason. This only becomes a problem if you are afraid that it may happen again. If your erection difficulty starts to occur more frequently, discuss the problem with your doctor. You may also find the advice on reducing sexual anxiety (opposite) helpful.

*Go to next page*

*Continued from previous page*

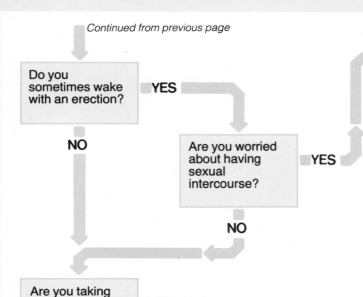

Do you sometimes wake with an erection?

**NO**

**YES**

Are you worried about having sexual intercourse?

**YES**

**NO**

Are you taking any medicines?

**YES**

**Certain drugs,** particularly antidepressants and anti-anxiety drugs, may prevent you from having an erection. The problem is usually only temporary, but discuss it with your doctor.

**NO**

**Consult your doctor** if you are unable to make a diagnosis from this chart.

**Anxiety** is a fairly common cause of erection difficulties and the fact that you sometimes wake with an erection means that there is no physical problem. Worry about premature ejaculation, making your partner pregnant, or catching a sexually transmitted disease, for example, are all common causes of sexual anxiety. In the majority of cases it is only a temporary difficulty.

***Self-help:*** Discuss your feelings with your partner. You may well find that your partner's reassurances are sufficient to help you overcome your difficulty. Meanwhile, try other forms of sexual contact such as mutual stimulation or oral sex. An erection may follow on from this when you begin to feel less anxious. Try also the advice given in *Reducing sexual anxiety* (below). If the problem persists and interferes with sexual enjoyment, consult your doctor, who may recommend *Sex counselling,* opposite.

---

### REDUCING SEXUAL ANXIETY

Many sexual difficulties arise out of anxiety in one or both partners, and most forms of *Sex counselling* (opposite) involve advice on reducing such anxiety as a basis for improving sexual enjoyment. The following technique, called sensate focus, is often successful in heightening sexual responsiveness without provoking anxiety about performance, and may help you overcome inhibitions and tensions that can mar sexual relationships. Usually the first step is for both partners to agree to abstain from sexual intercourse for, say, 3 weeks.

**Sensate focus**
Set aside at least 3 evenings (or a period at another time of day) in a week when you can be alone with your partner without fear of interruption for at least 2 hours. Try to create an atmosphere in which you both feel relaxed – for example, by playing some favourite music. During the time when you are trying this therapy you and your partner must stick to your agreement to refrain from full sexual intercourse.

**Stage 1**
On the first evening, each partner should take it in turns to gently massage and caress the other for a period of about 20 minutes. This is best carried out when you are both naked, and you can use a body lotion or oil, if you like. The massage should involve a gentle exploration of all parts of the body except the genital, breast, and anal areas. The partner being caressed should concentrate on finding pleasure from being touched, and the partner giving the caresses should concentrate on his or her own pleasure from contact with the partner's body. Once you have got over any awkwardness and are finding enjoyment from the experience – this may take several sessions – go to stage 2.

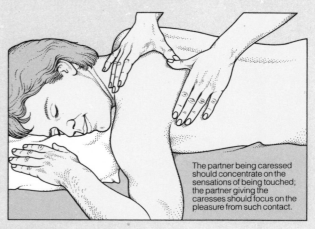

The partner being caressed should concentrate on the sensations of being touched; the partner giving the caresses should focus on the pleasure from such contact.

**Stage 2**
Stage 2 is similar to stage 1, but this time body massage may include genital, anal, and breast areas. Remember, however, to continue to include other parts of the body in your caresses, so that direct sexual stimulation can be felt in context with other body sensations.

**Stage 3**
Most couples find that soon after reaching stage 2 they are ready to resume sexual intercourse; and in most cases they find that they are more relaxed and are more able to enjoy a full range of physical and emotional sexual feelings.

---

### SEX IN LATER LIFE

The majority of men reach their sexual peak physically in their late teens or early twenties. During sexual intercourse they reach orgasm quickly, ejaculate powerfully, and are able to have another erection soon after. As a man gets older it may take him longer to get an erection, which may not be as stiff as in the past, and more stimulation may be necessary. Ejaculation may be delayed slightly (this can be beneficial for men who have previously suffered from premature ejaculation). The time it takes to develop another erection may be longer. However, there is usually no physical reason why a man should not continue to have an active and happy sex life until well into old age.

**Possible problems**
The changes described above occur only gradually and often go unnoticed. For many men, sexual activity becomes more enjoyable with increased experience and confidence. A reduction in the frequency of orgasm is often more than compensated for by the enhanced quality of the sexual experience.

However, some men become anxious about their sexual performance as they approach middle age. This usually occurs when anxiety or depression, possibly connected with other aspects of life – for example, lack of job satisfaction or concern about the future – lead a man to compare his current sex life unfavourably with how it was 20 or 30 years ago. Some men who have experienced sexual difficulties in the past use their advancing years as an excuse for avoiding sex altogether in later life. This is no cause for concern if both partners are happy not to have sex. But if a reduction in sexual activity causes unhappiness in either partner, it is never too late to seek *Sex counselling* (opposite) for this or any other sex problem.

# 119 Premature ejaculation

There are occasions when men ejaculate before they wish to. This becomes a problem only if you consistently ejaculate so quickly that you and your partner become frustrated by the curtailment of sexual intercourse. The anxiety that often accompanies premature ejaculation tends to make the problem worse, and may lead you to avoid sex which may result in disharmony between you and your partner. However, the tendency to ejaculate prematurely can usually be overcome with time, patience and self-help.

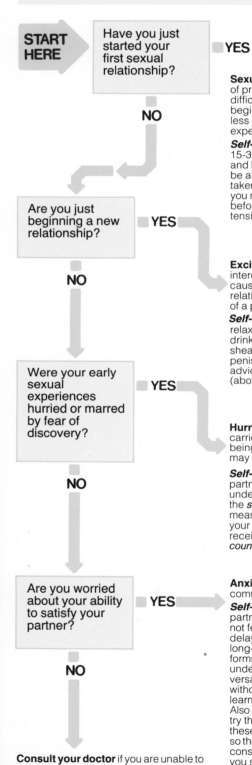

**START HERE** → Have you just started your first sexual relationship?

**YES** →

**Sexual inexperience** is a very common cause of premature ejaculation. Nearly all men have difficulty controlling orgasm when they are beginning to have sex. This usually becomes less of a problem with time and more experience.

*Self-help:* Try to get another erection about 15-30 minutes after you have your first orgasm and have intercourse again. You will probably be able to last longer once the edge has been taken off your sexual excitement. Alternatively, you may find it helpful to masturbate shortly before you have intercourse to reduce sexual tension, which will help you to delay orgasm.

**NO** ↓

Are you just beginning a new relationship?

**YES** →

**Excitement and anxiety** when you have intercourse with a new partner are common causes of premature ejaculation. As the relationship develops it is likely to become less of a problem.

*Self-help:* You and your partner should try to relax, perhaps by having one or two alcoholic drinks, before having intercourse. Using a sheath may help to dull the sensitivity of your penis and so delay ejaculation. See also the advice given under *sexual inexperience* (above).

**NO** ↓

Were your early sexual experiences hurried or marred by fear of discovery?

**YES** →

**Hurried or furtive sexual experiences,** carried out in an atmosphere of guilt or fear of being discovered by parents or passers by, may have caused the problem.

*Self-help:* Discuss the difficulty with your partner so that you both can develop an understanding of the problem. You can also try the *squeeze technique* (right). If these measures do not help the problem, consult your doctor, who may recommend that you receive some specialist advice (see *Sex counselling*, p. 240).

**NO** ↓

Are you worried about your ability to satisfy your partner?

**YES** →

**Anxiety about sexual performance** is a fairly common cause of premature ejaculation.

*Self-help:* Discuss the problem with your partner. You may very well find that she does not feel that enjoyable sex depends on your delaying ejaculation indefinitely or having a long-lasting erection. She may enjoy other forms of stimulation such as oral sex. Once you understand what your partner enjoys and vice versa, you will find it easier to have intercourse without feeling anxious and you will gradually learn to delay ejaculation as a matter of course. Also read *Reducing sexual anxiety* (p. 241) and try the *squeeze technique* described right. If these measures fail and the problem persists so that it interferes with your sexual enjoyment, consult your doctor, who may recommend that you seek specialist advice (see *Sex counselling*, p. 240).

**NO** ↓

**Consult your doctor** if you are unable to make a diagnosis from this chart or if self-help measures do not help the problem.

---

### THE SQUEEZE TECHNIQUE

The squeeze technique is one of the most widely accepted methods for helping a man to delay and control orgasm. It teaches both partners to recognize the sensations that immediately precede ejaculation, so increasing control. Many couples find that it helps to try the technique of sensate focus (see *Reducing sexual anxiety*, p. 241) before undertaking the squeeze technique.

**Stage 1**
Adopt a position that is comfortable for both you and your partner. Many couples find the best position is one in which the woman sits with her back to the headboard of the bed, her legs spread out in front, and the man lies facing her, with his body between her legs, his legs over hers. Your partner should then caress your penis to full erection and continue until you are close to orgasm. When you feel ready to ejaculate, signal to your partner, who then stops stimulating you and grips the penis firmly just below the glans until your erection subsides. After about half a minute, she can start to stimulate your penis again. Repeat this 2 or 3 times before allowing yourself to ejaculate. With practice, your partner will begin to sense without signal when you are near to orgasm. After a few sessions, when you both have gained confidence about controlling ejaculation, it is possible to move on to the next stage.

**Gripping below the glans delays orgasm**

**Stage 2**
Lie on your back with your partner astride you and your erect penis inside her vagina. Practise holding this position without moving for as long as possible. If you feel you are about to ejaculate, signal to your partner. She then lifts herself away and applies the squeeze grip as before. Repeat this 2 or 3 times. If your erection begins to subside, stimulation of the penis will restore it so that it can be once again inserted into your partner's vagina.

After a few sessions, when you feel control has improved, normal full intercourse can be attempted so that both partners can reach orgasm. You may find that positions in which your partner is on top allow you to control orgasm most easily. If at any time you feel ready to ejaculate before your partner is ready, she can use the squeeze technique.

# 120 Delayed ejaculation

Consult this chart if, although able to have a normal erection, you are unable to ejaculate as soon as you would like, or if you have lost the ability to ejaculate altogether. There may be physical or emotional reasons for this type of difficulty. Whatever you suspect may be the cause of the problem, frank discussion with your partner is essential, so that she can help you to overcome the difficulty.

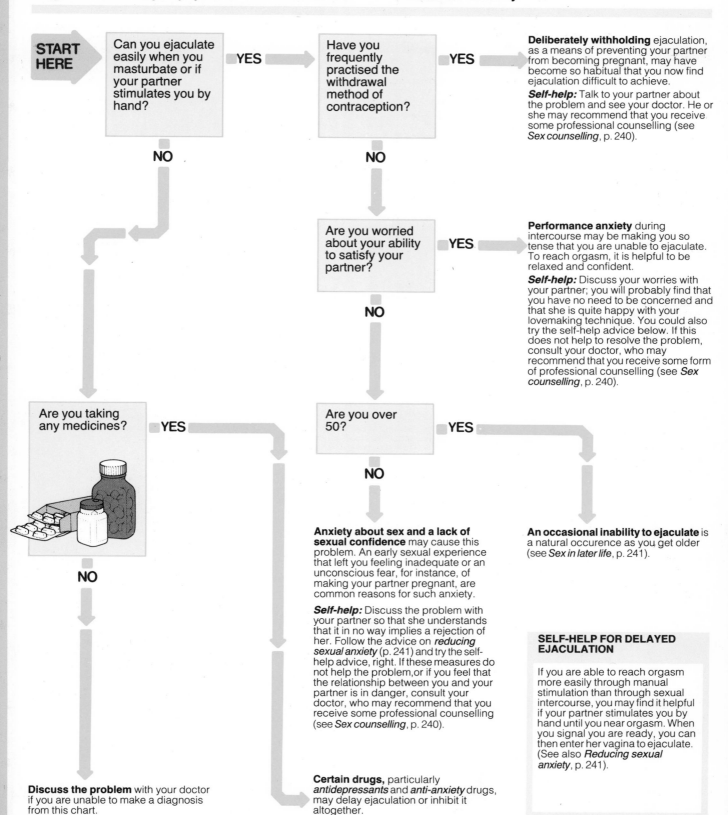

**START HERE**

**Can you ejaculate easily when you masturbate or if your partner stimulates you by hand?**
— YES → **Have you frequently practised the withdrawal method of contraception?**
— YES → **Deliberately withholding** ejaculation, as a means of preventing your partner from becoming pregnant, may have become so habitual that you now find ejaculation difficult to achieve.
*Self-help:* Talk to your partner about the problem and see your doctor. He or she may recommend that you receive some professional counselling (see *Sex counselling*, p. 240).

**Have you frequently practised the withdrawal method of contraception?** — NO →

**Are you worried about your ability to satisfy your partner?**
— YES → **Performance anxiety** during intercourse may be making you so tense that you are unable to ejaculate. To reach orgasm, it is helpful to be relaxed and confident.
*Self-help:* Discuss your worries with your partner; you will probably find that you have no need to be concerned and that she is quite happy with your lovemaking technique. You could also try the self-help advice below. If this does not help to resolve the problem, consult your doctor, who may recommend that you receive some form of professional counselling (see *Sex counselling*, p. 240).

**Are you worried about your ability to satisfy your partner?** — NO →

**Can you ejaculate easily when you masturbate or if your partner stimulates you by hand?** — NO →

**Are you taking any medicines?**
— YES → **Are you over 50?**
— YES → **An occasional inability to ejaculate** is a natural occurence as you get older (see *Sex in later life*, p. 241).

**Are you over 50?** — NO →

**Anxiety about sex and a lack of sexual confidence** may cause this problem. An early sexual experience that left you feeling inadequate or an unconscious fear, for instance, of making your partner pregnant, are common reasons for such anxiety.
*Self-help:* Discuss the problem with your partner so that she understands that it in no way implies a rejection of her. Follow the advice on *reducing sexual anxiety* (p. 241) and try the self-help advice, right. If these measures do not help the problem, or if you feel that the relationship between you and your partner is in danger, consult your doctor, who may recommend that you receive some professional counselling (see *Sex counselling*, p. 240).

**Are you taking any medicines?** — NO →

**Discuss the problem** with your doctor if you are unable to make a diagnosis from this chart.

**Certain drugs,** particularly *antidepressants* and *anti-anxiety* drugs, may delay ejaculation or inhibit it altogether.

---

**SELF-HELP FOR DELAYED EJACULATION**

If you are able to reach orgasm more easily through manual stimulation than through sexual intercourse, you may find it helpful if your partner stimulates you by hand until you near orgasm. When you signal you are ready, you can then enter her vagina to ejaculate. (See also *Reducing sexual anxiety*, p. 241).

# 121 Low sex drive

**Male sexual arousal is governed by both psychological factors and the male sex hormone testosterone. If a man has a very low level of testosterone he is unlikely to have a great interest in sex and may find it difficult to** **become sexually aroused. However, most cases of reduced sex drive have non-hormonal causes, including physical illness, stress, sexual difficulties, boredom, and discontent with a current relationship.**

**START HERE**

**Have you always had little interest in sex?** → **YES** →

**A naturally low level of interest in sex** is a normal part of the personality of some men. This is unlikely to be a cause for concern if you and your partner are happy with your present level of sexual activity. However, if your low sex drive is causing difficulties within your relationship, consult your doctor, who may recommend *sex counselling,* (p.240).

**NO**

**Have you been overtired and/or under stress recently?** → **YES** →

**Fatigue and stress** are very common reasons for making a man lose interest in sex.
*Self-help:* Discuss the problem with your partner and explain to her why you are feeling the way you do. This will help her to understand that it is not because you find her unattractive in any way. You will probably find that she agrees that there is little satisfaction for either of you from sex attempted out of duty. When you feel better, the desire for sex will almost certainly return. Meanwhile, see chart 55, *Tiredness,* and/or chart 73, *Anxiety,* for advice on tackling the underlying reason for your loss of sex drive.

**NO**

**Have you been feeling in low spirits recently?** → **YES** →

**Depression** is a possible cause of loss of interest in sex.
Go to chart

## 72 Depression

**NO**

### SEXUAL ORIENTATION

Sexual orientation – that is, whether you are heterosexual (attracted to people of the opposite sex), homosexual (attracted to people of the same sex), or bisexual (attracted to people of both sexes) is probably determined by a combination of inborn personality traits, upbringing, and family relationships. Some researchers have suggested that there may be hormonal factors that contribute to determining sexual orientation, but these findings have not been generally accepted. Few people are wholly heterosexual or homosexual. In particular, it is common for adolescents to go through a phase of experiencing homosexual feelings before becoming attracted to people of the opposite sex. Some people, however, remain homosexual in their sexual preferences.

**Have you been drinking heavily in recent weeks?** → **YES** →

**Regular consumption of large amounts of alcohol** is a common cause of loss of interest in sex and, in some cases, may lead to impotence. There is also the possibility of other health problems (see *The effects of alcohol,* p.146).
*Self-help:* Cutting out alcohol altogether should help to restore your interest in sex. If you find it difficult to cut down on your alcohol intake or your enthusiasm for sex does not return, consult your doctor.

**NO**

#### Homosexuality
This variation from the mainly heterosexual orientation of the majority is no cause for medical concern as long as the individual is happy with his homosexuality. Treatment to change sexual orientation is unlikely to be effective and is seldom recommended unless the individual is very determined to make the attempt and has at least some interest in the opposite sex. However, society's often intolerant attitude towards homosexuality frequently causes homosexuals to feel guilty and abnormal, and therefore leads them to repress their sexual feelings. This can be psychologically damaging. If you think that you are homosexual and are experiencing such problems, consult your doctor, who may be able to offer helpful advice and/or refer you to one of the voluntary organizations that specializes in advising homosexuals.

**Do you or your partner have a specific sexual difficulty?** → **YES** →

**A sexual problem** may unconsciously make you feel that you do not desire sex. When such an underlying problem is dealt with, sex drive usually returns to normal. Chart 118, *Erection difficulties,* chart 119, *Premature ejaculation,* and chart 120, *Delayed ejaculation,* deal with the most common sex difficulties in men. If your problem is not covered in this book, ask your doctor for advice, he or she may suggest that you and your partner receive some professional advice (see *Sex counselling,* (p.240).

**NO**

**Do you only fail to get aroused by your regular partner?** → **YES** →

**NO**

1 *Go to next page, column 1*

2 *Go to next page, column 2*

Continued from previous page, column 1

**Are you taking any medicines?**

**YES**

**Certain drugs,** particularly *diuretics, antidepressants* and *anti-anxiety* drugs may interfere with your sex drive. The problem is usually only temporary, but discuss it with your doctor.

**NO**

**Are you over 50?**

**YES**

**A need for less frequent sex** is common as men grow older, although this does not mean that your enjoyment of lovemaking is necessarily reduced (see *Sex in later life,* p.241).

**NO**

**Do you fail to be aroused by women, but find you are sexually attracted to men?**

**YES**

**Homosexuality** – being sexually aroused only by someone of the same sex – is a normal sexual preference for as many as 5 per cent of the population. While many homosexuals are aware of their sexual orientation from adolescence, some do not recognise their homosexuality until much later. See *Sexual orientation,* opposite.

**NO**

**Consult your doctor** if you are unable to make a diagnosis from this chart.

Continued from previous page, column 2

**Do you have any other cause for discontent in your relationship?**

**YES**

**NO**

**Loss of interest in a sexual relationship** once the excitement and novelty has worn off is a common cause of loss of sexual desire.

***Self-help:*** It may help to talk openly with your partner about how you feel so that there is no misunderstanding of the situation. If the relationship is a long-standing one, and sound in every other way, try to inject new life into it, for example, by going away for a weekend together or cooperating in some new venture. You may find trying new approaches to lovemaking helpful. If these measures do not help, consult your doctor, who may suggest that you and your partner receive some professional advice (see *Sex counselling,* p.240).

**Generalized antagonism or specific disagreements** can lead to tension in a relationship that also affects your sexual feelings for each other. There may also be some lack of communication so that you do not fully understand each other's feelings and attitudes towards sex and other matters; and this may produce conflict, and damage your sexual relationship.

***Self-help:*** Talk to your partner and explain how the problems with your relationship are affecting your feelings. If you find that things do not improve after full and frank discussion, consult your doctor, who will examine you to find out if there is an underlying physical problem. If there is no physical disorder he or she may suggest that you and your partner seek marriage guidance about your general difficulties and possibly *sex counselling,* (p.240) for any specific problem you may have.

---

## HORMONE DEFICIENCY AND LOW SEX DRIVE

In rare cases low sex drive may be a symptom of a deficiency of the male sex hormone testosterone. This type of hormone deficiency always causes additional symptoms such as loss of body hair and unusually small testes. If your lack of interest in sex is accompanied by such additional symptoms, consult your doctor.

### Treatment

If tests confirm the diagnosis, hormone treatment will be prescribed; this is usually successful in increasing sex drive and reversing such physical changes. Loss of sex drive that is not accompanied by the physical symptoms described here is not caused by lack of testosterone, and hormone supplements will have no beneficial effect.

---

## MEDICAL PROBLEMS ASSOCIATED WITH HOMOSEXUALITY

While homosexual activity is not in itself a danger to physical or mental health, some diseases seem to be particularly prevalent among male homosexuals. These include all the sexually transmitted diseases, but especially hepatitis (liver infection), syphilis, and the much-publicised, but nevertheless rare, disorder of the immune system – AIDS (acquired immune deficiency syndrome), see also *Sexually transmitted diseases,* (p.239).

The reason such diseases are more common among sexually active homosexuals is that they often have many different sexual partners and that most sexually transmitted diseases are passed on more easily by anal intercourse. Homosexual men who have many sexual contacts are therefore advised to read the information given under *Multiple sex partners,* (p.246) and to be especially vigilant for the following symptoms:

- inexplicable tiredness
- yellowing of the skin
- unexplained rashes or sores
- abnormally frequent and persistent respiratory and/or digestive-tract infections
- persistent swelling of the glands

If you notice any of the above symptoms, consult your doctor without delay. It is advisable to avoid sexual contact until the cause of the symptoms has been diagnosed and treated.

# 122 Fertility problems

Consult this chart if your partner has failed to become pregnant after you have had sexual intercourse without contraception for more than 12 months.Failure to conceive may be the result of a problem affecting the man or the woman; this chart deals only with possible problems affecting a man. Male infertility is nearly always the result of insufficient production of sperm or blockage of the passage of sperm during ejaculation. This may be caused by a temporary malfunction of the sperm-producing glands or by a longterm condition.

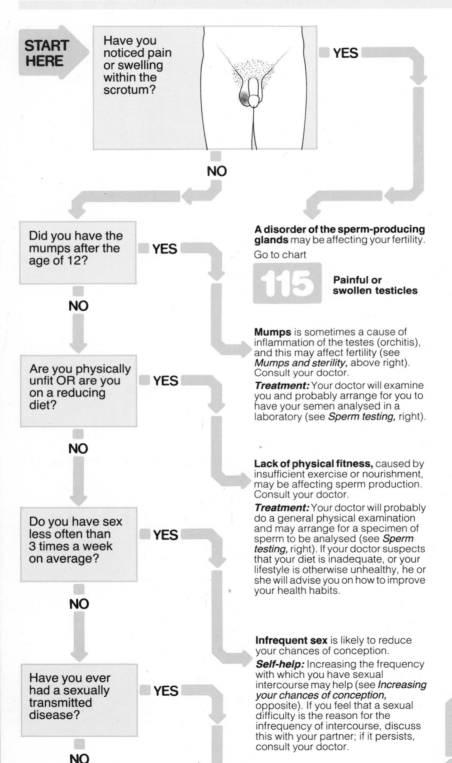

**START HERE**

Have you noticed pain or swelling within the scrotum?

YES

NO

Did you have the mumps after the age of 12?

YES

NO

Are you physically unfit OR are you on a reducing diet?

YES

NO

Do you have sex less often than 3 times a week on average?

YES

NO

Have you ever had a sexually transmitted disease?

YES

NO

*Go to next page*

**A disorder of the sperm-producing glands** may be affecting your fertility.

Go to chart

**115** Painful or swollen testicles

**Mumps** is sometimes a cause of inflammation of the testes (orchitis), and this may affect fertility (see *Mumps and sterility,* above right). Consult your doctor.

**Treatment:** Your doctor will examine you and probably arrange for you to have your semen analysed in a laboratory (see *Sperm testing,* right).

**Lack of physical fitness,** caused by insufficient exercise or nourishment, may be affecting sperm production. Consult your doctor.

**Treatment:** Your doctor will probably do a general physical examination and may arrange for a specimen of sperm to be analysed (see *Sperm testing,* right). If your doctor suspects that your diet is inadequate, or your lifestyle is otherwise unhealthy, he or she will advise you on how to improve your health habits.

**Infrequent sex** is likely to reduce your chances of conception.

**Self-help:** Increasing the frequency with which you have sexual intercourse may help (see *Increasing your chances of conception,* opposite). If you feel that a sexual difficulty is the reason for the infrequency of intercourse, discuss this with your partner; if it persists, consult your doctor.

## MUMPS AND STERILITY

If you had mumps after the age of 12 and your testicles became painful and/or swollen, a complication known as orchitis, there is a possibility that your ability to produce normal sperm may have been affected. Your doctor will arrange for you to have a sperm count (see *Sperm testing,* below) and offer you advice.

## SPERM TESTING

A sperm count is the standard test for male fertility – that is, whether or not a man has a chance of successfully conceiving. For this test you will need to attend a hospital clinic, where you will be asked to ejaculate into a container (by masturbation). For 2 days prior to the test you will need to refrain from sexual intercourse or masturbation so that the number of sperm in the semen is at its highest level. From this sample the number of active, healthy sperm can be assessed.

A count of 100 million sperm per cubic centimetre of semen makes conception likely, providing that your partner is fertile. A lower sperm count makes conception less likely. However, even if the count is as low as 20 million sperm per cubic centimetre, conception is still possible providing that a substantial proportion of sperm are active and healthy. Because the sperm count varies greatly from day to day, a man found to have a low sperm count may need to have another test to confirm whether or not the result of the low count was a temporary fluctuation in sperm production.

**Shape of a sperm**

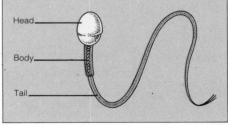

Head

Body

Tail

**Sexually transmitted diseases,** (see p.239) may sometimes cause infertility in both men and women. Consult your doctor.

**Treatment:** If you currently have symptoms, your doctor will examine you and take a sample from your urethra. This will be analysed in a laboratory and if a sexually transmitted disease is diagnosed you will probably be given *antibiotics.* If you have had such a disease in the past, tests on sperm (see *Sperm testing,* above) will determine whether or not it has affected your fertility.

*Continued from previous page*

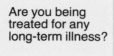

**Are you being treated for any long-term illness?**

**YES** →

**Certain illnesses** and the drugs used in their treatment may make it difficult for you to father a child. Liver and hormone disorders are particularly likely to have this effect. Discuss the problem with your doctor.

**NO** ↓

**Do you wear underpants that are tight-fitting or made of an artificial fibre or do you use saunas or steam baths frequently?**

**YES** →

**An increased temperature** within the scrotum may be making you less fertile. If the testes and the sperm they contain are not cooler than normal body temperature, fertility may be reduced (see *Sperm production*, below).

**Self-help:** Your chances of conception may be improved if you wear loose-fitting underpants made of a natural fibre such as cotton. This material allows air to circulate more freely so that the temperature around your testes does not get too high. Since there is some evidence that men who use saunas or steam baths often may have decreased sperm production due to high temperatures, it might be worthwhile to discontinue use of any saunas or steam baths for a while.

**NO** ↓

**Consult your doctor** if you are unable to make a diagnosis from this chart.

## INCREASING YOUR CHANCES OF CONCEPTION

Although prolonged delay in achieving conception requires professional tests and treatment, you may be able to increase your chances of conception by following the self-help advice given below:

- Try to ensure that both you and your partner are in good health; eat plenty of fresh, vitamin-rich foods, get plenty of rest, and keep alcohol consumption to a minimum.
- Have intercourse about 3 times a week; less frequent intercourse may mean that you miss your partner's fertile days, more frequent intercourse may reduce the number of sperm you ejaculate.
- Try to time intercourse to coincide with your partner's most fertile days (usually mid-way between menstrual periods).
- Following intercourse, encourage your partner to remain lying down for 10 to 15 minutes to allow the maximum number of sperm to enter the womb.
- Avoid wearing tight-fitting or nylon underpants, which may in some cases damage the sperm by increasing temperature within the scrotum.

## SPERM PRODUCTION

Inside the scrotum, the baggy pouch resting beneath the penis, are the two testes. Sperm cells are formed in the tiny tubes inside each testis at the rate of 10 to 30 billion each month. Behind each testis is a coiled tube called the epididymis. Sperm mature here over a period of 2 to 4 weeks before they are transferred to the seminal vesicles for storage. When you have an orgasm, the sperm pass into the urethra and are then ejaculated in the seminal fluid. Sperm comprise only a small part of this seminal fluid which is formed partly in the seminal vesicles and partly in the prostate. Neither the volume nor the appearance of the semen is any guide to fertility; after *vasectomy,* (p.248) when the sperm count is zero, the semen looks just the same.

Sperm production is most effective at a temperature 3-4°C (6°F) below normal body temperature. This is why the testes are suspended outside the body in the scrotum. A high temperature prevents new sperm from forming and may kill those already in storage. The effect of this is usually only temporary infertility. Very low temperature also prevents sperm from forming, but this does not damage those already in storage. Under normal conditions sperm production is continuous, though there may be seasonal variations – sperm concentration seems to be lower in the warm summer months.

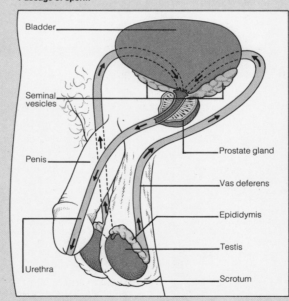

**Passage of sperm**

Bladder
Seminal vesicles
Penis
Urethra
Prostate gland
Vas deferens
Epididymis
Testis
Scrotum

The prostate gland (left) surrounds the urethra at the point where it leaves the bladder. The exact function of the gland is unclear, but it is thought that the secretions it produces stimulate the movement of sperm (right) after ejaculation.

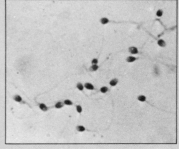

Bladder
Vas deferens
Seminal vesicles
Prostate gland
Urethra

**Where sperm forms and matures**

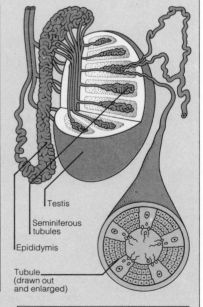

Testis
Seminiferous tubules
Epididymis
Tubule (drawn out and enlarged)

# 123 Contraception

The complex process by which sperm are produced makes it very difficult for an effective male contraceptive to be developed. It is hard to interfere with the production and development of sperm without affecting male sex drive or reducing the volume of semen ejaculated. Various drugs are being investigated to find a method of reducing sperm count without altering sexual desire or performance, but it will be some time before they can be guaranteed to be safe and effective. Until such a contraceptive has been tried and tested, it is up to you, after reading this chart and discussing contraception with your partner, to decide which is the best method for you or your partner to use (see Contraceptive methods, p. 271). The two methods currently available to you if you wish to take sole responsibility are the sheath and the vasectomy.

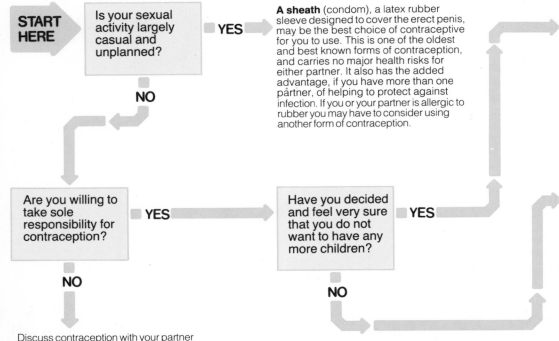

**START HERE**

Is your sexual activity largely casual and unplanned?

**YES** → **A sheath** (condom), a latex rubber sleeve designed to cover the erect penis, may be the best choice of contraceptive for you to use. This is one of the oldest and best known forms of contraception, and carries no major health risks for either partner. It also has the added advantage, if you have more than one partner, of helping to protect against infection. If you or your partner is allergic to rubber you may have to consider using another form of contraception.

**NO**

Are you willing to take sole responsibility for contraception?

**YES** → Have you decided and feel very sure that you do not want to have any more children?

**YES**

**NO**

**NO**

**A vasectomy** is becoming an increasingly popular method of birth control that will not interfere in any way with your own or your partner's sexual enjoyment. It involves a relatively minor operation that is virtually 100 per cent effective. Read the box below before deciding whether a vasectomy is the answer to your contraceptive needs.

**A sheath (or condom)** – a latex rubber sheath designed to cover the erect penis – may be the best choice of contraceptive for you to use. This is one of the oldest and best known forms of contraception and carries no major health risks for either partner. If you find that you or your partner are allergic to rubber, consider using another form of contraception.

Discuss contraception with your partner and read the information on *Contraceptive methods,* p. 271.

---

## VASECTOMY

### Who should consider it

If you feel that a vasectomy will solve your contraceptive problems it is important to discuss the implications with your partner. Vasectomy is usually irreversible, and so this is a permanent form of contraception. Therefore you and your partner need to be absolutely certain that you will not want to have any more children.

Remember that your present circumstances may change in the future: you may divorce and remarry, and want to start a family; you may lose the children you already have; or you may simply decide that you are no longer prepared to live without children. Couples under 30 years of age are usually discouraged from undertaking any form of sterilization. Your doctor may suggest that you receive some professional counselling before you make a final decision.

### The operation

Vasectomy is a straightforward operation that involves sealing off the vas deferens so that sperm are no longer present in the semen. Vasectomy does not interfere with sperm production; sperm continue to be produced, but because they cannot be ejaculated, eventually dissolve and are absorbed into the system (see *Sperm production*, p. 247). The operation does not affect sex drive or cause impotence. Ejaculation occurs normally because the blockage of the vas deferens does not affect the production of seminal fluid from the prostate gland. The only difference is that after the operation the seminal fluid contains no sperm.

The operation is usually carried out under local anaesthetic. Your pubic hair will be shaved and the surgeon will make two tiny cuts in the scrotum – one on each side, because you have two vas deferens, one for each testis. A loop of each vas is then tied in two places and the surgeon snips the short length between each knot. You may feel slight discomfort deep inside the lower abdomen, but this soon disappears. The whole operation lasts only a few minutes.

It is a safe procedure, but occasionally there is some bleeding within the scrotum, or a slight infection after the operation. If you notice any swelling in the scrotum in the days following a vasectomy, whether or not it is painful, consult your doctor, who may refer you back to hospital for treatment.

### After the operation

A vasectomy does not make you sterile at once. This is because sperm produced before the operation remain in the reproductive system beyond the break in the vas until they are all expelled by ejaculation over the course of the following months. In the meantime, you and your partner should use some alternative form of contraception until sperm counts (see *Sperm testing*, p. 246) taken during the next three months or so confirm that your seminal fluid is free of sperm.

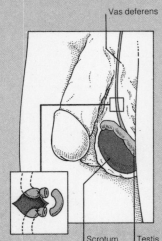

A tiny cut is made in the scrotum, and the vas deferens is tied in two places and snipped in between.

Vas deferens

Scrotum | Testis

# 4 Special problems: women

# Pregnancy and childbirth,

**page 273**

# 124 Breast problems

Each breast consists mainly of fatty tissues in which groups of milk-producing glands are embedded. The size and shape of the breast is determined by the amount of fatty tissue and the conditions of the muscles and ligaments that support it. It is common for a woman to have one breast slightly larger than the other. Problems affecting the breasts may include pain, tenderness, changes in shape or general appearance (including that of the overlying skin) or the development of one or more lumps in the usually soft breast tissue. Although most breast problems are minor and easily treated, it is essential to look out for any such changes and to report any change or obvious abnormality to your doctor so that the possibility of breast cancer (one of the commonest cancers affecting women) can be ruled out.

**START HERE** → Have you had a baby in the past few months?

**YES** → Go to chart **146** Breast-feeding problems

**NO** ↓

Have you recently noticed one or more lumps in the breast?

**YES** →

**NO** ↓

**CONSULT YOUR DOCTOR WITHOUT DELAY!**

**Any lump in the breast** should be examined by a doctor to exclude the possibility of breast cancer, although it is much more likely that there is a less alarming cause for the lump(s) such as a harmless cyst or a thickening of the fibrous breast tissue (fibro-adenosis).

*Treatment:* Your doctor will examine you, and if he or she thinks that there is any cause for concern, will refer you to hospital for tests such as those described under *Breast cancer* (opposite). If you are found to have a cyst, it will be treated by drawing off the fluid through a syringe – a procedure known as aspiration. Fibro-adenosis often needs no treatment, but it sometimes causes discomfort before periods, in which case you may be offered treatment as described under *Pre-menstrual breast tenderness* (opposite). Treatments for breast cancer are described in the box opposite.

---

### BREAST SELF-EXAMINATION

Every adult woman should make breast self-examination a regular part of her routine. This helps you to become familiar with the shape and feel of your breasts so that any changes will be quickly noticed and any problem dealt with promptly. Follow the routine described here once a month, ideally at the end of each menstrual period.

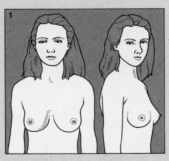

**1** Stand in front of a good mirror with your arms by your sides and look at your breasts and nipples from the front and sides for any change in their shape or in the appearance of the skin.

**2** Look again with your arms raised.

**3** With the left arm still raised, feel all over the left breast using the flat of the fingers of the right hand. Repeat using the left hand to examine the right breast.

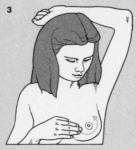

**4** Lie down with a pillow under your left shoulder and with your left arm behind your head. Using the right hand as before feel around the left breast, working from the outside towards the nipple at the centre.

**5** Check the area between the breast and the armpit and into the armpit itself, first with the left arm raised and then with it by your side.

**6** Gently squeeze the nipple to check for any discharge.

Repeat 4, 5 and 6 using the left hand to examine the right breast.

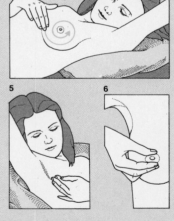

**When to consult your doctor**

If you notice any of the following during the course of your regular breast self-examination – or at any other time – consult your doctor without delay:

- a lump in the breast or armpit.
- a change in the outline of the breast.
- discharge from the nipple.
- retraction (indentation) of the nipple.
- any change in the skin of the breast – for example, puckering or dimpling.

Remember, the first few times you examine yourself, that you are still becoming familiar with your breasts and many of the lumps you find will be perfectly normal. However, if you are worried that you have found something abnormal, consult your doctor.

*Go to next page*

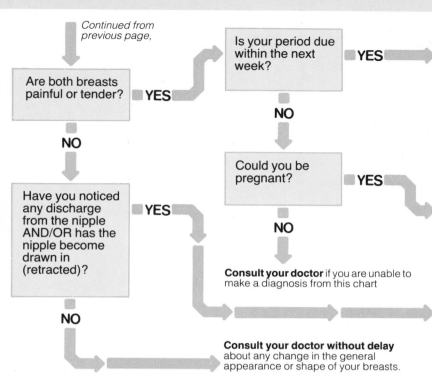

*Continued from previous page,*

**Are both breasts painful or tender?** → **YES** → **Is your period due within the next week?** → **YES**

**NO** ↓

**Have you noticed any discharge from the nipple AND/OR has the nipple become drawn in (retracted)?** → **YES**

**NO** ↓

**Is your period due within the next week?** → **NO** ↓

**Could you be pregnant?** → **YES**

**NO** ↓

  **Consult your doctor** if you are unable to make a diagnosis from this chart

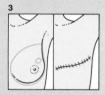 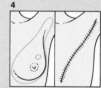 **Consult your doctor without delay** about any change in the general appearance or shape of your breasts.

**Pre-menstrual breast tenderness** is a common occurrence, and is most likely to affect women who have naturally lumpy breasts – a condition known as fibro-adenosis. (See also *The menstrual cycle,* (p.253). Consult your doctor.

*Treatment:* Your doctor will examine you. If he or she confirms the diagnosis, depending on the severity of your symptoms and whether you suffer from other unpleasant menstrual symptoms such as irritability or fluid retention, may suggest hormone treatment (see *Treatment for menstrual problems,* (p.255). Wearing a firm-support bra may also help to reduce discomfort.

**Tenderness of the breasts and nipples** is often one of the earliest signs of pregnancy and may continue for several months while your breasts prepare themselves to produce milk. If discomfort is severe, or you are not sure whether or not you are pregnant, consult your doctor. (See also *Diagnosis of pregnancy,* p.252).

**CONSULT YOU DOCTOR WITHOUT DELAY!**
**Nipple changes** may in some cases be a sign of *breast cancer* (below) and should always be brought to your doctor's attention.

*Treatment:* If your doctor thinks that there is any cause for concern after examining you, he or she will arrange for you to undergo tests as described in the box below.

---

## BREAST CANCER

Breast cancer is the most common cancer affecting women; about 1 woman in 20 develops the disease. Abnormal (cancerous) cells develop and multiply in the breast, forming a tumour. If untreated, the cancer may spread to other parts of the body.

### Risk factors
Several factors are now known to increase the risk of developing cancer of the breast. These affect women in the following categories:

- Women who have no children, or who had their first child late in life.
- Women who are overweight.
- Women with close relatives who have had the disease.

If you think you are in a high risk group, discuss this with your doctor, who may refer you to a breast clinic for regular screening (below), especially if you are over 40.

### Screening
Most of the risk factors for developing breast cancer are outside your control, but you can try to ensure that the disease is diagnosed early by regular screening for the disease. The basic form of screening that every adult woman should undertake is monthly *breast self-examination* (opposite). However, women in high risk groups may also be advised to undergo regular mammography (low-radiation X-ray of the breast). Another technique that is sometimes used is thermography, in which the temperature of the breast tissue is measured. "Hot spots" may indicate a cancer.

### Making the diagnosis
The most common sign of breast cancer is the appearance of a painless lump in the breast or armpit. However, any of the symptoms listed in the box on breast self-examination (opposite) could indicate cancer. If you notice any change in a breast, you should consult your doctor without delay. If the doctor suspects the slightest possibility of cancer, he or she will refer you to a hospital for examination by a specialist and for tests. These include:

**Mammography:** A low-radiation X-ray of the breast.
**Aspiration:** Used when a cyst is suspected. A fine needle is inserted into the lump to draw off a sample of fluid for examination.
**Needle biopsy:** A thick needle is inserted into the breast and a sample of tissue is removed for microscopic examination.
**Frozen-section biopsy:** Carried out under general anaesthetic. An incision is made in the breast and all or part of the lump is removed. While you are still under anaesthetic, a section of the lump is frozen and examined under a microscope. If cancerous cells are found, and if you have previously given permission, all or part of the breast may be removed (see *Breast surgery,* above right).

### Treatment
The best treatment in each case will depend largely on the nature of the cancer and the stage at which it is discovered – the earlier treatment is started the better the prospects of success – but the final choice should be a matter for joint decision between you and your doctors. The main forms of treatment are listed below:

#### Breast surgery

**1 Lumpectomy:** Removal of the growth alone.
**2 Partial mastectomy:** Removal of the growth and some of the surrounding breast tissue.
**3 Simple mastectomy:** Removal of the growth together with the whole breast.
**4 Radical mastectomy:** Removal of the growth, the breast, the underlying tissue and the nearby lymph nodes in the armpit.
**5 Subcutaneous mastectomy:** Occasionally, partial or simple mastectomies may be carried out leaving the overlying skin. Later on silicone can be implanted to restore breast appearance.

#### Radiotherapy
This may be used on its own or in conjunction with other treatments. The breast and armpit area is exposed to a series of short doses of radiation, usually during outpatient visits to the hospital. The aim is to kill off cancer cells. Radiotherapy may make you feel unusually tired, but this wears off when a course of treatment is completed.

#### Chemotherapy
Chemotherapy – treatment with *anti-cancer* drugs that inhibit multiplication of cancer cells or act on the hormone balance – may be the only treatment used or it may be used together with breast surgery and/or radiotherapy. Some forms of chemotherapy can produce side-effects of nausea, loss of hair and loss of energy.

#### After breast surgery
Any woman who loses a breast as a result of breast cancer is naturally upset and worried that it may affect her appearance and femininity. Doctors will normally try to ensure that as much breast tissue is preserved as possible, and may arrange for an implant to preserve breast shape. Following a mastectomy, you will be advised on the various types of artificial breast available. Many hospitals have counsellors who will advise on problems before and after surgery.

# 125 Absent periods

Menstruation normally starts between the ages of 11 and 14, although occasionally it does not start until some time later, especially in girls who are below-average height and/or weight. Once periods start they may be irregular for the first few years and may not settle down to a regular monthly cycle until the late teens. Once the menstrual cycle is established, it may vary in length between individual women from as little as 24 days between periods to about 35 days. Both extremes are normal. Absence of periods (amenorrhoea) may occur in healthy women for a variety of reasons, the most common of which is pregnancy. Other factors that may affect your monthly cycle include illness, stress, and strenuous physical activity. Only rarely is absence of periods a sign of an underlying disorder. It is normal for periods to cease permanently as you approach middle age. Consult this chart if you have never had a period or if your period is more than 2 weeks late.

**START HERE** → **Have you ever had a period?** → **YES**

**NO** ↓

**Primary amenorrhoea** is the term used to describe absence of periods in a woman (or girl) who has never started to menstruate. This is no cause for concern before the age of 14, but if you are older, you should discuss the problem with your doctor.

*Treatment:* Following a general physical examination, your doctor may arrange for you to undergo tests to discover the cause of the trouble. Often primary amenorrhoea needs no treatment, but if you want to become pregnant it is sometimes possible to start menstruation by hormone treatment.

**Might you be pregnant?** → **YES**

**NO** ↓

**Pregnancy** is the most common explanation for absence of periods in sexually active women of fertile years. Consider this possibility even if you think you have been taking reliable contraceptive precautions (including sterilization). Consult your doctor and/or try a "do-it-yourself" pregnancy test (see *Diagnosis of pregnancy*, above right).

**Have you had a baby recently?** → **YES**

**NO** ↓

**After childbirth** you are unlikely to start having periods again as long as you are breast-feeding regularly. Consult your doctor if you stopped breast-feeding more than three months ago.

**Have you been ill or under stress or have you undergone an upheaval such as moving house?** → **YES**

**NO** ↓

*Go to next page*

**Major physical or emotional upsets** often interfere with the complex chain of hormone interactions that control *The menstrual cycle* (opposite), causing periods to cease temporarily. This in itself is no cause for concern, but you should seek your doctor's advice if you are feeling generally unwell or if you are feeling anxious or depressed.

---

### DIAGNOSIS OF PREGNANCY

For most women the first indication of pregnancy is missing a menstrual period. However, you may also notice some of the following early signs of pregnancy:

- tenderness of the breasts or nipples
- increased frequency of urination
- unusual tiredness
- nausea and/or vomiting

**Pregnancy testing**
If you think that you may be pregnant you can either go to your doctor (or family planning clinic) for a pregnancy test, or try one of the "do-it-yourself" pregnancy testing kits that are widely available from chemists. If you go to your doctor, you are likely to be asked for a sample of the first urine you pass in the morning or a blood sample. This will be sent for tests that reveal the presence of certain hormones that occur only during pregnancy. Do-it-yourself pregnancy tests usually work in the same way.

---

### THE MENOPAUSE

The menopause is signalled by the end of menstrual periods and marks the time when a woman ceases to be fertile. The years surrounding this event are often referred to as the climacteric or change of life. The menopause usually occurs around the age of 50, but it can happen earlier or later. You can consider that you have reached the menopause if you are over 45 years old and have not had a period for 6 months. Hormonal fluctuations before and after the menopause often (though not always) give rise to a variety of physical and emotional symptoms. Emotional difficulties may be further complicated by social factors – for example, children growing up and leaving home – that also necessitate psychological adjustments as you approach middle age.

**Principal symptoms of the menopause**
These normally disappear within a year or so of the cessation of periods.

- irregularity and eventual cessation of periods
- hot flushes (attacks of increased heat and sweating)
- night sweats
- dryness of the vagina, as a result of thinning of the vaginal secretions, which may make intercourse uncomfortable
- emotional upset – depression, irritability, and tearfulness

**Treatment for menopausal symptoms**
Not all women need special medical treatment during the menopause. If your symptoms cause you no distress, treatment is unlikely to be beneficial. If you are suffering from uncomfortable or embarrassing symptoms, consult your doctor; much can be done to alleviate such symptoms.

**Hormone-replacement therapy (HRT)**
Supplements for female sex hormones may be prescribed for some women who are suffering from menopausal symptoms. However, because of the increased risk of blood clots, and therefore of heart attacks and strokes, such treatment is not suitable for all women. For this reason your doctor may also be unwilling to continue hormone treatment for more than a few years.

**Other treatments**
Hormone cream or lubricating jelly (for vaginal dryness), *anti-depressants* or *anti-anxiety* drugs (for psychological symptoms) and nonhormonal drugs (to control hot flushes) may also be prescribed in addition to or as an alternative to hormone-replacement therapy.

Continued from previous page

Are you underweight according to the chart on p.26, AND/OR have you recently lost more than 4kg (10lb) in weight?

**YES** ▶

**NO** ▼

Have you recently undertaken a rigorous programme of exercise?

**YES** ▶

**Loss of weight or regular strenuous exercise** often results in cessation of periods. In these circumstances absence of periods is not in itself a cause for concern, but it is advisable to discuss the problem with your doctor to check your general health.

See also chart

 **56** **Loss of weight**

**NO** ▼

Have you recently stopped taking the contraceptive pill?

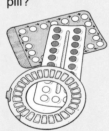

**YES** ▶

**Readjustment of your hormone balance** after stopping the contraceptive pill may take a month or so. Consult your doctor if normal menstrual periods have not started again after 3 months.

**NO** ▼

Are you over 40?

**YES** ▶

**Irregularity of periods** is normal in the years preceding the menopause (change of life) (see *The menopause*, opposite). Most women find that periods become increasingly infrequent until they stop altogether. Occasionally, periods continue normally until they suddenly cease. It is important to remember that while you continue to have periods you are probably still fertile. So if you are sexually active and have missed a period you should also consider the possibility of pregnancy.

**NO** ▼

**Consult your doctor** if you are unable to make a diagnosis from this chart.

## THE MENSTRUAL CYCLE

The menstrual cycle refers to the chain of hormone interactions that occurs in women during their childbearing years approximately every month. This series of events enables an egg to be released, and if it is fertilized this ensures that the womb provides a suitable environment for the egg to implant and for the fetus to develop. The most noticeable outward sign of the menstrual cycle is the monthly period of vaginal bleeding – menstruation – during which the lining of the womb is shed when the previous month's egg is not fertilized. However, many more body changes also take place during the course of the cycle.

**A typical cycle**
The typical menstrual cycle takes about 28 days, although this may vary between individual women. Conventionally, the first day of menstrual bleeding is counted as day 1.

**Days 1-5**
Falling levels of the hormone progesterone in the body trigger the start of menstruation – the shedding of the lining of the womb. During this time hormones produced in the pituitary gland, prompted by signals from the hypothalamus (part of the brain) stimulate the ripening of an egg in the ovary, which in turn produces increasing levels of another hormone, oestrogen.

**Days 5-14**
Menstrual bleeding normally ceases by day 5. For the next few days you may notice a slight vaginal discharge of mucus secretions from the cervix (neck of the womb). Between days 9 and 13, oestrogen levels reach their peak and the cervical mucus becomes clear and runny. This is the start of the potentially fertile period. On day 13 the levels of the pituitary hormones that stimulate the ripening and release of the egg also reach a peak, temperature rises by about ½°C (1°F), and ovulation takes place on day 14.

**Days 15-23**
Following ovulation, and if the egg is not fertilized, oestrogen levels drop markedly, and the follicle from which the egg has been released forms into a gland called the corpus luteum which secretes progesterone. On days 15-16 you may notice thick, jelly-like cervical mucus, after which there is likely to be little if any mucus for the remainder of the cycle.

**Days 24-28**
The activity of the corpus luteum begins to decline as the gland degenerates, and progesterone levels begin to fall. Some women may begin to notice pre-menstrual symptoms such as breast tenderness and mood changes – especially irritability and depression. There may be slight bloating due to fluid retention. The onset of menstruation may be signalled by a drop in temperature of about ½°C (1°F).

**Sequence of events**

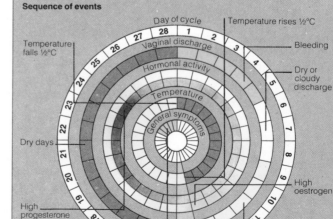

253

# 126 Heavy periods

Heavy periods, a condition sometimes called menorrhagia, are periods in which more than the average amount of blood is lost. Some women naturally lose more blood than others, but for most women bleeding lasts about 5 days, with the heaviest blood loss occurring in the first 3 days. Consult this chart if your periods last longer than this, if normal sanitary towels (or tampons) are not sufficient, or if your periods suddenly become heavier than you are used to. Various factors may cause unusually heavy periods, among them disorders of the lining of the womb and the intra-uterine contraceptive device (coil). However, whichever reason you suspect for your heavy periods, consult your doctor for treatment, because there is a risk that regular heavy bleeding may lead to anaemia (see, for example, p.147).

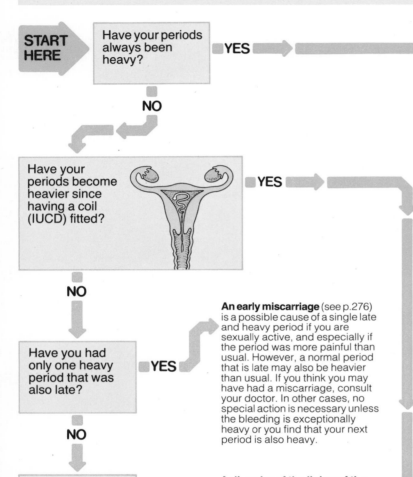

**START HERE**

**Have your periods always been heavy?**

**YES** →

**NO** ↓

**Have your periods become heavier since having a coil (IUCD) fitted?**

**YES** →

**NO** ↓

**Have you had only one heavy period that was also late?**

**YES** →

**An early miscarriage** (see p.276) is a possible cause of a single late and heavy period if you are sexually active, and especially if the period was more painful than usual. However, a normal period that is late may also be heavier than usual. If you think you may have had a miscarriage, consult your doctor. In other cases, no special action is necessary unless the bleeding is exceptionally heavy or you find that your next period is also heavy.

**NO** ↓

**Have your periods become more painful?**

**YES** →

**A disorder of the lining of the womb,** such as fibroids (benign growths) or endometriosis (formation of womb-lining tissue outside the womb) is a possible cause of increased pain and bleeding during periods. Consult your doctor.

**Treatment:** Your doctor will probably do a *vaginal examination* (p.258), and may arrange for you to have a *D and C,* (right) and possibly *laparoscopy,* (p.272). If you are found to have fibroids, these may be removed surgically. Occasionally, in cases of particularly troublesome fibroids, when a woman does not want to have children in the future, *hysterectomy,* (p.256) may be recommended. If you have endometriosis, you may be given long-term hormone treatment.

**NO** ↓

**Are your periods lasting longer than they used to?**

**YES** →

**NO** ↓

**Consult your doctor** if you are unable to make a diagnosis from this chart.

**A thicker than usual lining of the womb** is often the reason why some women tend to have heavier periods than others. This in itself is no cause for concern, but you should discuss the problem with your doctor, who may want to rule out the possibility of anaemia, and may suggest treatment.

**Treatment:** If after examining you your doctor suspects the possibility of anaemia, he or she will probably take a blood sample for analysis (see p.146). If you are found to be anaemic, your doctor will probably prescribe iron tablets and may advise a change of diet. Your doctor will also discuss the possibility of treating the heaviness of your periods using a hormone treatment. Or you may be advised to have a *D and C* (below).

---

### D AND C

D and C (dilatation and curettage) is a minor operation that is usually done in order to discover the cause of heavy periods, and may in some cases cure the problem. The technique may also be used for investigation of infertility, and for early termination of pregnancy (see p.271). D and C is carried out under general anaesthetic. The opening of the cervix (neck of the womb) is dilated (widened) and an instrument called a curette is used to scrape out the lining of the womb. These scrapings may then be taken for laboratory examination. Following the operation, you will have bleeding from the womb for a few days, and you are likely to experience backache and/or lower abdominal pain. You will probably also be advised not to use tampons and to refrain from sexual intercourse for a week or so.

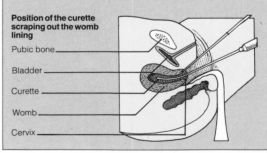

**Position of the curette scraping out the womb lining**

Pubic bone

Bladder

Curette

Womb

Cervix

---

**The coil** (intra-uterine contraceptive device) may cause heavier periods as a side-effect and this is no cause for concern if the increase in bleeding is slight. If the bleeding is much heavier than usual, consult your doctor, who may suggest an alternative method of contraception (see chart 136, *Choosing a contraceptive method*).

**Fibroids** (benign growths inside the womb) may cause periods to become heavier and longer. This is especially likely if you are over 35 years old. Consult your doctor.

**Treatment:** A doctor will usually be able to detect fibroids by a *vaginal examination,* (p.258). If the diagnosis is confirmed you may be prescribed hormone treatment to reduce bleeding. If this does not control your symptoms you may need to have a *D and C* (above). Large troublesome fibroids may need to be removed surgically. Occasionally, a *hysterectomy,* (p.256) is advised.

# 127 Painful periods

Many women experience some degree of pain or discomfort during menstrual periods. The pain – often called dysmenorrhoea – is usually cramping and is felt in the lower abdomen. In most cases painful periods are not a sign of ill health and do not disrupt everyday activities. However, if you suffer from severe pain or if your periods suddenly start to become much more painful, you may need treatment from your doctor.

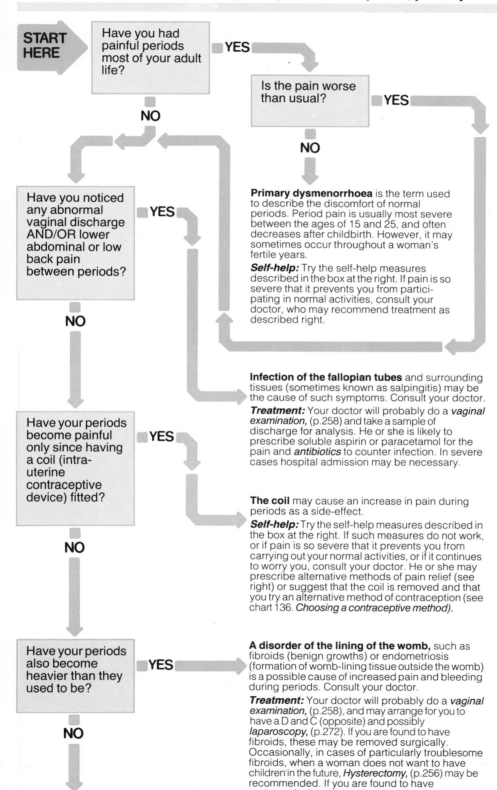

**START HERE**

Have you had painful periods most of your adult life?

**YES** → Is the pain worse than usual?

**YES** →

**NO** ↓

Have you noticed any abnormal vaginal discharge AND/OR lower abdominal or low back pain between periods?

**YES** →

**NO** ↓

**NO** ↓

**Primary dysmenorrhoea** is the term used to describe the discomfort of normal periods. Period pain is usually most severe between the ages of 15 and 25, and often decreases after childbirth. However, it may sometimes occur throughout a woman's fertile years.
**Self-help:** Try the self-help measures described in the box at the right. If pain is so severe that it prevents you from participating in normal activities, consult your doctor, who may recommend treatment as described right.

**Infection of the fallopian tubes** and surrounding tissues (sometimes known as salpingitis) may be the cause of such symptoms. Consult your doctor.
**Treatment:** Your doctor will probably do a *vaginal examination,* (p.258) and take a sample of discharge for analysis. He or she is likely to prescribe soluble aspirin or paracetamol for the pain and *antibiotics* to counter infection. In severe cases hospital admission may be necessary.

Have your periods become painful only since having a coil (intra-uterine contraceptive device) fitted?

**YES** →

**NO** ↓

**The coil** may cause an increase in pain during periods as a side-effect.
**Self-help:** Try the self-help measures described in the box at the right. If such measures do not work, or if pain is so severe that it prevents you from carrying out your normal activities, or if it continues to worry you, consult your doctor. He or she may prescribe alternative methods of pain relief (see right) or suggest that the coil is removed and that you try an alternative method of contraception (see chart 136. *Choosing a contraceptive method).*

Have your periods also become heavier than they used to be?

**YES** →

**NO** ↓

**A disorder of the lining of the womb,** such as fibroids (benign growths) or endometriosis (formation of womb-lining tissue outside the womb) is a possible cause of increased pain and bleeding during periods. Consult your doctor.
**Treatment:** Your doctor will probably do a *vaginal examination,* (p.258), and may arrange for you to have a D and C (opposite) and possibly *laparoscopy,* (p.272). If you are found to have fibroids, these may be removed surgically. Occasionally, in cases of particularly troublesome fibroids, when a woman does not want to have children in the future, *Hysterectomy,* (p.256) may be recommended. If you are found to have endometriosis, you may be given long-term hormone treatment.

**Consult your doctor** if you are unable to make a diagnosis from this chart.

**TREATMENT FOR MENSTRUAL PROBLEMS**
Unpleasant menstrual symptoms including premenstrual syndrome (see below), period pain and excessive bleeding, can often be successfully relieved by medical treatment. So it is worthwhile seeking your doctor's advice if you are distressed by such symptoms, even if these seem to be part of your normal menstrual cycle.

**Premenstrual syndrome**
In the week or so before a period, many women experience a variety of symptoms including tension, irritability, depression, a feeling of being bloated – especially in the breasts and abdomen, and headaches. Treatment will depend on your individual symptoms and their severity, but may include one or more of the following:

**Counselling** may be offered. This may be in the form of sympathetic discussion with your family doctor, or through self-help discussion groups.
**Progesterone (hormone supplements)** may be given in the last part of your *menstrual cycle* (p.253).
**Pyridoxine** (vitamin B6) is sometimes given daily to relieve premenstrual depression.
**Diuretics** (see p.296, 297) may be prescribed in the last half of your menstrual cycle to relieve bloating.

**Period pain**
If you have painful periods, first try the following self-help suggestions:
- Take soluble aspirin or paracetamol.
- When pain is severe, rest in bed with a well-wrapped hot-water bottle on your abdomen.

If pain continues to trouble you, consult your doctor, who may prescribe tablets to inhibit the muscle cramps that lead to period pain. Alternatively, you may be given hormone tablets. If you also require contraception, and there is no medical reason that makes it inadvisable, your doctor may suggest that you start taking hormones in the form of the contraceptive pill (see also chart 136, *Choosing a contraceptive method).*

**Excessive bleeding**
If you suffer from excessive blood loss during periods (menorrhagia), consult your doctor, who may advise a *D and C* (opposite) or may prescribe hormone treatment in the form of the contraceptive pill (see above) or in a non-contraceptive type of hormone.

# 128 Irregular vaginal bleeding

Irregular vaginal bleeding includes irregular menstrual periods and blood loss between normal periods. The latter type of bleeding may consist of occasional slight "spotting", or it may be heavier. Sometimes irregular periods may be the result of hormonal fluctuations – for example, in adolescence or as you approach the menopause. However, bleeding between periods, especially if accompanied by pain or if it occurs in an older woman, may occasionally be the sign of a serious underlying disorder and should be investigated by your doctor.

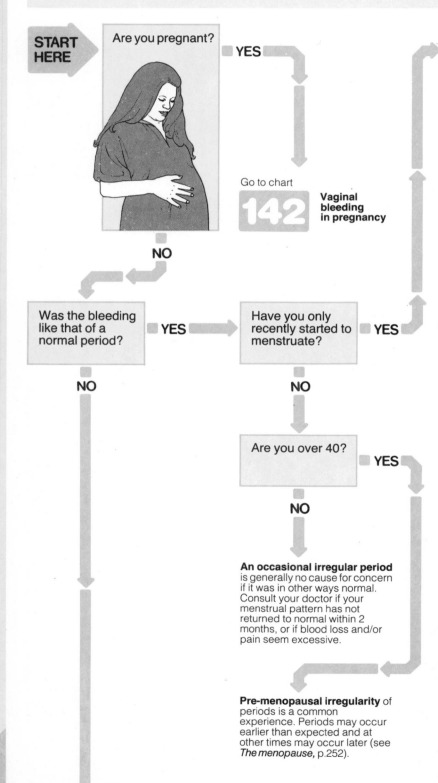

**START HERE**

**Are you pregnant?**

**YES** → Go to chart **142** **Vaginal bleeding in pregnancy**

**NO** ↓

**Was the bleeding like that of a normal period?**

**YES** → **Have you only recently started to menstruate?**

**YES** →

**NO** ↓ (from "Was the bleeding like that of a normal period?")

**NO** ↓ (from "Have you only recently started to menstruate?")

**Are you over 40?**

**YES** →

**NO** ↓

**An occasional irregular period** is generally no cause for concern if it was in other ways normal. Consult your doctor if your menstrual pattern has not returned to normal within 2 months, or if blood loss and/or pain seem excessive.

**Pre-menopausal irregularity** of periods is a common experience. Periods may occur earlier than expected and at other times may occur later (see *The menopause*, p.252).

*Go to next page*

**Irregular periods** are common in the first years of menstruation. They may occur sometimes as often as every two weeks, and then perhaps you may not have a period for several months. This is usually no cause for concern and a regular pattern will gradually establish itself. If you are worried, however, consult your doctor.

---

## HYSTERECTOMY

Hysterectomy – removal of the womb – is a major operation that may be carried out for a variety of reasons. It is a usual part of the treatment for cancer of the womb, but may also be carried out in cases of cervical cancer, severe fibroids (benign growths in the womb), or abnormal menstrual bleeding that cannot be controlled by other means. When there is no life-threatening disorder a hysterectomy will usually be recommended only after full discussion between the woman and her doctor and when she is certain she no longer wants children.

There are several types of hysterectomy, which depend on the site of the incision and whether or not the fallopian tubes and/or ovaries are removed. Doctors try to leave at least one ovary in place to prevent hormonal disturbance after the operation.

**Simple hysterectomy**
Removal of the womb only. It may be done through an incision in the lower abdomen or through the vagina (this leaves no scar).

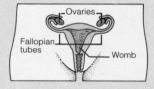

Ovaries · Fallopian tubes · Womb

**Hysterosalpingectomy**
Removal of the womb and fallopian tubes, usually through an incision in the lower abdomen.

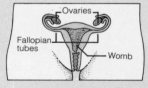

Ovaries · Fallopian tubes · Womb

**Hysterosalpingo-oöphorectomy**
Removal of the womb, fallopian tubes, and ovaries, usually through an incision in the lower abdomen.

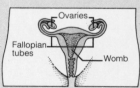

Ovaries · Fallopian tubes · Womb

**After a hysterectomy**
After a hysterectomy you will no longer be able to have children and you will cease to menstruate. However, you will be able to have a normal sex life, and most doctors encourage women who have had hysterectomies to resume sexual relations as soon as they have recovered from the operation itself. If you have had both ovaries removed and have not yet passed menopause, you will be given hormone-replacement treatment to prevent the symptoms of a premature menopause (see *The menopause*, p.252). Some women, especially younger women, find that it takes some time for them to adjust mentally and emotionally to the loss of the womb. They may feel that they have lost part of their femininity. Your doctor will be sympathetic to such feelings and may be able to offer counselling after the operation to help you overcome depression and other difficulties.

*Continued from previous page*

**Have you had sexual intercourse within the past 3 months AND have you missed a period?**

**YES** → 

**CALL YOUR DOCTOR NOW!**
**A serious complication of early pregnancy,** such as an ectopic pregnancy (pregnancy outside the womb), is possible, especially if your normal period is delayed and you also have abdominal pain.

***Treatment:*** If your doctor suspects an ectopic pregnancy, you will probably be admitted to hospital. If the diagnosis is confirmed, you will need to have an urgent operation to end the pregnancy.

**NO** ↓

**Does bleeding occur only within a few hours of intercourse?**

**YES** →

**CONSULT YOUR DOCTOR WITHOUT DELAY!**
**Post-coital bleeding** may be a sign of minor abnormality of the cells of the cervix (neck of the womb), or a sign of cancer of the cervix.

***Treatment:*** Your doctor will do a *vaginal examination,* (p.258) and will also take a smear (see *cervical screening,* right). If a smear shows the presence of abnormal cells you may need to have further investigations such as *colposcopy* (below right). Some cervical abnormalities can be treated by laser surgery, freezing, or by a minor operation called a cone biopsy. However, if you are found to have a cancer that seems to have spread you may require a *hysterectomy* (opposite) and/or radiotherapy (either in the form of X-ray treatment or by insertion of a radium pellet into the vagina). Treatment for cancer of the cervix is generally successful if started early.

**NO** ↓

**Are you over 40 AND is it more than six months since your last period?**

**YES** →

**CONSULT YOUR DOCTOR WITHOUT DELAY!**
**Post-menopausal bleeding** may be caused by a minor vaginal disorder, but it could also be a sign of cancer of the womb or cervix (neck of the womb).

***Treatment:*** Your doctor will do a *vaginal examination,* (p.258) and will probably take a smear of the cervix (see *Cervical screening,* right). He or she may also arrange for you to be admitted to hospital for a *D and C* (p.254). If cancer is diagnosed, you will probably need to have a *hysterectomy* (opposite). Radiotherapy or the insertion of a radium pellet into the vagina may also be part of your treatment. Hormones may also be prescribed. The earlier treatment is started, the greater the chances of a cure.

**NO** ↓

**Are you taking the contraceptive pill OR have you had the coil (intra-uterine contraceptive device) fitted?**

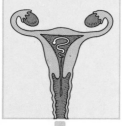

**YES** →

**Both these contraceptive methods** may cause spotting between periods. This is unlikely to be a cause for concern, but you should discuss the symptom with your doctor, who may suggest a change of pill, or an alternative form of contraception. (See also chart 136, *Choosing a contraceptive method.*)

**NO** ↓

**Consult your doctor without delay** if you are unable to make a diagnosis from this chart.

---

**CERVICAL SCREENING**

The cells that make up the outer surface of the cervix (neck of the womb) may sometimes undergo changes for reasons that are not yet fully understood. Such cell abnormalities often present no risk to general health, but in a small proportion of cases the abnormal cells may become cancerous. Cancer of the cervix, although rare compared with other cervical abnormalities, is one of the most common cancers affecting women. It is, however, also one of the most easily treated cancers if diagnosed early. For these reasons it is important for every adult woman to make sure that she has regular screening, so that any change in the cells of the cervix can be detected and, when necessary, treated as soon as possible.

**Cervical smear test**
The standard method of screening is the cervical smear (PAP) test. It is recommended that every sexually active woman should have this test every 3-5 years throughout adult life. The test can be carried out by your family doctor or by a family planning clinic. In the test, which is quite painless, the vagina is held open by an instrument called a speculum, and a spatula is used to scrape away a sample of cells from the surface of the cervix. The sample is then sent for laboratory examination.

If the smear shows up any cell abnormality, you will probably be asked to return for another smear test in a few months' time. This is because minor abnormalities often heal themselves without the need for further treatment. If the trouble persists you will probably be referred to an outpatient clinic for colposcopy.

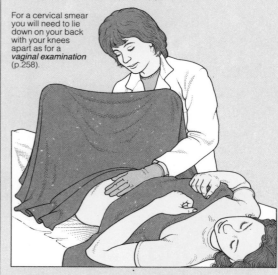

For a cervical smear you will need to lie down on your back with your knees apart as for a *vaginal examination* (p.258).

Spatula
Speculum
Cervix

The speculum holds the vagina open while the doctor uses the spatula to take a scraping of cells from the cervix.

**Colposcopy**
This is a technique that allows the doctor to take a close look at the surface of the cervix. An instrument with a magnifying lens and an eyepiece is inserted into the vagina. While the doctor is viewing the cervix, he or she will probably also take a *biopsy,* (p.159) of the cervical tissue for further examination. Minor abnormalities can often be treated during colposcopy by laser beam, burning or freezing. More serious abnormalities may require surgery.

# 129 Abnormal vaginal discharge

The vagina is normally kept moist and clean by secretions from the tissue lining the vagina. Such secretions may be apparent as a thin whitish discharge from the vagina. This normal discharge may vary in quantity and consistency according to the time of your menstrual cycle, and may increase at times of sexual arousal, during pregnancy, and in women using the contraceptive pill or intra-uterine contraceptive device (known as the IUCD or coil). A discharge that looks abnormal, especially if it is accompanied by itching or burning around the vagina, or pain during intercourse, may be a sign of infection and needs medical attention. Consult this chart if you notice any increase in discharge or change in its colour or consistency.

**For discharge containing blood, see chart 128, Irregular vaginal bleeding.**

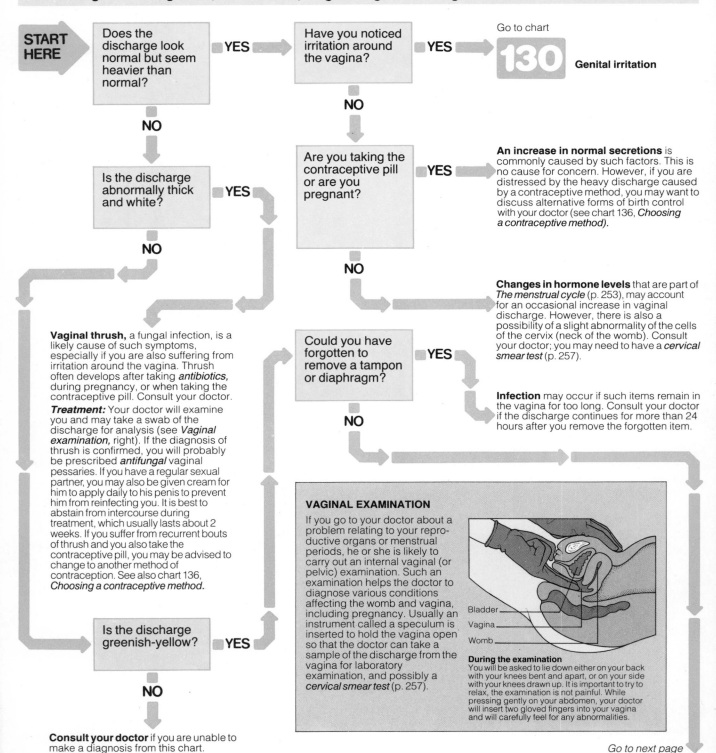

**START HERE**

Does the discharge look normal but seem heavier than normal? — **YES** → Have you noticed irritation around the vagina? — **YES** → Go to chart **130** **Genital irritation**

Does the discharge look normal but seem heavier than normal? — **NO** ↓

Have you noticed irritation around the vagina? — **NO** ↓

Is the discharge abnormally thick and white? — **YES** ↓

Is the discharge abnormally thick and white? — **NO**

Are you taking the contraceptive pill or are you pregnant? — **YES** → **An increase in normal secretions** is commonly caused by such factors. This is no cause for concern. However, if you are distressed by the heavy discharge caused by a contraceptive method, you may want to discuss alternative forms of birth control with your doctor (see chart 136, *Choosing a contraceptive method).*

Are you taking the contraceptive pill or are you pregnant? — **NO** ↓

**Changes in hormone levels** that are part of *The menstrual cycle* (p. 253), may account for an occasional increase in vaginal discharge. However, there is also a possibility of a slight abnormality of the cells of the cervix (neck of the womb). Consult your doctor; you may need to have a *cervical smear test* (p. 257).

Could you have forgotten to remove a tampon or diaphragm? — **YES** →

Could you have forgotten to remove a tampon or diaphragm? — **NO**

**Vaginal thrush,** a fungal infection, is a likely cause of such symptoms, especially if you are also suffering from irritation around the vagina. Thrush often develops after taking *antibiotics,* during pregnancy, or when taking the contraceptive pill. Consult your doctor.
*Treatment:* Your doctor will examine you and may take a swab of the discharge for analysis (see *Vaginal examination,* right). If the diagnosis of thrush is confirmed, you will probably be prescribed *antifungal* vaginal pessaries. If you have a regular sexual partner, you may also be given cream for him to apply daily to his penis to prevent him from reinfecting you. It is best to abstain from intercourse during treatment, which usually lasts about 2 weeks. If you suffer from recurrent bouts of thrush and you also take the contraceptive pill, you may be advised to change to another method of contraception. See also chart 136, *Choosing a contraceptive method.*

**Infection** may occur if such items remain in the vagina for too long. Consult your doctor if the discharge continues for more than 24 hours after you remove the forgotten item.

Is the discharge greenish-yellow? — **YES** ↑

Is the discharge greenish-yellow? — **NO** ↓

**Consult your doctor** if you are unable to make a diagnosis from this chart.

## VAGINAL EXAMINATION

If you go to your doctor about a problem relating to your reproductive organs or menstrual periods, he or she is likely to carry out an internal vaginal (or pelvic) examination. Such an examination helps the doctor to diagnose various conditions affecting the womb and vagina, including pregnancy. Usually an instrument called a speculum is inserted to hold the vagina open so that the doctor can take a sample of the discharge from the vagina for laboratory examination, and possibly a *cervical smear test* (p. 257).

Bladder
Vagina
Womb

**During the examination**
You will be asked to lie down either on your back with your knees bent and apart, or on your side with your knees drawn up. It is important to try to relax, the examination is not painful. While pressing gently on your abdomen, your doctor will insert two gloved fingers into your vagina and will carefully feel for any abnormalities.

*Go to next page*

*Continued from previous page*

**Do you have any lower abdominal or low back pain AND/OR do you feel generally unwell?**

**YES**

**Infection of the fallopian tubes and surrounding tissues** (sometimes known as salpingitis) may be the cause of such symptoms. Consult your doctor.

***Treatment:*** Your doctor will probably do a *vaginal examination* (opposite) and take a sample of discharge for analysis. He or she is likely to prescribe soluble aspirin or paracetamol for the pain and *antibiotics* to counter infection. In severe cases hospital admission may be necessary.

**NO**

**Trichomonal vaginitis,** or a similar vaginal infection that may be transmitted sexually, is a possibility. Consult your doctor.

***Treatment:*** Your doctor will examine you and will probably take a sample of the discharge from the vagina for analysis (see *Vaginal examination*, opposite). If the diagnosis is confirmed, you will be prescribed a course of antibacterial drugs. See also *Sexually transmitted diseases*, below.

## SEXUALLY TRANSMITTED DISEASES

Infections passed from one person to another during sexual contact (including sexual intercourse and anal or oral sex) are known as sexually transmitted (or venereal) diseases (VD). If you think you have caught a sexually transmitted disease and/or if your sexual partner has, consult your doctor, or go to a clinic that specializes in such diseases (genito-urinary clinic), where you will be treated in the strictest confidence. It is important to seek medical advice promptly because of the risk of serious damage to your reproductive organs from many such diseases, even when symptoms are not severe. Also you may unknowingly pass on the infection to someone else. If you are found to have a sexually transmitted disease, you will be asked to inform any recent sexual partners, so that they too may seek treatment if necessary. You should avoid sex until your doctor confirms that treatment has completely cleared your symptoms.

| Disease | Incubation period* | Symptoms | Treatment |
|---|---|---|---|
| Non-specific genital infection (including chlamydia) | 14-21 days | Often causes few or no symptoms. There may be an abnormal vaginal discharge. If untreated, the infection may spread to the fallopian tubes. Suspect the disease if you have a sexual partner who has non-specific urethritis (a disease usually caused by the chlamydia microbe). | Your doctor will take a swab from your vagina for culture (see *Vaginal examination*, opposite). Treatment is usually with *antibiotics*. |
| Trichomonal vaginitis | Variable | An infected-looking (greenish-yellow) vaginal discharge, usually causing irritation around the vagina. Pain on intercourse. | The diagnosis is confirmed by analysis of a sample of discharge taken from the vagina (see *Vaginal examination*, opposite). The usual treatment is a course of antibacterial drugs. |
| Gonorrhoea | 2 to 10 days | May be symptomless in women. It may sometimes cause abnormal vaginal or urethral discharge and/or painful urination. Persistent untreated infection may spread to womb and fallopian tubes causing lower abdominal pain. | The disease is diagnosed by a urethral vaginal swab (see *Vaginal examination*, opposite). Treatment consists of a course of *antibiotics*. |
| Herpes genitalis | 10 days or less | There is usually an itching feeling in the genital area followed by the appearance of a crop of small, painful blisters. Sometimes these also appear on the thighs and buttocks. The blisters burst after 24 hours, leaving small, red, moist, painful ulcers which sometimes crust over. The glands in the groin may become enlarged and painful. This may be accompanied by a feeling of being unwell and a raised temperature. Outbreaks of blisters are likely to recur. | There is no complete cure for this disorder, although outbreaks tend to become milder over the years. Your doctor may prescribe an *antiviral* drug or ointment to make the ulcers less sore and to speed healing. You will be advised to avoid close sexual contact while you have blisters or sores so that you do not transmit the infection to your partner. |
| Syphilis | 9-90 days | In the first stage a highly infectious, painless sore called a chancre develops in the genital area or inside the vagina. This disappears after a few weeks. In the second stage a rash which does not itch appears all over the body, including the palms and soles. There may also be painless swelling of the lymph glands and infectious wart-like lumps around the anus and/or mouth. | The disease is diagnosed by blood tests and samples taken from any sores. The usual treatment is a 2-week course of *antibiotic* injections. You will need to have regular blood tests for 2 years after treatment to check that the disease has not reappeared. |
| Pubic lice | 0-17 days | Usually there is intense itching in the pubic region, particularly at night. You may be able to see the lice; they are brown and 1 to 2mm long. | Your doctor will give you a lotion or ointment which kills lice and their eggs. At the same time he or she will check that you do not have any other sexually transmitted disease. Bedding and clothing should be thoroughly laundered. |

*Time between contact with the disease and the appearance of symptoms.

# 130 Genital irritation

Consult this chart if you have been suffering from itching and/or soreness in the vagina or around the vulva (external genital area). Such irritation may also cause stinging during urination and discomfort during intercourse. This symptom is known medically as pruritus vulvae. It may be brought on by infection in the vagina or urinary tract, by local irritation from soaps or deodorants, or by various skin conditions.

**Consult this diagnostic chart only after reading chart 8, Itching.**

**START HERE**

**Have you noticed a vaginal discharge that is abnormal in colour or consistency?**

YES → **A vaginal infection** is likely.

Go to chart

**129 Abnormal vaginal discharge**

NO ↓

**Have you noticed any abnormality in the skin of the genital area – for example, lumps, sores, or blisters?**

YES → **A skin condition affecting the vulva** is likely to be the cause of the irritation. Consult your doctor for a firm diagnosis and treatment.

NO ↓

**Have you been passing urine more frequently than usual?**

YES →

Go to chart

**133 Abnormally frequent urination**

NO ↓

**Do you use perfumed soap, bath salts, or deodorants in the genital area and/or vaginal douches?**

YES → **Irritation from perfumes and chemicals** in any of these may cause inflammation of the delicate skin of the vulva and the sensitive lining of the vagina.
*Self-help:* Avoid excessive use of soap in the genital area. Plain water is best. Because vaginal deodorants and douches are unnecessary for genital hygiene and may disrupt the skin's natural chemical balance, they should be avoided. See *Genital hygiene,* right.

NO ↓

**Are you over 45 AND have your periods become irregular?**

YES → **Pruritus vulvae** without obvious cause is a common problem for women.
*Self-help:* Try to resist the urge to scratch; scratching will only increase the irritation. Wash the genital area carefully once a day with plain water. Do not use talcum powders, soaps, bath salts or vaginal deodorants. Choose underpants made of cotton, wear stockings rather than tights, and avoid tight trousers. If irritation persists for more than 2 weeks, consult your doctor.

NO ↓

## GENITAL HYGIENE

### Everyday care
Cleansing the genital area should be part of your normal daily washing routine. However, the skin in this area is delicate and needs to be treated gently so that it does not become inflamed and irritated. Use only plain water; bath salts and soaps, even mild ones, may be irritating. It should only be necessary to wash the external skin of the vulva. The internal lining of the vagina is kept clean by its natural secretions, which also help to protect against infection. Vaginal douches and deodorants are unnecessary for hygiene and health and may cause irritation. They may also disrupt the chemical balance inside the vagina.

### Menstrual hygiene
Your choice of method of sanitary protection during menstrual periods is largely a matter of personal preference. In normal circumstances there is no medical reason for preferring external sanitary pads to internal tampons or vice versa. Sanitary pads may be more suitable for women who have heavy periods because they usually provide greater absorbency. Pads should also be used to absorb blood loss in the weeks following childbirth to minimise the chances of infection. Young girls may also find pads easier to use in the first years of menstruation. Tampons have the advantage of being unnoticeable even under close-fitting clothes, and do not interfere with participation in sports such as swimming. Whichever method you choose, you will need to change your pad or tampon every 3 to 6 hours depending on the heaviness of the menstrual flow.

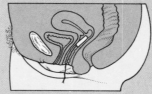

Choose the method that feels best for you – the easy-to-insert tampon or the absorbent press-on pad.

### Toxic shock
Some women may have been discouraged from using tampons by reports of women becoming seriously ill as a result of their use. This occurred when women using very high-absorbency tampons (no longer sold) failed to change them often enough, leading to bacterial growths in the vagina. Toxins (poisons) produced by the bacteria were absorbed into the bloodstream, leading to blood poisoning (toxic shock). Providing that you change your tampons regularly as recommended, there is no danger of being affected by this rare condition. A forgotten tampon of normal absorbency may cause an offensive discharge, but is most unlikely to be a serious risk to health.

**Falling levels of oestrogen** (a female hormone) as you approach *The menopause,* (p.252) may lead to genital irritation. Consult your doctor.

*Treatment:* If your doctor finds that your irritation is due to hormonal changes he or she may prescribe a hormone cream to apply to the vagina and vulva. Alternatively, the doctor may recommend hormone replacement therapy. If the irritation causes discomfort during sexual intercourse, a lubricating jelly may help.

# 131 Poor bladder control

Difficulty in controlling your bladder or involuntary passing of urine may be a sign of infection in the urinary tract or it may be due to weak muscle control. Always seek your doctor's advice about this symptom.

**START HERE** → **Do you have discomfort when passing urine?**

- **YES** → Go to chart **132** **Painful urination**
- **NO** ↓

**Do you often have a leakage of urine when you sneeze, laugh, cough, or run?**

- **YES** → **Have you noticed any feeling of heaviness or discomfort between your legs?**
  - **YES** → *Prolapse of the uterus (womb) or vagina* (see right)
  - **NO** ↓
- **NO** ↓

**Have you recently had a baby?**

- **YES** → *Childbirth* (see right)
- **NO** ↓

**Do you often have a sudden urge to pass urine which is difficult to control?**

- **YES** → **Unstable bladder** is a condition in which even small amounts of urine in the bladder produce a strong urge to urinate. Consult your doctor.
- **NO** ↓

**Do you find it hard to begin to urinate, and is the stream slow?**

- **YES** → **Narrowing of the urethra**
- **NO** ↓

**Consult your doctor** if you are unable to make a diagnosis from this chart.

---

**Prolapse of the uterus (womb) or vagina** may be causing these symptoms. Prolapse occurs when the muscles and ligaments supporting the womb become weak and slack. This is particularly likely if you are over 50. Consult your doctor.

*Treatment:* Your doctor will examine you and may ask you to provide a specimen of urine for analysis to rule out the possibility of infection. If you are suffering from prolapse, your doctor will probably recommend that you try *pelvic-floor exercises* (below). If you are overweight you will also be advised to lose weight (see *How to lose weight,* p.151). In some cases a specially-designed vaginal pessary will also be fitted. If these measures do not improve your condition, you may need to have an operation to strengthen your pelvic-floor muscles.

**Childbirth** may have temporarily weakened your pelvic-floor muscles. This is a common occurrence and nearly always improves within a few months without special treatment. Consult your doctor.

*Treatment:* Your doctor will examine you and may ask you to provide a urine sample for tests to rule out the possibility of infection. In most cases no treatment is necessary. However, *pelvic-floor exercises* (below) may help your muscle tone return to normal more quickly. Your condition will also improve if you lose any excess weight you may have gained during pregnancy (see *How to lose weight,* p.151).

**Stress incontinence** is a condition in which weakness of the pelvic-floor muscles results in leakage of urine when there is any pressure on the bladder. Consult your doctor.

*Treatment:* After examining you, your doctor may ask you to provide a specimen of urine to rule out the possibility of infection. Practising *pelvic-floor exercises* (below) may improve your bladder control. And it may be helpful to lose weight if you are overweight (see *How to lose weight,* p.151). If these measures do not help, your doctor may recommend an operation to strengthen the pelvic-floor muscles.

**Unstable bladder** is a condition in which even small amounts of urine in the bladder produce a strong urge to urinate. Consult your doctor.

*Treatment:* Your doctor will examine you and may ask you to provide a urine specimen for analysis. You may also be referred for *bladder function tests,* (p.264). Sometimes bladder control can be improved by practising holding your urine for as long as possible. The *pelvic-floor exercises* (right) may also be helpful. Your doctor may prescribe a drug to relax your bladder muscles and to calm the nerves that control bladder contraction. In rare cases an operation may be recommended.

**Narrowing of the urethra,** as a result of a difficult childbirth in the past or recurrent urinary-tract infections, may cause such symptoms. Consult your doctor.

*Treatment:* You will probably be referred to hospital for tests. If you are found to have a narrow urethra, a simple operation to enlarge the outlet will be carried out.

---

## WARNING

### INABILITY TO PASS URINE

If you find that you are unable to urinate even though you feel the urge, you need urgent medical attention. While waiting for medical help to arrive, try taking a warm bath, which may enable you to pass some urine.

### SUDDEN LOSS OF BLADDER CONTROL

Sudden inability to control urination may be a sign of damage to the spinal cord or nervous system, especially if you have recently had a back injury or have experienced weakness in your legs.

**Seek medical help at once!**

---

### PELVIC-FLOOR EXERCISES

These exercises are useful for toning up the pelvic-floor muscles, which support the bladder and reproductive organs. The exercises are particularly useful during pregnancy and after childbirth, or if you are suffering from weak bladder control, but they are worth practising at any time. When you go to the lavatory to pass urine, follow this procedure at least twice a day:

1 Contract the muscles around the vagina upwards and inwards so as to stop the flow of urine.

2 Hold this position for a count of 6.

3 Now let the flow of urine continue for another count of 6.

4 Finally, interrupt the flow again for a count of 6 before totally emptying your bladder.

# 132 Painful urination

Pain or discomfort when you pass urine is usually the result of infection in the urinary tract or inflammation around the urethral opening. Such disorders are common among women and in most cases they are easily cured in a short time by a combination of home and professional treatments.

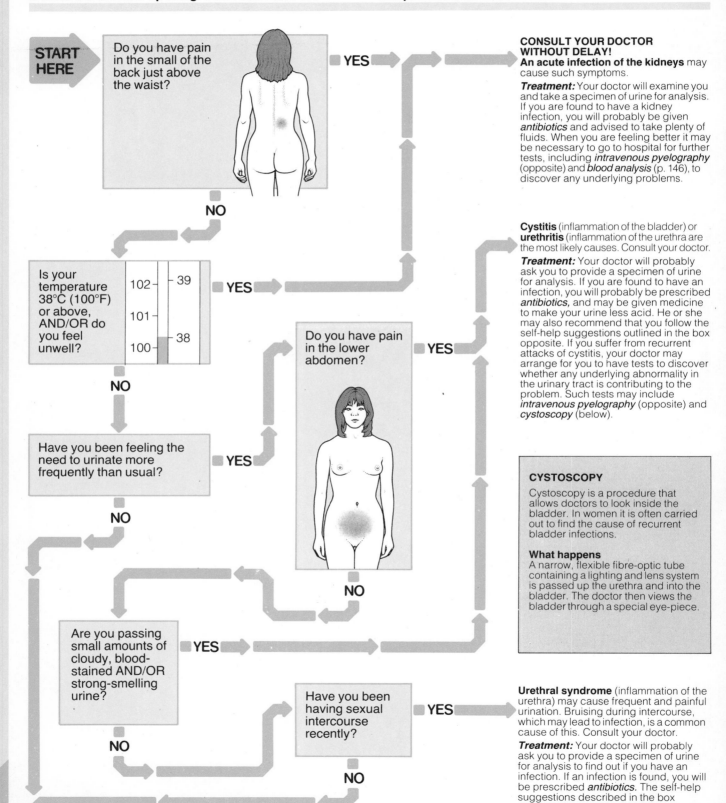

**START HERE**

Do you have pain in the small of the back just above the waist? **YES** →

**CONSULT YOUR DOCTOR WITHOUT DELAY!**
**An acute infection of the kidneys** may cause such symptoms.

*Treatment:* Your doctor will examine you and take a specimen of urine for analysis. If you are found to have a kidney infection, you will probably be given *antibiotics* and advised to take plenty of fluids. When you are feeling better it may be necessary to go to hospital for further tests, including *intravenous pyelography* (opposite) and *blood analysis* (p. 146), to discover any underlying problems.

**NO**

Is your temperature 38°C (100°F) or above, AND/OR do you feel unwell?

102 — 39
101
100 — 38

**YES** →

**Cystitis** (inflammation of the bladder) or **urethritis** (inflammation of the urethra are the most likely causes. Consult your doctor.

*Treatment:* Your doctor will probably ask you to provide a specimen of urine for analysis. If you are found to have an infection, you will probably be prescribed *antibiotics,* and may be given medicine to make your urine less acid. He or she may also recommend that you follow the self-help suggestions outlined in the box opposite. If you suffer from recurrent attacks of cystitis, your doctor may arrange for you to have tests to discover whether any underlying abnormality in the urinary tract is contributing to the problem. Such tests may include *intravenous pyelography* (opposite) and *cystoscopy* (below).

**NO**

Have you been feeling the need to urinate more frequently than usual?

Do you have pain in the lower abdomen? **YES** →

**YES**

**NO**

**CYSTOSCOPY**

Cystoscopy is a procedure that allows doctors to look inside the bladder. In women it is often carried out to find the cause of recurrent bladder infections.

**What happens**
A narrow, flexible fibre-optic tube containing a lighting and lens system is passed up the urethra and into the bladder. The doctor then views the bladder through a special eye-piece.

Are you passing small amounts of cloudy, blood-stained AND/OR strong-smelling urine? **YES** →

**NO**

Have you been having sexual intercourse recently? **YES** →

**Urethral syndrome** (inflammation of the urethra) may cause frequent and painful urination. Bruising during intercourse, which may lead to infection, is a common cause of this. Consult your doctor.

*Treatment:* Your doctor will probably ask you to provide a specimen of urine for analysis to find out if you have an infection. If an infection is found, you will be prescribed *antibiotics.* The self-help suggestions described in the box opposite may also be helpful.

**NO**

*Go to next page*

*Continued from previous page*

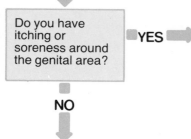

**Do you have itching or soreness around the genital area?** — **YES** → **Do you have a profuse thick, white vaginal discharge?** — **YES** → **Vaginal thrush,** a fungal infection, is a likely cause of such symptoms. Consult your doctor.

**NO** ↓

**NO** ↓

**Do you have a greenish-yellow vaginal discharge?** — **YES** →

**NO** ↓

**Urethral syndrome** (inflammation of the urethra), possibly caused by infection, is the most likely cause of painful urination without additional symptoms. Consult your doctor.

***Treatment:*** See *Urethral syndrome,* opposite.

**Vaginal thrush,** a fungal infection, is a likely cause of such symptoms. Consult your doctor.

***Treatment:*** Your doctor will examine you and may take a swab of the discharge from the inside of the vagina for analysis (see *Vaginal examination,* p. 258). If the diagnosis of thrush is confirmed, you will probably be prescribed *anti-fungal* vaginal pessaries. Thrush is not usually a sexually transmitted disorder, but if you have a regular sexual partner your doctor may give you some cream for him to apply daily to his penis to prevent him from reinfecting you. If you suffer from recurrent bouts of thrush and you also take the contraceptive pill, you may be advised to change to another method of contraception. This is because the pill sometimes causes an increase in vaginal secretions, which makes fungal infection more likely. See also chart 136, *Choosing a contraceptive method.*

**Trichomonal vaginitis,** a vaginal infection that may be transmitted sexually, is a possibility. Consult your doctor.

***Treatment:*** Your doctor will examine you and will probably take a sample of the discharge from the vagina for analysis (see *Vaginal examination,* p. 258). If trichomonal vaginitis is confirmed, you will be prescribed a course of *antibiotics.* Your sexual partner(s) should also receive treatment even if no symptoms are apparent. Otherwise it is likely that you will be reinfected. See also *Sexually transmitted diseases,* p. 259.

**Pruritus vulvae** (inflammation of the vulva) may cause urination to become painful. There is often no obvious cause for this condition, but in women past the menopause it may be linked to a drop in hormone levels, causing the vagina to become dry. In younger women an allergic reaction – to soap, for example – or sexual anxiety may be responsible.

***Self-help:*** Try not to scratch the irritated area, this will only aggravate the condition. Wash the genital area gently once a day and apply a soothing cream. Do not use soap, perfumed bath salts, talcum powder, vaginal deodorants, or douches, because these may increase irritation. Wear cotton underwear and avoid nylon tights and close-fitting trousers which restrict ventilation. If your vagina feels dry during intercourse, use a lubricating jelly. If the problem persists for more than a few days, consult your doctor.

---

### INTRAVENOUS PYELOGRAPHY

Intravenous pyelography (or urethography) is a procedure that provides doctors with a series of X-ray pictures of the urinary tract. A liquid containing chemicals that show up on X-rays is injected into the bloodstream. It travels around the body until it is absorbed by the kidneys. This process may take several hours. X-ray pictures are taken as the chemical works its way through the kidneys, down the ureters, and into the bladder.

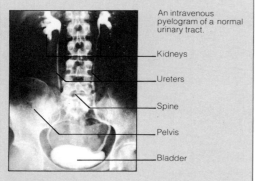

An intravenous pyelogram of a normal urinary tract.

— Kidneys
— Ureters
— Spine
— Pelvis
— Bladder

**Micturating cystogram**
This is a series of X-rays that shows the action of the bladder during urination. This is often done following an IVP when chemicals visible on X-ray are already in the bladder. However, sometimes the chemical solution is passed directly into the bladder through a fine tube (catheter) inserted into the urethra.

---

### SELF-HELP FOR INFECTIONS OF THE BLADDER AND URETHRA

If you are suffering from cystitis or the urethral syndrome, the following self-help suggestions, in addition to whatever treatment your doctor may prescribe, will help to relieve your symptoms, hasten recovery, and prevent the trouble from recurring.

- To relieve abdominal pain and fever, take soluble aspirin or paracetamol. A hot-water bottle on the abdomen is often comforting.
- Try to empty your bladder completely each time you pass urine to prevent a residue from remaining in the bladder and encouraging infection.
- Make sure that you drink plenty of fluids, but avoid heavily sweetened drinks. Reduce the acidity of your urine by adding a teaspoonful of bicarbonate of soda to each glass of

fruit juice or water that you drink; this helps discourage infection. Lemon barley water is also recommended.
- If sexual intercourse is sometimes painful, use a vaginal lubricant and experiment with different positions to find the one that is most comfortable for you.
- Always empty your bladder after sexual intercourse.

- If you use a diaphragm, ask your doctor or clinic to check that it fits properly; ill-fitting diaphragms may bruise the urethra, leading to infection.

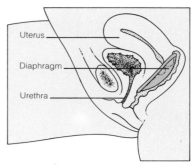

Uterus
Diaphragm
Urethra

- Keep the genital area clean and dry, but do not use vaginal douches or deodorants, or heavily scented soaps.
- Avoid wearing nylon tights or underpants. Cotton underpants are preferable because they absorb sweat and allow air to circulate more freely.
- When you go to the lavatory, always wipe from front to back to keep germs from the bowel away from the urethral opening.

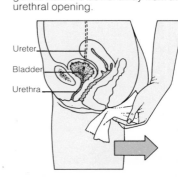

Ureter
Bladder
Urethra

# 133 Abnormally frequent urination

The number of times you need to pass urine each day depends on a number of factors including habit, the amount of fluid consumed, and the strength of your bladder muscles. Most women need to pass urine between 2 and 6 times a day. You will know what is normal for you. Consult this chart if you find that you are having to pass urine more often than usual. Frequency of urination is rarely a symptom of serious disease, but simple treatment can often clear up this disruptive and sometimes embarrassing symptom.

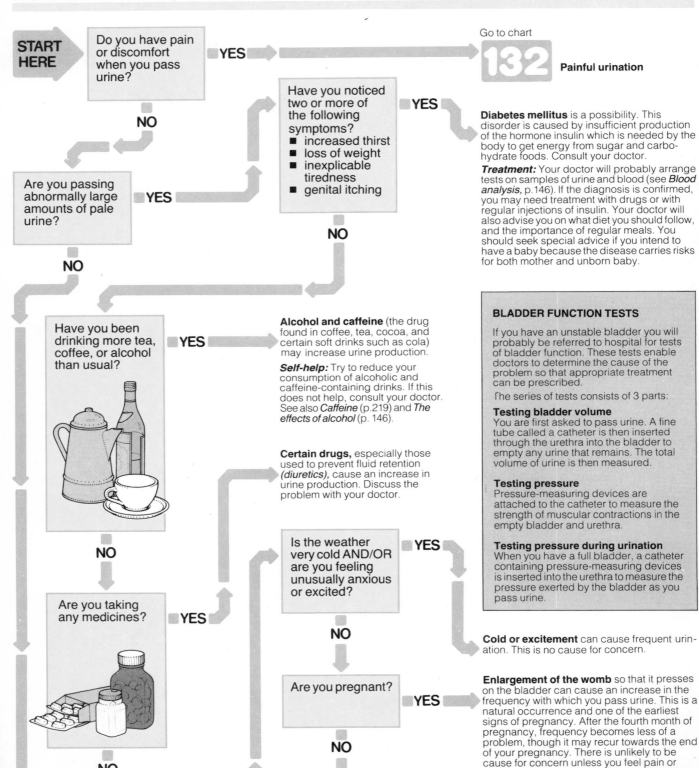

**START HERE**

**Do you have pain or discomfort when you pass urine?**

YES → Go to chart **132** Painful urination

NO

**Are you passing abnormally large amounts of pale urine?**

**Have you noticed two or more of the following symptoms?**
- increased thirst
- loss of weight
- inexplicable tiredness
- genital itching

YES →

**Diabetes mellitus** is a possibility. This disorder is caused by insufficient production of the hormone insulin which is needed by the body to get energy from sugar and carbohydrate foods. Consult your doctor.

*Treatment:* Your doctor will probably arrange tests on samples of urine and blood (see *Blood analysis,* p.146). If the diagnosis is confirmed, you may need treatment with drugs or with regular injections of insulin. Your doctor will also advise you on what diet you should follow, and the importance of regular meals. You should seek special advice if you intend to have a baby because the disease carries risks for both mother and unborn baby.

YES

NO

NO

**Have you been drinking more tea, coffee, or alcohol than usual?**

YES →

**Alcohol and caffeine** (the drug found in coffee, tea, cocoa, and certain soft drinks such as cola) may increase urine production.

*Self-help:* Try to reduce your consumption of alcoholic and caffeine-containing drinks. If this does not help, consult your doctor. See also *Caffeine* (p.219) and *The effects of alcohol* (p. 146).

**Certain drugs,** especially those used to prevent fluid retention *(diuretics),* cause an increase in urine production. Discuss the problem with your doctor.

---

**BLADDER FUNCTION TESTS**

If you have an unstable bladder you will probably be referred to hospital for tests of bladder function. These tests enable doctors to determine the cause of the problem so that appropriate treatment can be prescribed.

The series of tests consists of 3 parts:

**Testing bladder volume**
You are first asked to pass urine. A fine tube called a catheter is then inserted through the urethra into the bladder to empty any urine that remains. The total volume of urine is then measured.

**Testing pressure**
Pressure-measuring devices are attached to the catheter to measure the strength of muscular contractions in the empty bladder and urethra.

**Testing pressure during urination**
When you have a full bladder, a catheter containing pressure-measuring devices is inserted into the urethra to measure the pressure exerted by the bladder as you pass urine.

---

NO

**Are you taking any medicines?**

YES →

**Is the weather very cold AND/OR are you feeling unusually anxious or excited?**

YES →

NO

**Cold or excitement** can cause frequent urination. This is no cause for concern.

**Are you pregnant?**

YES →

**Enlargement of the womb** so that it presses on the bladder can cause an increase in the frequency with which you pass urine. This is a natural occurrence and one of the earliest signs of pregnancy. After the fourth month of pregnancy, frequency becomes less of a problem, though it may recur towards the end of your pregnancy. There is unlikely to be cause for concern unless you feel pain or discomfort. However, you should mention the symptom to your doctor, who may want to rule out the possibility of infection.

NO

NO

*Go to next page*

*Continued from previous page*

Do you often have a sudden, strong urge to pass urine, but pass only a small amount?

**YES**

**Unstable bladder** is a condition in which even small amounts of urine in the bladder produce a strong urge to urinate, and sometimes urine maybe passed before you can reach the lavatory. Consult your doctor.

*Treatment:* Your doctor will examine you and will probably ask you to provide a urine specimen for tests to exclude the possibility of infection. You may also be referred for *bladder function tests* (opposite). Sometimes bladder control can be improved by practising holding in your urine for as long as possible. *Pelvic-floor exercises* (p.261) may also be helpful. Your doctor may prescribe a drug to relax your bladder muscles and to calm the nerves that control bladder contraction. In rare cases an operation may be advised.

**NO**

Are you sometimes unable to prevent yourself from passing urine?

**YES**

Go to chart

**131** **Poor bladder control**

**NO**

**Consult your doctor** if you are unable to make a diagnosis from this chart and if the frequency of urination is such that it wakes you more than once or twice a night or continues for more than a week.

## THE STRUCTURE OF THE URINARY TRACT

The organs that comprise the urinary tract are responsible for filtering the blood and expelling the resulting waste fluid from the body. The tract is made up of the following elements: the 2 kidneys, which lie at the back of the abdomen just above the waist on either side of the spinal column; the 2 ureters, which connect the kidneys to the bladder; the bladder itself; and the tube that leads from the bladder to the outside (the urethra).

**How the tract works**
The outer part of the kidney, the cortex, contains tiny tubes that filter waste substances from the blood. The filtered liquid passes into the central section of the kidney, the medulla, which reabsorbs certain chemicals from the fluid. The remaining liquid (urine) flows down the ureters into the bladder, which is kept closed by a ring of muscles (sphincter). Periodically the collected urine is released from the body through the urethra.

Cortex
Medulla
Renal artery
Renal vein
Left kidney
Right kidney
Aorta
Urethra
Inferior vena cava
Ureters
Bladder
Bladder
Opening of ureters into the bladder
Sphincter
Urethra

## ABNORMAL-LOOKING URINE

| Colour of urine | Possible causes | What action is necessary |
|---|---|---|
| Pink, red or smoky | There is a chance that you may have blood in the urine, possibly caused by infection, inflammation, or a growth in the urinary tract. However, natural or artificial food colourings can also discolour the urine in this way. | Consult your doctor without delay. He or she may need to take samples of urine and blood for analysis (see *Blood analysis,* p.146) in order to make a firm diagnosis. Treatment will depend on the underlying problem. |
| Dark yellow or orange | Loss of fluid caused by diarrhoea, vomiting, or sweating can make your urine more concentrated and therefore darker than usual. Certain substances in senna-based laxatives and in rhubarb can also darken your urine temporarily. | This is no cause for concern, as soon as you compensate for any loss of fluid by drinking, your urine will return to its normal colour. Substances in laxatives and rhubarb will pass through your system within 24 hours. |
| Clear and dark brown | Jaundice caused by a disorder of the liver or gallbladder (most commonly hepatitis) is a possibility, especially if your faeces are very pale and your skin or the whites of your eyes have a yellow tinge. | Consult your doctor, who will need to take samples of urine and blood for analysis (see *Blood analysis,* p.146) in order to make a firm diagnosis. Treatment will depend on the underlying problem. |
| Green or blue | Artificial colouring in food or medicines is almost certainly the cause of this. | This is no cause for concern; the colouring will pass through without harmful effects. |

# 134 Painful intercourse

A woman may feel pain or discomfort in or around the vagina at the time of penetration, or during or following sexual intercourse. This symptom is known medically as dyspareunia. It is a relatively common problem among women of all ages, and may occur for a variety of physical or emotional reasons. Whatever cause you suspect, it is worthwhile seeking medical help, because if intercourse is repeatedly painful for you, there is a risk that it will affect your desire for sex and so damage your relationship with your partner.

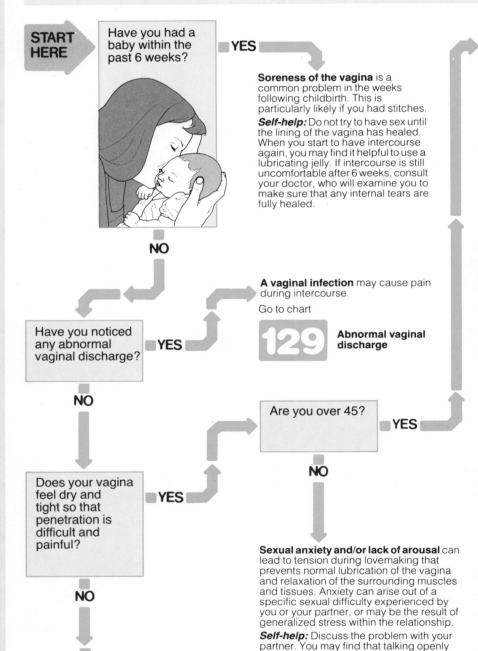

**START HERE**

**Have you had a baby within the past 6 weeks?**

**YES**

**Soreness of the vagina** is a common problem in the weeks following childbirth. This is particularly likely if you had stitches.

*Self-help:* Do not try to have sex until the lining of the vagina has healed. When you start to have intercourse again, you may find it helpful to use a lubricating jelly. If intercourse is still uncomfortable after 6 weeks, consult your doctor, who will examine you to make sure that any internal tears are fully healed.

**NO**

**Have you noticed any abnormal vaginal discharge?**

**YES**

**A vaginal infection** may cause pain during intercourse.

Go to chart

**129** **Abnormal vaginal discharge**

**NO**

**Does your vagina feel dry and tight so that penetration is difficult and painful?**

**YES**

**Are you over 45?**

**YES**

**NO**

**NO**

**Sexual anxiety and/or lack of arousal** can lead to tension during lovemaking that prevents normal lubrication of the vagina and relaxation of the surrounding muscles and tissues. Anxiety can arise out of a specific sexual difficulty experienced by you or your partner, or may be the result of generalized stress within the relationship.

*Self-help:* Discuss the problem with your partner. You may find that talking openly about the difficulty is in itself enough to reduce tension and help overcome the problem. Use of a lubricating jelly during intercourse may be helpful. You could also try the advice given opposite on reducing sexual anxiety. If the problem persists, consult your doctor. He or she will examine you to rule out the possibility of a physical cause for your difficulty, and may if necessary arrange for you and your partner to receive *sex counselling* (p.268). See also chart 135, *Loss of interest in sex.*

*Go to next page*

**Hormonal changes** around the time of the *menopause* (p.252) can cause the lining of the vagina to become thinner and less well lubricated, and this often makes intercourse uncomfortable. Consult your doctor.

*Treatment:* Your doctor will examine you and, depending on whether you are suffering from additional menopausal symptoms and on the state of your general health, may prescribe hormone-replacement therapy (see *The menopause*, p.252) and/or recommend that you use lubricating jelly. He or she may also advise you and your partner on sexual techniques to assist arousal and prevent discomfort. See also *Sex in later life,* below.

## SEX IN LATER LIFE

Most women who have enjoyed an active and happy sex life in the first part of their life continue to do so during middle and old age. Provided your relationship with your partner is sound, there is no physical reason why your capacity for enjoying the full range of physical and emotional sexual feelings should be diminished. In a loving relationship there is no reason why the physical changes associated with ageing should reduce the attraction you and your partner feel for each other. Many women find their sex life improves with greater experience and more leisure to enjoy their partner's company, and without the fear of pregnancy.

**Possible problems**

Although many women have no sex difficulties as they grow older, problems may arise. A common complaint of women past the menopause is discomfort during intercourse as a result of reduced vaginal lubrication. In the short-term this can sometimes be helped by hormone-replacement therapy (see *The menopause,* p.252). In the longer term, use of a lubricant jelly and adaptation of lovemaking techniques are usually the best solutions.

Obviously, if either partner has a disabling disease, this can inhibit sexual relations. In such cases experimenting with different positions and a variety of forms of sexual contact – for example, mutual caresses and oral sex – can be helpful. You should not be embarrassed to seek your doctor's advice about this.

Some women who have experienced sexual difficulties in the past use their advancing years as an excuse for avoiding sex altogether in later life. This is no cause for concern if both partners are happy not to have sex, but if a reduction in sexual activity causes unhappiness in either partner, it is never too late to seek *sex counselling* (p.268) for this or any other sex problem.

*Continued from previous page*

**Do you feel pain during intercourse only occasionally or only in certain positions?**

**YES** →

**Have your periods become increasingly painful in recent months?**

**YES** →

**Endometriosis,** a disorder in which womb-lining tissue forms outside the womb, is a possible, although rare, cause of increased pain during periods and pain during intercourse. Consult your doctor.

*Treatment:* Your doctor will probably do a *vaginal examination* (see p. 258) and may arrange for you to have a *D and C* (p. 254) and possibly *laparoscopy* (p. 272). If you are found to have endometriosis, you may be given long-term hormone treatment.

**NO** ↓     **NO** ↓

**Has intercourse only recently begun to be painful?**

**YES** →

**A cyst** (fluid-filled sac) around an ovary can sometimes cause pain if touched during intercourse. Such cysts may also cause abdominal swelling. Alternatively, such pain may be due to inflammation (erosion) of the cervix. Consult your doctor.

*Treatment:* Your doctor will examine your abdomen and probably do a vaginal examination (p.258). He or she may do a cervical smear test (see *Cervical screening,* p.257) and may arrange for you to have tests such as an X-ray, *ultrasound scan* (p.276), and possibly *laparoscopy* (p.272). If you are found to have an ovarian cyst, you may need to have an operation to remove it. This can sometimes be done without damaging the ovary, but in other cases it is necessary to remove the ovary and perhaps the fallopian tube as well. However, if the remaining ovary is healthy, you will still be able to have children. If you have a cervical erosion it may be treated by laser, freezing, or a minor operation.

**NO** ↓

**Have you just started your first or a new sexual relationship?**

**YES** →

**Bruising and soreness of the genital area** commonly follows unaccustomed or unusually enthusiastic sex. This is no cause for concern and the discomfort will soon pass. If soreness is severe, abstaining from sex for a day or so may help.

**Pressure on an ovary or on another tender spot** during deep penetration may be the cause of such pain. If you have always noticed such pain when you have intercourse in a certain position, this is unlikely to be a cause for concern; simply trying alternative positions may overcome the problem. However, it is wise to mention the symptom to your doctor, who may examine you to rule out the possibility of an underlying disorder.

**NO** ↓

**Consult your doctor** if you are unable to make a diagnosis from this chart.

---

## REDUCING SEXUAL ANXIETY

Many sexual difficulties arise out of anxiety in one or both partners, and most forms of sex counselling involve advice on reducing such anxiety as a basis for improving sexual enjoyment. Usually the first step in reducing anxiety is for both partners to agree to abstain from sexual intercourse for, say, 3 weeks. The following technique, called sensate focus, is often successful in heightening sexual responsiveness without provoking anxiety about performance, and may help you to overcome inhibitions and tensions that can mar sexual relationships:

### Sensate focus
Set aside at least 3 evenings (or a period at another time of day) when you can be alone with your partner without fear of interruption for at least 2 hours. Try to create an atmosphere in which you both feel relaxed – for example, by playing some favourite music or having a warm shower before beginning. During the time when you are trying this therapy you and your partner must stick to your agreement to refrain from full sexual intercourse.

### Stage 1
On the first couple of evenings, each partner should take it in turns to gently massage and caress the other for a period of about 20 minutes. This is best carried out when you are both naked, and you can use a body lotion or oil if you like. The massage should involve a gentle exploration of all parts of the body except the genitals, breast and anal areas. Both partners should concentrate on the pleasure they receive from this contact. Once you have got over any awkwardness and are finding enjoyment from the sensations you experience during this activity – this may take several sessions – go on to stage 2.

**Body massage**
The partner being caressed should concentrate on the sensations of being touched; the partner giving the caresses should focus on the pleasure from such contact.

### Stage 2
Stage 2 is similar to stage 1, but this time body massage may include genital, anal and breast areas. Remember, however, to continue to include other parts of the body in your caresses, so that direct sexual stimulation can be felt in context with other body sensations.

### Stage 3
Most couples find that soon after reaching stage 2 they are ready to resume sexual intercourse, and in most cases they find that they are more relaxed and are more able to enjoy a full range of physical and emotional sexual feelings.

# 135 Loss of interest in sex

The frequency with which a woman feels the need for sex is determined by a whole range of psychological and physiological factors, as well as being affected by experiences in early life. Some women feel the need for sex every day, others only once or twice a week or less. All points on the spectrum are normal. However, a sudden falling off in your normal level of sexual desire may be a sign of a number of problems. There may be a physical cause – for example, you may have had a baby recently, or suffered generalized ill health or an infection that makes intercourse painful – or the cause may be emotional – for example, overwork, depression, anxiety about a specific sexual difficulty, or discord within the relationship. Consult this chart if you are aware of a reduction in the frequency with which you want sex and/or if you notice that you are not as easily aroused as you used to be, which may lead to physical discomfort during intercourse.

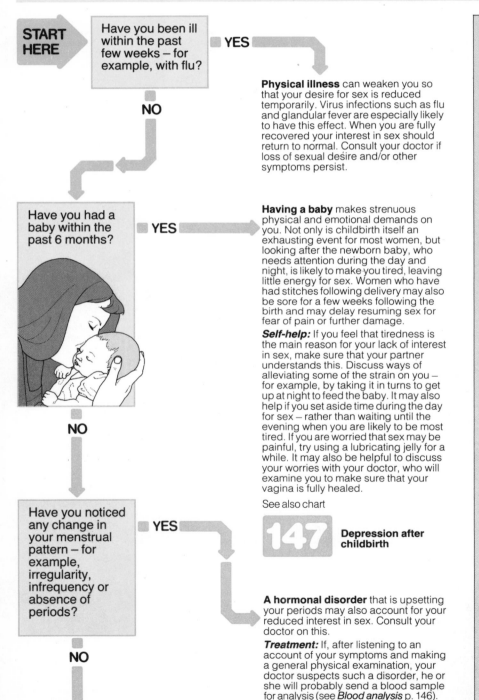

**START HERE**

Have you been ill within the past few weeks – for example, with flu?

**YES**

**Physical illness** can weaken you so that your desire for sex is reduced temporarily. Virus infections such as flu and glandular fever are especially likely to have this effect. When you are fully recovered your interest in sex should return to normal. Consult your doctor if loss of sexual desire and/or other symptoms persist.

**NO**

Have you had a baby within the past 6 months?

**YES**

**Having a baby** makes strenuous physical and emotional demands on you. Not only is childbirth itself an exhausting event for most women, but looking after the newborn baby, who needs attention during the day and night, is likely to make you tired, leaving little energy for sex. Women who have had stitches following delivery may also be sore for a few weeks following the birth and may delay resuming sex for fear of pain or further damage.

*Self-help:* If you feel that tiredness is the main reason for your lack of interest in sex, make sure that your partner understands this. Discuss ways of alleviating some of the strain on you – for example, by taking it in turns to get up at night to feed the baby. It may also help if you set aside time during the day for sex – rather than waiting until the evening when you are likely to be most tired. If you are worried that sex may be painful, try using a lubricating jelly for a while. It may also be helpful to discuss your worries with your doctor, who will examine you to make sure that your vagina is fully healed.

See also chart

**NO**

Have you noticed any change in your menstrual pattern – for example, irregularity, infrequency or absence of periods?

**YES**

# 147 Depression after childbirth

**A hormonal disorder** that is upsetting your periods may also account for your reduced interest in sex. Consult your doctor on this.

*Treatment:* If, after listening to an account of your symptoms and making a general physical examination, your doctor suspects such a disorder, he or she will probably send a blood sample for analysis (see *Blood analysis* p. 146). If this reveals a hormonal disorder, hormone supplements should correct the problem.

**NO**

*Go to next page*

## SEX COUNSELLING

Sex counselling can take many different forms. Most family doctors have experience of dealing with the more common types of sexual difficulty; if you are suffering from a problem in your sexual relationship, you should first consult your own doctor for advice. Depending on the nature of the problem and his or her experience in this field, your doctor may suggest treatment him- or herself, or may refer you to a specialist sex counsellor. Such counsellors may or may not be medically qualified – often they are specialists in psychology. Some large medical practices have sex counsellors attached to them. In other cases you may be referred to a clinic or hospital out-patient department.

**Treatments for sexual difficulties**
Treatments for all types of sexual difficulty have a greater chance of success if both partners attend counselling sessions. Usually a course of counselling starts with a discussion with the counsellor about the nature of the problem. In many cases this provides a couple with their first experience of talking together frankly about their sexual feelings, and this is often in itself of great help in clearing up misunderstandings and reducing anxiety. The counsellor may later suggest techniques for overcoming specific difficulties or he or she may give more generalized advice on sexual technique. The counsellor will also, if necessary, guide you through a prolonged therapy programme to be carried out at home, such as the sensate focus technique described under *Reducing sexual anxiety* (p. 266).

The success rate for couples who overcome their embarrassment sufficiently to seek sex counselling is high. So even if you feel that your problem is insoluble, it is worthwhile seeking your doctor's advice.

**Partners take part in sex counselling together**

*Continued from previous page*

**Have you any reason to feel under stress – for example, problems at work or upheavals at home?**

**YES** →

**Generalized stress** (see *What is stress?* p. 175) can easily affect your desire for sex. Once the cause of worry has been dealt with, you should find that your interest in sex revives. Meanwhile, make sure that your partner understands your feelings. If your difficulties cannot easily be resolved, or if your interest in sex does not return to normal, consult your doctor.

See also chart

 **73** **Anxiety**

**NO** ↓

**Have you been feeling in low spirits lately?**

**YES** →

**Depression** often causes loss of interest in sex.

Go to chart

 **72** **Depression**

**NO** ↓

**Are you worried that you may become pregnant?**

**YES** →

**Fear of pregnancy** can cause some women to reject sex. Consult your doctor.

**Treatment:** Your doctor will discuss your fears with you and the most reliable method of contraception in your case. There are several forms of contraception that provide excellent protection against pregnancy if used properly (see *Contraceptive methods,* p. 271). If your doctor is unable to allay your fears, or if reliable contraception is unsuitable or unacceptable, he or she may refer you for specialized counselling.

**NO** ↓

**Do you or your partner have a specific sexual difficulty?**

**YES** →

**Sexual difficulties** – for example, failure to achieve orgasm in a woman, or premature ejaculation in a man – can often cause one or both partners to lose interest in sex. Consult your doctor.

**Treatment:** Your doctor will want to discuss the problem with both you and your partner. Depending on the nature of the underlying difficulty, he or she may offer advice and treatment, and/or refer you for specialized *sex counselling* (opposite).

**NO** ↓

**Is it only your regular partner who fails to arouse you?**

**YES** →

**Do you have any other cause for discontent in your relationship?**

**YES** →

**NO** ↓

**Loss of interest in a sexual relationship,** once the excitement and novelty has worn off, is a common cause of loss of sexual desire.

**Self-help:** It may help to talk openly with your partner about how you feel so that there is no misunderstanding. If the relationship is a long-standing one and sound in every other way, try to inject new life into it – for example, by going away on holiday together or co-operating in some new venture. You may find adopting new approaches to lovemaking helpful. If these suggestions do not improve matters, consult your doctor, who may recommend *sex counselling* (opposite).

**NO** ↓

**Do you fail only to be aroused by men, but find you are sexually attracted to other women?**

**YES** →

**Homosexuality** – being sexually attracted only to those of the same sex – is a normal sexual perference for as much as 5 per cent of the population. While many homosexual women (lesbians) are aware of their orientation from adolescence, others do not recognize their homosexuality until much later. See *Sexual orientation,* right.

**NO** ↓

**Consult your doctor** if you are unable to make a diagnosis from this chart.

---

**Generalized antagonism** or specific disagreements can lead to tension in a relationship that also affects your sexual feelings for each other.

**Self-help:** Talk to each other and explain how the problems with your relationship are affecting your feelings. If you find that things do not improve after a full and frank discussion, consult your doctor. He or she will probably examine you to rule out any underlying physical problem, and may suggest that you and your partner seek marriage guidance about your general difficulties, and possibly *sex counselling* (opposite) for any specific sex problems you may have.

---

**SEXUAL ORIENTATION**

Sexual orientation – that is, whether you are heterosexual (attracted to people of the opposite sex), homosexual (attracted to people of the same sex), or bisexual (attracted to people of both sexes) is probably determined by a combination of inborn personality traits, upbringing, and family relationships. Some researchers have suggested that there may be hormonal factors that contribute to homosexuality, but these findings have not been generally accepted. Few people are wholly hetero- or homosexual. In particular, it is common for adolescents to go through a phase of experiencing homosexual feelings before becoming attracted to people of the opposite sex. Some, however, remain homosexual in their preferences. This variation from the mainly heterosexual orientation of the majority is no cause for medical concern as long as the individual woman is happy with her homosexuality. Treatment to change sexual orientation is unlikely to be effective and is seldom recommended. However, society's often intolerant attitude towards homosexuality frequently causes homosexuals to feel guilty and abnormal, and therefore leads them to repress their sexual feelings. This can be psychologically damaging. If you think that you are homosexual and are experiencing such problems, consult your doctor, who may be able to offer helpful advice and/or refer you to one of the voluntary organizations that specialize in advising homosexuals.

# 136 Choosing a contraceptive method

Although no method of contraception – the prevention of pregnancy – is problem-free, most couples with the right advice can find a method that suits them. Although contraceptive methods are available for use by both men and women, in most relationships it is the woman who takes prime responsibility for arranging contraception. This is probably because the fear of an unwanted pregnancy is far greater for most women, and therefore a woman who wants to be sure of avoiding pregnancy is likely to be more confident with a method

that she controls herself. However, some methods of contraception carry slight risks for a woman, and so a couple in a stable relationship may wish to consider the male options that are available. This chart is intended as a guide to help you decide which methods may be most suitable in your case, but the right decision can only be reached through discussion with your doctor and your partner, taking into account the possible side-effects and risks of each method, and your attitude to an unplanned pregnancy.

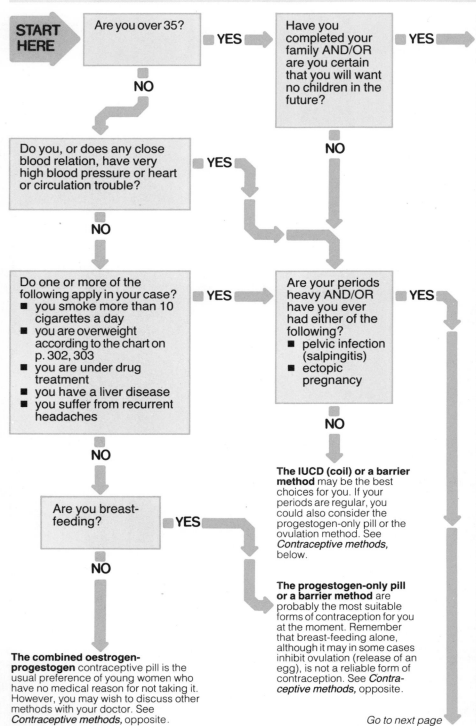

**START HERE**

Are you over 35?

YES →

Have you completed your family AND/OR are you certain that you will want no children in the future?

YES →

**Sterilization,** either for yourself or your partner, may be worth considering (see *Sterilization,* below). If this option is not acceptable to you, answer no to the previous question and follow the pathway.

**NO**

Do you, or does any close blood relation, have very high blood pressure or heart or circulation trouble?

**YES**

**NO**

Do one or more of the following apply in your case?
- you smoke more than 10 cigarettes a day
- you are overweight according to the chart on p. 302, 303
- you are under drug treatment
- you have a liver disease
- you suffer from recurrent headaches

**YES** →

Are your periods heavy AND/OR have you ever had either of the following?
- pelvic infection (salpingitis)
- ectopic pregnancy

**YES**

**NO**

**NO**

Are you breast-feeding?

**YES**

**NO**

**The IUCD (coil) or a barrier method** may be the best choices for you. If your periods are regular, you could also consider the progestogen-only pill or the ovulation method. See *Contraceptive methods,* below.

**The progestogen-only pill or a barrier method** are probably the most suitable forms of contraception for you at the moment. Remember that breast-feeding alone, although it may in some cases inhibit ovulation (release of an egg), is not a reliable form of contraception. See *Contraceptive methods,* opposite.

**The combined oestrogen-progestogen** contraceptive pill is the usual preference of young women who have no medical reason for not taking it. However, you may wish to discuss other methods with your doctor. See *Contraceptive methods,* opposite.

*Go to next page*

## STERILIZATION

Sterilization is a form of contraception that is usually irreversible and will prevent you from having children in the future. For this reason it is not a contraceptive option that should be chosen without careful consideration by both partners. Usually, couples thinking about sterilization are offered counselling before reaching a final decision. You will need to consider the possibility that you may change partners in the future and perhaps want to start a new family, and your reactions should anything happen to the children you already have. Those under 30 are generally discouraged from such a final step. Sterilization may be a good solution for an older couple who have completed their family and for whom the risks and inconveniences of other contraceptive methods no longer seem worthwhile, or for a couple for whom pregnancy presents a serious risk.

### Female sterilization
The usual method of sterilization for women is tubal ligation. This procedure is usually done under general anaesthetic using a laparoscope (see *Laparoscopy,* p. 272). Each fallopian tube is clipped or tied and sealed off. This prevents eggs from travelling down the tubes, being fertilized, and then entering the womb. Recovery from the operation usually takes only a few days and there are no lasting side-effects. In particular, sterilization has no physical effect on the production of female sex hormones, sexual desire or performance, or menstrual periods.

### Male sterilization
Male sterilization is achieved through an operation called vasectomy. It is a simpler operation than that required for female sterilization and carries fewer risks. Usually, 2 small incisions are made in the scrotum, and each vas deferens (the tube that links the testis to the urethra) is cut and sealed so that sperm cannot pass out of the body. Because sperm may remain in the male reproductive system for several months after the operation, you will need to take additional contraceptive precautions until test results confirm that the seminal fluid is free from sperm. Vasectomy has no effect on performance or ejaculation.

*Continued from previous page*

**Are your periods regular?** → **YES**

**NO**

**A barrier method** could be the best method for you. See *Contraceptive methods,* below.

**A barrier method,** ovulation method, or the progestogen-only pill may be suitable options in your case. See *Contraceptive methods,* below.

## MULTIPLE SEX PARTNERS

Many people enjoy an active and varied sex life with no ill-effects. However, there are certain medical risks associated with having sex with a large number of different partners. The chief risk for women is that of contracting a sexually transmitted disease (p. 259). There is also some evidence to suggest that women who have many different sex partners have a greater than average risk of developing cancer of the cervix, especially if they started having sex during their teens. This is because the viruses that are now thought to cause cervical cancer may be sexually transmitted. There are, however, several precautions you can take.

- Encourage your partner to wear a sheath. This may help to prevent the transmission of infection and may protect the cervix. Use of a diaphragm may also reduce the likelihood of cervical abnormalities.
- Make sure you have regular cervical smear tests (see *Cervical screening*, p. 257).
- Report any suspicious symptoms such as abnormal vaginal discharge or sores in the genital area to your doctor at once. If a partner mentions that he has had an infection consult your doctor.

## TERMINATION OF PREGNANCY

If you discover that you are pregnant and you are quite sure that you do not want the baby, you should discuss this with your doctor as soon as possible. Alternatively, a charitable pregnancy advisory service may be able to offer advice.

### Methods of terminating a pregnancy

Termination is best carried out before the 14th week of pregnancy when the usual procedure is similar to a *D and C* (p. 254). For a termination after the 14th week you will probably be given a hormone, prostaglandin, by vaginal pessary (suppository). This stimulates the womb to contract, as if in labour, to expel the fetus.

## CONTRACEPTIVE METHODS

### Combined oestrogen-progestogen pill

**How does it act?**
There are many different types of combined pill containing various dosages of oestrogen and progestogen (the synthetic form of the hormone progesterone). They all act primarily by increasing the level of these hormones in the body so as to prevent the release of an egg (ovulation).

**For whom is it recommended?**
The combined pill is the usual method recommended for young women. It is particularly useful for those who suffer from painful or heavy periods. The risk of side-effects is known to be greater for women over 35, who smoke, are overweight, who suffer from migraines, or who have a history of circulatory disorders, high blood pressure, heart or liver disease.

**Medical supervision**
The combined pill is only available on prescription from your doctor or family planning clinic. You will need to have regular medical checks (usually every 6 months).

**Possible side-effects and risks**
Possible side-effects include headaches, an increase in blood pressure, depression, loss of sex drive, and slight weight gain. The combined pill may cause spotting of blood between periods ("breakthrough bleeding"). If this is a nuisance you may need to change your prescription. Occasionally, it may take several months for ovulation to restart after stopping the pill. The main, but rare, medical risk associated with prolonged use of the pill is that of circulatory problems. In particular, there seems to be an increase in the frequency of blood clots (thromboembolisms) in regular pill-takers.

### Progestogen-only pill

**How does it act?**
Increased levels of progestogen (the synthetic form of the natural hormone progesterone) in the body may prevent eggs from implanting in the womb, but the most important contraceptive effect of this method is that it causes thickening of the mucus at the entrance to the cervix thus preventing penetration by sperm.

**For whom is it recommended?**
The progestogen-only pill is usually recommended for women who want to use an oral contraceptive but for whom an oestrogen-containing pill is unsuitable for any reason. In particular, it is useful for breast-feeding mothers because it does not reduce milk production. Because this type of pill needs to be taken at precisely the same time each day to be effective, it may not be suitable for those who have an irregular lifestyle or who tend to be forgetful.

**Medical supervision**
As for the combined oestrogen-progestogen contraceptive pill.

**Possible side-effects and risks**
There is a likelihood of irregular periods and spotting between periods (breakthrough bleeding). Health risks seem to be fewer than for the combined pill.

### Post-coital ("morning after") pill

**How does it act?**
The post-coital pill contains oestrogen and progestogen which, taken (usually in 2 separate doses) following intercourse without contraception, makes the lining of the womb hostile to implantation of the egg and so prevents a pregnancy from developing.

**For whom is it recommended?**
The post-coital pill can be taken by any woman who has had one occasion of sex without contraception in a cycle or for whom contraception may not have been effective – for example, if a sheath was damaged. To be effective the post-coital pill needs to be taken within 72 hours of intercourse. Because it contains high doses of hormones, it is only recommended as an emergency measure and should not be used as your regular method of contraception.

**Medical supervision**
The post-coital pill needs to be prescribed by a doctor.

**Possible side-effects and risks**
Some women experience nausea during the first few hours or or so after taking this type of pill.

### Intra-uterine contraceptive device (IUCD or coil)

**How does it act?**
The IUCD is a device, usually made of plastic and sometimes covered with copper wire, which is inserted in the womb and while in position prevents a fertilized egg from becoming implanted in the womb.

**For whom is it recommended?**
The IUCD is usually recommended for women in stable relationships who need effective and convenient contraception, but cannot or do not wish to use the combined pill. It may not be suitable for very young women, those who have never been pregnant, or those who have had pelvic infections in the past.

**Medical supervision**
An IUCD needs to be prescribed and fitted by a family-planning doctor. It can be inserted during a normal clinic visit. You will be taught to check that it remains in position and will need to have yearly check-ups. Depending on type, an IUCD needs to be replaced every 2-10 years.

**Possible side-effects and risks**
Most women who have an IUCD notice a slight increase in bleeding and sometimes pain during periods. There is also a slightly increased risk of pelvic infections and of ectopic pregnancy (pregnancy outside the womb). Occasionally, an IUCD may be displaced or expelled from the womb.

### Barrier methods

A barrier method is any device that prevents sperm from entering the womb and so fertilizing an egg. Barrier methods used by women include the diaphragm, cervical cap and contraceptive sponge. All these devices are placed over the entrance to the cervix. The sheath (condom) used by men is also a barrier method. For reliable contraception, all barrier methods, except the sponge and sheath, need to be used with spermicidal foam, cream, or jelly.

**For whom is it recommended?**
Barrier methods are suitable for use by almost all women, and may be the best method for women who cannot or do not want to use the pill or IUCD. Because a diaphragm, cap or sponge needs to be inserted in advance of intercourse, such methods may not be the best for the very young or those for whom sex is usually unplanned.

**Medical supervision**
A diaphragm or cap needs to be fitted by a trained family-planning doctor or nurse, who will also teach you how to use it properly together with spermicides. Subsequently, yearly checks are needed. You will also need to have your size checked again if you gain or lose a significant amount of weight or if you have a baby. Sheaths and contraceptive sponges can be bought over-the-counter and need no medical supervision. However, it is probably a good idea to ask your family-planning doctor or nurse to show you how to fit a sponge for the first time.

**Possible side-effects**
There are few adverse side-effects to barrier methods although some women find them inconvenient and they may be less reliable than the pill or IUCD. A few women are allergic to rubber or to certain chemicals in spermicides and may need to switch brands. Beneficial side-effects of using a barrier method include the possible protection they may provide to the cervix, and in the case of sheaths, some protection against sexually transmitted infections.

### Ovulation (rhythm) method

**How does it act?**
There are various ovulation methods of birth control, all of which are based on the principle of a woman being able to detect when ovulation (release of an egg) will occur, allowing her to abstain from sex on fertile days. Ovulation can be detected by monitoring changes in body temperature and observation of the appearance and consistency of the mucus produced by the cervix (see *The menstrual cycle*, p. 253).

**For whom is it recommended?**
Ovulation methods are the only form of contraception allowed by the Catholic Church. Women who are reluctant to use internal or barrier methods may also find these methods attractive. However, ovulation methods may be unreliable for women whose periods are irregular, and such methods may be unacceptable to couples who do not wish to abstain from sex for at least 7 days in each month.

**Medical supervision**
Women using ovulation methods of birth control need to be carefully taught by a doctor or other specialist trained in this method, how to monitor and record the changes that indicate ovulation.

**Possible side-effects and risks**
There are no physical side-effects, but the ovulation method can lead to frustration for both partners during the fertile period.

# 137 Failure to conceive

Consult this chart if you and your partner have been having regular sexual intercourse for more than 12 months without contraception and without your having become pregnant. Failure to conceive may be the result of a problem affecting the woman or man; this chart deals only with possible problems affecting the woman.

Female infertility is usually the result of a failure to produce eggs, or of a blockage in the fallopian tubes. Failure to conceive usually requires extensive investigation of both partners, usually in a specialist hospital clinic, to find the underlying reason for the problem.

**START HERE**

**Have you been suffering from any long-term illness such as diabetes, a thyroid disorder, or tuberculosis?**

YES

**Long-term diseases,** particularly hormonal disorders and chronic infections, may affect fertility. Specialist advice may be needed to help you conceive. Consult your doctor.

NO

**Do you have intercourse less often than three times a week on average?**

YES

**Infrequent intercourse** is a common cause of failure to conceive. If you have sex less than three times a week the chances of sperm being present in the womb when an egg is released are reduced.

*Self-help:* Try increasing the frequency with which you and your partner have intercourse. If you still have not conceived within a further 2 months or if a sexual difficulty prevents you from having intercourse more often, consult your doctor. See also *Increasing your chances of conception* (below).

NO

**Are your periods irregular or infrequent?**

YES

NO

**Have you ever had a pelvic infection (salpingitis)?**

YES

**Blockage of the fallopian tubes** may occur as a result of infection (which occasionally follows a termination of pregnancy) or an ectopic pregnancy, preventing fertilization of the egg. Consult your doctor.

*Treatment:* If your doctor suspects that this may be the cause of your difficulty in conceiving, he or she will probably arrange for you to see a specialist, who may arrange for you to have tests including *laparoscopy* (right), during which carbon dioxide may be passed up the tubes to check for blockages. Sometimes this also clears minor obstructions. Otherwise, surgery may be attempted to clear the tubes. If these treatments are unsuccessful, you may be offered in vitro (test tube) fertilization. This technique, which is not yet widely practised, involves the removal from the ovaries of one or more eggs which are then fertilized by your partner's sperm in a test tube. The developing embryo is then replaced in your womb where the pregnancy continues as normal.

NO

**Have you ever had a pregnancy terminated (an abortion) and/or an ectopic pregnancy (pregnancy outside the womb)?**

YES

NO

**Consult your doctor** if you are unable to make a diagnosis from this chart. The problem may be that you are not ovulating, even though your periods seem normal, or that your vaginal secretions are not compatible with your partner's sperm. Alternatively, the cause of the problem may lie with your partner. In all cases further investigations are needed.

**A hormone imbalance** that either prevents ovulation (release of an egg) or reduces the frequency with which you ovulate, may explain your failure to conceive. Consult your doctor.

*Treatment:* Your doctor will probably refer you to a hospital specialist for tests and treatment. If the tests, which may include *blood analysis* (p. 146), urine analysis, a *D and C* (p. 252) and *laparoscopy*, (below), show a hormone imbalance, you may be prescribed hormone supplements ("fertility drugs").

## LAPAROSCOPY

Laparoscopy is an endoscopic technique (see *Endoscopy*, p. 201) for investigating abdominal disorders. In women it is commonly used to discover the cause of gynaecological problems such as infertility or to assist in surgical procedures such as *sterilization* (p. 270). Laparascopy may also be used when other tests such as *barium X-rays* (p. 207) and *ultrasound scanning* (p. 276) fail to show the cause of symptoms such as recurrent abdominal pain.

The procedure is usually carried out under general anaesthetic. Two small slits are made in the abdomen, and carbon dioxide is passed through a hollow needle inserted into one slit to distend the abdomen. An endoscope is inserted into the second slit, enabling the surgeon to see inside and find the cause of the trouble.

## PREVIOUS PREGNANCY

If you have been pregnant before, by the same or by a different partner, the chances of your present failure to conceive being a result of a problem affecting you are reduced. However, it is possible for any one of the disorders discussed on this chart to develop after a previous pregnancy, so full investigation of both partners is still required.

## INCREASING YOUR CHANCES OF CONCEPTION

Although prolonged delay in achieving conception requires professional tests and treatment, you may increase your chances by following self-help advice given below:

- Ensure that both you and your partner are in good health; eat fresh foods, get plenty of rest, and keep alcohol consumption low.
- Have intercourse about 3 times a week; less may mean that you miss your fertile days, more may reduce the numbers of sperm.
- Try to have intercourse during your most fertile days (see *The menstrual cycle*, p. 253).
- Following intercourse, remain lying down for 10 to 15 minutes to allow the maximum number of sperm to enter your womb.
- Discourage your partner from wearing tight underpants, which may increase temperature inside the scrotum and damage sperm.

# Pregnancy and childbirth

# 138 Nausea and vomiting in pregnancy

Most women experience some nausea during the first three months of pregnancy and may actually vomit. Usually symptoms fade after the 12th week, but in some cases they may persist for longer. Morning sickness, as it is known, is probably the result of the dramatic increase in hormones in the blood. Although it commonly occurs in the morning, sickness can come on at any time, especially when you are tired or hungry. Most women control their nausea by self-help measures, but a few women who suffer from severe symptoms need medical treatment.

**Consult this diagnostic chart only after reading chart 94, Vomiting.**

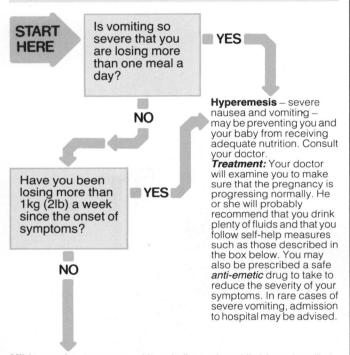

**START HERE**

Is vomiting so severe that you are losing more than one meal a day?

**YES** →

**NO** ↓

Have you been losing more than 1kg (2lb) a week since the onset of symptoms?

**YES** →

**NO** ↓

**Hyperemesis** – severe nausea and vomiting – may be preventing you and your baby from receiving adequate nutrition. Consult your doctor.
**Treatment:** Your doctor will examine you to make sure that the pregnancy is progressing normally. He or she will probably recommend that you drink plenty of fluids and that you follow self-help measures such as those described in the box below. You may also be prescribed a safe *anti-emetic* drug to take to reduce the severity of your symptoms. In rare cases of severe vomiting, admission to hospital may be advised.

**Mild to moderate nausea,** although distressing while it lasts, is unlikely to present a risk to your general health or to that of your baby.
**Self-help:** Try the self-help measures suggested in the box below. If these do not help, and especially if you find that nausea is preventing you from eating so that you are losing weight, consult your doctor.

### COPING WITH NAUSEA AND VOMITING

The following self-help suggestions may reduce the severity of nausea and vomiting during pregnancy:

- Have a light snack – for example, biscuits or toast – before you get out of bed in the morning.
- Eat small frequent meals of foods that seem to agree with you.
- Try to avoid sweet or fatty foods.
- Give up smoking and drinking alcohol.
- Get as much rest as possible.
- Take regular light exercise in the fresh air.
- Do not take any drugs or over-the-counter medicines without first consulting your doctor.

Consult your doctor if nausea and vomiting are so severe that you are unable to eat a proper diet or if you are losing weight.

# 139 Skin changes in pregnancy

The hormonal changes of pregnancy may have a variety of effects on your skin, including changes in colour. Some women find that their skin becomes more oily, others find that it becomes drier. Skin conditions such as eczema from which you have suffered before pregnancy may either improve or get worse. The way in which your skin is affected depends on the balance of hormones in your case, and on your basic skin type.

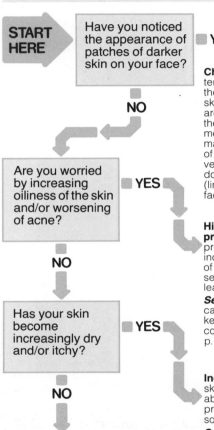

**START HERE** →

Have you noticed the appearance of patches of darker skin on your face?

**YES** →

**NO** ↓

Are you worried by increasing oiliness of the skin and/or worsening of acne?

**YES** →

**NO** ↓

Has your skin become increasingly dry and/or itchy?

**YES** →

**NO** ↓

**Chloasma** is the medical term used to describe these patches of increased skin pigmentation. They are due to an increase in the levels of the pigment melanin in the body. You may also notice darkening of the nipples and a dark vertical line extending downwards from your navel (linea nigra). This usually fades after childbirth.

**High levels of progesterone** during pregnancy can cause an increase in the production of sebum (oily skin secretions) which can also lead to acne.
**Self-help:** Normal skin-care measures should keep this trouble under control (see *Skin care,* p. 178, and *Acne,* p. 178).

**Increased dryness** of the skin, especially that of the abdomen, is common in pregnancy, and this can sometimes lead to itching.
**Self-help:** Regular applications of a simple moisturizing cream to the affected areas, especially after bathing, should relieve the dryness. Alternatively, you can add some baby oil to your bath.

**Your skin problem** may be unrelated to pregnancy.

Go to chart

**76** General skin problems

### STRETCH MARKS

Stretch marks are red marks on the skin that later fade, leaving silvery scar-like lines. They occur if the skin is stretched beyond its normal range of elasticity when weight is gained rapidly. In pregnancy stretch marks commonly occur on the breasts and on the abdomen. If too much weight is gained, they may also appear on the thighs, buttocks, and upper arms.

**Avoiding stretch marks**
Try to avoid putting on too much weight during pregnancy. However, even those who limit their weight gain to a healthy 9-13kg (22-28lb) may develop some marks. The regular application of any type of cream or oil does not prevent or heal stretch marks, although it may help to alleviate dryness of the skin.

# 140 Back pain in pregnancy

Backache is one of the commonest minor symptoms of pregnancy. It usually occurs as a dull pain and stiffness in the mid and lower back and may make it difficult to get up from a sitting or lying position. It is likely to become more troublesome as pregnancy progresses. Most such backaches do not signify any worrying condition.

However, occasionally the sudden onset of pain in the back, especially if accompanied by additional symptoms such as vaginal bleeding, may be a sign of an impending miscarriage. Towards the end of pregnancy, back pain may herald the onset of labour. Consult this diagnostic chart only after reading chart 107, Back pain.

Consult this chart only after reading chart 107, Back pain.

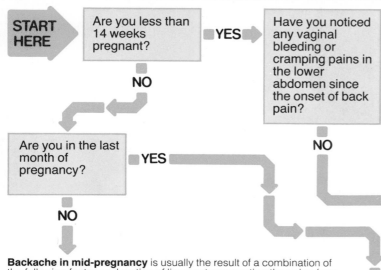

**START HERE**

**Are you less than 14 weeks pregnant?** — **YES** → **Have you noticed any vaginal bleeding or cramping pains in the lower abdomen since the onset of back pain?** — **YES** →

**NO** ↓

**Are you in the last month of pregnancy?** — **YES** →

**NO** ↓

**NO** ↓ (from vaginal bleeding question)

**CALL YOUR DOCTOR NOW!**
**A serious complication,** such as an impending miscarriage or ectopic pregnancy (pregnancy outside the womb), is a possibility.

**Treatment:** If your doctor suspects either of these possibilities, you will probably be admitted to hospital for rest and tests. If you have an ectopic pregnancy, an operation to end the pregnancy will need to be carried out. See also *Miscarriage*, p. 276.

**Relaxation of the ligaments** supporting the spine, as a result of hormonal changes, can lead to backache even in early pregnancy.

**Self-help:** Pay attention to the advice given under *Preventing backache* (p. 223). You may also find it helpful to try some gentle yoga-style exercises. Consult your doctor if pain becomes severe enough to restrict your day-to-day activities.

**Backache in mid-pregnancy** is usually the result of a combination of the following factors: relaxation of ligaments supporting the spine (see above right) and changes in posture to accommodate the increasing weight of the baby. Sometimes the enlarging womb puts pressure on a nerve and you may also experience a pain that shoots down the back of a leg (sciatica).

**Self-help:** Read the suggestions for preventing backache on p.223. Be careful about how you lift weights, such as young children. At this stage in pregnancy, good posture is especially important. You may find antenatal and gentle yoga-style exercises helpful. Consult your doctor if pain becomes severe enough to restrict your day-to-day activities.

**The start of labour** is sometimes marked by the onset of persistent back pain, especially if the pain is different from any backache you have experienced before.

Go to chart

**145** Am I in labour?

---

# 141 Heartburn in pregnancy

Heartburn, a burning pain in the centre of the chest or upper abdomen, is usually caused by the slight back-flow of acid juices from the stomach into the oeso-phagus (gullet). It is common throughout pregnancy,

but is likely to be more severe in the later months, when the growing baby and expanding womb take up more space. Heartburn may be uncomfortable, but it is never a danger to the general health of you or your baby.

**START HERE**

**Are you less than 5 months pregnant?** — **YES** →

**NO** ↓

**Pressure inside the abdomen** from the growing baby during the later stages of pregnancy can cause leakage of the stomach contents into the oesophagus. Laxity of the valve between the stomach and oesophagus (see right) also contributes to this problem, and there may be some degree of hiatus hernia (see p. 213).

**Self-help:** See *Self-help for heartburn*, right.

**Laxity of the muscular valve** (sphincter) between the stomach and the oesophagus commonly occurs together with the general relaxation of the ligaments experienced during pregnancy. This means that the stomach contents can more easily flow back up into the oesophagus, which becomes inflamed, leading to pain (heartburn).

**Self-help:** See *Self-help for heartburn,* right.

**SELF-HELP FOR HEARTBURN**

If you are suffering from heartburn, whatever the stage of your pregnancy, the following self-help measures should help to prevent and relieve the discomfort:

- Avoid eating large meals, especially of fried or highly spiced foods.
- Try to give up, or at least restrict, smoking and alcohol consumption.
- Do not wear tight maternity girdles.
- If heartburn is troublesome at night, drink a glass of milk before going to bed, and sleep propped up with pillows.

If such self-help measures do not help to alleviate the problem, consult your doctor, who may prescribe a safe antacid medicine for you to take.

# 142 Vaginal bleeding in pregnancy

Consult this chart if you notice any vaginal bleeding while you are pregnant, whether it consists of only slight spotting or more profuse blood loss. This is a serious symptom that should always be reported to your doctor promptly, although in a large proportion of cases there is no danger to the pregnancy. Whatever the suspected cause, if you notice vaginal bleeding, you should go to bed and rest until you have received medical attention.

**START HERE**

**Are you more than 28 weeks pregnant?**

NO

**Do you have pains in the abdomen and/or unaccustomed backache?**

NO

**Are you less than 14 weeks pregnant?**

NO

YES

YES

YES

**CALL YOUR DOCTOR NOW!**
**A miscarriage** is a strong possibility when cramping abdominal pains or persistent backache accompany vaginal bleeding in early or mid-pregnancy. There is also a possibility that you may have an ectopic pregnancy (pregnancy outside the womb) if you are less than 12 weeks pregnant and if the onset of pain preceded blood loss.

*Treatment:* If your doctor suspects either of these disorders, you will probably be admitted to hospital for rest and tests. If you have an ectopic pregnancy, an operation to end the pregnancy will be carried out. See also *Miscarriage,* right.

**In early pregnancy spotting of blood** is common and often occurs when a period would have been due and when the level of certain hormones produced by the placenta is not high enough to prevent slight shedding of the womb lining. Usually there is no risk to the pregnancy, but you should go to bed and consult your doctor.

*Treatment:* If your doctor confirms the diagnosis, he or she will probably advise you to rest until the bleeding stops. Hormone tablets or injections are sometimes given.

**CALL YOUR DOCTOR NOW!**
**A threatened miscarriage** is the usual diagnosis when bleeding occurs without pain in mid-pregnancy. However, bleeding may also occur as a result of an abnormality afflicting the cervix or inflammation of the vagina.

*Treatment:* See *Miscarriage,* right.

**CALL YOUR DOCTOR NOW!**
**Ante-partum haemorrhage** (bleeding before childbirth) is the term used to describe any vaginal bleeding in the later stages of pregnancy. It may be due to partial separation of the placenta from the wall of the womb, especially if the placenta is low-lying (placenta praevia), bleeding from a vein in the vagina, or abnormalities of the cervix. Sometimes the discharge of a blood-stained plug of mucus is the first sign of impending labour (see chart 145, *Am I in labour?*).

*Treatment:* Your doctor is likely to recommend hospital admission, where a careful examination and investigations which may include *ultrasound scanning* (below) will be carried out. Often no treatment other than bed rest is needed, but if bleeding is severe or continues, you may need to be delivered early by induction or caesarean section (see p. 279).

## MISCARRIAGE

Miscarriage (spontaneous abortion) is the expulsion of the fetus from the womb before the 28th week of pregnancy. It occurs in a significant proportion of pregnancies, often before a woman knows that she is pregnant.

**Causes**
The cause of miscarriage may not be easy to discover. Often it may be due to some abnormality or failure of the fetus to develop, so that pregnancy could never have been completed. Occasionally, miscarriages in mid-pregnancy are due to failure of the cervix to hold the fetus inside the womb (incompetent cervix).

**Symptoms**
The first sign of a threatened miscarriage is usually vaginal bleeding. Often this bleeding stops and the pregnancy continues as normal. However, bleeding may sometimes be followed by cramping pains in the abdomen, or, in some cases, backache. In such cases miscarriage is usually inevitable whatever treatment is carried out.

**Treatment**
A threatened miscarriage is usually treated by complete bed rest and you may be given hormone tablets or injections. Sometimes hospital admission is advised. If bleeding stops, you may need to have an ultrasound scan (left) to confirm that the pregnancy is continuing normally. If your doctor thinks that a miscarriage is inevitable or if you have already lost the baby, but some matter remains in the womb, you will probably be admitted to hospital where the contents of the womb may be removed under general anaesthetic (see also *D and C*, p. 254). Most women who have had a miscarriage are able to conceive again without difficulty and subsequently go through a normal pregnancy.

## ULTRASOUND SCANNING

Ultrasound provides a safe, painless way of examining internal organs and is often used during pregnancy to examine the womb, placenta, and fetus. The technique involves sending a beam of very high-pitched sound – ultrasound – through the tissues of the body. These sound waves are deflected off the internal organs and converted by computer into a picture that can be seen on a screen or printed on paper. Ultrasound may reveal cysts, tumours, or other swellings, and in pregnancy helps to determine the position of the placenta, the size of the fetus, and the stage of the pregnancy. Ultrasound scanning often reveals the presence of twins.

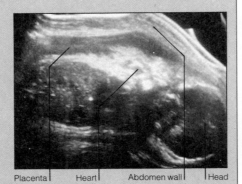

Placenta    Heart    Abdomen wall    Head

Ultrasound picture of fetus at 35 weeks.

# 143 Shortness of breath in pregnancy

Shortness of breath on exertion is noticed by many women after the 28th week of pregnancy. It is usually caused by restriction of the normal movement of the diaphragm and by expansion of the lungs as a result of the enlarged womb pushing the abdominal organs up into the chest cavity. Breathlessness is often reduced in the last month of pregnancy when the baby's head descends into the pelvis.

**Consult this diagnostic chart only after reading chart 90, Difficulty in breathing.**

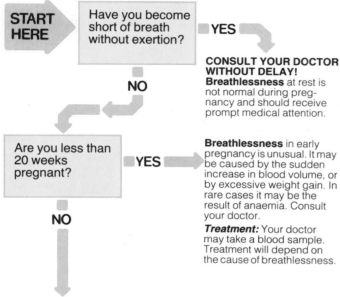

**START HERE** → Have you become short of breath without exertion?

**YES** →
**CONSULT YOUR DOCTOR WITHOUT DELAY!**
**Breathlessness** at rest is not normal during pregnancy and should receive prompt medical attention.

**NO** ↓

Are you less than 20 weeks pregnant?

**YES** →
**Breathlessness** in early pregnancy is unusual. It may be caused by the sudden increase in blood volume, or by excessive weight gain. In rare cases it may be the result of anaemia. Consult your doctor.

***Treatment:*** Your doctor may take a blood sample. Treatment will depend on the cause of breathlessness.

**NO** ↓

**Shortness of breath** after only moderate exertion is normal after the 28th week of pregnancy, but may occur earlier, especially if you are physically unfit, if you have gained too much weight, or if you smoke.

***Self-help:*** You cannot prevent a certain amount of breathlessness in late pregnancy, but you can minimize it. Try to control weight gain, give up or cut down on smoking and avoid tight clothes and girdles that constrict the abdomen. Consult your doctor if breathlessness restricts your daily activities or if you are also feeling unusually tired or unwell.

---

**ANTENATAL CHECK-UPS**

If you are pregnant, you should be sure to go to your doctor or midwife for regular antenatal check-ups where the progress of your pregnancy will be carefully monitored. In addition to a physical examination of your abdomen to assess the size of the womb and the position of the baby, the following checks are carried out:

- **Weight** Regular weighing enables you and your doctor to ensure that you are putting on enough, but not too much, weight. Most women can expect to gain 9-13kg (22-28lb) during pregnancy. During the first weeks of pregnancy little weight is usually gained and some may be lost (see *Weight loss in pregnancy*, p. 148). After the 12th week weight is usually gained at the rate of about 0.5kg (1lb) a week.
- **Urine** Urine is tested regularly for the presence of protein, which may be a sign of pre-eclampsia (below), and for the presence of sugar, which may indicate diabetes.
- **Blood pressure** This is tested at every antenatal visit. A sudden rise may be a sign of pre-eclampsia.
- **Blood tests** At the beginning of pregnancy your blood is tested to determine your blood group and whether you may be susceptible to anaemia. At 16-18 weeks a blood test for spina bifida (malformation of the spinal column) in the baby may also be carried out.
- **Ultrasound** Most women have at least one ultrasound scan during the course of their pregnancy (see *Ultrasound scanning*, opposite.
- **Amniocentesis** In this test a sample of the amniotic fluid surrounding the baby is drawn off by syringe. Analysis of the fluid reveals whether the baby is affected by abnormalities such as Down's syndrome or spina bifida. This test is normally carried out only when there is a higher than average risk of such disorders, because it may occasionally provoke a miscarriage.

---

# 144 Ankle-swelling in pregnancy

During pregnancy there is a tendency for the body to retain more water in the tissues than usual. This may cause the ankles to swell. Slight swelling is usually no cause for concern, but more marked swelling may occasionally be a sign of excessive fluid retention and high blood pressure.

**Consult this chart only after consulting chart 112, Painful or swollen joints.**

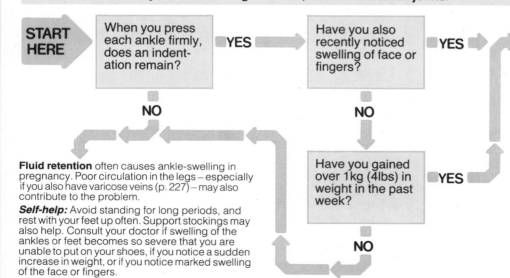

**START HERE** → When you press each ankle firmly, does an indentation remain?

**YES** → Have you also recently noticed swelling of face or fingers?

**YES** →
**CONSULT YOUR DOCTOR WITHOUT DELAY!**
**Pre-eclampsia** is a condition in which blood pressure rises, excessive fluid is retained, and protein leaks into the urine. It may be the cause of ankle-swelling, especially if accompanied by swelling elsewhere or sudden weight gain. Pre-eclampsia needs prompt treatment because it may develop into eclampsia (toxaemia), a disorder of pregnancy in which blood pressure reaches such high levels that the health of both mother and baby is threatened.

**NO** ↓

Have you gained over 1kg (4lbs) in weight in the past week?

**YES** →

**NO** ↓

**Fluid retention** often causes ankle-swelling in pregnancy. Poor circulation in the legs – especially if you also have varicose veins (p. 227) – may also contribute to the problem.

***Self-help:*** Avoid standing for long periods, and rest with your feet up often. Support stockings may also help. Consult your doctor if swelling of the ankles or feet becomes so severe that you are unable to put on your shoes, if you notice a sudden increase in weight, or if you notice marked swelling of the face or fingers.

***Treatment:*** Your doctor will examine you and take your blood pressure. You will also need to give a urine sample. If your doctor diagnoses pre-eclampsia you will probably be advised to rest and you may be given diuretics and/or a drug to reduce blood pressure. You may be advised to limit your salt intake. If your symptoms are severe, your baby may need to be delivered by *induction* (p. 278) or *caesarean section* (p. 279).

# 145 Am I in labour?

The average duration of pregnancy is 40 weeks, but it is quite normal for a baby to be born as early as 36 weeks or as late as 42 weeks. The onset of labour – the series of events leading to the expulsion of the baby from the womb – is heralded by a number of different signs, including abdominal or back pains, rupture of the amniotic sac (the "bag of waters") and the passage of a plug of thick,

perhaps blood-stained, mucus. The symptoms of labour experienced by each woman and the order in which they appear may vary. The diagnostic chart is designed to help you decide whether or not the symptoms you are experiencing indicate that labour has started and how urgently you should notify your doctor, midwife or hospital for further advice.

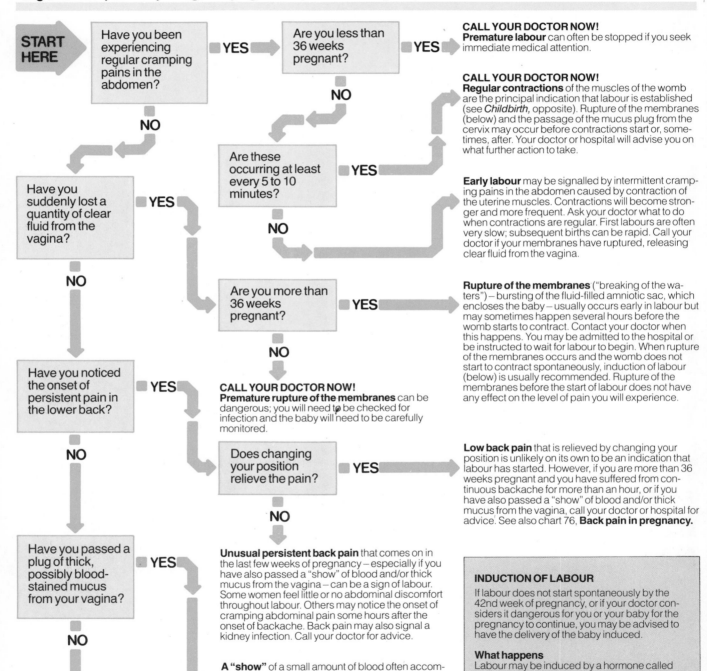

**START HERE**

**Have you been experiencing regular cramping pains in the abdomen?** — YES → **Are you less than 36 weeks pregnant?** — YES →

**CALL YOUR DOCTOR NOW!**
**Premature labour** can often be stopped if you seek immediate medical attention.

NO ↓

**Are these occurring at least every 5 to 10 minutes?** — YES →

**CALL YOUR DOCTOR NOW!**
**Regular contractions** of the muscles of the womb are the principal indication that labour is established (see *Childbirth,* opposite). Rupture of the membranes (below) and the passage of the mucus plug from the cervix may occur before contractions start or, sometimes, after. Your doctor or hospital will advise you on what further action to take.

NO ↓

**Have you suddenly lost a quantity of clear fluid from the vagina?** — YES →

**Early labour** may be signalled by intermittent cramping pains in the abdomen caused by contraction of the uterine muscles. Contractions will become stronger and more frequent. Ask your doctor what to do when contractions are regular. First labours are often very slow; subsequent births can be rapid. Call your doctor if your membranes have ruptured, releasing clear fluid from the vagina.

NO ↓

**Are you more than 36 weeks pregnant?** — YES →

**Rupture of the membranes** ("breaking of the waters") – bursting of the fluid-filled amniotic sac, which encloses the baby – usually occurs early in labour but may sometimes happen several hours before the womb starts to contract. Contact your doctor when this happens. You may be admitted to the hospital or be instructed to wait for labour to begin. When rupture of the membranes occurs and the womb does not start to contract spontaneously, induction of labour (below) is usually recommended. Rupture of the membranes before the start of labour does not have any effect on the level of pain you will experience.

NO ↓

**Have you noticed the onset of persistent pain in the lower back?** — YES →

**CALL YOUR DOCTOR NOW!**
**Premature rupture of the membranes** can be dangerous; you will need to be checked for infection and the baby will need to be carefully monitored.

NO ↓

**Does changing your position relieve the pain?** — YES →

**Low back pain** that is relieved by changing your position is unlikely on its own to be an indication that labour has started. However, if you are more than 36 weeks pregnant and you have suffered from continuous backache for more than an hour, or if you have also passed a "show" of blood and/or thick mucus from the vagina, call your doctor or hospital for advice. See also chart 76, **Back pain in pregnancy.**

NO ↓

**Have you passed a plug of thick, possibly blood-stained mucus from your vagina?** — YES →

**Unusual persistent back pain** that comes on in the last few weeks of pregnancy – especially if you have also passed a "show" of blood and/or thick mucus from the vagina – can be a sign of labour. Some women feel little or no abdominal discomfort throughout labour. Others may notice the onset of cramping abdominal pain some hours after the onset of backache. Back pain may also signal a kidney infection. Call your doctor for advice.

NO ↓

**None of the main indications of labour** are present in your case. Consult your doctor if you have any symptom that worries you.

**A "show"** of a small amount of blood often accompanies the expulsion of a thick plug of mucus that seals the cervix. This is usually an indication that labour is impending. However, because it may occur as much as 24 hours before labour starts, it is not necessary to notify your doctor immediately if you have no other symptoms. Seek medical advice as soon as you experience regular abdominal pains, persistent back pains or if your water breaks (see *Rupture of the membranes,* above right).

---

**INDUCTION OF LABOUR**

If labour does not start spontaneously by the 42nd week of pregnancy, or if your doctor considers it dangerous for you or your baby for the pregnancy to continue, you may be advised to have the delivery of the baby induced.

**What happens**

Labour may be induced by a hormone called oxytocin given intravenously. Alternatively, a vaginal gel or suppository containing prostaglandins may be given to soften and dilate the cervix, or the amniotic sac may be broken (artificial rupture of the membranes). Occasionally, if these procedures fail to bring about delivery or if your or the baby's medical condition requires very rapid delivery, a cesarean section will be performed.

# 146 Breast-feeding problems

All medical authorities agree that breast milk is the best form of nutrition for newborn babies. It contains all the essential nutrients in their ideal proportions and in the most easily assimilated form for your baby. Breast-fed babies develop fewer allergies than babies fed on artificial milk and are less subject to gastroenteritis. It is rare for a mother to be medically unable to breast-feed, but unfortunately many mothers are reluctant to start breast-feeding or are discouraged from continuing by minor difficulties during the first few weeks. However, once established, breast-feeding is usually a happy experience for both mother and baby. Consult this chart if you have had a baby in the past few months and have any problems related to breast-feeding such as pain in the breasts or nipples, overfull breasts, or inadequate milk supply.

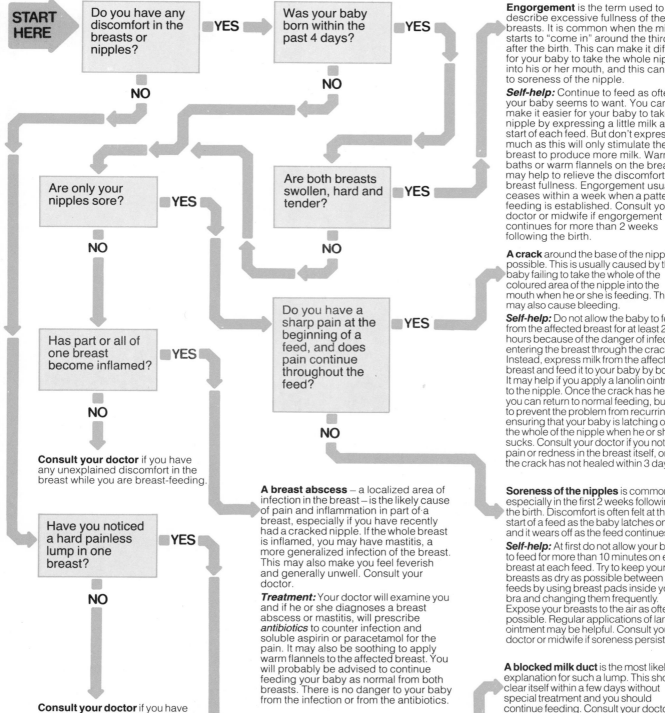

**START HERE**

Do you have any discomfort in the breasts or nipples?

Was your baby born within the past 4 days?

Are only your nipples sore?

Are both breasts swollen, hard and tender?

Has part or all of one breast become inflamed?

Do you have a sharp pain at the beginning of a feed, and does pain continue throughout the feed?

Have you noticed a hard painless lump in one breast?

**Consult your doctor** if you have any unexplained discomfort in the breast while you are breast-feeding.

**Consult your doctor** if you have a problem with breast-feeding that is not covered on this chart.

**Engorgement** is the term used to describe excessive fullness of the breasts. It is common when the milk starts to "come in" around the third day after the birth. This can make it difficult for your baby to take the whole nipple into his or her mouth, and this can lead to soreness of the nipple.

*Self-help:* Continue to feed as often as your baby seems to want. You can make it easier for your baby to take the nipple by expressing a little milk at the start of each feed. But don't express too much as this will only stimulate the breast to produce more milk. Warm baths or warm flannels on the breasts may help to relieve the discomfort of breast fullness. Engorgement usually ceases within a week when a pattern of feeding is established. Consult your doctor or midwife if engorgement continues for more than 2 weeks following the birth.

**A crack** around the base of the nipple is possible. This is usually caused by the baby failing to take the whole of the coloured area of the nipple into the mouth when he or she is feeding. This may also cause bleeding.

*Self-help:* Do not allow the baby to feed from the affected breast for at least 24 hours because of the danger of infection entering the breast through the crack. Instead, express milk from the affected breast and feed it to your baby by bottle. It may help if you apply a lanolin ointment to the nipple. Once the crack has healed you can return to normal feeding, but try to prevent the problem from recurring by ensuring that your baby is latching on to the whole of the nipple when he or she sucks. Consult your doctor if you notice pain or redness in the breast itself, or if the crack has not healed within 3 days.

**A breast abscess** – a localized area of infection in the breast – is the likely cause of pain and inflammation in part of a breast, especially if you have recently had a cracked nipple. If the whole breast is inflamed, you may have mastitis, a more generalized infection of the breast. This may also make you feel feverish and generally unwell. Consult your doctor.

*Treatment:* Your doctor will examine you and if he or she diagnoses a breast abscess or mastitis, will prescribe *antibiotics* to counter infection and soluble aspirin or paracetamol for the pain. It may also be soothing to apply warm flannels to the affected breast. You will probably be advised to continue feeding your baby as normal from both breasts. There is no danger to your baby from the infection or from the antibiotics.

**Soreness of the nipples** is common, especially in the first 2 weeks following the birth. Discomfort is often felt at the start of a feed as the baby latches on, and it wears off as the feed continues.

*Self-help:* At first do not allow your baby to feed for more than 10 minutes on each breast at each feed. Try to keep your breasts as dry as possible between feeds by using breast pads inside your bra and changing them frequently. Expose your breasts to the air as often as possible. Regular applications of lanolin ointment may be helpful. Consult your doctor or midwife if soreness persists.

**A blocked milk duct** is the most likely explanation for such a lump. This should clear itself within a few days without special treatment and you should continue feeding. Consult your doctor if the lump becomes painful or inflamed, or if it persists for more than a week.

# 147 Depression after childbirth

Childbirth is a traumatic event for a woman, both physically and emotionally. Not only is labour an exhausting physical experience, but it initiates a dramatic alteration in the body's hormone balance as you begin to readjust to no longer being pregnant. Your emotions are also likely to be in turmoil following this event which you have awaited with eager anticipation. You may not find it easy to come to terms with the reality of motherhood and the demands that a new baby will make on you. It is therefore natural that childbirth should be followed by a period of emotional instability. In the first day or so following the birth the most common feeling is that of elation, but in the subsequent days and sometimes weeks some women become sad, withdrawn, and apathetic, and they may also suffer from guilt that they cannot respond with more enthusiasm to the arrival of their baby. Consult this chart if you suffer from such feelings of depression.

**START HERE**

**Is it less than a week since your baby was born?**

**YES**

**The "third day blues"** is the common name for the feeling of tearfulness and depression that affects many women in the 7 days following the birth. It often coincides with the time when the milk "comes in" and when you may be suffering from engorgement and other breast-feeding problems. The cause of such feelings is probably mainly hormonal, and most women feel much better within a day or so.

*Self-help:* Try to keep the week following the birth as quiet as possible – especially around the third and fourth days. If you are in hospital, it may be helpful to restrict the number of visitors. If you are at home, try to have a friend or relative to help you in the house during this first week. Discuss any feeding difficulties or other problems related to your baby's progress with your doctor or visiting midwife. Consult your doctor if your depression lasts longer than 3 days.

**NO**

**Are you worried that you are unable to produce sufficient milk to feed your baby?**

**YES**

**Worry about being able to produce enough milk** is a common problem among new mothers. Very few women are unable to produce enough milk to meet their baby's needs. In particular, women with small breasts are just as able to produce large amounts of milk as women with larger breasts. As long as your baby gains weight as expected, there is unlikely to be cause for concern.

*Self-help:* You can ensure that your milk supply remains plentiful by feeding your baby as often as he or she seems to want. Make sure that you get plenty of rest and eat a nourishing diet (you may need up to 800 calories a day more than usual). Do not be tempted to start giving your baby extra bottles of artificial milk in the hope that it will help your baby to sleep through the night. If you feel that your milk supply is diminishing, express remaining milk after each feed.

**NO**

**Do you feel fine most of the time, but occasionally have days when you feel depressed and irritable?**

**YES**

**Periods of depression and irritability** are common in the months following childbirth, just as after any traumatic event. As well as being affected by hormonal changes and possible feelings of anti-climax, you may also be overtired as a result of frequent night feeds and may be worried about your competence as a mother or about your baby's general development. In addition, if you are used to working outside the home, it may be difficult for you to adjust to being at home all day with your baby. Consult your doctor.

*Treatment:* Your doctor will discuss your feelings with you and may carry out a physical examination to rule out any underlying disorder. In some cases no medical treatment is necessary and you may simply be advised to take care not to become overtired – for example, by allowing your partner to get up at night to feed the baby sometimes – and to make sure that you go out on your own regularly (your health visitor may be able to offer helpful advice about baby sitters). In other cases a course of *antidepressants* may be prescribed. You may also find it reassuring to join a local self-help support group for new mothers.

**NO**

**Do you often feel unable to cope with being a mother?**

**YES**

**NO**

**Consult your doctor** if you are unable to make a diagnosis from this chart.

**Post-natal depression** is a serious condition that often affects new mothers in the 6 months following childbirth. You may find it difficult to respond lovingly to your baby and to cope with day-to-day chores. You may also experience problems in your relationship with your partner. Consult your doctor.

*Treatment:* Your doctor will examine you to assess your general health and will talk to you about your feelings. Depending on the severity of your depression, you may be prescribed a course of *antidepressant* drugs and/or hormones. You may be referred to a specialist for treatment (see *Psychotherapy*, p.173). If you are found to be severely depressed you may be admitted to hospital with your baby, where drug treatment and other forms of therapy can be carefully monitored. When you are over the worst of your depression, you may find it helpful to join a self-help support group for women who have suffered from post-natal depression. Post-natal depression will not necessarily recur following a future pregnancy.

# Useful information

# Essential first aid

Most accidental injuries are minor and easily treated with simple first aid techniques. However, every person should be prepared for the possibility of a more serious accident that may require them to carry out lifesaving first aid treatment which may even involve resuscitating someone whose breathing has stopped. Accurate and rapid assessment of what must be done is therefore crucial and will require using good judgement and common sense. For instance, there would be little point in rushing to aid a victim of electric shock before eliminating the offending power source. It is equally important to know what must be done first, so an emergency action checklist is provided right. In any situation the goals of first aid are to preserve life, prevent the injury or condition from becoming worse and to promote recovery. The task of the person administering first aid is to find out what happened without endangering him or herself, to reassure and protect the person from any further danger, to deal with the injury or condition as required and to arrange for travel home or to a hospital as necessary. Ambulances are normally needed to take a casualty to hospital in any incident involving difficulty in breathing, heart failure, severe bleeding, unconsciousness, serious burns, shock or poisoning.

The more knowledge you have immediately at hand, the more useful you can be in an emergency. On the following pages you will find instructions on the major life-saving techniques. This can not substitute for the practical experience you can gain if you attend classes in first aid, but you should try to familiarize yourself with the techniques described here so that if you are ever faced with an emergency, you will be able to act swiftly and efficiently.

## Seeking emergency help

Usually, the quickest way of obtaining emergency medical treatment is to take the person by car to the accident department of your local hospital yourself. DO NOT attempt to take him, or her yourself in either of the following circumstances:
■ If the person has a suspected back injury and/or any other injury that makes moving him or her inadvisable without a stretcher (for example, broken leg).
■ If you are alone, and the person needs supervision because he or she is very distressed or unconscious.
In such cases, or if you have no means of transport, call for an ambulance at once. If you are in any doubt or live far away from a hospital call your doctor for advice.

## Emergency checklist

If a person has suffered any type of serious accident give emergency first aid treatment in the order listed below before seeking emergency help. If possible, send someone else for help while you carry out first aid.
**1** Check breathing. If this has stopped carry out mouth-to-mouth resuscitation (p. 283).
**2** Attempt to control any severe bleeding (p. 284).
**3** If the person is unconscious, place him or her in the recovery position (p.283).
**4** Treat any severe burns (p. 286).
**5** Watch for signs of shock (p. 285) and carry out treatment if necessary.

## First aid index

# Mouth-to-mouth resuscitation

A person may stop breathing after falling into water, being knocked unconscious by an electric shock or taking poisonous medicines. If you find someone unconscious and apparently not breathing, your first priority is to restart breathing by mouth-to-mouth resuscitation. Do this before summoning medical help , and before dealing with any other injury, except when the trouble is choking (see *Choking,* p. 285). Mouth-to-mouth resuscitation is suitable for older children, but for babies and young children the alternative methods described below should be used.

### Resuscitating an older child or adult

1 Lay the victim face upwards on a firm, rigid surface. Support the back of the neck and tip the head well back. Clear his or her mouth with your finger to remove any blockage from the windpipe.

2 Pinch the victim's nose shut and take a deep breath and seal your mouth around his or her mouth. Blow strongly into the lungs 4 times.

3 Continue to give a breath every 5 seconds, After each breath remove your mouth. Listen for air leaving the lungs and watch the chest fall. Continue until medical help arrives or until the victim is able to breathe on his or her own.

### Resuscitating babies and young children

1 Lay the baby on his or her back and clear the mouth as in step 1 above.

2 Tilt the baby's head back slightly, take a deep breath and seal your mouth over the baby's mouth and nose. Blow gently into the baby's lungs.

3 Remove your mouth and watch the baby's chest fall as air leaves the lungs. Repeat a breath every 2-3 seconds until medical help arrives or the baby starts to breathe on his or her own.

### Mouth-to-nose resuscitation

A facial injury may prevent you from breathing easily into the victim's mouth. In such cases, lay the victim on his or her back and quickly clear the mouth and airway of foreign material. Position the victim's head backwards (as in 1 and 2 of mouth-to-mouth resuscitation for an adult). Take a deep breath and seal your mouth around the victim's nose. Close the mouth by lifting the victim's chin. Blow strongly into the nose. Remove your mouth and hold the victim's mouth open with your hand, so that air can escape. Repeat as for mouth-to-mouth resuscitation, every five seconds.

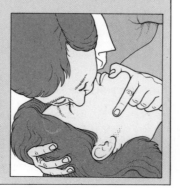

# The recovery position

The recovery position is a safe position for an unconscious person which allows him or her to breathe freely and prevents choking and inhalation of vomit. The position of the limbs supports the body in a stable and comfortable position. Place the victim in this position after you have ensured that he or she is breathing normally and have dealt with any obvious injury. DO NOT use the recovery position if you suspect a back injury.

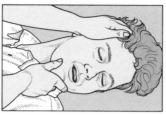
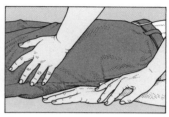
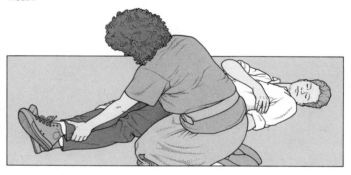

1 Check the mouth of an unconscious person to make sure there is no foreign matter or false teeth in the mouth.

2 Place the near arm of the victim close to his or her body, tucking the hand under the nearside leg.

3 Cross the far arm over the chest towards you and cross the far leg over the near one at the knee.

4 Protect and support the head with one hand. With the other hand, grasp the clothing at the hip furthest from you and pull the victim quickly towards you, keeping him or her supported against you.

5 Readjust the head to make certain the airway is still open.

6 Bend the victim's uppermost arm into a convenient position to support the upper body and his or her uppermost leg at the knee to bring the thigh well forward to support the lower body. Carefully pull the other arm out from under the victim working from the shoulder down. Leave it lying parallel to prevent the victim rolling on to the back.

# Drowning

In a drowning accident check breathing as soon as you reach the victim. If the victim is not breathing, start mouth-to-mouth resuscitation at once. Do not wait to get the victim out of the water or concern yourself about removing water from the lungs. Once you have managed to restore breathing and are out of the water, place the victim in the *recovery position* (see p. 283) and keep him or her warm, covered with blankets or clothes. Seek medical help.

1 Quickly remove any obstructions like seaweed from the victim's mouth and begin *mouth-to-mouth resuscitation* right away.

2 If the victim is still in the water and you are within your depth, use one arm to support the victim's body and the other hand to support his or her head and seal the nose.

# Bleeding

Bleeding, whether from a cut or more serious wound, is usually distressing and should be dealt with promptly and calmly. Treat bleeding as severe:

- If blood spurts forcefully from the wound.
- If you estimate that more than 250ml (½ pint) of blood has been lost.
- If bleeding continues for more than 5 minutes.

## Severe bleeding

While bleeding usually stops by itself after a short time with a minor wound, in a severe wound, blood may be flowing so freely that it cannot clot before spurting from the body. Your main aim is to reduce blood flow so as to encourage the clotting of blood in the wound to seal the damaged blood vessels. This can be done by applying pressure to the wound itself, as described below. As a general rule you should try to keep the injured part raised above the level of the heart. Do not try to clean a serious wound with water or antiseptic. As soon as you have carried out first aid, seek emergency medical help.

### How to stop severe bleeding

1 Lay the victim down and raise the injured part.

2 Remove any easily accessible foreign objects such as pieces of glass from the wound, but do not probe for anything that is deeply embedded.

3 Press hard on the wound with a cloth pad, holding any gaping edges together. If there is anything still embedded in the wound, avoid exerting direct pressure on it.

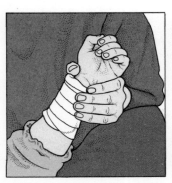

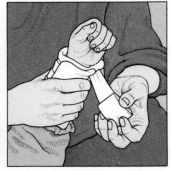

4 Maintain pressure on the wound by binding the pad firmly over the wound using a bandage or strips of material.

5 If the pad becomes soaked with blood, do not remove it. Instead apply more padding over the wound and hold this in place firmly with another bandage.

## Nosebleeds

Nosebleeds are a common occurrence and may be brought on by a minor injury to the nose.

If you have a nosebleed, sit down, leaning slightly forwards. Make sure that you breathe through the mouth and pinch both nostrils firmly closed for about 10 minutes. This pressure allows a blood clot to form and seal the damaged blood vessels. Do not blow your nose for several hours after the bleeding has stopped, as this may dislodge the blood clot.

Seek medical help if bleeding continues for longer than 20 minutes or if you suspect that the nose may be broken, for example, if bleeding followed a severe blow to the nose. Emergency medical attention should be sought if bleeding from the nose follows a blow to another part of the head; this may indicate a fractured skull.

## Minor cuts and grazes

Bleeding from a minor cut or graze helps to clean the wound and normally stops spontaneously after a few minutes. Pressing a clean pad over the wound for a few minutes helps to stop bleeding. When bleeding has stopped, clean around the cut wiping from the edges outwards with a clean gauze or cotton wool pad. There is no need to clean inside the wound itself. Small cuts and even quite large grazes heal most rapidly if left uncovered. You can hold gaping edges closed with strips of surgical tape, but any cut more than about 1 cm (½ in) long may need stitches to prevent scarring. Consult your doctor or local hospital accident department if you think that the wound might need stitching, if it is very dirty, or in the case of a deep puncture wound, for example, from a nail.

### Treating minor cuts

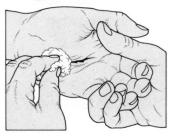

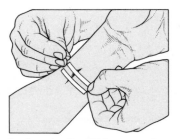

Wipe from the edges of the wound outwards, using a clean swab of cotton wool for each stroke. Put any antiseptics on the cleansing swab, not directly on the wound.

Small cuts heal best if left uncovered. However, if the edges of the cut gape, draw them together and put one or two strips of surgical tape across the wound ("butterfly strips").

## Puncture wounds

A deep wound caused by something dirty – a rusty nail or an animal's tooth – carries a high risk of infection, because dirt is carried deep into the tissues and the wound bleeds very little to carry it back out. If numbness, tingling or weakness in a limb follows a deep cut or puncture wound, underlying nerves or tendons may have been damaged. Antibiotics and a tetanus injection are advisable for all deep wounds.

# Choking

If your child chokes on a piece of food or any other object for example, an accidentally swallowed small toy – and is unable to cough it up, you should take action to remove the blockage without delay. The technique you use depends on the size of the child. Following successful removal of the blockage you should always seek medical advice promptly. Adults who are choking can be helped by an abdominal thrust (also known as the Heimlich manoeuvre) similar to that performed for older children. This technique is fully illustrated on page 199.

**Babies (under 1 year)**

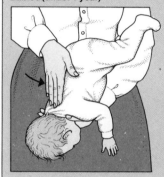

Lay the baby face down on your forearm, supporting the baby's chest, with the head lower than the body. Give several firm, but not forceful, blows with the heel of your hand between the shoulder blades.

**Small children (1 to 9 years)**

Sit down and place the child face down across your lap. Give several sharp blows with the heel of your hand between the shoulder blades. Be careful not to use excessive force. If the blockage is not dislodged, repeat.

**Older children (over 9 years)**

1 Hold the child up from behind in a standing position, pressing one fist with one thumb upward against the waist. Hold your other hand over the fist and thrust hard in and up under the rib cage. If this does not clear the blockage, repeat 3 more times.

2 If breathing does not restart following removal of the blockage, carry out mouth-to-mouth resuscitation (p. 283).

# Shock

Shock is a life-threatening condition that may be due to severe injuries, a large loss of blood, burns, or overwhelming infection. Its main feature is a dramatic drop in blood pressure. Suspect that a person is in shock if he or she becomes pale and sweaty, and possibly drowsy or confused following such an injury. A shock victim needs urgent medical attention. Do not give food or drink.

**Treating shock**
If the person seems to be in shock, lay him or her down on his or her back with legs raised. Loosen any tight clothing and cover to keep him or her warm. Offer plenty of reassurance.

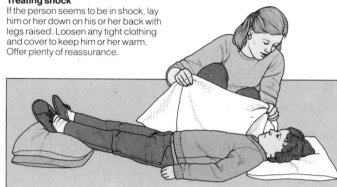

# Electric shock

A severe electric shock is likely to knock a person unconscious and breathing may stop. Deep burns at the point where the current entered the body and internal damage may result. Always seek medical advice after an electric shock even if the victim seems to have suffered only minor burns.

**What to do**
First switch off the current or break the contact between the victim and the appliance. Do not try to pull the victim away or you may receive a shock yourself. Instead, use an object such as a wooden broom handle to push away the source of the current. Check the victim's breathing. If this has stopped start mouth-to-mouth resuscitation (see p. 283) at once. You may need to continue with this for up to half an hour. Once the person is breathing, place him or her in the recovery position, treat any burns (see p.286) and summon medical help.

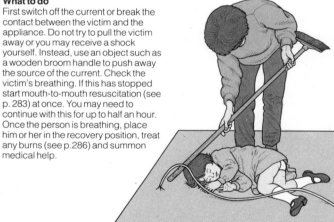

# Unconsciousness

Unconsciousness not only refers to unrousable coma, but also to a state in which someone is drowsy and confused and does not respond to your presence. It may result from such conditions as brain damage, loss of blood, lack of oxygen, chemical changes in the blood or overdose of certain drugs. The main danger with unconsciousness is obstruction of the airway, either because the tongue has become limp and flopped backwards blocking the airway, or because the victim can no longer cough to clear vomit or other matter from the back of the throat.

First check to see whether the unconscious person is breathing, if not, begin *mouth-to-mouth resuscitation* (see p.283). If the victim is breathing but respiration sounds noisy or gurgling, check deep inside the mouth to make certain there is no obstruction. Loosen any tight clothing around the victim's neck and chest as soon as normal breathing resumes. Place the victim in the *recovery position* (see p.283). If possible, place a coat or blanket under the victim to minimize heat loss and cover with another. Try not to leave the victim unattended until medical help arrives.

*Note:* If unconsciousness followed a fall or collision and a spinal injury is possible, do not place the victim in the recovery position unless he or she is vomiting. In such cases, try not to flex the victim's spine.

# Burns

Burns may be caused by dry heat (fire), moist heat (steam or hot liquids), electricity, or corrosive chemicals. For treatment of electric shock, see page 285.

To treat a burn, first remove the cause. For example, put out the flames. The affected area should then be cooled as rapidly as possible by immersing the area in cold water or by holding it beneath a running tap. DO NOT under any circumstance apply any type of ointment or cream to the burn or burst any blisters that may form on the skin.

Following first aid, seek emergency medical help if the burn affects an extensive area, if the skin is broken, severely blistered, or charred, or if the victim is in severe pain. Even small burns on the face or hands may cause a certain amount of scarring, so you should always seek medical advice about these without delay.

### Minor burns and scalds

A burn or scald can be treated safely at home even if it causes reddening and blistering if it damages only the superficial layer of skin over a fairly small area. Sunburn is normally considered a burn of this type.

Superficial burns are very painful, so first aid is aimed chiefly at cooling the area to relieve pain. If you can, keep the burned area in cold water or hold it under a cold running tap for at least 10 minutes, or until the pain stops. If blisters form over a burn, do not break them. If they are on a part of the skin which can be rubbed by clothing, cover them with a padded dressing. Do not put any cream, grease, or ointment on a burn. The exception is mild sunburn which is often soothed by covering it with calamine lotion.

### Dealing with burns

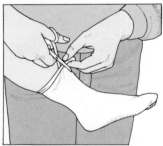

1 Remove clothing that has been soaked in hot fat, boiling water, or chemical agents from the burnt area unless it is firmly stuck to the skin. Dry, burnt clothing should be left.

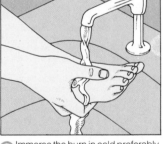

2 Immerse the burn in cold preferably running water for at least 10 minutes, if the area affected is large, cover it with a clean towel or sheet soaked in cold water.

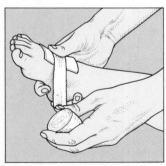

3 When you have cooled the burn, cover it with a clean dry gauze or cloth dressing. Do not use cotton wool or other fluffy materials. If you are taking the victim to hospital, do not cover the burn; any dressing will have to be removed, possibly causing him or her further pain.

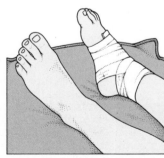

4 Keep a burnt limb raised and, if the victim is conscious, give sips of cold water while waiting for medical help.

# Poisoning

Accidental poisoning is one of the most common reasons for a child to need emergency treatment in hospital, especially among the under 5s. While in adults poisoning is more likely to be due to the overdose of drugs, deliberate as well as accidental, children are poisoned by having swallowed alcohol, medicines, household cleaning fluids or chemicals, poisonous plants or berries. In some cases a child will admit to having taken something poisonous, but you may also suspect that your child, or an older person, has swallowed poison if he or she suddenly and inexplicably starts to vomit, becomes drowsy or confused, loses consciousness, or if he or she starts to breathe abnormally.

If you think that your child or an older person may have taken any type of poison, even if he or she seems well at the moment, seek expert advice at once. Telephone your doctor or local hospital accident department. You should try and give the following information:
- What has been swallowed.
- How much has been swallowed. In the case of medicines, try to find out how many tablets were taken.
- When it was swallowed.
- If you take the victim to the hospital or to the doctor, take with you any containers that you think may be involved.

If you are unable to obtain expert advice and cannot easily get to a hospital, follow the advice given below.

### Chemical poisons
(including household cleaning fluids, paraffin, petrol, polishes and paint)

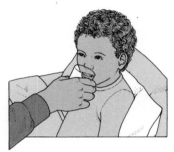

1 If the victim is conscious, give a glass of water to drink at once.

2 DO NOT try to induce vomiting, but if the victim vomits spontaneously, hold him or her face down over your lap to prevent inhalation of chemicals in the vomit. Keep an older person's head covered.

3 If the victim loses consciousness, place him or her in the *recovery position* (p. 283) and if breathing stops carry out *mouth-to-mouth resuscitation* (p. 283).

4 Seek medical help as soon as possible.

### Medicines, alcohol, poisonous plants and berries

1 If the victim is conscious, you may try to induce vomiting (see above).

2 If the victim is unconscious, do not give anything by mouth. Lay the victim down in the *recovery position* (p. 283) and if breathing stops carry out *mouth-to-mouth resuscitation* (p. 283).

3 Seek medical help as soon as possible.

### How to induce vomiting

Never try to induce vomiting in a person who is unconscious or who has swallowed chemical products such as cleaning fluids, paraffin or petrol (see below). Do not try to induce vomiting by giving salt water or by sticking a finger down the victim's throat.

In other cases, give 3 teaspoonfuls (15ml) of syrup of ipecac followed by 2 glasses of water or other liquid. If this does not lead to vomiting within 20 minutes, repeat the dose once only. When the person vomits, keep his or her face down with head lowered to prevent choking or inhalation of vomit.

# Hypothermia

Body temperature is normally constant at about 37°C (98°F). During prolonged exposure to cold, more body heat may be lost than can easily be replaced so the body temperature drops. This is known as hypothermia. Babies and old people are especially vulnerable to chilling. They may lose a dangerous amount of body heat in conditions that may not seem particularly cold to a younger adult. In fit people, hypothermia occurs after prolonged physical exertion in windy, cold conditions. The drop in body temperature causes a gradual physical and mental slowing down, once the stores of energy have been used up, although this may pass unnoticed. The victim will become increasingly clumsy, unreasonable, and irritable; there is confusion, drowsiness; the speech becomes slurred. Eventually, unconsciousness with slow, weak breathing and a barely discernible heartbeat results. Hypothermia needs urgent medical attention, but before professional help arrives you should be able to assist the victim following the steps below. If the victim is unconscious, he or she should be placed in the *recovery position* (see p. 283) if breathing is regular.

**Dealing with chilling**

1 If the victim is unconscious, begin *mouth-to-mouth resuscitation* (see p. 283) right away.

2 Once breathing is regular, shelter the victim from the cold, insulating him or her from the ground if you are outside. If you are indoors, remove any wet clothes and exchange for warm, dry ones or wrap the victim in warm blankets.

3 If the victim is conscious, give sips of warm, sweet liquids but do not give any alcohol. Do not immerse the victim in a hot bath, apply hot water bottles or electric blankets.

# Heat exhaustion

If someone who is not used to very hot conditions neglects to take plenty of salt and extra fluids, heat exhaustion can result from excessive sweating. The victim will become exhausted, with pale, clammy skin and may feel sick, dizzy, and faint. His or her pulse rate and breathing will become rapid and headache or muscle cramps may develop. Untreated, heat exhaustion may develop into the more serious condition, heat stroke, which always requires medical attention.

**Dealing with heat exhaustion**

1 Lay the victim down in a cool, quiet place with his or her feet raised a little.

2 Loosen any tight clothing and give water to drink, to which 1 teaspoonful of salt has been added for every 1 litre (about 1¾ pints).

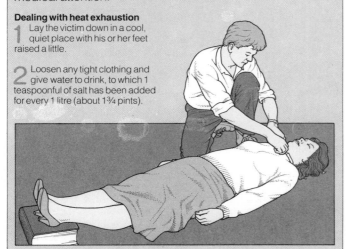

# Frostbite

This is a serious condition and needs urgent medical attention. Frostbitten skin is hard, pale, cold and painless; when thawed out, it becomes red and painful. Get the victim inside as soon as possible and summon medical help. Meanwhile, shelter the victim from the wind and give warm drinks. Cover the frozen part with extra clothing or blankets, or warm it against the body. The face can be covered with dry, gloved hands; hands should be tucked inside the victim's armpits; affected feet should be raised. Do not use direct heat and do not rub the affected area. Encourage the victim to exercise warmed up frostbitten parts.

# Bites and stings

Most animal and insect bites and stings in the British Isles are minor and are no threat to your general health. When abroad, know how to identify animals and insects that have poisonous bites or stings and seek advice about antidotes and treatments. Occasionally, a person may develop a severe allergic reaction to an apparently minor bite or sting. This situation requires emergency treatment (see *Anaphylactic shock,* below).

**Animal bites:** If you are bitten by an animal such as a dog, cat, or horse, seek medical help as most bite wounds may become septic if not quickly treated. You may need an anti-tetanus injection and/or stitches. If you receive any animal bite outside the British Isles, seek urgent medical advice; anti-rabies injections may be needed.

**Snake bites:** The only poisonous snake in the British Isles is the adder. In most cases its bite is not dangerous, but an adder bite may be serious for a young child. If you or your child receives a snake bite, wash around the wound, take (or give the child) liquid paracetamol to relieve any pain and encourage the child to rest. Seek medical advice.

**Insect bites and stings:** Bites and stings from most common insects – for example, gnats and mosquitoes – cause local itching, redness and swelling. Calamine lotion or surgical spirit should be applied to relieve discomfort. If stung by a bee or hornet, you should first try to remove the sting from the wound by gently scraping it out with a clean fingernail or knife blade. Watch for signs of anaphylactic shock (below).

**Jellyfish stings:** These are seldom dangerous, though they may cause painful burning and swelling. Calamine lotion or antihistamine cream are best for relieving burning and swelling. The Portuguese Man-of-War may cause a more serious reaction. The victim may suffer from shortness of breath and fainting. Scrape off the stings, which stick to the skin; use dry sand, if available. Place the victim in the *recovery position* (p. 283) and keep him or her warm while you send for medical help.

# Anaphylactic shock

In rare cases a person may become hypersensitive to a particular type of bite or sting – usually after having been bitten previously. If the person is bitten or stung again he or she develops a severe allergic reaction known as anaphylactic shock. Symptoms may include difficulty breathing as a result of narrowing of the air passages, and/or any of the signs of *shock* (p. 285). If a person shows such symptoms after receiving a bite or sting, treat as for shock and seek emergency medical help urgently.

# Nursing a sick child

A child who is ill is likely to be more anxious and in need of comfort than usual, even if the disease is not painful or serious. The reassurance of your presence is therefore an important part of nursing your child – whether he or she is at home or in hospital (see *Children in hospital,* opposite). If you learn a few basic ground rules (see *Treating the most common symptoms and disorders at home,* opposite) you will be able to remain calm and confident. Advice on dealing with specific disorders is given in the diagnostic charts (see *How to use the charts,* p. 38, On these pages you will find general advice on nursing a sick child at home.

### Telling when your child is unwell

Most parents can swiftly observe the signs of a child's illness. Apart from obvious symptoms such as rash, vomiting or pain, there are likely to be less specific indicators that all is not well, including loss of appetite (particularly in young babies), irritability and crying, or unusual lethargy. If you suspect that your baby or child is unwell, consult the appropriate diagnostic chart further on in this book (see *How to find the chart you need,* p. 40-48), to discover the possible cause of the trouble. If your child's symptoms are vague, try starting with chart 9, *Feeling generally unwell.*

### Bed rest

For most illnesses it is not essential for a child to stay in bed all day. If your child feels well enough to get up and play around the house, it is usually safe to allow this. However, if your child does not feel like getting out of bed or if the doctor has advised rest, you should try to prevent boredom by providing plenty of amusements. A sick child may not be able to concentrate for as long as usual and will not want to play games that are too demanding. He or she is likely to want extra attention and you may have to spend more time than usual with your child to prevent boredom occurring. Often, a child will be happier resting in a bed made up on the sofa in the sitting room where he or she can feel closely involved with other members of the family. This will also allow you to supervise your small patient more closely.

**Keeping a sick child occupied**
Keeping your child amused will help raise spirits. If your child needs or wants to stay in bed a variety of activities such as drawing, or sticking pictures in a scrapbook, may entertain him or her. Your child may be happier in a bed made up on a sofa in a room with other people.

## Lowering your child's temperature

You can safely try to reduce your child's high temperature in the following way:
- Remove as much clothing as possible.
- Keep the room temperature at about 15°C (60°F).
- Sponge your child repeatedly with tepid water, or put your child into a tepid bath.
- Give the recommended dose of paracetamol.
- Make sure your child drinks at least a litre (1½ pints) of fluid daily.

### Diet and drinks

A sick child is likely to have a reduced appetite, but this in itself is no cause for concern in the short term. No special diet is necessary for most illnesses, but if you are worrying that your child is not eating enough, you may be able to persuade him or her to eat a favourite meal. It does not matter if this does not happen to be particularly nourishing. Your doctor will advise you what to do if loss of appetite continues through a long illness. In most cases it is more important for a sick child to drink plenty of fluids, especially if he or she is feverish, has been vomiting or has diarrhoea. Although water or plain unsweetened fruit juices are preferable, offer whatever fluids your child enjoys, including fizzy drinks.

**Giving your child food and drink**
Your child will probably not feel like eating. You may successfully encourage him or her to eat a favourite food, and should make sure he or she drinks plenty of fluids.

### Fresh air

The room where your child is resting should be a comfortable temperature – around 18°C (65°F) and should be well ventilated. Do not overheat the room; this might increase any fever. If your child feels well enough to play around the house there is no reason why he or she should not be allowed to play outdoors providing the weather is not too cold and there is no fever. However, you may need to be careful if your child has an infectious disease (see opposite).

## Infectious diseases

If your child has an infectious illness there is a risk that it will be passed on to others. Keep any such child away from other children as well as from adults who may be vulnerable to infection in the early stages. In the case of German measles, you should be sure to keep your child away from public places, especially doctors' surgeries where there is risk that a pregnant woman may catch the disease, harming her baby. The table on p. 97 gives the infectious period of the common childhood infectious diseases. Your doctor will advise you on any disease not covered there. If your child is lonely, you could invite children who have already had the disease to play at your house. The danger of developing the disease a second time is remote.

## When to call your doctor

The charts further on in this book give advice on when to call a doctor about particular symptoms. However, as a general rule you should seek medical advice about your child's condition in the following cases:

- If you are unsure about the cause of the symptoms.
- If home treatment fails to help or if the symptoms start to get worse.
- If you are worried about a young baby.
- If your child refuses to drink or is excessively drowsy.

Remember that diseases tend to develop more quickly in a child than in an adult, so a delay in seeking medical help that may seem acceptable for an adult may not be safe for a young child. It is better to call your doctor needlessly than to risk serious complications.

## Medicines

Medicines are usually prescribed in easy-to-take fruit-flavoured liquid form for children. You can give a young baby accurately measured amounts of medicine in a dropper. For an older child, use an accurate measuring spoon available from chemists. If your child resists, however, try pouring the medicine down the back of the throat (the taste buds are at the front). It will also help if the child is not made to think that he or she needs to take it. (See also *Medication Guide,* p. 294).

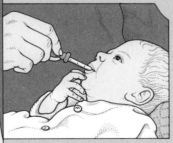

**Giving your child medicine**
To give your baby medicine fill a dropper with the exact dosage and empty it down the back of the throat. An older child should be given the medicine in a measuring spoon, whilst sitting up. Make sure that the dosage is accurate and that your child completes the whole course.

# Treating the most common symptoms and disorders at home

The boxes on the following pages give advice on what treatment you yourself can give to your child to combat childhood infection and on when to consult your doctor.

*Feverish fits,* babies under one, p. 54, children, p. 76
*Treating gastroenteritis in babies,* under one, p. 63
*Treating you child's gastroenteritis,* p. 121
*Relieving your child's headache,* p. 83
*Treating your child's cold,* p. 106
*Treatment for a sore throat,* p. 107
*How to relieve your child's toothache,* p. 112
*What to do when your child vomits,* p. 115

## Children in hospital

Admission to hospital – even for a short time – can be a frightening experience for a young child. It may be the first time he or she has been away from home without you and the surroundings are likely to be strange and impersonal. The fact that your child also feels unwell will obviously increase any distress. It is therefore extremely important for parents to spend as much time as possible in the hospital with their child. Most children's wards allow unlimited visiting for parents and are often able to provide overnight accommodation as well. You will usually be able to participate in the day-to-day care of your child – for example, feeding and bathing – and this will provide valuable reassurance for your child and may help to speed recovery. If your child needs to have an operation, it will help if you can arrange to be present when he or she is put under anaesthetic and when he or she wakes afterwards.

**Helping your child to settle**
You can prepare your child for a planned stay in hospital by talking about what is going to happen and by giving reassurance that he or she will then be returning home. Spending time with your child in hospital, taking familiar toys to him or her and making sure that he or she has plenty of amusement will help your child during the stay.

# When you are ill

Recovery from most illnesses is more speedy if you stop work, stay at home and take things easy. For the period that you feel unwell stop smoking and do not drink alcohol. Drink plenty of fluids, especially if you have a fever or diarrhoea. Unless your doctor has advised a particular kind of diet, you may safely eat whatever you choose but it is wise to eat small, frequent meals. There is no need to stay in bed if you are not seriously ill as long as you stay in a warm, well ventilated environment. If you are feverish, you may sweat profusely and quickly become hot, sticky and uncomfortable. This is because the sweat glands in the skin are more active than usual during illness. You will most certainly feel better if you are able to bathe yourself daily.

### Bed rest
If it is necessary to stay in bed while you are ill, make sure that the room is clean, reasonably warm – at about 21°C (70°F) during the day and 18°C (65°F) at night – and draught free. Try to place the bed near a pleasant view and if possible, have everything you may need within easy reach. The room should be free of unpleasant odours as the sense of smell is intensified during an illness. Smoking in bed is always dangerous, particularly if you are dozing on and off.

### Diet and drinks
Small helpings of simple, nutritious food may be all that you will feel like eating and it is wise to drink as much fluid (water, fresh juices and weak tea) as possible. It is particularly important when you are ill to ensure that your diet is well-balanced in all of the essential vitamins and nutrients (see *Safeguarding your health, diet*, p.35).

### Fresh air
When you are ill it may help you to feel more comfortable if a window is left slightly open. This will ensure that the room is properly ventilated and will clear the air of unpleasant odours. As long as the room is reasonably warm (especially if the patient is elderly) and free of draughts, a daily dose of fresh air can sometimes do wonders.

## Your temperature

Normal body temperature is about 37°C (98.5°F) but may vary by up to 1°C (1 to 2°F) throughout the day, dropping to its lowest in the early hours of the morning. A rise in temperature (a fever) is not in itself dangerous unless it exceeds 40°C (104°F), the level at which the body's own temperature control mechanism becomes inefficient.

### The clinical thermometer
The best way to take your temperature is by mouth with a clinical thermometer. This is a small glass tube marked by a scale and with a mercury-filled bulb at one end. As the mercury is heated by your body, it expands and rises up the tube to a point on the scale which has an arrow indicating normal body temperature. A small kink in the tube prevents the mercury sinking back into the bulb when the thermometer is removed from the warmth of your body. Before you buy a clinical thermometer examine it carefully, warming the bulb in your hand, to ensure that the mercury column and the markings are clearly visible.

A thermometer in the mouth gives a fairly accurate reading of body temperature, but it is easier to take the temperature of a young child by placing the thermometer bulb in the armpit. In this case the reading will be about ½°C (1°F) lower than that given when the thermometer is in the mouth. Never take a temperature immediately after a bath, a meal, a hot drink or a cigarette, because you will probably get a false reading.

### Temperature indicator strips
A temperature indicator strip is a re-usable plastic strip that is placed against the forehead. The strip is divided into chemically impregnated panels, each with a temperature printed on it. The different chemicals on each panel are heat-sensitive and change colour when they reach a certain temperature. This does not give the precise reading of a thermometer but rather an approximate indication of body temperature. The tendency is for the indicator strip to underestimate a fever and therefore, at least ½°C (1°F) should be added to a temperature-strip reading. You can read your own temperature by watching the strip in a mirror.

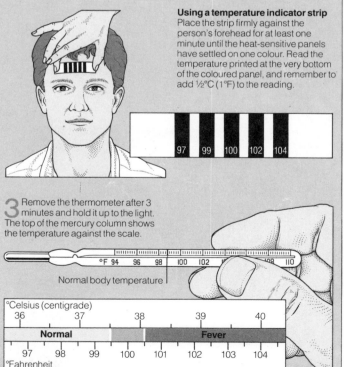

**Using a temperature indicator strip**
Place the strip firmly against the person's forehead for at least one minute until the heat-sensitive panels have settled on one colour. Read the temperature printed at the very bottom of the coloured panel, and remember to add ½°C (1°F) to the reading.

97   99   100   102   104

#### How to take your temperature

**1** Shake the thermometer towards the bulb with several sharp, downward flicks of the wrist until the mercury level is well below the normal mark.

**2** Place the thermometer under your tongue and make sure that your mouth is closed. Do not bite down on the thermometer.

**3** Remove the thermometer after 3 minutes and hold it up to the light. The top of the mercury column shows the temperature against the scale.

°F 94   96   98   100   102   104   106   108   110

Normal body temperature

| °Celsius (centigrade) | | | | |
|---|---|---|---|---|
| 36 | 37 | 38 | 39 | 40 |
| Normal | | Fever | | |
| 97   98   99 | 100 | 101   102 | 103 | 104 |
| °Fahrenheit | | | | |

**4** Finally, wash the thermometer in cool water with antiseptic added, and dry it so that it is ready for use.

Using this method, you can consider yourself feverish if your temperature is 38°C (100°F) or above.

# A raised temperature

It is important to know how to tell when you have a fever, and what measures to take to keep it under control. Aside from the most precise way of confirming a raised temperature by using a thermometer there are obvious signs to look for. If you have a fever you will probably feel very hot, flushed and sweaty. Your eyes will appear bright and may feel hot. You will probably experience dryness in the mouth, thirst and possibly headache. Because of increased fluid loss through sweating, you may pass smaller quantities than usual of dark urine. If headache is severe, a cold compress may be soothing.

## How to reduce fever

It is important to keep a raised temperature under control to promote recovery. The following self-help measures should help to reduce your fever, whatever the cause.
- Take the recommended dose of soluble aspirin or paracetamol.
- Drink plenty of cold, non-alcoholic fluids.
- Remove excess clothing and rest in a cool room.
- For a high fever, sponging the body with tepid water and/or fanning may be helpful.

Consult your doctor if your temperature continues to rise in spite of these measures.

### Applying a cold compress

**1** On a small tray put a bowl containing water and ice cubes. Fold a strip of linen in three and soak it in the bowl.

**2** Wring the linen out and apply to the forehead leaving a second piece to soak. Renew as necessary.

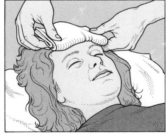

## Infectious diseases

Infectious diseases are caused by minute bacteria, viruses or fungi that invade and multiply within the body. Many of these organisms are contagious – that is they are spread between people in close contact or by sneezing or coughing into the air. In the early stages of an infection it is best to avoid vulnerable adults and children.

# When to call your doctor

The self-diagnosis charts contained within the body of this book give advice on when to call your doctor about particular symptoms. However, as a general rule, you should seek medical advice about your condition in the following cases:
- If your illness persists for more than 48 hours despite your efforts at self-help measures
- If your temperature exceeds 40°C (104°F)
- If after taking medicine you develop symptoms that seem unrelated to your illness
- If you have small children at home and are worried that you may be infectious.

It will help your doctor in his or her diagnosis if you record your temperature and the time it was taken. Keep specimens of faeces, vomit or urine, especially if they are black or bloodstained, and try to remember exactly when various symptoms started.

# Treating the most common symptoms and disorders at home

The following are boxes contained within the charts in the book which give advice on self-help measures for dealing with common symptoms and disorders at home. Listed in alphabetical order below they include self-help for:

# In hospital

Hospital treatment can not be obtained on demand, but only if your physician considers it necessary. In general, your consent to medical treatment given in hospital is taken as implied – implied by your request for help and non-refusal of the treatment offered.

When you go into hospital you will be issued a booklet explaining regular hospital routine and available services. You will also learn who's who in the hospital staff and the best person to discuss problems with. If the booklet is sent to you prior to your admission, it may include a list of what you should take into hospital with you, (see illustration below). You might want to bring something to read although most hospitals have a lending library for patient use. You will also need some money to buy items from the hospital shops, although many of the larger hospitals now provide banking services.

### Things to take to hospital

Soft holdall or case
Nightdress/pyjamas
Dressing gown
Towel
Flannel or sponge

Soap
Toothpaste
Toothbrush
Brush/comb
Slippers
Shaving equipment
Deodorant
Talcum powder
Sanitary towels (for women)
Cosmetics
Money

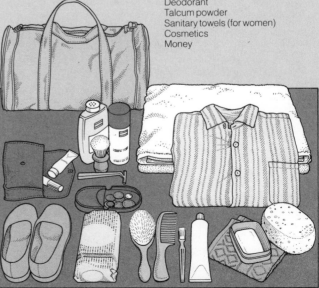

# Medical checks

Many people feel that they need only visit their physician when they are sick. However, certain conditions such as familial disorders of the blood fats (cholesterol and triglycerides) and blood sugar, high blood pressure, cervical cancer in women and testicular cancer in men, may be present in early stages without symptoms. When a disease has reached a fairly advanced stage, it is then far more difficult to treat. For this reason, early detection is the key to preventing disease and regular medical checkups may catch an illness in the beginning stages so that it can be either cured or controlled. Consult the relevant self-diagnosis charts in this book and inform your doctor without delay if you experience any of the following symptoms: change in bowel or bladder habits, a sore that does not heal, an unusual discharge or bleeding, thickening or lump underneath the skin, indigestion or persistent abdominal pain, obvious change in a wart or mole and nagging cough or hoarseness.

Talk to your physician about having regular medical checkups. The record from your first examination will serve as a guideline against which the significance of any further changes in your health can be measured. Your physician may use the checkup to assess your general life-style, to listen to your heart and breathing, to examine your eyes and ears and to perform a complete and thorough physical examination. It is especially important for women on the birth-control pill to have periodic checkups of blood pressure, and weight in order to monitor adverse effects.

## Testing blood pressure

Blood pressure is measured as systolic over diastolic pressure. Systolic pressure is the peak pressure at the moment when your heart contracts in the process of pumping out blood. Diastolic pressure is the pressure at a moment when your heart relaxes to permit the inflow of blood. A healthy young adult has a reading of about 110/75, which rises by age 60 to about 130/90.

**Measuring blood pressure**
Your doctor will place a soft, rubbery cuff around your upper arm and inflate it until it is tight enough to stop the flow of blood. The cuff is then slowly deflated until he or she can hear through a stethoscope blood forcing its way along the main artery. At this point your doctor can measure the amount of pressure – systolic pressure. Next, deflating the cuff until he or she can hear blood flowing steadily through the now open artery, the diastolic pressure is measured.

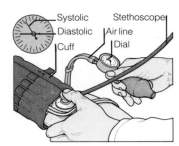

Systolic | Stethoscope
Diastolic | Air line
Cuff | Dial

## Table of medical checks

| NAME OF TEST AND PURPOSE | WHEN RECOMMENDED | WHEN TO BEGIN IF HEALTHY | FREQUENCY OF FOLLOW-UPS |
|---|---|---|---|
| **Complete physical examination** | | | |
| To check on the general health of your heart, lungs, brain and major internal organs | If you have a family history of disorders of any of these organs and as a preventative measure | From the age of 50 onwards | Every 3-5 years |
| **Blood pressure** (see above right) | | | |
| To check the condition of your heart and arteries. If there is any rise in blood pressure, this may cause serious medical problems | If you have a family history of high blood pressure, heart or kidney disease, stroke or diabetes, or if you are overweight or taking the contraceptive pill | From the age of 20 onwards | Every 3-5 years |
| **Stool tests** | | | |
| To detect blood in the faeces which may be caused by bowel cancer | If you have a family history of bowel cancer | From the age of 50 onwards | Annually |
| **Vaginal examination** (see also p.258) | | | |
| To examine the pelvic floor, perineum and pelvic organs | Before you start any new contraceptive, if you are pregnant or if you have a vaginal or pelvic infection | Regular checkups are not needed, unless stated otherwise | Not needed |
| **Cervical (Pap) smear** (see also p.32) | | | |
| To detect any premalignant or malignant changes in the cervix at an early stage | If you bleed between periods or have irregular periods | From the age of 25 onwards, or as soon as you are sexually active | Every 3-5 years |
| **Mammography** (breast X ray) | | | |
| To detect signs of breast cancer before it becomes noticeable through physical examination | If you have a family history of breast cancer | From the age of 40 (not available in all areas). | Every 1 to 2 years between the ages of 40 and 50; annually thereafter |
| **Eye tests** (see also p.186) | | | |
| Even if you can see well you should have regular vision tests | If you have difficulty with vision or a family history of glaucoma | From the age of 40 onward | Every 2 years |
| **Dental checkups** | | | |
| Regular inspections are vital to detect any early signs of decay, or for signs of infection of the mouth and gums | If you have not had regular checkups, start now rather than waiting until you have a toothache or painful gums | From childhood | Every 6 months before the age of 21, then every 1 to 2 years |
| **Serum cholesterol (blood) level** | | | |
| To detect people at high risk for development of coronary artery disease | If you have a family history of coronary artery disease before the age of 50 | In your 20s | No follow-up if first test is normal |

# Specialized tests

Some diagnostic tests, such as blood and urine tests, are routinely given to most patients, whereas others, such as X-rays or bronchoscopy, will only be given to confirm or rule out a particular disorder, suspected by the doctor. Recently, some tests that carried a risk to the patient or caused discomfort – for example, X-rays in pregnancy or cerebral angiography – have been replaced by new "non-invasive" tests that are risk free and painless – for example, ultrasound and the CAT scan. The introduction of fibre-optics has been a major advance in the field of specialized testing, allowing examination of various body cavities without major surgery. Many of the special tests listed below as well as those described within the body of the book (see Index of tests, below) utilize fibre-optic techniques.

## CHOLECYSTOGRAPHY
This is a special procedure for diagnosing disorders of the gallblader and bile duct.

### What happens
A special substance visible on X-rays is taken as a tablet and photographed as it passes through the gallbladder and bile duct. The X-ray below shows a gallbladder with gallstones.

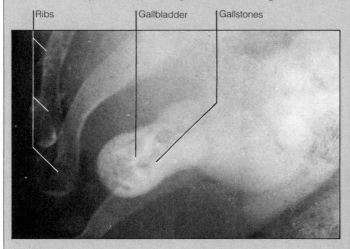

Ribs | Gallbladder | Gallstones

## CYSTOSCOPY
Cystoscopy is a procedure for diagnosing the cause of recurrent infections and other disorders of the bladder.

### What happens
Numbing medicine is usually applied to the urethra before insertion of a narrow, fibreoptic tube which contains a lighting and lens system. The physician then views the bladder using a special eyepiece.

## LAPAROTOMY
Laparotomy is an exploratory operation which allows the physician an inside view of the abdomen. It is usually carried out when there are signs of a severe abdominal disorder which can not be firmly diagnosed.

### What happens
An incision is made through the abdominal wall (the exact site depends on the suspected cause of the trouble). Treatment – for example, removal of an inflamed appendix – can usually be carried out at the same time.

## LAPAROSCOPY
Laparoscopy is an endoscopic technique (see Endoscopy, p.201) for investigating abdominal disorders. It is often used in women to discover the cause of gynecological problems such as infertility or to assist in sterilization procedures.

### What happens
The procedure is usually carried out under general anaesthetic. Two small slits are made in the abdomen, and carbon dioxide is passed through a hollow needle into one slit to distend the abdomen, while an endoscope is inserted into the second slit, enabling the surgeon to view the interior.

## MYELOGRAPHY
Myelography is a procedure that is used to diagnose disorders of the spine and spinal cord, such as prolapsed (slipped) disc. It can take up to an hour and requires sedation because it may be uncomfortable.

### What happens
A solution that is visible on X-rays is injected into the fluid-filled space which surrounds the spinal cord. The patient is then tilted into various positions so that the movement of the solution inside the spinal column can be recorded by X-ray.

## ULTRASOUND
Ultrasound provides a safe, painless way of examining internal organs, especially abdominal and pelvic organs such as the liver and kidneys. It is often used during pregnancy to examine the uterus, placenta and fetus.

### What happens
It involves sending a beam of very high-pitched sound – ultrasound – through the tissues of the body. These sound waves are deflected off the internal organs and converted into a picture that can be shown on a screen or printed on paper. Ultrasound may reveal any cysts, tumours or other swellings (see Ultrasound scan, Special problems: Women, p.276). The ultrasound scan below shows a healthy liver.

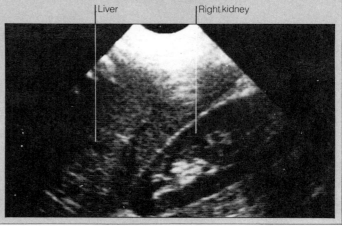

Liver | Right kidney

# Medication guide

New drugs are constantly being discovered. Many of the drugs in common use twenty years ago have been superseded by newer, safer compounds with broader applications. This medication guide is an index of major groups of drugs; it gives their uses and possible side-effects and, in many cases, special children's dose information and warnings about when medicines should not be taken. This is a selective list, it does not include chemicals of trade names, and it should not be used as a manual of self-prescription for you or your family.

When taking any medicine, a few precautionary measures can ensure the drug's effectiveness and safe use. Never exceed the stated dosage. Always check with your doctor or chemist if you are unsure exactly when or how frequently the medicine should be taken (for example, some drugs work most efficiently when taken with a meal). As a general rule, avoid drinking alcohol when taking medicine, as its effects are aggravated by certain drugs. Also, even if you think it unnecessary and you seem to have no more symptoms, complete the prescribed course of medicine. Failure to do so may prevent complete recovery. Keep all drugs locked in a medicine cabinet (see below left).

In general, the fewer drugs you take, the better. Except for minor symptoms (such as an occasional cough or headache), you are well advised to let your doctor discuss all the medicines you need. He or she will balance the potential benefits of medicine against its side-effects.

## Drugs in pregnancy

During pregnancy it is important to avoid any substances that could put the development of the fetus at risk. Most drugs pass from the mother's circulation to the fetus. While some are known to be harmless, there are others that can, in certain instances and at certain times during pregnancy, threaten the health of the fetus. Therefore, if you are pregnant or are contemplating pregnancy, you will need to ask your doctor for advice before taking any drugs, including those available over-the-counter. If you suffer from a chronic condition for which you are receiving medication, your doctor will advise you on the best treatment while you are pregnant. Both alcohol and smoking are known to have harmful effects on the developing fetus.

It is common practice during pregnancy to be prescribed iron tablets (to prevent anaemia) and vitamin supplements. In severe cases, a doctor may prescribe a safe anti-emetic.

## Drugs and breast-feeding

You should only take drugs while breast-feeding after discussion with your doctor. He or she will try to avoid prescribing at this time unless it is really very necessary. In practice, many drugs either pass into the breast milk in insignificant quantities or are known to be safe. When there is a risk of harm to the baby you can switch to bottle-feeding while you take the drugs. If you want to resume breast-feeding later, you will need to express, and discard, your milk to maintain the supply.

## Drugs for children

If your child becomes ill, part of the treatment may include giving prescribed or over-the counter drugs. Special care should be taken when giving drugs to babies and children because the liver, which processes chemicals from the bloodstream, is immature. Potentially dangerous levels of a drug may build up more quickly in a child than in an adult thus, it is important to use an accurate measure for liquid medicines and to give only the exact dose prescribed. Do not dilute or add medicines to your baby's bottle.

Never give a child any drug that has been prescribed for an adult or for another child. If you are giving over-the-counter medicines, make sure that you read the instructions carefully and ask your doctor or chemist for advice. Never give over-the-counter medicines for prolonged periods without seeking medical advice. And never use a drug to which your child has exhibited previous sensitivity such as nausea, vomiting, diarrhoea, rash or swollen joints. Replace over-the-counter drugs after 1 year.

### Tips for giving medicines
**Babies and toddlers.**
- Get the help of an older child or relative.
- If on your own, wrap a blanket around your baby's arms to stop any struggling and to hold him or her steady.
- Only put a little of the medicine in the baby's mouth at one time.
- If the baby spits out the medicine, put the medicine into the back of the mouth and then, gently but firmly, close the mouth.

### Older children
- Suggest your child hold his or her nose while taking the medicine to lessen the effect of the taste, but don't forcibly hold your child's nose as he or she may inhale some of the medicine.
- Crush tablets between two spoons and mix the powder with honey, jam or ice-cream, and make sure your child takes all.
- Mix liquid medicine with another syrup such as honey and give by spoonful.
- Have your child's favourite drink ready to wash the taste of the medicine away.

## Prescribed drugs

When your doctor prescribes a drug for you or your child, make sure that you ask the following:
- How much to take or give in each dose.
- How often a dose should be taken or given.
- If it matters when you take or give the drug in relation to meals and whether you should wake your child at night for medication.
- If there are any side-effects.
- If you should look out for any unusual or dangerous reactions to the drug.
- How soon you should expect to see an improvement in your or your child's condition.
- How long you should continue to take or give the drug before returning to your doctor.

## Over-the-counter medicines

There are many patent remedies available over-the-counter at chemists. They are available in tablets, capsules, liquids, drops, sprays, creams, ointments and inhalers. These seldom have any direct effect on the cause of a condition but they may relieve painful or uncomfortable symptoms. For instance, some of the remedies for coughs and colds are soothing, and mild analgesics such as aspirin and paracetamol relieve pain.

However, in most cases, the speed of your recovery depends more on your age and general health than on any such treatment. Nevertheless, if such "cures" make you feel better, they are unlikely to be harmful if you follow the instructions on the container. In some cases your doctor may actually recommend a particular over-the-counter preparation. If you are unsure about any aspect of an over-the-counter medication, consult your pharmacist or doctor.

# Home medical supplies

Below is a list of items to keep at home to deal with common problems such as indigestion and muscle strain and a list to deal with accidents and emergencies.

**Home medicine cabinet**
The best place to keep prescribed medications and common, over-the-counter remedies is in a section of a medicine cabinet that can be locked. This will keep the items dry and away from children. Many over-the-counter preparations have a shelf life of 1 year and should be replaced regularly. You are likely to need:

Clinical thermometer
Antiseptic cream (cuts and scrapes)
Insect-sting reliever
Antacid liquid or tablets (indigestion)
Kaolin (diarrhoea)
Oil of cloves (toothache)
Motion-sickness tablets
Protective sunscreen
Calamine lotion
Petroleum jelly (chafing)
Elastic bandages
Eye lotion
Aspirin or paracetamol

**Home first-aid kit**
In cases of emergency, you are likely to need additional supplies. These should be stored in a well-sealed metal or plastic box that is clearly labelled and easy for you to open. It should be kept in a dry place, out of reach of children and should include:

1 Packet of sterile cotton wool
2 Sterile prepared bandages (2 large, 2 medium, 2 small)
3 Sterile gauze squares in several sizes
4 Sterile triangular bandages (2)
5 Gauze bandages (2) and at least 1 crepe bandage
6 Tubular gauze with applicator
7 Surgical spirit
8 Waterproof plasters in assorted sizes
9 Surgical tape in wide and narrow widths
10 Safety pins
11 Small mirror
12 Tweezers
13 Scissors

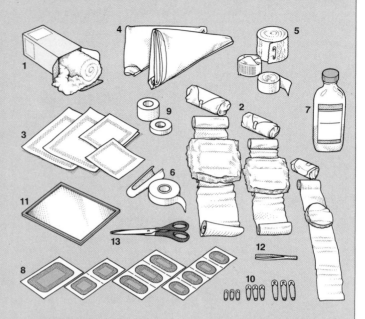

**Safety note:** Remember that it is important to keep all medicines safely out of the reach of children. A locked wall cabinet is usually the best place.

# Drug index

## ANALGESICS
Drugs that relieve pain. Many also reduce inflammation (see ANTI-INFLAMMATORIES) and fever (see ANTIPYRETICS). There are 3 main types: simple analgesics – usually containing aspirin or paracetamol – for mild pain; anti-inflammatories, often given for muscular aches and pains and arthritis; and narcotic analgesics – usually chemically related to morphine – for severe pain.
**Possible side-effects:** Nausea, constipation, dizziness, dependence and development of tolerance to the drug (narcotic analgesics only). For side-effects of other types, see ANTI-INFLAMMATORIES and ANTIPYRETICS.
**Children's doses:** Paracetamol in liquid form is the safest over-the-counter analgesic to use for painful and feverish symptoms in children. Aspirin, another analgesic often used by adults, is no longer considered entirely safe for children with certain viral infections because it may be linked with Reye's syndrome, a rare and dangerous condition affecting the brain and liver. For more severe pain – perhaps following an operation – a narcotic analgesic (e.g., codeine) may be prescribed. Analgesics may make a child sleepy and can cause transient constipation, nausea and dizziness.

## ANTACIDS
Drugs that neutralize stomach acid (relieving heartburn and similar conditions). They contain simple chemicals such as sodium bicarbonate, calcium carbonate, aluminium hydroxide and/or magnesium trisilicate.
**Possible side effects:** Belching (sodium bicarbonate preparations), constipation (aluminium or calcium pre-parations) and diarrhoea (magnesium preparations).
**Warning:** Seek medical advice if you are taking other drugs. Antacids should be taken by anyone with a kidney disorder only on medical advice.

## ANTI-ANXIETY DRUGS
(sometimes called anxiolytics, sedatives or minor tranquillizers). Drugs that reduce feelings of anxiety and relax muscles. May also be used as sleeping drugs and to relieve premenstrual tension.
**Possible side-effects:** Drowsiness, dizziness, confusion, unsteadiness and lack of coordination.
**Children's doses:** These drugs are rarely used to treat children. As an emergency treatment for convulsions, diazepam is used intravenously. The newer anti-anxiety drugs may occasionally be used to treat older children suffering from psychological stress. Side-effects include drowsiness and confusion, and these drugs may be habit-forming.
**Warning:** Not to be taken if you intend to drive or operate potentially dangerous machinery. Anti-anxiety drugs may increase the effects of alcohol. They can be habit-forming and should not be used for more than a few weeks. After prolonged use, withdrawal symptoms may occur if treatment is halted abruptly.

## ANTIBIOTICS
Substances (that are often derived from living organisms such as moulds or bacteria) that kill or inhibit the growth of bacteria in the body. Some of the newer antibiotics are synthetic versions of naturally occurring substances. Any one type of antibiotic is effective only against certain strains of bacteria, although some broad-spectrum anti-biotics combat a wide range of bacterial infections. Sometimes a strain of bacteria becomes resistant to a particular antibiotic and an alternative is chosen on the basis of laboratory tests. No antibiotic is effective against viruses.
**Possible side-effects:** Nausea, vomiting and diarrhoea. Some people may be allergic to certain antibiotics and may experience symptoms such as rashes, fever, joint pain, swelling and wheezing. Following treatment with broad-spectrum antibiotics, secondary fungal infection (thrush) – for example, of the mouth or vagina – may sometimes occur.
**Children's doses:** The following are the antibiotics most commonly used to treat children: ampicillin, amoxycillin, erythromycin and penicillin. When antibiotics are prescribed, always ensure that the full course of treatment is completed. Stopping treatment too soon may lead to a relapse and may encourage the emergence of resistant bacteria. Antibiotics may cause side-effects and some children may be particularly sensitive to penicillin and similar antibiotics. Side-effects may include rashes, nausea, vomiting, diarrhoea and wheezing. Always consult your doctor about any reaction to an antibiotic.
**Warning:** Always complete a prescribed course of antibiotics. Failure to do so, even when symptoms have cleared, may lead to a recurrence of infection that is more difficult to treat (due to resistance of the bacteria to the antibiotic).

## ANTICOAGULANTS
(including thrombolytics). Drugs that prevent and/or disperse blod clots.
**Possible side-effects:** Increased tendency to bleed from the nose or gums or under the skin (bruising). Blood may also appear in the urine or stool.
**Warning:** Anticoagulants may react more intensely with other drugs, including aspirin. Consult your doctor before taking any other medicines so that the effectiveness of the anticoagulant is not altered. If you are on regular anticoagulant treatment, you will be advised to carry a warning card:

## ANTICONVULSANTS
Drugs used to prevent and treat epileptic seizures. These usually are given at least twice a day. Careful calculation of the best dose for the individual is necessary to minimize side-effects. Blood or saliva tests are usually given to monitor drug concentrations in the blood. Usually the drug is given over a prolonged period until the person has gone 2 to 4 years without a seizure.
**Possible side-effects:** Drowsiness, rashes, dizziness, headache, nausea and thickening of the gums.
**Children's doses:** The drugs most commonly used to treat children who have grand mal seizures are phenytoin, sodium valproate and carbamazepine. Their side effects may include drowsiness, gastrointestinal disturbances, rashes, an increase in body hair, overgrowth of the gums, enlargement of the lymph glands, blood abnormalities and liver damage. Phenobarbital is less often prescribed for children because it may cause behaviour disturbances. Petit mal seizures (periods in which the child stares off into space and does not seem to hear or see) may be treated with sodium valproate or ethosuximide.
**Warning:** Alcohol may increase the likelihood and severity of side effects and is best avoided, as are ANTI-

HISTAMINES. Consult your doctor before operating potentially dangerous machinery.

## ANTIDEPRESSANTS

Drugs that counter depression. These fall into two main groups: tricyclics and their derivatives, and monoamine oxidase (MAO) inhibitors. Because their side effects are likely to be more serious, MAO inhibitors are usually only prescribed for those types of severe depression that are less likely to respond to treatment with tricylics.

**Possible side-effects:** Drowsiness, dry mouth, blurred vision, constipation, difficulty urinating, faintness, sweating, trembling, rashes, palpitations and headaches.

**Children's doses:** These may occasionally be prescribed for older children suffering from depression. In addition, some physicians may precribe antidepressant drugs such as amitriptyline for bed-wetting in children over the age of 6 when other forms of treatment have failed. This use of antidepressants is controversial, however. Side-effects may include behavioural disturbances and abnormal heart rate and rhythm.

**Warning:** MAO inhibitors react adversely with a number of foods and drugs, possibly leading to a serious rise in blood pressure. Your doctor will advise you and may recommend that you carry a warning card. During both types of antidepressant treatment, alcohol intake should be limited, ask your doctor whether it is advisable to drive or operate machinery.

## ANTIDIARRHOEALS

Drugs used to control and treat diarrhoea. There are two main types: those that absorb excess water and toxins in the bowel (for example, those containing kaolin, bismuth compounds, chalk or charcoal) and those that reduce the contractions of the bowel, thus decreasing the frequency with which stools are passed (including codeine, morphine and opium mixtures).

**Possible side-effects:** Constipation.

**Warning:** Antidiarrhoeals relieve symptoms but do not treat the underlying cause of diarrhoea and may prolong the course of toxic or infectious diarrhoea. They should not be taken for more than a day or so before seeking medical advice. When treating diarrhoea, always drink plenty of fluids. See also REHYDRATION TREATMENTS.

## ANTI-EMETICS

Drugs used to supress nausea and vomiting. Most also suppress vertigo (dizziness). The main groups of drugs in this category include certain ANTIHISTAMINES (especially for nausea caused by motion sickness or by ear disorders), ANTISPASMODICS, and certain tranquilizers. Because antiemetic treatment may hinder diagnosis, such drugs are not usually prescribed when the cause of vomiting is unknown or when vomiting is unlikely to persist for longer than a day or so, as in gastroenteritis. Anti-emetics are prescribed in pregnancy only when symptoms are severe.

**Possible side-effects:** These vary according to the drug group prescribed. Prolonged treatment with certain tranquillizers may cause involuntary movement of the facial muscles. These drugs should never be taken for more than a few days at a time.

**Warning:** Because most antiemetics may cause drowsiness, do not drink alcohol and seek your doctor's advice before driving or operating potentially dangerous machinery.

## ANTIFUNGALS

Drugs to treat fungal infections such as ringworm, athlete's foot, thrush and fungal nappy rash. They may be applied directly to the skin or administered orally over a prolonged period. The principal oral antifungal is griseofulvin. Antifungals applied to the skin include clotrimazole and miconazole.

**Possible side-effects:** Oral antifungals may cause nausea, vomiting, diarrhoea and/or headaches; locally applied (topical) preparations may cause irritation.

**Warning:** Always finish a course of antifungal treatment as prescribed; otherwise the infection may recur. Some infections, especially of the nails, may require treatment with oral antifungals for many months.

## ANTIHISTAMINES

Drugs to counteract allergic symptoms produced by the release of a substance called histamine in the body. Such symptoms may include runny nose and watering eyes (allergic rhinitis), itching and uticaria (hives). Anti-histamines may be given orally or applied to skin rashes in the form of creams or sprays. Antihistamine drugs also act on the organs of balance in the middle ear and therefore are often used to prevent motion sickness. Their sedative effect may also be used to treat sleeplessness (on your doctor's advice). They are also given as a medication before operations. They ensure that a person is in a relaxed, drowsy state prior to going to the operating theatre. Another class of antihistamine interferes with gastric acid secretion and is used to treat peptic ulcers.

**Possible side-effects:** Drowsiness, dry mouth and blurred vision.

**Children's doses:** The antihistamines most commonly given to children are trimeprazine tartate and promethazine hydrochloride. The main side-effect is drowsiness, but some children may become unusually excited instead.

**Warning:** Driving or drinking alcohol should be avoided after taking an antihistamine.

## ANTIHYPERTENSIVES

Drugs that lower blood pressure. BETA-BLOCKERS and DIURETICS and, more recently, enzyme inhibitors or receptor blockers (which affect the action of hormones controlling blood pressure), and calcium blockers (which affect the internal chemistry of the heart and arteries) are those most commonly used.

**Possible side-effects:** Dizziness, rashes, impotence, nightmares and lethargy.

## ANTI-INFLAMMATORIES

Drugs used to reduce inflammation. This is the redness, heat, swelling, pain and increased blood flow that is found in infections and in many chronic noninfective diseases such as rheumatoid arthritis and gout. Three main types of drugs are used as anti-inflammatories: ANALGESICS such as aspirin, CORTICOSTEROIDS and nonsteroidal antiinflammatory drugs such as indomethacin which is used especially in the treatment of arthritis and muscle disorders. CORTICOSTEROIDS may be applied locally as cream or eyedrops for inflammation of the skin or eyes, but they are not generally prescribed for chronic rheumatic conditions except in unusual circumstances.

**Possible side-effects:** Rashes and stomach irritation and occasionally bleeding, disturbances in hearing and wheezing.

**Children's doses:** There are two main categories of anti-inflammatory drugs used in the treatment of children: CORTI-COSTEROIDS and nonsteroidal anti-inflammatories. Commonly prescribed drugs of the latter type include aspirin (although this is now used with caution in the treatment of children – see ANALGESICS), ibuprofen and mefenamic acid. These drugs may cause transient constipation and often minor digestive disturbances.

## ANTIPYRETICS

Drugs that reduce fever. The most commonly used are aspirin and paracetamol, which are both also ANALGESICS. This double action makes them particularly effective for relieving the symptoms of an illness such as flu.

**Possible side-effects:** Rashes and stomach irritation and occasionally bleeding, disturbances in hearing, and wheezing.

## ANTISPASMODICS

Drugs for reducing spasm of the bowel to relieve the pain of conditions such as irritable colon or diverticular disease.

**Possible side-effects:** Dry mouth, palpitations, difficulty urinating, constipation and blurred vision.

## ANTIVIRALS

Drugs that combat viral infections. Effective drug treatment is not yet available for the majority of viral infections such as colds and flu. However, severe cold sores caused by the herpes simplex virus can be treated by the application of idoxuridine ointment – also used to treat shingles – to the skin as soon as symptoms appear. Another antiviral drug, acycolvir, may be given orally or by injection or applied directly to the skin in the form of a cream to treat most severe types of herpes infection.

**Possible side-effects:** Antivirals used to treat cold sores, herpes genitalis and shingles may cause a stinging sensation, rashes and occasionally loss of sensation in the skin.

## BETA-BLOCKERS

Beta-adrenergic blocking agents – beta-blockers for short – reduce oxygen needs of the heart by reducing heartbeat rate. They are used as ANTIHYPERTENSIVES and ANTIARRHYTHMICS, for treating angina due to exertion, and for easing symptoms such as palpitations and tremors in patients with anxiety states. Beta-blockers may be taken as tablets or given by injection.

**Possible side-effects:** Nausea, insomnia, physical weariness, diarrhoea.

**Warning:** Overdose can cause dizziness, and fainting spells. Discontinuance of treatment should be gradual, not abrupt. Beta-blockers are not prescribed for people with asthma or heart failure.

## BRONCHODILATORS

Drugs that open up bronchial tubes that have become narrowed by muscle spasm. Bronchodilators, which ease breathing in diseases such as asthma, are most often taken as aerosol sprays, but they are also available in tablet, liquid, or suppository form; in emergencies – for instance, severe attacks of asthma – they may be given by injection. Effects usually last for three to five hours.

**Possible side-effects:** Rapid heartbeat, palpitations, tremor, headache, dizziness.

**Children's doses:** In children narrowing of the bronchial tubes usually occurs as a result of asthma or respiratory infections (bronchitis and bronchiolitis). There are two primary groups of drugs used to treat asthma. First are those that treat an acute attack (bronchodilators), including terbutaline and the theophyllines. These may also be given routinely orally or by injection. Second are those that act to prevent an attack (sodium cromoglycate). These are not effective in an acute attack. CORTICOSTEROIDS (see ANTI-INFLAMMATORIES) are reserved for asthma that is resistant to the above mentioned drugs. Children over 3 can be taught to use inhalers very effectively. Side-effects of the anti-asthmatics include increased heart rate, tremor and irritability.

**Warning:** Because of possible effects on the heart, prescribed doses should never be exceeded; when asthma does not respond to the prescribed doses, emergency medical treatment is needed.

## COLD CURE REMEDIES

Although there is no drug that can cure a cold, symptoms can be relieved by aspirin or paracetamol, taken with plenty of fluid. The most effective cold cure remedies are those that contain either. For drying up nasal secretions and unblocking nasal passages, many preparations contain ANTIHISTAMINES and DECONGESTANTS. However, these drugs are unlikely to be effective, when taken by mouth, unless swallowed in doses high enough to produce side-effects which outweighs any benefits.

**Possible side-effects:** Drowsiness, giddiness, headache, nausea, vomiting, sweating, thirst, palpitations, difficulty in passing urine, weakness, trembling, anxiety, insomnia.

**Warning:** Cold cure remedies should be avoided by people suffering from angina, high blood pressure, diabetes, or thyroid disorders, and by anyone taking monoamineoxidase inhibitors. It is inadvisable to drive or use potentially dangerous machinery after taking a remedy containing an anti-histamine.

## CORTICOSTEROIDS

A group of anti-inflammatory drugs (see ANTI-INFLAMMATORIES) that is chemically similar to certain naturally produced hormones from the adrenal glands that help the body respond to stress. They may be given orally, injected, applied to the skin as a cream or inhaled into the lungs. Corticosteroid inhalations such as beclomethasone may be prescribed when other BRONCHODILATOR drugs have failed. There are few side-effects to such treatment when used for limited periods of time. Corticosteroids such as hydrocortisone

or prednisolone given orally or by injection are used for acute conditions (e.g., shock, severe allergic reactions or severe asthma). They are used in the long-term treatment of a wide variety of inflammatory conditions. They are not curative but do reduce inflammation, which sometimes enables the body to repair itself. Corticosteroids may be useful for treating certain types of cancer or in compensating for a deficiency of natural hormones.
**Possible side-effects:** Weight gain, redness of the face, stomach irritation, mental disturbances and increase in body hair.
**Children's doses:** The conditions of children who are prescribed these drugs should be carefully monitored because of the side-effects. These include fluid retention with excessive weight gain, a moon-shaped face, and growth retardation.

### COUGH SUPRESSANTS
Medicines that relieve coughing – usually as a result of a cold. There are many over-the-counter products, including lozenges and syrups, which contain soothing substances such as honey and glycerin to act on the surface of the throat, pleasant-tasting flavourings and minute doses of antiseptic chemicals. They may give temporary relief to a tickly throat and the taste may be comforting, but it is doubtful whether such products are any more effective than a home-made honey drink.

### CYTOTOXICS
Drugs that kill or damage multiplying cells. Cytotoxics are used in treatment of cancer and as IMMUNOSUPPRESSIVES. They are taken as tablets or given by injection or by intravenous drip, and several cytotoxics, with different types of action, may be used in combination.
**Possible side-effects:** Nausea, vomiting, loss of hair.
**Children's doses:** Cytotoxics are used in the treatment of some types of cancer in children, notably leukaemia. These powerful drugs are given under close specialist supervision. The most effective dosage is calculated, giving the minimum of side-effects.
**Warning:** Because cytotoxic action can affect healthy as well as cancerous cells, these drugs may also have dangerous side-effects: for example, they can damage bone marrow and affect the production of blood cells, causing anaemia, increased susceptibility to infection, and haemorrhage. Frequent blood counts are therefore advisable for anyone having treatment.

### DIURETICS
Drugs that increase the quantity of urine produced by the kidneys and passed out of the body, thus ridding the body of excess fluid. Diuretics reduce excess fluid that has collected in the tissues as a result of any disorder of the heart, kidneys and liver. They are useful in treating mildly raised blood pressure.
**Possible side-effects:** Rashes, dizziness, weakness, numbness, tingling in the hands and feet and excessive loss of potassium.

### DECONGESTANTS
Drugs that act on the mucous membranes lining the nose to reduce

mucous production and so relieve a runny or a blocked-up nose resulting from the common cold or an allergy. These drugs can be applied directly in the form of nose drops or spray or may be taken orally.
**Children's doses:** Decongestants are usually recommended only for occasional use on your doctor's advice – for example, when a blocked-up nose prevents a young baby from sucking. If used excessively or for prolonged periods, nose drops may cause increased congestion.

### HORMONES
Chemicals produced naturally by the endocrine (pituitary thyroid, adrenal, ovary/testis, pancreas or parathyroid) glands. When they are not produced naturally (because of some disorder), they can be replaced by natural or synthetic hormones. See SEX HORMONES.
**Possible side-effects:** There may be an exaggeration of the secondary sexual characteristics, so oestrogens given to a man may increase the size of his breasts, and androgens given to a women may cause increased body hair and deepening of the voice. Oestrogens also affect blood clotting and so may cause heart attack, stroke or thrombosis in the legs.
**Children's doses:** Hormones may occasionally be given to children when a glandular disorder prevents insufficient quantities of that hormone from being produced by the body. The most common deficiencies are in the thyroid-stimulating hormone, the growth hormone and insulin (diabetes). If your child needs to take supplements of any of these hormones, regular blood tests are likely to be taken so that the dosage can be accurately controlled.

### HYPOGLYCAEMICS
Drugs that lower the level of glucose in the blood. Oral hypoglycaemic drugs are used in the treatment of diabetes mellitus if it cannot be controlled by diet alone, and does not require treatment with injections of insulin.
**Possible side-effects:** Loss of appetite, nausea, indigestion, numbness or tingling in the skin, fever and rashes.
**Warning:** If the glucose level falls too low, weakness, dizziness, pallor, sweating, increased saliva flow, palpitations, irritability and trembling may result. If such symptoms occur several hours after eating, this may indicate that the dose is too high. Report symptoms to your doctor.

### IMMUNOSUPPRESSIVES
Drugs that prevent or reduce the body's normal reaction to invasion by disease or by foreign tissues. Immunosuppressives are used to treat autoimmune diseases (in which the body's defences work abnormally and attack the body's own tissues) and to help prevent rejection of organ transplants.
**Possible side-effects:** Susceptibility to infection (especially chest infections, fungal infections of the mouth and skin and virus infections) is increased. Some immunosuppressives may damage the bone marrow, causing anaemia, and may cause nausea and vomiting.

### LAXATIVES
Drugs that increase the frequency and

ease of bowel movements. They work by stimulating the bowel wall, by increasing the bulk of bowel contents, or by increasing the fluid content of the stool.
**Children's doses:** Laxatives should never be given to children except on the advice of your doctor.
**Warning:** Laxatives are not to be taken regularly; the bowel may become unable to work properly without them.

### REHYDRATING TREATMENTS
These specially formulated powders and solutions contain glucose and essential mineral salts in measured quantities that, when added to boiled water, can be used to prevent and treat dehydration resulting from diarrhoea or vomiting. These powders and solutions are useful for treating gastroenteritis in babies and children at home. Similar solutions may be given intravenously in the hospital.

### SEX HORMONES (FEMALE)
The hormones responsible for the development of secondary sexual characteristics and regulation of the menstrual cycle. There are two main types of hormone drugs: oestrogens and progestogens. Oestrogens may be used for treating breast or prostate cancer, progestogens may be used for treating endometriosis. Sex hormones may be taken as tablets, given by injection or implanted in muscle tissue.
**Possible side-effects:** Nausea, weight gain, headache, depression, breast enlargement and tenderness, rashes and skin pigmentation changes, alterations in sexual drive, abnormal blood-clotting causing heart disorders.
**Warning:** Oestrogens are not prescribed for anyone with circulatory or liver trouble, and oestrogen treatment must be carefully controlled for people who have had jaundice, diabetes, epilepsy, or kidney or heart disease. Progestogen treatment is not prescribed for people with liver trouble and must be carefully controlled for anyone who has asthma, epilepsy, or heart or kidney disease.

### SEX HORMONES (MALE)
Hormones, of which the most powerful is testosterone, responsible for development of male secondary sexual characteristics. Small quantities are also produced in females. As drugs, male sex hormones are given to compensate for hormonal deficiency in hypopituitarism or testicular disorders. They may be used for treating breast cancer in women, but synthetic derivatives, the anabolic steroids, which have less marked side-effects and specific anti-oestrogens are often preferable. Anabolic steroids also have a body building effect that has led to their usually illegal use in competitive sports, for both men and women. Male sex hormones can be taken as tablets, given by injection, or implanted in muscle tissue.
**Possible side-effects:** Oedema, weight gain, weakness, loss of appetite, drowsiness, nausea. High dose in women may cause cessation of menstruation, enlargement of the clitoris, deepening of the voice, shrinking of the breasts, hairiness, male-pattern baldness.
**Warning:** Treatment is inadvisable for people with kidney or liver trouble and

must be carefully controlled for anyone suffering from epilepsy or migraine.

### SKIN CREAMS
A wide variety of skin creams, ointments and lotions are available to treat and/or prevent skin disorders (for example, to combat infection or relieve irritation). They usually consist of a base to which various active ingredients are added. Creams commonly used include the following: antiseptic creams, containing a drug such as cetrimide to prevent infection of minor wounds; soothing barrier creams such as zinc and castor oil to prevent and treat nappy rash; ANTIBIOTIC creams to treat skin infections such as impetigo; CORTICOSTEROID creams; ANTIFUNGAL creams; acne preparations; local anaesthetic and antipruritic (itch-relieving) creams containing calamine, ANTIHISTAMINES or a local anaesthetic such as benzocaine.
**Children's doses:** When selecting a cream to treat a child's skin condition, always ask your doctor for advice.

### SLEEPING DRUGS
There are two main groups of drugs used for inducing sleep, ANTI-ANXIETY DRUGS and barbiturates. All such drugs have a sedative effect in low doses, and are effective sleeping pills, or potions, in higher doses. Anti-anxiety drugs are used more widely than barbiturates because they are safer, have fewer side-effects and there is less risk of eventual physical and psychological dependence.
**Possible side-effects:** "Hangover", dizziness, dry mouth, and, especially in the elderly, clumsiness and confusion.
**Children's doses:** Adult sleeping drugs are not used to treat sleeplessness in children. A young child who persistently wakes at night may be given ANTIHISTAMINES, which cause drowsiness. In rare cases an older child may be prescribed an ANTI-ANXIETY DRUG to promote sleep during a period of psychological distress.
**Warning:** Sleeping drugs are habit-forming, should be taken for short periods only, and should be discontinued gradually. Broken, restless sleep and vivid dreams may follow withdrawal and may persist for weeks. It is inadvisable to drive, handle dangerous machinery, or drink alcohol until the effects of a sleeping drug have completely worn off.

### VASODILATORS
Drugs that dilate blood vessels. Most widely used in prevention and treatment of angina, but also for treating heart failure and circulatory disorders.
**Possible side-effects:** Headache, palpitations, flushing, faintness, nausea, vomiting, diarrhoea and stuffy nose.

### VITAMINS
Vitamins are complex chemicals needed by the body in minute quantities. They are often prescribed routinely for babies and young children, especially if the children are breast-fed or premature, but are probably unnecessary for healthy children and adults receiving an adequate diet. Small doses of vitamin supplements are harmless, but exceeding the recommended daily dose may be dangerous.

# Growth charts

These growth charts and those on pages 300-301 are based on the standard growth charts used by doctors throughout the United Kingdom. You can use these charts to keep your own record of your child's growth from babyhood to adolescence. This will enable you to check that your child is gaining weight and height at the expected rate, and alert you at an early stage to possible problems such as obesity or growth disorders. Prompt treatment of all such problems gives the best chance of success.

The growth charts on this and the facing page are for recording the progress of babies of both sexes up to the age of one year. The charts on p.300-301 are for boys and girls from 1 to 18 years. All the charts allow you to record measurements in either metric or imperial equivalents.

### Standard growth curves
On each chart you will find 3 solid lines already drawn. These lines are the standard growth curves for small, average and large children of normal development. They show the

expected pattern of growth based on weight and head circumference at birth. The standard curves enable you to compare your child's progress with the expected growth of children of similar size at birth.

For example, if your baby's head circumference and weight at birth were average, you can expect his or her growth to follow the average curves throughout childhood. If your baby's measurements at birth fall somewhere between two of the standard curves, his or her growth should continue to follow a path between those curves. Weight and height (or head circumference) should both be in the same relationship to the standard curves – that is, if height is near average, weight too should be near average.

The dotted line on the growth charts for older children marks the lowest measurement likely in a normal child.

### Recording your child's growth
When you have weighed and measured your child (see *Weighing and measuring babies,* below, and *Weighing and*

**Weighing and measuring babies**
In the first few months of your baby's life you will probably be attending your local baby clinic regularly where your baby will be weighed for you. However, to enable you to confirm that your baby is growing in proportion, a record of weight gain needs to be combined with information about overall growth. It is often difficult to measure a baby's length or height accurately, so most doctors recommend regular checks on the head circumference instead. If this is not done at your clinic, you can measure your baby's head yourself at home as described below. For the first 2 months, your baby should be weighed and measured every 2 weeks, thereafter once every 4 weeks should be sufficient.

**Measuring a baby's head circumference**
To find the circumference of your baby's head, hold an accurate tape measure firmly, but not tightly, around the largest part of the head so that it rests just above the eyebrows and ears as shown.

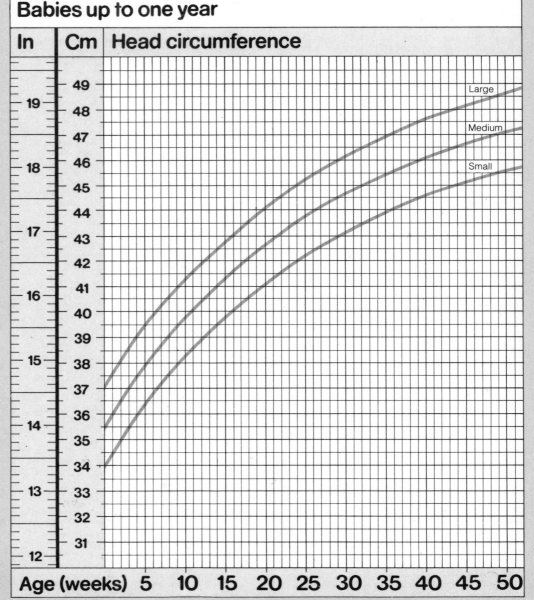

**Babies up to one year**

| In | Cm | Head circumference |
|---|---|---|

Age (weeks) 5 10 15 20 25 30 35 40 45 50

*measuring children,* right) mark the results on the appropriate chart. Use a ruler to help you read horizontally across from the scale on the left of the chart to the point where it meets the vertical line up from your child's age at the bottom of the chart. Mark the point where the two lines cross. By linking this mark with the previous result you will soon build up a curve showing your child's growth.

### Possible problems

If your child's increase in both weight and head circumference or height are following the standard growth curves as described, you have no cause for concern. If, however, either measurement increases significantly more or less than expected on two consecutive occasions, you may need to seek medical advice.

Also consult diagnostic chart 1, *Slow weight gain,* chart 10, *Slow growth,* chart 11, *Excessive weight gain,* or chart 53, *Adolescent weight problems* as appropriate.

**Weighing and measuring children**
After the age of one, you can reduce the frequency with which you weigh and measure your child; 6-monthly checks should be adequate. In this age range measurement of height takes the place of measurement of head circumference. For your children up to the age of two, accurate measurements of height and weight are best taken at your local baby clinic. However, if this is not possible, you can weigh and measure your child yourself at home as described below.

**Weighing**
If possible, use the same set of weighing scales each time you weigh your child. Your child should wear the minimum of clothing and stand as still and as straight as possible while you check the reading.

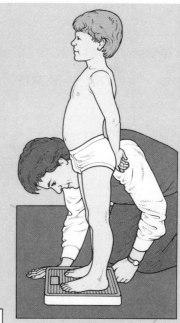

**Measuring height**
Choose a straight section of wall in a part of the house where you do not mind marking the paint. Your child should stand without shoes with feet together as close to the wall as possible. Try to make sure that he or she is standing upright and is looking straight ahead. Use a straight edge such as a ruler held at a right angle to measure from the top of the head to the wall and mark the height measures. You can then use an accurate ruler – a carpenter's rule is ideal – to measure the distance from the mark to the floor.

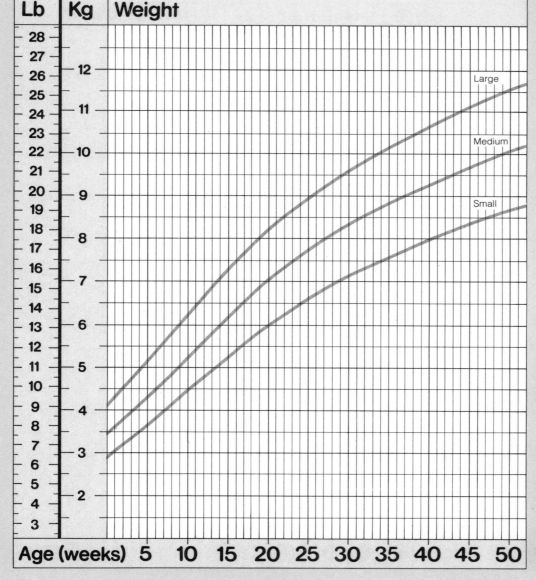

## Babies up to one year

| Lb | Kg | Weight |
|----|----|--------|

Large

Medium

Small

**Age (weeks)** 5 10 15 20 25 30 35 40 45 50

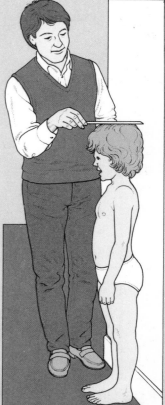

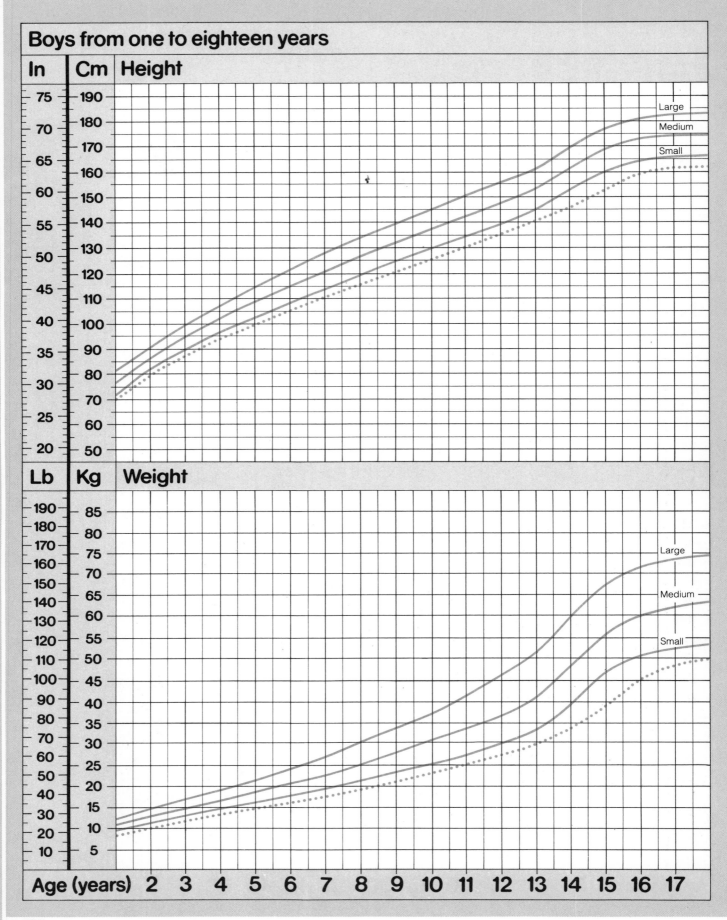

Boys from one to eighteen years

## Girls from one to eighteen years

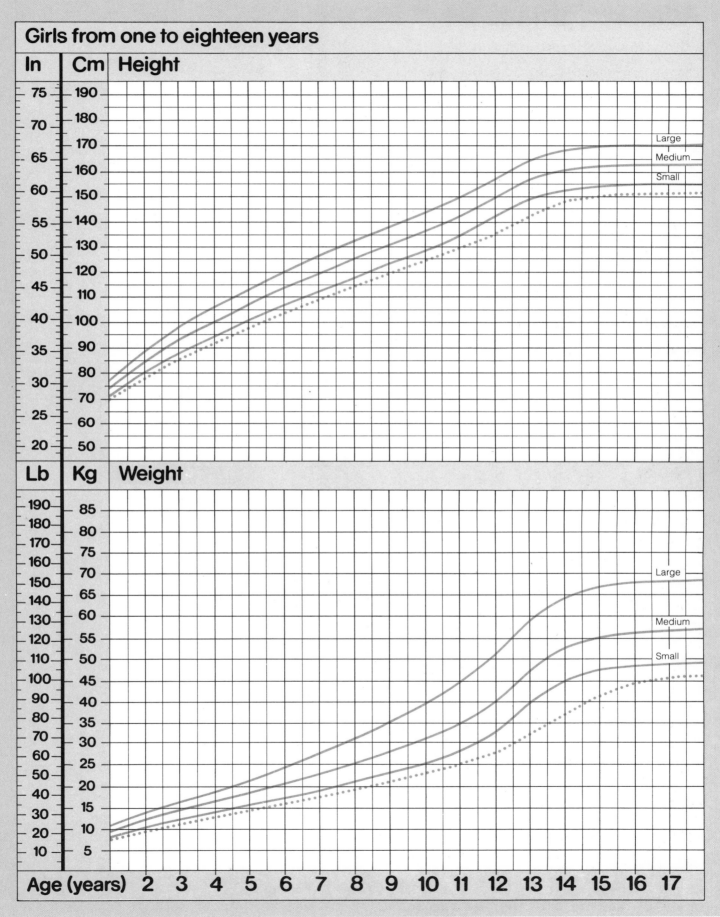

# Adult weight tables

Ordinarily, fat accounts for about 10 to 20 per cent of the weight of an adult male, and 25 per cent of the weight of an adult female. Any more than this is both unnecessary and unhealthy. The weight chart below shows "desirable" weight for different heights. Ideally, your weight should remain roughly constant after the age of 25. Most people gradually gain weight as they grow older, reaching their heaviest around 50. This is more than likely if you begin to exercise less at this time in life when the body is beginning to take longer to burn up food. Matching up food intake with energy output is the best way to maintain your weight over the years (see *Age and increasing weight,* p.150). If you fall into the "overweight" category on the weight chart, study the box on How to lose weight (p.151), so that you may be encouraged to drop the extra pounds sensibly. If you are not convinced that you need to lose weight, try the fat-fold thickness test as described on the opposite page. It is important to take a pinch of skin on the abdomen above the navel or on the side just over the lower ribs because both sexes have an equal amount of fat here, whereas in other areas such as the upper arm and thigh, women have more fat than men. To check your actual weight against the healthy "desirable" weight for someone of your height, first find your height on the left of the weight table below. Then rule a line across from your height and a line up from your weight on the bottom of the chart. If the point where your height and weight lines meet is in the coloured central band, your weight is healthy for someone of your height. If you are overweight, you are more susceptible than thinner people to coronary artery disease, high blood pressure, diabetes and a host of other disorders. For further information, consult the relevant self-diagnosis chart (see *Overweight,* p.150) and discuss the matter with your doctor. If you are seriously underweight, this too may be cause for concern (see *Loss of weight,* p.148) and you should discuss the matter with your doctor.

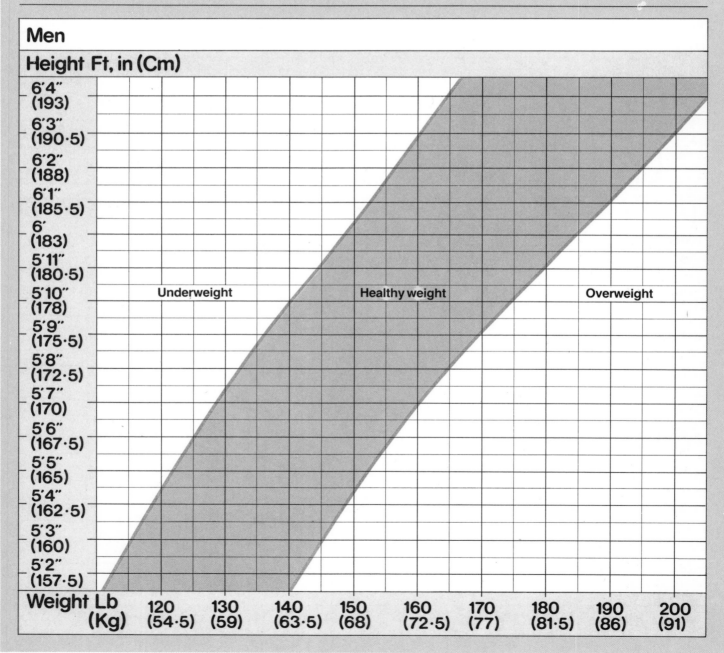

Fat is deposited in a layer underneath the skin and within the tissues in other parts of the body including the buttocks, breasts and inside the chest and abdominal cavities. Fat comprises more of a woman's weight as compared with a man's weight. It is distributed in such a way as to give male and female bodies their characteristic contours. Fat is laid down when food intake is greater than is needed to fuel the body's energy requirements. It is burned when food intake fails to equal the body's energy output. Fat also serves as insulation against the cold.

Both too much and too little fat can be unhealthy. Being too fat can lead to heart and circulation problems. Being too thin is less of a health risk, but may be a sign of undernourishment and can reduce your resistance to a variety of diseases. Fluctuations in the level of fat deposits are almost always the result of an imbalance between food intake and energy expenditure.

The most telling site to measure the thickness of a fold of fat for both men and women is the stomach, just above the navel. Alternatively, you can take a deep pinch of skin on your side just over the lower ribs. Most men and women have roughly the same amounts of fat here. If the distance between thumb and index finger is greater than 2.5cm (1in) thick, you are probably overweight and should adjust your diet now.

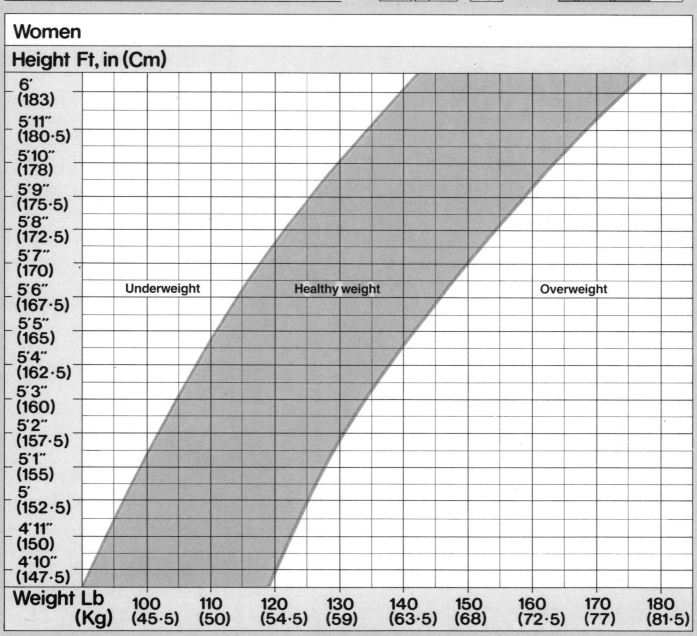

## Women

### Height Ft, in (Cm)

| | Underweight | Healthy weight | Overweight |
|---|---|---|---|

Height axis:
6′ (183)
5′11″ (180·5)
5′10″ (178)
5′9″ (175·5)
5′8″ (172·5)
5′7″ (170)
5′6″ (167·5)
5′5″ (165)
5′4″ (162·5)
5′3″ (160)
5′2″ (157·5)
5′1″ (155)
5′ (152·5)
4′11″ (150)
4′10″ (147·5)

**Weight Lb (Kg)**
100 (45·5) · 110 (50) · 120 (54·5) · 130 (59) · 140 (63·5) · 150 (68) · 160 (72·5) · 170 (77) · 180 (81·5)

# Children's medical records

## Birth record

Baby's name _____  Weight _____

Time of birth _____  Blood type _____

Date of birth _____  Type of feeding

Height _____      Breast _____ Bottle _____

## Details of pregnancy

Mothers health during pregnancy:

Illness _____

Medication _____

Problems _____

Delivery:

Type _____  Drugs _____

Monitoring _____  Consultant _____

Problems _____  Hospital _____

_____  Length of stay _____

## Illness, injury and allergy record

| Illness | Date/age | Duration |
| --- | --- | --- |
| _____ | _____ | _____ |
| _____ | _____ | _____ |
| _____ | _____ | _____ |

| Injuries | | Date/age |
| --- | --- | --- |
| _____ | | _____ |
| _____ | | _____ |

Allergies
_____
_____
_____

## Immunization record

| Disease | Date/age | Booster dates |
| --- | --- | --- |
| Diptheria, whooping cough, tetanus | _____ | _____ |
| Poliomyelitis _____ | _____ | _____ |
| Measles _____ | _____ | _____ |
| Tuberculosis _____ | _____ | _____ |
| German measles (girls only) _____ | _____ | |

## Birth record

Baby's name——————————— Weight————————————
Time of birth———————————— Blood type——————————
Date of birth———————————— Type of feeding
Height—————————————————    Breast————— Bottle—————

## Details of pregnancy

Mothers health during pregnancy:
Illness——————————————————————————————————
Medication—————————————————————————————————
Problems——————————————————————————————————

Delivery:
Type——————————————— Drugs———————————————
Monitoring————————————— Consultant—————————————
Problems——————————————— Hospital————————————————
——————————————————————— Length of stay————————————

## Illness, injury and allergy record

| Illness | Date/age | Duration |
|---|---|---|
|  |  |  |
|  |  |  |

| Injuries | | Date/age |
|---|---|---|
|  |  |  |

Allergies

## Immunization record

| Disease | Date/age | Booster dates |
|---|---|---|
| Diptheria, whooping cough, tetanus |  |  |
| Poliomyelitis |  |  |
| Measles |  |  |
| Tuberculosis |  |  |
| German measles (girls only) |  |  |

# Children's development records

Baby's name _____

| Milestone | Date/age |
|---|---|
| Smiles | |
| Rolls over | |
| Raises head and shoulders from a face down position | |
| Sits unsupported | |
| Passes toys from one hand to the other | |
| Crawls | |
| First tooth | |
| Starts solid foods | |
| Is weaned | |
| Stands unsupported | |
| Sleeps through the night | |
| Walks unaided | |
| First words | |
| Achieves bowel control | |
| Stays dry during the day | |
| Stays dry during the night | |
| Talks in simple sentences | |
| Gets dressed and undressed (with a little help) | |
| Draws a recognisable figure | |
| Starts playschool/nursery | |
| First visit to the dentist | |

Baby's name _____

| Milestone | Date/age |
|---|---|
| Smiles | |
| Rolls over | |
| Raises head and shoulders from a face down position | |
| Sits unsupported | |
| Passes toys from one hand to the other | |
| Crawls | |
| First tooth | |
| Starts solid foods | |
| Is weaned | |
| Stands unsupported | |
| Sleeps through the night | |
| Walks unaided | |
| First words | |
| Achieves bowel control | |
| Stays dry during the day | |
| Stays dry during the night | |
| Talks in simple sentences | |
| Gets dressed and undressed (with a little help) | |
| Draws a recognisable figure | |
| Starts playschool/nursery school | |
| First visit to the dentist | |

# Adult medical records

Name (female) ——————————————————————————

## Examinations

Date

Cervical (pap) smear ——————— ———————————————
Vaginal examination ——————— ———————————————
Mammography ——————— ———————————————
Eye test ——————— ———————————————
Dental check up ——————— ———————————————
Complete physical examination ——— ———————————————
Blood pressure ——————— ———————————————
Stool test ——————— ———————————————
Serum cholesterol blood level ——— ———————————————

## Medications

Dose                    Side effects

Drugs
——————————————   ——————————   ——————————
——————————————   ——————————   ——————————

Contraceptives
——————————————   ——————————   ——————————
——————————————   ——————————   ——————————

## Allergies

Treatment
——————————————   ——————————————————
——————————————   ——————————————————
——————————————   ——————————————————

## Injuries and/or illnesses

Date
——————————————————————   ——————————
——————————————————————   ——————————
——————————————————————   ——————————
——————————————————————   ——————————

## Operations and/or procedures

Date
——————————————————————   ——————————
——————————————————————   ——————————
——————————————————————   ——————————
——————————————————————   ——————————

Name (male)

| Examinations | Date |
|---|---|
| Eye test | |
| Dental check up | |
| Complete physical examination | |
| Blood pressure | |
| Stool test | |
| Serum cholesterol blood level | |

| Medications | Dose | Side effects |
|---|---|---|
| Drugs | | |
| | | |
| | | |
| | | |
| | | |
| | | |

| Allergies | Treatment |
|---|---|
| | |
| | |
| | |
| | |

| Injuries and/or illnesses | Date |
|---|---|
| | |
| | |
| | |
| | |

| Operations and/or procedures | Date |
|---|---|
| | |
| | |
| | |

## Immunization records

Name _____

| Disease | Date of Immunization/ illness | Date of booster |
|---|---|---|
| Measles | _____ | _____ |
| Mumps** | _____ | _____ |
| Rubella | _____ | _____ |
| Whooping cough (pertussis) | _____ | _____ |
| Diphtheria | _____ | _____ |
| BCG (for tuberculosis) | _____ | _____ |
| Tetanus | _____ | _____ |
| Poliomyelitis | _____ | _____ |
| Immunoglobulin* | _____ | _____ |
| Cholera* | _____ | _____ |
| Yellow fever* | _____ | _____ |
| TAB* | _____ | _____ |
| Other | _____ | _____ |

Name _____

| Measles | _____ | _____ |
|---|---|---|
| Mumps** | _____ | _____ |
| Rubella | _____ | _____ |
| Whooping cough (pertussis) | _____ | _____ |
| Diphtheria | _____ | _____ |
| BCG (for tuberculosis) | _____ | _____ |
| Tetanus | _____ | _____ |
| Poliomyelitis | _____ | _____ |
| Immunoglobulin* | _____ | _____ |
| Cholera* | _____ | _____ |
| Yellow fever* | _____ | _____ |
| TAB* | _____ | _____ |
| Other | _____ | _____ |

* These immunizations may be required when travelling abroad. It is always wise to check with your doctor if you intend to travel to a foreign country. He or she will advise on which vaccinations you need for which countries, the period of time that can elapse between vaccinations, and when the vaccinations need to be given. Your doctor will also provide you with the necessary immunization certificate. Some diseases – of which malaria is by far the most important – have no vaccines – protection requires that you take regular doses of a medicine. Again consult your doctor; up to date information is needed as the malaria parasites in some parts of the world are resistant to drugs which are effective elsewhere. No country now requires smallpox vaccination. Immunoglobulin (for hepatitis) and TAB (for typhoid) are never *required* but may be advisable in some countries. Vaccination against cholera, yellow fever, and very occasionally other diseases such as plague, are legally required from time to time depending on local conditions.

**Not recommended for routine use in Britain but may be advised in special circumstances.

# Useful addresses

## Alcohol

### ALCOHOL CONCERN
305 Gray's Inn Road,
London WC1X 8QF
Tel: 01-833 3471

The national agency on alcohol misuse. Supports local services and training initiatives, has a library and information service, and publishes a journal *Alcohol Concern*.

## Blind

### ROYAL NATIONAL INSTITUTE FOR THE BLIND
224/228 Great Portland Street,
London W1N 6AA
Tel: 01-388 1266

Provides an information and advisory service on accommodation, aids, education etc. RNIB has a library service, publishes material in ink-print and Braille, and administers the British Talking Book Service for the Blind.

## Broadcasting

### BROADCASTING SUPPORT SERVICES
Room 17,
252 Western Avenue,
London W3 6XJ
Tel: 01-992 5522

Provides follow-up services for programmes on BBC, Channel 4 and ITV. It publishes viewers' guides, runs telephone helplines, and letter-answering services. A standing order subscription service to all viewers' guides is now available.

## Cancer

### BACUP (BRITISH ASSOCIATION OF CANCER UNITED PATIENTS
121/3 Charterhouse Street,
London EC1M 6AA
Tel: 01-608 1661

National information service staffed by experienced cancer nurses. Provides information on treatment, research, support groups and practical help, and publishes leaflets.

### WOMEN'S NATIONAL CANCER CONTROL CAMPAIGN
1 South Audley Street,
London W1Y 5DQ.
Tel: 01-499 7532

An organisation which encourages measures for the early detection and prevention of cancer, particularly in women. The Campaign runs seven mobile clinics throughout the country offering simple tests to safeguard women's health. Health education material about cervical smear tests and breast self-examination is produced comprising a full range of posters, leaflets and audio visual aids.

## Children

### NATIONAL ASSOCIATION FOR THE WELFARE OF CHILDREN IN HOSPITAL (NAWCH)
Argyle House,
29/31 Euston Road,
London NW1 2SD
Tel: 01-833 2041

Information and advisory service for parents whose children are about to enter hospital. Initiates research and holds study days and conferences. Conducts surveys of hospital facilities. Publications list available. Publishes a newsletter *Update*.

### NATIONAL CHILDREN'S BUREAU
8 Wakley Street,
London EC1V 7QE
Tel: 01-278 9441

Multi-disciplinary centre concerned with children's needs in the family and society. Initiates a wide range of research. Provides information and library service. Publications list available. Publishes a journal *Concern* and produces an excellent series of lists and summaries of research (*Highlights*).

### NATIONAL LIBRARY FOR THE HANDICAPPED CHILD
Blyton Handi-Read Centre,
Lynton House,
Tavistock Square,
London WC1H 9LT.
Tel: 01-387 7016

Reference library and advisory service on all aspects of reading and the handicapped child. Includes books for and about children with reading handicaps, periodicals, audiovisual equipment, computer equipment and software.

## Deaf

### ROYAL NATIONAL INSTITUTE FOR THE DEAF
105 Gower Street,
London WC1E 6AH
Tel: 01-387 8033

Has a library and information service and a technical advisory service on hearing aids and other equipment. Publishes a journal *Soundbarrier.*

## Dentistry

### BRITISH DENTAL HEALTH FOUNDATION
88 Gurnards Avenue,
Fishermead,
Milton Keynes, MK6 2SL.

Aims are to promote better awareness of all dental hygiene for the general public. Answer enquiries from public is SAE enclosed. Make leaflets available to general public on all aspects of dental health care.

## Disability

### DISABILITY ALLIANCE
25 Denmark Street,
London WC2 8NJ
Tel: 01-240 0806

A federation of over 50 organisations of and for disabled people, campaigning for a comprehensive income scheme for disabled people as a right. Provides welfare rights information and advice, and sponsors local rights services. Publishes *Disability Rights Handbook.*

### DISABLED LIVING FOUNDATION
380/384 Harrow Road,
London W9 2HU
Tel: 01-289 6111

An information service on all aspects of disability. Specialist advisory services on Incontinence, Music, Clothing, Visual Handicap, and an Aids Centre. Aimed primarily at professionals but also helps disabled people and their relatives. Publications list available. Produces excellent information sheets as part of its information service.

## Family Planning

### FAMILY PLANNING INFORMATION SERVICES
27-35, Mortimer Street,
London W1N 7RJ.
Tel: 01-636 7866

Offers free information on all aspects of family planning and reproductive health care to the public, through answering personal telephone calls and letters (SAE appreciated), sending out leaflets, providing addresses, telephone numbers and opening times for NHS Family Planning Clinics, as well as specialist clinics for menopause, well woman, pre-menstrual, sub-fertility, psycho-sexual and youth services.

## Health information

### COLLEGE OF HEALTH
18 Victoria Park Square,
London E2 9PF
Tel: 01-980 6263
HEALTHLINE, 01-980 4848 2pm to 10pm, seven days a week.

Organisation for health care consumers, run along similar lines to the Consumers' Association. Publishes a quarterly magazine *Self Health* and a series of guides to health care services. The College of Health set up Healthline, the 'phone-in' tape library on more than 200 health topics. Members have access to a register of self help groups and an information service.

### HEALTH EDUCATION COUNCIL
78 New Oxford Street,
London WC1A 1AH
Tel: 01-631 0930

The Health Education Council is a national body funded largely by the DHSS and serving England, Wales and Northern Ireland. The HEC produces a wide range of free leaflets for the public on various aspects of keeping healthy. The HEC Resource Centre produces 22 invaluable Source Lists on topics such as

Cancer education and Mental Health, a monthly list of recent additions (books and audiovisual materials) and a monthly "Journal articles of interest." For Scotland, contact **SCOTTISH HEALTH EDUCATION GROUP,** Woodburn House, Canaan Lane, Edinburgh EH10 4SG.
Tel: 031 447 8044.

### WOMENS HEALTH INFORMATION CENTRE (WHIC)
52 Featherstone Street,
London EC1
Tel: 01-251 6580

National information and resource centre for women's health issues. Maintains a library of information materials and coordinates a network of women's health groups. Publishes *WHIC Newsletter* and fact sheets on individual topics.

## Mental handicap

### ROYAL SOCIETY FOR MENTALLY HANDICAPPED CHILDREN & ADULTS (MENCAP)
117/123 Golden Lane,
London EC1V 0RT
Tel: 01-253 9433

Specialist advisory and information services for the public and for professionals on all aspects of mental handicap. Finances research and holds conferences and meetings. Regional offices provide liaison for 450 local groups. Publications list available. Publishes a magazine *Parents' Voice* and a regular information pack *Communications.*

## Mental health

### MIND: NATIONAL ASSOCIATION FOR MENTAL HEALTH
22 Harley Street,
London W1N 2ED
Tel: 01-637 0741

Information and advisory service on all aspects of mental health (both mental illness and mental handicap). Legal and welfare rights service to protect the rights of patients and staff. Arranges conferences and short courses on a wide range of mental health issues. Publications list available. Publishes a journal *OpenMind.*

## Patients

### PATIENTS' ASSOCIATION
Room 33,
18 Charing Cross Road,
London WC2H 0HR
Tel: 01-240 0671

Represents and furthers the interests of patients through an individual advice service on patients' rights, and by spreading information on patients' interests. Publishes a newsletter *Patient Voice.*

## Pregnancy

### BRITISH PREGNANCY ADVISORY SERVICE (BPAS)
Head Office:
Austry Manor,
Wootton Wawen,
Solihull,
West Midlands B95 6BX.
Tel: 05642 3225

Non-profit making charity offering information, counselling, abortion advice and help, operations and services connected with contraception, pregnancy, infertility and sexuality. Has five nursing homes and 24 branches throughout Britain. For nearest branch, ring Head Office. Produces free leaflets on all services.

## Volunteers and voluntary organisations

### NATIONAL COUNCIL FOR VOLUNTARY ORGANISATIONS
26 Bedford Square,
London WC1B 3HU
Tel: 01-636 4066

National agency for the maintenance and promotion of voluntary social action. Information and resource centre providing training, legal, publishing, information and advisory services for voluntary organisations, nationally and locally. Publications list available (Bedford Square Press).

# Emergency telephone numbers

|  | Emergency Telephone | Name | Telephone/ address | Hours |
|---|---|---|---|---|
| GP or health centre |  |  |  |  |
| Local district general hospital |  |  |  |  |
| Hospital accident and emergency department |  |  |  |  |
| Dentist |  |  |  |  |
| Optician |  |  |  |  |
| Pharmacist |  |  |  |  |
| Family planning clinic |  |  |  |  |
| Clinic for sexually transmitted diseases |  |  |  |  |
| Samaritan's local office |  |  |  |  |
| Local police station |  |  |  |  |
| Others |  |  |  |  |

# INDEX

Each of the symptom charts in this book is designed to help you discover the possible reason for your, or your child's complaint. The book contains thousands of physiological references, and this index must of necessity be selective. For a full guide to the basic symptoms analyzed in the 147 charts and how to find the chart you need, see pp. 38-48. References within the following index are to page numbers of topics from the entire book, not just from the charts. Titles of information boxes within the charts and significant subtopics discussed in these boxes are *italicized* to emphasize their importance. Titles of the charts themselves are in **bold** typeface.

**Acknowledgements**
The publishers would like to thank the following for their help
during the preparation of this book: Georgina D'Angelo; Pi
Dorling; Debra Grayson; Andrew Parker; Amy Titcomb;
Cathy Tinknell; N. Edwards, Poisons Information Centre,
Guy's Hospital London; R. Goodchild, Family Planning
Association; Dr. J. Knight, Royal National Throat, Nose and
Ear Hospital, London; Dr M. Sidaway, Charing Cross
Hospital, London; Department of Medical Illustration, St.
Bartholomew's Hospital, London; Department of Nutrition
and Dietetics, St. Thomas's Hospital, London; Ultrasound
Department, St. Bartholomew's Hospital, London; X-ray
Department, St. Thomas's Hospital, London; The John Lewis
Partnership.

**Illustration**
Tony Graham
Edwina Keene
Andrew Popkiewicz

**Picture agencies**
Sally and Richard Greenhill
The Science Photo Library
Tim and Jennie Woodcock
Vision International

**Photographic Services**
W. Photo
Negs

**Typesetting**
Elements Ltd.
Foremost Typesetting Ltd.
The Letterbox Company (Woking) Ltd.

**Reproduction**
Repro Llovet, Barcelona